DEMOCRACY IN AMERICA

论美国的民主

（经典文库　汉英对照）

（法）托克维尔⊙著

吴　睿⊙译

台海出版社

Volume 2

下　卷

De Tocqueville's Preface To The Second Part

The Americans live in a democratic state of society, which has naturally suggested to them certain laws and a certain political character. This same state of society has, moreover, engendered amongst them a multitude of feelings and opinions which were unknown amongst the elder aristocratic communities of Europe: it has destroyed or modified all the relations which before existed, and established others of a novel kind. The—aspect of civil society has been no less affected by these changes than that of the political world. The former subject has been treated of in the work on the Democracy of America, which I published five years ago; to examine the latter is the object of the present book; but these two parts complete each other, and form one and the same work.

I must at once warn the reader against an error which would be extremely prejudicial to me. When he finds that I attribute so many different consequences to the principle of equality, he may thence infer that I consider that principle to be the sole cause of all that takes place in the present age: but this would be to impute to me a very narrow view. A multitude of opinions, feelings, and propensities are now in existence, which owe their origin to circumstances unconnected with or even contrary to the principle of equality. Thus if I were to select the United States as an example, I could easily prove that the nature of the country, the origin of its inhabitants, the religion of its founders, their acquired knowledge, and their former habits, have exercised, and still exercise, independently of democracy, a vast influence upon the thoughts and feelings of that people. Different causes, but no less distinct from the circumstance of the equality of conditions, might be traced in Europe, and would explain a

前　言

美国人之所以能够生活在民主社会，自然是有赖于他们的某些法律和政治特点。而且，正是这种社会状况令美国人产生了许多欧洲旧贵族社会中从未出现过的思想和观点。它打破并改变了昔日所有关系，建立起一种新型的关系。市民社会受到冲击而出现的变化丝毫不亚于政治世界。5年前出版的本书上卷里，我已就美国民主的主要问题进行了阐述，而本书将就一些次要问题进行探讨，两卷书互为补充，合成一部完整的著作。

我必须马上提醒读者，不要过度歪曲我的意图。在看到我将众多的不同后果都归因于平等之后，读者可能据此推断我认为平等是当今所发生的一切事情的唯一原因，但以这样的看法认定我的观点过于狭隘。如今，人们的众多观点、感情和倾向非但不是来自平等的原则，甚至还与之完全相反。因此，选择以美国为例，我可以轻易地证明这个国家的性质、居民的起源、早起定居者的宗教以及他们的既有知识和原有习惯，过去以及现在依然对除民主以外的这个国家人民的思想和感情产生的巨大影响。欧洲发生的许多事情也有各种不同的原因，尽管也适用于美国发生的大部分事情，但都与平等无关。

great portion of the occurrences taking place amongst us.

I acknowledge the existence of all these different causes, and their power, but my subject does not lead me to treat of them. I have not undertaken to unfold the reason of all our inclinations and all our notions: my only object is to show in what respects the principle of equality has modified both the former and the latter.

Some readers may perhaps be astonished that—firmly persuaded as I am that the democratic revolution which we are witnessing is an irresistible fact against which it would be neither desirable nor wise to struggle—I should often have had occasion in this book to address language of such severity to those democratic communities which this revolution has brought into being. My answer is simply, that it is because I am not an adversary of democracy, that I have sought to speak of democracy in all sincerity.

Men will not accept truth at the hands of their enemies, and truth is seldom offered to them by their friends: for this reason I have spoken it. I was persuaded that many would take upon themselves to announce the new blessings which the principle of equality promises to mankind, but that few would dare to point out from afar the dangers with which it threatens them. To those perils therefore I have turned my chief attention, and believing that I had discovered them clearly, I have not had the cowardice to leave them untold.

I trust that my readers will find in this Second Part that impartiality which seems to have been remarked in the former work. Placed as I am in the midst of the conflicting opinions between which we are divided, I have endeavored to suppress within me for a time the favorable sympathies or the adverse emotions with which each of them inspires me. If those who read this book can find a single sentence intended to flatter any of the great parties which have agitated my country, or any of those petty factions which now harass and weaken it, let such readers raise their voices to accuse me.

The subject I have sought to embrace is immense, for it includes the greater part of the feelings and opinions to which the new state of society has given birth. Such a subject is doubtless above my

我承认所有不同原因和力量的存在，但这并不是我研究的对象。我不打算探讨我们所有倾向和所有观念产生的原因，我唯一的目的就是说明平等原则对于所有倾向和思想改变发挥的作用。

一些读者可能感到惊讶，既然我如此坚决地认为我们所看到的民主革命不可抗拒，与之战斗既无希望也不明智，那么，我又为什么要在本书中不断用如此严厉的语言指责民主革命所创造的民主社会呢？我的回答很简单，正因为我不是民主的敌人，所以才要认真地对待民主。

人们不可能从敌人手中获得真理，而且也很难从朋友那里得到真理。这就是我要这样做的原因。我相信，许多人愿意出面大谈平等承诺带给人类的新的好处，但是却绝少有人敢指出平等带给人们的威胁。因此，我将自己的主要精力放在这些坏处上，而且认为既然我已经清楚地看到这些问题，就要敢于说出来。

我相信，读者在下卷中将会发现在上卷中似乎已经察觉到的我的不偏不倚。身处将我们分成不同派别的互相冲突的观点之中，我努力暂时压制自己对其中任何一种看法在我内心激起的同情或反感。如果读这本书的人看到任何一句话是讨好曾将我国弄得动荡不安的任何大党，或是现在令国家混乱国力衰弱的任何小党，那么请大声指责我。

我所要探讨的问题非常广泛，因为新的社会状态下所产生的绝大部分思想和观念都囊括其中。无疑，有些问题令我感到力不从心。但是，如果我未能实现我想要达到的目的，

strength, and in treating it I have not succeeded in satisfying myself. But, if I have not been able to reach the goal which I had in view, my readers will at least do me the justice to acknowledge that I have conceived and followed up my undertaking in a spirit not unworthy of success.

A. De T.
March, 1840

读者也会公允地认为，至少我以抛砖引玉的精神来计划和着手写这部书是正确的。

亚历克西·德·托克维尔
1840年3月

Section I: Influence of Democracy on the Action of Intellect in The United States.

Chapter I: Philosophical Method Among the Americans

I think that in no country in the civilized world is less attention paid to philosophy than in the United States. The Americans have no philosophical school of their own; and they care but little for all the schools into which Europe is divided, the very names of which are scarcely known to them. Nevertheless it is easy to perceive that almost all the inhabitants of the United States conduct their understanding in the same manner, and govern it by the same rules; that is to say, that without ever having taken the trouble to define the rules of a philosophical method, they are in possession of one, common to the whole people. To evade the bondage of system and habit, of family maxims, class opinions, and, in some degree, of national prejudices; to accept tradition only as a means of information, and existing facts only as a lesson used in doing otherwise, and doing better; to seek the reason of things for one's self, and in one's self alone; to tend to results without being bound to means, and to aim at the substance through the form;—such are the principal characteristics of what I shall call the philosophical method of the Americans. But if I go further, and if I seek amongst these characteristics that which predominates over and includes almost all the rest, I discover that in most of the operations of the mind, each American appeals to the individual exercise of his own understanding alone. America is therefore one of the countries in the world where philosophy is least

第一篇　民主对美国观念进步的影响

第一章　美国人的哲学方法

我认为，在文明世界没有一个国家像美国那样不重视哲学。美国人没有自己的哲学学派，对欧洲所有的哲学流派分支也毫不关心，甚至连它们的名字都不知道。但是，在美国，很容易发现，几乎所有的人都用同样的方式指导自己的思想，并运用同样的准则支配自己的思想，也就是说，虽然未曾下功夫定义他们的准则，但是所有人却有着一个共通的哲学方法。为了摆脱制度和习惯的束缚、家庭的清规、阶级的观念以及某种程度的国家的偏见，而只将传统视为一种习得的知识，将已有的事实视为改革和创新的经验教训，并只依靠自己找到事情的原因，也往往不拘泥于取得结果的手段，而且不管形式直接深入本质，这就是我所说的美国人哲学方法的主要特征。但是如果我进一步深入，想要从这些特征中找到一个足以概括所有其他特征的最主要特征，就会发现每个人在运用自己的头脑时，大多只会凭借自己的理解。因此，美国是世界上对哲学研究得最少的国家之一，却是

studied, and where the precepts of Descartes are best applied. Nor is this surprising. The Americans do not read the works of Descartes, because their social condition deters them from speculative studies; but they follow his maxims because this very social condition naturally disposes their understanding to adopt them. In the midst of the continual movement which agitates a democratic community, the tie which unites one generation to another is relaxed or broken; every man readily loses the trace of the ideas of his forefathers or takes no care about them. Nor can men living in this state of society derive their belief from the opinions of the class to which they belong, for, so to speak, there are no longer any classes, or those which still exist are composed of such mobile elements, that their body can never exercise a real control over its members. As to the influence which the intelligence of one man has on that of another, it must necessarily be very limited in a country where the citizens, placed on the footing of a general similitude, are all closely seen by each other; and where, as no signs of incontestable greatness or superiority are perceived in any one of them, they are constantly brought back to their own reason as the most obvious and proximate source of truth. It is not only confidence in this or that man which is then destroyed, but the taste for trusting the ipse dixit of any man whatsoever. Everyone shuts himself up in his own breast, and affects from that point to judge the world.

The practice which obtains amongst the Americans of fixing the standard of their judgment in themselves alone, leads them to other habits of mind. As they perceive that they succeed in resolving without assistance all the little difficulties which their practical life presents, they readily conclude that everything in the world may be explained, and that nothing in it transcends the limits of the understanding. Thus they fall to denying what they cannot comprehend; which leaves them but little faith for whatever is extraordinary, and an almost insurmountable distaste for whatever is supernatural. As it is on their own testimony that they are accustomed to rely, they like to discern the object which engages their attention with extreme clearness; they therefore strip off as much as possible all that covers it, they rid themselves of whatever separates them from it, they remove whatever conceals it from sight, in order to view it more closely and in the broad light of day.

将笛卡儿的哲学运用的最好的国家之一。这并没有什么值得惊讶。美国人之所以不读笛卡儿的著作，是因为他们的社会情况让他们打消进行思辨研究的想法，但是他们之所以会按照笛卡儿的理论行事，是因为同样的社会状况让他们自然而然地接纳他的思想。在搅动民主社会的接连不断的运动之中，一代人与另一代人之间的纽带逐渐松弛或断裂，每个人都很容易忘记祖先的观点，不然就是对这些观点丝毫不以为意。生活在这种社会状况中的人们不再固守他们所属阶级的信仰，因为可以这样说，阶级已经不复存在，或者依然存在的阶级也是由不稳定的成员构成，所以他们的团体根本无法具有真正控制其成员的能力。至于一个人的智慧对另一个人所产生的影响，在一个公民素质大致相同的国家里必定非常有限，因为彼此的能力非常接近，谁也不认可别人比自己更强大和优越，所以人人都依靠自己的理性，认为这才是真理最明显、最近的来源。这不仅说明对某一个人的信任尽毁，而且也表示没兴趣信任任何人。每个人将自己都封闭起来，并只从自己的角度看待世界。

美国人这种只从自身出发确定判断标准的做法，让他们形成另一种思维习惯。因为他们认为生活中出现的所有小难题都可以无须别人帮助成功得到解决，便想当然地认为，世界上的所有事情都是可以解释的，没有什么事情会超出人的理解力。因此，他们否认有他们所不能理解的事情，这让他们几乎不相信那些离奇的事情，而且对超自然的东西有着几乎难以抑制的厌恶。因为他们已经习惯于相信自己找到的证据，所以喜欢把自己关注的事情弄得清清楚楚。因此，他们尽其所能地抽丝剥茧，将所有使他们与事物隔开的东西剥除，把遮挡他们视线的一切移走，为的就是要在光天化日之下近距离地观察事物。他们的

This disposition of the mind soon leads them to contemn forms, which they regard as useless and inconvenient veils placed between them and the truth.

The Americans then have not required to extract their philosophical method from books; they have found it in themselves. The same thing may be remarked in what has taken place in Europe. This same method has only been established and made popular in Europe in proportion as the condition of society has become more equal, and men have grown more like each other. Let us consider for a moment the connection of the periods in which this change may be traced. In the sixteenth century the Reformers subjected some of the dogmas of the ancient faith to the scrutiny of private judgment; but they still withheld from it the judgment of all the rest. In the seventeenth century, Bacon in the natural sciences, and Descartes in the study of philosophy in the strict sense of the term, abolished recognized formulas, destroyed the empire of tradition, and overthrew the authority of the schools. The philosophers of the eighteenth century, generalizing at length the same principle, undertook to submit to the private judgment of each man all the objects of his belief.

Who does not perceive that Luther, Descartes, and Voltaire employed the same method, and that they differed only in the greater or less use which they professed should be made of it? Why did the Reformers confine themselves so closely within the circle of religious ideas? Why did Descartes, choosing only to apply his method to certain matters, though he had made it fit to be applied to all, declare that men might judge for themselves in matters philosophical but not in matters political? How happened it that in the eighteenth century those general applications were all at once drawn from this same method, which Descartes and his predecessors had either not perceived or had rejected? To what, lastly, is the fact to be attributed, that at this period the method we are speaking of suddenly emerged from the schools, to penetrate into society and become the common standard of intelligence; and that, after it had become popular among the French, it has been ostensibly adopted or secretly followed by all the nations of Europe?

The philosophical method here designated may have been engendered in the sixteenth century—it may have been more accurately defined and more extensively applied in the seventeenth; but neither

这种思想倾向不久就会让他们轻视形式，认为那不过是挡在他们和真理之间的一层毫无用处只会带来不便的面纱。

因此，美国人不会从书本上汲取哲学方法，他们要自己去发现。随着社会变得越来越平等，人们变得越来越相似，同样的方法已经在欧洲建立并普及起来。现在，让我们追溯一下欧洲发生的事件的时间联系。16世纪的宗教改革者开始用个人的理性判断去论证某些古老信仰的教义，但依旧对其余所有的教义避而不做论断。17世纪，培根在自然科学方面，笛卡儿在狭义哲学方面，颠覆了传统，推翻了权威。18世纪的哲学家们，将上述的原则推广，试图用每个人的个人判断论证其所有信仰。

路德、笛卡儿、伏尔泰使用同样的方法，只不过在运用上或多或少有些不同，这已被大家有目共睹。为什么宗教改革者们将自己仅仅束缚在宗教的范畴呢？为什么笛卡儿选择只将这种方式运用到特定事物，尽管他本可以将这种方法运用到一切事物，并宣称人们应自行判断的是哲学事物而不是政治事物。18世纪，源自这一方法的突然到来的普遍应用为什么笛卡儿及其先驱既没想到也没有反对呢？最后，为什么在这一时期，我们所说的这种方法突然走出学术界，深入到社会并成为思想活动的共同准则呢？而且又为什么在法国受到追捧之后，却又被欧洲所有国家公开采纳或暗中遵循呢？

我们所说的哲学方法虽然得以在16世纪诞生，却是在17世纪得到更为准确的定义和更广泛的应用，但是这两个世纪都没能让其得到普遍应用。政治法律，社会状况，以及这些主要原因造成的思维习惯还与其背道而驰。这种方法出现在人们开始趋于平等，彼此相差

in the one nor in the other could it be commonly adopted. Political laws, the condition of society, and the habits of mind which are derived from these causes, were as yet opposed to it. It was discovered at a time when men were beginning to equalize and assimilate their conditions. It could only be generally followed in ages when those conditions had at length become nearly equal, and men nearly alike.

The philosophical method of the eighteenth century is then not only French, but it is democratic; and this explains why it was so readily admitted throughout Europe, where it has contributed so powerfully to change the face of society. It is not because the French have changed their former opinions, and altered their former manners, that they have convulsed the world; but because they were the first to generalize and bring to light a philosophical method, by the assistance of which it became easy to attack all that was old, and to open a path to all that was new.

If it be asked why, at the present day, this same method is more rigorously followed and more frequently applied by the French than by the Americans, although the principle of equality be no less complete, and of more ancient date, amongst the latter people, the fact may be attributed to two circumstances, which it is essential to have clearly understood in the first instance. It must never be forgotten that religion gave birth to Anglo-American society. In the United States religion is therefore commingled with all the habits of the nation and all the feelings of patriotism; whence it derives a peculiar force. To this powerful reason another of no less intensity may be added: in American religion has, as it were, laid down its own limits. Religious institutions have remained wholly distinct from political institutions, so that former laws have been easily changed whilst former belief has remained unshaken. Christianity has therefore retained a strong hold on the public mind in America; and, I would more particularly remark, that its sway is not only that of a philosophical doctrine which has been adopted upon inquiry, but of a religion which is believed without discussion. In the United States Christian sects are infinitely diversified and perpetually modified; but Christianity itself is a fact so irresistibly established, that no one undertakes either to attack or to defend it. The Americans, having admitted the principal doctrines of the Christian religion without inquiry, are obliged to accept in like manner a great number of moral truths originating in it and connected with it. Hence the activity of individual analysis is restrained within narrow limits, and many of the most important

无几的时期，只有最终人们身份几乎平等，彼此几近相同的时代到来，才能被普遍遵从。

那么，18世纪的哲学方法并非法国人所独有，而是具有广泛的民主性，而且这也说明为什么它能够在整个欧洲得到认可，并使全欧洲的面貌为之一新。法国人之所以能够震动世界，并不是因为他们改变了原有的观点和民情，而是因为他们首先概括并推广了一种哲学方法，依靠它的帮助轻而易举地对所有旧事物发起攻击，并为所有新事物的到来铺平道路。

如果要问现在为什么法国人比平等已相当完备且由来已久的美国人更严格、更经常地使用这一方法，我认为原因主要来自下述两种情况，而这是我们首先要弄清楚的。我们千万不能忘记，是宗教让英裔美国人的社会得以诞生。因此，在美国，宗教与这个民族的所有习惯和所有爱国主义情感交织在一起，因此宗教拥有特殊的力量。除了这个强有力的原因之外，另外一个原因的作用也丝毫不逊色。正如我们所了解的那样，在美国宗教只在自己的范围内活动。政教完全分离，所以旧的法律很容易被改变，而旧的信仰却可以岿然不动。因此，基督教对美国人的思想有很强的控制力，而且我还要特别指出，基督教并不仅仅是作为一门经过论证并被接受的哲学在发挥支配作用，而是作为一种无须论证即被信仰的宗教在发挥作用。在美国，基督教的教派多如牛毛而且一直变换，但是基督教本身不可抗拒的存在既无人能撼动也无须他人的捍卫。美国人毫不置疑地承认基督教的基本教义，所以同样会接受基督教提出或支持的大量道德真理。因此，个人的分析活动被限制在狭小的范围，从而使得许多人类最为重要的观点免受个人分析的影响。

of human opinions are removed from the range of its influence.

The second circumstance to which I have alluded is the following: the social condition and the constitution of the Americans are democratic, but they have not had a democratic revolution. They arrived upon the soil they occupy in nearly the condition in which we see them at the present day; and this is of very considerable importance.

There are no revolutions which do not shake existing belief, enervate authority, and throw doubts over commonly received ideas. The effect of all revolutions is therefore, more or less, to surrender men to their own guidance, and to open to the mind of every man a void and almost unlimited range of speculation. When equality of conditions succeeds a protracted conflict between the different classes of which the elder society was composed, envy, hatred, and uncharitableness, pride, and exaggerated self-confidence are apt to seize upon the human heart, and plant their sway there for a time. This, independently of equality itself, tends powerfully to divide men—to lead them to mistrust the judgment of others, and to seek the light of truth nowhere but in their own understandings. Everyone then attempts to be his own sufficient guide, and makes it his boast to form his own opinions on all subjects. Men are no longer bound together by ideas, but by interests; and it would seem as if human opinions were reduced to a sort of intellectual dust, scattered on every side, unable to collect, unable to cohere.

Thus, that independence of mind which equality supposes to exist, is never so great, nor ever appears so excessive, as at the time when equality is beginning to establish itself, and in the course of that painful labor by which it is established. That sort of intellectual freedom which equality may give ought, therefore, to be very carefully distinguished from the anarchy which revolution brings. Each of these two things must be severally considered, in order not to conceive exaggerated hopes or fears of the future.

I believe that the men who will live under the new forms of society will make frequent use of their private judgment; but I am far from thinking that they will often abuse it. This is attributable to a cause of more general application to all democratic countries, and which, in the long run, must needs restrain in them the independence of individual speculation within fixed, and sometimes narrow, limits. I shall proceed to point out this cause in the next chapter.

我前面所说的两个情况中的第二个是美国社会状况和宪法的民主性，尽管这里从未出现过民主革命。美国人来到他们所占据的这片土地时的样子跟他们今天的面貌差不多，而这一点非常重要。

所有的革命都会动摇旧有的信仰，削弱当局的权威，并质疑原先普遍存在的思想。因此，所有的革命都会起到或多或少让人们能够自主，或是为人们开辟广阔无限的精神活动空间的作用。当经过旧社会各阶级之间旷日持久的斗争平等随之出现的时候，嫉妒、憎恨、轻蔑、骄傲和过分的自信往往会蛊惑人心，并在一段时间内对人起支配作用。这往往会促使人们不相信他人的判断，而只依靠自己的理解力寻求真理。于是，每个人都试图充分自主，并以对所有事情都有自己的见解为荣。人们不再靠思想而是靠利益来联系，似乎人类的观点已经犹如一堆智慧之尘，散落四处，无法再凝聚起来。

因此，随平等而来的精神独立，从未像在平等确立之初，以及为巩固平等而艰苦奋斗期间那样强烈。所以，要特别小心地对平等带来的精神自由和革命带来的无政府状态加以区分。要对两者分别进行深入研究，才不会对未来有过高的期望或是过度的恐惧。

我相信，生活在新社会中的人们将会常常运用个人的判断力，但我一点也不认为他们会滥用个人的判断力。这要归功于一个能最广泛地适用于所有民主国家的因素，而且从长期来看，这一因素还将会把个人思想的独立性限定在一个固定的乃至有时候很狭小的范围之内。在下一章我将就这一原因进行论述。

Chapter II: Of The Principal Source Of Belief Among Democratic Nations

At different periods dogmatical belief is more or less abundant. It arises in different ways, and it may change its object or its form; but under no circumstances will dogmatical belief cease to exist, or, in other words, men will never cease to entertain some implicit opinions without trying them by actual discussion. If everyone undertook to form his own opinions and to seek for truth by isolated paths struck out by himself alone, it is not to be supposed that any considerable number of men would ever unite in any common belief. But obviously without such common belief no society can prosper—say rather no society can subsist; for without ideas held in common, there is no common action, and without common action, there may still be men, but there is no social body. In order that society should exist, and, a fortiori, that a society should prosper, it is required that all the minds of the citizens should be rallied and held together by certain predominant ideas; and this cannot be the case, unless each of them sometimes draws his opinions from the common source, and consents to accept certain matters of belief at the hands of the community.

If I now consider man in his isolated capacity, I find that dogmatical belief is not less indispensable to him in order to live alone, than it is to enable him to co-operate with his fellow-creatures. If man were forced to demonstrate to himself all the truths of which he makes daily use, his task would never end. He would exhaust his strength in preparatory exercises, without advancing beyond them. As, from the shortness of his life, he has not the time, nor, from the limits of his intelligence, the capacity, to accomplish this, he is reduced to take upon trust a number of facts and opinions which he has not had either the time or the power to verify himself, but which men of greater ability have sought out, or which the world adopts. On this groundwork he raises for himself the structure of his own thoughts; nor is he led to proceed in this manner by choice so much as he is constrained by the inflexible law of his condition. There is no philosopher of such great parts in the world, but that he believes a million of things on the faith of other people, and supposes a great many more truths than he demonstrates. This is not only necessary but desirable. A man who should undertake to inquire into everything for himself, could devote to each thing but little time and attention. His task

第二章　民主国家信仰的主要来源

在不同的时期，教条式信仰也会有多有少。这些信仰的产生方式不同，其对象和形式也会有所改变。但是，教条式的信仰绝不会消失，换句话说，人们永远不会停止对某些信仰不加论证便欣然接受。如果每个人都力图形成自己的观点，并独自沿着自己开辟的道路寻求真理，那么就不会有很多人愿意团结在任何一个共同的信仰之下。但是，显然没有这样一个共同的信仰社会就无法发展，也许说社会就无法存在更为合适。因为没有共同的思想就不会有共同的行动，而没有共同的行动，尽管依然可能会有人的存在，但无法构成社会。为了社会的存在，特别是为了能让社会欣欣向荣，就需要通过某种主导观念将所有公民的思想集中并团结起来。但是，除非每个人的观念都系出同源，并愿意接受既有信仰中的一部分，否则是无法做到这一点的。

如果我现在单就一个人而论，会发现无论是为了单独一个人生活还是为了与他人共同协作，教条式信仰都是不可或缺的。如果一个人每天都要亲自证明日常自己所用到的所有真理，那么他的工作将永远没完没了，而且他还会因为验证前面的真理而精疲力竭无法再验证后面出现的真理。因为人的一生是短暂的，所以他没有时间，而且由于智力有限，也没有能力去那样做，结果他不得不信任许多自己没有时间也无力去证明却已经被人证实或大众认可的事实和真理。他只能在这个基础上构筑自己的思想大厦。他之所以采用这样的方式并非自愿而是迫于自身现有的状况不得已而为之。世界上没有一个哲学家不是通过相信别人的论断而认识许多事物，并接受大量未经自己验证的真理的。这样做不但有必要

would keep his mind in perpetual unrest, which would prevent him from penetrating to the depth of any truth, or of grappling his mind indissolubly to any conviction. His intellect would be at once independent and powerless. He must therefore make his choice from amongst the various objects of human belief, and he must adopt many opinions without discussion, in order to search the better into that smaller number which he sets apart for investigation. It is true that whoever receives an opinion on the word of another, does so far enslave his mind; but it is a salutary servitude which allows him to make a good use of freedom.

A principle of authority must then always occur, under all circumstances, in some part or other of the moral and intellectual world. Its place is variable, but a place it necessarily has. The independence of individual minds may be greater, or it may be less: unbounded it cannot be. Thus the question is, not to know whether any intellectual authority exists in the ages of democracy, but simply where it resides and by what standard it is to be measured.

I have shown in the preceding chapter how the equality of conditions leads men to entertain a sort of instinctive incredulity of the supernatural, and a very lofty and often exaggerated opinion of the human understanding. The men who live at a period of social equality are not therefore easily led to place that intellectual authority to which they bow either beyond or above humanity. They commonly seek for the sources of truth in themselves, or in those who are like themselves. This would be enough to prove that at such periods no new religion could be established, and that all schemes for such a purpose would be not only impious but absurd and irrational. It may be foreseen that a democratic people will not easily give credence to divine missions; that they will turn modern prophets to a ready jest; and they that will seek to discover the chief arbiter of their belief within, and not beyond, the limits of their kind.

When the ranks of society are unequal, and men unlike each other in condition, there are some individuals invested with all the power of superior intelligence, learning, and enlightenment, whilst the multitude is sunk in ignorance and prejudice. Men living at these aristocratic periods are therefore naturally induced to shape their opinions by the superior standard of a person or a class of persons,

而且正是他之所想。一个凡事要亲自求证的人，只能给每件事情投入非常有限的时间和精力。这就会让他的思想始终处于不安的状态，从而无法深入研究任何一个真理，或是坚定不移地信守任何一种信仰。他的才智尽管独立，却也变得软弱了。因此，他必须在人类各种各样的信仰之中进行选择，并不加置疑地接受，而后选出少数几个问题留待深入研究。的确，仅听从他人一面之词便接受一个观点的人，只会让自己的精神受到奴役，但这却是可以让他充分利用自由的有益奴役。

无论何时，在智慧和道德的世界，权威的原则始终会存在。它的位置可能会有所不同，但是必定会有一席之地。个人思想的独立性可以有大有小，但不会不受控制。因此，问题不在于了解民主时代是否有智力权威，而是要知道它在哪里以及它的力量有多大。我在前面的一章中已经说明身份平等会让人们对超自然的东西产生本能的怀疑，并对人的判断力给予过高而且往往过分的评价。因此，生活在平等时代的人们不会将他们所信奉的智力权威放在超人的位置。他们通常会从自己或自己同类的身上寻找真理之源。这将足以证明在这样的时期不会产生新的宗教，而且所有创立新宗教的企图不但被视为亵渎神灵，而且还被认为荒谬不合理。可以预见，一个民主国家的人们不会轻易相信神的使者，还会让现代的先知成为笑柄，并将在他们之中而不是之外去寻找自己信仰的主宰。

当社会等级不平等的时候，人们的状况彼此不同，有一些人会集所有超群的智慧、知识和见识于一身，而同时，大批人会非常无知而狭隘。因此，生活在贵族制度时代的人自然会将某一个人或是一个阶级的高级标准作为自己的思想指南，同时还不愿承认群众永远

whilst they are averse to recognize the infallibility of the mass of the people.

The contrary takes place in ages of equality. The nearer the citizens are drawn to the common level of an equal and similar condition, the less prone does each man become to place implicit faith in a certain man or a certain class of men. But his readiness to believe the multitude increases, and opinion is more than ever mistress of the world. Not only is common opinion the only guide which private judgment retains amongst a democratic people, but amongst such a people it possesses a power infinitely beyond what it has elsewhere. At periods of equality men have no faith in one another, by reason of their common resemblance; but this very resemblance gives them almost unbounded confidence in the judgment of the public; for it would not seem probable, as they are all endowed with equal means of judging, but that the greater truth should go with the greater number.

When the inhabitant of a democratic country compares himself individually with all those about him, he feels with pride that he is the equal of any one of them; but when he comes to survey the totality of his fellows, and to place himself in contrast to so huge a body, he is instantly overwhelmed by the sense of his own insignificance and weakness. The same equality which renders him independent of each of his fellow-citizens taken severally, exposes him alone and unprotected to the influence of the greater number. The public has therefore among a democratic people a singular power, of which aristocratic nations could never so much as conceive an idea; for it does not persuade to certain opinions, but it enforces them, and infuses them into the faculties by a sort of enormous pressure of the minds of all upon the reason of each.

In the United States the majority undertakes to supply a multitude of ready-made opinions for the use of individuals, who are thus relieved from the necessity of forming opinions of their own. Everybody there adopts great numbers of theories, on philosophy, morals, and politics, without inquiry, upon public trust; and if we look to it very narrowly, it will be perceived that religion herself holds her sway there, much less as a doctrine of revelation than as a commonly received opinion. The fact that the political laws of the Americans are such that the majority rules the community with sovereign sway, materially increases the power which that majority naturally exercises over

是正确的。而在平等的时代，情形与此恰恰相反。公民间越是日益平等和彼此趋同，人们就越不会盲目相信某一个人或是某一个阶级。于是相信群众的趋势会不断加强，而且将成为主宰社会的观点。公众的观点不但是民主社会个人判断力的唯一指导，而且拥有比任何社会都要强大的力量。在平等的时代，因为彼此相似，所以并不信赖他人，但是这种相似性却让他们无限信任公众的判断力，而且因为他们都拥有同等的认识水平，所以真理掌握在大多数人手中。

当民主国家的居民拿自己与身边的人比较的时候，会骄傲地感到他与每个人一样平等。但是当他审视全体同胞的时候，自己与如此大的一个团体形成鲜明对比，又往往会因自己的微不足道和渺小而自惭形秽。同样的平等让他觉得自己能独立于每个同胞的面前，但也让他感到在多数面前孤立无援。因此，民主国家的大众拥有贵族国家无法想象的强大力量。因为它不是用说服的办法，而是通过给每个人的理性施加强大的压力，将观点加诸并渗透到人们的头脑。

在美国，多数提供大量现成的观点给个人使用，因此人们没有必要再酝酿自己的观点。在这里，每个人基于对公众的信任，毫不置疑地大量采用公众的哲学、道德和政治观点。如果再进一步观察，会发现宗教本身更多是作为共同的既有观念而不是神启的教条在社会中发挥统治作用。美国人的政治法律是多数对社会进行绝对统治的法律，这就使得多数对人思想的自然支配力量得到极大加强。因为，人们最习惯于认为压迫自己的人在智慧上高于

the mind. For nothing is more customary in man than to recognize superior wisdom in the person of his oppressor. This political omnipotence of the majority in the United States doubtless augments the influence which public opinion would obtain without it over the mind of each member of the community; but the foundations of that influence do not rest upon it. They must be sought for in the principle of equality itself, not in the more or less popular institutions which men living under that condition may give themselves. The intellectual dominion of the greater number would probably be less absolute amongst a democratic people governed by a king than in the sphere of a pure democracy, but it will always be extremely absolute; and by whatever political laws men are governed in the ages of equality, it may be foreseen that faith in public opinion will become a species of religion there, and the majority its ministering prophet.

Thus intellectual authority will be different, but it will not be diminished; and far from thinking that it will disappear, I augur that it may readily acquire too much preponderance, and confine the action of private judgment within narrower limits than are suited either to the greatness or the happiness of the human race. In the principle of equality I very clearly discern two tendencies; the one leading the mind of every man to untried thoughts, the other inclined to prohibit him from thinking at all. And I perceive how, under the dominion of certain laws, democracy would extinguish that liberty of the mind to which a democratic social condition is favorable; so that, after having broken all the bondage once imposed on it by ranks or by men, the human mind would be closely fettered to the general will of the greatest number.

If the absolute power of the majority were to be substituted by democratic nations, for all the different powers which checked or retarded overmuch the energy of individual minds, the evil would only have changed its symptoms. Men would not have found the means of independent life; they would simply have invented (no easy task) a new dress for servitude. There is—and I cannot repeat it too often—there is in this matter for profound reflection for those who look on freedom as a holy thing, and who hate not only the despot, but despotism. For myself, when I feel the hand of power lie heavy on my brow, I care but little to know who oppresses me; and I am not the more disposed to pass beneath the yoke, because it is held out to me by the arms of a million of men.

自己。在美国多数的无限政治权威无疑增强了公众舆论原本对每个社会成员思想的影响力，但是这并不是这种影响力的基础。它们应该去平等原则本身中寻找，而不是在平等的人们建立的或多或少人拥护的制度中寻找。绝大多数的精神统治可能在国王统治的民主社会不如在纯粹的民主社会来得绝对，但毕竟是非常绝对的。而且在民主时代，无论人们采用什么样的法律进行统治，都可以预见对公众舆论的信仰将成为一种以多数为先知的宗教。

因此，智力权威虽然会有所不同，但绝不会被削弱，而且我认为它非但不会消失，反而会强大起来，并将个人判断力限定在与人类的伟大和幸福不相称的更狭小的范围。我非常清楚地看到平等有两个趋势：一个将人的思想引向未经实验的想法，另一个趋向于让人不去思考。我注意到，在某些特定法律的统治下，民主将会使有利于民主社会状况的思想自由覆灭，所以，人类思想在打破某个阶级或某个人原先加诸它的束缚之后，将被大多数人的普遍一直牢牢禁锢起来。

如果多数的绝对权力在民主国家取代所有阻碍或推迟个人思想飞速发展的不同力量，那么这只是换汤不换药。人们依然没有找到独立生活的办法，不过是给奴役换上一件新衣罢了。因此，我不免在这里再次重复，凡是将自由视为神圣事业的人，凡是那些不但憎恨暴君而且憎恨专制的人，都应该三思而行。于我自己，当我感到权力之手在我面前飞舞的时候，我并不在意是谁压迫我，而是打算俯首听命套上枷锁，因为在我面前有千万只举着枷锁的手。

Chapter III: Why The Americans Display More Readiness And More Taste For General Ideas Than Their Forefathers, The English.

The Deity does not regard the human race collectively. He surveys at one glance and severally all the beings of whom mankind is composed, and he discerns in each man the resemblances which assimilate him to all his fellows, and the differences which distinguish him from them. God, therefore, stands in no need of general ideas; that is to say, he is never sensible of the necessity of collecting a considerable number of analogous objects under the same form for greater convenience in thinking. Such is, however, not the case with man. If the human mind were to attempt to examine and pass a judgment on all the individual cases before it, the immensity of detail would soon lead it astray and bewilder its discernment: in this strait, man has recourse to an imperfect but necessary expedient, which at once assists and demonstrates his weakness. Having superficially considered a certain number of objects, and remarked their resemblance, he assigns to them a common name, sets them apart, and proceeds onwards.

General ideas are no proof of the strength, but rather of the insufficiency of the human intellect; for there are in nature no beings exactly alike, no things precisely identical, nor any rules indiscriminately and alike applicable to several objects at once. The chief merit of general ideas is, that they enable the human mind to pass a rapid judgment on a great many objects at once; but, on the other hand, the notions they convey are never otherwise than incomplete, and they always cause the mind to lose as much in accuracy as it gains in comprehensiveness. As social bodies advance in civilization, they acquire the knowledge of new facts, and they daily lay hold almost unconsciously of some particular truths. The more truths of this kind a man apprehends, the more general ideas is he naturally led to conceive. A multitude of particular facts cannot be seen separately, without at last discovering the common tie which connects them. Several individuals lead to the perception of the species; several species to that of the genus. Hence the habit and the taste for general ideas will always be greatest amongst a people of ancient cultivation and extensive knowledge.

But there are other reasons which impel men to generalize their ideas, or which restrain them from it.

The Americans are much more addicted to the use of general ideas than the English, and entertain

第三章　为什么美国人比其祖先英国人更倾向和喜好一般观念

上帝不会从头到脚地看待人类。他只需一瞥就可以看清人性中包含的一切东西，他能从每个人身上看到人们的相似点和不同点。因此，上帝不需要一般的观念，也就是说上帝从未感到有必要将大量的类似的对象置于同样的形式下，以便于更好地思考。但是，人类并非如此。如果人的头脑想要对其面前的所有的个例进行观察并加以判断，庞杂的细枝末节不久就会令他误入歧途或是如坠云雾。在这样的窘境中，人便求助于一种虽不完美却很有必要的办法，这一办法在补救人类弱点的同时也暴露了人的弱点。在对一定量的对象进行表面观察，发现他们的相似之后，给它们起一个共同的名称，而后搁置一边继续考察其他对象。

一般观点非但无法证明人类智慧的强大，反而证明了人类智慧的不足。因为在大自然中，没有完全一样的东西，绝没有两个一模一样的事情，也没有可以不加区分同时适用于多个对象的规则。一般观点的主要优势在于它可以让人类思想同时对大量事物做出迅速判断，但另一方面，它从来无法给予完整的概念，让人们理解到的东西总是不够准确。随着社会开化，他们获得新的认知，而且几乎每天在不知不觉中获得某些个别真理。人们领悟的这种真理越多，就越能够自然而然地得到更多的一般观念。找不到将这些大量个别事实联系起来的纽带，就无法将它们分开单独观察。几个个体可以形成种的概念，几个种则可以形成类的概念。因此，越是文化历史悠久知识广泛的国家，越是习惯和偏爱一般观念。

但是也有一些其他原因可以促使或阻碍人们把观念一般化。

a much greater relish for them: this appears very singular at first sight, when it is remembered that the two nations have the same origin, that they lived for centuries under the same laws, and that they still incessantly interchange their opinions and their manners. This contrast becomes much more striking still, if we fix our eyes on our own part of the world, and compare together the two most enlightened nations which inhabit it. It would seem as if the mind of the English could only tear itself reluctantly and painfully away from the observation of particular facts, to rise from them to their causes; and that it only generalizes in spite of itself. Amongst the French, on the contrary, the taste for general ideas would seem to have grown to so ardent a passion, that it must be satisfied on every occasion. I am informed, every morning when I wake, that some general and eternal law has just been discovered, which I never heard mentioned before. There is not a mediocre scribbler who does not try his hand at discovering truths applicable to a great kingdom, and who is very ill pleased with himself if he does not succeed in compressing the human race into the compass of an article. So great a dissimilarity between two very enlightened nations surprises me. If I again turn my attention to England, and observe the events which have occurred there in the last half-century, I think I may affirm that a taste for general ideas increases in that country in proportion as its ancient constitution is weakened.

The state of civilization is therefore insufficient by itself to explain what suggests to the human mind the love of general ideas, or diverts it from them. When the conditions of men are very unequal, and inequality itself is the permanent state of society, individual men gradually become so dissimilar that each class assumes the aspect of a distinct race: only one of these classes is ever in view at the same instant; and losing sight of that general tie which binds them all within the vast bosom of mankind, the observation invariably rests not on man, but on certain men. Those who live in this aristocratic state of society never, therefore, conceive very general ideas respecting themselves, and that is enough to imbue them with an habitual distrust of such ideas, and an instinctive aversion of them. He, on the contrary, who inhabits a democratic country, sees around him, one very hand, men differing but little from each other; he cannot turn his mind to any one portion of mankind, without expanding and dilating his thought till it embrace the whole. All the truths which are applicable to

美国人比英国人更沉溺于使用一般观念，也更喜欢一般观念。两个同宗的国家，在同样的法律下生活几个世纪，至今依然不断有思想和民情的交流，这使得这种情况初看起来让人觉得非常奇怪。如果我们将眼光集中在居住在欧洲这里的两个最开化的民族，其对比会更为鲜明惊人。看上去英国人的思想只是极不情愿、非常痛苦地脱离对个别事物的观察，因为他们要通过这种观察寻找原因，而且英国人接受一般观念也并非出于自愿。法国人则与之相反，他们对一般观念的爱好已经达到凡事都要满足这种热爱的地步。我每天早上一起床，总会有人告诉我人们发现了我以前从未听说过的某个普遍的永久法则。哪怕是一个平庸的三流作家也试图要发现可用于治国的大道理，如果他没能在文章中把全人类都写进去，一定会对自己很不满意。两个最开化民族之间如此巨大的差异让我震惊。如果我再将注意力转向英国，观察最近半个世纪这里发生的事情，我可以肯定，随着古老制度的削弱，这个国家对于一般观念的爱好得到加强。

因此，仅凭文明状态不足以解释人们对一般观念的喜爱和回避。当人们处于非常不平等的状况，而且这种不平等状态将一直存在下去时，人与人会逐渐变得越来越不同，以至于有多少种不同的人就有多少个阶级，而人们只会同时注意一个阶级，而看不到将所有阶级汇集于广大人群中的一般纽带，无疑人们只注意到个别人，而忽略了一般的人。所以，在贵族社会生活过的人们不会产生有关自己的一般观念，而且足以让他们习惯性地产生对一般观念的不信任，以及对一般观念的本能厌恶。相反，生活在民主社会的人环顾身边，人们彼此没有太大差别，所以不会只专注任何一部分人，而是将他的视野扩展到全人

himself, appear to him equally and similarly applicable to each of his fellow-citizens and fellow-men. Having contracted the habit of generalizing his ideas in the study which engages him most, and interests him more than others, he transfers the same habit to all his pursuits; and thus it is that the craving to discover general laws in everything, to include a great number of objects under the same formula, and to explain a mass of facts by a single cause, becomes an ardent, and sometimes an undiscerning, passion in the human mind.

Nothing shows the truth of this proposition more clearly than the opinions of the ancients respecting their slaves. The most profound and capacious minds of Rome and Greece were never able to reach the idea, at once so general and so simple, of the common likeness of men, and of the common birthright of each to freedom: they strove to prove that slavery was in the order of nature, and that it would always exist. Nay, more, everything shows that those of the ancients who had passed from the servile to the free condition, many of whom have left us excellent writings, did themselves regard servitude in no other light.

All the great writers of antiquity belonged to the aristocracy of masters, or at least they saw that aristocracy established and uncontested before their eyes. Their mind, after it had expanded itself in several directions, was barred from further progress in this one; and the advent of Jesus Christ upon earth was required to teach that all the members of the human race are by nature equal and alike.

In the ages of equality all men are independent of each other, isolated and weak. The movements of the multitude are not permanently guided by the will of any individuals; at such times humanity seems always to advance of itself. In order, therefore, to explain what is passing in the world, man is driven to seek for some great causes, which, acting in the same manner on all our fellow-creatures, thus impel them all involuntarily to pursue the same track. This again naturally leads the human mind to conceive general ideas, and superinduces a taste for them.

I have already shown in what way the equality of conditions leads every man to investigate truths for himself. It may readily be perceived that a method of this kind must insensibly beget a tendency to general ideas in the human mind. When I repudiate the traditions of rank, profession, and birth;

类。凡是可以应用于自身的真理，在他看来似乎都可以同样应用到他的每一个同胞或同类的身上。他只要在自己最投入、最感兴趣的研究中染上喜欢一般概念的习惯，就会把这种习惯带到所有的工作中。因此，发现所有事物的共同法则，将大量的事物概括在同一形式之下，并用同一个原因解释大量事物的渴望成为人们思想的一种强烈有时甚至是盲目的热情。

古代人对奴隶的看法能够最清晰地表明这一真理。古罗马和希腊最深刻最渊博的头脑也没有参透如此普遍又如此简单的一个道理，即人是相似的，自由是共同的与生俱来的权利。他们试图证明奴隶制符合自然规律，而且将永久存在下去。然而，所有的一切都在证明古代那些在获得自由前曾是奴隶的人之中，有很多都曾给我们留下不朽的名作。

古代所有的伟大作家都属于奴隶主贵族阶级，或者至少是见证了当时贵族制度的建立并认为无可厚非的人。尽管他们的思想向四面八方延伸，但就是没能超出原有的圈子。只有耶稣基督降生之后，他才教导人们说：所有人类成员生下来是一样的，平等的。

在平等的时代，所有人都各自独立，孤独而无力。多数的活动不应一直受到任何个人意志的左右，在这样的时代，人类似乎自行前进。因此，为了解释世界上发生的事情，人们不得不去寻找某些重要的原因，这些原因会对我们所有人产生同样的影响并让我们自愿地走上同一条道路。而这又会让人类的头脑自然而然地去追求一般观念，并让人们爱上一般观念。

我已经说过平等是如何引导每个人亲自寻求真理的。不难看出，这种方法必然会不知

when I escape from the authority of example, to seek out, by the single effort of my reason, the path to be followed, I am inclined to derive the motives of my opinions from human nature itself; which leads me necessarily, and almost unconsciously, to adopt a great number of very general notions.

All that I have here said explains the reasons for which the English display much less readiness and taste or the generalization of ideas than their American progeny, and still less again than their French neighbors; and likewise the reason for which the English of the present day display more of these qualities than their forefathers did. The English have long been a very enlightened and a very aristocratic nation; their enlightened condition urged them constantly to generalize, and their aristocratic habits confined them to particularize. Hence arose that philosophy, at once bold and timid, broad and narrow, which has hitherto prevailed in England, and which still obstructs and stagnates in so many minds in that country.

Independently of the causes I have pointed out in what goes before, others may be discerned less apparent, but no less efficacious, which engender amongst almost every democratic people a taste, and frequently a passion, for general ideas. An accurate distinction must be taken between ideas of this kind. Some are the result of slow, minute, and conscientious labor of the mind, and these extend the sphere of human knowledge; others spring up at once from the first rapid exercise of the wits, and beget none but very superficial and very uncertain notions. Men who live in ages of equality have a great deal of curiosity and very little leisure; their life is so practical, so confused, so excited, so active, that but little time remains to them for thought. Such men are prone to general ideas because they spare them the trouble of studying particulars; they contain, if I may so speak, a great deal in a little compass, and give, in a little time, a great return. If then, upon a brief and inattentive investigation, a common relation is thought to be detected between certain obtects, inquiry is not pushed any further; and without examining in detail how far these different objects differ or agree, they are hastily arranged under one formulary, in order to pass to another subject.

One of the distinguishing characteristics of a democratic period is the taste all men have at such ties for easy success and present enjoyment. This occurs in the pursuits of the intellect as well as in

不觉令人类思维倾向于一般观念。当我批判阶级、职业和出身的传统时，当我脱离先例的影响而完全靠自己的理性努力寻求自己的道路时，我倾向于从人类的本性中发现自己的观念产生的原因，这必然在不知不觉之中用到大量的一般观念。

上述所有内容，就是要说明英国人为什么不如他们的后裔美国人和邻居法国人那样愿意且热衷将概念一般化，以及今天的英国人为什么在这方面比他们的祖先走得远。英国长久以来是一个非常开化，恪守贵族制度的国家。他们的文明程度促使他们不断追求一般观念，而他们的贵族习惯又将他们限制于个别观念。因此，英国人的哲学既大胆又羞怯，既豁达又狭隘。时至今日，这样的哲学依旧在英国盛行，并阻碍、限制很多人的思想。

除了我前面已经提到过的原因，还有另外一些不十分明显但作用不容小觑的原因会令几乎每个民主国家的人们热爱并不断追求一般观念。所以必须对这些一般观念加以准确区分。有些一般观念是人类长期细致自觉的智力活动的结果，人类知识的延伸就属于这一类。另一些一般观念则是智慧灵光一现的结果，但形成的观念往往非常肤浅也靠不住。生活在平等时代的人们好奇心多而闲心少，他们生活得如此务实、复杂、紧张和活跃，以至于几乎没有时间用来思考。这样的人往往喜欢一般观念，因为可以不用去操心个别事物。如果可以，我甚至会这样说，他们将大量的东西保存在一个小的容器中，用有限的时间取得巨大的回报。那么，人们就会在做过一次短暂而不够深入的考察之后，便认为已经发现两个特定事物之间的共同联系，于是不再做进一步的深入研究，也不详细考察这些不同的事物之间有多少的区别和相似，为了能够进行下一个主题，而是匆匆将它们归为一类。

all others. Most of those who live at a time of equality are full of an ambition at once aspiring and relaxed: they would fain succeed brilliantly and at once, but they would be dispensed from great efforts to obtain success. These conflicting tendencies lead straight to the research of general ideas, by aid of which they flatter themselves that they can figure very importantly at a small expense, and draw the attention of the public with very little trouble. And I know not whether they be wrong in thinking thus. For their readers are as much averse to investigating anything to the bottom as they can be themselves; and what is generally sought in the productions of the mind is easy pleasure and information without labor.

If aristocratic nations do not make sufficient use of general ideas, and frequently treat them with inconsiderate disdain, it is true, on the other hand, that a democratic people is ever ready to carry ideas of this kind to excess, and to espouse the with injudicious warmth.

Chapter IV: Why The Americans Have Never Been So Eager As The French For General Ideas In Political Matters

I observed in the last chapter, that the Americans show a less decided taste for general ideas than the French; this is more especially true in political matters. Although the Americans infuse into their legislation infinitely more general ideas than the English, and although they pay much more attention than the latter people to the adjustment of the practice of affairs to theory, no political bodies in the United States have ever shown so warm an attachment to general ideas as the Constituent Assembly and the Convention in France. At no time has the American people laid hold on ideas of this kind with the passionate energy of the French people in the eighteenth century, or displayed the same blind confidence in the value and absolute truth of any theory. This difference between the Americans and the French originates in several causes, but principally in the following one. The Americans form a democratic people, which has always itself directed public affairs. The French are a democratic people, who, for a long time, could only speculate on the best manner of conducting them. The social condition of France led that people to conceive very general ideas on the subject of government, whilst its political

民主时代的显著特征之一就是所有人都喜欢轻而易举地获得成功，贪图眼前的享乐。对知识的追求是如此，对其他的一切也是如此。生活在平等时代的大多数人野心勃勃，失败了会立即萎靡，成功后则更加活跃。他们希望能够立即取得辉煌的胜利，但是又不愿为成功付出巨大努力。这样矛盾的倾向促使他们直接寻求一般观念，他们会自夸通过利用一般观念没费多大功夫就描绘出大千世界的图景，而且不费吹灰之力就得到公众的关注。我不知道他们的想法到底是不是错的。因为他们的读者跟他们一样，讨厌追根究底，而总是希望不经努力就可以痛快享受并获得知识。

如果贵族制度的国家说没有充分利用一般观念，并不断对其不屑一顾，那么，民主国家则刚好相反，它随时想要滥用一般观念，并对其盲目追捧。

第四章　为什么美国人从来没有像法国人那样如此热衷于政治上的一般观念

在上一章中我说过美国人不像法国人那样热衷于一般观念，这特别表现在政治上。尽管美国人在立法上注入的一般观念比英国人多得不计其数，尽管他们比英国人注重用实践武装理论，但是在美国却没有任何政治机构对一般观念曾表现出如法国制宪会议和国民公会一样的热情。美利坚民族对一般观念从未表现出如18世纪法国人一般的激情能量，或是表现出对任何理论的价值和真实性的盲目信任。美国人和法国人之间的不同原因有很多，但主要原因如下：美国人形成的一个民主民族，一直由自己管理公共事务。法国人也是一个民主的民族，但是长期以来只停留在口头上议论如何管理公共事务。法国的社会状况引

constitution prevented it from correcting those ideas by experiment, and from gradually detecting their insufficiency; whereas in America the two things constantly balance and correct each other.

It may seem, at first sight, that this is very much opposed to what I have said before, that democratic nations derive their love of theory from the excitement of their active life. A more attentive examination will show that there is nothing contradictory in the proposition. Men living in democratic countries eagerly lay hold of general ideas because they have but little leisure, and because these ideas spare them the trouble of studying particulars. This is true; but it is only to be understood to apply to those matters which are not the necessary and habitual subjects of their thoughts. Mercantile men will take up very eagerly, and without any very close scrutiny, all the general ideas on philosophy, politics, science, or the arts, which may be presented to them; but for such as relate to commerce, they will not receive them without inquiry, or adopt them without reserve. The same thing applies to statesmen with regard to general ideas in politics. If, then, there be a subject upon which a democratic people is peculiarly liable to abandon itself, blindly and extravagantly, to general ideas, the best corrective that can be used will be to make that subject a part of the daily practical occupation of that people. The people will then be compelled to enter upon its details, and the details will teach them the weak points of the theory. This remedy may frequently be a painful one, but its effect is certain.

Thus it happens, that the democratic institutions which compel every citizen to take a practical part in the government, moderate that excessive taste for general theories in politics which the principle of equality suggests.

Chapter V: Of The Manner In Which Religion In The United States Avails Itself Of Democratic Tendencies

I have laid it down in a preceding chapter that men cannot do without dogmatical belief; and even that it is very much to be desired that such belief should exist amongst them. I now add, that of all the kinds of dogmatical belief the most desirable appears to me to be dogmatical belief in matters

导我们想出一些有关政府工作的一般观念，而其政治制度却阻碍通过实践慢慢发现其不足并予以纠正。但是在美国，这两者相互适应，互相修正。

初看起来，这跟我之前所说的民主国家对理论的热爱源自积极生活带来的兴奋的观点大相径庭，但是只要仔细观察就会发现其间并不矛盾。生活在民主国家的人们之所以非常渴望一般观念，是因为他们没有闲暇时间，而且这样的观念可以不用操心去考察个别事物。这固然是事实，但这样的说法只适用于那些他们不常想不必想的问题。商人会非常热衷于接受，同时也不会细致推敲，那些别人提供给他们的有关哲学、政治、科学或艺术方面的一般观念，但是，对那些与商业相关的一般观念他们则不会无条件接受，而是会有保留地接受。政治家对有关政治的一般观念也持有相同的态度。那么，如果民主国家针对一个特别危险的问题盲目过分地追求一般观念，最好的办法就是让它成为人们民日常时间活动的一部分。这样，人们就不得不深入到问题的细节，而这些细节会让他们发现理论的缺陷。这样的解决办法往往会令人痛苦不堪，但却非常有效。

因此，强迫每个公民实际参与政府管理的民主制度能够中和平等带来的人们对政治上的一般观念的过度热衷。

第五章　在美国宗教采用何种方式利用民主的倾向

在前面的一章里，我已经说过没有教条式信仰人们无法生活下去，而且人们甚至对这样的信仰非常渴望。现在我还要补充，在各式各样的教条式信仰中，我认为有关宗教方面

of religion; and this is a very clear inference, even from no higher consideration than the interests of this world. There is hardly any human action, however particular a character be assigned to it, which does not originate in some very general idea men have conceived of the Deity, of his relation to mankind, of the nature of their own souls, and of their duties to their fellow-creatures. Nor can anything prevent these ideas from being the common spring from which everything else emanates. Men are therefore immeasurably interested in acquiring fixed ideas of God, of the soul, and of their common duties to their Creator and to their fellow-men; for doubt on these first principles would abandon all their actions to the impulse of chance, and would condemn them to live, to a certain extent, powerless and undisciplined.

This is then the subject on which it is most important for each of us to entertain fixed ideas; and unhappily it is also the subject on which it is most difficult for each of us, left to himself, to settle his opinions by the sole force of his reason. None but minds singularly free from the ordinary anxieties of life—minds at once penetrating, subtle, and trained by thinking—can even with the assistance of much time and care, sound the depth of these most necessary truths. And, indeed, we see that these philosophers are themselves almost always enshrouded in uncertainties; that at every step the natural light which illuminates their path grows dimmer and less secure; and that, in spite of all their efforts, they have as yet only discovered a small number of conflicting notions, on which the mind of man has been tossed about for thousands of years, without either laying a firmer grasp on truth, or finding novelty even in its errors. Studies of this nature are far above the average capacity of men; and even if the majority of mankind were capable of such pursuits, it is evident that leisure to cultivate them would still be wanting. Fixed ideas of God and human nature are indispensable to the daily practice of men's lives; but the practice of their lives prevents them from acquiring such ideas.

The difficulty appears to me to be without a parallel. Amongst the sciences there are some which are useful to the mass of mankind, and which are within its reach; others can only be approached by the few, and are not cultivated by the many, who require nothing beyond their more remote applications: but the daily practice of the science I speak of is indispensable to all, although the study

的教条式信仰人们最为渴望，哪怕只是从现世利益出发，也能轻松得出这一结论。人类的行为，无论其特殊性如何，都源自他对上帝、对自己与人类关系、对自己灵魂的本性以及对同类应承担的义务所持的一般观念。没有什么能够阻止这些观念成为所有事物产生的共同源泉。因此，人们极度渴望获得与上帝、灵魂以及对造物主和同类应承担责任有关的确定无疑的观念。因为对这些基本问题的怀疑会令自己的行动听任偶然因素的摆布，并在一定程度上，会让他们变得虚弱且混乱不堪。

那么，在这些问题上拥有确定无疑的观念对我们每个人至关重要，而且不幸的是，有关这些问题一般观念也是仅靠我们个人一己之力只运用个人的理性最难以取得的。只有摆脱日常琐事的困扰，细致入微、训练有素的人，经过长期细心的思考之后，才能发现那些最必不可少的真理。而且，我们看到那些哲学家自己也总是满腹狐疑，他们每前进一步，照耀前路的自然之光总是忽明忽暗，尽管他们已经倾尽全力，发现的也不过是些自相矛盾的观点。几千年来，人们反复琢磨这些观念，既无法将真理牢牢握紧，甚至也没能发现新的错误。这样的研究远非一般人能力所及，而即使大部分人有能力做这样的研究，显然，他们也没有这份闲暇。有关上帝和人性的固定观念是人日常生活实践所不可或缺的，但是他们的日常生活实践又妨碍他们获得这样的观念。

在我看来，其困难程度绝无仅有。在人类科学中，有一些知识对人类有益而且依靠自己的能力可以学会，而其他的一些只有少数人才能学会，并远远超越了大多数人的理解能力。尽管大多数人无法研究这样的科学，但是每个人又不可避免地要在日常生活实践中用

of it is inaccessible to the far greater number.

General ideas respecting God and human nature are therefore the ideas above all others which it is most suitable to withdraw from the habitual action of private judgment, and in which there is most to gain and least to lose by recognizing a principle of authority. The first object and one of the principal advantages of religions, is to furnish to each of these fundamental questions a solution which is at once clear, precise, intelligible to the mass of mankind, and lasting. There are religions which are very false and very absurd; but it may be affirmed, that any religion which remains within the circle I have just traced, without aspiring to go beyond it (as many religions have attempted to do, for the purpose of enclosing on every side the free progress of the human mind), imposes a salutary restraint on the intellect; and it must be admitted that, if it do not save men in another world, such religion is at least very conducive to their happiness and their greatness in this. This is more especially true of men living in free countries. When the religion of a people is destroyed, doubt gets hold of the highest portions of the intellect, and half paralyzes all the rest of its powers. Every man accustoms himself to entertain none but confused and changing notions on the subjects most interesting to his fellow-creatures and himself. His opinions are ill-defended and easily abandoned: and, despairing of ever resolving by himself the hardest problems of the destiny of man, he ignobly submits to think no more about them. Such a condition cannot but enervate the soul, relax the springs of the will, and prepare a people for servitude. Nor does it only happen, in such a case, that they allow their freedom to be wrested from them; they frequently themselves surrender it. When there is no longer any principle of authority in religion any more than in politics, men are speedily frightened at the aspect of this unbounded independence. The constant agitation of all surrounding things alarms and exhausts them. As everything is at sea in the sphere of the intellect, they determine at least that the mechanism of society should be firm and fixed; and as they cannot resume their ancient belief, they assume a master.

For my own part, I doubt whether man can ever support at the same time complete religious independence and entire public freedom. And I am inclined to think, that if faith be wanting in him, he must serve; and if he be free, he must believe.

到它。

因此，有关上帝和人性的一般观念是所有观念中首当其冲应该避免个人理性的习惯性行为的观念。而且对于个人理性而言，承认权威的存在，得之甚多而失之甚少。宗教的首要目的和主要优势之一就是能够给这些基本问题提供清晰、准确、人人都理解以及永久的解答。有一些宗教虚伪而荒谬，但是可以肯定，任何宗教只要保持在我所说的范围之内，而不妄图逾越这个范围（因为有些宗教试图从各方面压制人类思想的自由发展），就会对智力活动进行有益的规范，而且必须承认，即使宗教不能在来世拯救人们，至少会对他们今生的幸福和高尚大有裨益。对于生活在自由国家的人们来说尤其如此。当一个国家的宗教受到破坏时，智力最高的那部分人会满腹狐疑，而其余的所有人则多半处于麻痹状态。每个人习惯对于那些与自己和同胞最有利害关系的事物持混乱、变化不定的观念。个人观点无法得到捍卫，很容易被弃之一边。他们因无法独自解决有关人类命运的重大问题而感到绝望，于是便自暴自弃不再去想它们。然而，这样的情况只能令人精神萎靡，意志松懈，成为任人奴役的民族。当一个民族陷入这样的窘境，他们不但会听凭自己的自由被剥夺，往往还会自愿献出自由。当在宗教界和政界一样权威不复存在，人们马上会对这种无限独立的状况感到恐慌。周边所有事物的持续动荡会令人们惊恐不安，精疲力竭。因为在精神世界一切都发生了动摇，所以人们下决心要在物质世界建立牢固不变的秩序，但是他们已经无法再重拾往日的信仰，把自己交付给一个人。

就我而言，我不确定人是否能够永远做到在保持宗教完全独立的同时保持政治的完全

Perhaps, however, this great utility of religions is still more obvious amongst nations where equality of conditions prevails than amongst others. It must be acknowledged that equality, which brings great benefits into the world, nevertheless suggests to men (as will be shown hereafter) some very dangerous propensities. It tends to isolate them from each other, to concentrate every man's attention upon himself; and it lays open the soul to an inordinate love of material gratification. The greatest advantage of religion is to inspire diametrically contrary principles. There is no religion which does not place the object of man's desires above and beyond the treasures of earth, and which does not naturally raise his soul to regions far above those of the senses. Nor is there any which does not impose on man some sort of duties to his kind, and thus draws him at times from the contemplation of himself. This occurs in religions the most false and dangerous. Religious nations are therefore naturally strong on the very point on which democratic nations are weak; which shows of what importance it is for men to preserve their religion as their conditions become more equal.

I have neither the right nor the intention of examining the supernatural means which God employs to infuse religious belief into the heart of man. I am at this moment considering religions in a purely human point of view: my object is to inquire by what means they may most easily retain their sway in the democratic ages which we are entering. It has been shown that, at times of general cultivation and equality, the human mind does not consent to adopt dogmatical opinions without reluctance, and feels their necessity acutely in spiritual matters only. This proves, in the first place, that at such times religions ought, more cautiously than at any other, to confine themselves within their own precincts; for in seeking to extend their power beyond religious matters, they incur a risk of not being believed at all. The circle within which they seek to bound the human intellect ought therefore to be carefully traced, and beyond its verge the mind should be left in entire freedom to its own guidance. Mahommed professed to derive from Heaven, and he has inserted in the Koran, not only a body of religious doctrines, but political maxims, civil and criminal laws, and theories of science. The gospel, on the contrary, only speaks of the general relations of men to God and to each other—beyond which it inculcates and imposes no point of faith. This alone, besides a thousand other reasons,

自由。我一向认为，如果人没有信仰，必然遭到奴役，而如果人想要获得自由，就必须信仰宗教。

所以，宗教的这种巨大功效在趋向人人平等的国家比在其他国家都要更为显著。必须承认，给世界带来诸多好处的平等也让人们养成一些后面我将要谈到的非常危险的嗜好。它让人们日趋孤立，只关注自身，并向人们的灵魂敞开喜欢物质享受的大门。宗教的最大优势是能唤起与此相反的嗜好。没有任何一种宗教不是将人类追求的目标置于现世的物质财富之上，并让人的灵魂自然而然超越感觉世界来到更高尚的地方。也没有任何一种宗教不是教化人们要对人类承担某种责任，从而能够让他时常不是只顾自己。哪怕是最虚伪荒谬的宗教也是如此。因此，虔诚信奉宗教的国家的长处自然成为民主国家的弱点。这表明人们在实现平等的同时维护宗教是多么重要。

我既无权利也没有打算考察上帝所运用的将宗教深植人心的超自然手段。此刻我只是从纯粹的人类观点看待宗教。我的目的是探讨要通过什么样的手段它们才能最为轻而易举地在我们即将进入的民主时代保持自己的影响力。我已经说过，在普遍文明平等的时代，人类的头脑不会满足于毫无保留地接受教条式信仰，而让人的精神感到对这种信仰迫切需要的正是宗教。这首先证明在这样的时代，宗教要比在任何其他时代都要小心谨慎，不要让自己越出自己的领地。因为在寻求让自己的力量延伸到宗教范围之外的时候，要冒着失去所有信任的危险。因此，宗教应该小心划定自己的活动范围，并只在这一范围内对人类精神施以影响，而在这个范围之外，则应任其独立自主。穆罕默德自称从天而降，而其不

would suffice to prove that the former of these religions will never long predominate in a cultivated and democratic age, whilst the latter is destined to retain its sway at these as at all other periods.

But in continuation of this branch of the subject, I find that in order for religions to maintain their authority, humanly speaking, in democratic ages, they must not only confine themselves strictly within the circle of spiritual matters: their power also depends very much on the nature of the belief they inculcate, on the external forms they assume, and on the obligations they impose. The preceding observation, that equality leads men to very general and very extensive notions, is principally to be understood as applied to the question of religion. Men living in a similar and equal condition in the world readily conceive the idea of the one God, governing every man by the same laws, and granting to every man future happiness on the same conditions. The idea of the unity of mankind constantly leads them back to the idea of the unity of the Creator; whilst, on the contrary, in a state of society where men are broken up into very unequal ranks, they are apt to devise as many deities as there are nations, castes, classes, or families, and to trace a thousand private roads to heaven.

It cannot be denied that Christianity itself has felt, to a certain extent, the influence which social and political conditions exercise on religious opinions. At the epoch at which the Christian religion appeared upon earth, Providence, by whom the world was doubtless prepared for its coming, had gathered a large portion of the human race, like an immense flock, under the sceptre of the Caesars. The men of whom this multitude was composed were distinguished by numerous differences; but they had thus much in common, that they all obeyed the same laws, and that every subject was so weak and insignificant in relation to the imperial potentate, that all appeared equal when their condition was contrasted with his. This novel and peculiar state of mankind necessarily predisposed men to listen to the general truths which Christianity teaches, and may serve to explain the facility and rapidity with which they then penetrated into the human mind. The counterpart of this state of things was exhibited after the destruction of the empire. The Roman world being then as it were shattered into a thousand fragments, each nation resumed its pristine individuality. An infinite scale of ranks very soon grew up in the bosom of these nations; the different races were more sharply

仅将宗教信条还将政治原则、民法和刑法，以及科学理论嵌入《古兰经》。相反，《福音书》则只涉及人与上帝以及人与人的一般关系，除此之外并没有灌入任何观念信仰。抛开其他诸多理由不谈，仅此一点就足以证明前者的宗教不可能长期统治开化的民主时代，而后者在开化的民主时代注定会同在任何时代一样保有其影响力。

但是继续研究这一问题，就会发现从人类的立场来说为了能够让宗教在民主时代保持其权威，它们不但要严格地将自己限定在宗教的范畴之内，而且宗教的力量还很大程度上取决于它们所灌输的宗教信仰的性质、外在形式及其规定的义务。前面所说的平等会引导人们形成的非常一般和广泛的观念应主要从宗教方面来理解。生活在彼此相同平等世界中的人们很容易产生单一神的观念，认为他给每个人制定了同样的法则，并赋予每个人来世同样的幸福。人类一致性的观念不单促使他们产生造物主一致性的观念。与之相反，在一个人们被分成三六九等的社会，有多少民族、种姓、阶级就有多少神，并衍生出千万条通向天国之路。

不可否认，基督教本身在一定程度上感受到社会政治状况对宗教产生的影响。当基督教诞生的时候，上帝无疑已经为其到来做好准备，已将大部分人类聚集起来，置于罗马帝国的麾下。这一大群人虽然彼此有众多不同之处，但是有一点相同，他们都遵守同样的法律，而且相对于皇帝的伟大，每个人都很弱小微不足道，而在皇帝的面前，他们似乎又全部平等。这种全新的特殊的人类状态必然会令基督教宣扬的真理更容易为人所接受，这就能够解释为什么基督教能够如此顺利迅速地深入人心。在罗马帝国崩溃后，则出现了与

defined, and each nation was divided by castes into several peoples. In the midst of this common effort, which seemed to be urging human society to the greatest conceivable amount of voluntary subdivision, Christianity did not lose sight of the leading general ideas which it had brought into the world. But it appeared, nevertheless, to lend itself, as much as was possible, to those new tendencies to which the fractional distribution of mankind had given birth. Men continued to worship an only God, the Creator and Preserver of all things; but every people, every city, and, so to speak, every man, thought to obtain some distinct privilege, and win the favor of an especial patron at the foot of the Throne of Grace. Unable to subdivide the Deity, they multiplied and improperly enhanced the importance of the divine agents. The homage due to saints and angels became an almost idolatrous worship amongst the majority of the Christian world; and apprehensions might be entertained for a moment lest the religion of Christ should retrograde towards the superstitions which it had subdued. It seems evident, that the more the barriers are removed which separate nation from nation amongst mankind, and citizen from citizen amongst a people, the stronger is the bent of the human mind, as if by its own impulse, towards the idea of an only and all-powerful Being, dispensing equal laws in the same manner to every man. In democratic ages, then, it is more particularly important not to allow the homage paid to secondary agents to be confounded with the worship due to the Creator alone.

Another truth is no less clear—that religions ought to assume fewer external observances in democratic periods than at any others. In speaking of philosophical method among the Americans, I have shown that nothing is more repugnant to the human mind in an age of equality than the idea of subjection to forms. Men living at such times are impatient of figures; to their eyes symbols appear to be the puerile artifice which is used to conceal or to set off truths, which should more naturally be bared to the light of open day: they are unmoved by ceremonial observances, and they are predisposed to attach a secondary importance to the details of public worship. Those whose care it is to regulate the external forms of religion in a democratic age should pay a close attention to these natural propensities of the human mind, in order not unnecessarily to run counter to them. I firmly

此相反的情景。那时的罗马世界四分五裂，每个民族恢复了往日的独立。不久，在这些国家内便出现阶级林立的状况，从而出现种族差别，并将国家分成不同的种族集团。在这种共同努力的作用下，人类社会好像要被分成无数的小块，而基督教并没有对这种世界上主导的一般观念视而不见，而是尽可能地让自己顺应这些人类分裂后出现的新趋势。于是，人们继续崇拜创造庇护万物的唯一的上帝，但是每个民族、每个城市，可以说每个人都认为自己能够得到某些特权，并能赢得至高无上的上帝的保护。因为无法把一个神分成许多个，他们只能增加神使的数量并过度夸大他们的权力。于是在大多数基督徒之中对于圣徒和天使的崇拜几乎成为一种偶像崇拜，以至于一时之间人们担心基督教是否会退化成为它原来所战胜的那些宗教。显然，随着各民族之间以及公民间的壁垒的消除，人们的这种思想倾向就变得越来越强，单一而万能的存在的观念能够平等地以同样的方式将法律施予每个人。那么，在民主的时代，特别重要的是防止将人们对神使的崇敬和对造物主的崇拜混淆起来。

另外一个非常清楚的真理是在民主时代，宗教应该采取比别的时代更少的表面仪式。在谈到美国人的哲学方法的时候，我说道，在平等时代，最令人的精神厌恶的莫过于让自己的观念服从形式的思想。生活在平等时代的人，不愿接受图像的渲染，在他们看来这只是用来掩盖真相的幼稚手段，不让真相大白于天下。他们对宗教仪式无动于衷，认为礼拜的细节只有次要的意义。那些在民主时代规定宗教表面仪式的人应特别注重人类思想的自然倾向，从而避免与之发生冲突。我坚定地认为，必要的形式能够让人们的精神专注于对

believe in the necessity of forms, which fix the human mind in the contemplation of abstract truths, and stimulate its ardor in the pursuit of them, whilst they invigorate its powers of retaining them steadfastly. Nor do I suppose that it is possible to maintain a religion without external observances; but, on the other hand, I am persuaded that, in the ages upon which we are entering, it would be peculiarly dangerous to multiply them beyond measure; and that they ought rather to be limited to as much as is absolutely necessary to perpetuate the doctrine itself, which is the substance of religions of which the ritual is only the form. A religion which should become more minute, more peremptory, and more surcharged with small observances at a time in which men are becoming more equal, would soon find itself reduced to a band of fanatical zealots in the midst of an infidel people.

I anticipate the objection, that as all religions have general and eternal truths for their object, they cannot thus shape themselves to the shifting spirit of every age without forfeiting their claim to certainty in the eyes of mankind. To this I reply again, that the principal opinions which constitute belief, and which theologians call articles of faith, must be very carefully distinguished from the accessories connected with them. Religions are obliged to hold fast to the former, whatever be the peculiar spirit of the age; but they should take good care not to bind themselves in the same manner to the latter at a time when everything is in transition, and when the mind, accustomed to the moving pageant of human affairs, reluctantly endures the attempt to fix it to any given point. The fixity of external and secondary things can only afford a chance of duration when civil society is itself fixed; under any other circumstances I hold it to be perilous.

We shall have occasion to see that, of all the passions which originate in, or are fostered by, equality, there is one which it renders peculiarly intense, and which it infuses at the same time into the heart of every man: I mean the love of well-being. The taste for well-being is the prominent and indelible feature of democratic ages. It may be believed that a religion which should undertake to destroy so deep seated a passion, would meet its own destruction thence in the end; and if it attempted to wean men entirely from the contemplation of the good things of this world, in order to devote their faculties exclusively to the thought of another, it may be foreseen that the soul would

抽象真理的思考，并激发人们追求真理的热情，同时鼓舞他们更坚定地相信真理。而且我并不认为一种宗教可以没有表面仪式而存在下去。但是另一方面，我又认为，在我们即将进入的时代，过分追求表面仪式则是极为危险的，我们要将表面仪式限定在教义本身绝对需要的范围之内，因为宗教的仪式只是形式而已。在人们越来越平等的时代，拘泥于细节，顽固不化，迫使信徒遵守清规戒律的宗教不久就会发现它的身边只剩下一些狂热的信徒，而大多数人已经不再信奉它。

我想一定有人会反驳说因为所有的宗教都以一般永久的真理作为其追求目标，所以它们不会随着时代精神的变化而改变其目标，从而在人们眼中失去可信性。对此我的回答是，形成信仰的主要观点以及神学家们所说的信条得以建立的那些主要观点必须要跟与其相关的从属观点严格区分开。无论时代特点如何，宗教都应该牢牢坚持前者。但是在万物都在变换，人们思想已习惯事物的千变万化而不愿墨守成规的时候，宗教要小心与后者的经常联系。表面次要事物的固定不变，只有在市民社会固定不变的情况下，才有可能维持下去，而在其他任何情况下，我认为这种固定不变只会带来危险。

我们可以看到，来源于平等或由其促成的所有激情之中，有一种激情特别强烈，同时还能深入每个人的心灵。这就是人们对幸福的热爱。热爱幸福是民主时代永远不可磨灭的特征。可以认为，旨在摧毁如此深植人心激情的宗教最终会引火自焚。如果它企图完全断掉人们对现世世界美好事物的念头，从而让人们能够全身心地追求来世幸福，可以预见人们最终将摆脱它的束缚，为的是能够完全投入到对眼前物质享受的追求。宗教的主要任务

at length escape from its grasp, to plunge into the exclusive enjoyment of present and material pleasures. The chief concern of religions is to purify, to regulate, and to restrain the excessive and exclusive taste for well-being which men feel at periods of equality; but they would err in attempting to control it completely or to eradicate it. They will not succeed in curing men of the love of riches: but they may still persuade men to enrich themselves by none but honest means.

This brings me to a final consideration, which comprises, as it were, all the others. The more the conditions of men are equalized and assimilated to each other, the more important is it for religions, whilst they carefully abstain from the daily turmoil of secular affairs, not needlessly to run counter to the ideas which generally prevail, and the permanent interests which exist in the mass of the people. For as public opinion grows to be more and more evidently the first and most irresistible of existing powers, the religious principle has no external support strong enough to enable it long to resist its attacks. This is not less true of a democratic people, ruled by a despot, than in a republic. In ages of equality, kings may often command obedience, but the majority always commands belief: to the majority, therefore, deference is to be paid in whatsoever is not contrary to the faith.

I showed in my former volumes how the American clergy stand aloof from secular affairs. This is the most obvious, but it is not the only, example of their self-restraint. In America religion is a distinct sphere, in which the priest is sovereign, but out of which he takes care never to go. Within its limits he is the master of the mind; beyond them, he leaves men to themselves, and surrenders them to the independence and instability which belong to their nature and their age. I have seen no country in which Christianity is clothed with fewer forms, figures, and observances than in the United States; or where it presents more distinct, more simple, or more general notions to the mind. Although the Christians of America are divided into a multitude of sects, they all look upon their religion in the same light. This applies to Roman Catholicism as well as to the other forms of belief. There are no Romish priests who show less taste for the minute individual observances for extraordinary or peculiar means of salvation, or who cling more to the spirit, and less to the letter of the law, than the Roman Catholic priests of the United States. Nowhere is that doctrine of the Church,

是净化、规范、限制人们在平等时代对幸福过分专注的热爱，但如果宗教要试图将其完全控制或根除，则是大错而特错。宗教无法治愈人们的爱财之心，但是可以说服人们用诚实的手段致富。

现在，我来进行最后的思考，这将涵盖上述所有的内容。人们彼此越是相近越是平等，宗教就越是重要，它们小心谨慎地与每日不断变化的世俗事务保持距离，也不与那些普遍为人们所接受的观念和在大众中起到支配作用的利益做不必要的对抗。因为随着公众意见成为越来越首要和不可抵制的力量，宗教的原则得不到能够长期抵抗其所受攻击的强大支持。这无论是在一个由暴君统治的民主国家还是共和制的民主国家都是如此。在平等的时代，国王虽然可以迫使人服从，但是多数才能让人信服，因此，只要不与自己的信仰相悖，人们总是倾向多数。

在本书上卷中，我已经说明美国的神职人员是如何的不问俗世。这是最鲜明的一个他们自制的例子，但绝不是唯一的一个。在美国，宗教有其独立的一片天地，这里由神职人员统治，而且他们从不想走出这片天地。在这里他们是精神的主宰，离开这里他们任凭人们做自己，任凭属于这个时代和人们自己本性的独立和动荡将他们左右。我从未见过哪个国家的基督教能跟美国的基督教一样不拘于形式和繁文缛节，或是能够提供如此清楚、简明和一般的观念。尽管美国的基督教教派众多，但是他们对所有的教派一视同仁。无论是对罗马的天主教还是其他的宗教信仰都是一样。没有任何地方的天主教神职人员能够向美国的天主教神职人员那样不在意信徒个人的额外特殊的礼拜方式，更重教义的精神，而不

which prohibits the worship reserved to God alone from being offered to the saints, more clearly inculcated or more generally followed. Yet the Roman Catholics of America are very submissive and very sincere.

Another remark is applicable to the clergy of every communion. The American ministers of the gospel do not attempt to draw or to fix all the thoughts of man upon the life to come; they are willing to surrender a portion of his heart to the cares of the present; seeming to consider the goods of this world as important, although as secondary, objects. If they take no part themselves in productive labor, they are at least interested in its progression, and ready to applaud its results; and whilst they never cease to point to the other world as the great object of the hopes and fears of the believer, they do not forbid him honestly to court prosperity in this. Far from attempting to show that these things are distinct and contrary to one another, they study rather to find out on what point they are most nearly and closely connected.

All the American clergy know and respect the intellectual supremacy exercised by the majority; they never sustain any but necessary conflicts with it. They take no share in the altercations of parties, but they readily adopt the general opinions of their country and their age; and they allow themselves to be borne away without opposition in the current of feeling and opinion by which everything around them is carried along. They endeavor to amend their contemporaries, but they do not quit fellowship with them. Public opinion is therefore never hostile to them; it rather supports and protects them; and their belief owes its authority at the same time to the strength which is its own, and to that which they borrow from the opinions of the majority. Thus it is that, by respecting all democratic tendencies not absolutely contrary to herself, and by making use of several of them for her own purposes, religion sustains an advantageous struggle with that spirit of individual independence which is her most dangerous antagonist.

Chapter VI: Of The Progress Of Roman Catholicism In The United States

America is the most democratic country in the world, and it is at the same time (according to

拘泥于教义的文字。而在美国宣讲得最清晰，人们遵行得最好的是天主教只对天主礼拜而禁止对圣徒进行礼拜的教义。然而，美国的天主教徒则最驯服，最虔诚。

适用于美国各教派神职人员的另外一个特点是，美国的神职人员并不将人的思想完全引向或禁锢于来世，而是更愿意让人将一部分心思放在现世，似乎认为次要的现世的幸福也并非完全不重要。即使他们并不参与生产劳动，但是至少也会对其发展进步表示关心和赞赏。在他们不断向信徒宣扬来世并勾起人们的希望和害怕的时候，也并不阻止人们诚实地追求现世的荣华。他们并不多讲来世与今生的不同，而宁愿研究找到它们之间的相似和联系。

所有的美国神职人员都认可并尊重多数对人们思想的支配作用，而且除非必要，他们绝不反对多数。他们不参与党派斗争，却愿意随时接受国家和时代的一般观念，他们会不加抵制地跟着引领周围所有人的情感和思想潮流前进。他们努力引导同时代的人向善，从不与同时代的人脱离。因此公众舆论非但从不与他们为敌，反而给予他们支持和保护。他们信仰的权威依靠的不单是他们自身的力量，而且还借助了多数的力量。因此，通过尊重所有的不与其相悖的民主倾向，并将其中的一部分为自己所用，宗教在与其最危险的敌人个人独立精神的斗争中占据了优势。

第六章　罗马天主教在美国的发展

美国是世界上最民主的国家，同时（根据可信的报告）也是天主教最发达的国家。

reports worthy of belief) the country in which the Roman Catholic religion makes most progress. At first sight this is surprising. Two things must here be accurately distinguished: equality inclines men to wish to form their own opinions; but, on the other hand, it imbues them with the taste and the idea of unity, simplicity, and impartiality in the power which governs society. Men living in democratic ages are therefore very prone to shake off all religious authority; but if they consent to subject themselves to any authority of this kind, they choose at least that it should be single and uniform. Religious powers not radiating from a common centre are naturally repugnant to their minds; and they almost as readily conceive that there should be no religion, as that there should be several. At the present time, more than in any preceding one, Roman Catholics are seen to lapse into infidelity, and Protestants to be converted to Roman Catholicism. If the Roman Catholic faith be considered within the pale of the church, it would seem to be losing ground; without that pale, to be gaining it. Nor is this circumstance difficult of explanation. The men of our days are naturally disposed to believe; but, as soon as they have any religion, they immediately find in themselves a latent propensity which urges them unconsciously towards Catholicism. Many of the doctrines and the practices of the Romish Church astonish them; but they feel a secret admiration for its discipline, and its great unity attracts them. If Catholicism could at length withdraw itself from the political animosities to which it has given rise, I have hardly any doubt but that the same spirit of the age, which appears to be so opposed to it, would become so favorable as to admit of its great and sudden advancement. One of the most ordinary weaknesses of the human intellect is to seek to reconcile contrary principles, and to purchase peace at the expense of logic. Thus there have ever been, and will ever be, men who, after having submitted some portion of their religious belief to the principle of authority, will seek to exempt several other parts of their faith from its influence, and to keep their minds floating at random between liberty and obedience. But I am inclined to believe that the number of these thinkers will be less in democratic than in other ages; and that our posterity will tend more and more to a single division into two parts—some relinquishing Christianity entirely, and others returning to the bosom of the Church of Rome.

初看之下，这令人大吃一惊。在这里有两件事必须进行严格区分。平等促使人们希望形成自己的观念，但是另一方面平等又让人们喜欢和向往统一、单一和公平的权力观念。因此，生活在民主国家的人们非常想要摆脱所有宗教的权威，但是如果他们想服从某一个宗教权威，那么他们至少会选择一个单一的唯一的权威。从一个共同中心辐射出来的多个宗教力量自然会令他们产生敌意，于是他们几乎会轻易地认为与其有几个宗教不如没有宗教。与以往的任何时代相比，现代的罗马天主教徒最不虔诚，但是基督教徒却都纷纷改信天主教。从天主教的内部来看，它似乎衰退了，但是从外部来看，却是进步了。这种现象不难解释。我们这个时代的人们天生不笃信宗教，但是一旦他们信奉某一宗教，便会立即发现在他们内心有一种潜在的力量将他们不知不觉地推向天主教。罗马教的许多教义和教规令他们震惊，但他们却发自内心地钦佩它的纪律，被它的统一所吸引。如果天主教最终能够从它所引起的政治恩怨中撤出来，那么我敢肯定，似乎与其背道而驰的我们这个时代的精神，会对其非常有利，并使之瞬间取得巨大的成功。人类智力活动常见的弱点之一就是试图调节相互对立的原则，而且不惜以逻辑为代价求得和平。因此，过去和未来都是如此，总是有人在让自己的部分宗教信仰服从一个权威之后，试图保全自己的其他信仰免受其影响，让自己的精神不断在自由和服从之间飘忽不定。但是我趋向于认为在民主时代有这样想法的人比任何其他时代都要少，而且我们的后代将越来越趋向于两极分化，一类人会完全脱离基督教，而另一类人则会投入罗马教会的怀抱。

Chapter VII: Of The Cause Of A Leaning To Pantheism Amongst Democratic Nations

I shall take occasion hereafter to show under what form the preponderating taste of a democratic people for very general ideas manifests itself in politics; but I would point out, at the present stage of my work, its principal effect on philosophy. It cannot be denied that pantheism has made great progress in our age. The writings of a part of Europe bear visible marks of it: the Germans introduce it into philosophy, and the French into literature. Most of the works of imagination published in France contain some opinions or some tinge caught from pantheistical doctrines, or they disclose some tendency to such doctrines in their authors. This appears to me not only to proceed from an accidental, but from a permanent cause.

When the conditions of society are becoming more equal, and each individual man becomes more like all the rest, more weak and more insignificant, a habit grows up of ceasing to notice the citizens to consider only the people, and of overlooking individuals to think only of their kind. At such times the human mind seeks to embrace a multitude of different objects at once; and it constantly strives to succeed in connecting a variety of consequences with a single cause. The idea of unity so possesses itself of man, and is sought for by him so universally, that if he thinks he has found it, he readily yields himself up to repose in that belief. Nor does he content himself with the discovery that nothing is in the world but a creation and a Creator; still embarrassed by this primary division of things, he seeks to expand and to simplify his conception by including God and the universe in one great whole. If there be a philosophical system which teaches that all things material and immaterial, visible and invisible, which the world contains, are only to be considered as the several parts of an immense Being, which alone remains unchanged amidst the continual change and ceaseless transformation of all that constitutes it, we may readily infer that such a system, although it destroy the individuality of man—nay, rather because it destroys that individuality—will have secret charms for men living in democracies. All their habits of thought prepare them to conceive it, and predispose them to adopt it. It naturally attracts and fixes their imagination; it fosters the pride, whilst it soothes the indolence, of their minds. Amongst the different systems by whose aid philosophy endeavors to explain the

第七章　民主国家倾向于泛神论的原因

我虽然准备在后面才来谈民主国家对一般观念的绝对爱好是如何表现在政治方面的，但是此刻我就想要指出这种绝对爱好对哲学的主要影响。不可否认，泛神论已经在我们这个时代有了很大的发展。欧洲的部分作品已经带有明显的泛神论的色彩。德国人把它引入哲学，法国人则将它带进文学。法国出版的大部分虚构作品都包含来自泛神论的一些观点和色彩，或者在他们的作品中暴露出泛神论的某种倾向。这在我看来绝非偶然，而且有其久远的原因。

当社会状况变得越来越平等，人与人越来越相似，同时也变得越来越弱小、无足轻重的时候，人们便养成不重视公民个人只注重全体人民，以及忽视个体只考虑人类整体的习惯。在这样的时代，人们的头脑想要同时包罗万象，并试图将各种各样的结果归于同一原因。统一的思想占据每个人的头脑，人们到处寻找统一的观念，以至于他们认为只要能够找到它，自己便可以躺在上面高枕无忧。人们不再满足于发现世界上只有一个造物主，而且对万物的这种初级分类也令他们感到尴尬，于是他们便通过将上帝和宇宙汇成一个整体来升华和简化自己的概念。如果有一个哲学体系可以将世间万物无论是物质还是非物质、可见还是不可见都视为一个巨大存在的不同组成部分，而且这个巨大的存在能在其内在组成部分不断变化和无休止的转换中保持不变，那么我们就可以推定，这样的一个哲学体系，尽管会破坏人的个性，但也正是因为如此才会对生活在民主制度下的人们具有隐秘的魅力。人们所有的思维习惯都引导人们去理解这一哲学体系，并让人们做好接受它的准

universe, I believe pantheism to be one of those most fitted to seduce the human mind in democratic ages. Against it all who abide in their attachment to the true greatness of man should struggle and combine.

Chapter VIII: The Principle Of Equality Suggests To The Americans The Idea Of The Indefinite Perfectibility Of Man

Equality suggests to the human mind several ideas which would not have originated from any other source, and it modifies almost all those previously entertained. I take as an example the idea of human perfectibility, because it is one of the principal notions that the intellect can conceive, and because it constitutes of itself a great philosophical theory, which is every instant to be traced by its consequences in the practice of human affairs. Although man has many points of resemblance with the brute creation, one characteristic is peculiar to himself—he improves: they are incapable of improvement. Mankind could not fail to discover this difference from its earliest period. The idea of perfectibility is therefore as old as the world; equality did not give birth to it, although it has imparted to it a novel character.

When the citizens of a community are classed according to their rank, their profession, or their birth, and when all men are constrained to follow the career which happens to open before them, everyone thinks that the utmost limits of human power are to be discerned in proximity to himself, and none seeks any longer to resist the inevitable law of his destiny. Not indeed that an aristocratic people absolutely contests man's faculty of self-improvement, but they do not hold it to be indefinite; amelioration they conceive, but not change: they imagine that the future condition of society may be better, but not essentially different; and whilst they admit that mankind has made vast strides in improvement, and may still have some to make, they assign to it beforehand certain impassable limits. Thus they do not presume that they have arrived at the supreme good or at absolute truth (what people or what man was ever wild enough to imagine it?) but they cherish a persuasion that they have pretty nearly reached that degree of greatness and knowledge which our imperfect nature

备。它能够自然而然地引起和加强人们的想象力，在提高人精神自豪感的同时满足精神的愉悦。在帮助哲学努力解释世界的所有不同体系中，我相信泛神论最适合笼络民主时代的人心。所有坚信人类真正伟大的人们都应当团结起来反对泛神论。

第八章　平等令美国人产生人可以无限完美的想法

平等在人的思想中激发起几个源自它的观念后，要改变已存在的几乎所有的观念。我以人类的可完善性为例，因为它只是人脑所能想出的主要观点之一，还因为它本身就是一个伟大的哲学理论，是一个时刻接受人类验证的哲学理论。尽管人与野生动物在很多方面非常相似，但是有一个特点则是人类所独有。这就是人能自我完善。在人类出现伊始，人类就已发现这个不同。因此，人可完善的观念跟世界一样古老，所以它并不是由平等造就的，但是平等令它产生了新的特点。

当社会的公民根据其所属阶级、职业和出生的不同分为三六九等，所有人不得不沿着偶然出现在自己面前的道路前进的时候，每个人都会认为人力量的极限大概就在自己身上，于是没有人再试图与这个不可避免的命运进行抗争。事实上，贵族制国家的人民并非绝对没有自我完善的能力，但他们并不认为人的自我完善是无限的。他们想改进，但不想改变。他们希望未来的社会越来越好，但本质上没有差别。然而，当他们在承认人类至今已经取得巨大进步并仍将继续有所进步的同时，却又提前在人类面前划定一个不可逾越的界限。因此，他们并不认为自己已经达到至善或是已经获得绝对真理（又有哪个民族或是

admits of; and as nothing moves about them they are willing to fancy that everything is in its fit place. Then it is that the legislator affects to lay down eternal laws; that kings and nations will raise none but imperishable monuments; and that the present generation undertakes to spare generations to come the care of regulating their destinies.

In proportion as castes disappear and the classes of society approximate—as manners, customs, and laws vary, from the tumultuous intercourse of men—as new facts arise—as new truths are brought to light—as ancient opinions are dissipated, and others take their place—the image of an ideal perfection, forever on the wing, presents itself to the human mind. Continual changes are then every instant occurring under the observation of every man: the position of some is rendered worse; and he learns but too well, that no people and no individual, how enlightened soever they may be, can lay claim to infallibility;—the condition of others is improved; whence he infers that man is endowed with an indefinite faculty of improvement. His reverses teach him that none may hope to have discovered absolute good—his success stimulates him to the never-ending pursuit of it. Thus, forever seeking—forever falling, to rise again—often disappointed, but not discouraged—he tends unceasingly towards that unmeasured greatness so indistinctly visible at the end of the long track which humanity has yet to tread. It can hardly be believed how many facts naturally flow from the philosophical theory of the indefinite perfectibility of man, or how strong an influence it exercises even on men who, living entirely for the purposes of action and not of thought, seem to conform their actions to it, without knowing anything about it. I accost an American sailor, and I inquire why the ships of his country are built so as to last but for a short time; he answers without hesitation that the art of navigation is every day making such rapid progress, that the finest vessel would become almost useless if it lasted beyond a certain number of years. In these words, which fell accidentally and on a particular subject from a man of rude attainments, I recognize the general and systematic idea upon which a great people directs all its concerns.

Aristocratic nations are naturally too apt to narrow the scope of human perfectibility; democratic nations to expand it beyond compass.

哪个人曾敢有这样的妄想呢？），但是他们却怀有一种信念，认为自己已经非常接近人类不完美的本性所能达到的最高程度，而且因为他们身边一切照旧，于是很容易产生一切均已各就其位的想法。于是，立法者们喜欢制定永久性法律，国王和人民只愿树立永久的丰碑，而现代人则愿意为了让后代免受操劳而为他们安排好命运。

随着种姓的消失，社会各阶级的接近，随着人们不断的交流而带来的民情、风俗和法律的变化，随着新事物的出现、新真理的发现，以及随着古老观念的渐行渐远并被其他新的观念所取代，一个理想的但又无法固定的完美形象出现在人们的头脑中。不断的变化时刻呈现在人们的眼前。有些人的处境变得糟糕，于是人们开始清晰地认识到一个民族或一个人无论其多么文明开化，都不可能永远不犯错误。另一些人的命运得到改善，于是他们由此断定，人具有无限自我完善的能力。而受挫的人则对他们说没有人能够达到至善，因为一个人的成功会令他不断追求下一个从成功，永无止境。因此，人们始终在追求，跌倒，再爬起来，常常会感到失望，但不会泄气。人总是永无休止地朝着他们尚未踏上的那条漫长道路尽头的隐约可见的无限伟大前进。难以令人置信这种人可无限完善的哲学理论自然而然衍生出多少事实，甚至对那些行动上与它有关思想上与其无涉，但在活动中又好像不知不觉与其吻合的人们产生的影响又是那么巨大。我遇到过一位美国水手，曾经问他为什么你们国家造的船不那么坚固耐用。他毫不犹豫地回答我，航海技术日新月异，制造最精良的船只几年之后也几乎无法再派上用场。一个粗人就某一问题偶然脱口而出的一番言论，让我认识到一个伟大民族凡事都会遵循的一套一般观念。

Chapter IX: The Example Of The Americans Does Not Prove That A Democratic People Can Have No Aptitude And No Taste For Science, Literature, Or Art

It must be acknowledged that amongst few of the civilized nations of our time have the higher sciences made less progress than in the United States; and in few have great artists, fine poets, or celebrated writers been more rare. Many Europeans, struck by this fact, have looked upon it as a natural and inevitable result of equality; and they have supposed that if a democratic state of society and democratic institutions were ever to prevail over the whole earth, the human mind would gradually find its beacon-lights grow dim, and men would relapse into a period of darkness. To reason thus is, I think, to confound several ideas which it is important to divide and to examine separately: it is to mingle, unintentionally, what is democratic with what is only American.

The religion professed by the first emigrants, and bequeathed by them to their descendants, simple in its form of worship, austere and almost harsh in its principles, and hostile to external symbols and to ceremonial pomp, is naturally unfavorable to the fine arts, and only yields a reluctant sufferance to the pleasures of literature. The Americans are a very old and a very enlightened people, who have fallen upon a new and unbounded country, where they may extend themselves at pleasure, and which they may fertilize without difficulty. This state of things is without a parallel in the history of the world. In America, then, every one finds facilities, unknown elsewhere, for making or increasing his fortune. The spirit of gain is always on the stretch, and the human mind, constantly diverted from the pleasures of imagination and the labors of the intellect, is there swayed by no impulse but the pursuit of wealth. Not only are manufacturing and commercial classes to be found in the United States, as they are in all other countries; but what never occurred elsewhere, the whole community is simultaneously engaged in productive industry and commerce. I am convinced that, if the Americans had been alone in the world, with the freedom and the knowledge acquired by their forefathers, and the passions which are their own, they would not have been slow to discover that progress cannot long be made in the application of the sciences without cultivating the theory of them; that all the arts are perfected by one another: and, however absorbed they might have been by the pursuit of the

贵族制国家自然倾向于限定人可完善的范围，而民主制国家又有将其过分扩大的趋势。

第九章　美国的例子并不能证明民主国家不具有科学、文学和艺术方面的才能和爱好

必须承认，在我们这个时代为数不多的几个文明国家中，美国在高级科学方面进步不大，而且伟大的艺术家、优秀的诗人和著名的作家也寥寥无几。许多欧洲人注意到这个事实，于是便认定这是平等造成的不可避免的自然结果，而且还据此认定，如果民主社会状况和民主制度一旦席卷整个世界，指引人类思想的开化之光将逐渐暗淡，人类也将重回黑暗时代。我认为，做出这样推论的人错将一些本应分开单独研究的观念混在一起，也就是说无意之中将民主的东西和美国所独有的东西混在了一起。

随第一代移民而来并被世代相传的宗教，仪式简单，教义严格甚至几近苛责，反对外表的浮夸和繁文缛节，这自然不利于艺术的发展，也只有消遣性文学才能获得些许空间。美国人是一个非常古老和开化的民族，他们来到一片辽阔的新土地，在这里他们可以肆意扩张，而且富饶的土地能够轻易地结出硕果。这样的事情简直史无前例。因此，在美国每个人都有其他地方的人们所没有的发财致富的便利条件。这里的人们总是有着很强的贪欲，因此人们的思想，总是被从想象的乐趣和理性活动上转移开，只被追求财富的欲望所左右。在美国，不但向其他国家一样有工业和商业阶层，而且还有其他国家所没有的一种

principal object of their desires, they would speedily have admitted, that it is necessary to turn aside from it occasionally, in order the better to attain it in the end.

The taste for the pleasures of the mind is moreover so natural to the heart of civilized man, that amongst the polite nations, which are least disposed to give themselves up to these pursuits, a certain number of citizens are always to be found who take part in them. This intellectual craving, when once felt, would very soon have been satisfied. But at the very time when the Americans were naturally inclined to require nothing of science but its special applications to the useful arts and the means of rendering life comfortable, learned and literary Europe was engaged in exploring the common sources of truth, and in improving at the same time all that can minister to the pleasures or satisfy the wants of man. At the head of the enlightened nations of the Old World the inhabitants of the United States more particularly distinguished one, to which they were closely united by a common origin and by kindred habits. Amongst this people they found distinguished men of science, artists of skill, writers of eminence, and they were enabled to enjoy the treasures of the intellect without requiring to labor in amassing them. I cannot consent to separate America from Europe, in spite of the ocean which intervenes. I consider the people of the United States as that portion of the English people which is commissioned to explore the wilds of the New World; whilst the rest of the nation, enjoying more leisure and less harassed by the drudgery of life, may devote its energies to thought, and enlarge in all directions the empire of the mind. The position of the Americans is therefore quite exceptional, and it may be believed that no democratic people will ever be placed in a similar one. Their strictly Puritanical origin—their exclusively commercial habits—even the country they inhabit, which seems to divert their minds from the pursuit of science, literature, and the arts—the proximity of Europe, which allows them to neglect these pursuits without relapsing into barbarism—a thousand special causes, of which I have only been able to point out the most important—have singularly concurred to fix the mind of the American upon purely practical objects. His passions, his wants, his education, and everything about him seem to unite in drawing the native of the United States earthward: his religion alone bids him turn, from time to time, a transient and distracted glance to heaven. Let us

现象，即整个社会都参与工业和商业活动。我可以肯定，如果全世界只剩下美国人，而且能依然保留着从祖先那里继承的自由和知识以及他们自身的热情，那么，他们不久就会发现没有自己的理论科学的应用的进步是无法长久的，而且所有艺术也应相辅相成地得到完善。不管美国人多么执著于他们追求的主要目标，他们很快就会承认为了能够实现最终的目标，时不时地还要绕绕弯子。

此外，对精神享受的喜爱也是文明人自然而然的心之所向。所以在高度文明的国家中，人们不但热衷于追求精神享受，而且还有一批人对其进行专门研究。这种精神上的渴望一旦出现便会很快得到满足。但是，当美国人只顾科学的实际运用，专注于寻找让生活过得舒适的方法时，精通学术和文艺的欧洲正埋头探索真理的共同来源，并致力于同时完善所有可以带给人们享乐和满足人们需要的一切。美国人认为，在旧大陆的开化民族之中，有一个民族鹤立鸡群，而且因为与自己同宗同俗，所以关系非常密切。他们注意到这个民族拥有杰出的科学家、富于才情的艺术家和显赫的作家，而且自己可以不费吹灰之力便可以从他们那里汲取知识财富。尽管美洲和欧洲远隔重洋，但我不认为两者互不相干。我将美国人视为英国人的一部分，是这部分人承担了开发新大陆的任务，而剩下的人则留在英国乐享安逸，不必为生活奔波，从而能够专注于思索，全方位地扩展人的思维。因此，美国人的地位非常特殊，而且我认为不会再有任何一个民主国家能拥有类似的地位。他们是清一色的清教徒，有专门从商的习惯，而且他们所居住的这个国家似乎也并没有让他们分神去研究科学、文学和艺术，欧洲的邻居让他们哪怕不研究这些也不会退回到野蛮

cease then to view all democratic nations under the mask of the American people, and let us attempt to survey them at length with their own proper features.

It is possible to conceive a people not subdivided into any castes or scale of ranks; in which the law, recognizing no privileges, should divide inherited property into equal shares; but which, at the same time, should be without knowledge and without freedom. Nor is this an empty hypothesis: a despot may find that it is his interest to render his subjects equal and to leave them ignorant, in order more easily to keep them slaves. Not only would a democratic people of this kind show neither aptitude nor taste for science, literature, or art, but it would probably never arrive at the possession of them. The law of descent would of itself provide for the destruction of fortunes at each succeeding generation; and new fortunes would be acquired by none. The poor man, without either knowledge or freedom, would not so much as conceive the idea of raising himself to wealth; and the rich man would allow himself to be degraded to poverty, without a notion of self-defence. Between these two members of the community complete and invincible equality would soon be established.

No one would then have time or taste to devote himself to the pursuits or pleasures of the intellect; but all men would remain paralyzed by a state of common ignorance and equal servitude. When I conceive a democratic society of this kind, I fancy myself in one of those low, close, and gloomy abodes, where the light which breaks in from without soon faints and fades away. A sudden heaviness overpowers me, and I grope through the surrounding darkness, to find the aperture which will restore me to daylight and the air.

But all this is not applicable to men already enlightened who retain their freedom, after having abolished from amongst them those peculiar and hereditary rights which perpetuated the tenure of property in the hands of certain individuals or certain bodies. When men living in a democratic state of society are enlightened, they readily discover that they are confined and fixed within no limits which constrain them to take up with their present fortune. They all therefore conceive the idea of increasing it; if they are free, they all attempt it, but all do not succeed in the same manner. The legislature, it is true, no longer grants privileges, but they are bestowed by nature. As natural

状态。令美国人特别专注纯物质方面事物的独特原因数以千计，而我只能就其中最重要的列举一二。美国人的热情、需要、教育乃至环境都在驱使他们面对现世。只有宗教能够令他时不时地分神仰望一下天堂。所以，我们不应该据此推断所有民主国家的表现都跟美国一样，而是应该根据每个民族的特点来研究它们。

我们可以想象有这样一个民族，没有种姓和阶级之分，法律也不认可任何特权并规定遗产应由继承人平分，但同时它并没有让人民享有知识和自由。这并不是一个没有根据的假设。一个暴君可能会出于自己的利益而让所有臣民平等的同时让他们愚昧无知，这样更便于奴役他们。这样的民主国家不但不会在科学、文学或艺术方面表现出才华和爱好，而且甚至可以让人相信它永远不会有这样的表现。它的继承法以一代接一代地将财产分化变小为己任，而新的财富也没有人去创造。穷人既没知识也没自由，根本连发财致富的想法都没有，而有钱人则任凭自己堕入贫困也不知自救。这样的社会中的这两类成员很快就会确立起无法克服的完全的平等。

那么，没有任何人会有时间和兴趣再去追求精神享受，所有人都处于麻木不仁的状态，同样的无知，同样的受奴役。我一想到这样的民主社会，立刻觉得自己如坠入一个低矮、密闭昏暗的小房子，尽管时不时会有光线照射进来，但不久又会变暗消失。突然之间我觉得心情沉闷，于是在黑暗中四处摸索，想要找到一个能够令我重新沐浴阳光呼吸新鲜空气的出口。

但是，所有这些假设都不适用于已经开化的，并废除那些规定财产永久归属某个人或

inequality is very great, fortunes become unequal as soon as every man exerts all his faculties to get rich. The law of descent prevents the establishment of wealthy families; but it does not prevent the existence of wealthy individuals. It constantly brings back the members of the community to a common level, from which they as constantly escape: and the inequality of fortunes augments in proportion as knowledge is diffused and liberty increased.

A sect which arose in our time, and was celebrated for its talents and its extravagance, proposed to concentrate all property into the hands of a central power, whose function it should afterwards be to parcel it out to individuals, according to their capacity. This would have been a method of escaping from that complete and eternal equality which seems to threaten democratic society. But it would be a simpler and less dangerous remedy to grant no privilege to any, giving to all equal cultivation and equal independence, and leaving everyone to determine his own position. Natural inequality will very soon make way for itself, and wealth will spontaneously pass into the hands of the most capable.

Free and democratic communities, then, will always contain a considerable number of people enjoying opulence or competency. The wealthy will not be so closely linked to each other as the members of the former aristocratic class of society: their propensities will be different, and they will scarcely ever enjoy leisure as secure or as complete: but they will be far more numerous than those who belonged to that class of society could ever be. These persons will not be strictly confined to the cares of practical life, and they will still be able, though in different degrees, to indulge in the pursuits and pleasures of the intellect. In those pleasures they will indulge; for if it be true that the human mind leans on one side to the narrow, the practical, and the useful, it naturally rises on the other to the infinite, the spiritual, and the beautiful. Physical wants confine it to the earth; but, as soon as the tie is loosened, it will unbend itself again.

Not only will the number of those who can take an interest in the productions of the mind be enlarged, but the taste for intellectual enjoyment will descend, step by step, even to those who, in aristocratic societies, seem to have neither time nor ability to in indulge in them. When hereditary wealth, the privileges of rank, and the prerogatives of birth have ceased to be, and when every man

某个团体的特殊法令和继承法后依旧保持自由的国家。生活在民主社会的人们已经开化，他们随时能够发现没有任何东西能够限制并强迫他们安于现状。因此，每个人都想要改变现状，而且如果他们是自由的，每个人都会想要试上一试，尽管并不是所有人都能获得成功。当然，立法也不再授予人们特权，但是天赋会赋予人们特权。当天赋的差别巨大时，尽管每个人都倾尽所能发财致富，但是获得的财富并不平等。继承法可以避免一个家族世世代代富裕下去，但是却无法阻止富人的存在。继承法不断将社会所有成员拉回同一水平线，而人们则不断试图逃离。随着知识的传播和自由的扩大，财富的不平等不断加剧。

在我们这个时代，出现一个教派，因其才华和狂妄而出名，它主张将所有的财富都集中到中央当局的手中，再由其依据个人能力的大小将财富分配到个人。这好像是一个办法，可以令民主社会摆脱完全永久的平等的威胁。但是还有一种更简单、危险更小的解决之道，不但可以不给任何人特权，而且还能赋予所有人平等的知识和独立，让每个人自己决定自己的位置。天赋的不平等不久便会显现出威力，而财富自然会落入最能干者之手。

因此，在自由和民主社会里，总会有一大批富裕且有能力的人。这些有钱人之间的联系并不像原来社会的贵族阶级成员间那么密切。他们与贵族阶级的爱好不同，也不像贵族那样有时间去享乐，但是他们的数量将远远超过以往社会的富裕阶层。这些人不只关心物质生活，也会追求精神享受，尽管程度上不及贵族。他们投入在那些享受上的时间是合理的，因为如果人的精神上一方面要有一个有限的目标，即物质的实用的目标，另一方面还要有一个无限的目标，即非物质的审美的目标。物质需要使人的精神倾向现世，然而一旦

derives his strength from himself alone, it becomes evident that the chief cause of disparity between the fortunes of men is the mind. Whatever tends to invigorate, to extend, or to adorn the mind, instantly rises to great value. The utility of knowledge becomes singularly conspicuous even to the eyes of the multitude: those who have no taste for its charms set store upon its results, and make some efforts to acquire it. In free and enlightened democratic ages, there is nothing to separate men from each other or to retain them in their peculiar sphere; they rise or sink with extreme rapidity. All classes live in perpetual intercourse from their great proximity to each other. They communicate and intermingle every day—they imitate and envy one other: this suggests to the people many ideas, notions, and desires which it would never have entertained if the distinctions of rank had been fixed and society at rest. In such nations the servant never considers himself as an entire stranger to the pleasures and toils of his master, nor the poor man to those of the rich; the rural population assimilates itself to that of the towns, and the provinces to the capital. No one easily allows himself to be reduced to the mere material cares of life; and the humblest artisan casts at times an eager and a furtive glance into the higher regions of the intellect. People do not read with the same notions or in the same manner as they do in an aristocratic community; but the circle of readers is unceasingly expanded, till it includes all the citizens.

As soon as the multitude begins to take an interest in the labors of the mind, it finds out that to excel in some of them is a powerful method of acquiring fame, power, or wealth. The restless ambition which equality begets instantly takes this direction as it does all others. The number of those who cultivate science, letters, and the arts, becomes immense. The intellectual world starts into prodigious activity: everyone endeavors to open for himself a path there, and to draw the eyes of the public after him. Something analogous occurs to what happens in society in the United States, politically considered. What is done is often imperfect, but the attempts are innumerable; and, although the results of individual effort are commonly very small, the total amount is always very large.

It is therefore not true to assert that men living in democratic ages are naturally indifferent to science, literature, and the arts: only it must be acknowledged that they cultivate them after their own

物质需要不那么迫切，人的精神就要自我崛起。

不但那些能够欣赏精神食粮的人数大大增加，而且对于智力活动的爱好也将逐步渗透到在贵族社会中似乎既没时间也没能力从事这类活动的人群之中。当世袭财产、阶级特权以及出身优势都已不再，当每个人都要凭自己的力量前进，人们之间财富的分配显然主要取决于智力。凡是可以激励、扩大或是发挥智力的东西，立刻身价倍增。知识的功用极其明显地呈现在人们眼前。那些不懂得欣赏知识魅力的人，也要付出努力才能获得知识的成果。在自由文明的民主时代，没有任何东西能够将人们分隔开来，或是限制在各自的位置，人们的际遇快速变幻。所有阶级比邻而居交往不断，每天不断地交流融合，互相模仿倾慕。这让人们产生许多等级森严社会停滞时代不曾有过的想法、见解和欲望。在这样的国家，仆人可以与主人同享乐共劳动，穷人也可以跟富人如此，乡下人会模仿城里人，地方会模仿首都。所以，没有任何一个人会轻易让自己只关注物质生活，哪怕是最卑微的匠人也会时不时地向高级的智力活动世界偷偷地投上关切的目光。人们不再用与贵族社会相同的观点和方法读书，但是读书人的圈子不断地扩大，最终涵盖所有公民。

人们一旦开始关注精神劳动，便会发现获得名誉、权力和财富最有利的方法就是要胜过他人。

平等带来的无休止的野心立即会从其他方面转向这里。研究科学、文学和艺术的人将会骤增。知识界将呈现出惊人的活跃性，每个人都努力为自己开辟一条通往那里的道路，并吸引人们追随自己。这与美国政界发生的事情类似。尽管美国人做得并不完美，但是却

fashion, and bring to the task their own peculiar qualifications and deficiencies.

Chapter X: Why The Americans Are More Addicted To Practical Than To Theoretical Science

If a democratic state of society and democratic institutions do not stop the career of the human mind, they incontestably guide it in one direction in preference to another. Their effects, thus circumscribed, are still exceedingly great; and I trust I may be pardoned if I pause for a moment to survey them. We had occasion, in speaking of the philosophical method of the American people, to make several remarks which must here be turned to account.

Equality begets in man the desire of judging of everything for himself: it gives him, in all things, a taste for the tangible and the real, a contempt for tradition and for forms. These general tendencies are principally discernible in the peculiar subject of this chapter. Those who cultivate the sciences amongst a democratic people are always afraid of losing their way in visionary speculation. They mistrust systems; they adhere closely to facts and the study of facts with their own senses. As they do not easily defer to the mere name of any fellow-man, they are never inclined to rest upon any man's authority; but, on the contrary, they are unremitting in their efforts to point out the weaker points of their neighbors' opinions. Scientific precedents have very little weight with them; they are never long detained by the subtilty of the schools, nor ready to accept big words for sterling coin; they penetrate, as far as they can, into the principal parts of the subject which engages them, and they expound them in the vernacular tongue. Scientific pursuits then follow a freer and a safer course, but a less lofty one.

The mind may, as it appears to me, divide science into three parts. The first comprises the most theoretical principles, and those more abstract notions whose application is either unknown or very remote. The second is composed of those general truths which still belong to pure theory, but lead, nevertheless, by a straight and short road to practical results. Methods of application and means of execution make up the third. Each of these different portions of science may be separately cultivated, although reason and experience show that none of them can prosper long, if it be absolutely cut off

做了无数的尝试，而且尽管个人奋斗的成果往往都很小，但是总量却往往非常惊人。

因此，断言生活在民主国家的人与生俱来不关心科学、文学和艺术并不正确，而且应该承认他们是按照自己的方式进行科学、文学和艺术研究，尽管他们的做法有其固有的特点和不足。

第十章　为什么美国人更注重实践而不是理论

尽管民主的社会状况和民主制度不会阻碍人类的精神发展，但是却无可争辩地将人类的精神发展引向一个方向而不是其他方向。因此，尽管它们的作用受到一定的限制，但是依旧十分强大。我相信如果在此我稍作停留谈一谈它们的作用人们应该可以理解。在谈到美国人的哲学方法的时候我们曾经提到过一些观点，它们可以用来解释这种情形。

平等促使人们产生凡事想要自行判断的愿望，所以这让人们喜欢所有那些看得见摸得着的真实的东西，而轻视传统和形式。这些普遍的特性就是本章想要特别论述的内容。在民主国家研究科学的人，总是担心会陷入空想而迷失方向。他们无法信任已有的体系，紧紧抓住事实以及亲自研究的事实不放。他们既不会轻易相信同行的空名，也从不盲目信赖任何权威，而是不断地力图指出这些人的理论的弱点。科学的先例对他们来说无足轻重，他们也不会长期驻足一个学派进行琐碎的讨论，更不会听信别人的豪言壮语。他们会竭尽所能深入所研究问题的主要部分，并用通俗的语言加以表述。于是，科学研究变得更为自由，更为确切，也不再遥不可及。

from the two others.

In America the purely practical part of science is admirably understood, and careful attention is paid to the theoretical portion which is immediately requisite to application. On this head the Americans always display a clear, free, original, and inventive power of mind. But hardly anyone in the United States devotes himself to the essentially theoretical and abstract portion of human knowledge. In this respect the Americans carry to excess a tendency which is, I think, discernible, though in a less degree, amongst all democratic nations.

Nothing is more necessary to the culture of the higher sciences, or of the more elevated departments of science, than meditation; and nothing is less suited to meditation than the structure of democratic society. We do not find there, as amongst an aristocratic people, one class which clings to a state of repose because it is well off; and another which does not venture to stir because it despairs of improving its condition. Everyone is actively in motion: some in quest of power, others of gain. In the midst of this universal tumult—this incessant conflict of jarring interests—this continual stride of men after fortune—where is that calm to be found which is necessary for the deeper combinations of the intellect? How can the mind dwell upon any single point, when everything whirls around it, and man himself is swept and beaten onwards by the heady current which rolls all things in its course? But the permanent agitation which subsists in the bosom of a peaceable and established democracy, must be distinguished from the tumultuous and revolutionary movements which almost always attend the birth and growth of democratic society. When a violent revolution occurs amongst a highly civilized people, it cannot fail to give a sudden impulse to their feelings and their opinions. This is more particularly true of democratic revolutions, which stir up all the classes of which a people is composed, and beget, at the same time, inordinate ambition in the breast of every member of the community. The French made most surprising advances in the exact sciences at the very time at which they were finishing the destruction of the remains of their former feudal society; yet this sudden fecundity is not to be attributed to democracy, but to the unexampled revolution which attended its growth. What happened at that period was a special incident, and

在我看来，根据人的精神追求，科学可以被分成三个部分。第一部分是最纯的理论原则，是最为抽象的观点，不是没有就是几乎没有应用价值。第二部分是普遍真理，依然属于纯理论范畴，但是可以直接或间接得到应用。第三部分则是应用方法和执行手段。科学的每个不同部分都可以进行单独研究，尽管理性和经验证明如果其中的一个被与其他两个割裂开来，根本无法长期繁荣。

在美国，人们潜心研究科学的纯应用部分，并特别注重理论方面与应用有直接关系的部分。在这方面，美国人总是表现出求真、自由、大胆和创新的精神，但是在美国却很难找到有人致力于人类知识中的基本理论和抽象部分的研究。在这方面，美国人表现出所有民主国家所共有的倾向，尽管我认为它们的这种倾向不及美国人突出。

对于高级科学或是科学的高级部分而言，最必不可少的就是静心沉思，而民主社会的结构则与静心沉思最不合拍。在这里，我们无法像在贵族制社会中那样找到一个因为有钱而可以高枕无忧的阶层，也无法找到一个因为改善环境无望而安于现状的阶层。每个人都积极向上，一些人追求权力，另一些人则追求财富。在这样普遍存在的动荡，频繁的利害冲突，以及人们不断追求财富的环境下，哪里能有可以让人们进行深刻思考必不可少的平静可寻呢？当你周围的一切都在不停变幻，而自己也被卷入席卷万物的洪流，人又怎能停下来思考高级科学呢？但是必须将建立已久的安定的民主社会中存在的这种永久的激荡与几乎伴随民主社会出生成长的动荡和革命运动断然分开。当一个高度文明的国家中发生暴力革命的时候，无一例外人们的情感和思想都会受到突然的冲击。而且在民主国家尤其如

it would be unwise to regard it as the test of a general principle. Great revolutions are not more common amongst democratic nations than amongst others: I am even inclined to believe that they are less so. But there prevails amongst those populations a small distressing motion—a sort of incessant jostling of men—which annoys and disturbs the mind, without exciting or elevating it. Men who live in democratic communities not only seldom indulge in meditation, but they naturally entertain very little esteem for it. A democratic state of society and democratic institutions plunge the greater part of men in constant active life; and the habits of mind which are suited to an active life, are not always suited to a contemplative one. The man of action is frequently obliged to content himself with the best he can get, because he would never accomplish his purpose if he chose to carry every detail to perfection. He has perpetually occasion to rely on ideas which he has not had leisure to search to the bottom; for he is much more frequently aided by the opportunity of an idea than by its strict accuracy; and, in the long run, he risks less in making use of some false principles, than in spending his time in establishing all his principles on the basis of truth. The world is not led by long or learned demonstrations; a rapid glance at particular incidents, the daily study of the fleeting passions of the multitude, the accidents of the time, and the art of turning them to account, decide all its affairs.

In the ages in which active life is the condition of almost everyone, men are therefore generally led to attach an excessive value to the rapid bursts and superficial conceptions of the intellect; and, on the other hand, to depreciate below their true standard its slower and deeper labors. This opinion of the public influences the judgment of the men who cultivate the sciences; they are persuaded that they may succeed in those pursuits without meditation, or deterred from such pursuits as demand it.

There are several methods of studying the sciences. Amongst a multitude of men you will find a selfish, mercantile, and trading taste for the discoveries of the mind, which must not be confounded with that disinterested passion which is kindled in the heart of the few. A desire to utilize knowledge is one thing; the pure desire to know is another. I do not doubt that in a few minds and far between, an ardent, inexhaustible love of truth springs up, self-supported, and living in ceaseless fruition without ever attaining the satisfaction which it seeks. This ardent love it is—this proud, disinterested

此，这样一场革命会将国家中所有阶级同时都发动起来，在每个公民的胸中激起勃勃的野心。在法国人毁灭旧封建社会残余的同时，精密科学得到惊人的发展，但是这些突如其来的成果并不是源于民主，而是应该归功于这场史无前例发展起来的革命。那时所发生的事是一个偶然现象，如果将其视为一般规律则有失明智。民主国家发生的伟大革命并不比其他国家更多，我甚至趋向于认为会更少一些。但是在民主国家却普遍存在令人感到不快的小的不和谐，即人与人之间的不断排斥，这只会扰乱和涣散人们的精神，而无法激发和振奋人心。生活在民主社会的人很少静心沉思，所以自然不会重视它。民主的社会状况和民主制度让绝大部分人勇于投入积极的生活，然而适合积极生活的思维习惯并不总适用于沉思。按照这样的习惯活动的人，往往满足于不求甚解，因为如果他们选择让每个细节都趋于完美，那么永远也无法实现自己的目标。他们经常要依赖他们无暇深入研究的思想，因为不失时机地利用这一思想往往比这个思想的严密性对他们更为重要，而且从长远来看，与花时间论证其所有原理的真实性相比，利用某些错误原理的风险还要小些。世界也并非靠长久和确凿无疑的论点来推动，而是通过对特殊现象的快速一瞥，对群众转瞬即逝的热情的日常观察，以及对所发生事实的随时掌握，来处理所有的事物。

所以，在几乎每个人都积极生活的时代，人们普遍过于重视智力的快速成果和肤浅的概念，而另一方面对缓慢深刻的智力劳动则非常轻视。这样的公众舆论影响了科学研究人员的判断，让他们相信即使不静心沉思也可以取得成果，或是根本无须研究那些需要沉思的科学。

love of what is true—which raises men to the abstract sources of truth, to draw their mother-knowledge thence. If Pascal had had nothing in view but some large gain, or even if he had been stimulated by the love of fame alone, I cannot conceive that he would ever have been able to rally all the powers of his mind, as he did, for the better discovery of the most hidden things of the Creator. When I see him, as it were, tear his soul from the midst of all the cares of life to devote it wholly to these researches, and, prematurely snapping the links which bind the frame to life, die of old age before forty, I stand amazed, and I perceive that no ordinary cause is at work to produce efforts so extra-ordinary.

The future will prove whether these passions, at once so rare and so productive, come into being and into growth as easily in the midst of democratic as in aristocratic communities. For myself, I confess that I am slow to believe it. In aristocratic society, the class which gives the tone to opinion, and has the supreme guidance of affairs, being permanently and hereditarily placed above the multitude, naturally conceives a lofty idea of itself and of man. It loves to invent for him noble pleasures, to carve out splendid objects for his ambition. Aristocracies often commit very tyrannical and very inhuman actions; but they rarely entertain grovelling thoughts; and they show a kind of haughty contempt of little pleasures, even whilst they indulge in them. The effect is greatly to raise the general pitch of society. In aristocratic ages vast ideas are commonly entertained of the dignity, the power, and the greatness of man. These opinions exert their influence on those who cultivate the sciences, as well as on the rest of the community. They facilitate the natural impulse of the mind to the highest regions of thought, and they naturally prepare it to conceive a sublime—nay, almost a divine—love of truth. Men of science at such periods are consequently carried away by theory; and it even happens that they frequently conceive an inconsiderate contempt for the practical part of learning. "Archimedes," says Plutarch, "was of so lofty a spirit, that he never condescended to write any treatise on the manner of constructing all these engines of offence and defence. And as he held this science of inventing and putting together engines, and all arts generally speaking which tended to any useful end in practice, to be vile, low, and mercenary, he spent his talents and his studious hours

研究科学有几个方法。对于智力活动的成果，人们存在一种利己主义的爱好，即要将其应用于商业。这种爱好与少数人内心燃起的追求真理的无私热情不可混为一谈。一个只是希望利用知识，而另一个则完全出于对知识的渴望。我并不怀疑，随着时间的流转，在一些人心中会呈现出对真理的无限热爱，而这种热爱靠着自己不断壮大成长，而且永远不会自我满足。正是对真理这种自豪无私的热爱，才能够让人们找到真理的抽象之源，并从中汲取最根本的观念。如果帕斯卡尔的眼中只有名利别无其他，或者只为荣誉而行动的话，我无法想象他能倾尽所有才智，就像他做的那样，揭开造物主隐藏的最深的奥秘。当我看到，他摆脱所有杂念的束缚，倾尽所有精力投入这些研究，不到40岁便英年早逝时，不禁为之惊叹。而且我认为通常的原因绝无法令他做出如此非凡的努力。

未来将证明贵族社会中的如此罕见多产的求知热情能否在民主社会同样能够存在和发展。至于我自己，我承认我很难相信这一点。在贵族制社会，拥有话语权的阶级对政务有绝对的指导权，永远骑在人民的头上，所以，他们自然而然会对自身和人类抱有一种优越的观念。这个阶级热衷于为自己制造高尚的享受，并为自己设定宏伟的目标。贵族的行为常常很残暴不人道，却少有下流的思想，而且贵族对小型娱乐往往表现得不屑一顾，尽管他们也很喜欢。他们的举止间接地提高了整个社会的格调。在贵族时代，对于人的尊严、力量和伟大普遍有着很高的看法。这些看法不但影响着那些研究科学的人，而且也影响着其余的人，会促进人们的精神达到思想的最高境界，并令人们产生对真理的崇高乃至神圣的热爱。因此，这个时代科学的研究者们都潜心研究理论，而且甚至对于理论的实践应用

in writing of those things only whose beauty and subtilty had in them no admixture of necessity."
Such is the aristocratic aim of science; in democratic nations it cannot be the same.

The greater part of the men who constitute these nations are extremely eager in the pursuit of
actual and physical gratification. As they are always dissatisfied with the position which they occupy,
and are always free to leave it, they think of nothing but the means of changing their fortune, or
of increasing it. To minds thus predisposed, every new method which leads by a shorter road to
wealth, every machine which spares labor, every instrument which diminishes the cost of production,
every discovery which facilitates pleasures or augments them, seems to be the grandest effort of the
human intellect. It is chiefly from these motives that a democratic people addicts itself to scientific
pursuits—that it understands, and that it respects them. In aristocratic ages, science is more particularly
called upon to furnish gratification to the mind; in democracies, to the body. You may be sure that the
more a nation is democratic, enlightened, and free, the greater will be the number of these interested
promoters of scientific genius, and the more will discoveries immediately applicable to productive
industry confer gain, fame, and even power on their authors. For in democracies the working class
takes a part in public affairs; and public honors, as well as pecuniary remuneration, may be awarded
to those who deserve them. In a community thus organized it may easily be conceived that the
human mind may be led insensibly to the neglect of theory; and that it is urged, on the contrary,
with unparalleled vehemence to the applications of science, or at least to that portion of theoretical
science which is necessary to those who make such applications. In vain will some innate propensity
raise the mind towards the loftier spheres of the intellect; interest draws it down to the middle zone.
There it may develop all its energy and restless activity, there it may engender all its wonders. These
very Americans, who have not discovered one of the general laws of mechanics, have introduced into
navigation an engine which changes the aspect of the world.

Assuredly I do not content that the democratic nations of our time are destined to witness the
extinction of the transcendent luminaries of man's intelligence, nor even that no new lights will ever
start into existence. At the age at which the world has now arrived, and amongst so many cultivated

往往持不屑一顾的态度。普卢塔克曾经说过："阿基米德的治学精神如此崇高以至于不肯
自贬身价撰写任何有关进攻和防御性武器如何制造的内容。在他看来，有关发明和机器组
装的所有科学，以及一般来说最终会应用于实践的所有技艺，都是毫无价值、卑贱且市侩
的。他把自己的才情和研究都用在撰写那些与实际毫无关系的美和精妙之上。"这就是贵
族在科学上的追求，而在民主国家绝无可能出现。

民主国家的大部分人非常热衷于追求实际的和物质的享乐。因为他们总是对自己的
处境感到不满，而且可以随意摆脱这样的处境，所以他们满脑子想的都是如何改变命运增
加财富。因此，对于抱有这样想法的人来说，一切可以成为发财致富的新捷径，一切可以
节省劳力的机器，一切可以降低生产成本的工具，一切有助于享乐或增加享乐的新发现，
似乎才是人类智慧最伟大的成果。民主国家人们对科学的追求、尊重和认识都是出于这些
动机。在贵族时代，科学研究主要为了获得精神上的满足，而在民主社会则是为了身体的
享受。可以想见，一个国家越是民主、文明和自由，以利为先的科学天才的催生者也就越
多，能直接应用于工业生产的发明也就越多，而且这些发明还能给发明人带来名、利乃至
权。因为在民主社会劳动阶级参与国家事务，而且公共荣誉和金钱的报酬会奖给那些值得
奖励的人。所以，不难想象在如此架构的社会中，人们的精神不但会不知不觉中忽视理
论，而且会无比强烈地促进应用科学，或者至少是那部分应用必不可少的理论科学。即使
天生的求知欲会将人们的思想推向最高的智力活动领域，也毫无用处，因为利益会将人的
智力活动拉回到中等的地带。在这里，可以激发出人所有的能量和积极性，可以创造出所

nations, perpetually excited by the fever of productive industry, the bonds which connect the different parts of science together cannot fail to strike the observation; and the taste for practical science itself, if it be enlightened, ought to lead men not to neglect theory. In the midst of such numberless attempted applications of so many experiments, repeated every day, it is almost impossible that general laws should not frequently be brought to light; so that great discoveries would be frequent, though great inventors be rare. I believe, moreover, in the high calling of scientific minds. If the democratic principle does not, on the one hand, induce men to cultivate science for its own sake, on the other it enormously increases the number of those who do cultivate it. Nor is it credible that, from amongst so great a multitude no speculative genius should from time to time arise, inflamed by the love of truth alone. Such a one, we may be sure, would dive into the deepest mysteries of nature, whatever be the spirit of his country or his age. He requires no assistance in his course—enough that he be not checked in it.

All that I mean to say is this:—permanent inequality of conditions leads men to confine themselves to the arrogant and sterile research of abstract truths; whilst the social condition and the institutions of democracy prepare them to seek the immediate and useful practical results of the sciences. This tendency is natural and inevitable: it is curious to be acquainted with it, and it may be necessary to point it out. If those who are called upon to guide the nations of our time clearly discerned from afar off these new tendencies, which will soon be irresistible, they would understand that, possessing education and freedom, men living in democratic ages cannot fail to improve the industrial part of science; and that henceforward all the efforts of the constituted authorities ought to be directed to support the highest branches of learning, and to foster the nobler passion for science itself. In the present age the human mind must be coerced into theoretical studies; it runs of its own accord to practical applications; and, instead of perpetually referring it to the minute examination of secondary effects, it is well to divert it from them sometimes, in order to raise it up to the contemplation of primary causes. Because the civilization of ancient Rome perished in consequence

有奇迹。这些美国人，尽管连一个力学基本定理都没有发现，却推出一部可以使整个世界航运业面貌为之一新的新机器。

当然，我并不是说我们这个时代的民主国家注定只能眼睁睁地看着人类智慧之光渐渐熄灭，甚至不会再有新的光芒绽放。世界发展到现在这个时代，许多开化的国家都在不懈地努力发展工业，所以将科学的不同部分联系起来的纽带便不可能不引起人们的注意，而对实践科学的爱好本身，如果它开化到一定的程度，必然会引导人们重视理论。在数不胜数的每日不断重复的应用实验之中，不可能不常常发现一般法则。所以，尽管伟大的发明家不常见，但是伟大的发明必然层出不穷。此外，我还相信科学的崇高使命。一方面，即使民主原则不能促使人们为了科学而研究科学，而另一方面，它可以促使研究科学的人数大幅增长。不要不相信，在如此众多的研究人员中会时不时地冒出个真正热爱真理的天才来进行理论研究。我们可以肯定，这样的天才无论他所处的国家和时代受到何种精神的支配，必然会努力探索大自然最深的奥秘。在他前进的道路上他不需要别人的帮助，只要没有人阻碍他，便已心满意足。

在这里我想说的是：永久的不平等会将人们限制在高尚却一无所获的抽象真理的研究，而民主的社会和制度则让人们时刻追求科学的直接实际的应用。这种趋势是自然而然的也是不可避免的。了解这种趋势能够满足好奇心，但是指出这种趋势则非常必要。如果负责引领我们这个时代国家的人能够有远见卓识，清楚地认识到这些不可阻挡的新趋势，他们就能明白，生活在民主时代的人在获得教育和自由之后，必然会发展科学的工业应用部分，所以从今往后政府当局应倾尽全力支持高级科学的研究并培养研究科学的高尚的热

of the invasion of the barbarians, we are perhaps too apt to think that civilization cannot perish in any other manner. If the light by which we are guided is ever extinguished, it will dwindle by degrees, and expire of itself. By dint of close adherence to mere applications, principles would be lost sight of; and when the principles were wholly forgotten, the methods derived from them would be ill-pursued. New methods could no longer be invented, and men would continue to apply, without intelligence, and without art, scientific processes no longer understood.

When Europeans first arrived in China, three hundred years ago, they found that almost all the arts had reached a certain degree of perfection there; and they were surprised that a people which had attained this point should not have gone beyond it. At a later period they discovered some traces of the higher branches of science which were lost. The nation was absorbed in productive industry: the greater part of its scientific processes had been preserved, but science itself no longer existed there. This served to explain the strangely motionless state in which they found the minds of this people. The Chinese, in following the track of their forefathers, had forgotten the reasons by which the latter had been guided. They still used the formula, without asking for its meaning: they retained the instrument, but they no longer possessed the art of altering or renewing it. The Chinese, then, had lost the power of change; for them to improve was impossible. They were compelled, at all times and in all points, to imitate their predecessors, lest they should stray into utter darkness, by deviating for an instant from the path already laid down for them. The source of human knowledge was all but dry; and though the stream still ran on, it could neither swell its waters nor alter its channel. Notwithstanding this, China had subsisted peaceably for centuries. The invaders who had conquered the country assumed the manners of the inhabitants, and order prevailed there. A sort of physical prosperity was everywhere discernible: revolutions were rare, and war was, so to speak, unknown.

It is then a fallacy to flatter ourselves with the reflection that the barbarians are still far from us; for if there be some nations which allow civilization to be torn from their grasp, there are others who trample it themselves under their feet.

情。在今天这个时代，必须促使人们的精神注重进行理论研究，并使其自然转化为实践应用，而不应该让它总是追求详细研究带来的次要功效。为了能够将人的精神提升到静心沉思最初原因的水准，最好时不时地暂时放弃一下这样的详细研究。因为古罗马文明的灭亡是蛮夷民族的入侵造成的，于是我们过于相信文明的灭亡不会有其他的方式。如果引导我们的前进之光会熄灭，那它必然只会逐渐暗淡，而最终自行熄灭。只注重应用，就会忽视原理，而当原理完全被人们遗忘的时候，由此而生的方法也不会太多。结果，人们再也无法发现新的方法，只是继续无知，不熟练地使用他们不明就里的科学方法。

当欧洲人三百年前第一次来到中国时，他们觉得几乎所有的技艺在这里都达到近乎完美的地步，并认为不会再有任何一个国家能够超越它。不久之后，他们发现中国的一些已经失传的高级知识的蛛丝马迹。这个国家注重实业，大部分的科学方法已经被保存下来，但是科学本身已经不复存在。这恰好可以说明这个民族的精神已经陷入不可思议的停滞状态。中国人，追随着祖先的脚步，却忘记了引领他们祖先前进的原理。他们依然在用公式，却不再追究其真意。他们继承了生产工具，却不再设法对其进行改进和更新。于是，中国人失去了变革的力量，所以也无法再进步。他们不得不时刻完全模仿他们的祖先，不敢偏离祖先留下的道路半步，唯恐会误入歧途。人的知识之源近乎干涸，因此，尽管依旧流水潺潺，但是已无法再掀起波澜，也不可能改变河道。尽管如此，中国已经平静地存在了几个世纪。征服这里的入侵者们接受了居住在这里的人们的习俗，一切依旧井然有序。一种物质繁荣依旧随处可见，革命已实属罕见，战争更是闻所未闻的事情。

所以，不要错误地以为蛮族离我们尚远而高枕无忧，因为如果说有些国家文明的火把

Chapter XI: Of The Spirit In Which The Americans Cultivate The Arts

It would be to waste the time of my readers and my own if I strove to demonstrate how the general mediocrity of fortunes, the absence of superfluous wealth, the universal desire of comfort, and the constant efforts by which everyone attempts to procure it, make the taste for the useful predominate over the love of the beautiful in the heart of man. Democratic nations, amongst which all these things exist, will therefore cultivate the arts which serve to render life easy, in preference to those whose object is to adorn it. They will habitually prefer the useful to the beautiful, and they will require that the beautiful should be useful. But I propose to go further; and after having pointed out this first feature, to sketch several others.

It commonly happens that in the ages of privilege the practice of almost all the arts becomes a privilege; and that every profession is a separate walk, upon which it is not allowable for everyone to enter. Even when productive industry is free, the fixed character which belongs to aristocratic nations gradually segregates all the persons who practise the same art, till they form a distinct class, always composed of the same families, whose members are all known to each other, and amongst whom a public opinion of their own and a species of corporate pride soon spring up. In a class or guild of this kind, each artisan has not only his fortune to make, but his reputation to preserve. He is not exclusively swayed by his own interest, or even by that of his customer, but by that of the body to which he belongs; and the interest of that body is, that each artisan should produce the best possible workmanship. In aristocratic ages, the object of the arts is therefore to manufacture as well as possible—not with the greatest despatch, or at the lowest rate.

When, on the contrary, every profession is open to all—when a multitude of persons are constantly embracing and abandoning it—and when its several members are strangers to each other, indifferent, and from their numbers hardly seen amongst themselves; the social tie is destroyed, and each workman, standing alone, endeavors simply to gain the greatest possible quantity of money at the least possible cost. The will of the customer is then his only limit. But at the same time a corresponding revolution takes place in the customer also. In countries in which riches as well as

是被别人从手中夺走的，那么还有另一些国家他们是用自己的脚把文明的火把踩灭的。

第十一章　美国人用什么样的精神对待艺术

如果我力图说明，每个人的财富普遍相等，谁也没有过多剩余，人人希望过上舒适的生活，于是大家不懈地努力追求，从而在人们心中形成爱好实用胜过热爱美的状况，不但是在浪费读者的时间也是浪费自己的时间。因为民主国家都有这些情况存在，所以相对于那些用来装点生活的艺术，他们会优先发展让生活变得舒适的艺术。他们习惯上对实用的爱好要胜过美，所以要求美的东西也必须实用。但是我想要更进一步，在指出这第一个特征之后，再简述一下其他的几个特征。

一般来说，在特权时代，几乎所有的艺术实践都成为特权，而且每种职业都是一个不允许他人涉足的独立领域。甚至当各行各业已经自由的时候，贵族制国家的固有特征会逐渐让从事同一行业的所有人形成一个不同的阶级，总是由固定的几个家族组成，成员之间彼此非常熟悉，于是不久便形成同行业间的共同的民意和自尊。在这样一个阶级或行会的内部，每个手艺人不但要挣钱，而且要维护声誉。他们不只为自己的利益、为顾客的利益所左右，而且受到其所属团体利益的左右，而所谓的团体利益指的是每个手艺人都应该制造出尽可能好的产品。因此，在贵族时代，艺术的目标就是尽可能制造出精美的产品，而不是加快速度或是降低成本。

相反，当每个行业都向所有人开放，当所有人都可以随时进入或离开这个行业时，

power are concentrated and retained in the hands of the few, the use of the greater part of this world's goods belongs to a small number of individuals, who are always the same. Necessity, public opinion, or moderate desires exclude all others from the enjoyment of them. As this aristocratic class remains fixed at the pinnacle of greatness on which it stands, without diminution or increase, it is always acted upon by the same wants and affected by them in the same manner. The men of whom it is composed naturally derive from their superior and hereditary position a taste for what is extremely well made and lasting. This affects the general way of thinking of the nation in relation to the arts. It often occurs, among such a people, that even the peasant will rather go without the object he covets, than procure it in a state of imperfection. In aristocracies, then, the handicraftsmen work for only a limited number of very fastidious customers: the profit they hope to make depends principally on the perfection of their workmanship.

Such is no longer the case when, all privileges being abolished, ranks are intermingled, and men are forever rising or sinking upon the ladder of society. Amongst a democratic people a number of citizens always exist whose patrimony is divided and decreasing. They have contracted, under more prosperous circumstances, certain wants, which remain after the means of satisfying such wants are gone; and they are anxiously looking out for some surreptitious method of providing for them. On the other hand, there are always in democracies a large number of men whose fortune is upon the increase, but whose desires grow much faster than their fortunes: and who gloat upon the gifts of wealth in anticipation, long before they have means to command them. Such men eager to find some short cut to these gratifications, already almost within their reach. From the combination of these causes the result is, that in democracies there are always a multitude of individuals whose wants are above their means, and who are very willing to take up with imperfect satisfaction rather than abandon the object of their desires.

The artisan readily understands these passions, for he himself partakes in them: in an aristocracy he would seek to sell his workmanship at a high price to the few; he now conceives that the more expeditious way of getting rich is to sell them at a low price to all. But there are only two ways of

而且当行业成员之间彼此不再熟悉，漠不关心，甚至互不相讽的地步，行业的纽带不复存在，每个匠人都各自为政，只想着用尽可能少的成本获取尽可能大的利润，于是顾客的意志成为他们唯一的忌惮。但是同时消费者身上也相应地发生了巨大的变化。在财富如同权力一样集中到少数人手中的国家中，这个世界大多数的财富将为同一些为数不多的个人所享用。贫困、习俗和自我节制将其余所有人排除在这样的享受之外。当这个贵族阶级始终处于巅峰不动，而且既不扩大也不缩小的时候，他们的需求也总是一成不变，享用的方式也始终如一。形成这个阶级的人们因为高人一等的世袭地位自然喜好精工细作耐用的东西。这影响着这个国家对于艺术品的普遍看法。在这样的国家中，甚至农民也常常觊觎最好的物品，而不愿将就买一些次货。于是，在贵族制国家，手艺人只为数量非常有限的非常挑剔的顾客服务。他们之所以能赚钱完全仰赖他们精湛的手艺。

但如果所有的特权都被废除，等级的界限消失，人们在社会的阶梯上下浮沉的时候，情况就不会再是这个样子。在一个民主国家，公民的财产不断地被分化缩小。他们家业兴旺时催生的某些需要，在他们无法再得到满足之后依旧存在，于是他们迫切地想要找到某种能够满足这种需要的隐秘手段。另一方面，民主国家中还有大批人的财富不断增加，但是他们的欲望比他们的财富增长得更快。在得到满足之前，他们贪婪的目光早已盯上了这笔唾手可得的财富。这些人热衷于寻找某种捷径来获得满足，尽管财富已经近在咫尺。在这些原因的共同作用下，于是就出现了这样的结果：在民主国家，总是有很多人的需求超出自己的能力范围，而且宁可勉强地满足自己的愿望，也不愿放弃他们渴望的对象。

lowering the price of commodities. The first is to discover some better, shorter, and more ingenious method of producing them: the second is to manufacture a larger quantity of goods, nearly similar, but of less value. Amongst a democratic population, all the intellectual faculties of the workman are directed to these two objects: he strives to invent methods which may enable him not only to work better, but quicker and cheaper; or, if he cannot succeed in that, to diminish the intrinsic qualities of the thing he makes, without rendering it wholly unfit for the use for which it is intended. When none but the wealthy had watches, they were almost all very good ones: few are now made which are worth much, but everybody has one in his pocket. Thus the democratic principle not only tends to direct the human mind to the useful arts, but it induces the artisan to produce with greater rapidity a quantity of imperfect commodities, and the consumer to content himself with these commodities.

Not that in democracies the arts are incapable of producing very commendable works, if such be required. This may occasionally be the case, if customers appear who are ready to pay for time and trouble. In this rivalry of every kind of industry—in the midst of this immense competition and these countless experiments, some excellent workmen are formed who reach the utmost limits of their craft. But they have rarely an opportunity of displaying what they can do; they are scrupulously sparing of their powers; they remain in a state of accomplished mediocrity, which condemns itself, and, though it be very well able to shoot beyond the mark before it, aims only at what it hits. In aristocracies, on the contrary, workmen always do all they can; and when they stop, it is because they have reached the limit of their attainments.

When I arrive in a country where I find some of the finest productions of the arts, I learn from this fact nothing of the social condition or of the political constitution of the country. But if I perceive that the productions of the arts are generally of an inferior quality, very abundant and very cheap, I am convinced that, amongst the people where this occurs, privilege is on the decline, and that ranks are beginning to intermingle, and will soon be confounded together.

The handicraftsmen of democratic ages endeavor not only to bring their useful productions within the reach of the whole community, but they strive to give to all their commodities attractive qualities

　　手艺人很能理解这样的感情，因为他们自己也是其中的一分子。在贵族制国家，他们向少数人高价出售自己的产品，而现在他们知道最快速的致富之路是低价向大众出售自己的产品。然而，要想降低商品价格，只有两种方法：第一种是找到某种更好、更快和更精巧的生产方法，第二种则是大批量生产质量相似但是价格较低的产品。在民主国家，手工业者的所有精力都用在这两方面。他们努力发明能够做得更好、更快、更经济的新方法。如果他们做不到这一点，便会降低产品的品质，但同时还不能降低产品的实用性。在只有富人戴得起表的时代，所有的表都价值不菲。而现在，表已经不再是稀罕东西，几乎每个人口袋中都有一块。因此，民主的原则不但会促使人们的思想专注实用工艺，而且还会引导手艺人快速生产出大量不完美的商品，而消费者对这样的商品也表示满意。

　　这并不是说，民主国家，在必要的时候，无法生产出可以为人所称道的产品。如果顾客愿意付出时间和金钱，手艺人也可以生产出高水平产品。在各行各业参与的这场竞赛中，经过大量的竞争和无数的实验，自然会出现一些优秀的手艺人，他们的技艺登峰造极，却鲜有机会一试身手。他们对自己的手艺吝啬到极点，表现得庸庸碌碌，而且尽管他们的能力已经大大超出所承担的任务，却只满足于完成任务。相反，在贵族国家，手艺人总是精益求精，而且只有做到最好的时候才肯停手。

　　当我来到一个国家，看到最精致的艺术品，我无法据此知晓这个国家的社会和政治状况。但是，如果我发现这个国家的艺术品一般来说质量不高、数量众多且价格便宜，我便可以肯定在这个国家正在发生的事情：特权正在消失，阶级开始混合而且不久便会融为一体。

which they do not in reality possess. In the confusion of all ranks everyone hopes to appear what he is not, and makes great exertions to succeed in this object. This sentiment indeed, which is but too natural to the heart of man, does not originate in the democratic principle; but that principle applies it to material objects. To mimic virtue is of every age; but the hypocrisy of luxury belongs more particularly to the ages of democracy.

To satisfy these new cravings of human vanity the arts have recourse to every species of imposture: and these devices sometimes go so far as to defeat their own purpose. Imitation diamonds are now made which may be easily mistaken for real ones; as soon as the art of fabricating false diamonds shall have reached so high a degree of perfection that they cannot be distinguished from real ones, it is probable that both one and the other will be abandoned, and become mere pebbles again.

This leads me to speak of those arts which are called the fine arts, by way of distinction. I do not believe that it is a necessary effect of a democratic social condition and of democratic institutions to diminish the number of men who cultivate the fine arts; but these causes exert a very powerful influence on the manner in which these arts are cultivated. Many of those who had already contracted a taste for the fine arts are impoverished: on the other hand, many of those who are not yet rich begin to conceive that taste, at least by imitation; and the number of consumers increases, but opulent and fastidious consumers become more scarce. Something analogous to what I have already pointed out in the useful arts then takes place in the fine arts; the productions of artists are more numerous, but the merit of each production is diminished. No longer able to soar to what is great, they cultivate what is pretty and elegant; and appearance is more attended to than reality. In aristocracies a few great pictures are produced; in democratic countries, a vast number of insignificant ones. In the former, statues are raised of bronze; in the latter, they are modelled in plaster.

When I arrived for the first time at New York, by that part of the Atlantic Ocean which is called the Narrows, I was surprised to perceive along the shore, at some distance from the city, a considerable number of little palaces of white marble, several of which were built after the models

　　民主时代的手艺人不仅努力生产每个人都能买得起的具有实用价值的产品，而且还想方设法让他们的产品看上去具有本来不具备的诱人品质。在各阶级相互混杂的社会，每个人都希望自己看起来不是自己真实的样子，并不惜为此大费周章。这种情感完全是人心的自然流露，而并非民主的原则使然，但民主的原则的确让人们把这种情感应用到物质方面。虚伪的美德每个时代都有，但是虚伪的奢侈则是民主时代所独有。

　　为了满足人虚荣心的这些新渴望，于是便在工艺上进行种种欺骗，而且有时候这样的伎俩已经过分地影响到工艺本身。现在，假钻石已经足以乱真，一旦假钻石的制作工艺达到登峰造极真假难辨的地步，人们便可能对两者都不感兴趣，只把它们视为普通的石子罢了。

　　这又令我想要谈一谈那些我们称之为"美术"的独特艺术。我不认为民主的社会状况和制度必然导致从事美术的人的数量减少，但是肯定会对这些美术工作者的培养方式产生巨大的影响。一方面，已经沾染上美术这一爱好的人，大多数都会变穷；另一方面，一些还没富起来的人开始附庸风雅爱好美术。因此，美术品消费者的数量增加了，但是识货的有钱人则越来越少。我曾说过的发生在实用艺术上的类似情形也发生在美术方面。艺术家们的产量与日俱增，但每件美术品的价值则在下降。人们不再追求伟大，而只关注优美和悦目，表面比实质更重要。在贵族制国家，涌现出很多伟大的画作，而在民主国家，大量的平庸之作层出不穷。在前者，建造的是青铜像；而在后者，则多的是石膏的仿制品。

　　当我从大西洋驶入伊斯特河第一次来到纽约的时候，很惊讶地看到沿着河岸离市中心不远的地方，有一些白色大理石建造的小宫殿，其中的几个还颇具古风遗韵。当我第二天

of ancient architecture. When I went the next day to inspect more closely the building which had particularly attracted my notice, I found that its walls were of whitewashed brick, and its columns of painted wood. All the edifices which I had admired the night before were of the same kind.

The social condition and the institutions of democracy impart, moreover, certain peculiar tendencies to all the imitative arts, which it is easy to point out. They frequently withdraw them from the delineation of the soul to fix them exclusively on that of the body: and they substitute the representation of motion and sensation for that of sentiment and thought: in a word, they put the real in the place of the ideal. I doubt whether Raphael studied the minutest intricacies of the mechanism of the human body as thoroughly as the draughtsmen of our own time. He did not attach the same importance to rigorous accuracy on this point as they do, because he aspired to surpass nature. He sought to make of man something which should be superior to man, and to embellish beauty's self. David and his scholars were, on the contrary, as good anatomists as they were good painters. They wonderfully depicted the models which they had before their eyes, but they rarely imagined anything beyond them: they followed nature with fidelity: whilst Raphael sought for something better than nature. They have left us an exact portraiture of man; but he discloses in his works a glimpse of the Divinity. This remark as to the manner of treating a subject is no less applicable to the choice of it. The painters of the Middle Ages generally sought far above themselves, and away from their own time, for mighty subjects, which left to their imagination an unbounded range. Our painters frequently employ their talents in the exact imitation of the details of private life, which they have always before their eyes; and they are forever copying trivial objects, the originals of which are only too abundant in nature.

Chapter XII: Why The Americans Raise Some Monuments So Insignificant, And Others So Important

I have just observed, that in democratic ages monuments of the arts tend to become more

前往其中一个特别吸引我的地方想要仔细看看的时候，结果却发现这里哪有什么大理石，不过是砖墙涂了一层白粉，高大的柱子则是涂了漆的木头。我昨晚倾慕不已的所有广厦，原来都是这样的货色。

　　民主的社会状况和制度让所有的仿制艺术品具有一眼便能看穿的特性。这样的特性往往使艺术只关注描摹表象而不注重刻画灵魂，并用动作和感触的表现代替了情感和思想的表现。一句话，他们用现实取代了理想。我怀疑拉斐尔是否像我们这个时代的画家那样细致入微地研究过人体的结构。在这一点上，他的想法一定不同于我们的画家，要描摹得不差分毫，因为他所追求的神似而不是形似。他要把人画得像人而且还要超越人，要把美画得比美本身更美。相反，大卫和他的学生们不但是优秀的画家也同样是优秀的解剖家。他们完美地描绘出他们眼前的模特，但是仅此而已。他们精确地描摹自然，而拉斐尔则追求更高的东西。他们虽然给我们留下了精准的人像画，但是拉斐尔在他的作品中则让我们得窥天堂的一隅。我上述有关绘画方法的评论同样适用于绘画题材的选择。中世纪的画家普遍追求超越自身及所处时代的恢宏题材，并能够让他们的想象力尽情发挥。我们这个时代的画家则往往把他们的才华用来分毫不差地表现呈现在他们眼前的日常生活的细节，他们始终在复制大自然中随处可见的平凡题材。

第十二章　为什么美国人建造的建筑物有些是那么平庸，有些又是那么恢宏

　　我刚刚已经说过，在民主时代，艺术品往往变得越来越多但同时也越来越平庸。但我

numerous and less important. I now hasten to point out the exception to this rule. In a democratic community individuals are very powerless; but the State which represents them all, and contains them all in its grasp, is very powerful. Nowhere do citizens appear so insignificant as in a democratic nation; nowhere does the nation itself appear greater, or does the mind more easily take in a wide general survey of it. In democratic communities the imagination is compressed when men consider themselves; it expands indefinitely when they think of the State. Hence it is that the same men who live on a small scale in narrow dwellings, frequently aspire to gigantic splendor in the erection of their public monuments.

The Americans traced out the circuit of an immense city on the site which they intended to make their capital, but which, up to the present time, is hardly more densely peopled than Pontoise, though, according to them, it will one day contain a million of inhabitants. They have already rooted up trees for ten miles round, lest they should interfere with the future citizens of this imaginary metropolis. They have erected a magnificent palace for Congress in the centre of the city, and have given it the pompous name of the Capitol. The several States of the Union are every day planning and erecting for themselves prodigious undertakings, which would astonish the engineers of the great European nations. Thus democracy not only leads men to a vast number of inconsiderable productions; it also leads them to raise some monuments on the largest scale: but between these two extremes there is a blank. A few scattered remains of enormous buildings can therefore teach us nothing of the social condition and the institutions of the people by whom they were raised. I may add, though the remark leads me to step out of my subject, that they do not make us better acquainted with its greatness, its civilization, and its real prosperity. Whensoever a power of any kind shall be able to make a whole people co-operate in a single undertaking, that power, with a little knowledge and a great deal of time, will succeed in obtaining something enormous from the co-operation of efforts so multiplied. But this does not lead to the conclusion that the people was very happy, very enlightened, or even very strong.

The Spaniards found the City of Mexico full of magnificent temples and vast palaces; but that did

现在要赶快指出，事情也有例外。在一个民主社会，个人往往无能为力，但是代表他们统治众人的国家则非常强大。世界上没有任何一个国家的公民像民主国家的公民那样渺小，没有哪个国家能像民主国家那样自身拥有强大的力量，而且也没有任何一个国家的精神能够如民主国家的精神那样具有如此开阔的视野。在民主社会，当人们只考虑自己的时候，想象力就会受到抑制；而当他想到国家的时候，想象力便无限广阔。因此，住在小房子里过惯平凡生活的人，总是力求建造巨大辉煌的公共建筑物。

美国人在他们打算设立首都的地方规划一座巨大的城市，但是现在这个地方的人口还不及法国的蓬图瓦兹多，尽管根据他们的计划，有一天这里的居民人口将达到百万。他们已将方圆10英里以内的树木连根拔起，为的就是不妨碍这座想象中的大都市未来居民的生活。在这座城市的中心，他们建造了供国会使用的恢宏建筑，并给它起个了好听的名字：国会大厦。联邦的各州每天都在各自计划建造一些甚至会令欧洲大国的工程师感到震撼的巨大工程。因此，民主不但促使人们大量生产微不足道的产品，还会促使人们兴建一些宏伟的建筑物，但在这两个极端之间则是一片空白。因此，散建在各地的巨大建筑物根本无法向我们透露将它们兴建起来的这个国家的社会状况和制度。尽管这句话有点离题，但是我想说：这些宏伟的建筑物无法让我们更好地理解这个国家的伟大、文明和真正的繁荣。无论何时，只要任何一个政权能够让全体人民合作共同承担一项任务，哪怕科学水平不高，时间也不充分，它必然能够在众人如此的帮助下，成功取得某些恢宏的成果。但是不能据此得出结论认为这个国家非常幸福、高度文明乃至异常强大。

not prevent Cortes from conquering the Mexican Empire with 600 foot soldiers and sixteen horses. If the Romans had been better acquainted with the laws of hydraulics, they would not have constructed all the aqueducts which surround the ruins of their cities—they would have made a better use of their power and their wealth. If they had invented the steam-engine, perhaps they would not have extended to the extremities of their empire those long artificial roads which are called Roman roads. These things are at once the splendid memorials of their ignorance and of their greatness. A people which should leave no other vestige of its track than a few leaden pipes in the earth and a few iron rods upon its surface, might have been more the master of nature than the Romans.

Chapter XIII: Literary Characteristics Of Democratic Ages

When a traveller goes into a bookseller's shop in the United States, and examines the American books upon the shelves, the number of works appears extremely great; whilst that of known authors appears, on the contrary, to be extremely small. He will first meet with a number of elementary treatises, destined to teach the rudiments of human knowledge. Most of these books are written in Europe; the Americans reprint them, adapting them to their own country. Next comes an enormous quantity of religious works, Bibles, sermons, edifying anecdotes, controversial divinity, and reports of charitable societies; lastly, appears the long catalogue of political pamphlets. In America, parties do not write books to combat each others' opinions, but pamphlets which are circulated for a day with incredible rapidity, and then expire. In the midst of all these obscure productions of the human brain are to be found the more remarkable works of that small number of authors, whose names are, or ought to be, known to Europeans.

Although America is perhaps in our days the civilized country in which literature is least attended to, a large number of persons are nevertheless to be found there who take an interest in the productions of the mind, and who make them, if not the study of their lives, at least the charm of their leisure hours. But England supplies these readers with the larger portion of the books which they require. Almost all important English books are republished in the United States. The literary

西班牙人当年来到墨西哥城的时候，看到这里到处是宏伟的庙宇和巨大的宫殿，但这并没能阻止西班牙人仅靠600名士兵和16匹骏马就将墨西哥帝国征服。如果罗马人能够多懂一点水力学原理，他们必定会更好地利用自己的人力和物力，而不会在如今已为一片废墟的城市周围建造如此多的水道。如果他们已经发明了蒸汽机，也许就不会修茸向四面八方延伸开来的长长的被称为"罗马大道"的人造石路。如今这些恢宏的建筑仅供后人凭吊，在证明罗马人无知的同时也在证明他们的伟大。一个除了在地下铺设几段铅灰色管道，在地面搭起一些铁架之外，没有留下任何恢宏建筑物的国家，也许比罗马人更能成为自然之主。

第十三章　民主时代的文学特征

当一个旅行者来到美国的书店，看着书架上美国出版的书，会感到书籍的数量的确很可观，但是知名作家却寥寥无几。在这里，人们首先看到的是一些介绍基本原理的初级读物，其中的大多数都是在欧洲出版后，美国人依据自己的国情再版的。随后，就是数不胜数的宗教书籍，如圣经、布道集、醒世故事集、教义辩论书以及慈善团体报告等。最后则是各式各样的政治小册子。在美国，各党派并不出版专门著作互相攻击对方的观点，却以难以置信的速度印发小册子，以至于在其出版后的当天就会被人们遗忘。在所有这些乌七八糟的人类精神产品中，时不时地也会发现几个为数不多的欧洲人知晓的能称得起名家的作品。

尽管美国也许是我们这个时代文明国家中最不关心文学的国家，然而在这里却有很多人关注精神食粮，尽管他们并非终身致力于此，但至少会将自己所有的业余时间完全用

genius of Great Britain still darts its rays into the recesses of the forests of the New World. There is hardly a pioneer's hut which does not contain a few odd volumes of Shakespeare. I remember that I read the feudal play of Henry V for the first time in a loghouse.

Not only do the Americans constantly draw upon the treasures of English literature, but it may be said with truth that they find the literature of England growing on their own soil. The larger part of that small number of men in the United States who are engaged in the composition of literary works are English in substance, and still more so in form. Thus they transport into the midst of democracy the ideas and literary fashions which are current amongst the aristocratic nation they have taken for their model. They paint with colors borrowed from foreign manners; and as they hardly ever represent the country they were born in as it really is, they are seldom popular there. The citizens of the United States are themselves so convinced that it is not for them that books are published, that before they can make up their minds upon the merit of one of their authors, they generally wait till his fame has been ratified in England, just as in pictures the author of an original is held to be entitled to judge of the merit of a copy. The inhabitants of the United States have then at present, properly speaking, no literature. The only authors whom I acknowledge as American are the journalists. They indeed are not great writers, but they speak the language of their countrymen, and make themselves heard by them. Other authors are aliens; they are to the Americans what the imitators of the Greeks and Romans were to us at the revival of learning—an object of curiosity, not of general sympathy. They amuse the mind, but they do not act upon the manners of the people.

I have already said that this state of things is very far from originating in democracy alone, and that the causes of it must be sought for in several peculiar circumstances independent of the democratic principle. If the Americans, retaining the same laws and social condition, had had a different origin, and had been transported into another country, I do not question that they would have had a literature. Even as they now are, I am convinced that they will ultimately have one; but its character will be different from that which marks the American literary productions of our time, and that character will be peculiarly its own. Nor is it impossible to trace this character beforehand.

上。这些人所需要的书籍大部分来自英国，英国的一些重要著作几乎全部被美国再版。英国文学巨匠还将他们的光芒折射到新大陆的密林深处。几乎所有拓荒者的小屋里都能找到基本莎士比亚的作品。我记得，我第一次读历史剧《亨利五世》还是在一间原木小屋。

美国人不但总是汲取英国文学宝藏中的精华，而且甚至可以说他们让英国文学在自己土地上得到发展。在美国为数不多的从事文学创作的人之中，绝大部分原来就是英国人，所采用的表现手法也是英国式的。而且他们将贵族国家盛行的文学思想和风潮视为自己的楷模，并将其引入自己的民主制度。他们借用外来的色彩渲染自己的作品，而且因为无法呈现自己出生的这片土地的真实面貌，所以很难受到人们的欢迎。美国的公民自己也意识到这些书籍并非为他们而写，通常只是在他们的某一位作家在英国得到认可之后，他们才会对其大加赞赏，这就好像是画作的原作者被迫放弃判断自己画作真伪的权利。可以说，美国的居民没有文学。我认为在美国称得上作家的只有新闻记者而已。的确，他们并不是伟大的作家，但是他们是在用美国人的语言来说给美国人听。而其余的作家都可以算成外国人，他们对于美国人而言，就如同文艺复兴时期模仿希腊罗马文学的作家之于我们一样，对他们只有好奇，而没有共鸣。他们的作品可以供大众消遣，但是不会起到移风易俗的作用。

我已经说过，现在的这种状况不能仅归因于民主制度，还应从与民主无关的几个独特的环境条件中去找寻原因。如果美国人保留同样的法律和社会状况不变，但是其来源有所不同，而且移居到另一个地方，我绝不置疑他们会有自己的文学。甚至他们目前虽然如

I suppose an aristocratic people amongst whom letters are cultivated; the labors of the mind, as well as the affairs of state, are conducted by a ruling class in society. The literary as well as the political career is almost entirely confined to this class, or to those nearest to it in rank. These premises suffice to give me a key to all the rest. When a small number of the same men are engaged at the same time upon the same objects, they easily concert with one another, and agree upon certain leading rules which are to govern them each and all. If the object which attracts the attention of these men is literature, the productions of the mind will soon be subjected by them to precise canons, from which it will no longer be allowable to depart. If these men occupy a hereditary position in the country, they will be naturally inclined, not only to adopt a certain number of fixed rules for themselves, but to follow those which their forefathers laid down for their own guidance; their code will be at once strict and traditional. As they are not necessarily engrossed by the cares of daily life— as they have never been so, any more than their fathers were before them—they have learned to take an interest, for several generations back, in the labors of the mind. They have learned to understand literature as an art, to love it in the end for its own sake, and to feel a scholar-like satisfaction in seeing men conform to its rules. Nor is this all: the men of whom I speak began and will end their lives in easy or in affluent circumstances; hence they have naturally conceived a taste for choice gratifications, and a love of refined and delicate pleasures. Nay more, a kind of indolence of mind and heart, which they frequently contract in the midst of this long and peaceful enjoyment of so much welfare, leads them to put aside, even from their pleasures, whatever might be too startling or too acute. They had rather be amused than intensely excited; they wish to be interested, but not to be carried away.

Now let us fancy a great number of literary performances executed by the men, or for the men, whom I have just described, and we shall readily conceive a style of literature in which everything will be regular and prearranged. The slightest work will be carefully touched in its least details; art and labor will be conspicuous in everything; each kind of writing will have rules of its own, from which it will not be allowed to swerve, and which distinguish it from all others. Style will be thought

此，我依然肯定他们最终会有自己的文学，但必然会呈现出与我们这个时代美国文学完全不同的特点，而且是他们所独有的特点。想预先给这个特点画出一个大致轮廓则是根本不可能的。

假设有一个文学很发达的贵族制国家，其智力劳动与国家事务一样都被统治阶级所垄断。文学和政务几乎完全为这一阶级或与之过从甚密的几个阶级所独掌。这样的前提让我足以能够得到解决所有问题的钥匙。当为数不多的同一些人同时进行同样工作的时候，彼此之间很容易协调一致，共同制定他们自己及所有人都应遵守的原则。如果这些人的工作对象是文学，他们不久便会将这种精神生产置于明确的规则之下，而且不得违反。如果这些人在国家中拥有世袭地位，他们自然不但会给自己定下一定数量的固定规则，还会遵从祖先留给他们的教诲，他们的规章制度必定严格又传统。因为他们从不需要为生活操劳，实际上他们也从未为此操劳，而他们的祖辈更是如此，所以他们能够连续几辈人专注精神劳动。他们将文学视为艺术，并为艺术而艺术，而且当看到人们按照其规则行事的时候感受到学者般的快感。而这还并不是全部，我所说的这些人从生到死都过着舒适富裕的生活，因此自然热衷于选择最好的享乐，爱好精致优雅的消遣。此外，长期地安享富裕生活往往会让他们养成某种精神和心灵的安逸，令他们远离太过突然和刺激的享乐。他们想要的是安逸而不是刺激，他们希望从享乐中得到乐趣，而不是为之癫狂。

现在，让我们设想，我方才所说的这些人创作或是有人为他们创作了大量的文学作品，我们会发现这些文学作品都是一种风格，不敢有违任何前人的规范。最微不足道的作

of almost as much importance as thought; and the form will be no less considered than the matter: the diction will be polished, measured, and uniform. The tone of the mind will be always dignified, seldom very animated; and writers will care more to perfect what they produce than to multiply their productions. It will sometimes happen that the members of the literary class, always living amongst themselves and writing for themselves alone, will lose sight of the rest of the world, which will infect them with a false and labored style; they will lay down minute literary rules for their exclusive use, which will insensibly lead them to deviate from common-sense, and finally to transgress the bounds of nature. By dint of striving after a mode of parlance different from the vulgar, they will arrive at a sort of aristocratic jargon, which is hardly less remote from pure language than is the coarse dialect of the people. Such are the natural perils of literature amongst aristocracies. Every aristocracy which keeps itself entirely aloof from the people becomes impotent—a fact which is as true in literature as it is in politics.

Let us now turn the picture and consider the other side of it; let us transport ourselves into the midst of a democracy, not unprepared by ancient traditions and present culture to partake in the pleasures of the mind. Ranks are there intermingled and confounded; knowledge and power are both infinitely subdivided, and, if I may use the expression, scattered on every side. Here then is a motley multitude, whose intellectual wants are to be supplied. These new votaries of the pleasures of the mind have not all received the same education; they do not possess the same degree of culture as their fathers, nor any resemblance to them—nay, they perpetually differ from themselves, for they live in a state of incessant change of place, feelings, and fortunes. The mind of each member of the community is therefore unattached to that of his fellow-citizens by tradition or by common habits; and they have never had the power, the inclination, nor the time to concert together. It is, however, from the bosom of this heterogeneous and agitated mass that authors spring; and from the same source their profits and their fame are distributed. I can without difficulty understand that, under these circumstances, I must expect to meet in the literature of such a people with but few of those strict conventional rules which are admitted by readers and by writers in aristocratic ages. If it should

品也会着力在细节上大下功夫，力求一切都要突出作者的技巧和功力。每种文学体裁都有其各自不可逾越的独特规则。文体被视为与思想几乎同等重要，形式被认为与内容几乎同等重要。措辞必须洗练、慎重、统一。思想的基调必须高贵，极少表现出轻狂。而作家更注重的是作品的打磨，而不是作品的层出不穷。有时候，文学界的成员会因为一直生活在自己的圈子，只为他们自己而创作，而看不到其余的世界，以至于作品显得矫揉造作。他们会专门为自己制定烦琐的写作规则，这不知不觉之间会让他们有违人们的常识，最终将脱离现实。他们尽量避免使用通俗的语言，而是力求使用与人民大众的粗俗言语相去甚远的贵族腔调。这是贵族社会为文学发展自己设置的障碍。凡是与人民完全隔离的贵族必然软弱无力，无论是文学还是政治都是如此。

现在让我们翻转到图画的另一面看一看，让我们穿越到民主社会，在这里无论是古老的传统还是现代的文化都可以让人们获得精神上的享乐。在这里各阶级混合并融为一体，知识和权力都被无限分割，而如果让我说的话，我得说已经分散到各个角落。这里五行八作的人们都要求获得精神上的满足，这些爱好精神享受的新人物，并没有接受过同样的教育，文化水平也不相同，与他们的祖先相似但又与他们没有任何相同之处，而且他们自己也时刻处在变化之中，因为他们的住所、情感和财富都在不断地变化。因此，社会成员彼此之间的精神并未能通过传统和共同习惯联系起来，而且他们也没有力量、意愿和时间来彼此协调。然而，作家正是从这群形形色色激动不已的人们之中产生，并依靠他们成名得利。我不必费力就可以知道，在这样的情形下，想要在这样的国家的文学作品中找到哪

happen that the men of some one period were agreed upon any such rules, that would prove nothing for the following period; for amongst democratic nations each new generation is a new people. Amongst such nations, then, literature will not easily be subjected to strict rules, and it is impossible that any such rules should ever be permanent.

In democracies it is by no means the case that all the men who cultivate literature have received a literary education; and most of those who have some tinge of belles-lettres are either engaged in politics, or in a profession which only allows them to taste occasionally and by stealth the pleasures of the mind. These pleasures, therefore, do not constitute the principal charm of their lives; but they are considered as a transient and necessary recreation amidst the serious labors of life. Such man can never acquire a sufficiently intimate knowledge of the art of literature to appreciate its more delicate beauties; and the minor shades of expression must escape them. As the time they can devote to letters is very short, they seek to make the best use of the whole of it. They prefer books which may be easily procured, quickly read, and which require no learned researches to be understood. They ask for beauties, self-proffered and easily enjoyed; above all, they must have what is unexpected and new. Accustomed to the struggle, the crosses, and the monotony of practical life, they require rapid emotions, startling passages—truths or errors brilliant enough to rouse them up, and to plunge them at once, as if by violence, into the midst of a subject.

Why should I say more? or who does not understand what is about to follow, before I have expressed it? Taken as a whole, literature in democratic ages can never present, as it does in the periods of aristocracy, an aspect of order, regularity, science, and art; its form will, on the contrary, ordinarily be slighted, sometimes despised. Style will frequently be fantastic, incorrect, overburdened, and loose—almost always vehement and bold. Authors will aim at rapidity of execution, more than at perfection of detail. Small productions will be more common than bulky books; there will be more wit than erudition, more imagination than profundity; and literary performances will bear marks of an untutored and rude vigor of thought—frequently of great variety and singular fecundity. The object of authors will be to astonish rather than to please, and to stir the

怕仅是几个贵族时代读者和作家一致认可的严格的传统规则都是不可能的事情。即使在某一时期这个国家的人们同意采用某几个这样的规则，也不证明他们会一直采用这些规则。因为，在民主国家每一代新人如同一个新的民族。因此，在这样的国家中，文学很难服从严格的规则，而任何一种规则也都不可能持久。

在民主制度下，所有从事文学的人也并不一定都受过文学教育，而大多数搞纯文学的人也都参与政治或从事其他职业，只是偶尔抽空得暇的时候才体验精神上的享受。因此，这样的满足并不是他们生活的主要乐趣，而被视为忙碌生活的短暂而必要的消遣。这些人对于文学艺术的理解不会深刻到足以欣赏文艺之美的地步，更无法体会文笔间的细微差别。因为他们能用来写作的时间很少，所以想要充分利用这段时间。他们喜欢购买可以很快读完、浅显易懂的书籍，他们希望的美要直观浅显，而且最重要的是要有出人意料的新鲜的东西。已经习惯于既有冲突又很乏味的现实生活，人们需要的是快速的情感，惊人的段落，是真伪足够鲜明，能激发他们立即投入其中，并好像有一股力量驱使他们马上动笔的故事情节。

我还需要再多说吗？不用解释，谁都知道接下来我要说什么。总的来说，民主时代的文学永远不会呈现出贵族时代那样的秩序、规则、科学和艺术。相反，它往往不注重形式，甚至有时候对此不屑一顾。文体也往往是天马行空、杂乱无章，啰唆冗长，而且还几乎总是大胆奔放。作家只求快速，而不愿完善细节描写，短篇小品远远超过鸿篇巨制，凭才气而不靠实学，重想象而缺乏深度，而且文学活动带有粗野未开化的思想活力的痕迹，

passions more than to charm the taste. Here and there, indeed, writers will doubtless occur who will choose a different track, and who will, if they are gifted with superior abilities, succeed in finding readers, in spite of their defects or their better qualities; but these exceptions will be rare, and even the authors who shall so depart from the received practice in the main subject of their works, will always relapse into it in some lesser details.

I have just depicted two extreme conditions: the transition by which a nation passes from the former to the latter is not sudden but gradual, and marked with shades of very various intensity. In the passage which conducts a lettered people from the one to the other, there is almost always a moment at which the literary genius of democratic nations has its confluence with that of aristocracies, and both seek to establish their joint sway over the human mind. Such epochs are transient, but very brilliant: they are fertile without exuberance, and animated without confusion. The French literature of the eighteenth century may serve as an example.

I should say more than I mean if I were to assert that the literature of a nation is always subordinate to its social condition and its political constitution. I am aware that, independently of these causes, there are several others which confer certain characteristics on literary productions; but these appear to me to be the chief. The relations which exist between the social and political condition of a people and the genius of its authors are always very numerous: whoever knows the one is never completely ignorant of the other.

Chapter XIV: The Trade Of Literature

Democracy not only infuses a taste for letters among the trading classes, but introduces a trading spirit into literature. In aristocracies, readers are fastidious and few in number; in democracies, they are far more numerous and far less difficult to please. The consequence is, that among aristocratic nations, no one can hope to succeed without immense exertions, and that these exertions may bestow a great deal of fame, but can never earn much money; whilst among democratic nations, a writer may flatter himself that he will obtain at a cheap rate a meagre reputation and a large fortune. For this

作品往往多种多样而且产量惊人。作者的目的与其说是让读者感到愉悦不如说是惊奇，与其说是让人体验到美的享受不如说是激动着他们的情绪。的确，偶然也会出现一些另辟蹊径的作家，而且如果他们才华出众，无论其作品优劣都能赢得一批读者。但是这样的特例很少，而且甚至那些作品主题偏离常规实践的作家最终在细节方面依旧要回归。

我刚刚对两种极端的情况进行了描述。一个国家从一个极端向另一个极端的转化不可能一蹴而就，而是一个有着无数阶段的渐进的过程。在一个尚文民族由一个极端走向另一个极端的过程中，总会有那么一段时间民主国家的文学天才和贵族国家的文学天才汇于一处，共同影响着人们的精神。这样的时期很短暂，却非常辉煌。作品丰富但没有滥竽充数，活跃而不混乱。18世纪的法国文学就是这样的一个例子。

我的意思绝不是说，一个国家的文学永远取决于其社会状况和政治制度。我意识到，除去这两个因素外，还有一些其他原因会令文学作品产生某种特定的特征。但是在我看来这两个是主要因素。一个国家的社会和政治状况与作家们的才华有着千丝万缕的联系，无论是谁只要了解了其中的一个就不会完全对另一个一无所知。

第十四章　文学的商业性

民主不但促使商业阶层爱好文学，而且还将商业精神引入文学。在贵族制国家，读者挑剔且数量不多。在民主国家，读者群庞大而且容易取悦。于是，在贵族制国家，没有人能够不付出巨大努力而获得成功，这份努力让他们能够赢得很高的荣誉，但是无法给他们

purpose he need not be admired; it is enough that he is liked. The ever-increasing crowd of readers, and their continual craving for something new, insure the sale of books which nobody much esteems.

In democratic periods the public frequently treat authors as kings do their courtiers; they enrich, and they despise them. What more is needed by the venal souls which are born in courts, or which are worthy to live there? Democratic literature is always infested with a tribe of writers who look upon letters as a mere trade: and for some few great authors who adorn it you may reckon thousands of idea-mongers.

Chapter XV: The Study Of Greek And Latin Literature Peculiarly Useful In Democratic Communities

What was called the People in the most democratic republics of antiquity, was very unlike what we designate by that term. In Athens, all the citizens took part in public affairs; but there were only 20,000 citizens to more than 350,000 inhabitants. All the rest were slaves, and discharged the greater part of those duties which belong at the present day to the lower or even to the middle classes. Athens, then, with her universal suffrage, was after all merely an aristocratic republic in which all the nobles had an equal right to the government. The struggle between the patricians and plebeians of Rome must be considered in the same light: it was simply an intestine feud between the elder and younger branches of the same family. All the citizens belonged, in fact, to the aristocracy, and partook of its character.

It is moreover to be remarked, that amongst the ancients books were always scarce and dear; and that very great difficulties impeded their publication and circulation. These circumstances concentrated literary tastes and habits amongst a small number of men, who formed a small literary aristocracy out of the choicer spirits of the great political aristocracy. Accordingly nothing goes to prove that literature was ever treated as a trade amongst the Greeks and Romans.

These peoples, which not only constituted aristocracies, but very polished and free nations, of course imparted to their literary productions the defects and the merits which characterize the

带来很多的金钱。然而，在民主国家，作家则可以通过推销廉价作品换来小小的声誉和大大的财富。为了达到这个目的，他们不需要人们的崇拜，只要受到人们的喜欢就可以了。不断增长的读者群，以及他们日新月异的渴望，确保了没有什么价值的书籍也能畅销。

在民主时期，大众对待作者的态度往往和国王对待朝臣的态度一样，他们令作家们富裕起来，却又看不起他们。试问对待出生在宫廷或是蒙宠而在宫廷生活的御用文人，不如此还能怎样呢？民主国家的文学界总是充斥着一批将文学视为生意的文人，装点其间的为数不多的伟大作家可以胜过千万的思想贩子。

第十五章　为什么研究希腊和拉丁文学在民主国家特别有用

古代的民主共和国所说的人民与我们今天的含义大不相同。在雅典城，所有的公民都参与公共事务，但是在其35万的人口中只有2万是公民，其余的全部是奴隶，他们干的大部分是我们今天下层阶级甚至是中产阶级的活。所以，雅典人尽管实行普选制，但毕竟只是一个贵族的共和国，只是所有贵族对政府拥有平等的权利。古罗马贵族与平民的斗争也应该用同样的观点来看待，只能将其看作是同一个家族内部老一辈与少壮派的内讧。实际上，所有的公民都是贵族，都具有贵族的特性。

此外，还要指出在古代书籍总是很稀有很昂贵，而其出版和流通也是阻力重重。这样的情况让对文学的爱好和习惯集中出现在少数人身上，并在大的政治贵族集团之中形成一个小的文学贵族圈子。因此，没有任何证据证明在古希腊和古罗马文学曾经被视为一种商业。

literature of aristocratic ages. And indeed a very superficial survey of the literary remains of the ancients will suffice to convince us, that if those writers were sometimes deficient in variety, or fertility in their subjects, or in boldness, vivacity, or power of generalization in their thoughts, they always displayed exquisite care and skill in their details. Nothing in their works seems to be done hastily or at random: every line is written for the eye of the connoisseur, and is shaped after some conception of ideal beauty. No literature places those fine qualities, in which the writers of democracies are naturally deficient, in bolder relief than that of the ancients; no literature, therefore, ought to be more studied in democratic ages. This study is better suited than any other to combat the literary defects inherent in those ages; as for their more praiseworthy literary qualities, they will spring up of their own accord, without its being necessary to learn to acquire them.

It is important that this point should be clearly understood. A particular study may be useful to the literature of a people, without being appropriate to its social and political wants. If men were to persist in teaching nothing but the literature of the dead languages in a community where everyone is habitually led to make vehement exertions to augment or to maintain his fortune, the result would be a very polished, but a very dangerous, race of citizens. For as their social and political condition would give them every day a sense of wants which their education would never teach them to supply, they would perturb the State, in the name of the Greeks and Romans, instead of enriching it by their productive industry.

It is evident that in democratic communities the interest of individuals, as well as the security of the commonwealth, demands that the education of the greater number should be scientific, commercial, and industrial, rather than literary. Greek and Latin should not be taught in all schools; but it is important that those who by their natural disposition or their fortune are destined to cultivate letters or prepared to relish them, should find schools where a complete knowledge of ancient literature may be acquired, and where the true scholar may be formed. A few excellent universities would do more towards the attainment of this object than a vast number of bad grammar schools, where superfluous matters, badly learned, stand in the way of sound instruction in necessary studies.

古希腊和古罗马的人民，不但都是贵族，而且是非常文明自由的民族，自然他们的文学作品都带有贵族时代文学所特有的优点和缺点。实际上，只需对古代流传下来的文学作品肤浅地浏览一下就足以让我们确信，尽管这些作者有时候缺乏多样性，产量也不高，思想上普遍不够大胆、活跃和概括，但在细节上他们总是表现得细腻而有技巧。他们的作品完全没有匆忙或是随意下笔的痕迹。他们的每一行文字都是写给行家看的，字里行间都流露着对纯美学的追求。后来的文学作品中再也没有像古代文学那样突出地表现出这样优秀的特点，而民主时代的作家自然也不会有这样的优点。因此，民主时代如果不深入研究古代文学就不会有文学可言。这样的研究比任何其他的研究都更适合克服民主时代文学的固有缺陷。至于其更为人称道的文学特点，根本不用学习如何使之产生它们便会自己冒出来。

清楚地认识到这一点非常重要。专门的研究可能对一个国家的文学有帮助，但是对其社会和政治需要却无助。在一个人人都习惯于通过暴力来增加和维护财富的社会，如果人们坚持只进行纯文学教育，则必然会造就非常文雅，而又非常危险的公民。因为，他们的社会和政治状况让他们不断产生新的需要而他们的教育并没有教会他们如何满足这些需要。于是，他们会以古希腊和古罗马的名义扰乱国家，从而使国家的产业经济无法得到发展。

显然，在民主社会，个人的利益和国家的安全都需要对大多数人优先进行科学、商业、工业教育而不是文学教育。所有的学校都不讲授希腊文和拉丁文，但是对于那些由于出身或命运注定要学习文学或是爱好文学的人来说，开设一些能够让他们全面掌握古代文学和培养真正学者的学校非常重要。为了达到这样的目的，办几所优秀的大学远胜于开办

All who aspire to literary excellence in democratic nations, ought frequently to refresh themselves at the springs of ancient literature: there is no more wholesome course for the mind. Not that I hold the literary productions of the ancients to be irreproachable; but I think that they have some especial merits, admirably calculated to counterbalance our peculiar defects. They are a prop on the side on which we are in most danger of falling.

Chapter XVI: The Effect Of Democracy On Language

If the reader has rightly understood what I have already said on the subject of literature in general, he will have no difficulty in comprehending that species of influence which a democratic social condition and democratic institutions may exercise over language itself, which is the chief instrument of thought.

American authors may truly be said to live more in England than in their own country; since they constantly study the English writers, and take them every day for their models. But such is not the case with the bulk of the population, which is more immediately subjected to the peculiar causes acting upon the United States. It is not then to the written, but to the spoken language that attention must be paid, if we would detect the modifications which the idiom of an aristocratic people may undergo when it becomes the language of a democracy.

Englishmen of education, and more competent judges than I can be myself of the nicer shades of expression, have frequently assured me that the language of the educated classes in the United States is notably different from that of the educated classes in Great Britain. They complain not only that the Americans have brought into use a number of new words—the difference and the distance between the two countries might suffice to explain that much—but that these new words are more especially taken from the jargon of parties, the mechanical arts, or the language of trade. They assert, in addition to this, that old English words are often used by the Americans in new acceptations; and lastly, that the inhabitants of the United States frequently intermingle their phraseology in the strangest manner, and sometimes place words together which are always kept apart in the language

大量的文法学校，因为文法学校的质量不高的肤浅教育会成为日后必要深造的障碍。

在民主国家，凡是想要在文学上有所建树的人，都应不断从古代文学之泉中汲取营养，这是最有益的办法。我并不是说古代文学作品毫无缺点，但是我认为它们有很多独特的优点，可以很好地抵消我们特有的缺点。它们是避免我们落入深渊的支柱。

第十六章　民主对语言的影响

如果读者已经完全理解前面我就文学所说的一切，那就不难理解民主的社会状况和民主制度对于思想的主要表达工具——语言本身产生的影响。

事实上，可以说美国的作者更多的是生活在英国的环境下，而不是他们自己的国家。因为他们不断研究英国作家，并终日将其视为自己的楷模。但是人民大众则不这么认为，因为对美国产生影响的那些特殊原因会对人民产生直接影响。如果我们想要发现贵族的惯用语在成为大众语言时经历了怎样的变化，就必须将注意力集中到口头语言而不是书面语言。

有教养的英国人，和那些使我望尘莫及有能力辨别出语言细微差别的人，不断地向我保证，美国有教养阶层的语言与英国有教养阶层使用的语言有明显的不同。他们不但指责美国人大量使用新词（两个国家之间的不同和彼此遥远的距离足以造成这样的现象），而且指出这些新词还大多来自各党派、行业，以及业务术语。除此之外，他们还说美国人往往会给旧的英语词汇赋予新的含义。最后他们称美国的居民的措辞常常令人感到莫名其妙，有时候会将母国中一直分开使用的词汇放到一起用。一些值得我信任的人不断地跟我

of the mother-country. These remarks, which were made to me at various times by persons who appeared to be worthy of credit, led me to reflect upon the subject; and my reflections brought me, by theoretical reasoning, to the same point at which my informants had arrived by practical observation.

In aristocracies, language must naturally partake of that state of repose in which everything remains. Few new words are coined, because few new things are made; and even if new things were made, they would be designated by known words, whose meaning has been determined by tradition. If it happens that the human mind bestirs itself at length, or is roused by light breaking in from without, the novel expressions which are introduced are characterized by a degree of learning, intelligence, and philosophy, which shows that they do not originate in a democracy. After the fall of Constantinople had turned the tide of science and literature towards the west, the French language was almost immediately invaded by a multitude of new words, which had all Greek or Latin roots. An erudite neologism then sprang up in France which was confined to the educated classes, and which produced no sensible effect, or at least a very gradual one, upon the people. All the nations of Europe successively exhibited the same change. Milton alone introduced more than six hundred words into the English language, almost all derived from the Latin, the Greek, or the Hebrew. The constant agitation which prevails in a democratic community tends unceasingly, on the contrary, to change the character of the language, as it does the aspect of affairs. In the midst of this general stir and competition of minds, a great number of new ideas are formed, old ideas are lost, or reappear, or are subdivided into an infinite variety of minor shades. The consequence is, that many words must fall into desuetude, and others must be brought into use.

Democratic nations love change for its own sake; and this is seen in their language as much as in their politics. Even when they do not need to change words, they sometimes feel a wish to transform them. The genius of a democratic people is not only shown by the great number of words they bring into use, but also by the nature of the ideas these new words represent. Amongst such a people the majority lays down the law in language as well as in everything else; its prevailing spirit is as manifest in that as in other respects. But the majority is more engaged in business than in

说这样的话，促使我开始思考这个问题。我依据理论做出的结论和他们通过观察给我的信息不谋而合。

在贵族制社会，语言同其他事物一样，都处于停滞状态。因为几乎没有什么新事物出现，所以也几乎没有新词产生。而且即使有新事物出现，他们也会用含义已经固定的已知词汇来表示。如果碰巧人们的思想终于得到振奋，或是被外部射入的光芒照射惊醒，他们所创造出的全新表达方式必定带有一定程度的学究气、辞藻色和哲学味，以表明它们绝非民主的出身。君士坦丁堡陷落之后科学和文学的大潮开始向西方袭来，源自希腊文和拉丁文的词汇立即大量侵入法语。于是在法国有教养的阶层开始出现使用新词的风气，其影响也并不大，很长一段时间之后才开始普及人民大众。所有的欧洲国家都接连出现相同的现象。仅弥尔顿一个人就将600多个新词引入英语，而这些词几乎无一例外都来自拉丁文、希腊文和希伯来文。相反，民主社会普遍存在的永不休止的变化往往会不断促使语言和事物的面貌发生改变。在事事都在变化和竞争思想作用下，形成大量的新观念，而老观念则逐渐消失，或是失而复得，然而更多的则是不断发生微小的变化。于是，许多词遭到废弃，而另一些词则被拿来使用。

民主国家热衷于为自己而变，这既表现在他们的语言上也表现在他们的政治上。甚至当他们没有必要改用新词的时候，他们有时候也想改用新词。民主国家人民的才华不仅表现在他们使用的大量新词上，还表现在这些新词所代表的观念的本质上。在这样的一个国家，多数不但制定语言的规则，而且制定一切一切的规则，多数致上的思想不仅表现于此

study—in political and commercial interests than in philosophical speculation or literary pursuits. Most of the words coined or adopted for its use will therefore bear the mark of these habits; they will mainly serve to express the wants of business, the passions of party, or the details of the public administration. In these departments the language will constantly spread, whilst on the other hand it will gradually lose ground in metaphysics and theology.

As to the source from which democratic nations are wont to derive their new expressions, and the manner in which they go to work to coin them, both may easily be described. Men living in democratic countries know but little of the language which was spoken at Athens and at Rome, and they do not care to dive into the lore of antiquity to find the expression they happen to want. If they have sometimes recourse to learned etymologies, vanity will induce them to search at the roots of the dead languages; but erudition does not naturally furnish them with its resources. The most ignorant, it sometimes happens, will use them most. The eminently democratic desire to get above their own sphere will often lead them to seek to dignify a vulgar profession by a Greek or Latin name. The lower the calling is, and the more remote from learning, the more pompous and erudite is its appellation. Thus the French rope-dancers have transformed themselves into acrobates and funambules.

In the absence of knowledge of the dead languages, democratic nations are apt to borrow words from living tongues; for their mutual intercourse becomes perpetual, and the inhabitants of different countries imitate each other the more readily as they grow more like each other every day.

But it is principally upon their own languages that democratic nations attempt to perpetrate innovations. From time to time they resume forgotten expressions in their vocabulary, which they restore to use; or they borrow from some particular class of the community a term peculiar to it, which they introduce with a figurative meaning into the language of daily life. Many expressions which originally belonged to the technical language of a profession or a party, are thus drawn into general circulation.

The most common expedient employed by democratic nations to make an innovation in language

还表现在其他方方面面。但是多数更愿意参与实业而不是进行研究，对政治和商业利益的追求超过对哲学思辨和文学的重视。因此，大多数创造和采用的新词都带有这些习惯的烙印。这些词主要用来表达商业的需要、党派的热情或是公共行政的细节。这样一方面语言将来还会不断发展，而另一反面，形而上学和神学方面的语言将逐渐失去根基。

至于民主国家出现的新的表达方式的来源以及他们所采用的造词方式，也并不难说明。生活在民主国家的人们对于雅典人和罗马人使用的语言知之甚少，而且也不想一头扎到古代文献中寻找他们需要的词汇。即使他们有时候会求助于高深的词源学，也不过是虚荣心在作祟，驱使他们去已经死去的语言中寻根溯源，而并非是他们的头脑天生博学多才。所以往往最无知的人才最愿意这样做。民主特别想要拔高自己的愿望常常令他们想要通过使用希腊或是拉丁的名字来显耀自己并不高尚的职业。他们认为，职业越是低下，就越没学问，而名字则越是好听，为的就是彰显自己学识的渊博。因此，法国的走索演员用希腊语Acrobate和拉丁文funambale来称呼自己。

因为对已经死去的语言一无所知，民主国家往往从正在使用的语言中借用词汇。因为各国人民之间不断往来，彼此互相模仿，变得越来越相似。

但是，民主国家的人民主要还是深入自己的语言进行革新。有时候，他们会将人们已经遗忘的词再拿出来用，或是借用社会某个特定阶层的专用术语，将其喻义引入日常用语。许多表达方式最初都源自某一职业和党派的专门用语，就是这样成为一般用语的。

民主国家进行语言革新最常见的方法就是赋予已经使用的词汇新的意义。这样的方法

consists in giving some unwonted meaning to an expression already in use. This method is very simple, prompt, and convenient; no learning is required to use it aright, and ignorance itself rather facilitates the practice; but that practice is most dangerous to the language. When a democratic people doubles the meaning of a word in this way, they sometimes render the signification which it retains as ambiguous as that which it acquires. An author begins by a slight deflection of a known expression from its primitive meaning, and he adapts it, thus modified, as well as he can to his subject. A second writer twists the sense of the expression in another way; a third takes possession of it for another purpose; and as there is no common appeal to the sentence of a permanent tribunal which may definitely settle the signification of the word, it remains in an ambiguous condition. The consequence is that writers hardly ever appear to dwell upon a single thought, but they always seem to point their aim at a knot of ideas, leaving the reader to judge which of them has been hit. This is a deplorable consequence of democracy. I had rather that the language should be made hideous with words imported from the Chinese, the Tartars, or the Hurons, than that the meaning of a word in our own language should become indeterminate. Harmony and uniformity are only secondary beauties in composition; many of these things are conventional, and, strictly speaking, it is possible to forego them; but without clear phraseology there is no good language.

The principle of equality necessarily introduces several other changes into language. In aristocratic ages, when each nation tends to stand aloof from all others and likes to have distinct characteristics of its own, it often happens that several peoples which have a common origin become nevertheless estranged from each other, so that, without ceasing to understand the same language, they no longer all speak it in the same manner. In these ages each nation is divided into a certain number of classes, which see but little of each other, and do not intermingle. Each of these classes contracts, and invariably retains, habits of mind peculiar to itself, and adopts by choice certain words and certain terms, which afterwards pass from generation to generation, like their estates. The same idiom then comprises a language of the poor and a language of the rich—a language of the citizen and a language of the nobility—a learned language and a vulgar one. The deeper the

简单、快捷、方便，也不需要什么学识就可以做到，甚至没有学识的人用起来更方便，但是这样的方法会给语言带来极大的危害。当民主国家的人通过这样的方式让一个词具有双重含义时，往往会让人们在使用哪个含义时感到有些无措。一个作家会先让一个已知词汇稍微偏离原义，经过这样的修改使之适合自己的目的；第二个作家会用另一种方式来曲解词义；而第三个作家还会将其另作他用。因为没有一个常设的法庭能够最终确定该词的意义，所以这个词的含义依旧模棱两可。结果，作家们表达的思想可以有不同的解释，而到底作者的真意如何，就只能留给读者在这一大堆解释中自己去寻找。这是民主的一大可悲的后果。我宁可我们的语言充斥着中国语、鞑靼语或休伦语的词汇，也不愿自己的语言变得含混不清。谐声和押韵只是文章次要的美，而且对此也有一些传统惯例，但是严格来说也可以不遵守，然而如果没有明确的词义，就不会有好的语言。

平等必然会给语言带来一些其他的变化。在贵族时代，每个国家都习惯于对其他国家敬而远之，喜欢有自己的特点，所以经常会出现同一起源的多个国家将彼此视为异族，无法再团结一致，最终连语言也不再相同。在那样的时代，每个民族都被分成若干个阶级，彼此互不往来，不相融合。每个阶级都形成并保有自己特有的思维习惯，选择使用特定的词汇和术语，并让其如遗产一般代代相传。同样的话，有穷人用语和富人用语，公民用语和贵族用语，文人用语和通俗用语。阶级界限越深，社会壁垒就越难以逾越，在语言方面也是如此。我打赌，在印度的不同种姓之间，存在惊人的语言差异，贱民语言跟婆罗门语言之间的差别跟他们所穿衣服的差别一样大。相反，当人们不再受到阶级的限制，可以不

divisions, and the more impassable the barriers of society become, the more must this be the case. I would lay a wager, that amongst the castes of India there are amazing variations of language, and that there is almost as much difference between the language of the pariah and that of the Brahmin as there is in their dress. When, on the contrary, men, being no longer restrained by ranks, meet on terms of constant intercourse—when castes are destroyed, and the classes of society are recruited and intermixed with each other, all the words of a language are mingled. Those which are unsuitable to the greater number perish; the remainder form a common store, whence everyone chooses pretty nearly at random. Almost all the different dialects which divided the idioms of European nations are manifestly declining; there is no patois in the New World, and it is disappearing every day from the old countries.

The influence of this revolution in social conditions is as much felt in style as it is in phraseology. Not only does everyone use the same words, but a habit springs up of using them without discrimination. The rules which style had set up are almost abolished: the line ceases to be drawn between expressions which seem by their very nature vulgar, and other which appear to be refined. Persons springing from different ranks of society carry the terms and expressions they are accustomed to use with them, into whatever circumstances they may pass; thus the origin of words is lost like the origin of individuals, and there is as much confusion in language as there is in society.

I am aware that in the classification of words there are rules which do not belong to one form of society any more than to another, but which are derived from the nature of things. Some expressions and phrases are vulgar, because the ideas they are meant to express are low in themselves; others are of a higher character, because the objects they are intended to designate are naturally elevated. No intermixture of ranks will ever efface these differences. But the principle of equality cannot fail to root out whatever is merely conventional and arbitrary in the forms of thought. Perhaps the necessary classification which I pointed out in the last sentence will always be less respected by a democratic people than by any other, because amongst such a people there are no men who are permanently disposed by education, culture, and leisure to study the natural laws of language, and who cause

断碰面交往的时候，当种姓被废除，社会不同阶级彼此交互融合的时候，语言的所有词汇也会完全混合。那些不适用于大多数使用的词汇被淘汰，留下来的词汇形成一个公共的词汇储备，供人们根据需要随意选择。几乎所有成为欧洲地方习语的不同方言都明显出现下滑的趋势。在新大陆没有方言土语，而旧大陆上的方言土语也正在消失。

社会情况的革命，影响的不仅是措辞，还有文体。每个人不仅使用同样的词汇，而且还养成同样的使用习惯。文体原有的规则几乎被全部废除。表达也不再有粗俗和文雅之分。在各种场合下，来自社会不同阶层的人们使用他们已经习惯的术语和措辞。因此，词汇的出身就好像人的出身一样被淡忘，语言如同整个社会一样已经浑然一体。

我注意到，词汇的分类规则并不取决于任何社会形式，而是源自事物的本性。有些词语及句子之所以粗俗，是因为它们本身表达的意思就是如此低级下流；而另一些词语和句子之所以文雅，是因为它们所描绘的对象本来就高尚。阶级的融合并不能抹杀这样的差异。但是平等却不会将思想上的武断和硬性规定的东西连根拔起。也许我刚刚所说的词汇的必要分类在民主国家受到的重视远不及在其他国家，因为在这样的国家，没有人会在教育、知识和时间的驱使下长期地研究语言的自然规则，也没有人会通过自己对这些规则的考察而使之受到尊重。

没有讲民主国家语言与其他国家语言最不同的一个特点，我是不会就此罢手的。前面已经说过，民主国家有一种对一般观念的爱好，有时候可以说是一种热情，而这也源自其固有的优点和缺点。对一般观念的爱好在民主语言上面则是通过不断使用通用词汇和抽

those laws to be respected by their own observance of them.

I shall not quit this topic without touching on a feature of democratic languages, which is perhaps more characteristic of them than any other. It has already been shown that democratic nations have a taste, and sometimes a passion, for general ideas, and that this arises from their peculiar merits and defects. This liking for general ideas is displayed in democratic languages by the continual use of generic terms or abstract expressions, and by the manner in which they are employed. This is the great merit and the great imperfection of these languages. Democratic nations are passionately addicted to generic terms or abstract expressions, because these modes of speech enlarge thought, and assist the operations of the mind by enabling it to include several objects in a small compass. A French democratic writer will be apt to say capacites in the abstract for men of capacity, and without particularizing the objects to which their capacity is applied: he will talk about actualities to designate in one word the things passing before his eyes at the instant; and he will comprehend under the term eventualities whatever may happen in the universe, dating from the moment at which he speaks. Democratic writers are perpetually coining words of this kind, in which they sublimate into further abstraction the abstract terms of the language. Nay, more, to render their mode of speech more succinct, they personify the subject of these abstract terms, and make it act like a real entity. Thus they would say in French, "La force des choses veut que les capacites gouvernent."

I cannot better illustrate what I mean than by my own example. I have frequently used the word "equality" in an absolute sense—nay, I have personified equality in several places; thus I have said that equality does such and such things, or refrains from doing others. It may be affirmed that the writers of the age of Louis XIV would not have used these expressions: they would never have thought of using the word "equality" without applying it to some particular object; and they would rather have renounced the term altogether than have consented to make a living personage of it.

These abstract terms which abound in democratic languages, and which are used on every occasion without attaching them to any particular fact, enlarge and obscure the thoughts they are intended to convey; they render the mode of speech more succinct, and the idea contained in it less

象表达，以及对这些词汇和表达的使用方式来体现的。这既是民主语言的一大优点也是它的一大缺陷。民主国家特别热衷于通用词汇和抽象表达，因为这样的表达方式可以开阔思想，并通过把大量对象涵盖在一个小小的范畴来促进思维活动。一位法国民主作家往往喜欢用"才干"一词来抽象说明人有才干，而不会具体到他们有何种才干。他会用"现实"一词来概括此刻他眼前发生的一切；会用"偶然性"一词解释世界上在他说话那一刻可能发生的一切。民主作家总是能造出这样的词，或者让语言中抽象名词的含义更抽象。此外，为了让语言风格更加简洁，他们还将这些抽象词汇代表的东西拟人化，让它看上去像真人活动一般。因此，在法语里他们会说："物力喜欢人才支配它。"

用我自己的例子来说明我的这个想法最好不过。一直以来我常常使用"平等"一词的绝对意义，而且我在许多地方还会将"平等"一词拟人化。因此，我会说平等可以使某事如何，或是不会使某事如何。可以断言，路易十四时期的作家绝不会说出这样的话。他们甚至都不会想到用"平等"这个词，因为他们不曾享受过平等。与其说他们不用平等这个词不如说他们没有亲身体验过平等。

这些抽象的词语在民主国家的语言中比比皆是，而且人们在使用的时候也并不将其与任何具体事实联系起来，所以它们在扩大思想的同时又使思想模糊不清。它们虽然使语言的表达简洁，但表达的思想则不再清晰。但是就语言来说，民主国家更喜欢含糊不清而不愿花工夫推敲。我不知道这种含糊的语言对于使用它们讲话和写作的那些民主国家的人们是否有某种隐秘的魅力。因为生活在民主国家的人要不断地靠自己头脑的努力进行判断，

clear. But with regard to language, democratic nations prefer obscurity to labor. I know not indeed whether this loose style has not some secret charm for those who speak and write amongst these nations. As the men who live there are frequently left to the efforts of their individual powers of mind, they are almost always a prey to doubt; and as their situation in life is forever changing, they are never held fast to any of their opinions by the certain tenure of their fortunes. Men living in democratic countries are, then, apt to entertain unsettled ideas, and they require loose expressions to convey them. As they never know whether the idea they express to-day will be appropriate to the new position they may occupy to-morrow, they naturally acquire a liking for abstract terms. An abstract term is like a box with a false bottom: you may put in it what ideas you please, and take them out again without being observed.

Amongst all nations, generic and abstract terms form the basis of language. I do not, therefore, affect to expel these terms from democratic languages; I simply remark that men have an especial tendency, in the ages of democracy, to multiply words of this kind—to take them always by themselves in their most abstract acceptation, and to use them on all occasions, even when the nature of the discourse does not require them.

Chapter XVII: Of Some Of The Sources Of Poetry Amongst Democratic Nations

Various different significations have been given to the word "poetry." It would weary my readers if I were to lead them into a discussion as to which of these definitions ought to be selected: I prefer telling them at once that which I have chosen. In my opinion, poetry is the search and the delineation of the ideal. The poet is he who, by suppressing a part of what exists, by adding some imaginary touches to the picture, and by combining certain real circumstances, but which do not in fact concurrently happen, completes and extends the work of nature. Thus the object of poetry is not to represent what is true, but to adorn it, and to present to the mind some loftier imagery. Verse, regarded as the ideal beauty of language, may be eminently poetical; but verse does not, of itself, constitute poetry.

所以他们总是犹豫不决，而且因为他们的生活状况不断发生变化，所以即使他们的财产没有变化，他们的思想也永远不会停留在一点不动。生活在民主国家的人思想往往不稳定，所以需要泛泛的表达。因为他们不知道今天所表达的思想是否适合自己明天的新处境，所以自然喜欢抽象的词语。一个抽象的词汇就像一个有假底子的箱子，你可以随意将自己的观点放进去，还能不为人知地将其取出来。

笼统和抽象的词语是所有国家语言的基础。因此，我不认为只有民主国家的语言有这样的词汇。我只是说，在民主时代，人有一种特别的倾向喜欢增加此类词汇，经常孤立地使用它们最抽象的意义，而且将它们用于各种情形，甚至根本无须使用抽象词汇进行交谈时也想要使用。

第十七章　民主国家诗歌的某些源泉

人们赋予"诗歌"一词各种不同的含义。如果我将读者引入一个有关哪个定义最适合诗歌的讨论，必然会令其感到厌倦，所以我更愿意马上告诉他们我的选择。在我看来，诗歌是对理想的探索和描绘。诗人是通过剔除一些真实的东西，融入一些想象的成分，并通过将实际上并没有真正同时出现的一些特定真实情况的结合来表达自然的壮丽的人。因此，诗歌的目的不是表现真实，而是美化现实，并呈现给人们一个崇高的形象。韵文，作为语言的理想美，显然很有诗意，但是韵文就其本身而言并不是诗。

现在，我要继续探讨的是在民主国家的行动、情绪和观念中，是否有什么能够让人产

I now proceed to inquire whether, amongst the actions, the sentiments, and the opinions of democratic nations, there are any which lead to a conception of ideal beauty, and which may for this reason be considered as natural sources of poetry. It must in the first place, be acknowledged that the taste for ideal beauty, and the pleasure derived from the expression of it, are never so intense or so diffused amongst a democratic as amongst an aristocratic people. In aristocratic nations it sometimes happens that the body goes on to act as it were spontaneously, whilst the higher faculties are bound and burdened by repose. Amongst these nations the people will very often display poetic tastes, and sometimes allow their fancy to range beyond and above what surrounds them. But in democracies the love of physical gratification, the notion of bettering one's condition, the excitement of competition, the charm of anticipated success, are so many spurs to urge men onwards in the active professions they have embraced, without allowing them to deviate for an instant from the track. The main stress of the faculties is to this point. The imagination is not extinct; but its chief function is to devise what may be useful, and to represent what is real.

The principle of equality not only diverts men from the description of ideal beauty—it also diminishes the number of objects to be described. Aristocracy, by maintaining society in a fixed position, is favorable to the solidity and duration of positive religions, as well as to the stability of political institutions. It not only keeps the human mind within a certain sphere of belief, but it predisposes the mind to adopt one faith rather than another. An aristocratic people will always be prone to place intermediate powers between God and man. In this respect it may be said that the aristocratic element is favorable to poetry. When the universe is peopled with supernatural creatures, not palpable to the senses but discovered by the mind, the imagination ranges freely, and poets, finding a thousand subjects to delineate, also find a countless audience to take an interest in their productions. In democratic ages it sometimes happens, on the contrary, that men are as much afloat in matters of belief as they are in their laws. Scepticism then draws the imagination of poets back to earth, and confines them to the real and visible world. Even when the principle of equality does not disturb religious belief, it tends to simplify it, and to divert attention from secondary agents, to fix it

生理想美的概念，或者可以被视为诗歌的源泉。首先，必须承认民主国家的人们对于理想美的爱好以及由此而来的享受从未曾像贵族制国家那样深刻和广泛。在贵族制国家中，有时候身体的活动可以不由自主，而精神活动则离不开安宁。在这些国家中，人民总是表现出对诗歌的爱好，而且有时候他们会让自己的想象超越身边的现实。但是在民主国家，对于物质满足的热爱、改善现状的愿望、彼此的竞争、马到成功的热望，如此多的刺激促使人们每走一步都要迈向自己笃定的事业，不允许自己有一时半刻从这条道路上偏离。人们将所有的精力用在这些方面。人们的想象力并未枯竭，而是完全被用来想象实用的东西和表现真实。

平等不但让人们轻视对理想美的描绘，而且还将其所描绘对象的范围缩小。贵族制度通过将社会维持在一个固定的状态，促进正统宗教的安定和持久以及政治制度的稳定。它不仅能够使人的精神限定在一种信仰之内，还能让人们更容易接受一种信仰而不是其他的信仰。贵族制国家的人们总是想要在上帝和人之间设置一些中间权力。就此来看，可以说贵族制度非常有利于诗歌的创作。当宇宙的一切都是感官无法感知只有精神才能发现的超自然的存在时，想象力可以天马行空自由发挥，而诗人会发现他们可以描绘的事物数以千计，而能够欣赏他们作品的读者则数不胜数。相反，在民主时代，有时候会看到人们的信仰跟他们的法律一样飘忽不定。于是，怀疑论让诗人的想象力回归现实，并将其封闭在可见的现实世界。平等尽管不能动摇宗教信仰，却可以使宗教趋于简化，将信徒的注意力从次要的崇拜对象转移开，而主要崇拜至高的上帝。贵族制度会自然而然地将人们的精神引

principally on the Supreme Power. Aristocracy naturally leads the human mind to the contemplation of the past, and fixes it there. Democracy, on the contrary, gives men a sort of instinctive distaste for what is ancient. In this respect aristocracy is far more favorable to poetry; for things commonly grow larger and more obscure as they are more remote; and for this twofold reason they are better suited to the delineation of the ideal.

After having deprived poetry of the past, the principle of equality robs it in part of the present. Amongst aristocratic nations there are a certain number of privileged personages, whose situation is, as it were, without and above the condition of man; to these, power, wealth, fame, wit, refinement, and distinction in all things appear peculiarly to belong. The crowd never sees them very closely, or does not watch them in minute details; and little is needed to make the description of such men poetical. On the other hand, amongst the same people, you will meet with classes so ignorant, low, and enslaved, that they are no less fit objects for poetry from the excess of their rudeness and wretchedness, than the former are from their greatness and refinement. Besides, as the different classes of which an aristocratic community is composed are widely separated, and imperfectly acquainted with each other, the imagination may always represent them with some addition to, or some subtraction from, what they really are. In democratic communities, where men are all insignificant and very much alike, each man instantly sees all his fellows when he surveys himself. The poets of democratic ages can never, therefore, take any man in particular as the subject of a piece; for an object of slender importance, which is distinctly seen on all sides, will never lend itself to an ideal conception. Thus the principle of equality; in proportion as it has established itself in the world, has dried up most of the old springs of poetry. Let us now attempt to show what new ones it may disclose.

When scepticism had depopulated heaven, and the progress of equality had reduced each individual to smaller and better known proportions, the poets, not yet aware of what they could substitute for the great themes which were departing together with the aristocracy, turned their eyes to inanimate nature. As they lost sight of gods and heroes, they set themselves to describe streams

向对过往的沉思而不再离开，与之相反，民主制度让人们产生对古代事物的本能反感。从这一方面来看，贵族制度特别有利于诗歌，因为当事物越来越遥远时，往往会变得越来越壮丽恢宏，由于这两个原因的共同作用，它更适合成为描写理想的对象。

平等在剥夺了诗歌描写过去的权利之后，还抢走了它表现现在的部分权利。在贵族制国家中，有一定数量的特权人士的存在，他们的地位在一般人之上或之外。权力、财富、荣誉、智慧、文雅和高尚，总之所有好的东西似乎都属于他们。群众从未走的他们身边近距离地观察他们，或者说细致入微地观察他们，所以可以毫不费力地对他们进行富有诗意的描写。另一方面，这些国家中有一些无知卑贱甘愿受奴役的阶层，因为他们过于粗野和悲惨也非常适合作为诗歌描写的对象，这跟前者因为其高尚和文雅成为诗歌描写对象的原因如出一辙。此外，由于贵族社会各不同阶级彼此隔离，无法识得对方的庐山真面目，所以想象力在表现它们的时候总是要添加或剔除一些东西。在民主社会，每个人都微不足道，彼此相近，所以每个人只要审视一下自己就可以立即知道别人的情况。因此，民主时代的诗人决不会只将一个人作为其描写对象，因为一个无足轻重且在众目睽睽之下的对象，无法成为抒发理想的题材。因此，随着平等在世界上的确立，诗歌大多数的古老源泉都已干涸。现在，让我们来看一看平等带给诗歌的新源泉。

当怀疑使人不再向往天堂，平等的发展让人越来越相似、越来越渺小的时候，还没有找到可以替代与贵族制度一同消失的大题材的诗人们，将他们的目光转向没有生命的自然界。因为他们已经看不到上帝和英雄，于是便开始描写山川河流。于是，从上个世纪，便

and mountains. Thence originated in the last century, that kind of poetry which has been called, by way of distinction, the descriptive. Some have thought that this sort of delineation, embellished with all the physical and inanimate objects which cover the earth, was the kind of poetry peculiar to democratic ages; but I believe this to be an error, and that it only belongs to a period of transition.

I am persuaded that in the end democracy diverts the imagination from all that is external to man, and fixes it on man alone. Democratic nations may amuse themselves for a while with considering the productions of nature; but they are only excited in reality by a survey of themselves. Here, and here alone, the true sources of poetry amongst such nations are to be found; and it may be believed that the poets who shall neglect to draw their inspirations hence, will lose all sway over the minds which they would enchant, and will be left in the end with none but unimpassioned spectators of their transports. I have shown how the ideas of progression and of the indefinite perfectibility of the human race belong to democratic ages. Democratic nations care but little for what has been, but they are haunted by visions of what will be; in this direction their unbounded imagination grows and dilates beyond all measure. Here then is the wildest range open to the genius of poets, which allows them to remove their performances to a sufficient distance from the eye. Democracy shuts the past against the poet, but opens the future before him. As all the citizens who compose a democratic community are nearly equal and alike, the poet cannot dwell upon any one of them; but the nation itself invites the exercise of his powers. The general similitude of individuals, which renders any one of them taken separately an improper subject of poetry, allows poets to include them all in the same imagery, and to take a general survey of the people itself. Democractic nations have a clearer perception than any others of their own aspect; and an aspect so imposing is admirably fitted to the delineation of the ideal.

I readily admit that the Americans have no poets; I cannot allow that they have no poetic ideas. In Europe people talk a great deal of the wilds of America, but the Americans themselves never think about them: they are insensible to the wonders of inanimate nature, and they may be said not to perceive the mighty forests which surround them till they fall beneath the hatchet. Their eyes

诞生了人们特称为"山水诗"的诗歌。有些人认为，这种描绘大地上有形而无生命的物体的诗，是民主时代所特有的，但是我认为这样的看法不正确，它只属于一个过渡时期。

我肯定，最终民主必然将想象力从人之外的事物转向人本身，并最终专注于人。民主国家的人民可能为了消遣而一段时间向往大自然的产物，但是他们真正向往的则是认识自己。这里，而且只有这里才能在这些国家之中找到诗歌之源，而且可以肯定凡是不想从此处汲取灵感的诗人将不会打动那些他试图感动的人的心灵，而且最终留下的不过是看过他的大作后无动于衷的人们。我已经说过，人类不断进步和无限完善的思想特属于民主时代。民主国家的人民几乎完全不关心过去怎样，在他们心中挥之不去的是未来会如何。于是，一想到未来他们的想象力便开始天马行空一发不可收拾。这便给诗人开辟了无尽的广阔天地，极大地开阔了他们的视野。民主向诗人关闭了通向过去的大门，但是为他们敞开了面向未来的窗户。因为民主社会的所有公民几乎完全平等和相同，诗人不能专门描绘他们中的任何一个，但是民族本身却可以让诗人大展拳脚。人与人的普遍相似，使得他们之中的任何一个都不适合作为诗歌描写的对象，但同时可以让诗人将所有人合成一个统一的形象，从而对整个民族本身进行描绘。民主国家对自身的认识比任何其他国家对它们自身的认识都要清晰。这就使其成为理想描述的最好素材。

我同意美国没有诗人的说法，但是我不认为他们没有富于诗意的思想。在欧洲，人们谈到美国总会说是一片荒野，但是美国人自己从来没有这样的感觉。他们对无生命大自然的奇迹无动于衷，而且可以说，直到他们周围的森林被伐光后，才会意识到森林的壮丽。

are fixed upon another sight: the American people views its own march across these wilds—drying swamps, turning the course of rivers, peopling solitudes, and subduing nature. This magnificent image of themselves does not meet the gaze of the Americans at intervals only; it may be said to haunt every one of them in his least as well as in his most important actions, and to be always flitting before his mind. Nothing conceivable is so petty, so insipid, so crowded with paltry interests, in one word so anti-poetic, as the life of a man in the United States. But amongst the thoughts which it suggests there is always one which is full of poetry, and that is the hidden nerve which gives vigor to the frame.

In aristocratic ages each people, as well as each individual, is prone to stand separate and aloof from all others. In democratic ages, the extreme fluctuations of men and the impatience of their desires keep them perpetually on the move; so that the inhabitants of different countries intermingle, see, listen to, and borrow from each other's stores. It is not only then the members of the same community who grow more alike; communities are themselves assimilated to one another, and the whole assemblage presents to the eye of the spectator one vast democracy, each citizen of which is a people. This displays the aspect of mankind for the first time in the broadest light. All that belongs to the existence of the human race taken as a whole, to its vicissitudes and to its future, becomes an abundant mine of poetry. The poets who lived in aristocratic ages have been eminently successful in their delineations of certain incidents in the life of a people or a man; but none of them ever ventured to include within his performances the destinies of mankind—a task which poets writing in democratic ages may attempt. At that same time at which every man, raising his eyes above his country, begins at length to discern mankind at large, the Divinity is more and more manifest to the human mind in full and entire majesty. If in democratic ages faith in positive religions be often shaken, and the belief in intermediate agents, by whatever name they are called, be overcast; on the other hand men are disposed to conceive a far broader idea of Providence itself, and its interference in human affairs assumes a new and more imposing appearance to their eyes. Looking at the human race as one great whole, they easily conceive that its destinies are regulated by the same design; and

他们的眼睛完全被另一番景象所吸引。美国人一心只想穿越这片荒野，他们排干沼泽，改变河道，开垦荒地，征服自然。他们自己描画出的这幅图画，不仅逐渐映入美国人的眼帘，甚至可以说烙印在每个人的一举一动，并始终在他们的脑海中浮现。人们所能想象到的再没有什么比美国人的生活更加渺小、更加无趣、更加乏味，总之一句话：完全没有诗意。但是在指引人们前进的思想之中，始终有一个充满诗情画意，它就好像是隐藏在人体内支配整个身体的神经。

在贵族时代，每个民族每个人都处于静止不动的状态，并与其他的民族和个人隔离。在民主时代，人们的波动和强烈的愿望让他们不断迁徙，以至于不同国家的人们杂居相处、彼此往来，取长补短。于是，不仅仅是同一社会的成员之间越来越相似，社会与社会彼此之间也越来越相似，以至于人们眼前呈现出一个巨大的民主共和国，它的每一个公民都是一个民族。这是有史以来第一次将人类的本来面貌呈现出来。所有属于全人类生存、演变和未来的一切都成为充裕的诗歌之源。生活在贵族时代的诗人显然在描绘一个民族和一个人的事迹上取得辉煌的成就，但是他们之中没有任何一个人曾敢将人类的命运作为自己的创作题材，而这正是民主时代诗人所做的尝试。在每个人都可以放眼世界开始关注全人类的时代，神也越来越充分全面地将其威严表现在人的精神之中。如果在民主时代，人们对正统宗教的信仰会时常被动摇，那么对一些无论他们姓甚名谁的次要权威的信仰就更是被丢到一边。而另一方面，人们对神意本身又有了更为广泛深刻的认识，在他们看来，神意对人类事务的干预会进一步加深。因为他们将整个人类视为一个整体，所以很容易产生人类命运是受同一神意支

in the actions of every individual they are led to acknowledge a trace of that universal and eternal plan on which God rules our race. This consideration may be taken as another prolific source of poetry which is opened in democratic ages. Democratic poets will always appear trivial and frigid if they seek to invest gods, demons, or angels, with corporeal forms, and if they attempt to draw them down from heaven to dispute the supremacy of earth. But if they strive to connect the great events they commemorate with the general providential designs which govern the universe, and, without showing the finger of the Supreme Governor, reveal the thoughts of the Supreme Mind, their works will be admired and understood, for the imagination of their contemporaries takes this direction of its own accord.

It may be foreseen in the like manner that poets living in democratic ages will prefer the delineation of passions and ideas to that of persons and achievements. The language, the dress, and the daily actions of men in democracies are repugnant to ideal conceptions. These things are not poetical in themselves; and, if it were otherwise, they would cease to be so, because they are too familiar to all those to whom the poet would speak of them. This forces the poet constantly to search below the external surface which is palpable to the senses, in order to read the inner soul: and nothing lends itself more to the delineation of the ideal than the scrutiny of the hidden depths in the immaterial nature of man. I need not to ramble over earth and sky to discover a wondrous object woven of contrasts, of greatness and littleness infinite, of intense gloom and of amazing brightness—capable at once of exciting pity, admiration, terror, contempt. I find that object in myself. Man springs out of nothing, crosses time, and disappears forever in the bosom of God; he is seen but for a moment, staggering on the verge of the two abysses, and there he is lost. If man were wholly ignorant of himself, he would have no poetry in him; for it is impossible to describe what the mind does not conceive. If man clearly discerned his own nature, his imagination would remain idle, and would have nothing to add to the picture. But the nature of man is sufficiently disclosed for him to apprehend something of himself; and sufficiently obscure for all the rest to be plunged in thick darkness, in which he gropes forever—and forever in vain—to lay hold on some completer notion of

配的想法，并能从每个人的行动上认识到上帝将依据其伟大的计划而引领人类所走的道路。这样的想法可以被认为是民主时代为诗歌开辟的另一个充沛的源泉。如果民主时代的诗人试图赋予上帝、鬼神或是天使以肉身，并试图将他们从天上拉到地上看他们斗法，那么他们必然会显得软弱无力。但是如果他们试图将自己要纪念的重大事件与统治宇宙的神的宗旨联系起来，并且不将至高无上的主的手示于人前，而只揭示神的思想，他们的作品将可以得到赞扬和人们的共鸣。因为这与他们同时代人想象力的发展方向一致。

可以预见，生活在民主时代的诗人会更喜欢描写人们的激情和思想，而不是人的行动本身和其成就。民主时代人们的语言、衣着以及日常行为都与人们对于理想的向往南辕北辙。这些事情就其本身而言丝毫没有诗情画意，而且也不能入诗，因为诗人所要感动的那些人对这些东西再熟悉不过。这就迫使诗人不断深入到感官所能感知的表象之下去阅读人类的灵魂。最能深入灵魂深处的人，也最能塑造理想。我没有必要上天入地去寻找冲突交织、兼具伟大与渺小、黑暗与光明，且能够让人顿生怜悯、赞美、恐怖和轻视之心的惊人题材。我发现人本身就是这样的题材。人从无中来，穿越时空，最终永远投入上帝的怀抱。人生在世，从出生到死亡不过转瞬即逝。人如果对自己一无所知，也就永远不会有诗意，因为人不可能描绘其无法想象的东西。如果人可以清楚地认识到自己的本质，那么他的想象力也会毫无用武之地，无法给他的描绘增加任何东西。但是人的本性足以让他能够认识到自己的某些部分，也足以始终将其余部分隐藏在黑暗之中让他无法看清，他会一直在这片黑暗中摸索，却始终毫无进展。

his being.

Amongst a democratic people poetry will not be fed with legendary lays or the memorials of old traditions. The poet will not attempt to people the universe with supernatural beings in whom his readers and his own fancy have ceased to believe; nor will he present virtues and vices in the mask of frigid personification, which are better received under their own features. All these resources fail him; but Man remains, and the poet needs no more. The destinies of mankind—man himself, taken aloof from his age and his country, and standing in the presence of Nature and of God, with his passions, his doubts, his rare prosperities, and inconceivable wretchedness—will become the chief, if not the sole theme of poetry amongst these nations. Experience may confirm this assertion, if we consider the productions of the greatest poets who have appeared since the world has been turned to democracy. The authors of our age who have so admirably delineated the features of Faust, Childe Harold, Rene, and Jocelyn, did not seek to record the actions of an individual, but to enlarge and to throw light on some of the obscurer recesses of the human heart. Such are the poems of democracy. The principle of equality does not then destroy all the subjects of poetry: it renders them less numerous, but more vast.

Chapter XVIII: Of The Inflated Style Of American Writers And Orators

I have frequently remarked that the Americans, who generally treat of business in clear, plain language, devoid of all ornament, and so extremely simple as to be often coarse, are apt to become inflated as soon as they attempt a more poetical diction. They then vent their pomposity from one end of a harangue to the other; and to hear them lavish imagery on every occasion, one might fancy that they never spoke of anything with simplicity. The English are more rarely given to a similar failing. The cause of this may be pointed out without much difficulty. In democratic communities each citizen is habitually engaged in the contemplation of a very puny object, namely himself. If he ever raises his looks higher, he then perceives nothing but the immense form of society at large, or the still more imposing aspect of mankind. His ideas are all either extremely minute and clear, or extremely

在民主国家，即不会充斥着传奇叙事诗，也不会充斥纪念传统的诗作。诗人不会试图将读者及自己都已不再相信的超自然的存在，以及本身善恶已分的东西再拟人化后呈现给世人。因为所有这些诗歌之源都不能让他获得成功。但是人依旧存在，这对于诗人来说就已足够。人类的命运、人本身，无论其所处的时代和国家，伫立于大自然和神的面前，他们的热情、怀疑、罕见的得志和难以想象的悲惨，都会成为民主国家诗歌的主要或者说是唯一的来源。如果我们看一下世界自民主以来那些伟大诗人的作品，便可知此言不虚。我们这个时代的作家在惟妙惟肖地刻画恰尔德·哈罗德、勒内、若斯兰等人的形象时，并没有试图描绘个人的行为，而是试图照亮隐藏在人们内心的东西。这就是民主时代的诗。所以，民主并没有破坏所有的诗歌题材，只是减少了它们的数目，同时却令其范围更加广泛。

第十八章　为什么美国的作家和演说家爱夸张

我经常看到，美国人平时说话清晰明了，不加任何修饰，而且极为直白，有时候甚至有些粗俗，然而他们一旦想要发表一段富于诗意的言论时，往往总爱夸大其词。于是，他们的慷慨陈词从头到尾都是华丽的辞藻，听着他们大肆渲染一切其想象时，你会以为他们讲话从来不会是直率的。而英国人则不会有这样的问题。这种现象出现的原因很容易找到。在民主社会，每个公民都习惯于对一个微不足道的对象煞费苦心，也就是他自己。如果他们一旦开阔视野，就会看到整个社会的庞大身形，或是更为高大的全人类的形象。所以，他们的思想不是极为具体和清晰，就是极为笼统和模糊，而在这两个极端之间则是一

general and vague: what lies between is an open void. When he has been drawn out of his own sphere, therefore, he always expects that some amazing object will be offered to his attention; and it is on these terms alone that he consents to tear himself for an instant from the petty complicated cares which form the charm and the excitement of his life. This appears to me sufficiently to explain why men in democracies, whose concerns are in general so paltry, call upon their poets for conceptions so vast and descriptions so unlimited.

The authors, on their part, do not fail to obey a propensity of which they themselves partake; they perpetually inflate their imaginations, and expanding them beyond all bounds, they not unfrequently abandon the great in order to reach the gigantic. By these means they hope to attract the observation of the multitude, and to fix it easily upon themselves: nor are their hopes disappointed; for as the multitude seeks for nothing in poetry but subjects of very vast dimensions, it has neither the time to measure with accuracy the proportions of all the subjects set before it, nor a taste sufficiently correct to perceive at once in what respect they are out of proportion. The author and the public at once vitiate one another.

We have just seen that amongst democratic nations, the sources of poetry are grand, but not abundant. They are soon exhausted: and poets, not finding the elements of the ideal in what is real and true, abandon them entirely and create monsters. I do not fear that the poetry of democratic nations will prove too insipid, or that it will fly too near the ground; I rather apprehend that it will be forever losing itself in the clouds, and that it will range at last to purely imaginary regions. I fear that the productions of democratic poets may often be surcharged with immense and incoherent imagery, with exaggerated descriptions and strange creations; and that the fantastic beings of their brain may sometimes make us regret the world of reality.

Chapter XIX: Some Observations On The Drama Amongst Democratic Nations

When the revolution which subverts the social and political state of an aristocratic people begins

片真空地带。因此，当他们脱离自己的圈子时，总是希望能有一些惊人的东西引起自己的注意，而且只有如此他们才同意暂时不考虑那些激励和鼓舞其生活的琐碎小事。在我看来，这足以充分说明为什么民主国家普遍只关注与己有关的小事的人民，却要求他们的诗人拥有无限开阔的视野和极尽夸张的描绘。

就作者本身而言，他们本身也有这种夸张的倾向，所以自然乐于遵命。于是，作家的想象力不断膨胀，甚至膨胀得过度，以至于常常为了夸张而放弃伟大的真实。通过这些方式诗人们希望能够吸引广大读者的视线，并将注意力集中在自己身上。他们的希望并没有落空，因为读者希望从诗歌中找到的是海阔天空，他们既没有时间去探寻诗歌内容的真伪，而且也没有足够的鉴赏力能够一下子指出哪些不合实际。就这样作家害了读者，读者也害了作家。

我们刚刚已经看到，在民主国家中，诗歌的来源很宏大，但不够丰富。诗歌的源泉不久便会干涸，而诗人们因为无法从真和实中找到理想的素材，于是便将其完全抛弃，创造出一些怪诞的东西。我并不害怕民主国家的诗歌变得乏味，或是太贴近现实，而是担心它会一直如坠云里雾里，并只描写想象的国度被牢牢地困在那里。我害怕民主诗人的作品总是充满空洞不连贯的想象，华丽的辞藻和怪诞的描写；而且也害怕他们的奇思异想会让我们时不时地为现实而感到遗憾。

第十九章　略论民主国家的戏剧

当颠覆一个贵族国家社会和政治状况的革命开始深入到文学，一般会首先表现在戏剧

to penetrate into literature, it generally first manifests itself in the drama, and it always remains conspicuous there. The spectator of a dramatic piece is, to a certain extent, taken by surprise by the impression it conveys. He has no time to refer to his memory, or to consult those more able to judge than himself. It does not occur to him to resist the new literary tendencies which begin to be felt by him; he yields to them before he knows what they are. Authors are very prompt in discovering which way the taste of the public is thus secretly inclined. They shape their productions accordingly; and the literature of the stage, after having served to indicate the approaching literary revolution, speedily completes its accomplishment. If you would judge beforehand of the literature of a people which is lapsing into democracy, study its dramatic productions.

The literature of the stage, moreover, even amongst aristocratic nations, constitutes the most democratic part of their literature. No kind of literary gratification is so much within the reach of the multitude as that which is derived from theatrical representations. Neither preparation nor study is required to enjoy them: they lay hold on you in the midst of your prejudices and your ignorance. When the yet untutored love of the pleasures of the mind begins to affect a class of the community, it instantly draws them to the stage. The theatres of aristocratic nations have always been filled with spectators not belonging to the aristocracy. At the theatre alone the higher ranks mix with the middle and the lower classes; there alone do the former consent to listen to the opinion of the latter, or at least to allow them to give an opinion at all. At the theatre, men of cultivation and of literary attainments have always had more difficulty than elsewhere in making their taste prevail over that of the people, and in preventing themselves from being carried away by the latter. The pit has frequently made laws for the boxes.

If it be difficult for an aristocracy to prevent the people from getting the upper hand in the theatre, it will readily be understood that the people will be supreme there when democratic principles have crept into the laws and manners—when ranks are intermixed—when minds, as well as fortunes, are brought more nearly together—and when the upper class has lost, with its hereditary wealth, its power, its precedents, and its leisure. The tastes and propensities natural to democratic nations, in

上，而且对其影响会一直非常显著。戏剧观众的情绪，在一定程度上，会随戏剧的起伏而波动。他们在观看戏剧时既没有时间玩味剧情，也没时间与比自己高明的人讨论剧情。而对于自己已经感受到的文学新趋势，他们也并没有加以抑制的想法，在还没有弄清它们是什么之前，便已经倒戈。作家们很快就发现大众爱好暗藏的倾向。于是，他们让自己的创作投其所好，而舞台文学，在预示了即将到来的文学革命之后，迅速将其完成。如果你想要预测一个正在走向民主的国家的文学发展，研究一下它的戏剧就可以了。

此外，甚至在贵族制国家，舞台文学也是其文学中最具民主性的部分。在所有的文艺享乐中，戏剧带给群众的满足感最大。既不用做准备也无须研究，人们就可以欣赏戏剧。无论你有什么样的偏见，如何的无知，戏剧都会将你紧紧抓牢。当一种雅俗参半的精神享乐开始在人民群众中受到欢迎时，它便会被立即带上舞台。贵族国家的剧院中总是有很多不属于贵族阶级的观众出入。剧院是唯一一个上层阶级与中下层阶级有所接触的地方，也只有在这里前者愿意倾听后者的观点，或至少允许他们发表自己的意见。在剧院，有教养的人和学识渊博的人最难以让自己的爱好不被群众追随，也最难以防止自己被群众的爱好所吸引。因此，上层阶级往往在剧院里订包厢。

既然贵族难以阻止人民群众进入剧院，所以不难知道，当民主原则被法律和民情所认可，各阶级融为一体，人们的思想和财富彼此接近，而且上层阶级失去其世袭的财富、权力、传统和舒适生活的时候，人民群众将成为这里的主导。因此，民主国家人民对文艺的天然爱好和本性将首先表现在戏剧方面，而且可以预见，他们的这种爱好和本性还将更有

respect to literature, will therefore first be discernible in the drama, and it may be foreseen that they will break out there with vehemence. In written productions, the literary canons of aristocracy will be gently, gradually, and, so to speak, legally modified; at the theatre they will be riotously overthrown. The drama brings out most of the good qualities, and almost all the defects, inherent in democratic literature. Democratic peoples hold erudition very cheap, and care but little for what occurred at Rome and Athens; they want to hear something which concerns themselves, and the delineation of the present age is what they demand.

When the heroes and the manners of antiquity are frequently brought upon the stage, and dramatic authors faithfully observe the rules of antiquated precedent, that is enough to warrant a conclusion that the democratic classes have not yet got the upper hand of the theatres. Racine makes a very humble apology in the preface to the "Britannicus" for having disposed of Junia amongst the Vestals, who, according to Aulus Gellius, he says, "admitted no one below six years of age nor above ten." We may be sure that he would neither have accused himself of the offence, nor defended himself from censure, if he had written for our contemporaries. A fact of this kind not only illustrates the state of literature at the time when it occurred, but also that of society itself. A democratic stage does not prove that the nation is in a state of democracy, for, as we have just seen, even in aristocracies it may happen that democratic tastes affect the drama; but when the spirit of aristocracy reigns exclusively on the stage, the fact irrefragably demonstrates that the whole of society is aristocratic; and it may be boldly inferred that the same lettered and learned class which sways the dramatic writers commands the people and governs the country.

The refined tastes and the arrogant bearing of an aristocracy will rarely fail to lead it, when it manages the stage, to make a kind of selection in human nature. Some of the conditions of society claim its chief interest; and the scenes which delineate their manners are preferred upon the stage. Certain virtues, and even certain vices, are thought more particularly to deserve to figure there; and they are applauded whilst all others are excluded. Upon the stage, as well as elsewhere, an aristocratic audience will only meet personages of quality, and share the emotions of kings. The

力地渗透其中。贵族给文艺写作订立的清规戒律将逐步分阶段地被改变，而且可以说被合法地改变，在剧场它们将被人民大张旗鼓地推翻。戏剧会将民主文学固有的大部分优点和几乎所有缺点都表现出来。民主国家的人民对于学识并不注重，也毫不关心罗马和雅典曾经发生过什么，他们只想听与自己有关的事情，要的是对现在的描绘。

当古代的英雄和故事不断地被搬上舞台，戏剧作家忠实地恪守古代的传统，这就足以断定，民主阶层还没有在剧院占据上风。拉辛在《布里塔尼居斯》的前言中，为把儒尼叶作为侍奉女灶神维斯塔的一名贞女来进行艺术加工一事，进行了十分谦逊的辩解。他依据格列乌斯的记叙说："那里绝不收不满6岁或是超过10岁的女孩。"我们可以肯定，如果他今天写这个剧本，肯定不会为这样的错误而自责或辩解。这样的事实不仅表现出那个时代的文艺状况，而且表现出那个时代的社会状况。一个民主的舞台并不能证明那个国家处于民主状态，因为正如我们所见，甚至在贵族制国家，民主的爱好也会影响到戏剧。但是当贵族精神绝对统治舞台的时候，则无可辩驳地证明整个社会处于贵族制度，而且可以大胆推断，影响着戏剧作家的那个有学识有教养的阶级，同样也在号令着人民统治着这个国家。

当贵族掌控戏剧舞台和表演的时候，他们总是会从自己的文雅爱好和高尚气质出发判断人的本性。他们对有一定社会地位的人物感兴趣，喜欢让这样的人物出现在舞台上。他们认为特定的善，甚至是特定的恶，都特别适合出现在这里，而其他的一切，则都应排除在外。贵族在剧院跟在其他地方一样，只愿意跟大领主们交谈，只会对宫廷的悲欢离合产生共鸣。对于剧本的体裁，他们的态度也是一样。贵族总是要求剧作家按照他们规定的调

same thing applies to style: an aristocracy is apt to impose upon dramatic authors certain modes of expression which give the key in which everything is to be delivered. By these means the stage frequently comes to delineate only one side of man, or sometimes even to represent what is not to be met with in human nature at all—to rise above nature and to go beyond it.

In democratic communities the spectators have no such partialities, and they rarely display any such antipathies: they like to see upon the stage that medley of conditions, of feelings, and of opinions, which occurs before their eyes. The drama becomes more striking, more common, and more true. Sometimes, however, those who write for the stage in democracies also transgress the bounds of human nature—but it is on a different side from their predecessors. By seeking to represent in minute detail the little singularities of the moment and the peculiar characteristics of certain personages, they forget to portray the general features of the race.

When the democratic classes rule the stage, they introduce as much license in the manner of treating subjects as in the choice of them. As the love of the drama is, of all literary tastes, that which is most natural to democratic nations, the number of authors and of spectators, as well as of theatrical representations, is constantly increasing amongst these communities. A multitude composed of elements so different, and scattered in so many different places, cannot acknowledge the same rules or submit to the same laws. No concurrence is possible amongst judges so numerous, who know not when they may meet again; and therefore each pronounces his own sentence on the piece. If the effect of democracy is generally to question the authority of all literary rules and conventions, on the stage it abolishes them altogether, and puts in their place nothing but the whim of each author and of each public.

The drama also displays in an especial manner the truth of what I have said before in speaking more generally of style and art in democratic literature. In reading the criticisms which were occasioned by the dramatic productions of the age of Louis XIV, one is surprised to remark the great stress which the public laid on the probability of the plot, and the importance which was attached to the perfect consistency of the characters, and to their doing nothing which could not be easily

调写台词，希望一切都合乎他们的腔调。就这样，戏剧总是描绘人的一个侧面，有时甚至是人性中根本不存在的东西，也就是那些超乎人性或是不符合人性的东西。

在民主社会，观众没有这样的偏好，也罕有贵族那样的反感。他们喜欢在舞台上看到各种不同出身的人物，形形色色的情感和思想，而这些都曾是他们亲眼所见。戏剧变得更具冲击力、更通俗，而且更真实。然而，有时候在民主国家，写戏剧的人有时候也会脱离人的本性，但是初衷与他们的前辈们并不相同。由于力求惟妙惟肖地描绘再现当代的小人物、小事和某些人的特征，他们忽略了对人类普遍特征的描写。

当民主阶级控制戏剧的时候，他们在题材的选择和处理上给予作家充分的自由。因为在民主国家所有的文艺爱好之中，对戏剧的热爱是其最自然的倾向，所以在这样的社会，剧作家和观众，乃至演出，都与日俱增。作者和观众的人数众多，形形色色，分散在各地，所以不可能制定同样的规则，或是让他们遵守同样的规则。而且评论戏剧的人数量庞大，彼此也互不相识，所以他们也无法做出一致的评论，因此每个人不过是表达自己的看法。如果说民主制度的影响让人们普遍质疑所有文学方面的规则和章法，那么在舞台上，民主制度则将其全部废除，取而代之的是每个作家和观众的心血来潮。

我在前面概括地谈到民主文学的体裁和技巧时所做的评述，也特别适用于戏剧。在阅读路易十四时期剧评家对当时戏剧作品的评论时，有一处令人惊讶的评价称：观众特别重视情节的真实性，剧中人物行为的得体性，即不能做出使人难以理解或是无法解释的举止。当时人们对于语言表达形式十分重视，以至于作家台词上的一点小毛病也会受到苛

explained and understood. The value which was set upon the forms of language at that period, and the paltry strife about words with which dramatic authors were assailed, are no less surprising. It would seem that the men of the age of Louis XIV attached very exaggerated importance to those details, which may be perceived in the study, but which escape attention on the stage. For, after all, the principal object of a dramatic piece is to be performed, and its chief merit is to affect the audience. But the audience and the readers in that age were the same: on quitting the theatre they called up the author for judgment to their own firesides. In democracies, dramatic pieces are listened to, but not read. Most of those who frequent the amusements of the stage do not go there to seek the pleasures of the mind, but the keen emotions of the heart. They do not expect to hear a fine literary work, but to see a play; and provided the author writes the language of his country correctly enough to be understood, and that his characters excite curiosity and awaken sympathy, the audience are satisfied. They ask no more of fiction, and immediately return to real life. Accuracy of style is therefore less required, because the attentive observance of its rules is less perceptible on the stage. As for the probability of the plot, it is incompatible with perpetual novelty, surprise, and rapidity of invention. It is therefore neglected, and the public excuses the neglect. You may be sure that if you succeed in bringing your audience into the presence of something that affects them, they will not care by what road you brought them there; and they will never reproach you for having excited their emotions in spite of dramatic rules.

The Americans very broadly display all the different propensities which I have here described when they go to the theatres; but it must be acknowledged that as yet a very small number of them go to theatres at all. Although playgoers and plays have prodigiously increased in the United States in the last forty years, the population indulges in this kind of amusement with the greatest reserve. This is attributable to peculiar causes, which the reader is already acquainted with, and of which a few words will suffice to remind him. The Puritans who founded the American republics were not only enemies to amusements, but they professed an especial abhorrence for the stage. They considered it as an abominable pastime; and as long as their principles prevailed with undivided sway, scenic

责，这也让我们吃惊不小。路易十四时期的人们似乎对这些在舞台上无须留意而只有在书斋里才会细细玩味的细节太过重视。戏剧的主要目的是表演，主要的价值在于感动观众。但是那个时代的观众和读者都是同一群人，他们在看完演出后，会将作家请到家中在火炉边当面品评。在民主国家，戏剧是听的，而不是读的。不断出入剧院看演出的大多数人并不是为寻求精神享乐而来，而是为追求感性刺激而来。他们并不指望能够听到华丽的台词，而只是希望戏演得够热闹。只要作者能够正确地使用本国语言，人们能够理解，而且剧中人物可以激起人们的好奇，唤起人们的共鸣，观众就会感到满意。观众知道戏剧是虚构的，所以看完之后便立即回归现实。因此，戏剧的文体并不重要，因为在舞台上人们意识不到它是否合乎规定。至于情节的真实性，则不可能和新奇、意外和剧情的急转直下兼具。因此，剧作家不重视真实性，而观众也对此不以为意。可以肯定，如果你能成功地让观众为你写的戏所感动，他们根本不会在乎你使用了什么样的方法，而且他们也不会因为你没有遵守写作的规则却可以感动观众而指责你。

当美国人走进剧院时，会将我所说过的所有这些不同的特点表现得淋漓尽致，但是必须承认，在美国到剧院看戏的人还为数不多。尽管40年来，美国的戏剧观众和演出与日俱增，但是人们对这种娱乐方式依旧持非常谨慎的态度。出现这种情况的原因我在前面已经说过，为了帮助读者回忆，我再稍作补充。在美国建立最初几个定居点的清教徒不但反对娱乐，而且对戏剧特别痛恨。他们认为戏剧是一种可憎的消遣，而且只要是在他们的教义盛行的地方，人们就不知道戏剧演出为何物。殖民地初代移民的这些观点在其后代的精神上留下

performances were wholly unknown amongst them. These opinions of the first fathers of the colony have left very deep marks on the minds of their descendants. The extreme regularity of habits and the great strictness of manners which are observable in the United States, have as yet opposed additional obstacles to the growth of dramatic art. There are no dramatic subjects in a country which has witnessed no great political catastrophes, and in which love invariably leads by a straight and easy road to matrimony. People who spend every day in the week in making money, and the Sunday in going to church, have nothing to invite the muse of Comedy.

A single fact suffices to show that the stage is not very popular in the United States. The Americans, whose laws allow of the utmost freedom and even license of language in all other respects, have nevertheless subjected their dramatic authors to a sort of censorship. Theatrical performances can only take place by permission of the municipal authorities. This may serve to show how much communities are like individuals; they surrender themselves unscrupulously to their ruling passions, and afterwards take the greatest care not to yield too much to the vehemence of tastes which they do not possess.

No portion of literature is connected by closer or more numerous ties with the present condition of society than the drama. The drama of one period can never be suited to the following age, if in the interval an important revolution has changed the manners and the laws of the nation. The great authors of a preceding age may be read; but pieces written for a different public will not be followed. The dramatic authors of the past live only in books. The traditional taste of certain individuals, vanity, fashion, or the genius of an actor may sustain or resuscitate for a time the aristocratic drama amongst a democracy; but it will speedily fall away of itself—not overthrown, but abandoned.

Chapter XX: Characteristics Of Historians In Democratic Ages

Historians who write in aristocratic ages are wont to refer all occurrences to the particular will or temper of certain individuals; and they are apt to attribute the most important revolutions to very slight accidents. They trace out the smallest causes with sagacity, and frequently leave the greatest

了深深的烙印。美国人一成不变的生活习惯和死板严肃的民情至今对美国戏剧的发展依然有着不利的影响。一个国家从未见证过巨大政治变故，男女相爱便无一例外、毫无曲折地径直走入婚姻，就不会有戏剧的题材，而每个周日都上教堂礼拜的人，也不会与喜剧女神结缘。

仅举一例，就足以证明戏剧在美国并不是很受欢迎。美国的法律承认公民在一切方面享有言论自由，却对剧作家实行审查制度。戏剧只有在获得地方当局的认可后方可演出。这一事实清楚地表明，全体人民和个人对于戏剧态度完全一致。他们完全被自己的热情所左右，对于他们最关心的无比热情，而对于他们不爱好的则千方百计地阻止其侵入。

没有任何一种文学样式与戏剧一样跟社会现状的联系如此紧密和复杂。如果两个时代之间发生令国家的民情和法律为之改变的重大革命，那么前一个时代的戏剧绝不会适合于后一个时代。前一个时代伟大作家的作品也许人们还会拜读，但是人们不会再观看为另一个时代的人们所写的戏剧。过去的剧作家只能留在书本里。某些人对于传统的爱好、虚荣心、时尚，或是演员的才华，也许可以让贵族时代的戏剧在民主国家上演或是复兴上一段时间，但很快便会销声匿迹。它们并没有被人推翻，而是被人抛弃。

第二十章　民主时代历史学家的特点

贵族时代的历史学家总是把所有的史实与某个人的独特意志和性格联系起来，而且往往把最重大的革命归因于一些非常偶然的事件。他们可以远见卓识地找到一些最不起眼的原因，却总是将最重大的原因忽略。生活在民主时代的历史学家，则完全表现出与他们

unperceived. Historians who live in democratic ages exhibit precisely opposite characteristics. Most of them attribute hardly any influence to the individual over the destiny of the race, nor to citizens over the fate of a people; but, on the other hand, they assign great general causes to all petty incidents. These contrary tendencies explain each other.

When the historian of aristocratic ages surveys the theatre of the world, he at once perceives a very small number of prominent actors, who manage the whole piece. These great personages, who occupy the front of the stage, arrest the observation, and fix it on themselves; and whilst the historian is bent on penetrating the secret motives which make them speak and act, the rest escape his memory. The importance of the things which some men are seen to do, gives him an exaggerated estimate of the influence which one man may possess; and naturally leads him to think, that in order to explain the impulses of the multitude, it is necessary to refer them to the particular influence of some one individual.

When, on the contrary, all the citizens are independent of one another, and each of them is individually weak, no one is seen to exert a great, or still less a lasting power, over the community. At first sight, individuals appear to be absolutely devoid of any influence over it; and society would seem to advance alone by the free and voluntary concurrence of all the men who compose it. This naturally prompts the mind to search for that general reason which operates upon so many men's faculties at the same time, and turns them simultaneously in the same direction.

I am very well convinced that even amongst democratic nations, the genius, the vices, or the virtues of certain individuals retard or accelerate the natural current of a people's history: but causes of this secondary and fortuitous nature are infinitely more various, more concealed, more complex, less powerful, and consequently less easy to trace in periods of equality than in ages of aristocracy, when the task of the historian is simply to detach from the mass of general events the particular influences of one man or of a few men. In the former case the historian is soon wearied by the toil; his mind loses itself in this labyrinth; and, in his inability clearly to discern or conspicuously to point out the influence of individuals, he denies their existence. He prefers talking about the characteristics

完全相反的特征。大多数民主时代的历史学家认为，个人几乎不会对人类命运产生什么影响，而少数的公民也不会对国家的命运产生重大影响。而另一方面，他们却总是喜欢用一般原因去解释所有特殊的小事件。这些对立的倾向并不难理解。

当贵族时代的历史学家纵观世界舞台时，他会立刻注意到站在舞台中央表演的为数不多的几个引人注目的演员。这几个站在舞台前面的人立刻吸引了他们的目光，于是他们便目不转睛地盯着这些人。他们专心研究这些人一言一行的隐秘动机，而完全没有注意到其他的一切。由于一些人做了一些重要的事情，于是他们便夸大了个人可能发生的影响，进而便顺理成章地用某个人的特殊影响力来解释人民大众的冲动。

相反，当所有的公民都彼此独立，每个人都势单力薄，那么没有人能够拥有对人民大众强大而永久的权力。乍一看，个人似乎对于社会完全没有任何影响力，而社会似乎是在所有人自由和自发行为的共同作用下自行前进。这就自然促使人的精神去探索能够同时将众人能力激发起来并自发朝同一方向前进的一般原因。

我非常肯定，即使在民主国家，某些个人的才华、恶行和美德也会推迟和加速人类历史的自然进程。但这些次要的和偶然的原因天性变化无常、隐秘、复杂、力量也不大，所以在平等时代比在贵族时代更难发现它们的蛛丝马迹。当历史学家的任务就是简单地从大量一般事件中找出单独某一个人或几个人的活动进行研究时，不久他们就会对这样的苦活感到厌烦，思想很快就好像迷失在迷宫之中，因为无力弄清并指出个人的影响力，所以便否定其存在，于是便更喜欢谈论人类的特征、国家的自然环境、文明的精神面貌，这可以

of race, the physical conformation of the country, or the genius of civilization, which abridges his own labors, and satisfies his reader far better at less cost.

M. de Lafayette says somewhere in his "Memoirs" that the exaggerated system of general causes affords surprising consolations to second-rate statesmen. I will add, that its effects are not less consolatory to second-rate historians; it can always furnish a few mighty reasons to extricate them from the most difficult part of their work, and it indulges the indolence or incapacity of their minds, whilst it confers upon them the honors of deep thinking.

For myself, I am of opinion that at all times one great portion of the events of this world are attributable to general facts, and another to special influences. These two kinds of cause are always in operation: their proportion only varies. General facts serve to explain more things in democratic than in aristocratic ages, and fewer things are then assignable to special influences. At periods of aristocracy the reverse takes place: special influences are stronger, general causes weaker—unless indeed we consider as a general cause the fact itself of the inequality of conditions, which allows some individuals to baffle the natural tendencies of all the rest. The historians who seek to describe what occurs in democratic societies are right, therefore, in assigning much to general causes, and in devoting their chief attention to discover them; but they are wrong in wholly denying the special influence of individuals, because they cannot easily trace or follow it.

The historians who live in democratic ages are not only prone to assign a great cause to every incident, but they are also given to connect incidents together, so as to deduce a system from them. In aristocratic ages, as the attention of historians is constantly drawn to individuals, the connection of events escapes them; or rather, they do not believe in any such connection. To them the clew of history seems every instant crossed and broken by the step of man. In democratic ages, on the contrary, as the historian sees much more of actions than of actors, he may easily establish some kind of sequency and methodical order amongst the former. Ancient literature, which is so rich in fine historical compositions, does not contain a single great historical system, whilst the poorest of modern literatures abound with them. It would appear that the ancient historians did not make

让他们的劳动事半功倍，也能令读者感到满意。

拉法夷特先生在其《回忆录》的某处曾经这样说：过分夸大一般原因的研究方法，会带给二流的政客莫大的安慰。而我要补充一句，这也能给二流的历史学家带来不小的安慰。这可以让他们总是能用一些冠冕堂皇的理由来回避他们最难以处理的问题，掩盖他们的懒惰和无能，同时还能安享思想深刻的荣誉。

至于我自己，我认为在任何时代，这个世界大事件中的一大部分都可以归因于一般事实，而其余部分则来自个别的影响。这两种原因总是互相交织，只是所占比例各自不同。与贵族时代相比，在民主时代一般原因可以用来解释更多的事情，只有很少的事情受到个别影响。在贵族时代，情况刚好相反：个别影响更强大，一般原因相对更弱，甚至很少承认身份不平等这个事实，正是准许某些个人压制其他一切人的天赋意愿的一般原因。因此，试图描绘民主社会所发生的一切事情的历史学家利用一般原因去解释大部分问题，并专注于发现这些原因是正确的，但因为他们无法轻易地发现个人的个别影响而将其完全否定又是错误的。

生活在民主时代的历史学家不但喜欢为每个事件找到一般原因，而且还努力将各个事件联系起来，并演绎出一个体系。在贵族时代，因为历史学家的注意力不断被吸引到个人身上，于是便看不到事件之间的联系，或者说他们并不相信有这样的联系存在。在他们看来，历史的进程似乎时刻会因为一个人的逝去而中断。相反，在民主时代，因为历史学家更注重的是演出而不是演员，所以能够轻易地在各场演出之间建立起某种系统的联系和秩

sufficient use of those general theories which our historical writers are ever ready to carry to excess.

Those who write in democratic ages have another more dangerous tendency. When the traces of individual action upon nations are lost, it often happens that the world goes on to move, though the moving agent is no longer discoverable. As it becomes extremely difficult to discern and to analyze the reasons which, acting separately on the volition of each member of the community, concur in the end to produce movement in the old mass, men are led to believe that this movement is involuntary, and that societies unconsciously obey some superior force ruling over them. But even when the general fact which governs the private volition of all individuals is supposed to be discovered upon the earth, the principle of human free-will is not secure. A cause sufficiently extensive to affect millions of men at once, and sufficiently strong to bend them all together in the same direction, may well seem irresistible: having seen that mankind do yield to it, the mind is close upon the inference that mankind cannot resist it.

Historians who live in democratic ages, then, not only deny that the few have any power of acting upon the destiny of a people, but they deprive the people themselves of the power of modifying their own condition, and they subject them either to an inflexible Providence, or to some blind necessity. According to them, each nation is indissolubly bound by its position, its origin, its precedents, and its character, to a certain lot which no efforts can ever change. They involve generation in generation, and thus, going back from age to age, and from necessity to necessity, up to the origin of the world, they forge a close and enormous chain, which girds and binds the human race. To their minds it is not enough to show what events have occurred: they would fain show that events could not have occurred otherwise. They take a nation arrived at a certain stage of its history, and they affirm that it could not but follow the track which brought it thither. It is easier to make such an assertion than to show by what means the nation might have adopted a better course.

In reading the historians of aristocratic ages, and especially those of antiquity, it would seem that, to be master of his lot, and to govern his fellow-creatures, man requires only to be master of himself. In perusing the historical volumes which our age has produced, it would seem that man

序。古代文学为我们留下众多美丽的史诗，却未能描绘出一个伟大的历史体系，而如此简陋的现代文学则为我们提供了这样的体系。古代的历史学家似乎并未能充分利用那些有点被我们这个时代历史学家滥用的一般理论。

民主时代的历史学者还有另外一种更加危险的倾向。当个人行为对国家的影响消失的时候，尽管无法看到隐藏的动力，但世界往往依旧继续运动。因为很难发现并分析那些作用于社会每个成员意志并最终促使全民共同运动的原因，人们便认为这样的运动并不是自发的，社会必然在冥冥之中受到某种最高力量的支配。但是甚至当世界上确实有能够支配个人意志的一般原因存在的时候，人类的自由意志的原则就无法得到保障。一个广泛的足以同时影响到千百万人，强大得足以让所有人朝同一方向前进的原因，也将会是难以抗拒的。人们一旦服从这一原因，精神也随之认可人类无法抗拒。

于是，生活在民主时代的历史学家不但否认少数个人对国家命运的影响，而且否定人民自己有力量改善自己的处境。他们有时认为人民受到不可改变的天意的影响，有时又认为人民受到盲目需要的支配。在他们看来，每个民族不可改变的命运与其地理位置、起源、历史和性格有着非常紧密的联系。他们考察了一代又一代人，一个时代又一个时代，并从一个必然事件到另一个必然事件，一直追溯到世界的起源，他们打造出一个环环相扣的巨大链条，将整个人类束缚捆绑起来。他们并不满足于指出事件是怎样发生的，而且还乐于指明未来将如何发展。他们在研究一个发展到一定阶段的民族的历史之后，便断言这个民族将按照他们一路走来的这条道路继续下去。做这样的论断显然会比指出采用什么样

is utterly powerless over himself and over all around him. The historians of antiquity taught how to command: those of our time teach only how to obey; in their writings the author often appears great, but humanity is always diminutive. If this doctrine of necessity, which is so attractive to those who write history in democratic ages, passes from authors to their readers, till it infects the whole mass of the community and gets possession of the public mind, it will soon paralyze the activity of modern society, and reduce Christians to the level of the Turks. I would moreover observe, that such principles are peculiarly dangerous at the period at which we are arrived. Our contemporaries are but too prone to doubt of the human free-will, because each of them feels himself confined on every side by his own weakness; but they are still willing to acknowledge the strength and independence of men united in society. Let not this principle be lost sight of; for the great object in our time is to raise the faculties of men, not to complete their prostration.

Chapter XXI: Of Parliamentary Eloquence In The United States

Amongst aristocratic nations all the members of the community are connected with and dependent upon each other; the graduated scale of different ranks acts as a tie, which keeps everyone in his proper place and the whole body in subordination. Something of the same kind always occurs in the political assemblies of these nations. Parties naturally range themselves under certain leaders, whom they obey by a sort of instinct, which is only the result of habits contracted elsewhere. They carry the manners of general society into the lesser assemblage.

In democratic countries it often happens that a great number of citizens are tending to the same point; but each one only moves thither, or at least flatters himself that he moves, of his own accord. Accustomed to regulate his doings by personal impulse alone, he does not willingly submit to dictation from without. This taste and habit of independence accompany him into the councils of the nation. If he consents to connect himself with other men in the prosecution of the same purpose, at least he chooses to remain free to contribute to the common success after his own fashion. Hence it is that in democratic countries parties are so impatient of control, and are never manageable except in

的方法这个民族才能走上更好的道路要简单得多。

在阅读贵族时代历史学家著作，特别是那些古代著作时，似乎人只要自己管理好自己，就能成为自己命运的主宰，管理好自己的同胞。而在阅读我们这个时代的人所撰写的历史书籍时，会感到似乎人对自己和身边的一切完全无能为力。古代的历史学家教导人们如何掌控，而我们这个时代的历史学家则只教导人们如何服从。在他们的著作中，总是让自己看起来很伟大，而人类很渺小。如果民主时代书写历史的人如此醉心于这个有害的学说并将其传递给读者，随后深入人民大众并掌控人们的思想，那么，不久便会令现代社会处于麻痹状态，并让基督教徒变回成土耳其人。此外，我注意到这样的原则对于我们现在所处的时代特别危险。我们这个时代的人特别怀疑意志自由，因为他们觉得自己在每个方面都软弱无力，但是他们依然愿意承认团结起来的人们是独立的、有力量的。我们不应该对这样的思想视而不见，因为我们这个时代的主要目标是提升人们的士气，而不是压抑人们的精神。

第二十一章　美国议会的辩才

在贵族制国家中，社会所有成员相互牵连彼此依靠，等级制度就像一条纽带让人各安其位。同样的事情也不断在这些国家的政治团体中出现。贵族制国家的党派自然要有首领来领导，而党员对首脑的服从则是出于一种习惯成自然的本能。他们将大社会里的行事方式带到这个小团体中。

在民主国家，大多数公民往往朝着同一目标前进，但是每个公民只是自行前进，或

moments of great public danger. Even then, the authority of leaders, which under such circumstances may be able to make men act or speak, hardly ever reaches the extent of making them keep silence.

Amongst aristocratic nations the members of political assemblies are at the same time members of the aristocracy. Each of them enjoys high established rank in his own right, and the position which he occupies in the assembly is often less important in his eyes than that which he fills in the country. This consoles him for playing no part in the discussion of public affairs, and restrains him from too eagerly attempting to play an insignificant one.

In America, it generally happens that a Representative only becomes somebody from his position in the Assembly. He is therefore perpetually haunted by a craving to acquire importance there, and he feels a petulant desire to be constantly obtruding his opinions upon the House. His own vanity is not the only stimulant which urges him on in this course, but that of his constituents, and the continual necessity of propitiating them. Amongst aristocratic nations a member of the legislature is rarely in strict dependence upon his constituents: he is frequently to them a sort of unavoidable representative; sometimes they are themselves strictly dependent upon him; and if at length they reject him, he may easily get elected elsewhere, or, retiring from public life, he may still enjoy the pleasures of splendid idleness. In a democratic country like the United States a Representative has hardly ever a lasting hold on the minds of his constituents. However small an electoral body may be, the fluctuations of democracy are constantly changing its aspect; it must, therefore, be courted unceasingly. He is never sure of his supporters, and, if they forsake him, he is left without a resource; for his natural position is not sufficiently elevated for him to be easily known to those not close to him; and, with the complete state of independence prevailing among the people, he cannot hope that his friends or the government will send him down to be returned by an electoral body unacquainted with him. The seeds of his fortune are, therefore, sown in his own neighborhood; from that nook of earth he must start, to raise himself to the command of a people and to influence the destinies of the world. Thus it is natural that in democratic countries the members of political assemblies think more of their constituents than of their party, whilst in aristocracies they think more of their party than of their

者至少自认为是在自行前进。因为人们习惯于只遵从自己的意志来行动，所以不愿接受外来的指导。这种独立自主的爱好和习惯也伴随他们来到国家议会。即使他同意与其他人联合起来推行相同的计划，他至少会选择可以自由地按照自己的方式来取得共同的成果。因此，在民主国家，除非国家遭遇重大危机，否则政党绝不愿受制于他人任人摆布。在这样的情况下，即使国家首脑有权命令各党派的一言一行，但是依旧无法让他们闭口不言。

在贵族制国家，政治议会的成员同时也是贵族成员。每个人原本就有很高的官职和权力，而在他们眼中，自己在议会中占据的位置往往不如在国家中的位置重要。这让他们不愿在议会中对公共事务进行积极讨论，也不肯在议会中热烈争辩一般问题。

在美国，一般来说议员只有在议会中才成为重要的人。因此，他总是想着如何在这里占据重要的位置，并迫不及待地在这里推行自己的观点。他之所以这样做不仅仅是出于个人的虚荣心，而且也是为了选民的荣誉，以及可以持续得到选民的支持。在贵族制国家，立法机构的成员很少严格地依附于选民，因为他一直以来是他们的不二人选，而且有时候反而是选民完全依附于他。即使选民最终不再选举他做代表，他也可以很容易地在其他地方当选，或是完全从公众视线中退下来乐享悠闲的生活。像在美国这样的民主国家，议员不可能长期掌控选民的思想。不论一个选区有多小，民主的波动性会令它不断发生变化。因此，议员必须时刻讨好选民，因为他对此没有把握。如果选民放弃他，他便会失去支持，因为他的地位并没有高到远近皆知的地步。而且在公民完全自由的情况下，他也不能寄希望于自己的朋友或政府将自己送到一个自己所不熟悉的选区当选。因此，他飞黄

constituents.

But what ought to be said to gratify constituents is not always what ought to be said in order to serve the party to which Representatives profess to belong. The general interest of a party frequently demands that members belonging to it should not speak on great questions which they understand imperfectly; that they should speak but little on those minor questions which impede the great ones; lastly, and for the most part, that they should not speak at all. To keep silence is the most useful service that an indifferent spokesman can render to the commonwealth. Constituents, however, do not think so. The population of a district sends a representative to take a part in the government of a country, because they entertain a very lofty notion of his merits. As men appear greater in proportion to the littleness of the objects by which they are surrounded, it may be assumed that the opinion entertained of the delegate will be so much the higher as talents are more rare among his constituents. It will therefore frequently happen that the less constituents have to expect from their representative, the more they will anticipate from him; and, however incompetent he may be, they will not fail to call upon him for signal exertions, corresponding to the rank they have conferred upon him.

Independently of his position as a legislator of the State, electors also regard their Representative as the natural patron of the constituency in the Legislature; they almost consider him as the proxy of each of his supporters, and they flatter themselves that he will not be less zealous in defense of their private interests than of those of the country. Thus electors are well assured beforehand that the Representative of their choice will be an orator; that he will speak often if he can, and that in case he is forced to refrain, he will strive at any rate to compress into his less frequent orations an inquiry into all the great questions of state, combined with a statement of all the petty grievances they have themselves to complain to; so that, though he be not able to come forward frequently, he should on each occasion prove what he is capable of doing; and that, instead of perpetually lavishing his powers, he should occasionally condense them in a small compass, so as to furnish a sort of complete and brilliant epitome of his constituents and of himself. On these terms they will vote for him at the next election. These conditions drive worthy men of humble abilities to despair, who, knowing their

腾达的种子必须播种在自己的地方。他必须从这个角落开始，然后高升可以对人民发号施令，并最终影响世界的命运。因此，在民主国家，政治议会的代表自然会更多地考虑自己的选民而不是自己的党派。然而，在贵族制国家，他们想得更多的则是自己的党派而不是选民。

但是为了满足选民才说的话并不总是服务于议员所属党派。为了维护党派的利益，一般而言要求所属成员不对尚不清楚的重大问题发表言论，少谈会影响到大问题的小问题，而大多数情况下，则什么都不谈。缄口不语是一个平庸的议员对国家的最大贡献。然而，选民则不这么想。一个地区的人从中选出一个代表参与国家管理，是因为他们深知这个人的优点。因为人在周围的人都很渺小的时候才显得越发高大，所以可以想象，对于代表的要求越高，就越难从选民中找到这样的天才。因此，往往实际情况是他们对代表的要求不高，但是期望却很高。而且无论选出的议员如何的无能，选民都会要求他做出与其名誉地位相称的努力。

议员除了是一个国家立法机构的成员外，选民还将其视为本选区立法方面的天然保护人，而且他还被支持者们视为自己的代理人，并深信他会用不亚于像维护国家利益那样的热情来维护他们的个人利益。因此，选民早就想好，他们选出的议员要是一个演说家，只要有机会他就会发言，而万一他不得不有所克制，也会力争在有限的发言时间就所有国家大事提出质疑，而且还会在其中加上本区的小小不满。尽管他的发言机会有限，但是每次发言他都会努力证明自己的能力。为了不浪费每次机会，他有时会将所有的问题都浓缩，

own powers, would never voluntarily have come forward. But thus urged on, the Representative begins to speak, to the great alarm of his friends; and rushing imprudently into the midst of the most celebrated orators, he perplexes the debate and wearies the House.

All laws which tend to make the Representative more dependent on the elector, not only affect the conduct of the legislators, as I have remarked elsewhere, but also their language. They exercise a simultaneous influence on affairs themselves, and on the manner in which affairs are discussed.

There is hardly a member of Congress who can make up his mind to go home without having despatched at least one speech to his constituents; nor who will endure any interruption until he has introduced into his harangue whatever useful suggestions may be made touching the four-and-twenty States of which the Union is composed, and especially the district which he represents. He therefore presents to the mind of his auditors a succession of great general truths (which he himself only comprehends, and expresses, confusedly), and of petty minutia, which he is but too able to discover and to point out. The consequence is that the debates of that great assembly are frequently vague and perplexed, and that they seem rather to drag their slow length along than to advance towards a distinct object. Some such state of things will, I believe, always arise in the public assemblies of democracies.

Propitious circumstances and good laws might succeed in drawing to the legislature of a democratic people men very superior to those who are returned by the Americans to Congress; but nothing will ever prevent the men of slender abilities who sit there from obtruding themselves with complacency, and in all ways, upon the public. The evil does not appear to me to be susceptible of entire cure, because it not only originates in the tactics of that assembly, but in its constitution and in that of the country. The inhabitants of the United States seem themselves to consider the matter in this light; and they show their long experience of parliamentary life not by abstaining from making bad speeches, but by courageously submitting to hear them made. They are resigned to it, as to an evil which they know to be inevitable.

We have shown the petty side of political debates in democratic assemblies—let us now exhibit

以求完整卓越地表达出选民及他本人的见解。只有这样，他才能再次当选。这样的状况让那些受人尊敬却自知能力不足的人不再自告奋勇。如果这样的人当上议员，他可以在他的朋友面前侃侃而谈，但要是让他去全是杰出演说家的议员中演讲，恐怕只会弄得一塌糊涂令人无比厌烦。

令议员越来越依赖选民的所有法律，不但会像我所说的那样改变立法者的行为，还会改变他们的语言。这些法律不但会影响到国家事务还会影响到讨论事务的方式。

几乎每一个决定告老还乡的国会议员都会至少准备好一份讲稿给他的选民，其间会长篇大论地诉说自己为24个州特别是自己所代表的州做了哪些好事。因此，他带给听众的不会一个接一个的大道理，而是一些人们难以察觉或不屑一顾的琐碎小事。结果，这个大会上的讨论空洞而混乱，他们似乎是在故意拖延时间而并不想朝着明确的目标前进。我认为，民主国家的议会都有这样的情况。

良好的政治环境和法律也许可以成功地将比美国现任国会议员更优秀的人才吸引到民主国家的立法机构，但是什么也无法阻止能力不高的人在国会高谈阔论，到处招摇过市。在我看来，美国人的问题已经无药可救，因为这并不仅是国会的组织问题，而且还有宪法和国家制度的问题。对此，美国的居民似乎也这么认为。他们对国会的活动已经习以为常，多么拙劣的演讲都不会让他们退场，而是勇气可嘉的继续听下去。他们心甘情愿地忍受，就好像忍受无法医治的顽疾。

我们所说的都是民主议会政治辩论的细节，现在让我们来看看更为重要的问题。英国

the more imposing one. The proceedings within the Parliament of England for the last one hundred and fifty years have never occasioned any great sensation out of that country; the opinions and feelings expressed by the speakers have never awakened much sympathy, even amongst the nations placed nearest to the great arena of British liberty; whereas Europe was excited by the very first debates which took place in the small colonial assemblies of America at the time of the Revolution. This was attributable not only to particular and fortuitous circumstances, but to general and lasting causes. I can conceive nothing more admirable or more powerful than a great orator debating on great questions of state in a democratic assembly. As no particular class is ever represented there by men commissioned to defend its own interests, it is always to the whole nation, and in the name of the whole nation, that the orator speaks. This expands his thoughts, and heightens his power of language. As precedents have there but little weight-as there are no longer any privileges attached to certain property, nor any rights inherent in certain bodies or in certain individuals, the mind must have recourse to general truths derived from human nature to resolve the particular question under discussion. Hence the political debates of a democratic people, however small it may be, have a degree of breadth which frequently renders them attractive to mankind. All men are interested by them, because they treat of man, who is everywhere the same. Amongst the greatest aristocratic nations, on the contrary, the most general questions are almost always argued on some special grounds derived from the practice of a particular time, or the rights of a particular class; which interest that class alone, or at most the people amongst whom that class happens to exist. It is owing to this, as much as to the greatness of the French people, and the favorable disposition of the nations who listen to them, that the great effect which the French political debates sometimes produce in the world, must be attributed. The orators of France frequently speak to mankind, even when they are addressing their countrymen only.

下院150多年以来的议事经过从未在国外引起任何轰动。发言人们所表达的观点和情感从未唤起人们的共鸣，甚至是在距离英国自由大舞台最近的邻国也从未有过。但是，在革命时期美洲殖民地召开的几次小会议的最初辩论，就轰动了整个欧洲。这并不仅仅是一些偶然和特殊的原因使然，而且还有其一般和必然的原因。我认为，在民主国家议会中就国家大事辩论的伟大演说家最值得敬佩，最有力量。因为，没有哪个特定阶级可以派代表在国会捍卫自己的利益，所以议员们总是以全民族和国家的名义发言。这增强了思想，加重了发言分量。因为在这里，先例没有太大的作用，特权也不再与特定的财富相关，任何世袭的权利也不再与特定的团体或个人相关，所以人们的思想必须依靠源自人本性的一般真理去解决个别问题。因此，民主国家的政治辩论，无论其规模多么小，总是具有关系到人类命运的普遍意义。所有人都对此感兴趣，因为他们讨论的是世界各地都一样的人。相反，在最伟大的贵族制国家中，一般来说，重要的问题都会根据某些特殊理由来进行处理，而这些特殊理由则源自特定时代的习惯做法或是特定阶级的权利。所以，对此感兴趣的只有相关的阶级，至多还有这些相关阶级所在的民族。正是基于这个原因，法兰西民族的政治辩论有时才能在世界引起巨大的反响，当然，法兰西民族的伟大和其他国家的愿意倾听也同样重要。法国演说家的演讲总是面向全人类，甚至当他们只对同胞演讲时也是如此。

Section 2: Influence of Democracy on the Feelings of Americans

Chapter I: Why Democratic Nations Show A More Ardent And Enduring Love Of Equality Than Of Liberty

The first and most intense passion which is engendered by the equality of conditions is, I need hardly say, the love of that same equality. My readers will therefore not be surprised that I speak of its before all others. Everybody has remarked that in our time, and especially in France, this passion for equality is every day gaining ground in the human heart. It has been said a hundred times that our contemporaries are far more ardently and tenaciously attached to equality than to freedom; but as I do not find that the causes of the fact have been sufficiently analyzed, I shall endeavor to point them out.

It is possible to imagine an extreme point at which freedom and equality would meet and be confounded together. Let us suppose that all the members of the community take a part in the government, and that each of them has an equal right to take a part in it. As none is different from his fellows, none can exercise a tyrannical power: men will be perfectly free, because they will all be entirely equal; and they will all be perfectly equal, because they will be entirely free. To this ideal state democratic nations tend. Such is the completest form that equality can assume upon earth; but there are a thousand others which, without being equally perfect, are not less cherished by those nations.

The principle of equality may be established in civil society, without prevailing in the political world. Equal rights may exist of indulging in the same pleasures, of entering the same professions, of frequenting the same places—in a word, of living in the same manner and seeking wealth by the

第二篇　民主对美国人情感的影响

第一章　为什么民主国家爱平等比爱自由更热烈更持久

身份平等造就的最首要也是最强烈的激情，不用说，理所当然是对平等本身的热爱。因此，在这里我首先将它提出来，读者一定不会感到意外。每个人都已经察觉到，在我们这个时代，而且特别是在法国，对于平等的这份热爱在人们心中与日俱增。人们总是说，我们这个时代的人对平等那份炙热执著的爱胜过对自由的热爱千百倍，但是我还没有看到有任何人对其原因进行过充分的分析，所以现在我想要试着指出这些原因。

可以想象一个自由和平等汇合并融为一体的极端情形。让我们假设，所有的社会成员都参与政府管理，而且每个人都拥有平等的权利。没有任何人与众不同，没有任何人能运用专制权力。因为人人都完全平等，所以人人都绝对自由。这就是民主国家人们所追求的完美状态。这是地球上平等的最完美形式，但是也有其他各式各样的形式存在，尽管不是那么完美，但依旧为民主国家的人民所珍惜。

平等原则可以在市民社会建立，却不能在政界推行。尽管人们不能在政界享有同等

same means, although all men do not take an equal share in the government. A kind of equality may even be established in the political world, though there should be no political freedom there. A man may be the equal of all his countrymen save one, who is the master of all without distinction, and who selects equally from among them all the agents of his power. Several other combinations might be easily imagined, by which very great equality would be united to institutions more or less free, or even to institutions wholly without freedom. Although men cannot become absolutely equal unless they be entirely free, and consequently equality, pushed to its furthest extent, may be confounded with freedom, yet there is good reason for distinguishing the one from the other. The taste which men have for liberty, and that which they feel for equality, are, in fact, two different things; and I am not afraid to add that, amongst democratic nations, they are two unequal things.

Upon close inspection, it will be seen that there is in every age some peculiar and preponderating fact with which all others are connected; this fact almost always gives birth to some pregnant idea or some ruling passion, which attracts to itself, and bears away in its course, all the feelings and opinions of the time: it is like a great stream, towards which each of the surrounding rivulets seems to flow. Freedom has appeared in the world at different times and under various forms; it has not been exclusively bound to any social condition, and it is not confined to democracies. Freedom cannot, therefore, form the distinguishing characteristic of democratic ages. The peculiar and preponderating fact which marks those ages as its own is the equality of conditions; the ruling passion of men in those periods is the love of this equality. Ask not what singular charm the men of democratic ages find in being equal, or what special reasons they may have for clinging so tenaciously to equality rather than to the other advantages which society holds out to them: equality is the distinguishing characteristic of the age they live in; that, of itself, is enough to explain that they prefer it to all the rest.

But independently of this reason there are several others, which will at all times habitually lead men to prefer equality to freedom. If a people could ever succeed in destroying, or even in

的地位，但是平等的权利可以使人们能够在社会上有同样的享乐，从事同样的行业，居住在同样的地方，简而言之，就是人们可以选择同样的生活方式，可以采用同样的方式发财致富。有一种平等可以在政界建立，尽管那里没有政治自由。所有人都是平等的，除了一个人以外，而这个人正是所有人的主宰，他在所有人中用同样的标准选择自己的权力代理人。还可以做一些其他的假设，比如，高度的平等可以与或多或少的自由制度相结合，或者与完全没有自由的制度相结合。尽管没有绝对自由就不可能有绝对平等，而且在平等到达极限时会与自由融合，但我们还是有理由把两者区分开来。实际上，人们对自由的爱好和对平等的爱好是两回事。而且我还要斗胆补充一句，在民主国家，自由和平等还是两件不调和的事情。

仔细研究就会发现在每个时代都有一个关系到所有事情的居于支配地位的独特事实。那个时代的基本思想，或由此引起并将人的感情和思想汇集起来的主要激情，几乎都源自这个事实。这就像一条大河，周边的小溪流都向它汇拢过来。自由曾经在不同的时代以不同的形式出现在世界上，它不只在特定的社会里出现，不只属于民主制度。因此，自由并不是民主时代的独特的特征。彰显民主时代特点的居于支配地位的独特事实是身份平等，在这样的时代，人们的主要激情是对平等的热爱。不要问民主时代的人们平等的独特吸引力是什么，或者是什么原因让他们宁可放弃社会提供的其他福利，也要如此地执著于平等。因为平等是他们生活的这个时代的基本特征。仅凭这一点，就足以解释为什么人们爱平等胜过其他一切。

但是，除了这个原因之外，还有其他几个原因促使人们在任何时代对平等的热爱都要胜过自由。即使一个民族可以成功地破坏或削弱其内部享有的平等，也必然要经过长期艰

diminishing, the equality which prevails in its own body, this could only be accomplished by long and laborious efforts. Its social condition must be modified, its laws abolished, its opinions superseded, its habits changed, its manners corrupted. But political liberty is more easily lost; to neglect to hold it fast is to allow it to escape. Men therefore not only cling to equality because it is dear to them; they also adhere to it because they think it will last forever.

That political freedom may compromise in its excesses the tranquillity, the property, the lives of individuals, is obvious to the narrowest and most unthinking minds. But, on the contrary, none but attentive and clear-sighted men perceive the perils with which equality threatens us, and they commonly avoid pointing them out. They know that the calamities they apprehend are remote, and flatter themselves that they will only fall upon future generations, for which the present generation takes but little thought. The evils which freedom sometimes brings with it are immediate; they are apparent to all, and all are more or less affected by them. The evils which extreme equality may produce are slowly disclosed; they creep gradually into the social frame; they are only seen at intervals, and at the moment at which they become most violent habit already causes them to be no longer felt. The advantages which freedom brings are only shown by length of time; and it is always easy to mistake the cause in which they originate. The advantages of equality are instantaneous, and they may constantly be traced from their source. Political liberty bestows exalted pleasures, from time to time, upon a certain number of citizens. Equality every day confers a number of small enjoyments on every man. The charms of equality are every instant felt, and are within the reach of all; the noblest hearts are not insensible to them, and the most vulgar souls exult in them. The passion which equality engenders must therefore be at once strong and general. Men cannot enjoy political liberty unpurchased by some sacrifices, and they never obtain it without great exertions. But the pleasures of equality are self-proffered: each of the petty incidents of life seems to occasion them, and in order to taste them nothing is required but to live.

Democratic nations are at all times fond of equality, but there are certain epochs at which the

苦的努力。它的社会状况必定会发生变化，其法律会被废除，其观念会被淘汰，其习惯会被改变，民情也会堕落。但是，想要废除政治自由则很简单，只要不实行它就好了。因此人们不但因为平等弥足珍贵而依恋它，而且因为认定平等将永世长存而拥护它。

过分运用政治自由会危害个人的安全、财产乃至生命，这一点哪怕最狭隘、最没有思想的人也能看得出。但是与之相反，只有头脑清晰观察力强的人才能洞悉平等给我们带来的危险，而他们往往对此避而不谈。他们知道这种危险带来的灾难还很遥远，于是便说什么这是以后几代人该操心的事，而现在的一代大可高枕无忧。自由带来的灾难往往很直接，显而易见，所有人都会或多或少受到其影响。然而，极度平等带来的灾难则只会慢慢显现，一点一点地侵害社会结构。只有在很长一段时间之后，人们才会注意到它，而此时它俨然已经幻化成为可怕的习惯，人们已经对其视而不见。自由带来的好处则只有经过许久之后才能被发现，而且这种好处的来源也往往不易被人们辨认。而平等的好处会立竿见影，而且人们能一下子发现它的来源。政治自由会时不时带给特定的公民尊贵的享受。而平等则能每天带给每个人大量的小小的享受，所以平等的魅力能够时刻感受到，惠及每个人，最高贵的人也不会感受不到，最卑贱的人也能从中获得欢乐。因此，平等带来的激情必定强烈而普遍。不付出一些代价，人享受不到政治自由，而要获得政治自由必须做出巨大的努力。然而平等带来的乐趣则是自动的，生活中的每件小事上都能感到，只要活着就能享受到它所带来的快乐。

民主国家的人民任何时候都热爱平等，但是在某些时期，他们对平等的热情会达到狂热的地步。这种情况往往发生在长期受到威胁的旧的社会体系在经历最后一次内部斗争之后终被毁灭，而且社会等级壁垒最终坍塌的时刻。在这样的时刻，人们会将平等视为战

passion they entertain for it swells to the height of fury. This occurs at the moment when the old social system, long menaced, completes its own destruction after a last intestine struggle, and when the barriers of rank are at length thrown down. At such times men pounce upon equality as their booty, and they cling to it as to some precious treasure which they fear to lose. The passion for equality penetrates on every side into men's hearts, expands there, and fills them entirely. Tell them not that by this blind surrender of themselves to an exclusive passion they risk their dearest interests: they are deaf. Show them not freedom escaping from their grasp, whilst they are looking another way: they are blind—or rather, they can discern but one sole object to be desired in the universe.

What I have said is applicable to all democratic nations: what I am about to say concerns the French alone. Amongst most modern nations, and especially amongst all those of the Continent of Europe, the taste and the idea of freedom only began to exist and to extend themselves at the time when social conditions were tending to equality, and as a consequence of that very equality. Absolute kings were the most efficient levellers of ranks amongst their subjects. Amongst these nations equality preceded freedom: equality was therefore a fact of some standing when freedom was still a novelty: the one had already created customs, opinions, and laws belonging to it, when the other, alone and for the first time, came into actual existence. Thus the latter was still only an affair of opinion and of taste, whilst the former had already crept into the habits of the people, possessed itself of their manners, and given a particular turn to the smallest actions of their lives. Can it be wondered that the men of our own time prefer the one to the other?

I think that democratic communities have a natural taste for freedom: left to themselves, they will seek it, cherish it, and view any privation of it with regret. But for equality, their passion is ardent, insatiable, incessant, invincible: they call for equality in freedom; and if they cannot obtain that, they still call for equality in slavery. They will endure poverty, servitude, barbarism—but they will not endure aristocracy. This is true at all times, and especially true in our own. All men and all powers seeking to cope with this irresistible passion, will be overthrown and destroyed by it. In our age,

利品朝它猛扑过去，并紧紧抓住不放，就好像抓着生怕会丢失的宝藏一样。平等的热情从四面八方涌入人们的心灵，在这里扩展直至占据人们的整个心灵。此时，告诉他们这种盲目的热情会让他们失去最宝贵的利益，他们只会充耳不闻。而在他们死盯着别的地方的时候，也无法展示给他们自由正在从他们的指间溜走。他们对此视而不见，或者说天地之间他们所唯一想要看到的东西就只有平等。

我所说的适用于所有民主国家。而接下来我想专门说一说法国。在大部分现代国家，特别是那些欧洲大陆的国家，对自由的爱好和观念只有在社会状况趋于平等的时候才会出现和发展，而且是作为平等的结果而出现。专制的君主是最致力于拉平所有臣民等级的人。在这些国家平等先于自由出现。因此，在平等已经成为既成事实的时候，自由还是新鲜事物。当自由第一次真实存在的时候，平等已经建立起自己的习俗、观念和法律。因此，在自由还是观念和爱好中的事物时，平等已经悄然成为人们的习惯和民情，甚至影响着人们生活中最细小的行动。所以，我们这个时代的人爱平等胜于爱自由有什么好奇怪的呢？

我认为，民主国家的人民天生热爱自由，不用去管他们，他们会自己去寻找自由，珍惜它，会因为失去它而遗憾不已。但是对于平等，他们的热情则更为炙热，永无止境，源源不断，所向披靡。他们希望自由地享受平等，而如果不能如此，他们也愿意在奴役中享有平等。他们可以忍受贫困、奴役和野蛮，但是他们无法忍受贵族制度。在任何时代都是如此，而且在我们这个时代尤其如此。所有那些试图与这种不可抗拒的热情抗衡的人和权

freedom cannot be established without it, and despotism itself cannot reign without its support.

Chapter II: Of Individualism In Democratic Countries

I have shown how it is that in ages of equality every man seeks for his opinions within himself: I am now about to show how it is that, in the same ages, all his feelings are turned towards himself alone. Individualism is a novel expression, to which a novel idea has given birth. Our fathers were only acquainted with egotism. Egotism is a passionate and exaggerated love of self, which leads a man to connect everything with his own person, and to prefer himself to everything in the world. Individualism is a mature and calm feeling, which disposes each member of the community to sever himself from the mass of his fellow-creatures; and to draw apart with his family and his friends; so that, after he has thus formed a little circle of his own, he willingly leaves society at large to itself. Egotism originates in blind instinct: individualism proceeds from erroneous judgment more than from depraved feelings; it originates as much in the deficiencies of the mind as in the perversity of the heart. Egotism blights the germ of all virtue; individualism, at first, only saps the virtues of public life; but, in the long run, it attacks and destroys all others, and is at length absorbed in downright egotism. Egotism is a vice as old as the world, which does not belong to one form of society more than to another: individualism is of democratic origin, and it threatens to spread in the same ratio as the equality of conditions.

Amongst aristocratic nations, as families remain for centuries in the same condition, often on the same spot, all generations become as it were contemporaneous. A man almost always knows his forefathers, and respects them: he thinks he already sees his remote descendants, and he loves them. He willingly imposes duties on himself towards the former and the latter; and he will frequently sacrifice his personal gratifications to those who went before and to those who will come after him. Aristocratic institutions have, moreover, the effect of closely binding every man to several of his fellow-citizens. As the classes of an aristocratic people are strongly marked and permanent, each of them is regarded by its own members as a sort of lesser country, more tangible and more

力，最终都会被它推翻并毁灭。在我们的时代，没有平等自由无法确立，而没有平等的支持专制制度本身也无法统治下去。

第二章　民主国家的个人主义

我已经说过在民主时代每个人如何靠自己确定信念。现在，我要阐述一下在这样的时代，人们如何让所有的感情以自己为中心。个人主义是源自一个全新观念的一个全新的词汇。我们的祖先只知道利己主义。利己主义是一种对自己过分偏激的爱，会让人只关心自己，爱自己胜于爱世上一切事物。个人主义则是一种成熟且平静的情感，会令每个公民与其同胞大众分离，让他与亲人朋友疏远。于是，在他个人的小圈子形成以后，他便任由大社会随意发展。利己主义出于盲目的本能，个人主义则是来自错误的判断，而不是不良的情感。个人主义的根源既有思想的缺陷，又有人心的险恶。利己主义会令所有美德的萌芽枯萎，个人主义开始只会令公德的源泉干涸，但是长此以往，它会攻击破坏所有一切，最终沦为利己主义。利己主义是自古有之的恶习，不属于任何一种社会形态；个人主义则源于民主，并随着平等的加强而扩大。

在贵族制国家中，因为家庭情况可以历经几个世纪而不变，而且一直在同一地方生活，几世同堂，几乎每个人都了解自己的祖先并尊重他们。人们在世的时候已经看到曾孙的出生，而且很爱自己的后代。人们心甘情愿地承担责任，而且常常会为已经逝去的先人和尚未出生的后代牺牲自己的享乐。此外，贵族制度往往会把每个人和其他同胞紧密联系

cherished than the country at large. As in aristocratic communities all the citizens occupy fixed positions, one above the other, the result is that each of them always sees a man above himself whose patronage is necessary to him, and below himself another man whose co-operation he may claim. Men living in aristocratic ages are therefore almost always closely attached to something placed out of their own sphere, and they are often disposed to forget themselves. It is true that in those ages the notion of human fellowship is faint, and that men seldom think of sacrificing themselves for mankind; but they often sacrifice themselves for other men. In democratic ages, on the contrary, when the duties of each individual to the race are much more clear, devoted service to any one man becomes more rare; the bond of human affection is extended, but it is relaxed.

Amongst democratic nations new families are constantly springing up, others are constantly falling away, and all that remain change their condition; the woof of time is every instant broken, and the track of generations effaced. Those who went before are soon forgotten; of those who will come after no one has any idea: the interest of man is confined to those in close propinquity to himself. As each class approximates to other classes, and intermingles with them, its members become indifferent and as strangers to one another. Aristocracy had made a chain of all the members of the community, from the peasant to the king: democracy breaks that chain, and severs every link of it. As social conditions become more equal, the number of persons increases who, although they are neither rich enough nor powerful enough to exercise any great influence over their fellow-creatures, have nevertheless acquired or retained sufficient education and fortune to satisfy their own wants. They owe nothing to any man, they expect nothing from any man; they acquire the habit of always considering themselves as standing alone, and they are apt to imagine that their whole destiny is in their own hands. Thus not only does democracy make every man forget his ancestors, but it hides his descendants, and separates his contemporaries from him; it throws him back forever upon himself alone, and threatens in the end to confine him entirely within the solitude of his

起来。因为贵族国家阶级固定差别明显，每个阶级的成员都将自己的阶级视为一个小国家，而且对这个小国家比对他们的大国家还要亲近，还要珍惜。因为在贵族社会所有的公民都有固定不变的位置，等级分明，以至于每个人都将位于自己之上的那个人视为自己当然的保护人，而将位于自己之下的人视为理所应当的扶助对象。因此，生活在贵族时代的人几乎总是与本身以外的某些事物有着紧密的联系，并往往为了这些东西而忘我地牺牲。的确，在那样的时代同胞的一般观念很淡薄，人们也很少想到为人类而牺牲自我。但是他们却常常为了他人而做出牺牲。而在民主时代则刚好相反，每个人对于全体的义务非常明确，而对于某一个人的奉献义务则很罕见，人类互爱的纽带不断加宽，但是越来越松弛。

在民主国家，新的家庭不断出现，而另一些家庭又不断衰败，所有的家庭都处在变化之中。时代的联系随时都会断开，前代的事迹逐渐被抹去。离开的人很快就会被遗忘，而对于即将到来的人则没有人去考虑。人们只关心自己最亲近的人。因为每个阶层与其他阶层都很接近，并与之融为一体，其成员变得对彼此漠不关心，形同路人。贵族制度用一根链条将从农民到国王的所有社会成员联系起来；而民主则将这根链条打破，将每一环割裂开。因为社会状况变得更加平等，所以个人的数量增加了，尽管他们这些人并没有有钱或有权到可以影响其他同胞的地步，却足以拥有或获得充分的教育和财富来满足自己的需要。他们不欠任何人什么，也不指望从任何人那里得到什么。他们养成自己的独立思考的习惯，总认为自己的命运掌握在自己手中。因此，民主不但让每个人忘记自己的祖先，还让他们不顾后代，并与同时代的人疏远，把他永久丢进一个人的孤单，最终完全陷入内心

own heart.

Chapter III: Individualism Stronger At The Close Of A Democratic Revolution Than At Other Periods

The period when the construction of democratic society upon the ruins of an aristocracy has just been completed, is especially that at which this separation of men from one another, and the egotism resulting from it, most forcibly strike the observation. Democratic communities not only contain a large number of independent citizens, but they are constantly filled with men who, having entered but yesterday upon their independent condition, are intoxicated with their new power. They entertain a presumptuous confidence in their strength, and as they do not suppose that they can henceforward ever have occasion to claim the assistance of their fellow-creatures, they do not scruple to show that they care for nobody but themselves.

An aristocracy seldom yields without a protracted struggle, in the course of which implacable animosities are kindled between the different classes of society. These passions survive the victory, and traces of them may be observed in the midst of the democratic confusion which ensues. Those members of the community who were at the top of the late gradations of rank cannot immediately forget their former greatness; they will long regard themselves as aliens in the midst of the newly composed society. They look upon all those whom this state of society has made their equals as oppressors, whose destiny can excite no sympathy; they have lost sight of their former equals, and feel no longer bound by a common interest to their fate: each of them, standing aloof, thinks that he is reduced to care for himself alone. Those, on the contrary, who were formerly at the foot of the social scale, and who have been brought up to the common level by a sudden revolution, cannot enjoy their newly acquired independence without secret uneasiness; and if they meet with some of their former superiors on the same footing as themselves, they stand aloof from them with an expression of triumph and of fear. It is, then, commonly at the outset of democratic society that citizens are

的寂寞。

第三章　个人主义在民主革命完成之后比在其他时期强烈

当民主社会在贵族制度的废墟上刚刚建立起来的时候，人们之间彼此孤立和随之而来的利己主义表现得特别明显。民主社会不但有大批已经独立的公民，还不断有刚刚获得独立并陶醉于新获得的权力的人补充进来。他们对自己的力量过于自信，而且因为觉得自己从今往后不再需要别人的帮忙，于是便肆无忌惮地表现出只关心自己。

不经历长期的斗争，贵族制度不会屈服，而在这一过程中，不同阶级间不可调和的仇恨被点燃。胜利过后，这些仇恨并未消失，会在随后的民主混乱时期继续兴风作浪。那些曾经高高在上的人不会立即忘记他们昔日的辉煌，在这个新社会中，他们会在很长一段时间将自己视为异类，会将社会里所有与他们平等的人视为命运未卜不值得同情的压迫者。他们不去看曾经与他们一样的人，不想因为共同利益而与这些人的命运联系起来。他们每个人形单影只，认为除了自己不用去管别人。与之相反，那些原先处于社会底层的人，革命过后地位提升到与众人平等，在享受刚刚得到的独立之时难免感到内心的不安。如果他们遇到如今与自己平起平坐的原来的上级，总是带着胜利又胆怯的表情远远地避开。所以，在民主社会的初期公民往往喜欢独善其身。民主制度不让人们与自己的同胞接近，而民主革命则让人们彼此回避，并将不平等带来的仇恨永远地留在平等之内。美国人的最大优势在于他们没有经历民主革命便直接进入民主状态，而且生来平等而非后来变为平等。

most disposed to live apart. Democracy leads men not to draw near to their fellow-creatures; but democratic revolutions lead them to shun each other, and perpetuate in a state of equality the animosities which the state of inequality engendered. The great advantage of the Americans is that they have arrived at a state of democracy without having to endure a democratic revolution; and that they are born equal, instead of becoming so.

Chapter IV: That The Americans Combat The Effects Of Individualism By Free Institutions

Despotism, which is of a very timorous nature, is never more secure of continuance than when it can keep men asunder; and all is influence is commonly exerted for that purpose. No vice of the human heart is so acceptable to it as egotism: a despot easily forgives his subjects for not loving him, provided they do not love each other. He does not ask them to assist him in governing the State; it is enough that they do not aspire to govern it themselves. He stigmatizes as turbulent and unruly spirits those who would combine their exertions to promote the prosperity of the community, and, perverting the natural meaning of words, he applauds as good citizens those who have no sympathy for any but themselves. Thus the vices which despotism engenders are precisely those which equality fosters. These two things mutually and perniciously complete and assist each other. Equality places men side by side, unconnected by any common tie; despotism raises barriers to keep them asunder; the former predisposes them not to consider their fellow-creatures, the latter makes general indifference a sort of public virtue.

Despotism then, which is at all times dangerous, is more particularly to be feared in democratic ages. It is easy to see that in those same ages men stand most in need of freedom. When the members of a community are forced to attend to public affairs, they are necessarily drawn from the circle of their own interests, and snatched at times from self-observation. As soon as a man begins to treat of public affairs in public, he begins to perceive that he is not so independent of his fellow-men as he had at first imagined, and that, in order to obtain their support, he must often lend them his co-operation.

第四章　美国人如何用自由制度对抗个人主义

本质上非常害怕被统治者的专制，认为将人们隔绝是其永世长存的最可靠保障，于是将自己所有的力量都用在这上面。人心的所有险恶之中，只有利己主义容易为人所接受。只要人们不互相爱护，专制者很容易原谅他们不热爱自己。他不要求他们辅助自己治理国家，只要他们没有自己当家做主统治国家的想法便已心满意足。他颠倒黑白，给那些想要共同努力促进社会繁荣的人贴上乱民歹徒的标签，而授予那些只顾自己的人好公民称号。因此，专制造就的恶，刚好是平等所助长的恶。专制和平等以一种有害的方式相辅相成。平等让人们并肩而立，却没有任何共同纽带将他们联系起来；专制竖起层层壁垒将人们隔开。前者让人只顾自己不考虑其他同胞，后者将漠不关心视为一种公共美德。

所以，专制制度在任何时代都是危险的，而且在民主时代尤其危险。不难看到，在这样的时代，人们最需要的是自由。当社会成员必须参与国家事务时，必然会走出个人的利益圈子，还时不时地要放弃自己的观点。一旦人们开始参与公共事务，便会注意到自己无法像最初想象的那样完全离开他人而独立，于是为了赢得他人的支持，必须时刻准备帮助他人。

当国家由公众治理时，每个人都能感到公众相互照顾的好处，而且所有人都努力互相照顾以赢得周围人的尊重和爱戴。于是，一些令人心冷漠和产生隔阂的情绪必然要收回隐藏起来。高傲必须被掩饰起来，轻蔑也不敢露头，利己主义本身也感到恐惧。在一个自由

When the public is supreme, there is no man who does not feel the value of public goodwill, or who does not endeavor to court it by drawing to himself the esteem and affection of those amongst whom he is to live. Many of the passions which congeal and keep asunder human hearts, are then obliged to retire and hide below the surface. Pride must be dissembled; disdain dares not break out; egotism fears its own self. Under a free government, as most public offices are elective, the men whose elevated minds or aspiring hopes are too closely circumscribed in private life, constantly feel that they cannot do without the population which surrounds them. Men learn at such times to think of their fellow-men from ambitious motives; and they frequently find it, in a manner, their interest to forget themselves.

I may here be met by an objection derived from electioneering intrigues, the meannesses of candidates, and the calumnies of their opponents. These are opportunities for animosity which occur the oftener the more frequent elections become. Such evils are doubtless great, but they are transient; whereas the benefits which attend them remain. The desire of being elected may lead some men for a time to violent hostility; but this same desire leads all men in the long run mutually to support each other; and if it happens that an election accidentally severs two friends, the electoral system brings a multitude of citizens permanently together, who would always have remained unknown to each other. Freedom engenders private animosities, but despotism gives birth to general indifference.

The Americans have combated by free institutions the tendency of equality to keep men asunder, and they have subdued it. The legislators of America did not suppose that a general representation of the whole nation would suffice to ward off a disorder at once so natural to the frame of democratic society, and so fatal: they also thought that it would be well to infuse political life into each portion of the territory, in order to multiply to an infinite extent opportunities of acting in concert for all the members of the community, and to make them constantly feel their mutual dependence on each other. The plan was a wise one. The general affairs of a country only engage the attention of leading politicians, who assemble from time to time in the same places; and as they often lose sight of each other afterwards, no lasting ties are established between them. But if the object be to have the local

的政体下，由于大多数的公职人员经选举产生，所以那些自视才高志远将自己封闭在个人生活小圈子的人，会不断感到没有周围人的支持，自己无所作为。此时，人们出于自己的野心开始考虑他人，而且不断发现忘记自己往往能给自己带来好处。

也许有人会用选举的阴谋、候选人的卑鄙和相互中伤来反驳我。选举中的确有敌对的情形，而且选举的次数越多，敌对的程度就越强。毫无疑问这是很大的弊端，但这不过是暂时的，但是由此而来的好处却是永久的。当选的愿望让一些人在一段时间内极端敌对，但从长期来看这样的愿望会让人们彼此互相支持。而且即使一次选举偶然间让两个朋友反目成仇，选举制度也会让原本互不相识的众多公民长久地在一起。自由制造私人恩怨，但是专制则造就普遍的冷漠。

美国人用自由制度对抗平等带来的个人主义倾向，并取得成功。美国的立法者认为，在全国实行代议制不足以抵挡民主社会体制自然产生的致命危机。他们还认为最好让国内每个部分都享有独立的政治生活，以便于无限增加所有社会成员共同行动的机会，从而时刻感到彼此相互的依赖。这是一个明智的计划。国家的一般事务由政界要员参与，他们会时不时地聚在一起开会，而会后则很少见面，所以他们之间无法形成永久的联系。但是如果是让当地居民管理自己的地方事务，居民自然要经常接触，于是他们不得不彼此相识彼此适应。

很难让一个人走出自己的圈子关心国家命运，因为他不理解国家命运会对自己的命运产生什么样的影响。但是如果计划修一条通往他家的道路，他马上就会看到这件小公事和

affairs of a district conducted by the men who reside there, the same persons are always in contact, and they are, in a manner, forced to be acquainted, and to adapt themselves to one another.

It is difficult to draw a man out of his own circle to interest him in the destiny of the State, because he does not clearly understand what influence the destiny of the State can have upon his own lot. But if it be proposed to make a road cross the end of his estate, he will see at a glance that there is a connection between this small public affair and his greatest private affairs; and he will discover, without its being shown to him, the close tie which unites private to general interest. Thus, far more may be done by intrusting to the citizens the administration of minor affairs than by surrendering to them the control of important ones, towards interesting them in the public welfare, and convincing them that they constantly stand in need one of the other in order to provide for it. A brilliant achievement may win for you the favor of a people at one stroke; but to earn the love and respect of the population which surrounds you, a long succession of little services rendered and of obscure good deeds—a constant habit of kindness, and an established reputation for disinterestedness—will be required. Local freedom, then, which leads a great number of citizens to value the affection of their neighbors and of their kindred, perpetually brings men together, and forces them to help one another, in spite of the propensities which sever them.

In the United States the more opulent citizens take great care not to stand aloof from the people; on the contrary, they constantly keep on easy terms with the lower classes: they listen to them, they speak to them every day. They know that the rich in democracies always stand in need of the poor; and that in democratic ages you attach a poor man to you more by your manner than by benefits conferred. The magnitude of such benefits, which sets off the difference of conditions, causes a secret irritation to those who reap advantage from them; but the charm of simplicity of manners is almost irresistible: their affability carries men away, and even their want of polish is not always displeasing. This truth does not take root at once in the minds of the rich. They generally resist it as long as the democratic revolution lasts, and they do not acknowledge it immediately after that revolution is accomplished. They are very ready to do good to the people, but they still choose to keep them at arm's length; they think that is sufficient, but they are mistaken. They might spend fortunes thus

自己的大私事之间的联系，而且不必告诉他，他自己就会发现个人利益和公共利益之间的紧密关系。因此，如果让公民多参与小事务，少理大事务，他们反而会关心公益，而且还能意识到为了实现公益他们不断需要彼此支持。一个辉煌的成果能够帮你一下子赢得人们的支持，但如果想要赢得周围人对你的热爱和尊重，则需要长期不断地为人们做些点滴的小事，养成与人为善的习惯，并赢得廉洁奉公的名声才能获得。于是，地方自由可以引导公民重视邻里友爱和家人亲情，能将人们永久地联系起来，并迫使他们互相帮助，抵制让人们彼此隔离的本性。

在美国，越是富裕的公民越注意不脱离群众，而且会不断保持与下层人民的接触，倾听他们的意见并常常与之交谈。他们知道在民主制度下，富人需要不断帮助穷人，而且在民主时代，争取穷人的最好方式不是小恩小惠而是对他们友好。给予的恩惠越大，贫富的对比就越强烈，受惠人的内心反而会暗生反感。但是与人为善的魅力却难以抵挡，他们的亲切总是能令人感动。而这个道理富人也不是一下子就领悟到的。只要民主革命在继续，他们就会一直抵制它，而且在民主革命结束之后，他们也不会一下子就接受这种思想。虽然他们时刻想要为人民做点好事，但是依然要与人民保持一定距离。他们认为这样就足够了，但是他们却错了。如果不能温暖周围人的心，他们可能会倾家荡产，人们并不想让他们牺牲金钱，而是想让他们放下傲气。

似乎在美国，人们的想象力全部用来创造发财致富的手段和满足公众的愿望。每个地

without warming the hearts of the population around them;—that population does not ask them for the sacrifice of their money, but of their pride.

It would seem as if every imagination in the United States were upon the stretch to invent means of increasing the wealth and satisfying the wants of the public. The best-informed inhabitants of each district constantly use their information to discover new truths which may augment the general prosperity; and if they have made any such discoveries, they eagerly surrender them to the mass of the people.

When the vices and weaknesses, frequently exhibited by those who govern in America, are closely examined, the prosperity of the people occasions—but improperly occasions—surprise. Elected magistrates do not make the American democracy flourish; it flourishes because the magistrates are elective.

It would be unjust to suppose that the patriotism and the zeal which every American displays for the welfare of his fellow-citizens are wholly insincere. Although private interest directs the greater part of human actions in the United States as well as elsewhere, it does not regulate them all. I must say that I have often seen Americans make great and real sacrifices to the public welfare; and I have remarked a hundred instances in which they hardly ever failed to lend faithful support to each other. The free institutions which the inhabitants of the United States possess, and the political rights of which they make so much use, remind every citizen, and in a thousand ways, that he lives in society. They every instant impress upon his mind the notion that it is the duty, as well as the interest of men, to make themselves useful to their fellow-creatures; and as he sees no particular ground of animosity to them, since he is never either their master or their slave, his heart readily leans to the side of kindness. Men attend to the interests of the public, first by necessity, afterwards by choice: what was intentional becomes an instinct; and by dint of working for the good of one's fellow citizens, the habit and the taste for serving them is at length acquired.

Many people in France consider equality of conditions as one evil, and political freedom as a second. When they are obliged to yield to the former, they strive at least to escape from the latter. But I contend that in order to combat the evils which equality may produce, there is only one effectual remedy—namely, political freedom.

方最有学识的居民不断地用他们的知识去发现可以促进地方共同繁荣的新真理，而且他们一旦有任何新发现，便会积极拿来与众人分享。

当仔细考察美国当政者的缺点和弱点时，会让人对美国人民的日益繁荣感到吃惊。民选的行政官员不能让美国的民主制度昌盛，美国的民主制度之所以昌盛是因为这些官员是经过选举产生的。

如果认为每个美国人为同胞谋福利所表现出的爱国精神和热情并非出自真心，未免有失公正。尽管在美国和在其他地方一样，个人利益支配人的大多数行动，但并不是支配人所有的行动。我必须说我常常会看到美国人为了公共利益做出巨大的真诚的牺牲，而且我还能举出上百个例子证明人们彼此真诚地互相帮助。美国居民享有的自由制度，以及他们充分行使的政治权利，用各种方式在提醒美国人他们生活在社会之中。他们时刻牢记有助于他人不但是自己的责任也是自己的利益之所在。而且他们也没有任何的理由互相憎恨，因为从没有人是谁的主人，也从没有人是谁的奴隶，他们的心很容易同情他人。人们关注公共利益，最初是被迫，后来则变成自愿，于是故意而为之变成本能。通过为同胞幸福而努力，最终人们养成为同胞服务的习惯和爱好。

在法国，许多人视平等为第一大恶，而自由则紧随其后。当他们不得不接受前者时，至少会想方设法逃避后者。但是我要说，只有一种有效的方式能够对抗平等可能带来的危险，那就是政治自由。

Chapter V: Of The Use Which The Americans Make Of Public Associations In Civil Life

I do not propose to speak of those political associations—by the aid of which men endeavor to defend themselves against the despotic influence of a majority—or against the aggressions of regal power. That subject I have already treated. If each citizen did not learn, in proportion as he individually becomes more feeble, and consequently more incapable of preserving his freedom single-handed, to combine with his fellow-citizens for the purpose of defending it, it is clear that tyranny would unavoidably increase together with equality.

Those associations only which are formed in civil life, without reference to political objects, are here adverted to. The political associations which exist in the United States are only a single feature in the midst of the immense assemblage of associations in that country. Americans of all ages, all conditions, and all dispositions, constantly form associations. They have not only commercial and manufacturing companies, in which all take part, but associations of a thousand other kinds—religious, moral, serious, futile, extensive, or restricted, enormous or diminutive. The Americans make associations to give entertainments, to found establishments for education, to build inns, to construct churches, to diffuse books, to send missionaries to the antipodes; and in this manner they found hospitals, prisons, and schools. If it be proposed to advance some truth, or to foster some feeling by the encouragement of a great example, they form a society. Wherever, at the head of some new undertaking, you see the government in France, or a man of rank in England, in the United States you will be sure to find an association. I met with several kinds of associations in America, of which I confess I had no previous notion; and I have often admired the extreme skill with which the inhabitants of the United States succeed in proposing a common object to the exertions of a great many men, and in getting them voluntarily to pursue it. I have since travelled over England, whence the Americans have taken some of their laws and many of their customs; and it seemed to me that the principle of association was by no means so constantly or so adroitly used in that country. The English often perform great things singly; whereas the Americans form associations for the smallest undertakings. It is evident that the former people consider association as a powerful means of action,

第五章　美国人在市民生活中对结社的运用

在这一章，我并不打算探讨为抵制多数专制或王权入侵而进行的政治结社。因为这个问题我已经讲过了。随着个人的力量日益微不足道以至于无法独自捍卫自己的自由，此时如果每个公民不懂得与同胞联合起来对抗专制，显然暴政会随平等的扩大不可避免地加强。

这里我只想谈的是跟政治无关的市民生活中的社团。美国的政治结社只是这个国家五花八门的结社中的一种。在美国各种年龄、各种社会地位以及拥有各种不同兴趣的人不断地结成社团。这里不但有人人都可以组织的工商团体，还有数以千计的其他团体，既有宗教道德团体，还有十分认真的团体，也有非常无聊的团体，而且还有大小规模各异的不同团体。美国人会为娱乐、创办学院、开设旅馆、修葺教堂、出售图书乃至向边远地区派遣教士而创建社团。用这样的方式，他们建立起医院、监狱和学校。在想要传播真理或是用示范来感化人的时候，他们也会创建社团。在法国，凡是要创办新的事业，政府都会出面；在英国，则是权贵出面；而在美国，可以肯定会是社团来牵头。在美国我看到过各种各样的社团，而且我承认我原先对社团一无所知，而且常常会为美国居民能够成功动员大多数人共同努力奔赴同一目标或是能够令他们自发前进的技巧而赞叹不已。我曾经到英国游历，尽管美国人承袭了英国人的许多法律和习惯，但是在我看来，英国人在结社原则的运用上，远没有美国人那样频繁和熟练。英国人通常只会在办大事的时候才成立社团，而美国人为一点点小事也要成立社团。显然，前者将社团视为强有力的行动手段，而后者似乎将其视为采取行动的唯一方式。

but the latter seem to regard it as the only means they have of acting.

Thus the most democratic country on the face of the earth is that in which men have in our time carried to the highest perfection the art of pursuing in common the object of their common desires, and have applied this new science to the greatest number of purposes. Is this the result of accident? or is there in reality any necessary connection between the principle of association and that of equality? Aristocratic communities always contain, amongst a multitude of persons who by themselves are powerless, a small number of powerful and wealthy citizens, each of whom can achieve great undertakings single-handed. In aristocratic societies men do not need to combine in order to act, because they are strongly held together. Every wealthy and powerful citizen constitutes the head of a permanent and compulsory association, composed of all those who are dependent upon him, or whom he makes subservient to the execution of his designs. Amongst democratic nations, on the contrary, all the citizens are independent and feeble; they can do hardly anything by themselves, and none of them can oblige his fellow-men to lend him their assistance. They all, therefore, fall into a state of incapacity, if they do not learn voluntarily to help each other. If men living in democratic countries had no right and no inclination to associate for political purposes, their independence would be in great jeopardy; but they might long preserve their wealth and their cultivation: whereas if they never acquired the habit of forming associations in ordinary life, civilization itself would be endangered. A people amongst which individuals should lose the power of achieving great things single-handed, without acquiring the means of producing them by united exertions, would soon relapse into barbarism.

Unhappily, the same social condition which renders associations so necessary to democratic nations, renders their formation more difficult amongst those nations than amongst all others. When several members of an aristocracy agree to combine, they easily succeed in doing so; as each of them brings great strength to the partnership, the number of its members may be very limited; and when the members of an association are limited in number, they may easily become mutually acquainted, understand each other, and establish fixed regulations. The same opportunities do not occur

因此，在我们这个地球上最民主的国家就是能令我们这个时代的人们善于共同奔赴共同的目标并能将这样的新方法应用到最多对象的国家。这到底是偶然现象还是结社和平等之间真的存在某种必然联系呢？贵族制社会，大多数的人民群众都毫无力量，而为数不多的一些有钱有势的公民能够仅凭一己之力做出一番大事业。所以，在贵族社会，人们不需要共同行动，因为他们本来已经紧密地联系在一起。每个有钱有权的公民都是一个永久的强制社团的领导，所有的成员都依附于他，或者说都按照他的意愿行动。与之相反，在民主社会，所有的公民都是独立的、软弱的，只靠他们自己几乎什么也干不成，而且也没有任何人能够迫使他人帮助自己。因此，如果他们不学会自愿地互相帮助，就会完全陷入无能为力的状态。如果生活在民主国家的人们没有权利和意愿为政治目的结社，尽管他们的财富和知识能够长期保全，但是他们的独立却将处于极大的危险之中。然而如果他们没有在日常生活中养成结社的习惯，文明本身也会受到威胁。一个民族，如果其个人失去了单枪匹马完成大事业的力量，也没有学会共同努力完成大事业的方法，不久便会退回到野蛮状态。

不幸的是，让社团对民主国家而言必不可少的社会状况，同时也让结社在民主国家变得比在任何其他国家都困难。当贵族中的几个人想要联合时，他们可以轻而易举地办到。因为他们每个人都能带给自己的伙伴巨大的力量，所以成员人数无须太多。而当一个社团的成员数量非常有限的时候，他们就很容易认识彼此，理解对方，并确立固定的规章制度。然而，同样的事情不会发生在民主国家，因为在这里，只有社团成员数量足够庞大，

amongst democratic nations, where the associated members must always be very numerous for their association to have any power.

I am aware that many of my countrymen are not in the least embarrassed by this difficulty. They contend that the more enfeebled and incompetent the citizens become, the more able and active the government ought to be rendered, in order that society at large may execute what individuals can no longer accomplish. They believe this answers the whole difficulty, but I think they are mistaken. A government might perform the part of some of the largest American companies; and several States, members of the Union, have already attempted it; but what political power could ever carry on the vast multitude of lesser undertakings which the American citizens perform every day, with the assistance of the principle of association? It is easy to foresee that the time is drawing near when man will be less and less able to produce, of himself alone, the commonest necessaries of life. The task of the governing power will therefore perpetually increase, and its very efforts will extend it every day. The more it stands in the place of associations, the more will individuals, losing the notion of combining together, require its assistance: these are causes and effects which unceasingly engender each other. Will the administration of the country ultimately assume the management of all the manufacturers, which no single citizen is able to carry on? And if a time at length arrives, when, in consequence of the extreme subdivision of landed property, the soil is split into an infinite number of parcels, so that it can only be cultivated by companies of husbandmen, will it be necessary that the head of the government should leave the helm of state to follow the plough? The morals and the intelligence of a democratic people would be as much endangered as its business and manufactures, if the government ever wholly usurped the place of private companies.

Feelings and opinions are recruited, the heart is enlarged, and the human mind is developed by no other means than by the reciprocal influence of men upon each other. I have shown that these influences are almost null in democratic countries; they must therefore be artificially created, and this can only be accomplished by associations.

When the members of an aristocratic community adopt a new opinion, or conceive a new

他们的社团才拥有足够的力量。

我注意到，我们国家的许多人完全没有注意到这个困难。他们认为，公民越是软弱无能，政府就要更能干和积极，让政府去完成个人无法完成的事业。他们认为这可以解决所有问题，但我认为他们错了。政府也许可以代替美国的某些大的社团，而且联邦内部的几个州已经这样做了。但是有哪个政府能够承担那些美国人依靠社团推进的数量庞大而规模很小的事业呢？不难预见，人们越来越无法单靠自己获得日常生活必需品的时代，正在到来。因此，政府的任务会持续增加，而政府为此而做的努力又会将其任务日益扩大。政府越是要取代社团的位置，个人就越没有联合起来的意愿，也就越需要政府的帮助。这些因果将会不断相互作用恶性循环下去。最终，行政当局将承担起所有个人无法独立经营的事业吗？而如果这样的时代最终到来，由于土地的过度分割，导致土地被分成无数小块，而只能由农夫社团来耕作的时候，政府首脑是否要挂冠而去扶犁耕田？如果政府完全取代社团，那么一个民主国家的道德和知识面临的危险绝不会比它的工商业面临的危险小。

人们只有在相互影响下，才能使情感和观念焕然一新，才能让心胸开阔，才能发挥自己的才智。我曾经说过，这些影响在民主国家几乎为零，因此，民主国家必须人为地将其创造出来，而这只能通过结社来实现。

当贵族社会的成员接受一个新的观念，或是体会到一种新感情时，他们会将这些观念和感情放到自己活动的主要舞台，让所有群众能够一下子注意到这些观念和感情，从而深入到周围人的心里和头脑里。在民主国家，从性质上来说，唯一有条件这样行事的就是政

sentiment, they give it a station, as it were, beside themselves, upon the lofty platform where they stand; and opinions or sentiments so conspicuous to the eyes of the multitude are easily introduced into the minds or hearts of all around. In democratic countries the governing power alone is naturally in a condition to act in this manner; but it is easy to see that its action is always inadequate, and often dangerous. A government can no more be competent to keep alive and to renew the circulation of opinions and feelings amongst a great people, than to manage all the speculations of productive industry. No sooner does a government attempt to go beyond its political sphere and to enter upon this new track, than it exercises, even unintentionally, an insupportable tyranny; for a government can only dictate strict rules, the opinions which it favors are rigidly enforced, and it is never easy to discriminate between its advice and its commands. Worse still will be the case if the government really believes itself interested in preventing all circulation of ideas; it will then stand motionless, and oppressed by the heaviness of voluntary torpor. Governments therefore should not be the only active powers: associations ought, in democratic nations, to stand in lieu of those powerful private individuals whom the equality of conditions has swept away.

As soon as several of the inhabitants of the United States have taken up an opinion or a feeling which they wish to promote in the world, they look out for mutual assistance; and as soon as they have found each other out, they combine. From that moment they are no longer isolated men, but a power seen from afar, whose actions serve for an example, and whose language is listened to. The first time I heard in the United States that 100,000 men had bound themselves publicly to abstain from spirituous liquors, it appeared to me more like a joke than a serious engagement; and I did not at once perceive why these temperate citizens could not content themselves with drinking water by their own firesides. I at last understood that 300,000 Americans, alarmed by the progress of drunkenness around them, had made up their minds to patronize temperance. They acted just in the same way as a man of high rank who should dress very plainly, in order to inspire the humbler orders with a contempt of luxury. It is probable that if these 100,000 men had lived in France, each of them would singly have memorialized the government to watch the public-houses all over the kingdom.

府。但是不难发现，政府的行为总是不够充分，而且往往很危险。一个政府不能只靠自己的力量维持和更新人们的思想和感情交流，就好像它不能依靠自己的力量去管理所有的实业部门一样。一旦政府试图超越政治领域，踏上这条新的道路，便会不由自主地实行令人难以忍受的暴政。因为政府只有颁布严格的制度，其支持的观念才能得以严格奉行，而人们则难以分清它到底是在建议还是在命令。更糟糕的是，如果政府认为自己的真正利益在于禁止人们的思想流通，那么政府将会无所作为，并听任自己迟钝下去。因此，不能让政府包办所有社会活动。在民主国家，社团应该代替那些平等所消灭的能力强大的个人。

只要美国的一些居民产生一种想要推广给世人的观念或情感，他们会立即寻找同道中人，而且他们一旦找到彼此，便立即结成社团。从那一刻起，他们不再是孤身一人，而是一股力量，是一股人们远远就能看见，行动被人仿效，言论有人倾听的力量。我第一次听说在美国有10万人公开宣誓不饮烈酒的时候，还以为这只是开玩笑而并非严肃的承诺。最初，我也并不理解为什么这些有节制的公民能够心甘情愿地坐在自家的炉火边只喝白水。最后我明白10万美国人是因为惊讶于身边的酒鬼越来越多，所以才痛下决心戒酒。他们的行为就好比一个高高在上的人衣着朴素，为的就是引导广大的群众杜绝奢侈。如果这10万人生活在法国，他们每个人可能会各自向政府请愿要求在全国禁酒。

在我看来，最值得我们注意的是美国智力和道德方面的结社。尽管这个国家的政治和工商业的结社最能吸引我们的眼球，但是其他的结社却总是逃过我们的注意，或者说，即使我们发现了它们，也无法对其完全理解，因为我们以前从未见过这种结社。然而，必

Nothing, in my opinion, is more deserving of our attention than the intellectual and moral associations of America. The political and industrial associations of that country strike us forcibly; but the others elude our observation, or if we discover them, we understand them imperfectly, because we have hardly ever seen anything of the kind. It must, however, be acknowledged that they are as necessary to the American people as the former, and perhaps more so. In democratic countries the science of association is the mother of science; the progress of all the rest depends upon the progress it has made. Amongst the laws which rule human societies there is one which seems to be more precise and clear than all others. If men are to remain civilized, or to become so, the art of associating together must grow and improve in the same ratio in which the equality of conditions is increased.

Chapter VI: Of The Relation Between Public Associations And Newspapers

When men are no longer united amongst themselves by firm and lasting ties, it is impossible to obtain the cooperation of any great number of them, unless you can persuade every man whose concurrence you require that this private interest obliges him voluntarily to unite his exertions to the exertions of all the rest. This can only be habitually and conveniently effected by means of a newspaper; nothing but a newspaper can drop the same thought into a thousand minds at the same moment. A newspaper is an adviser who does not require to be sought, but who comes of his own accord, and talks to you briefly every day of the common weal, without distracting you from your private affairs.

Newspapers therefore become more necessary in proportion as men become more equal, and individualism more to be feared. To suppose that they only serve to protect freedom would be to diminish their importance: they maintain civilization. I shall not deny that in democratic countries newspapers frequently lead the citizens to launch together in very ill-digested schemes; but if there were no newspapers there would be no common activity. The evil which they produce is therefore much less than that which they cure.

The effect of a newspaper is not only to suggest the same purpose to a great number of persons,

须要承认，对于美国人而言，这样的结社与政治和工商业的结社一样必不可少，甚至可能还要更加重要。在民主国家，科学的学问是一切学问之源，所有其他一切学问的进步都依赖于它的发展。在规范人类社会的所有法则之中，有一条最为明确清晰。如果人要保持文明，或者变得文明，结社艺术的成长和进步必须要能够与平等的发展同步。

第六章　结社与报刊的关系

当人们之间不再有牢固持久的纽带时，就不可能让大量的人携手共同行动，除非可以从个人利益的角度说服每个需要参与其中的人，从而让他们自愿地与其他人联合起来共同努力。而利用报纸往往可以顺利地做到这一点。只有报纸能够同时将同样的思想灌输到无数人的脑海。报纸就好比是一位不请自来的顾问，每天都会简明扼要地向你报告国家大事，同时还不会干扰到你的私人生活。

因此，随着人们越来越平等，个人主义日趋强大，报刊变得越来越必不可少。假设报刊的作用只在于维护自由，那么其重要性将大打折扣。因为报刊还能维护文明。我并不否认，在民主国家报刊往往会将公民一起引向一些非常欠妥的计划。但是如果没有报刊就不会有共同的行动。因此，报刊所带来的问题远比它们所解决的问题要少得多。

报刊的作用不但在于为大多数人提出共同的计划，而且还在于为这一共同的计划提供了共同的执行办法。生活在贵族社会的一些主要公民，彼此熟悉，如果他们想要把自己的力量团结起来，只要接近彼此并同时吸引一大批自己的追随者便可。而民主社会的情况往

but also to furnish means for executing in common the designs which they may have singly conceived. The principal citizens who inhabit an aristocratic country discern each other from afar; and if they wish to unite their forces, they move towards each other, drawing a multitude of men after them. It frequently happens, on the contrary, in democratic countries, that a great number of men who wish or who want to combine cannot accomplish it, because as they are very insignificant and lost amidst the crowd, they cannot see, and know not where to find, one another. A newspaper then takes up the notion or the feeling which had occurred simultaneously, but singly, to each of them. All are then immediately guided towards this beacon; and these wandering minds, which had long sought each other in darkness, at length meet and unite.

The newspaper brought them together, and the newspaper is still necessary to keep them united. In order that an association amongst a democratic people should have any power, it must be a numerous body. The persons of whom it is composed are therefore scattered over a wide extent, and each of them is detained in the place of his domicile by the narrowness of his income, or by the small unremitting exertions by which he earns it. Means then must be found to converse every day without seeing each other, and to take steps in common without having met. Thus hardly any democratic association can do without newspapers. There is consequently a necessary connection between public associations and newspapers: newspapers make associations, and associations make newspapers; and if it has been correctly advanced that associations will increase in number as the conditions of men become more equal, it is not less certain that the number of newspapers increases in proportion to that of associations. Thus it is in America that we find at the same time the greatest number of associations and of newspapers.

This connection between the number of newspapers and that of associations leads us to the discovery of a further connection between the state of the periodical press and the form of the administration in a country; and shows that the number of newspapers must diminish or increase amongst a democratic people, in proportion as its administration is more or less centralized. For amongst democratic nations the exercise of local powers cannot be intrusted to the principal members

往与之相反，大批希望或是有联合意愿的人们无法联合起来，因为他们太过于渺小，分散在各处，彼此谁也看不到谁，也不知道去哪里找到对方。于是报刊将人们各自产生的观点和情感同时报道出来。接着，所有人立即被这座灯塔所吸引，那些长久以来在黑暗中摸索寻找彼此的人们最终相遇并团结在一起。

报刊将人们吸引到一起，但还需要将人们团结起来。在民主国家一个社团要想拥有力量，必须还要人多势众。因此，由于社团的成员为数众多，而且分散在各地，每个人又由于个人有限的收入或是需要不断操劳的小事所累，无法离开他们生活的地方。所以必须找到一个能够让彼此不见面也能每天对话，不开会也能共同行动的手段，而这一手段就是报刊。所以，在民主国家没有报刊，社团寸步难行。由此可见，社团和报刊之间存在着必然的联系。报刊造就社团，而社团也造就报刊。如果说社团的数量必然会随平等的发展而增加，那么可以肯定，报刊会随社团的增加而增加。因此，我们看到在美国报刊和社团的数量都是最多的。

报刊数量和社团数量之间的关系让我们发现期刊的发行情况和国家行政组织形式之间的关系，并揭示出在民主国家报刊的数量必定会随行政集权的强弱而减少或增加。因为在民主国家，地方权力不可能像在贵族制国家那样委托给社会主要成员来执行。而民主国家则将这些权力取消，而交给当地大多数人来行使，而事实上，这些人会依法组织一个常设机构处理本地的行政事务。这样，他们就需要一份报纸，以便于每天能够了解地方及国家的大事小情。地方权力机构越多，依法行使这些权力的人也就越多，就越是需要随时了解

of the community as in aristocracies. Those powers must either be abolished, or placed in the hands of very large numbers of men, who then in fact constitute an association permanently established by law for the purpose of administering the affairs of a certain extent of territory; and they require a journal, to bring to them every day, in the midst of their own minor concerns, some intelligence of the state of their public weal. The more numerous local powers are, the greater is the number of men in whom they are vested by law; and as this want is hourly felt, the more profusely do newspapers abound.

The extraordinary subdivision of administrative power has much more to do with the enormous number of American newspapers than the great political freedom of the country and the absolute liberty of the press. If all the inhabitants of the Union had the suffrage—but a suffrage which should only extend to the choice of their legislators in Congress—they would require but few newspapers, because they would only have to act together on a few very important but very rare occasions. But within the pale of the great association of the nation, lesser associations have been established by law in every country, every city, and indeed in every village, for the purposes of local administration. The laws of the country thus compel every American to co-operate every day of his life with some of his fellow-citizens for a common purpose, and each one of them requires a newspaper to inform him what all the others are doing.

I am of opinion that a democratic people, without any national representative assemblies, but with a great number of small local powers, would have in the end more newspapers than another people governed by a centralized administration and an elective legislation. What best explains to me the enormous circulation of the daily press in the United States, is that amongst the Americans I find the utmost national freedom combined with local freedom of every kind. There is a prevailing opinion in France and England that the circulation of newspapers would be indefinitely increased by removing the taxes which have been laid upon the press. This is a very exaggerated estimate of the effects of such a reform. Newspapers increase in numbers, not according to their cheapness, but according to the more or less frequent want which a great number of men may feel for intercommunication and combination.

In like manner I should attribute the increasing influence of the daily press to causes more general

本地和全国的情况，也就越需要更多的报刊。

行政权力的过度分散对于这个国家庞大的报刊数量的影响要比其政治的广泛自由和出版业的绝对自由要大得多。如果联邦的所有居民都有选举权，但是只能用于选举全国的立法机构，那么他们需要的报刊数量就会非常有限。因为选民们只有少数几次非常重要的共同行动的机会。但是在美国，除了大型的全国性集会外，还有依据法律规定的在各州、各市和各乡镇处理地方行政的许多小型的集会。因此，国家的法律迫使每个美国公民为共同的目的每天与其他同胞共同协作，于是，每个人都需要一份报纸告诉他们别人都在做些什么。

我认为，一个民主国家如果没有全国性的议会，而只有大量的地方性权力机关，其报刊数量最终一定会超过另一个集权制的由选举产生立法机构的民主国家。对我而言，美国每日出版的报刊数量之所以如此庞大，是因为美国人享有最广泛的全国性自由以及各种各样的地方自由。在法国和英国存在一种普遍的观点认为，只要取消出版业的苛捐杂税，报刊的种类必将无限增加。这样的观点过分夸大了税制改革的作用。报刊数量的增加，不仅与报刊价格的低廉有关，而且还与大多数人是否需要互动信息和共同行动有关。

所以，同样地，我会将日报与日俱增的影响力归因于更普遍的原因而不是人们常常提到的原因。一份报纸只有能够反映大多数人共同的情感和思想才能存在下去。因此，报纸总是要代表其长期读者所在的社团。这个社团的宗旨可高可低，范围可宽可窄，人数可多可少，但是只要有一份报纸存在，就至少证明一个社团的萌芽已经在读者的心中存在。

than those by which it is commonly explained. A newspaper can only subsist on the condition of publishing sentiments or principles common to a large number of men. A newspaper therefore always represents an association which is composed of its habitual readers. This association may be more or less defined, more or less restricted, more or less numerous; but the fact that the newspaper keeps alive, is a proof that at least the germ of such an association exists in the minds of its readers.

This leads me to a last reflection, with which I shall conclude this chapter. The more equal the conditions of men become, and the less strong men individually are, the more easily do they give way to the current of the multitude, and the more difficult is it for them to adhere by themselves to an opinion which the multitude discard. A newspaper represents an association; it may be said to address each of its readers in the name of all the others, and to exert its influence over them in proportion to their individual weakness. The power of the newspaper press must therefore increase as the social conditions of men become more equal.

Chapter VII: Connection Of Civil And Political Associations

There is only one country on the face of the earth where the citizens enjoy unlimited freedom of association for political purposes. This same country is the only one in the world where the continual exercise of the right of association has been introduced into civil life, and where all the advantages which civilization can confer are procured by means of it. In all the countries where political associations are prohibited, civil associations are rare. It is hardly probable that this is the result of accident; but the inference should rather be, that there is a natural, and perhaps a necessary, connection between these two kinds of associations. Certain men happen to have a common interest in some concern—either a commercial undertaking is to be managed, or some speculation in manufactures to be tried; they meet, they combine, and thus by degrees they become familiar with the principle of association. The greater is the multiplicity of small affairs, the more do men, even without knowing it, acquire facility in prosecuting great undertakings in common. Civil associations, therefore, facilitate political association: but, on the other hand, political association singularly strengthens and improves associations for civil purposes. In civil life every man may, strictly

说到此处，我将要做最后一次反思来结束这一章。人们变得越平等，个人就变得越软弱，就越容易跟随大众的潮流，就越是难以坚持遭到多数反对的意见。一份报刊就代表一个社团，可以说它在以所有读者的名义向每个读者发言，而且读者的个人能力越弱，越容易对其产生影响。因此，报刊的力量必定随社会状况越来越平等而逐渐增强。

第七章　民间结社和政治结社的关系

世界上只有一个国家的公民能够享受政治结社的无限自由，而且世界上也只有这个国家的公民能够将结社权不断的应用于日常生活，并由此享受到文明所带来的一切好处。在所有政治结社遭到禁止的国家，民间结社也很罕见。这很可能并非偶然现象，而更可能是在这两种结社之间存在某种天然的必然联系。一些人可能出于偶然因素在某一事业上有共同的利害关系，也许是要共同进行一项商业，也许是要经营一项工业，于是他们碰面并联合起来，逐步了解到结社的好处。人们共同处理的这种小事越多，甚至在不知不觉之中，共同办大事的能力就越来越得到加强。因此，民间结社会促进政治结社，但是另一反面，政治结社也会让民间结社得到进一步加强和发展。严格来说，在日常生活中每个人都觉得自己能够满足自己的需要，但是在政治上，他则不这么认为。因此，当人们参与公共生活的时候，结社的想法和愿望便在全社会所有人的头脑中日日浮现。所以无论人们对共同行动有什么样固有的反感，他们会随时为了党派而联合。因此，政治生活让人们对于结社的

speaking, fancy that he can provide for his own wants; in politics, he can fancy no such thing. When a people, then, have any knowledge of public life, the notion of association, and the wish to coalesce, present themselves every day to the minds of the whole community: whatever natural repugnance may restrain men from acting in concert, they will always be ready to combine for the sake of a party. Thus political life makes the love and practice of association more general; it imparts a desire of union, and teaches the means of combination to numbers of men who would have always lived apart.

Politics not only give birth to numerous associations, but to associations of great extent. In civil life it seldom happens that any one interest draws a very large number of men to act in concert; much skill is required to bring such an interest into existence: but in politics opportunities present themselves every day. Now it is solely in great associations that the general value of the principle of association is displayed. Citizens who are individually powerless, do not very clearly anticipate the strength which they may acquire by uniting together; it must be shown to them in order to be understood. Hence it is often easier to collect a multitude for a public purpose than a few persons; a thousand citizens do not see what interest they have in combining together—ten thousand will be perfectly aware of it. In politics men combine for great undertakings; and the use they make of the principle of association in important affairs practically teaches them that it is their interest to help each other in those of less moment. A political association draws a number of individuals at the same time out of their own circle: however they may be naturally kept asunder by age, mind, and fortune, it places them nearer together and brings them into contact. Once met, they can always meet again.

Men can embark in few civil partnerships without risking a portion of their possessions; this is the case with all manufacturing and trading companies. When men are as yet but little versed in the art of association, and are unacquainted with its principal rules, they are afraid, when first they combine in this manner, of buying their experience dear. They therefore prefer depriving themselves of a powerful instrument of success to running the risks which attend the use of it. They are, however, less reluctant to join political associations, which appear to them to be without danger, because they adventure no money in them. But they cannot belong to these associations for any length of

热爱和习惯更普遍, 并让一直以来独立行动的人们产生团结的愿望, 学会联合的技巧。

政治不但造就众多的社团, 而且造就规模庞大的社团。在日常生活中, 很少有任何一种利益能够吸引数量如此庞大的人们共同行动, 所以需要采取某种技巧来制造这样的共同利益。但是在政治上, 却每天都有这样的机会。而结社的普遍价值只有在规模巨大的社团才能表现出来。个人力量有限的公民对他们联合起来后所拥有的力量并不清楚, 所以必须通过示范来让他们明白。因此, 为一个公共目的结社时, 人数越多示范作用越强。一千个公民联合起来可能看不到利益, 但是一万个公民就能够清楚地看到。在政治上, 人们联合起来是为了做大事, 而在重大事务上运用结社原则实际上又教会他们在小事上互相帮助是彼此的利益之所在。政治结社能够将许多人同时拉出自己的小圈子。无论年龄、思想和贫富带给人们的隔阂有多大, 结社都能够让人们彼此接近, 互相接触。只要一次相会, 他们就会想要再次相会。

人们往往会拿出自己的一部分财产来参与民间结社, 例如所有的工业和商业公司就是这样的情况。当人们对于结社的艺术知之甚少, 不了解结社基本原则的时候, 他们会害怕一旦自己以这样的方式联合, 难免会付出高昂的代价。因此, 他们宁可放弃这种可以带来成功的有力手段, 而不肯冒合作给他们带来的风险。然而, 人们却常常毫不犹豫地参加政治社团, 因为在他们看来政治社团没有风险, 不需要金钱投入。但是如果他们不知道在这样的一大群人中应该遵守什么样的规则, 应该采取什么样的步骤来有条不紊地奔向共同目标, 他们便无法长期属于这样的社团。因此, 人们愿意让个人意志服从集体意志, 让自己的

time without finding out how order is maintained amongst a large number of men, and by what contrivance they are made to advance, harmoniously and methodically, to the same object. Thus they learn to surrender their own will to that of all the rest, and to make their own exertions subordinate to the common impulse—things which it is not less necessary to know in civil than in political associations. Political associations may therefore be considered as large free schools, where all the members of the community go to learn the general theory of association.

But even if political association did not directly contribute to the progress of civil association, to destroy the former would be to impair the latter. When citizens can only meet in public for certain purposes, they regard such meetings as a strange proceeding of rare occurrence, and they rarely think at all about it. When they are allowed to meet freely for all purposes, they ultimately look upon public association as the universal, or in a manner the sole means, which men can employ to accomplish the different purposes they may have in view. Every new want instantly revives the notion. The art of association then becomes, as I have said before, the mother of action, studied and applied by all.

When some kinds of associations are prohibited and others allowed, it is difficult to distinguish the former from the latter, beforehand. In this state of doubt men abstain from them altogether, and a sort of public opinion passes current which tends to cause any association whatsoever to be regarded as a bold and almost an illicit enterprise.

It is therefore chimerical to suppose that the spirit of association, when it is repressed on some one point, will nevertheless display the same vigor on all others; and that if men be allowed to prosecute certain undertakings in common, that is quite enough for them eagerly to set about them. When the members of a community are allowed and accustomed to combine for all purposes, they will combine as readily for the lesser as for the more important ones; but if they are only allowed to combine for small affairs, they will be neither inclined nor able to effect it. It is in vain that you will leave them entirely free to prosecute their business on joint-stock account: they will hardly care to avail themselves of the rights you have granted to them; and, after having exhausted your strength in vain efforts to put down prohibited associations, you will be surprised that you cannot persuade men

努力配合共同的行动。这些事情无论对于民间结社还是政治结社都是必不可少的。因此，政治结社可以被视为一所免费大学，所有社会成员都可以到这里学习结社的一般理论。

即使政治结社不能直接促进民间结社的发展，但是对前者的破坏依旧会给后者带来损害。当公民只能由于特定原因才能结社的时候，他们会将这样的结社视为罕见的情况，而不把它放在心上。当公民能够出于各种原因自由结社的时候，便会将结社视为自己可以实现各种目的的通用或是唯一的手段。于是，只要有新的需要，人们会立刻想到结社。于是，正如我前面所说，结社的艺术成为人人都应学会并应用的所有行动的基本知识。

当某种形式的社团被禁止，而其他形式的社团依旧被允许时，很难说清依旧存在的社团何时遭到禁止。在这样的情况下，满腹狐疑的人们必然对结社敬而远之，同时社会上还会盛行一种看法，认为无论什么样的结社都是胆大妄为和非法的活动。

因此，如果认为结社精神只在某一点上受到限制，而并不会影响到它在其他方面的继续发展，或者认为只要允许人们在某些事情上共同行动，就足以让人们对共同行动乐此不疲，这些想法都是不切实际的。当社会成员被允许，或是习惯于出于各种原因结社时，他们在小事上的结社热情绝不会比在大事上低。但是如果只允许他们为小事结社，那么他们结社的热情和才干都将消失。所以只允许他们在商业上自由结社，你只会徒劳无功。因为他们会对你赋予他们的权利不屑一顾，而在你费尽九牛二虎之力劝说他们不要组织会被查禁的社团后，你会惊讶地发现也无法说服他们去组织你所鼓励的社团。

我并不是说，在一个禁止政治结社的国家就没有民间结社，因为在社会中没有共同

to form the associations you encourage.

I do not say that there can be no civil associations in a country where political association is prohibited; for men can never live in society without embarking in some common undertakings: but I maintain that in such a country civil associations will always be few in number, feebly planned, unskillfully managed, that they will never form any vast designs, or that they will fail in the execution of them.

This naturally leads me to think that freedom of association in political matters is not so dangerous to public tranquillity as is supposed; and that possibly, after having agitated society for some time, it may strengthen the State in the end. In democratic countries political associations are, so to speak, the only powerful persons who aspire to rule the State. Accordingly, the governments of our time look upon associations of this kind just as sovereigns in the Middle Ages regarded the great vassals of the Crown: they entertain a sort of instinctive abhorrence of them, and they combat them on all occasions. They bear, on the contrary, a natural goodwill to civil associations, because they readily discover that, instead of directing the minds of the community to public affairs, these institutions serve to divert them from such reflections; and that, by engaging them more and more in the pursuit of objects which cannot be attained without public tranquillity, they deter them from revolutions. But these governments do not attend to the fact that political associations tend amazingly to multiply and facilitate those of a civil character, and that in avoiding a dangerous evil they deprive themselves of an efficacious remedy.

When you see the Americans freely and constantly forming associations for the purpose of promoting some political principle, of raising one man to the head of affairs, or of wresting power from another, you have some difficulty in understanding that men so independent do not constantly fall into the abuse of freedom. If, on the other hand, you survey the infinite number of trading companies which are in operation in the United States, and perceive that the Americans are on every side unceasingly engaged in the execution of important and difficult plans, which the slightest revolution would throw into confusion, you will readily comprehend why people so well employed are

的事业，人就无法生存。但是我坚持认为，在这样的国家民间结社必然数量有限，组织松散，而且缺乏技巧，将永远无法谋求或实现任何宏图大业。

这自然令我想到，政治结社自由对社会安定并没有想象中的那样危险，而且很可能，在给社会带来一段时间的动荡之后，最终会巩固国家的统治。在民主国家，可以说政治结社是企图统治国家的强大个体。由此可见，在我们这个时代的政府眼中，这种社团俨然就是中世纪的诸侯，所以他们本能地对这种社团有一种恐惧感，而且一有机会就对其予以打击。与之相反，各国政府对民间社团则有着与生俱来的好感，因为它们已经充分意识到，这些组织能够将人们的注意力从公共事务上转移开，而且人们对于国家安定才能得以实现的目标的不断追求，还会让人们远离革命。但是这些政府忽略了这样一个事实，政治结社可以极大地加强和促进民间结社，所以他们在避免一种危险的同时丧失了一种有效规避这种危险的手段。

当你看到美国人为了鼓吹某个政治观点，推捧某个政客参与政府，或是从另一位政客手中篡夺权力而随时自由结社的时候，你也许会很难理解如此独立不羁的人怎么没有滥用自由。但是，从另一方面，如果你看到在美国人们共同经营着如此数不胜数的商业团体，并意识到美国人在各方面时刻推行着宏伟的计划，哪怕最轻微的革命也会令这些前功尽弃的时候，便不难理解为什么如此繁忙的人们一点都没有给这个国家带来混乱，也没有对所有人都能从中受益的社会安定带来丝毫破坏。

只对这些事情进行孤立的观察就足够吗？还是我们应该进一步去探寻他们之间的内在联系呢？正是在政治结社的过程中，美国人才逐步养成不问出身、思想和年龄的结社的

by no means tempted to perturb the State, nor to destroy that public tranquillity by which they all profit.

Is it enough to observe these things separately, or should we not discover the hidden tie which connects them? In their political associations, the Americans of all conditions, minds, and ages, daily acquire a general taste for association, and grow accustomed to the use of it. There they meet together in large numbers, they converse, they listen to each other, and they are mutually stimulated to all sorts of undertakings. They afterwards transfer to civil life the notions they have thus acquired, and make them subservient to a thousand purposes. Thus it is by the enjoyment of a dangerous freedom that the Americans learn the art of rendering the dangers of freedom less formidable.

If a certain moment in the existence of a nation be selected, it is easy to prove that political associations perturb the State, and paralyze productive industry; but take the whole life of a people, and it may perhaps be easy to demonstrate that freedom of association in political matters is favorable to the prosperity and even to the tranquillity of the community.

I said in the former part of this work, "The unrestrained liberty of political association cannot be entirely assimilated to the liberty of the press. The one is at the same time less necessary and more dangerous than the other. A nation may confine it within certain limits without ceasing to be mistress of itself; and it may sometimes be obliged to do so in order to maintain its own authority." And further on I added: "It cannot be denied that the unrestrained liberty of association for political purposes is the last degree of liberty which a people is fit for. If it does not throw them into anarchy, it perpetually brings them, as it were, to the verge of it." Thus I do not think that a nation is always at liberty to invest its citizens with an absolute right of association for political purposes; and I doubt whether, in any country or in any age, it be wise to set no limits to freedom of association. A certain nation, it is said, could not maintain tranquillity in the community, cause the laws to be respected, or establish a lasting government, if the right of association were not confined within narrow limits. These blessings are doubtless invaluable, and I can imagine that, to acquire or to preserve them, a nation may impose upon itself severe temporary restrictions: but still it is well that the nation should know at what price these blessings are purchased. I can understand that it may be advisable to cut off

普遍爱好和习惯。在这里，他们大多数人彼此结识，交谈、互相倾听，并共同开创各种事业。随后，他们将在这里获得的观念引入日常生活，应用到各个方面。因此，正是通过享有一种危险的自由，美国人掌握了如何让这种危险的自由不危险的技巧。

如果我们只对某一民族的某一历史时刻进行考察，不难证明政治结社给国家带来危害，并令工商业处于瘫痪状态。但是如果考察一个民族的整个历史，便可轻而易举地证明政治结社自由不但有利于国家的繁荣，甚至有利于社会的安定。

在本书的上卷中我曾经说过："政治结社的绝对自由与出版自由不尽相同。前者的必要性不如后者，而其危险性则远大于后者。一个国家也许能够对结社自由进行限制并令其完全处于自己的掌控之中，而且有时候为了维持结社自由的存在还不得不要一些手段。"而且我还补充道："不可否认，政治结社的无限自由是最不适合人民的一种自由。也就是说它不是让人民陷入无政府状态，就是让他们始终在无政府状态的边缘徘徊。"因此，我不认为一个国家会让公民享有绝对的政治结社自由，我甚至怀疑，在任何国家或是时代，不对结社自由加以限制会是明智之举。有人说，如果不将结社权限制在狭小的范围，一个国家就无法维护社会安定、法律的尊严或是政府的持久。毫无疑问这些都是无价之宝。而且一个国家为了得到和保留这些珍贵的东西，宁愿给自己暂时戴上沉重的枷锁，但是如果一个国家知道为了换取这些宝贵的东西自己应该付出怎样的代价那就更好了。我可以理解为了保住一个人的性命可以将他的手臂斩断，但如果说他还能像原来一样活动自如那简直就是荒谬之极。

a man's arm in order to save his life; but it would be ridiculous to assert that he will be as dexterous as he was before he lost it.

Chapter VIII: The Americans Combat Individualism By The Principle Of Interest Rightly Understood

When the world was managed by a few rich and powerful individuals, these persons loved to entertain a lofty idea of the duties of man. They were fond of professing that it is praiseworthy to forget one's self, and that good should be done without hope of reward, as it is by the Deity himself. Such were the standard opinions of that time in morals. I doubt whether men were more virtuous in aristocratic ages than in others; but they were incessantly talking of the beauties of virtue, and its utility was only studied in secret. But since the imagination takes less lofty flights and every man's thoughts are centred in himself, moralists are alarmed by this idea of self-sacrifice, and they no longer venture to present it to the human mind. They therefore content themselves with inquiring whether the personal advantage of each member of the community does not consist in working for the good of all; and when they have hit upon some point on which private interest and public interest meet and amalgamate, they are eager to bring it into notice. Observations of this kind are gradually multiplied: what was only a single remark becomes a general principle; and it is held as a truth that man serves himself in serving his fellow-creatures, and that his private interest is to do good.

I have already shown, in several parts of this work, by what means the inhabitants of the United States almost always manage to combine their own advantage with that of their fellow-citizens: my present purpose is to point out the general rule which enables them to do so. In the United States hardly anybody talks of the beauty of virtue; but they maintain that virtue is useful, and prove it every day. The American moralists do not profess that men ought to sacrifice themselves for their fellow-creatures because it is noble to make such sacrifices; but they boldly aver that such sacrifices are as necessary to him who imposes them upon himself as to him for whose sake they are made. They

第八章　美国人用正确理解的利益的原则与个人主义做斗争

当世界由一些有钱有势的人把持时，他们很愿意培养人们对义务的崇高思想。他们喜欢主张忘我是值得大加赞赏的，人们应该向上帝那样行善而不图回报。这就是那个时代的道德标准。难道说贵族时代的人会比其他时代的人都更加道德？对此我深表怀疑。但是他们的确总是将德行之美挂在口头，至于其功用则只做私下讨论。但是，因为想象力的枯竭，人们便开始只关注自己，道德高尚的人也对这样的自我牺牲的思想望而却步，于是不敢再向人们宣扬这种精神。因此，他们只满足于研究每个社会成员的个人利益是否在于为全体造福。而当他们发现在个人利益和公共利益之间存在某种契合点时，便迫不及待地公之于众。后来这样的发现与日俱增，原本孤立的观点成为普遍原理。最后人们发现了这个真理，服务他人就是服务自己，个人利益就在于为善。

在这本书的很多地方，我已经说过美国居民几乎总是设法将自己的幸福与同胞的幸福结合起来。而我现在就是要指出促使他们这样做的一般原理。在美国，几乎没有人谈论德行之美，但是他们坚信德行是有用的，而且每天都在证明这一点。美国的道德家们不会公开宣称，由于为同胞而牺牲自我很高尚，所以人们应该这样做。但是他们会大胆宣称，这种牺牲，无论是对牺牲者本人还是对受益者都同样必要。他们已经发现，在他们的国家和他们的时代，人们在一种不可抗拒力量的驱使下关注自己，而因为完全无望制止这股力量，他们便决定因势利导。因此，他们不否认每个人都可以根据自己的利益做出选择，但同时他们力图证明行善是每个人的利益之所在。在这里我并不想离题去探讨他们这样说的

have found out that in their country and their age man is brought home to himself by an irresistible force; and losing all hope of stopping that force, they turn all their thoughts to the direction of it. They therefore do not deny that every man may follow his own interest; but they endeavor to prove that it is the interest of every man to be virtuous. I shall not here enter into the reasons they allege, which would divert me from my subject: suffice it to say that they have convinced their fellow-countrymen.

Montaigne said long ago: "Were I not to follow the straight road for its straightness, I should follow it for having found by experience that in the end it is commonly the happiest and most useful track." The doctrine of interest rightly understood is not, then, new, but amongst the Americans of our time it finds universal acceptance: it has become popular there; you may trace it at the bottom of all their actions, you will remark it in all they say. It is as often to be met with on the lips of the poor man as of the rich. In Europe the principle of interest is much grosser than it is in America, but at the same time it is less common, and especially it is less avowed; amongst us, men still constantly feign great abnegation which they no longer feel. The Americans, on the contrary, are fond of explaining almost all the actions of their lives by the principle of interest rightly understood; they show with complacency how an enlightened regard for themselves constantly prompts them to assist each other, and inclines them willingly to sacrifice a portion of their time and property to the welfare of the State. In this respect I think they frequently fail to do themselves justice; for in the United States, as well as elsewhere, people are sometimes seen to give way to those disinterested and spontaneous impulses which are natural to man; but the Americans seldom allow that they yield to emotions of this kind; they are more anxious to do honor to their philosophy than to themselves.

I might here pause, without attempting to pass a judgment on what I have described. The extreme difficulty of the subject would be my excuse, but I shall not avail myself of it; and I had rather that my readers, clearly perceiving my object, should refuse to follow me than that I should leave them in suspense. The principle of interest rightly understood is not a lofty one, but it is clear and sure. It does not aim at mighty objects, but it attains without excessive exertion all those at which

原因，只要指出他们的同胞已经接受他们的理念就可以了。

很久以前，蒙坦就曾经说过："我走上一条捷径并不是因为它笔直，而是从经验得知它会是我到达目的地最便捷最适合的道路。"所以，正确理解的利益的原则并不是什么新东西，而不过是得到我们这个时代美国人的普遍认可。在这里，这一原则得到普遍推广，深入到人们的所有行动，表现在人们的所有言论。无论是穷人还是富人张口闭口都离不开这个原则。在欧洲，利益原则没有在美国那样完善，而且也没有那么普遍，特别是很少有人公开主张。在我们之中，人们依然不断表现出一副极具献身精神的样子，尽管他们内心已经不再这么想。与之相反，美国人则喜欢用正确理解的利益的原则来解释他们生活中的几乎一切行为，并自鸣得意地展示一种文明的自爱如何不断地促使他们互相帮助并心甘情愿地为了国家的福祉牺牲一部分自己的时间和财富。在这一点上，我认为他们对自己的评价并不客观，因为无论是在美国还是在别的国家，人们往往会服从于与生俱来的某些自发的无私的激情，但是美国人则绝不承认自己会受到这种激情的左右，他们宁愿让自己的哲学生辉而不是为自身增光。

我本可以就此停笔，不再对我所述的一切进行评价，并以题目太难作为我的托词，但我并不想以此为借口。我宁可读者在清楚理解我的意图之后不跟着我走，也不愿让读者悬在那里。正确理解的利益的原则并不高深，相反它很清晰易懂。它并不旨在高尚的目标，而旨在不费太大力气实现其追求的所有目标。因为每个人都能理解它，所以都可以毫无困难地学会并掌握。因为它与人类的弱点相吻合，可以轻松对人产生巨大的影响，而且这种

it aims. As it lies within the reach of all capacities, everyone can without difficulty apprehend and retain it. By its admirable conformity to human weaknesses, it easily obtains great dominion; nor is that dominion precarious, since the principle checks one personal interest by another, and uses, to direct the passions, the very same instrument which excites them. The principle of interest rightly understood produces no great acts of self-sacrifice, but it suggests daily small acts of self-denial. By itself it cannot suffice to make a man virtuous, but it disciplines a number of citizens in habits of regularity, temperance, moderation, foresight, self-command; and, if it does not lead men straight to virtue by the will, it gradually draws them in that direction by their habits. If the principle of interest rightly understood were to sway the whole moral world, extraordinary virtues would doubtless be more rare; but I think that gross depravity would then also be less common. The principle of interest rightly understood perhaps prevents some men from rising far above the level of mankind; but a great number of other men, who were falling far below it, are caught and restrained by it. Observe some few individuals, they are lowered by it; survey mankind, it is raised. I am not afraid to say that the principle of interest, rightly understood, appears to me the best suited of all philosophical theories to the wants of the men of our time, and that I regard it as their chief remaining security against themselves. Towards it, therefore, the minds of the moralists of our age should turn; even should they judge it to be incomplete, it must nevertheless be adopted as necessary.

I do not think upon the whole that there is more egotism amongst us than in America; the only difference is, that there it is enlightened—here it is not. Every American will sacrifice a portion of his private interests to preserve the rest; we would fain preserve the whole, and oftentimes the whole is lost. Everybody I see about me seems bent on teaching his contemporaries, by precept and example, that what is useful is never wrong. Will nobody undertake to make them understand how what is right may be useful? No power upon earth can prevent the increasing equality of conditions from inclining the human mind to seek out what is useful, or from leading every member of the community to be wrapped up in himself. It must therefore be expected that personal interest will become more than ever the principal, if not the sole, spring of men's actions; but it remains to be

影响还会持续下去，因为它以个人利益来对抗个人本身，并在引导个人激情时产生同样的作用。正确理解的利益的原则并不鼓励自我牺牲，只是促使人们每天做出小小的牺牲。仅凭它自己并不足以让一个人变成有德之人，但是它可以使大多数公民的循规蹈矩、自我克制、温和稳健、深谋远虑、严于律己。而且即使它不能引导人们直接靠意志来修德，也可以逐渐通过习惯来让他们走上修德之路。如果正确理解的利益的原则影响到整个道德世界，非凡的美德无疑会难得一见。但是我认为，普遍的邪恶也将不再多见。正确理解的利益的原则也许会妨碍某些人从人们的一般水平中脱颖而出，但是在这个水平之下的大量其他人会对这个原则紧抓不放。尽管会看到有个别人因为这一原则而德行下降，但是纵观整体，人类的德行得到了提高。我敢说正确理解的利益的原则依我看是最适合我们这个时代的人们需要的哲学理论，也是我们与自己对抗的最有力保障。因此，我们这个时代的道德学家们应该将注意力投向这一理论。即使他们认为这个理论还不够完美，但必须将其视为必须而采纳。

我不认为，从总体上看，我们法国人的利己主义倾向比美国人强。我们与美国人的利己主义的唯一不同在于，美国人公开主张利己主义，而我们刚好相反嘴上不说但实际上这样做。每个美国人都愿意牺牲一部分个人利益成全其他，而我们则想保住全部利益却往往什么都得不到。我看到我身边的每一个人都致力于用自己的言行教导同时代的人追求功利没有错。难道就没有人教导大家正派的行为也可能是追求功利吗？世界上，没有任何力量能够阻止不断发展的平等去引导人们追求功利，或是让每个社会成员以自己为中心。因此，必须承认个人利益将成为即使不是唯一，也会是最主要的人们行动的动力，但是这依

seen how each man will understand his personal interest. If the members of a community, as they become more equal, become more ignorant and coarse, it is difficult to foresee to what pitch of stupid excesses their egotism may lead them; and no one can foretell into what disgrace and wretchedness they would plunge themselves, lest they should have to sacrifice something of their own well-being to the prosperity of their fellow-creatures. I do not think that the system of interest, as it is professed in America, is, in all its parts, self-evident; but it contains a great number of truths so evident that men, if they are but educated, cannot fail to see them. Educate, then, at any rate; for the age of implicit self-sacrifice and instinctive virtues is already flitting far away from us, and the time is fast approaching when freedom, public peace, and social order itself will not be able to exist without education.

Chapter IX: That The Americans Apply The Principle Of Interest Rightly Understood To Religious Matters

If the principle of interest rightly understood had nothing but the present world in view, it would be very insufficient; for there are many sacrifices which can only find their recompense in another; and whatever ingenuity may be put forth to demonstrate the utility of virtue, it will never be an easy task to make that man live aright who has no thoughts of dying. It is therefore necessary to ascertain whether the principle of interest rightly understood is easily compatible with religious belief. The philosophers who inculcate this system of morals tell men, that to be happy in this life they must watch their own passions and steadily control their excess; that lasting happiness can only be secured by renouncing a thousand transient gratifications; and that a man must perpetually triumph over himself, in order to secure his own advantage. The founders of almost all religions have held the same language. The track they point out to man is the same, only that the goal is more remote; instead of placing in this world the reward of the sacrifices they impose, they transport it to another. Nevertheless I cannot believe that all those who practise virtue from religious motives are only actuated by the hope of a recompense. I have known zealous Christians who constantly forgot

然有赖于每个人对其个人利益的理解。如果随着社会成员越来越平等，他们依旧无知和粗野，那么就很难预见他们的利己主义会令他们做出怎样愚蠢的行为。而且如果他们不能为了同胞而牺牲自己的某些福利，也没人能够预言他们会陷入怎样耻辱悲惨的境地。我并不认为，美国人口口声声宣扬的利益原则的所有部分都已明明白白，但是它包含的众多真理已经昭然若揭，只要对人进行启发教育，每个人都能理解。于是，要不遗余力地进行教育。因为在盲目的自我牺牲和本能行善的时代已经离我们远去之后，自由、公共安宁和社会秩序本身只有通过教育才能实现的时代正在快速到来。

第九章　美国人的正确理解的利益的原则在宗教上的应用

如果正确理解的利益的原则只着眼于现世，将远远不够，因为有许多牺牲只有在来世才能得到补偿。无论你用什么样的技巧来证明德行的功用，想让一个活得好好的从未想过死的人去行善也始终是件难事。因此，有必要确认正确理解的利益的原则是否能够与宗教信仰顺利融合。不断向人们灌输这一道德原则的哲学家们告诉大家，要想过得幸福就必须节制自己的激情并将其牢牢控制在适度的范围，要想获得持久的幸福就必须放弃无数转瞬即逝的享乐，而且为了保障自己的利益必须始终能够战胜自己。几乎所有宗教的创始人都曾经说过相同的话，也为世人指出过相同的道路，只不过目标更为遥远，即他们的牺牲不是为了现世而是为了来生。然而我绝不认为出于宗教动机行善的所有人都是为了得到报偿。我就见到过一些虔诚忘我的基督徒，他们热诚地为所有人造福，而且我还听到他们

themselves, to work with greater ardor for the happiness of their fellow-men; and I have heard them declare that all they did was only to earn the blessings of a future state. I cannot but think that they deceive themselves; I respect them too much to believe them.

Christianity indeed teaches that a man must prefer his neighbor to himself, in order to gain eternal life; but Christianity also teaches that men ought to benefit their fellow-creatures for the love of God. A sublime expression! Man, searching by his intellect into the divine conception, and seeing that order is the purpose of God, freely combines to prosecute the great design; and whilst he sacrifices his personal interests to this consummate order of all created things, expects no other recompense than the pleasure of contemplating it. I do not believe that interest is the sole motive of religious men: but I believe that interest is the principal means which religions themselves employ to govern men, and I do not question that this way they strike into the multitude and become popular. It is not easy clearly to perceive why the principle of interest rightly understood should keep aloof from religious opinions; and it seems to me more easy to show why it should draw men to them. Let it be supposed that, in order to obtain happiness in this world, a man combats his instinct on all occasions and deliberately calculates every action of his life; that, instead of yielding blindly to the impetuosity of first desires, he has learned the art of resisting them, and that he has accustomed himself to sacrifice without an effort the pleasure of a moment to the lasting interest of his whole life. If such a man believes in the religion which he professes, it will cost him but little to submit to the restrictions it may impose. Reason herself counsels him to obey, and habit has prepared him to endure them. If he should have conceived any doubts as to the object of his hopes, still he will not easily allow himself to be stopped by them; and he will decide that it is wise to risk some of the advantages of this world, in order to preserve his rights to the great inheritance promised him in another. "To be mistaken in believing that the Christian religion is true," says Pascal, "is no great loss to anyone; but how dreadful to be mistaken in believing it to be false!"

The Americans do not affect a brutal indifference to a future state; they affect no puerile pride in despising perils which they hope to escape from. They therefore profess their religion without shame

说，他们所做的一切只为来世能得到善报。对此，我只能认为他们是在自欺欺人。但由于我对他们非常尊重，所以只好相信他们。

的确，基督教教诲人们，为了能获得永生，人爱他人要胜于爱自己。但是基督教也教诲人们，人是由于爱上帝才施惠于他人。多么崇高的说法！人凭借自己的智慧领会上帝的意旨，认为秩序是上帝的目的，并毅然参与上帝这一伟大的计划，然而当他为了实现万物有序而情愿牺牲个人利益时，他不求任何回报想的只有这一计划带来的快乐。我不相信，利益是宗教人士的唯一动机，但是我认为，利益是宗教本身用来控制人行动的手段，而且我丝毫不怀疑宗教能够深入人心并广为流传靠的就是这个办法。要清楚地弄明白为什么正确理解的利益的原则会令人们远离宗教并不容易。但是在我看来，说明为什么这一原则能够让人们与宗教更接近反而是更容易的事情。让我们假设，为了获得现世的幸福，一个人要时刻与自己的本能斗争，冷静地算计生活中的一举一动，不为一时出现的盲目冲动所左右，为此他学会了克制的技巧，让自己养成了为了长久利益而牺牲暂时享受的习惯。如果这样的一个人一旦皈依他所信奉的宗教，遵守宗教本身的清规戒律将不会给他造成任何麻烦。理智本身会劝导他服从，习惯也已为他遵守这些清规戒律做好准备。即使他对所期望的目标表示怀疑，也不会轻易放弃，而会认为以现世的利益为赌注来换得来世继承巨额财富的权利是明智之举。帕斯卡尔说过："误信基督教是真的，并没有什么损失；而误信基督教是假的，则损失严重。"

美国人既不装作对未来漠不关心，也不对他们想要逃避的危险天真地采取满不在乎的态度。因此，他们对自己信教既不感觉可耻，也不感觉软弱，而往往是在他们的虔诚之

and without weakness; but there generally is, even in their zeal, something so indescribably tranquil, methodical, and deliberate, that it would seem as if the head, far more than the heart, brought them to the foot of the altar. The Americans not only follow their religion from interest, but they often place in this world the interest which makes them follow it. In the Middle Ages the clergy spoke of nothing but a future state; they hardly cared to prove that a sincere Christian may be a happy man here below. But the American preachers are constantly referring to the earth; and it is only with great difficulty that they can divert their attention from it. To touch their congregations, they always show them how favorable religious opinions are to freedom and public tranquillity; and it is often difficult to ascertain from their discourses whether the principal object of religion is to procure eternal felicity in the other world, or prosperity in this.

Chapter X: Of The Taste For Physical Well-Being In America

In America the passion for physical well-being is not always exclusive, but it is general; and if all do not feel it in the same manner, yet it is felt by all. Carefully to satisfy all, even the least wants of the body, and to provide the little conveniences of life, is uppermost in every mind. Something of an analogous character is more and more apparent in Europe. Amongst the causes which produce these similar consequences in both hemispheres, several are so connected with my subject as to deserve notice.

When riches are hereditarily fixed in families, there are a great number of men who enjoy the comforts of life without feeling an exclusive taste for those comforts. The heart of man is not so much caught by the undisturbed possession of anything valuable as by the desire, as yet imperfectly satisfied, of possessing it, and by the incessant dread of losing it. In aristocratic communities, the wealthy, never having experienced a condition different from their own, entertain no fear of changing it; the existence of such conditions hardly occurs to them. The comforts of life are not to them the end of life, but simply a way of living; they regard them as existence itself—enjoyed, but scarcely thought of. As the natural and instinctive taste which all men feel for being well off is thus satisfied

中表现出难以名状的淡定，按部就班和胸有成竹，以至于让人们觉得似乎引导他们走到圣坛之前的并不是他们的心灵而是他们的理智。美国人信奉宗教不仅是出于利益，而且还往往把他们可以从宗教中获得的利益放在现世。在中世纪，神职人员只谈来世，从未想过证明一个虔诚的基督徒可以在现世也做一个幸福的人。但是，美国的传教士，则不断谈及现世，只有大费周章才能让信徒的注意力从现世转移。为了能够打动听众，他们不断地向信徒们证明宗教的观念如何有利于自由和公共秩序。所以在听他们布道的时候常常会弄不清宗教的主旨到底是求得来世的永久幸福，还是现世的安乐。

第十章　美国人对物质利益的爱好

在美国，对于物质利益的热爱并不是个别现象，而是普遍现象。尽管不是所有人都用同样的方式去热爱，但至少每个人都有这样的热爱。在这里，小心翼翼地满足所有需要，哪怕是身体最微不足道的需要，带给生活的小小便利，都是每个人心中的头等大事。在欧洲，具有类似特点的现象也越来越多。导致两个洲产生相似结果的原因之中，有一些与我所讨论的问题有关，所以值得注意。

当财富固定在一些家族世代相传的，很多这样享受着舒适生活的人并不认为自己是在独享这份舒适。人心之所以激动不是因为他们毫无阻碍、如愿以偿地得到某个珍贵的东西，而是因为未能完全如愿，而在获得部分满足后又时刻担惊受怕唯恐再失去它。在贵族制社会，有钱人从未有过与自己现状完全不同的经历，所以根本不担心生活会有变化，几

without trouble and without apprehension, their faculties are turned elsewhere, and cling to more arduous and more lofty undertakings, which excite and engross their minds. Hence it is that, in the midst of physical gratifications, the members of an aristocracy often display a haughty contempt of these very enjoyments, and exhibit singular powers of endurance under the privation of them. All the revolutions which have ever shaken or destroyed aristocracies, have shown how easily men accustomed to superfluous luxuries can do without the necessaries of life; whereas men who have toiled to acquire a competency can hardly live after they have lost it.

If I turn my observation from the upper to the lower classes, I find analogous effects produced by opposite causes. Amongst a nation where aristocracy predominates in society, and keeps it stationary, the people in the end get as much accustomed to poverty as the rich to their opulence. The latter bestow no anxiety on their physical comforts, because they enjoy them without an effort; the former do not think of things which they despair of obtaining, and which they hardly know enough of to desire them. In communities of this kind, the imagination of the poor is driven to seek another world; the miseries of real life inclose it around, but it escapes from their control, and flies to seek its pleasures far beyond. When, on the contrary, the distinctions of ranks are confounded together and privileges are destroyed—when hereditary property is subdivided, and education and freedom widely diffused, the desire of acquiring the comforts of the world haunts the imagination of the poor, and the dread of losing them that of the rich. Many scanty fortunes spring up; those who possess them have a sufficient share of physical gratifications to conceive a taste for these pleasures—not enough to satisfy it. They never procure them without exertion, and they never indulge in them without apprehension. They are therefore always straining to pursue or to retain gratifications so delightful, so imperfect, so fugitive.

If I were to inquire what passion is most natural to men who are stimulated and circumscribed by the obscurity of their birth or the mediocrity of their fortune, I could discover none more peculiarly appropriate to their condition than this love of physical prosperity. The passion for physical comforts

乎想象不到还会有另外一种生活。生活的舒适对他们来说并不是生活的目的，只不过是一种生活方式，是理所应当享有的东西，所以从未对此多加思考。因为人们对于物质满足与生俱来的本能爱好如此轻而易举无忧无虑地得到满足，于是他们便将精力用到其他地方，执著于某些能让他们激动并全神贯注的更困难更高尚的事业。因此，贵族成员虽然身处物质享乐之中，但往往会对这些享乐表现出一种傲慢的轻视，而且在不得不放弃这些享乐的时候还会表现出惊人的忍耐力。所有曾经撼动或是摧毁贵族制度的革命，已经向我们证明过惯奢华生活的人忍受清贫的生活对他们而言不是什么难事，然而历经千辛万苦才过上好日子的人往往在失去之后则很难生活下去。

如果我将注意力从上层阶级转向下层阶级，也会发现类似的现象，但是其产生的原因会有所不同。在一个贵族制度居于统治地位，社会稳定的国家，人民最终会习惯于贫穷，就好像富人习惯于他们的富裕一样。后者之所以无须为物质享受担忧，是因为他们不必为此而努力；而前者之所以没有物质享乐的念头，是因为他们根本没有希望获得或是没有强烈的物质欲望。在这样的社会，穷人的想象力完全用于来世，现实生活的悲惨虽然将他的想象力包围，但是他可以摆脱它们的控制，想象来世的安乐。相反，当不同阶级相互融合，特权被取消，财产日益分散，教育和自由广泛传播的时候，渴望获得现世舒适生活的愿望开始在穷人的想象中不断浮现，而富人则开始不断害怕失去它。于是许多小康之家开始出现，这些过着小康生活的人已经充分体验到这样的物质享受，但是还不能让他们感到这种爱好已经得到完全满足。他们只有付出才能获得这样的享乐，而且在尽情享乐的时候还总是战战兢兢。因此，他们总是在努力追求或是保持一种如此令人愉悦却又无法获得充分满足的无常的享乐。

is essentially a passion of the middle classes: with those classes it grows and spreads, with them it preponderates. From them it mounts into the higher orders of society, and descends into the mass of the people. I never met in America with any citizen so poor as not to cast a glance of hope and envy on the enjoyments of the rich, or whose imagination did not possess itself by anticipation of those good things which fate still obstinately withheld from him. On the other hand, I never perceived amongst the wealthier inhabitants of the United States that proud contempt of physical gratifications which is sometimes to be met with even in the most opulent and dissolute aristocracies. Most of these wealthy persons were once poor; they have felt the sting of want; they were long a prey to adverse fortunes; and now that the victory is won, the passions which accompanied the contest have survived it: their minds are, as it were, intoxicated by the small enjoyments which they have pursued for forty years. Not but that in the United States, as elsewhere, there are a certain number of wealthy persons who, having come into their property by inheritance, possess, without exertion, an opulence they have not earned. But even these men are not less devotedly attached to the pleasures of material life. The love of well-being is now become the predominant taste of the nation; the great current of man's passions runs in that channel, and sweeps everything along in its course.

Chapter XI: Peculiar Effects Of The Love Of Physical Gratifications In Democratic Ages

It may be supposed, from what has just been said, that the love of physical gratifications must constantly urge the Americans to irregularities in morals, disturb the peace of families, and threaten the security of society at large. Such is not the case: the passion for physical gratifications produces in democracies effects very different from those which it occasions in aristocratic nations. It sometimes happens that, wearied with public affairs and sated with opulence, amidst the ruin of religious belief and the decline of the State, the heart of an aristocracy may by degrees be seduced to the pursuit of sensual enjoyments only. At other times the power of the monarch or the weakness of the people, without stripping the nobility of their fortune, compels them to stand aloof from

如果有人问我，对于受到出身卑微和家业平庸的影响和制约的人而言，哪种激情是最自然不过的，我的发现是人对物质享乐的爱好，而且除此之外无出其右。对于物质享受的热情是中产阶级最本质的激情。它随这个阶级的成长而成长，壮大而壮大，举足轻重而举足轻重。来自中产阶级的这种激情不断向社会上层阶级和下层人民大众之中扩散。在美国，我从未遇到一个不会对富人的享乐产生向往和羡慕的穷人，而且他们的想象也从未放弃期待，期待那份上天未曾赐予他们的财富。而另一方面，在美国的富有居民中，我从未察觉到他们表现出最富有最不羁的贵族身上时不时出现的那种对于物质享受的傲慢和不屑。在美国，这些有钱人大多原本贫困，曾经饱尝辛酸，长期与逆境斗争，如今取得胜利，而那份战斗的激情依旧没有退去，似乎依然陶醉于40年来他们始终追求的小小享乐。这并不是说美国与其他国家完全不同，在这里，也有一些富人，他们靠继承遗产毫不费力地过上奢侈的生活。但甚至是这些人对于物质生活享受的热情依旧不减。热爱物质享乐如今已经成为整个国家的主要爱好。这股人心所向的激情的狂潮将所有人卷入其中。

第十一章　物质享乐的爱好在民主时代的特殊影响

通过我刚刚的描述，人们可能会认为，对物质享乐的爱好必定会不断驱使美国人道德败坏、家庭不稳，最终危及社会安定。但事实并非如此。在民主社会对于物质享受的爱好产生的影响与其在贵族社会引起的后果大不相同。有时候，厌烦政务、贪财过度、失去信仰、国家衰败，会令贵族的心完全倒向物质享乐的追求。而另一些时候，由于王权的强大或是人民的软弱，贵族不得不远离政务，尽管他们依旧拥有财富，但是飞黄腾达之路却

the administration of affairs, and whilst the road to mighty enterprise is closed, abandons them to the inquietude of their own desires; they then fall back heavily upon themselves, and seek in the pleasures of the body oblivion of their former greatness. When the members of an aristocratic body are thus exclusively devoted to the pursuit of physical gratifications, they commonly concentrate in that direction all the energy which they derive from their long experience of power. Such men are not satisfied with the pursuit of comfort; they require sumptuous depravity and splendid corruption. The worship they pay the senses is a gorgeous one; and they seem to vie with each other in the art of degrading their own natures. The stronger, the more famous, and the more free an aristocracy has been, the more depraved will it then become; and however brilliant may have been the lustre of its virtues, I dare predict that they will always be surpassed by the splendor of its vices.

The taste for physical gratifications leads a democratic people into no such excesses. The love of well-being is there displayed as a tenacious, exclusive, universal passion; but its range is confined. To build enormous palaces, to conquer or to mimic nature, to ransack the world in order to gratify the passions of a man, is not thought of: but to add a few roods of land to your field, to plant an orchard, to enlarge a dwelling, to be always making life more comfortable and convenient, to avoid trouble, and to satisfy the smallest wants without effort and almost without cost. These are small objects, but the soul clings to them; it dwells upon them closely and day by day, till they at last shut out the rest of the world, and sometimes intervene between itself and heaven.

This, it may be said, can only be applicable to those members of the community who are in humble circumstances; wealthier individuals will display tastes akin to those which belonged to them in aristocratic ages. I contest the proposition: in point of physical gratifications, the most opulent members of a democracy will not display tastes very different from those of the people; whether it be that, springing from the people, they really share those tastes, or that they esteem it a duty to submit to them. In democratic society the sensuality of the public has taken a moderate and tranquil course,

被关闭，所以他们满腹牢骚。于是，只好重回自己的小圈子，寻求身体上的享受而将曾经的伟大抛诸脑后。因此，当贵族成员只追求物质享受的时候，往往会将长期掌权积蓄的所有精力都用在享乐上。这样的人不会只满足于追求享乐，他们需要的是穷奢极侈，腐败堕落。他们极度崇拜感觉，似乎在互相攀比自我堕落之术。一个贵族越是强大，越是荣耀，越是自由，就变得越发堕落。而且无论他的德行曾经多么光芒四射，我敢断言，这些光芒迟早会被其邪恶的魔光所掩盖。

物质享乐的爱好则不会让民主国家的人们做出如此过分的举动。在这里，对幸福的热爱尽管是强烈的独一无二的普遍激情，却受到一定限制。在这里，为了满足一人享乐耗尽天下之财兴建宏大宫殿、修葺巧夺天工花园的事情不会发生。人们想的不过是多买几亩良田，经营一个果园，扩建一下宅邸，不过是让生活更加舒适便捷，少生是非，能够毫不费力少花钱满足小小的需要，仅此而已。这些都是小事情，但是人人梦寐以求。人们天天想的时时念的就是这些，最终将世间其他的一切抛诸脑后，有时候，甚至成为仅次于上帝的存在。

也许有人会说，这样的说法只适合那些生活环境不好的社会成员，而富裕的人会表现出与贵族时代类似的爱好。对此我不敢苟同。就物质享受的爱好而言，民主社会最富有的人与这些人不会有丝毫的不同，因为他们不是来自人民，就是认为自己应当服从人民的爱好。在民主社会，公众的欲望以一种温和平静的方式表现出来，而且所有人都要与此保持一致。在这里，偏离常规去做坏事或是好事都同样困难。因此，生活在民主社会的富人更注重满足小小的需要，而不是纵情享乐。他们只求满足各种小愿望，而不放情纵欲。因此，他们往往表现得活力不足而不会放荡不羁。民主时代人们对物质享受的特殊爱好，与

to which all are bound to conform: it is as difficult to depart from the common rule by one's vices as by one's virtues. Rich men who live amidst democratic nations are therefore more intent on providing for their smallest wants than for their extraordinary enjoyments; they gratify a number of petty desires, without indulging in any great irregularities of passion: thus they are more apt to become enervated than debauched. The especial taste which the men of democratic ages entertain for physical enjoyments is not naturally opposed to the principles of public order; nay, it often stands in need of order that it may be gratified. Nor is it adverse to regularity of morals, for good morals contribute to public tranquillity and are favorable to industry. It may even be frequently combined with a species of religious morality: men wish to be as well off as they can in this world, without foregoing their chance of another. Some physical gratifications cannot be indulged in without crime; from such they strictly abstain. The enjoyment of others is sanctioned by religion and morality; to these the heart, the imagination, and life itself are unreservedly given up; till, in snatching at these lesser gifts, men lose sight of those more precious possessions which constitute the glory and the greatness of mankind. The reproach I address to the principle of equality, is not that it leads men away in the pursuit of forbidden enjoyments, but that it absorbs them wholly in quest of those which are allowed. By these means, a kind of virtuous materialism may ultimately be established in the world, which would not corrupt, but enervate the soul, and noiselessly unbend its springs of action.

Chapter XII: Causes Of Fanatical Enthusiasm In Some Americans
Although the desire of acquiring the good things of this world is the prevailing passion of the American people, certain momentary outbreaks occur, when their souls seem suddenly to burst the bonds of matter by which they are restrained, and to soar impetuously towards heaven. In all the States of the Union, but especially in the half-peopled country of the Far West, wandering preachers may be met with who hawk about the word of God from place to place. Whole families—old men, women, and children—cross rough passes and untrodden wilds, coming from a great distance, to join

公共秩序当然并不对立。甚至有时候这种需要的满足还往往需要秩序。而且它也并不与道德为敌，因为良好的道德有助于公共安定，有利于工业发展。它甚至往往可以和宗教道德结合起来。人们希望他们在现世能够尽量得到满足，也不放弃到来世寻找机会。有些物质享乐只有通过犯罪才能获得，对此人们必须时刻克制。还有其他一些物质享乐是宗教和道德所允许的，人们对于这类享乐毫无例外地去追求、想象并促其实现，但是他们在努力获得这些享乐的过程中，却忽略了那些可以让人类荣耀和伟大的更为宝贵的享乐。我之所以斥责平等，并不是因为它促使人们追求不被允许的享乐，而是因为它让人们太过于投入追求获得允许的享乐。这样，一种温存的唯物主义最终会在世界上出现，它不会腐蚀而是净化人们的灵魂，并悄无声息地缓解一切紧张的精神。

第十二章　一些美国人唯灵主义的原因
尽管获得现世幸福的渴望是美国人的普遍热情，但是这个渴望也有暂时中断的时候。此时，人们的灵魂似乎突然冲破将它们牢牢捆绑的枷锁，冲向天堂。在联邦的所有各州，特别是在人烟稀少的西部各州，巡回教士不断从一个地方到另一个地方向人们宣讲上帝的福音。全家人，老人、妇女和儿童，不惜跋山涉水，去很远的地方听教士们布道。在那里，他们专心于教士的布道，一听就是几天几夜，完全把正常的工作丢到一边，甚至忘记了吃喝和睡眠。在美国社会里，你到处都会看到一些几乎在欧洲都看不到的唯灵主义者。在美国，一些奇怪的教派会时不时出现，他们试图开辟一条直通永久乐境的特别之路。宗教的狂热在美国非常普遍。

a camp-meeting, where they totally forget for several days and nights, in listening to these discourses, the cares of business and even the most urgent wants of the body. Here and there, in the midst of American society, you meet with men, full of a fanatical and almost wild enthusiasm, which hardly exists in Europe. From time to time strange sects arise, which endeavor to strike out extraordinary paths to eternal happiness. Religious insanity is very common in the United States.

Nor ought these facts to surprise us. It was not man who implanted in himself the taste for what is infinite and the love of what is immortal: those lofty instincts are not the offspring of his capricious will; their steadfast foundation is fixed in human nature, and they exist in spite of his efforts. He may cross and distort them—destroy them he cannot. The soul has wants which must be satisfied; and whatever pains be taken to divert it from itself, it soon grows weary, restless, and disquieted amidst the enjoyments of sense. If ever the faculties of the great majority of mankind were exclusively bent upon the pursuit of material objects, it might be anticipated that an amazing reaction would take place in the souls of some men. They would drift at large in the world of spirits, for fear of remaining shackled by the close bondage of the body.

It is not then wonderful if, in the midst of a community whose thoughts tend earthward, a small number of individuals are to be found who turn their looks to heaven. I should be surprised if mysticism did not soon make some advance amongst a people solely engaged in promoting its own worldly welfare. It is said that the deserts of the Thebaid were peopled by the persecutions of the emperors and the massacres of the Circus; I should rather say that it was by the luxuries of Rome and the Epicurean philosophy of Greece. If their social condition, their present circumstances, and their laws did not confine the minds of the Americans so closely to the pursuit of worldly welfare, it is probable that they would display more reserve and more experience whenever their attention is turned to things immaterial, and that they would check themselves without difficulty. But they feel imprisoned within bounds which they will apparently never be allowed to pass. As soon as they have passed these bounds, their minds know not where to fix themselves, and they often rush unrestrained beyond the range of common-sense.

　　对此我们无须惊讶。人们对于永生的爱好和不死的热爱并非是后天的。这些崇高的本能并不是人意志的产物，它们的基础甚至已经在人性之中，而且不依人的努力而存在。人们也许可以阻止它们的发展或是改变它们的形式，但是无法摧毁它们。心灵有必须获得满足的需要，而且无论你做出怎样的努力想要分散其注意力，但不久它就会因感官活动的影响表现出厌烦、不安或是激动。如果大多数人都致力于追求物质享受，可以料想一些人的心灵必然会做出惊人的反应。他们将会驰骋在广阔的精神世界，唯恐再受到肉体的束缚。

　　因此，在只考虑现世的社会中，出现少数一些一心只向往天堂的人并不足为奇。让我感到惊讶的是，为什么神秘主义未能很快在一个只顾自身现世幸福的国家中有所作为。有人说，这是迫害和大屠杀的结果，就好像罗马的皇帝把他们的迫害和在圆形大剧场的屠杀带到埃及的底比斯沙漠一般。而我宁可说这是罗马的奢侈和希腊的伊壁鸠鲁哲学使然。即使美国人的社会平等、地理位置以及法律并没有将美国人的思想紧紧束缚于对物质幸福的追求，无论他们的注意力转向对任何非物质东西的追求，他们可能会日益积累起知识和经验，轻而易举地实现自我改进。但是，他们已经明显感到自己被一些不可逾越的东西束缚。然而一旦跨过这些束缚，他们的精神又不知该何去何从，于是他们往往会胡乱冲撞，以致做出些有违常理的事。

第十三章　美国人身处幸福却心神不安的原因

　　在旧大陆某些偏远的角落，有时依然可以看到一些在普遍的动荡中被人们所遗忘的小

Chapter XIII: Causes Of The Restless Spirit Of Americans In The Midst Of Their Prosperity

In certain remote corners of the Old World you may still sometimes stumble upon a small district which seems to have been forgotten amidst the general tumult, and to have remained stationary whilst everything around it was in motion. The inhabitants are for the most part extremely ignorant and poor; they take no part in the business of the country, and they are frequently oppressed by the government; yet their countenances are generally placid, and their spirits light. In America I saw the freest and most enlightened men, placed in the happiest circumstances which the world affords: it seemed to me as if a cloud habitually hung upon their brow, and I thought them serious and almost sad even in their pleasures. The chief reason of this contrast is that the former do not think of the ills they endure—the latter are forever brooding over advantages they do not possess. It is strange to see with what feverish ardor the Americans pursue their own welfare; and to watch the vague dread that constantly torments them lest they should not have chosen the shortest path which may lead to it. A native of the United States clings to this world's goods as if he were certain never to die; and he is so hasty in grasping at all within his reach, that one would suppose he was constantly afraid of not living long enough to enjoy them. He clutches everything, he holds nothing fast, but soon loosens his grasp to pursue fresh gratifications.

In the United States a man builds a house to spend his latter years in it, and he sells it before the roof is on: he plants a garden, and lets it just as the trees are coming into bearing: he brings a field into tillage, and leaves other men to gather the crops: he embraces a profession, and gives it up: he settles in a place, which he soon afterwards leaves, to carry his changeable longings elsewhere. If his private affairs leave him any leisure, he instantly plunges into the vortex of politics; and if at the end of a year of unremitting labor he finds he has a few days' vacation, his eager curiosity whirls him over the vast extent of the United States, and he will travel fifteen hundred miles in a few days, to shake off his happiness. Death at length overtakes him, but it is before he is weary of his bootless chase of that complete felicity which is forever on the wing.

村镇，在周围的一切都不断前进的时候，它依旧平静如水。在这些地方，大部分居民都极为无知和贫穷，他们不参与国家事务，不断受到政府的压迫，但是他们表情依旧平静，心情保持舒畅。在美国，我见到一些最自由最文明的人，生活在世界上最幸福的环境，但是在我看来他们的眉宇之间似乎总是阴云密布，甚至在他们享乐的时候也总是满脸凝重，心事重重。之所以会出现这样的对比，主要是因为前者根本不考虑自己不幸的处境，而后者却一直想着自己没有得到的好处。看着美国人追求自身幸福的那份狂热，以及不断折磨着他们的唯恐找不到致富捷径的隐忧，实在让人觉得奇怪。美国人对世界上所有美好东西的那份执著，让人觉得似乎他们可以长生不老；他们急于一下子把握住所有的东西，却又好像他们总是唯恐此生没有命享用。他想要把握一切，却没有一样能抓牢，于是不久便松手开始追求新的满足。

在美国，一个人建造一所房子原打算在此养老，却在房子封顶前将其出售；他开辟一片果园，却又在树木即将结果的时候将其租出去；他耕种一片土地，却在行将收获的时候让别人来收割；他从事一项事业，但随后又会放弃；在一个地方定居，不久便又离开，带着不断变换的渴望迁往他处。在料理私人事务之余，他还会涉足政界；如果在一年辛苦劳作之后有几天闲暇，他还会让自己度几天假，强烈好奇心的驱使他游历美国各地，在短短几天内行程数千里大饱眼福。死亡最终降临，让他不得不在尚无倦意之前，眼看着追求完美幸福的事业未尽而撒手人寰。

乍一看，生活在如此富裕环境中的如此幸福的人们表现得如此不安很是令人惊讶。然

At first sight there is something surprising in this strange unrest of so many happy men, restless in the midst of abundance. The spectacle itself is however as old as the world; the novelty is to see a whole people furnish an exemplification of it. Their taste for physical gratifications must be regarded as the original source of that secret inquietude which the actions of the Americans betray, and of that inconstancy of which they afford fresh examples every day. He who has set his heart exclusively upon the pursuit of worldly welfare is always in a hurry, for he has but a limited time at his disposal to reach it, to grasp it, and to enjoy it. The recollection of the brevity of life is a constant spur to him. Besides the good things which he possesses, he every instant fancies a thousand others which death will prevent him from trying if he does not try them soon. This thought fills him with anxiety, fear, and regret, and keeps his mind in ceaseless trepidation, which leads him perpetually to change his plans and his abode. If in addition to the taste for physical well-being a social condition be superadded, in which the laws and customs make no condition permanent, here is a great additional stimulant to this restlessness of temper. Men will then be seen continually to change their track, for fear of missing the shortest cut to happiness. It may readily be conceived that if men, passionately bent upon physical gratifications, desire eagerly, they are also easily discouraged: as their ultimate object is to enjoy, the means to reach that object must be prompt and easy, or the trouble of acquiring the gratification would be greater than the gratification itself. Their prevailing frame of mind then is at once ardent and relaxed, violent and enervated. Death is often less dreaded than perseverance in continuous efforts to one end.

The equality of conditions leads by a still straighter road to several of the effects which I have here described. When all the privileges of birth and fortune are abolished, when all professions are accessible to all, and a man's own energies may place him at the top of any one of them, an easy and unbounded career seems open to his ambition, and he will readily persuade himself that he is born to no vulgar destinies. But this is an erroneous notion, which is corrected by daily experience. The same equality which allows every citizen to conceive these lofty hopes, renders all the citizens less able to realize them: it circumscribes their powers on every side, whilst it gives freer scope to their desires.

而这样的情形却是自古有之，但是整个民族都是如此却是第一例。他们对于物质享受的爱好被认为是美国人一举一动所暴露的内心不安和每天用实际行动证明的反复无常的原始来源。一心追求现世幸福的人总是显得迫不及待，因为他可供自己支配的用来寻求、抓住和享用幸福的时间有限。一想到人生苦短，他就要快马加鞭。除了他本已拥有的美好事物，他时刻惦记着数以千计的美好东西，害怕如不赶快，死亡会让自己永远失去享有的机会。这样的想法让他满心忧虑、恐惧和遗憾，让他的精神始终处于不安的状态，促使他不断地改变自己的计划和居所。除了对物质生活享乐的爱好，法律和习惯始终变换的社会状况，也是人心不安的另一大刺激。于是，人们不断变换人生轨迹，唯恐找不到获得幸福的最佳捷径。不难设想，如果热情地专注于物质享受的人们期望很高，那么他们也很容易感到失望。因为他们的终极目标是享受，所以达到目的的手段必须简单快捷，否则获得享乐的付出要超过享乐本身。于是，人们的心情普遍是既狂热又萎靡，既紧张又消极。死亡往往不及为实现目标不断努力的坚持来得可怕。

平等会对我上述所说的各种效果产生更加直接的影响。当所有出身和财富带来的特权被全部废除，各行各业对所有人平等开放，任何人都能凭借自己的能力在本行业出类拔萃时，拥有雄心的人感到无限光明的前程在面前展开，感到自己命中注定能干出一番大事业。但这是一个可以靠经验矫正的错误想法。让每个公民产生这种高尚想法的平等，让所有人无法感觉到自己的存在，从各方面限制着人们的力量，但同时却让他们的欲望不断扩大。人们不但本身软弱无力，而且每迈出一步都会碰到以前从未料到的巨大阻碍。他们虽

Not only are they themselves powerless, but they are met at every step by immense obstacles, which they did not at first perceive. They have swept away the privileges of some of their fellow-creatures which stood in their way, but they have opened the door to universal competition: the barrier has changed its shape rather than its position. When men are nearly alike, and all follow the same track, it is very difficult for any one individual to walk quick and cleave a way through the dense throng which surrounds and presses him. This constant strife between the propensities springing from the equality of conditions and the means it supplies to satisfy them, harasses and wearies the mind.

It is possible to conceive men arrived at a degree of freedom which should completely content them; they would then enjoy their independence without anxiety and without impatience. But men will never establish any equality with which they can be contented. Whatever efforts a people may make, they will never succeed in reducing all the conditions of society to a perfect level; and even if they unhappily attained that absolute and complete depression, the inequality of minds would still remain, which, coming directly from the hand of God, will forever escape the laws of man. However democratic then the social state and the political constitution of a people may be, it is certain that every member of the community will always find out several points about him which command his own position; and we may foresee that his looks will be doggedly fixed in that direction. When inequality of conditions is the common law of society, the most marked inequalities do not strike the eye: when everything is nearly on the same level, the slightest are marked enough to hurt it. Hence the desire of equality always becomes more insatiable in proportion as equality is more complete.

Amongst democratic nations men easily attain a certain equality of conditions: they can never attain the equality they desire. It perpetually retires from before them, yet without hiding itself from their sight, and in retiring draws them on. At every moment they think they are about to grasp it; it escapes at every moment from their hold. They are near enough to see its charms, but too far off to enjoy them; and before they have fully tasted its delights they die. To these causes must be attributed that strange melancholy which oftentimes will haunt the inhabitants of democratic countries in the midst of their abundance, and that disgust at life which sometimes seizes upon them in the midst of

然已经将阻碍自己前进的某些同胞的特权扫荡一空，却开启了普遍竞争的大门。曾经的障碍不过是换了个形式卷土重来而已。当人们越来越接近彼此，走在同一条道路上的时候，任何一个人都难以快速前进，在四周密集的人群中开辟一条道路穿行而过。平等带来的对享乐的追求和用以满足这些享乐的手段之间的不断冲突，折磨着人们的精神。

可以想象，人一旦到达能令自己完全满足的一定自由的地步，必然可以无忧无虑地立即享受他们的独立自主。但是人永远也无法得到能令自己感到满足的平等。无论一个民族多么努力，他们始终无法成功建立起完全平等的社会条件。即使有一天真的出现这种完全平等的局面，源自上帝之手的思想不平等依然会存在，任何人间法律都会对其无可奈何。于是，无论一个国家的社会状况和政治制度多么民主，可以肯定每个社会成员依然会始终感到在某些方面受制于人。我们可以预见，他们的视线会始终盯着这个方向。当不平等成为社会的普遍法则，最显眼的不平等也不会引起人们的注意。当所有一切几乎处在同一水平，哪怕最微不足道的不平等也让人难以忍受。因此，随着平等越来越趋于完美，平等的愿望则越来越难以满足。

在民主国家，人们很容易获得的一定程度的平等，但永远无法得到他们渴望的平等。这样的平等在人们眼前溜走，但又没有离开人们的视线，就在不远处。人们时刻觉得它唾手可得，却又总是在最后一刻让它溜走。人们离它近得可以看到它熠熠的光芒，却又远得无法弄到手，于是人们在即将尝到它甜头的时候离开人世。时常萦绕在民主国家富裕居民心头的奇怪忧郁，以及他们在平静安逸生活中所表现出的厌世情绪，都应当归因于此。在

calm and easy circumstances. Complaints are made in France that the number of suicides increases; in America suicide is rare, but insanity is said to be more common than anywhere else. These are all different symptoms of the same disease. The Americans do not put an end to their lives, however disquieted they may be, because their religion forbids it; and amongst them materialism may be said hardly to exist, notwithstanding the general passion for physical gratification. The will resists—reason frequently gives way. In democratic ages enjoyments are more intense than in the ages of aristocracy, and especially the number of those who partake in them is larger: but, on the other hand, it must be admitted that man's hopes and his desires are oftener blasted, the soul is more stricken and perturbed, and care itself more keen.

Chapter XIV: Taste For Physical Gratifications United In America To Love Of Freedom And Attention To Public Affairs

When a democratic state turns to absolute monarchy, the activity which was before directed to public and to private affairs is all at once centred upon the latter: the immediate consequence is, for some time, great physical prosperity; but this impulse soon slackens, and the amount of productive industry is checked. I know not if a single trading or manufacturing people can be cited, from the Tyrians down to the Florentines and the English, who were not a free people also. There is therefore a close bond and necessary relation between these two elements—freedom and productive industry. This proposition is generally true of all nations, but especially of democratic nations. I have already shown that men who live in ages of equality continually require to form associations in order to procure the things they covet; and, on the other hand, I have shown how great political freedom improves and diffuses the art of association. Freedom, in these ages, is therefore especially favorable to the production of wealth; nor is it difficult to perceive that despotism is especially adverse to the same result. The nature of despotic power in democratic ages is not to be fierce or cruel, but minute and meddling. Despotism of this kind, though it does not trample on humanity, is directly opposed to the genius of commerce and the pursuits of industry.

法国，人们抱怨自杀的人数不断上升，而在美国则很罕见，但这里的精神失常者却比任何地方的都多。这些都是同一种顽疾的不同症状。无论美国人多么心神不安，都不会终结自己的生命，因为他们的信仰不允许这样做。尽管人们普遍追求物质享受，但是在他们中间几乎从来没有唯物主义。人们的意志坚强但是往往理性薄弱。在民主时代，享乐比贵族时代更多，而且特别是可以参加享乐的人数更多。但是另一方面，必须承认，在民主时代人们的希望和欲望更容易破灭，灵魂也更容易激动和不安，忧郁感也更为深重。

第十四章　美国人如何将对物质享受的爱好和对自由的热爱以及对公共事务的关注结合起来

当一个民主国家退变回专制君主国家，人们原来在公私事务上表现的积极性立刻集中到后者。在最初的一段时间，会立即呈现出巨大的物质繁荣，但是不久这股冲劲就会放缓，生产的发展也会停滞。我不知道是否能从泰尔人到佛罗伦萨人和英国人之中，找到一个经营工商业的民族不是自由民族的例子。因此，自由和实业之间一定存在和某种紧密的必然联系。对于所有国家一般都是如此，而且民主国家尤其如此。我已经说过，生活在平等时代的人需要不断通过结社来获得他们觊觎的东西，而另一方面，我也说过，广大的政治自由会完善和普及结社艺术。因此，在这样的时代，特别有利于财富的生产，而且也很容易注意到专制对财富生产特别有害。在民主时代，专制权力本质并非是凶狠和残暴，而是烦琐和干扰。这种形式的专制，尽管不会践踏人性，是会直接压制商业精神和对工业的追求。

Thus the men of democratic ages require to be free in order more readily to procure those physical enjoyments for which they are always longing. It sometimes happens, however, that the excessive taste they conceive for these same enjoyments abandons them to the first master who appears. The passion for worldly welfare then defeats itself, and, without perceiving it, throws the object of their desires to a greater distance.

There is, indeed, a most dangerous passage in the history of a democratic people. When the taste for physical gratifications amongst such a people has grown more rapidly than their education and their experience of free institutions, the time will come when men are carried away, and lose all self-restraint, at the sight of the new possessions they are about to lay hold upon. In their intense and exclusive anxiety to make a fortune, they lose sight of the close connection which exists between the private fortune of each of them and the prosperity of all. It is not necessary to do violence to such a people in order to strip them of the rights they enjoy; they themselves willingly loosen their hold. The discharge of political duties appears to them to be a troublesome annoyance, which diverts them from their occupations and business. If they be required to elect representatives, to support the Government by personal service, to meet on public business, they have no time—they cannot waste their precious time in useless engagements: such idle amusements are unsuited to serious men who are engaged with the more important interests of life. These people think they are following the principle of self-interest, but the idea they entertain of that principle is a very rude one; and the better to look after what they call their business, they neglect their chief business, which is to remain their own masters.

As the citizens who work do not care to attend to public business, and as the class which might devote its leisure to these duties has ceased to exist, the place of the Government is, as it were, unfilled. If at that critical moment some able and ambitious man grasps the supreme power, he will find the road to every kind of usurpation open before him. If he does but attend for some time to the material prosperity of the country, no more will be demanded of him. Above all he must insure public tranquillity: men who are possessed by the passion of physical gratification generally find out that the

因此，民主国家的人们需要获得自由，才能得到他们长久以来梦寐以求的物质享受。然而，有时候，他们对这些享乐的过度爱好，一旦遭遇强权便会屈服。于是，追求现世幸福的激情便会消失，不知不觉中将原来的渴望丢到一边。

的确，在民主国家的历史上有一个极为危险的阶段。当对物质享受的爱好的发展大大超越教育和自由的习惯时，人们就会失控，无法自制的时代就会到来，于是他们一看到新的东西就想要据为己有。因为他们一心一意想要发财，便对个人财富和共同繁荣之间的密切关系视而不见。对于这样的民族，无须使用暴力剥夺他们享有的权利，他们会心甘情愿地自动奉上。政治义务似乎对他们而言不过是让人心烦的事情，让他们无法专注于自己的职业和生意。如果他们需要选出代表亲自帮助政府做事或是负担一些公共工作，他们会说没时间，因为他们不愿将自己宝贵的时间浪费在参与毫无收益的事情上。在他们看来，这不过是无聊的消遣，根本不适合认真追求生活中重大利益的人。这些人认为他们是在遵循个人利益的原则，但是他们对这一原则的理解实在是粗浅。而且他们对自己的事业照顾得越好，他们就越是会忽略他们的头等大事，即自己做自己的主人。

因为人们只关注个人工作，不参与公共事务，还因为可以奉献自己的时间投入这些工作的阶级已经不复存在，政府中的许多职位出现空缺，无人填补。如果在这样至关重要的时刻，某个有能力的野心家大权在握，他会发现篡夺各项大权的道路已经在他面前敞开。如果他在一段时间内能够专注搞好国家的物质繁荣，所有一切就会迎刃而解。首先他必须要确保社会安定。已被物质享受的热情所掌控的人们，普遍会在注意到自由可以促进物质

turmoil of freedom disturbs their welfare, before they discover how freedom itself serves to promote it. If the slightest rumor of public commotion intrudes into the petty pleasures of private life, they are aroused and alarmed by it. The fear of anarchy perpetually haunts them, and they are always ready to fling away their freedom at the first disturbance.

I readily admit that public tranquillity is a great good; but at the same time I cannot forget that all nations have been enslaved by being kept in good order. Certainly it is not to be inferred that nations ought to despise public tranquillity; but that state ought not to content them. A nation which asks nothing of its government but the maintenance of order is already a slave at heart—the slave of its own well-being, awaiting but the hand that will bind it. By such a nation the despotism of faction is not less to be dreaded than the despotism of an individual. When the bulk of the community is engrossed by private concerns, the smallest parties need not despair of getting the upper hand in public affairs. At such times it is not rare to see upon the great stage of the world, as we see at our theatres, a multitude represented by a few players, who alone speak in the name of an absent or inattentive crowd: they alone are in action whilst all are stationary; they regulate everything by their own caprice; they change the laws, and tyrannize at will over the manners of the country; and then men wonder to see into how small a number of weak and worthless hands a great people may fall.

Hitherto the Americans have fortunately escaped all the perils which I have just pointed out; and in this respect they are really deserving of admiration. Perhaps there is no country in the world where fewer idle men are to be met with than in America, or where all who work are more eager to promote their own welfare. But if the passion of the Americans for physical gratifications is vehement, at least it is not indiscriminating; and reason, though unable to restrain it, still directs its course. An American attends to his private concerns as if he were alone in the world, and the next minute he gives himself up to the common weal as if he had forgotten them. At one time he seems animated by the most selfish cupidity, at another by the most lively patriotism. The human heart cannot be thus divided. The inhabitants of the United States alternately display so strong and so similar a passion for their own welfare and for their freedom, that it may be supposed that these passions are united and

享受之前，便首先发现自由的混乱会影响到他们的利益。如果公众小小的骚动对他们私人生活的小安乐稍有影响，他们便会立刻警觉起来，坐卧不宁。由于对无政府状态的恐惧不断困扰着他们，所以一旦出现骚乱他们便随时准备放弃自由。

我完全认同，社会的安宁是一件大好事。但是同时我不会忘记所有的国家在被奴役之前都曾有一段秩序良好的时期。当然，并不能够据此推断，所有的国家都可以轻视社会安定，但是一个国家只有安定社会还并不够。如果一个民族对于政府的要求只有维护秩序，那么他们就已经有了一颗奴隶的心，即他们已成为自己财富的奴隶，等待着束手就擒。这样的一个国家不但要提防个人专制还要提防党派专制。当社会大众只专注个人私利的时候，最微不足道的政党也有机会在公共事务中取得上风。这样的事情在世界政治大舞台上也绝非罕见，就好像在我们自己的政治舞台看到的那样，少数几个人代表大多数站在舞台上，他们以未出席或是不关心政治的群众的名义发言，他们是唯一活跃的人，至于其他人都静止不动。他们随心所欲地规定一切，改变法律，肆意践踏民情，于是人们会惊讶于一个如此伟大的民族竟然会被这几个无能之辈玩弄于股掌。

迄今为止，美国人已经幸运地避过我所指出的所有的危机，在这一点上，他们的确值得羡慕。世界上也许没有哪个国家能够像美国一样游手好闲的人如此少，所有工作的人都如此积极地追求物质财富。但是尽管美国人追求物质享受的热情非常强烈，他们却很少肆意妄为。他们的理智虽然无法抑制他们的热情，但是可以对他们的热情加以指导。一个美国人在关注自己事情的时候，似乎这世界上只有他自己，而下一刻当他热心公益的时候，

mingled in some part of their character. And indeed the Americans believe their freedom to be the best instrument and surest safeguard of their welfare: they are attached to the one by the other. They by no means think that they are not called upon to take a part in the public weal; they believe, on the contrary, that their chief business is to secure for themselves a government which will allow them to acquire the things they covet, and which will not debar them from the peaceful enjoyment of those possessions which they have acquired.

Chapter XV: That Religious Belief Sometimes Turns The Thoughts Of The Americans To Immaterial Pleasures

In the United States, on the seventh day of every week, the trading and working life of the nation seems suspended; all noises cease; a deep tranquillity, say rather the solemn calm of meditation, succeeds the turmoil of the week, and the soul resumes possession and contemplation of itself. Upon this day the marts of traffic are deserted; every member of the community, accompanied by his children, goes to church, where he listens to strange language which would seem unsuited to his ear. He is told of the countless evils caused by pride and covetousness: he is reminded of the necessity of checking his desires, of the finer pleasures which belong to virtue alone, and of the true happiness which attends it. On his return home, he does not turn to the ledgers of his calling, but he opens the book of Holy Scripture; there he meets with sublime or affecting descriptions of the greatness and goodness of the Creator, of the infinite magnificence of the handiwork of God, of the lofty destinies of man, of his duties, and of his immortal privileges. Thus it is that the American at times steals an hour from himself; and laying aside for a while the petty passions which agitate his life, and the ephemeral interests which engross it, he strays at once into an ideal world, where all is great, eternal, and pure.

I have endeavored to point out in another part of this work the causes to which the maintenance of the political institutions of the Americans is attributable; and religion appeared to be one of the most prominent amongst them. I am now treating of the Americans in an individual capacity, and I again observe that religion is not less useful to each citizen than to the whole State. The Americans show,

似乎又完全忘记了自己。有时他好像受到最强烈的利己主义的驱使，有时又受到崇高的爱国主义的推动。照常理，人心是不能这样一分为二的。美国的居民却将他们如此强烈的热情不断交替地用于追求自己的个人利益和自由。也许可以认为这些热情已经合二为一融为一体，成为他们性格的一部分。而且美国人的确认为他们的自由是他们获得幸福的最佳工具和最有力的保障。他们将两者联系起来。他们从不认为参与公益事业是分外的事，恰恰相反，他们认为自己的主要事情就是确保能够有一个政府，它不但可以让他们的追求得到满足，而且不会妨碍他们宁静地享受获得的财富。

第十五章　宗教信仰有时会让美国人的心灵转向非物质享乐

在美国，每周第七天，全国的工商业活动似乎都处于停滞状态，所有的喧闹消失，迎来一片宁静，也许说是一段庄严的凝思时刻更合适。在喧闹的一周之后，灵魂回归自我，进行沉思自省。在这一天，市场上一片萧瑟，每个社会成员都在孩子的陪伴下前往教堂，在这里他倾听似乎与他并不相称的布道，聆听骄傲和贪婪带来的无数害处。传教士的话会提醒他，人要抑制自己的欲望，只有美德能让人获得高尚的享乐，应该追求真正的幸福。当他回到家里，并不会先打开自己的账簿，而是会翻开《圣经》，看到对造物主的伟大与善良，对上帝无限壮丽的丰功伟绩，乃至对人类的最后归宿、职责和追求永生的权利的美好动人的描绘。因此，美国人就是这样时不时地挤出一些时间，暂时将生活上的小小欲望和转瞬即逝的利益搁置一边，让自己沉浸在一个伟大、永生、纯净的理想世界。

by their practice, that they feel the high necessity of imparting morality to democratic communities by means of religion. What they think of themselves in this respect is a truth of which every democratic nation ought to be thoroughly persuaded.

I do not doubt that the social and political constitution of a people predisposes them to adopt a certain belief and certain tastes, which afterwards flourish without difficulty amongst them; whilst the same causes may divert a people from certain opinions and propensities, without any voluntary effort, and, as it were, without any distinct consciousness, on their part. The whole art of the legislator is correctly to discern beforehand these natural inclinations of communities of men, in order to know whether they should be assisted, or whether it may not be necessary to check them. For the duties incumbent on the legislator differ at different times; the goal towards which the human race ought ever to be tending is alone stationary; the means of reaching it are perpetually to be varied.

If I had been born in an aristocratic age, in the midst of a nation where the hereditary wealth of some, and the irremediable penury of others, should equally divert men from the idea of bettering their condition, and hold the soul as it were in a state of torpor fixed on the contemplation of another world, I should then wish that it were possible for me to rouse that people to a sense of their wants; I should seek to discover more rapid and more easy means for satisfying the fresh desires which I might have awakened; and, directing the most strenuous efforts of the human mind to physical pursuits, I should endeavor to stimulate it to promote the well-being of man. If it happened that some men were immoderately incited to the pursuit of riches, and displayed an excessive liking for physical gratifications, I should not be alarmed; these peculiar symptoms would soon be absorbed in the general aspect of the people.

The attention of the legislators of democracies is called to other cares. Give democratic nations education and freedom, and leave them alone. They will soon learn to draw from this world all the benefits which it can afford; they will improve each of the useful arts, and will day by day render life more comfortable, more convenient, and more easy. Their social condition naturally urges them in

在这部著作的上卷我曾着重指出美国人政治制度长久稳定的原因，并将宗教视为主要原因之一。现在，我要研究的是宗教对于个人的影响，而且我发现宗教对于每个公民的作用丝毫不亚于整个国家。美国人用自己的行动证明，宗教是将道德引入民主社会极为必要的手段。他们对这一问题的看法，应该是每个民主国家都应领悟的真理。

我不怀疑，一个国家的社会和政治制度，会注定他们产生一定的信仰和爱好，而且在产生之后会迅速发展壮大。然而这些因素同样也可以不费吹灰之力甚至在不知不觉之中让一个国家放弃某些观念和倾向。立法者的才华就在于能够提前认识到人类社会这些天然趋势，从而了解到底是应该推波助澜，还是应该加以遏制。在不同的时代立法者担负的职责也不尽相同，因为人类所追求的目标并非一成不变，而且用以实现目标的手段也不断变化。

如果我出生在贵族时代，一个一些人世代荣华而另一些人辈辈贫困的国家，以至于所有的人都不再想要改变自己的境遇，麻木不仁，将所有的希望寄托于来世。那么，我真想挺身而出唤起人们认识到自己的需要，我会试图找到更快捷方便的手段来满足我刚刚所唤起的人们的这些新的欲望，并引导他们全情投入追求物质满足，并鼓励他们去创造财富。如果有一天有些人会不遗余力地追求财富，并对物质享受表现出极度的热爱，我不会感到任何不安，因为这些个别现象在整个社会所有人都普遍追求物质财富的时候就不再个别。

民主国家的立法者们还有其他需要注意的地方。在民主国家，人们被赋予教育和自由的权利后，应该放手让人们自己去大干一场。他们不久就会得到现世世界能够提供给他们的一切。他们会不断地完善有用的技术，让生活变得一天比一天舒适、便捷和轻松。他们的社会状况自然会促使他们朝这个方向走，我一点都不担心他们会停滞不前。

this direction; I do not fear that they will slacken their course.

But whilst man takes delight in this honest and lawful pursuit of his wellbeing, it is to be apprehended that he may in the end lose the use of his sublimest faculties; and that whilst he is busied in improving all around him, he may at length degrade himself. Here, and here only, does the peril lie. It should therefore be the unceasing object of the legislators of democracies, and of all the virtuous and enlightened men who live there, to raise the souls of their fellow-citizens, and keep them lifted up towards heaven. It is necessary that all who feel an interest in the future destinies of democratic society should unite, and that all should make joint and continual efforts to diffuse the love of the infinite, a sense of greatness, and a love of pleasures not of earth. If amongst the opinions of a democratic people any of those pernicious theories exist which tend to inculcate that all perishes with the body, let men by whom such theories are professed be marked as the natural foes of such a people.

The materialists are offensive to me in many respects; their doctrines I hold to be pernicious, and I am disgusted at their arrogance. If their system could be of any utility to man, it would seem to be by giving him a modest opinion of himself. But these reasoners show that it is not so; and when they think they have said enough to establish that they are brutes, they show themselves as proud as if they had demonstrated that they are gods. Materialism is, amongst all nations, a dangerous disease of the human mind; but it is more especially to be dreaded amongst a democratic people, because it readily amalgamates with that vice which is most familiar to the heart under such circumstances. Democracy encourages a taste for physical gratification: this taste, if it become excessive, soon disposes men to believe that all is matter only; and materialism, in turn, hurries them back with mad impatience to these same delights: such is the fatal circle within which democratic nations are driven round. It were well that they should see the danger and hold back.

Most religions are only general, simple, and practical means of teaching men the doctrine of the immortality of the soul. That is the greatest benefit which a democratic people derives, from its belief, and hence belief is more necessary to such a people than to all others. When therefore any

但是当人们乐于诚实合法地追求幸福的时候，最终往往会让自己的非凡才能无用武之地；而当他只是忙于改善周边一切的时候，则很有可能令自己堕落。危机就在这里，而且只在这里。因此，民主国家的立法者和所有的有德有才之人都应该始终致力于提升人们的灵魂，并将人们的灵魂引入天堂。凡是关心民主社会未来命运的人都应该联合起来，不断共同努力传播永恒的爱、崇高的情感，以及对非物质享乐的热爱。如果民主国家中存在有害的观念，认为一切将随肉体的消失而消失，那么，我们就应该将散播这种观念的人视为人民的敌人。

唯物主义者在很多方面都让我反感，我认为他们的学说是有害的，而且对他们的妄自尊大很厌恶。如果说他们的理论还有什么用处的话，那大概就是它让人对自身有了一个朴素的认识。但是这些唯物主义者本身并不这样认为。当他们认为自己已经充分论证自己也不过是兽类的时候，往往表现得很高傲，就好像已经证明自己就是上帝一般。在所有国家，唯物主义都是一种人类思想的危险疾病，而且在民主国家尤为可怕，因为它随时可以和民主国家人心常有的邪恶合而为一。民主制度孤立追求物质满足，这种爱好，一旦变得极端，不久便会驱使人们认为一切都是物而已，而唯物主义便会促使人们迫不及待地追求这种享受。这就会让民主国家陷入一个致命的循环。如果他们能够看到这一危险并加以遏制，就再好不过了。

大多数的宗教不过是向人们宣传灵魂不灭的一般、简单和实用的工具。而一个民主国家之所以能够有信仰，主要得益于宗教，所以民主国家比任何其他国家都需要宗教。因此，当任何宗教开始在民主国家扎根的时候，一定小心不要干涉它，而是要将其视为贵族

religion has struck its roots deep into a democracy, beware lest you disturb them; but rather watch it carefully, as the most precious bequest of aristocratic ages. Seek not to supersede the old religious opinions of men by new ones; lest in the passage from one faith to another, the soul being left for a while stripped of all belief, the love of physical gratifications should grow upon it and fill it wholly.

The doctrine of metempsychosis is assuredly not more rational than that of materialism; nevertheless if it were absolutely necessary that a democracy should choose one of the two, I should not hesitate to decide that the community would run less risk of being brutalized by believing that the soul of man will pass into the carcass of a hog, than by believing that the soul of man is nothing at all. The belief in a supersensual and immortal principle, united for a time to matter, is so indispensable to man's greatness, that its effects are striking even when it is not united to the doctrine of future reward and punishment; and when it holds no more than that after death the divine principle contained in man is absorbed in the Deity, or transferred to animate the frame of some other creature. Men holding so imperfect a belief will still consider the body as the secondary and inferior portion of their nature, and they will despise it even whilst they yield to its influence; whereas they have a natural esteem and secret admiration for the immaterial part of man, even though they sometimes refuse to submit to its dominion. That is enough to give a lofty cast to their opinions and their tastes, and to bid them tend with no interested motive, and as it were by impulse, to pure feelings and elevated thoughts.

It is not certain that Socrates and his followers had very fixed opinions as to what would befall man hereafter; but the sole point of belief on which they were determined—that the soul has nothing in common with the body, and survives it—was enough to give the Platonic philosophy that sublime aspiration by which it is distinguished. It is clear from the works of Plato, that many philosophical writers, his predecessors or contemporaries, professed materialism. These writers have not reached us, or have reached us in mere fragments. The same thing has happened in almost all ages; the greater part of the most famous minds in literature adhere to the doctrines of a supersensual philosophy. The

时代遗留的最宝贵财富。不要试图用新的宗教观念取代旧的宗教观念，以免在从一种信仰皈依另一种信仰的过程中，心灵会出现信仰真空，此时对物质满足的爱好便会乘虚而入，不断壮大最终占据整个人心。

轮回转生说也并不比唯物主义强多少。然而，当民主国家不得不从中选其一的时候，我会毫不犹豫地认为，它会选择前者，因为让人们相信人的灵魂会脱生为猪，总比让他们相信根本不存在灵魂要少暴露出一些残暴。信仰与物暂时结合的非物质的永恒原则，是人高尚所必不可少的。甚至当人们并不相信因果报应，而只相信神赐的灵魂将在人死后归还给神或是转移到某些其他神所创造的物上时，这种信仰依然可以发挥显著的作用。拥有如此并不完美的新信仰的人依旧会认为肉体是人本质中次要的低级的部分，而且在承认肉体影响的同时也会轻视肉体。然而他们对人非物质的部分有着一种与生俱来的尊重和赞美，尽管有时候他们会拒绝非物质部分的指令。仅此一点就足以让他们的观念和爱好看上去很崇高，让他们不受利益的驱动而是自动地接近纯洁的情感和高尚的思想。

苏格拉底和他的追随者们对于人死后是否有来世的观点并不确定，但是有一点他们很笃定，就是灵魂和肉体毫无共同之处而且人死后灵魂依旧存在。仅此一点就足以给柏拉图的哲学提供令其独具特色的强大动力。从柏拉图的著作中可以清楚地看到，许多在他之前或是与其同时代的哲学家都鼓吹唯物主义。这些哲学家的著作并没有流传至今，或者说只流传下来只字片语。同样的事情几乎在所有时代都有发生，得以传世的大部分名著都主张唯心主义。人类的本能和爱好让这些学说得以保留，而且它们往往不以人的意志为转移地被留存下来，并让捍卫它们的人名垂青史。因此，千万不要相信，在任何时代或是任何

instinct and the taste of the human race maintain those doctrines; they save them oftentimes in spite of men themselves, and raise the names of their defenders above the tide of time. It must not then be supposed that at any period or under any political condition, the passion for physical gratifications, and the opinions which are superinduced by that passion, can ever content a whole people. The heart of man is of a larger mould: it can at once comprise a taste for the possessions of earth and the love of those of heaven: at times it may seem to cling devotedly to the one, but it will never be long without thinking of the other.

If it be easy to see that it is more particularly important in democratic ages that spiritual opinions should prevail, it is not easy to say by what means those who govern democratic nations may make them predominate. I am no believer in the prosperity, any more than in the durability, of official philosophies; and as to state religions, I have always held, that if they be sometimes of momentary service to the interests of political power, they always, sooner or later, become fatal to the Church. Nor do I think with those who assert, that to raise religion in the eyes of the people, and to make them do honor to her spiritual doctrines, it is desirable indirectly to give her ministers a political influence which the laws deny them. I am so much alive to the almost inevitable dangers which beset religious belief whenever the clergy take part in public affairs, and I am so convinced that Christianity must be maintained at any cost in the bosom of modern democracies, that I had rather shut up the priesthood within the sanctuary than allow them to step beyond it.

What means then remain in the hands of constituted authorities to bring men back to spiritual opinions, or to hold them fast to the religion by which those opinions are suggested? My answer will do me harm in the eyes of politicians. I believe that the sole effectual means which governments can employ in order to have the doctrine of the immortality of the soul duly respected, is ever to act as if they believed in it themselves; and I think that it is only by scrupulous conformity to religious morality in great affairs that they can hope to teach the community at large to know, to love, and to observe it in the lesser concerns of life.

政治状况下，对于物质满足的爱好，以及由此而生的观念，能够始终满足全体人民。人心比人们想象的要宽敞，它既能容纳对于世间享受的爱好又能容下对天国幸福的向往。有时候，它似乎疯狂热衷于其中之一，但是它绝不会将另一个永远忘记。

如果说指出在民主时代唯心主义观点应该占据主导非常重要并不是难事，那么，要说明民主国家的领导人应该采用什么样的方式使其占据主导则并不简单。我不相信官方的哲学能够繁荣和长存。至于国教，我则一直认为，即使它们可以在某段时间为政权利益服务，但是这样迟早会给教会带来致命损害。而且我不同意某些人的观点，认为为了提高宗教在人们心中的地位，让人们尊重宗教提倡的唯心主义，最好间接授予神职人员法律未赋予他们的政治影响力。我认为，无论何时只要神职人员参与公共事务，信仰就会不可避免地陷入危机。而且我认为，现代民主国家应该不惜一切代价维护基督教。于是，我宁愿将神职人员困在教堂也不愿他们跨出圣殿一步。

那么，政府当局有什么办法能够让人们相信唯心主义观点，或是让他们牢牢皈依主张唯心主义观点的宗教呢？我的观点可能会遭到政客们的反对。我认为，为了让灵魂永生的主张得到人们的充分尊重，政府能够行使的唯一行之有效的手段就是，用自己的行动证明自己对此深信不疑。而且我认为，政府只有在大事上认真遵循宗教道德，才能寄希望于教导社会大众在日常小事上承认、热爱和遵守宗教道德。

第十六章　过分热爱福利会给福利带来损害

在灵魂的提升和肉体享受的改善之间，存在着人们意想不到的紧密关系。人也许可

Chapter XVI: That Excessive Care Of Worldly Welfare May Impair That Welfare

There is a closer tie than is commonly supposed between the improvement of the soul and the amelioration of what belongs to the body. Man may leave these two things apart, and consider each of them alternately; but he cannot sever them entirely without at last losing sight of one and of the other. The beasts have the same senses as ourselves, and very nearly the same appetites. We have no sensual passions which are not common to our race and theirs, and which are not to be found, at least in the germ, in a dog as well as in a man. Whence is it then that the animals can only provide for their first and lowest wants, whereas we can infinitely vary and endlessly increase our enjoyments?

We are superior to the beasts in this, that we use our souls to find out those material benefits to which they are only led by instinct. In man, the angel teaches the brute the art of contenting its desires. It is because man is capable of rising above the things of the body, and of contemning life itself, of which the beasts have not the least notion, that he can multiply these same things of the body to a degree which inferior races are equally unable to conceive. Whatever elevates, enlarges, and expands the soul, renders it more capable of succeeding in those very undertakings which concern it not. Whatever, on the other hand, enervates or lowers it, weakens it for all purposes, the chiefest, as well as the least, and threatens to render it almost equally impotent for the one and for the other. Hence the soul must remain great and strong, though it were only to devote its strength and greatness from time to time to the service of the body. If men were ever to content themselves with material objects, it is probable that they would lose by degrees the art of producing them; and they would enjoy them in the end, like the brutes, without discernment and without improvement.

Chapter XVII: That In Times Marked By Equality Of Conditions And Sceptical Opinions, It Is Important To Remove To A Distance The Objects Of Human Actions

In the ages of faith the final end of life is placed beyond life. The men of those ages therefore naturally, and in a manner involuntarily, accustom themselves to fix their gaze for a long course of years on some immovable object, towards which they are constantly tending; and they learn by insensible degrees to

以将两者分开，轮流给予关注，但是却无法将两者完全分开，而只见其一。野兽与我们有同样的感官感受，和几乎相同的欲望。对于感官需求的激情兽类与我们并没有什么不同之处，这种激情的萌芽无论是在狗身上还是在人身上都可以找到。那么，为什么动物只能满足自己最基本最低级的需要，而人却可以不断改变和提高我们的需要呢？

在这方面，我们比野兽高级，因为我们用自己的灵魂寻找物质福利，而野兽只是靠本能的驱使。在人类社会，善良的人会教会愚笨的人满足自己需要的技能。因为人有能力超越肉体享受，甚至轻视生命本身，而野兽则根本没有这样的观念，所以人能够成倍地将肉体感受提高到兽类根本无法想象的地步。凡是能够提升、充实或扩大心灵的东西，都能使心灵更成功地完成与心灵本身无关的事情。另一方面，凡是削弱贬低心灵的东西，会让它对一切都失去兴趣，无论大小事情都无法做成。因此，人的心灵必须始终强大有力，尽管它的力量和强大只是时不时地为肉体服务。如果人们始终以追求物质财富为目标，他们将很有可能逐渐失去创造物质财富的才能，最终会变得跟野兽一样不再有鉴别能力，不再有发展。

第十七章　在平等和怀疑论观念盛行的时期应当把人的行动目标放长远一些

在宗教信仰影响强大的时代，人们将生命的终极目标放在来世。因此，这样时代的人自然而然地，也可以说是心甘情愿地习惯于许多年将目光锁定在某个一成不变的目标，并不断向这个目标靠近，而且为了能够让心中那个伟大永恒的愿望可以得到满足，他们在不知不觉中学会抑制自己转瞬即逝的小欲望。当这些人忙于现世事务的时候，同样的习惯也在指

repress a multitude of petty passing desires, in order to be the better able to content that great and lasting desire which possesses them. When these same men engage in the affairs of this world, the same habits may be traced in their conduct. They are apt to set up some general and certain aim and end to their actions here below, towards which all their efforts are directed: they do not turn from day to day to chase some novel object of desire, but they have settled designs which they are never weary of pursuing. This explains why religious nations have so often achieved such lasting results: for whilst they were thinking only of the other world, they had found out the great secret of success in this. Religions give men a general habit of conducting themselves with a view to futurity: in this respect they are not less useful to happiness in this life than to felicity hereafter; and this is one of their chief political characteristics.

But in proportion as the light of faith grows dim, the range of man's sight is circumscribed, as if the end and aim of human actions appeared every day to be more within his reach. When men have once allowed themselves to think no more of what is to befall them after life, they readily lapse into that complete and brutal indifference to futurity, which is but too conformable to some propensities of mankind. As soon as they have lost the habit of placing their chief hopes upon remote events, they naturally seek to gratify without delay their smallest desires; and no sooner do they despair of living forever, than they are disposed to act as if they were to exist but for a single day. In sceptical ages it is always therefore to be feared that men may perpetually give way to their daily casual desires; and that, wholly renouncing whatever cannot be acquired without protracted effort, they may establish nothing great, permanent, and calm.

If the social condition of a people, under these circumstances, becomes democratic, the danger which I here point out is thereby increased. When everyone is constantly striving to change his position—when an immense field for competition is thrown open to all—when wealth is amassed or dissipated in the shortest possible space of time amidst the turmoil of democracy, visions of sudden and easy fortunes—of great possessions easily won and lost—of chance, under all its forms—haunt the mind. The instability of society itself fosters the natural instability of man's desires. In the midst of these perpetual fluctuations of his lot, the present grows upon his mind, until it conceals futurity

导着他们的行动。他们往往会为自己现世的一切行动设定一个明确的总的目标，并竭尽所能奔向这一目标。他们不会日复一日地变换新目标，而是会制定好计划孜孜不倦地追求。这就是笃信宗教的民族往往能够完成远大事业的原因所在。因为当他们一心想着来世的时候，也发现了在现世取得成功的重大秘密。宗教引导人们养成站在来世的角度立身的习惯。就这一点而言，宗教对于现世幸福的好处不亚于来世，而且这也是宗教的主要政治特征之一。

但是随着信仰之光日渐暗淡，人们的目光日益短浅，似乎人们活动的目标每天都摆在眼前。当人们一旦不再考虑死后将会如何的时候，便很容易对未来采取漠不关心的态度，这与人的某些本性不谋而合。他们只要失去将自己的主要希望置于长远目标的习惯，就会自然而然地想要小的欲望能够马上得到满足。而且在对于永生的希望破灭之后，他们的行为举止变得好像自己只能活一天似的。因此，在怀疑论盛行的时代，可怕的往往是人们会一直为其每天偶然出现的欲望所左右，而完全放弃需要持久努力才能实现的目标，他们不会完成任何伟大、永久和稳妥的事业。

如果处于这种社会状态的民族，有一天变得民主，我刚刚所指出的危险将进一步加大。当每个人不断努力试图改变自己的处境，广泛的竞争空间对所有人敞开，财富在民主的动荡中可以一夜时间积聚或是散尽的时候，各式各样的幻想就开始在人们的脑海浮现，会想到一夜暴富，来财容易，会想到钱财来得容易去得快。社会的不稳定本身就会让人们欲望多变。在命运的变幻莫测之中，现在不断在人们的头脑中膨胀，直到人们再也看不见未来，于是人们再也不去想明天。

from his sight, and his looks go no further than the morrow.

In those countries in which unhappily irreligion and democracy coexist, the most important duty of philosophers and of those in power is to be always striving to place the objects of human actions far beyond man's immediate range. Circumscribed by the character of his country and his age, the moralist must learn to vindicate his principles in that position. He must constantly endeavor to show his contemporaries, that, even in the midst of the perpetual commotion around them, it is easier than they think to conceive and to execute protracted undertakings. He must teach them that, although the aspect of mankind may have changed, the methods by which men may provide for their prosperity in this world are still the same; and that amongst democratic nations, as well as elsewhere, it is only by resisting a thousand petty selfish passions of the hour that the general and unquenchable passion for happiness can be satisfied.

The task of those in power is not less clearly marked out. At all times it is important that those who govern nations should act with a view to the future: but this is even more necessary in democratic and sceptical ages than in any others. By acting thus, the leading men of democracies not only make public affairs prosperous, but they also teach private individuals, by their example, the art of managing private concerns. Above all they must strive as much as possible to banish chance from the sphere of politics. The sudden and undeserved promotion of a courtier produces only a transient impression in an aristocratic country, because the aggregate institutions and opinions of the nation habitually compel men to advance slowly in tracks which they cannot get out of. But nothing is more pernicious than similar instances of favor exhibited to the eyes of a democratic people: they give the last impulse to the public mind in a direction where everything hurries it onwards. At times of scepticism and equality more especially, the favor of the people or of the prince, which chance may confer or chance withhold, ought never to stand in lieu of attainments or services. It is desirable that every advancement should there appear to be the result of some effort; so that no greatness should be of too easy acquirement, and that ambition should be obliged to fix its gaze long upon an object before it is gratified. Governments must apply themselves to restore to men that love of the future

在那些很不幸不信教的思想和民主制度共存的国家，哲学家和执政者最重要的责任就是要始终致力于让人们的行动目标不再鼠目寸光。道德学家们在潜心研究自己所处国家和时代特征的时候，必须学会保护这种特征。他们必须要努力向同时代的人证明，哪怕他们一直身处动荡之中，规划和推行长期的事业也并没有想象中的那样困难。他们还要教会人们，尽管人类的某一方面可能已经发生变化，但是人们用来促进现世繁荣的手段依然没有发生改变。而且在民主国家和在其他国家一样，只有能够时刻抵抗住数以千计的自私的小小欲望，才能使渴望幸福的共同激情得到满足。

执政者的任务已经非常明确。在所有时代，国家的执政者们都应该高瞻远瞩，而在民主和怀疑论盛行的时代，应该尤其如此。通过这样做，民主国家的领导人不但可以使国家昌盛，而且还能引导每个人以他们为例学会处理私人事务的技巧。首先，执政者必须在为政的过程中尽最大努力避免侥幸心理。在贵族时代，突然得宠和无功受禄的大臣的影响不会长远，因为国家的这个制度和舆论已经让人们习惯于循规蹈矩慢慢腾腾地前进。但是，在民主国家，同样的事情会产生极大的恶果，因为民主国家的人们丝毫不关心这样的事情，只各自忙于自己的私事。因此，特别是在怀疑论和平等盛行的时代，要首先防止人民和君主的随心所欲，让人尽其才。每一次晋升都应该是努力的结果，所有的大事都不会轻易实现，有抱负的人必须为实现自己的目标做出长久的努力。政府必须要努力恢复宗教和社会状况已无法再激起的人们对于未来的热爱，不是空喊，而是必须以身作则引导公民明白财富、名誉和权力都是劳动的奖励，伟大的成功在于对渴望的长久追求，持久的东西只

with which religion and the state of society no longer inspire them; and, without saying so, they must practically teach the community day by day that wealth, fame, and power are the rewards of labor—that great success stands at the utmost range of long desires, and that nothing lasting is obtained but what is obtained by toil. When men have accustomed themselves to foresee from afar what is likely to befall in the world and to feed upon hopes, they can hardly confine their minds within the precise circumference of life, and they are ready to break the boundary and cast their looks beyond. I do not doubt that, by training the members of a community to think of their future condition in this world, they would be gradually and unconsciously brought nearer to religious convictions. Thus the means which allow men, up to a certain point, to go without religion, are perhaps after all the only means we still possess for bringing mankind back by a long and roundabout path to a state of faith.

Chapter XVIII: That Amongst The Americans All Honest Callings Are Honorable

Amongst a democratic people, where there is no hereditary wealth, every man works to earn a living, or has worked, or is born of parents who have worked. The notion of labor is therefore presented to the mind on every side as the necessary, natural, and honest condition of human existence. Not only is labor not dishonorable amongst such a people, but it is held in honor: the prejudice is not against it, but in its favor. In the United States a wealthy man thinks that he owes it to public opinion to devote his leisure to some kind of industrial or commercial pursuit, or to public business. He would think himself in bad repute if he employed his life solely in living. It is for the purpose of escaping this obligation to work, that so many rich Americans come to Europe, where they find some scattered remains of aristocratic society, amongst which idleness is still held in honor.

Equality of conditions not only ennobles the notion of labor in men's estimation, but it raises the notion of labor as a source of profit. In aristocracies it is not exactly labor that is despised, but labor with a view to profit. Labor is honorific in itself, when it is undertaken at the sole bidding of ambition or of virtue. Yet in aristocratic society it constantly happens that he who works for honor is not insensible to the attractions of profit. But these two desires only intermingle in the innermost depths

有经过艰苦努力才能获得。当人们习惯于从长远出发预见现在所做事情的发展并对其进行仔细筹划的时候，就不会将自己的思想局限于现实生活，而能随时冲破束缚并放眼未来。我丝毫不怀疑，通过训练社会成员对现世世界未来的思考，人们会在不知不觉中逐渐接近宗教信仰。因此，在没有宗教的帮助下，让人们达到指定目标的方法也许只有这一种，即经过漫长曲折的道路让人们最终树立起信念。

第十八章　美国人认为所有正当职业都是高尚的

在民主国家，没有世袭的财富，每个人都要靠劳动，靠劳动的积蓄，或是靠父母的劳动生活。劳动是人生存的必要、自然和正常的条件，因此劳动的观念从四面八方涌入人们的思想。在这样的国家，劳动不但不可耻，而且是光荣的事情。人们对劳动没有丝毫偏见，反而予以支持。在美国，一个有钱人认为，应该利用自己的余暇投身工商业或是公益事业。他认为，如果自己只为自己活，必定会声名狼藉。于是许多美国有钱人为了逃避这种义务便来到欧洲，在这里依然还存有贵族制度的残余，依然把无所事事视为光荣。

平等不但让人们产生尊重劳动的观念，而且提出劳动牟利的观点。在贵族社会，受到鄙视的不仅仅是劳动，还有牟利的劳动。当劳动是为了实现伟大抱负或修德时，劳动本身依旧是高尚行为。所以在贵族制社会，也常常出现为荣誉而劳动的人也不知不觉受到利益驱使的情形。但他们将这两种已经融合起来的欲望一起埋藏在内心最深处。他们会小心翼翼地不被别人识破，甚至不想让自己发现。在贵族制国家，几乎没有一个官员在为国家服

of his soul: he carefully hides from every eye the point at which they join; he would fain conceal it from himself. In aristocratic countries there are few public officers who do not affect to serve their country without interested motives. Their salary is an incident of which they think but little, and of which they always affect not to think at all. Thus the notion of profit is kept distinct from that of labor; however they may be united in point of fact, they are not thought of together.

In democratic communities these two notions are, on the contrary, always palpably united. As the desire of well-being is universal—as fortunes are slender or fluctuating—as everyone wants either to increase his own resources, or to provide fresh ones for his progeny, men clearly see that it is profit which, if not wholly, at least partially, leads them to work. Even those who are principally actuated by the love of fame are necessarily made familiar with the thought that they are not exclusively actuated by that motive; and they discover that the desire of getting a living is mingled in their minds with the desire of making life illustrious.

As soon as, on the one hand, labor is held by the whole community to be an honorable necessity of man's condition, and, on the other, as soon as labor is always ostensibly performed, wholly or in part, for the purpose of earning remuneration, the immense interval which separated different callings in aristocratic societies disappears. If all are not alike, all at least have one feature in common. No profession exists in which men do not work for money; and the remuneration which is common to them all gives them all an air of resemblance. This serves to explain the opinions which the Americans entertain with respect to different callings. In America no one is degraded because he works, for everyone about him works also; nor is anyone humiliated by the notion of receiving pay, for the President of the United States also works for pay. He is paid for commanding, other men for obeying orders. In the United States professions are more or less laborious, more or less profitable; but they are never either high or low: every honest calling is honorable.

Chapter XIX: That Almost All The Americans Follow Industrial Callings

Agriculture is, perhaps, of all the useful arts that which improves most slowly amongst democratic

务的时候是出于利益的驱使。他们的薪俸对于他们来说微不足道，往往根本不会考虑这个问题。因此，牟利的观点和劳动观念仍有区别，然而从现实的角度来看，它们又联系在一起，但在思想上，它们还是分开的。

与之相反，在民主社会，这两个观念始终被公开联系起来。因为对幸福的渴望是普遍的，因为每个人的财富不多而且变化无常，而且还因为每个人都既想增加自己的财富也想为子孙后代多积累财富，所以人们清楚地认识到，正是利益，即使不是全部也是部分，在驱使人们劳动。甚至是那些主要为了名誉而工作的人，也不得不承认名并不是他们唯一的动机，并发现在他们的头脑中已经将谋生与求名合二为一。

一方面，只要劳动被全社会视为人生光荣的必要条件，而另一方面只要劳动表面上是完全或部分以获得酬劳为目的，那么，贵族社会职业之间存在的巨大鸿沟便会消失。尽管各行各业并不相同，但至少有一个共同点。即没有任何一个行业不是为赚钱而劳动。每个人都领工资成为所有人的相似之处。这足以说明美国人对各行各业的看法。在美国，没有人因为工作而低人一等，因为每个人都工作；也没有人会觉得领工资抬不起头，因为美国总统也领工资。在美国，各行业或多或少都很辛苦，也或多或少都有报酬，所以它们并没有高低贵贱之分，所有正当的职业都是光荣的。

第十九章　是什么让几乎所有美国人热衷于实业

农业也许是民主国家中发展得最慢的实用技术。甚至有人常常会说，农业似乎处于停

nations. Frequently, indeed, it would seem to be stationary, because other arts are making rapid strides towards perfection. On the other hand, almost all the tastes and habits which the equality of condition engenders naturally lead men to commercial and industrial occupations.

Suppose an active, enlightened, and free man, enjoying a competency, but full of desires: he is too poor to live in idleness; he is rich enough to feel himself protected from the immediate fear of want, and he thinks how he can better his condition. This man has conceived a taste for physical gratifications, which thousands of his fellow-men indulge in around him; he has himself begun to enjoy these pleasures, and he is eager to increase his means of satisfying these tastes more completely. But life is slipping away, time is urgent—to what is he to turn? The cultivation of the ground promises an almost certain result to his exertions, but a slow one; men are not enriched by it without patience and toil. Agriculture is therefore only suited to those who have already large, superfluous wealth, or to those whose penury bids them only seek a bare subsistence. The choice of such a man as we have supposed is soon made; he sells his plot of ground, leaves his dwelling, and embarks in some hazardous but lucrative calling. Democratic communities abound in men of this kind; and in proportion as the equality of conditions becomes greater, their multitude increases. Thus democracy not only swells the number of workingmen, but it leads men to prefer one kind of labor to another; and whilst it diverts them from agriculture, it encourages their taste for commerce and manufactures.

This spirit may be observed even amongst the richest members of the community. In democratic countries, however opulent a man is supposed to be, he is almost always discontented with his fortune, because he finds that he is less rich than his father was, and he fears that his sons will be less rich than himself. Most rich men in democracies are therefore constantly haunted by the desire of obtaining wealth, and they naturally turn their attention to trade and manufactures, which appear to offer the readiest and most powerful means of success. In this respect they share the instincts of the poor, without feeling the same necessities; say rather, they feel the most imperious of all necessities, that of not sinking in the world.

滞状态，因为其他行业都在快速大踏步地前进。另一方面，平等带来的几乎所有的爱好和习惯会自然而然将人们引向实业。

假设有一个人，他积极、聪明、自由而且很有才干，充满希望。但是他并不富裕无法过优哉的生活，而另一方面，他又可以说足够富裕能够衣食无忧，他总是想着如何改变自己的境遇。这个人已经产生对物质享受的爱好，于是他开始追求这些爱好，并努力增加满足这些爱好的手段。但是人生苦短，时间紧迫，他该怎么做呢？种地，会让他的付出必然有所收获，但是太慢，想要以此致富的人必须有耐心肯吃苦。因此，农业只适合家财万贯的有钱人或是只求糊口的穷人。我们假设的这个人不久便做出选择，他将土地出卖，离开家乡，开始从事某种有风险却获利颇丰的行业。在民主社会这样的人很多，而且随着平等的日益普及，他们的人数还在不断攀升。因此，民主不但让劳动者的数量增加，还让人们可以选择自己更喜欢的工作。而民主制度在将人们从农业上引开的同时，鼓励了人们对工商业的爱好。

这种精神甚至在最富有的公民中也能看到。在民主国家，无论一个人多么的富有，他总是不会满足于现有财富，因为他觉得自己不如祖辈富有，而且害怕后代子孙不如自己富有。因此，民主国家的大部分富人不断想着如何更富，于是便自然而然将目光投向工商业，因为这似乎是最快捷、最有效的成功方式。就此而言，他们跟穷人有着同样的本能，尽管需求并不相同，或者说他们也受到最迫切的需求支配。

在贵族社会，富人同时也是统治者。他们不断将注意力投向重要的公共事务，让他们无暇顾及工商业。即使他们之中有人有志从商，其所属阶级的意志也会立即挡住他的道

In aristocracies the rich are at the same time those who govern. The attention which they unceasingly devote to important public affairs diverts them from the lesser cares which trade and manufactures demand. If the will of an individual happens, nevertheless, to turn his attention to business, the will of the body to which he belongs will immediately debar him from pursuing it; for however men may declaim against the rule of numbers, they cannot wholly escape their sway; and even amongst those aristocratic bodies which most obstinately refuse to acknowledge the rights of the majority of the nation, a private majority is formed which governs the rest.

In democratic countries, where money does not lead those who possess it to political power, but often removes them from it, the rich do not know how to spend their leisure. They are driven into active life by the inquietude and the greatness of their desires, by the extent of their resources, and by the taste for what is extraordinary, which is almost always felt by those who rise, by whatsoever means, above the crowd. Trade is the only road open to them. In democracies nothing is more great or more brilliant than commerce: it attracts the attention of the public, and fills the imagination of the multitude; all energetic passions are directed towards it. Neither their own prejudices, nor those of anybody else, can prevent the rich from devoting themselves to it. The wealthy members of democracies never form a body which has manners and regulations of its own; the opinions peculiar to their class do not restrain them, and the common opinions of their country urge them on. Moreover, as all the large fortunes which are to be met with in a democratic community are of commercial growth, many generations must succeed each other before their possessors can have entirely laid aside their habits of business.

Circumscribed within the narrow space which politics leave them, rich men in democracies eagerly embark in commercial enterprise: there they can extend and employ their natural advantages; and indeed it is even by the boldness and the magnitude of their industrial speculations that we may measure the slight esteem in which productive industry would have been held by them, if they had been born amidst an aristocracy.

A similar observation is likewise applicable to all men living in democracies, whether they be poor or rich. Those who live in the midst of democratic fluctuations have always before their eyes the

路。因为，无论人们如何激烈抨击阶级的多数统治，却依旧无法逃脱他们的影响，而且甚至在那些坚决拒绝认可人民多数权利的贵族集团内部，也存在一个专门进行统治的多数。

在民主国家，金钱并不能导致有钱人掌权，甚至往往会令他们远离政界，所以有钱人不知道该如何消磨他们的闲暇时间。他们在远大希望、大量财产以及某些不管用什么方法致富的人常有的特别爱好的激励下积极生活。但是经商是唯一向他们敞开的大路。在民主时代，最伟大最辉煌的事业就是经商。它吸引着公众的目光，是大众向往的目标，所有活力四射的激情全部指向它。无论是富人自己的偏见还是他人的偏见，都不能阻止有钱人投身商业。民主社会的有钱人并没有形成具有自己独特民情和制度的团体，他们这一阶层所特有的观念对他们没有任何约束力，反而是国家的一般观念会不断推动他们。此外，因为民主国家所有的巨富都是靠经商而来，所以在财富的持有人完全失去经商习惯之前，一代一代的人还要一直经营下去。

在民主国家，因为政治留给富人的空间非常狭小，所以他们特别热衷于经商。在这里，他们可以尽情发挥和运用自己得天独厚的优势。而且这确实应归功于他们大胆创办实业的精神，但是如果他们生在贵族时代，恐怕很难想象他们会有如此的作为。

在民主国家我们会看到所有人都有这样的表现，无论他们是贫穷还是富有。生活在民主时代动荡之中的人们眼前一直浮现着变幻莫测的偶然因素，所以喜欢从事所有具有偶然因素的事业。因此，他们都愿意从商，但并不仅仅是为了牟利，而是因为喜欢商业不断带

phantom of chance; and they end by liking all undertakings in which chance plays a part. They are therefore all led to engage in commerce, not only for the sake of the profit it holds out to them, but for the love of the constant excitement occasioned by that pursuit.

The United States of America have only been emancipated for half a century [in 1840] from the state of colonial dependence in which they stood to Great Britain; the number of large fortunes there is small, and capital is still scarce. Yet no people in the world has made such rapid progress in trade and manufactures as the Americans: they constitute at the present day the second maritime nation in the world; and although their manufactures have to struggle with almost insurmountable natural impediments, they are not prevented from making great and daily advances. In the United States the greatest undertakings and speculations are executed without difficulty, because the whole population is engaged in productive industry, and because the poorest as well as the most opulent members of the commonwealth are ready to combine their efforts for these purposes. The consequence is, that a stranger is constantly amazed by the immense public works executed by a nation which contains, so to speak, no rich men. The Americans arrived but as yesterday on the territory which they inhabit, and they have already changed the whole order of nature for their own advantage. They have joined the Hudson to the Mississippi, and made the Atlantic Ocean communicate with the Gulf of Mexico, across a continent of more than five hundred leagues in extent which separates the two seas. The longest railroads which have been constructed up to the present time are in America. But what most astonishes me in the United States, is not so much the marvellous grandeur of some undertakings, as the innumerable multitude of small ones. Almost all the farmers of the United States combine some trade with agriculture; most of them make agriculture itself a trade. It seldom happens that an American farmer settles for good upon the land which he occupies: especially in the districts of the Far West he brings land into tillage in order to sell it again, and not to farm it: he builds a farmhouse on the speculation that, as the state of the country will soon be changed by the increase of population, a good price will be gotten for it. Every year a swarm of the inhabitants of the North arrive in the Southern States, and settle in the parts where the cotton plant and the sugar-cane grow. These men cultivate the soil in order to make it produce in a few years enough to enrich them; and they already

给他们的刺激。

美国被从英国殖民地状态解放出来不过只有半个世纪，所以并没有多少大富之家，而且资本也很有限。但是，世界上却没有任何一个民族像美国人那样能够在工商业上取得如此快速的进步。今天，他们已经是世界上第二大海运国家。尽管他们的制造业还要克服一些几乎无法克服的天然障碍，但这并不妨碍他们每天取得新的进展。在美国，经营大型的工业企业没有任何困难，因为全民都从事工业生产，而且为此最贫穷的人和最富有的人已随时准备好团结起来共同奋斗。所以，当你看到这样一个可以说并不富强的国家不断开展大型工程的时候，必然会感到很惊讶。美国人不过是昨天才踏上这片他们生活的土地，但他们已经改变了整个自然秩序使之为自己服务。他们将赫德森河和密西西比河连通，并在陆地上建设500多英里的道路将大西洋和墨西哥湾连接起来。美国已经建成几条大铁路。但是美国人最令我惊讶的不是他们规模惊人的大企业，而是他们大大小小的企业数不胜数。在美国几乎所有的农民都将农业和商业联合经营，而且大多数已经将农业商业化。美国的农民很少老守田园，特别是在那些西部的新州，在那里人们开垦土地不是为了耕种而是为了出售。人们建设农场是为了投机，因为随着这个州人口的不断增长，不久就能卖上一个好价钱。每年北方的居民都会蜂拥而来，在盛产棉花和蔗糖的地方定居。这些人来到这里耕种土地，希望能够在几年之内发财致富，并期待着有一天带着在这里赚来的财富回老家享受。因此，美国人将商业精神带入农业，并将他们经营实业的激情在农业上表现出来。

look forward to the time when they may return home to enjoy the competency thus acquired. Thus the Americans carry their business-like qualities into agriculture; and their trading passions are displayed in that as in their other pursuits.

The Americans make immense progress in productive industry, because they all devote themselves to it at once; and for this same reason they are exposed to very unexpected and formidable embarrassments. As they are all engaged in commerce, their commercial affairs are affected by such various and complex causes that it is impossible to foresee what difficulties may arise. As they are all more or less engaged in productive industry, at the least shock given to business all private fortunes are put in jeopardy at the same time, and the State is shaken. I believe that the return of these commercial panics is an endemic disease of the democratic nations of our age. It may be rendered less dangerous, but it cannot be cured; because it does not originate in accidental circumstances, but in the temperament of these nations.

Chapter XX: That Aristocracy May Be Engendered By Manufactures

I have shown that democracy is favorable to the growth of manufactures, and that it increases without limit the numbers of the manufacturing classes: we shall now see by what side road manufacturers may possibly in their turn bring men back to aristocracy. It is acknowledged that when a workman is engaged every day upon the same detail, the whole commodity is produced with greater ease, promptitude, and economy. It is likewise acknowledged that the cost of the production of manufactured goods is diminished by the extent of the establishment in which they are made, and by the amount of capital employed or of credit. These truths had long been imperfectly discerned, but in our time they have been demonstrated. They have been already applied to many very important kinds of manufactures, and the humblest will gradually be governed by them. I know of nothing in politics which deserves to fix the attention of the legislator more closely than these two new axioms of the science of manufactures.

When a workman is unceasingly and exclusively engaged in the fabrication of one thing, he

美国人之所以在工业上取得巨大发展，是因为所有人都投身其中。而且正是因为这一原因，他们也经常陷入意外的、可怕的尴尬境地。因为他们所有人都经商，而商业活动往往会受到各种复杂因素的影响，所以无法预见可能遇到的困难。而且因为所有人都或多或少地参与工业生产，所以哪怕是商业上最轻微的冲击，所有人的财富都会同时受到损害，以至整个国家都会受到震动。我认为，周而复始的商业危机是我们这个时代民主国家的通病。它也许并没有那么危险，但是无法治愈，因为它的出现并非偶然，而是民主国家的本性使然。

第二十章　实业为什么可能产生贵族制度

我已经说过民主制度有利于实业的发展，会让从事实业的人数无限增长。现在，我们要看一看实业会通过什么样的旁门左道让人们重回贵族社会。我们已经看到，若一个工人每天都做着同样一个零部件，那么整个商品的生产会更加方便、快速和经济。我们同样也看到，一个企业越大，资本越多，信用越好，商品生产的成本也就越低。人们早已对这些真理有所察觉，但是在我们这个时代它们得到清楚的证明。人们已经将这两个真理应用在非常重要的工业部门，而且最微不足道的部门也将逐渐被其所掌控。我认为，在政治方面，立法者最应该注意这两个工业科学的新原理。

如果一个工人不停地只生产一种产品，最终手艺必然会炉火纯青，但同时会失去利用自己的头脑全面指导工作的一般能力。日复一日，他变得越来越熟练，却越来越不动脑筋。以至于可以说，随着他作为一个工人技术上的日臻完善，他作为一个人的本质却在日

ultimately does his work with singular dexterity; but at the same time he loses the general faculty of applying his mind to the direction of the work. He every day becomes more adroit and less industrious; so that it may be said of him, that in proportion as the workman improves the man is degraded. What can be expected of a man who has spent twenty years of his life in making heads for pins? and to what can that mighty human intelligence, which has so often stirred the world, be applied in him, except it be to investigate the best method of making pins' heads? When a workman has spent a considerable portion of his existence in this manner, his thoughts are forever set upon the object of his daily toil; his body has contracted certain fixed habits, which it can never shake off: in a word, he no longer belongs to himself, but to the calling which he has chosen. It is in vain that laws and manners have been at the pains to level all barriers round such a man, and to open to him on every side a thousand different paths to fortune; a theory of manufactures more powerful than manners and laws binds him to a craft, and frequently to a spot, which he cannot leave: it assigns to him a certain place in society, beyond which he cannot go: in the midst of universal movement it has rendered him stationary.

In proportion as the principle of the division of labor is more extensively applied, the workman becomes more weak, more narrow-minded, and more dependent. The art advances, the artisan recedes. On the other hand, in proportion as it becomes more manifest that the productions of manufactures are by so much the cheaper and better as the manufacture is larger and the amount of capital employed more considerable, wealthy and educated men come forward to embark in manufactures which were heretofore abandoned to poor or ignorant handicraftsmen. The magnitude of the efforts required, and the importance of the results to be obtained, attract them. Thus at the very time at which the science of manufactures lowers the class of workmen, it raises the class of masters.

Whereas the workman concentrates his faculties more and more upon the study of a single detail, the master surveys a more extensive whole, and the mind of the latter is enlarged in proportion as that of the former is narrowed. In a short time the one will require nothing but physical strength without intelligence; the other stands in need of science, and almost of genius, to insure success. This

益下降。你能指望一个20年来一直制作别针帽的人会有什么作为呢？往往能够做出惊天动地大事业的人类的伟大智慧，于他除了用来研究制造别针帽的最好方法以外，还能用在哪里呢？当一个工人一生大部分时间都是这样度过的时候，他的思想会一直想着自己终日制作的东西，身体也养成无法改变的固定习惯。一句话，他不再属于自己，而是属于他所选择的行业。无论法律和民情如何想方设法将围在这样一个人身边的篱笆移除，为其开辟条条致富之路，都是枉然。实业的原理比法律和民情都更有力量将他牢牢绑在一个行业以至于往往无法离开。实业的原理为他安排了一个他无法变换的位置，尽管整个世界都在运动，但是实业原理却让他原地不动。

随着劳动分工原则的普遍应用，工人变得越来越弱小，思想越来越狭隘，越来越具有依附性。技术在进步，手艺人则在退化。而另一方面，随着工业生产规模越大资本越雄厚，产品就越物美价廉的道理越来越清晰，有钱和有知识的人也开始从事原来只有物质贫困的手艺人从事的行业。巨大的需求量和无限的收益吸引着他们。因此，实业科学在贬低工人阶级的同时，不断抬高雇主阶级。

当工人的所有精力越来越集中到小事的研究上时，老板们则每天都要纵观全局。于是后者的思想越来越广阔，而前者的思想却越来越狭窄。用不了多久，一个将只会用力而不会用脑，另一个则不但需要科学还需要才干方能成功。于是，老板越来越像一个大帝国的行政长官，而工人则越来越像牛马。所以，老板和工人不再有相同之处，而不同之处则与日俱增。他们好像是一根长长的链条上两端的两个环，各自占据各自的位置，谁也不能

man resembles more and more the administrator of a vast empire—that man, a brute. The master and the workman have then here no similarity, and their differences increase every day. They are only connected as the two rings at the extremities of a long chain. Each of them fills the station which is made for him, and out of which he does not get: the one is continually, closely, and necessarily dependent upon the other, and seems as much born to obey as that other is to command. What is this but aristocracy?

As the conditions of men constituting the nation become more and more equal, the demand for manufactured commodities becomes more general and more extensive; and the cheapness which places these objects within the reach of slender fortunes becomes a great element of success. Hence there are every day more men of great opulence and education who devote their wealth and knowledge to manufactures; and who seek, by opening large establishments, and by a strict division of labor, to meet the fresh demands which are made on all sides. Thus, in proportion as the mass of the nation turns to democracy, that particular class which is engaged in manufactures becomes more aristocratic. Men grow more alike in the one—more different in the other; and inequality increases in the less numerous class in the same ratio in which it decreases in the community. Hence it would appear, on searching to the bottom, that aristocracy should naturally spring out of the bosom of democracy.

But this kind of aristocracy by no means resembles those kinds which preceded it. It will be observed at once, that as it applies exclusively to manufactures and to some manufacturing callings, it is a monstrous exception in the general aspect of society. The small aristocratic societies which are formed by some manufacturers in the midst of the immense democracy of our age, contain, like the great aristocratic societies of former ages, some men who are very opulent, and a multitude who are wretchedly poor. The poor have few means of escaping from their condition and becoming rich; but the rich are constantly becoming poor, or they give up business when they have realized a fortune. Thus the elements of which the class of the poor is composed are fixed; but the elements of which the class of the rich is composed are not so. To say the truth, though there are rich men, the class of rich men does not exist; for these rich individuals have no feelings or purposes in common, no mutual

离开。一个始终必须紧密依附于另一个，似乎一个生来就要服从，另一个生来就要发号施令。这难道不是贵族制度吗？

随着一个国家的人们越来越平等，对于工业产品的需求也变得越来越普遍和广泛。让这些产品走入寻常人家的低廉价格则是成功的关键要素。因此，每天都可以看到越来越多的富裕有知识的人将他们的财富和知识用于工业生产，并通过开办大型企业，进行严格的劳动分工，来满足人们各方面的新需要。因此，随着人民大众转向民主制度，专门从事工业的阶层则越来越贵族化。人与人在一方面变得越来越相似，而在另一方面则越来越不同。在全社会的不平等越来越少的同时，少数人与大多数人的不平等反而在加剧。因此，究其根本就会发现贵族阶层自然而然从民主社会之中诞生。

但是这种贵族与以往的贵族完全不同。初看起来，这些贵族制专心于实业或是某些实业部门，是与整个社会完全不同的怪物。在我们这个高度民主化时代中，一些实业家形成贵族小社会，就像以往的贵族大社会一样，一些人非常富有，而大多数人则穷得可怜。穷人几乎没有任何可以摆脱命运发财致富的手段，但是富人则随时有可能变回穷人，或者致富之后再弃商。因此，穷人阶层的成员几乎相对固定，而富人阶层则常常变化。事实上，尽管有富人存在，但是却没有富人阶层。因为这些富有的个人并没有共同的情感或目标，也没有相同的传统和希望，因此只是一伙人，而不是一个团体。

不但富人之间没有牢固的联系，富人和穷人之前也不存在真正的纽带。他们之间关系也并非一成不变。因为利害关系他们不断分分合合。一般来说，工人需要依靠老板，但并

traditions or mutual hopes; there are therefore members, but no body.

Not only are the rich not compactly united amongst themselves, but there is no real bond between them and the poor. Their relative position is not a permanent one; they are constantly drawn together or separated by their interests. The workman is generally dependent on the master, but not on any particular master; these two men meet in the factory, but know not each other elsewhere; and whilst they come into contact on one point, they stand very wide apart on all others. The manufacturer asks nothing of the workman but his labor; the workman expects nothing from him but his wages. The one contracts no obligation to protect, nor the other to defend; and they are not permanently connected either by habit or by duty. The aristocracy created by business rarely settles in the midst of the manufacturing population which it directs; the object is not to govern that population, but to use it. An aristocracy thus constituted can have no great hold upon those whom it employs; and even if it succeed in retaining them at one moment, they escape the next; it knows not how to will, and it cannot act. The territorial aristocracy of former ages was either bound by law, or thought itself bound by usage, to come to the relief of its serving-men, and to succor their distresses. But the manufacturing aristocracy of our age first impoverishes and debases the men who serve it, and then abandons them to be supported by the charity of the public. This is a natural consequence of what has been said before. Between the workmen and the master there are frequent relations, but no real partnership.

I am of opinion, upon the whole, that the manufacturing aristocracy which is growing up under our eyes is one of the harshest which ever existed in the world; but at the same time it is one of the most confined and least dangerous. Nevertheless the friends of democracy should keep their eyes anxiously fixed in this direction; for if ever a permanent inequality of conditions and aristocracy again penetrate into the world, it may be predicted that this is the channel by which they will enter.

不总是固定的一个。他们彼此在工厂相识，一离开工厂就如同陌生人一般；他们只在一个点上接触，而在其他所有点上，则毫不相干。工厂主只要求工人为他工作，而工人只希望获得工资。一方没有保护的义务，另一方也不需要保护，他们彼此之间无论是从习惯上还是从义务上都没有任何永久的关系。来自商业的贵族很少扎根在他们所统领的实业大军，他们的目的不是统治这些人，而是利用这些人。因此，这样的贵族并不想牢牢控制被雇佣者，即使能够一时将这些人控制住，但是过不了多久他们就会溜走。所以这些贵族既不想也不能这样做。旧时代的地方贵族，不但依据法律规定而且自己也习惯上认为，应该对自己的下属负有救济和援助他们苦难的义务。但是我们这个时代的实业贵族，则在把为其服务的人变穷变蠢之后，将他们推出去丢给社会福利救济。这是事情发展的必然结果。工人和雇主之间虽然时常有联系，却不是真正的伙伴。

总之，在我看来，我们亲眼看其成长起来的实业贵族是世界上有史以来最残酷的贵族，但同时他们又是最受限制和危险性最小的贵族。然而民主的朋友则不安地将视线集中到这一方向，因为一旦不平等和贵族制度要再次入侵这个世界，可以预见，这将是成为它们的通道。

Book Three: Influence Of Democracy On Manners, Properly So Called

Chapter I: That Manners Are Softened As Social Conditions Become More Equal

We perceive that for several ages social conditions have tended to equality, and we discover that in the course of the same period the manners of society have been softened. Are these two things merely contemporaneous, or does any secret link exist between them, so that the one cannot go on without making the other advance? Several causes may concur to render the manners of a people less rude; but, of all these causes, the most powerful appears to me to be the equality of conditions. Equality of conditions and growing civility in manners are, then, in my eyes, not only contemporaneous occurrences, but correlative facts. When the fabulists seek to interest us in the actions of beasts, they invest them with human notions and passions; the poets who sing of spirits and angels do the same; there is no wretchedness so deep, nor any happiness so pure, as to fill the human mind and touch the heart, unless we are ourselves held up to our own eyes under other features.

This is strictly applicable to the subject upon which we are at present engaged. When all men are irrevocably marshalled in an aristocratic community, according to their professions, their property, and their birth, the members of each class, considering themselves as children of the same family, cherish a constant and lively sympathy towards each other, which can never be felt in an equal degree by the citizens of a democracy. But the same feeling does not exist between the several classes

第三篇　民主对所谓民情的影响

第一章　民情随平等的加深而日趋温和

我们注意到几个世纪以来，社会状况不断趋于平等，而同时我们还发现，在这一过程中社会民情也日趋温和。这两件事到底只是刚好同时发生，还是它们之间有什么潜在的关系，以至于没有一个的发展另一个也无法前进呢？许多因素都可以让一个国家的民情变得温和，但是，在我看来其中最有力的因素就是平等。因此，在我眼中，平等和民情的温和不但是同时发生的事情，而且是彼此联系的事实。当寓言家试图用动物的故事来开导我们的时候，便把人的观念和情感加诸动物。歌颂精灵和天使的诗人也在做着相同的事情。如果他们不用借喻的手法来再现我们人本身，那我们就无法感受到那种能够触动我们精神、打动我们心灵的深刻的痛苦和纯净的幸福。

这特别适用于我们现在正在讨论的内容。当所有人按照自己的职业、财产和出身，在等级森严的贵族社会各就各位的时候，在每个阶级的内部成员都视彼此为同一家族的子女，彼此之间总是怀有民主社会公民从来未曾感受过的深切同情，但是在不同阶级之间则

towards each other. Amongst an aristocratic people each caste has its own opinions, feelings, rights, manners, and modes of living. Thus the men of whom each caste is composed do not resemble the mass of their fellow-citizens; they do not think or feel in the same manner, and they scarcely believe that they belong to the same human race. They cannot, therefore, thoroughly understand what others feel, nor judge of others by themselves. Yet they are sometimes eager to lend each other mutual aid; but this is not contrary to my previous observation. These aristocratic institutions, which made the beings of one and the same race so different, nevertheless bound them to each other by close political ties. Although the serf had no natural interest in the fate of nobles, he did not the less think himself obliged to devote his person to the service of that noble who happened to be his lord; and although the noble held himself to be of a different nature from that of his serfs, he nevertheless held that his duty and his honor constrained him to defend, at the risk of his own life, those who dwelt upon his domains.

It is evident that these mutual obligations did not originate in the law of nature, but in the law of society; and that the claim of social duty was more stringent than that of mere humanity. These services were not supposed to be due from man to man, but to the vassal or to the lord. Feudal institutions awakened a lively sympathy for the sufferings of certain men, but none at all for the miseries of mankind. They infused generosity rather than mildness into the manners of the time, and although they prompted men to great acts of self-devotion, they engendered no real sympathies; for real sympathies can only exist between those who are alike; and in aristocratic ages men acknowledge none but the members of their own caste to be like themselves.

When the chroniclers of the Middle Ages, who all belonged to the aristocracy by birth or education, relate the tragical end of a noble, their grief flows apace; whereas they tell you at a breath, and without wincing, of massacres and tortures inflicted on the common sort of people. Not that these writers felt habitual hatred or systematic disdain for the people; war between the several classes of the community was not yet declared. They were impelled by an instinct rather than by a

并没有这样的感情。在贵族制国家，每个阶层都有自己的观念、情感、权利、民情和生活方式。因此，贵族阶级与人民大众毫无共同之处。他们之间没有共同的思想和情感，以至于很难相信他们同属一个国家。因此，他们无法完全理解对方的感受，也无从设身处地为他人考虑。但是，他们有时候很乐于互相帮助，而这一点与我上面所说的并不矛盾。尽管贵族制度将人与人划分为不同的等级，但是又通过政治纽带将他们彼此紧密联系起来。尽管农奴天生不关心贵族的命运，但他依然认为自己有义务效忠刚好成为自己主人的贵族；而贵族尽管认为自己与农奴天生并非同类，却也出于自己的责任和荣誉愿意不顾生命危险保护生活在自己领地上的人们。

显然，这种相互的义务并非源自自然法则，而是来自社会制度，所以这样的义务是社会的迫切要求而不是人性。这些义务并不是对自认为应该互助的人所尽，而是主人对家奴和家奴对主人应尽的义务。封建制度唤起了人们对于某些人所受痛苦的同情心，但并不是对所有人。封建时代唤起的民情是慷慨而不是如今的温和，而且尽管它鼓励人们自我牺牲，但并没有让人们产生真正的同情。因为真正的同情只会出现在彼此相近的人们之间，而在贵族时代，只有同一阶级的人才认为彼此相同。

中世纪的编年史家们，按照他们的出身和教育都属于贵族阶层，所以在描写贵族的悲惨结局的时候都流露出深切的悲伤。然而对于老百姓惨遭屠杀和折磨，他们则只是轻描淡写，无动于衷。这并不是因为这些作家一贯仇视或历来轻视人民，而且社会各阶层之间也并未宣战。他们之所以如此并非是出于感情而是本能，因为他们对于穷人的痛苦根本没有

passion; as they had formed no clear notion of a poor man's sufferings, they cared but little for his fate. The same feelings animated the lower orders whenever the feudal tie was broken. The same ages which witnessed so many heroic acts of self-devotion on the part of vassals for their lords, were stained with atrocious barbarities, exercised from time to time by the lower classes on the higher. It must not be supposed that this mutual insensibility arose solely from the absence of public order and education; for traces of it are to be found in the following centuries, which became tranquil and enlightened whilst they remained aristocratic. In 1675 the lower classes in Brittany revolted at the imposition of a new tax. These disturbances were put down with unexampled atrocity. Observe the language in which Madame de Sevigne, a witness of these horrors, relates them to her daughter:—

"Aux Rochers, 30 Octobre, 1675.

"Mon Dieu, ma fille, que votre lettre d'Aix est plaisante! Au moins relisez vos lettres avant que de les envoyer; laissez-vous surpendre a leur agrement, et consolez-vous par ce plaisir de la peine que vous avez d'en tant ecrire. Vous avez donc baise toute la Provence? il n'y aurait pas satisfaction a baiser toute la Bretagne, a moins qu'on n'aimat a sentir le vin. . . . Voulez-vous savoir des nouvelles de Rennes? On a fait une taxe de cent mille ecus sur le bourgeois; et si on ne trouve point cette somme dans vingt-quatre heures, elle sera doublee et exigible par les soldats. On a chasse et banni toute une grand rue, et defendu de les recueillir sous peine de la vie; de sorte qu'on voyait tous ces miserables, veillards, femmes accouchees, enfans, errer en pleurs au sortir de cette ville sans savoir ou aller. On roua avant-hier un violon, qui avait commence la danse et la pillerie du papier timbre; il a ete ecartele apres sa mort, et ses quatre quartiers exposes aux quatre coins de la ville. On a pris soixante bourgeois, et on commence demain les punitions. Cette province est un bel exemple pour les autres, et surtout de respecter les gouverneurs et les gouvernantes, et de ne point jeter de pierres dans leur jardin."

"Madame de Tarente etait hier dans ces bois par un temps enchante: il n'est question ni de chambre ni de collation; elle entre par la barriere et s'en retourne de meme. . . ."

清楚的认识，所以也不关心他们的命运。一旦封建的关系被打破，下层阶级也会有同样的情感。在这样的时代，我们见证过许多奴仆为了自己的主子甘愿自我牺牲的英勇行为，但时不时地也会出现一些下层阶级对上层阶级施加暴行的事情。千万不要认为这种互不关心的现象完全是因为缺乏公共秩序和文化，因为在接下来的几个世纪里，在社会安定、文化发达的贵族社会，依然能够看到这样的现象。1675年，布列塔尼的下层阶级曾发起暴动反对新税。这次暴动被当局无比残酷地镇压下去。我们可以看一看亲历这一恐怖事件的塞文夫富人在信中是如何跟她的女儿描述的：

"我的亲爱的女儿：你从埃克斯寄来的信，写得太可笑了！在把信寄出之前，至少要再看一遍，你会对你写的那么多赞美之词表示吃惊，但你又会因为喜欢这样不厌其烦地写了这么多而感到安慰。可见，你已经吻遍了普罗旺斯地方的所有的人，是不是？不过，只要你不爱闻葡萄酒的香味，就是你吻遍了布列塔尼地方的所有的人，也不会令他们满意。……你喜欢听雷恩地方的消息吗？那里下令征税10万银币，如果不在24小时内交出，就把税额翻一番，并派兵去征收。当局已把整条大街的所有居民都撵出家门，而且不准任何人收留，违者处死。因此，一大群倒霉的人，其中有孕妇、老人和小孩，在恋恋不舍地离开这个城市时号啕大哭，他们不知何去何从，既没有吃的，又没有栖身之处。前天，一个开舞厅的小提琴师，因偷印花税而被车裂。他被五马分尸，……而且他的四肢还被放在城市的四个角上示众。……已有60名市民被捕，明天开始治罪。这个地方为其他地方树立了良好的榜样，叫其他地方也尊重总督及其夫人，……不得往他们的花园里投石头。

"……昨天，天气很好，塔朗特夫人来到她的林园小憩。当然要为她准备下榻之处和

In another letter she adds:—

"Vous me parlez bien plaisamment de nos miseres; nous ne sommes plus si roues; un en huit jours, pour entretenir la justice. Il est vrai que la penderie me parait maintenant un refraichissement. J'ai une tout autre idee de la justice, depuis que je suis en ce pays. Vos galeriens me paraissent une societe d'honnetes gens qui se sont retires du monde pour mener une vie douce."

It would be a mistake to suppose that Madame de Sevigne, who wrote these lines, was a selfish or cruel person; she was passionately attached to her children, and very ready to sympathize in the sorrows of her friends; nay, her letters show that she treated her vassals and servants with kindness and indulgence. But Madame de Sevigne had no clear notion of suffering in anyone who was not a person of quality.

In our time the harshest man writing to the most insensible person of his acquaintance would not venture wantonly to indulge in the cruel jocularity which I have quoted; and even if his own manners allowed him to do so, the manners of society at large would forbid it. Whence does this arise? Have we more sensibility than our forefathers? I know not that we have; but I am sure that our insensibility is extended to a far greater range of objects. When all the ranks of a community are nearly equal, as all men think and feel in nearly the same manner, each of them may judge in a moment of the sensations of all the others; he casts a rapid glance upon himself, and that is enough. There is no wretchedness into which he cannot readily enter, and a secret instinct reveals to him its extent. It signifies not that strangers or foes be the sufferers; imagination puts him in their place; something like a personal feeling is mingled with his pity, and makes himself suffer whilst the body of his fellow-creature is in torture. In democratic ages men rarely sacrifice themselves for one another; but they display general compassion for the members of the human race. They inflict no useless ills; and they are happy to relieve the griefs of others, when they can do so without much hurting themselves; they are not disinterested, but they are humane.

Although the Americans have, in a manner, reduced egotism to a social and philosophical theory,

饮食。她从柴扉走进来，又从原路回去。"

在另一封信里，她又补充说：

"你总是喜欢跟我谈论我们这里的悲惨事件。我们这里已经不再实行车裂了。为了维护正义，每周只杀一个人。不错，我现在认为判处绞刑已经算宽大了。自从到了这里以后，我对于正义的观点已经完全改变了。在我看来，你的那些曳船奴隶，真是一群不问世事令生活安宁的好人。"

如果认为写下这些文字的塞文涅夫人是一个自私残忍的人就大错特错了。她深爱着自己的孩子，对朋友的不幸甚是同情，从她的信中也能看出她对自己的农奴和仆人也很和蔼包容。但是塞文涅夫人对于贵族圈以外任何人的疾苦一无所知。

在我们这个时代，最残暴的人在给最无情的人所写的信件中，也不会坦然自若地说出上面的那番话。即使个人的态度促使他这样做，社会的大民情也不会允许他如此。为什么会这样呢？难道我们比我们的祖先感情更丰富吗？我知道事实并非如此。但是我敢肯定我们的无动于衷已经扩展到更多的事物。当社会的所有阶层几乎平等，所有人的所想所感几近相同的时候，每个人都能立即判断出其他所有人的感受。也就是说，他只要迅速地审视一下自己就已足够。因此，他可以感知他人所有苦难，而且潜在的本能还能让他立刻察觉这种苦难的加剧。这意味着在对待陌生人和敌人的时候，他也能感同身受。个人感情和同情交织起来，让他在看到同类身体受到折磨的时候也同样感到痛苦。在民主时代，人们很少为了彼此自我牺牲，却对人类有着普遍的同情心。他们不会制造无谓的伤害，而且在对自己没有太大损害的时候很乐于帮助他人减轻痛苦。他们虽不无私，但是仁慈。

they are nevertheless extremely open to compassion. In no country is criminal justice administered with more mildness than in the United States. Whilst the English seem disposed carefully to retain the bloody traces of the dark ages in their penal legislation, the Americans have almost expunged capital punishment from their codes. North America is, I think, the only one country upon earth in which the life of no one citizen has been taken for a political offence in the course of the last fifty years. The circumstance which conclusively shows that this singular mildness of the Americans arises chiefly from their social condition, is the manner in which they treat their slaves. Perhaps there is not, upon the whole, a single European colony in the New World in which the physical condition of the blacks is less severe than in the United States; yet the slaves still endure horrid sufferings there, and are constantly exposed to barbarous punishments. It is easy to perceive that the lot of these unhappy beings inspires their masters with but little compassion, and that they look upon slavery, not only as an institution which is profitable to them, but as an evil which does not affect them. Thus the same man who is full of humanity towards his fellow-creatures when they are at the same time his equals, becomes insensible to their afflictions as soon as that equality ceases. His mildness should therefore be attributed to the equality of conditions, rather than to civilization and education.

What I have here remarked of individuals is, to a certain extent, applicable to nations. When each nation has its distinct opinions, belief, laws, and customs, it looks upon itself as the whole of mankind, and is moved by no sorrows but its own. Should war break out between two nations animated by this feeling, it is sure to be waged with great cruelty. At the time of their highest culture, the Romans slaughtered the generals of their enemies, after having dragged them in triumph behind a car; and they flung their prisoners to the beasts of the Circus for the amusement of the people. Cicero, who declaimed so vehemently at the notion of crucifying a Roman citizen, had not a word to say against these horrible abuses of victory. It is evident that in his eyes a barbarian did not belong to the same human race as a Roman. On the contrary, in proportion as nations become more like each other, they become reciprocally more compassionate, and the law of nations is mitigated.

尽管美国人在某种程度上已经将利己主义幻化为一种社会哲学理论，但是他们的同情心也丝毫没有减少。没有一个国家的刑事法庭像美国那样从轻治罪。当英国人还在小心翼翼地保存刑法中暗黑时代的嗜血遗风的时候，美国人几乎已经将死刑从他们的法典中剔除。我认为，北美是过去50年来世界上唯一一个没有政治犯被判死刑的国家。美国人的这种特别温和的态度主要是因为他们的社会状况，这从他们对待奴隶的态度上便可以得到证明。从总体来看，新大陆没有任何一个欧洲殖民地黑人奴隶的物质条件比美国还好，然而在这里，奴隶依然要忍受可怕的痛苦，不断受到残暴的惩罚。不难发现，这些可怜人的不幸遭遇并没有引起他们的丝毫同情。在他们的眼中，奴隶制不仅是有利于他们的制度，而且是不会影响到自己的罪恶。因此，当同类与之平等时充满人性的人们，在平等消失之后便会对同类的疾苦麻木不仁。因此，他们的温和是源自平等，而不是文明和教育。

这里我对于个人所做的评述，在一定程度上也适用于国家。当每个国家形成自己独特的观念、信仰、法律和习惯时，便会将自己视同为整个人类，只会为自己的悲伤而悲伤。如果战争在两个秉持这种观念的国家间爆发，必定会非常残酷。罗马人在他们文化最辉煌的时候，在将敌人拖在战车后面炫耀之后才会将他们屠杀，还会把俘虏扔进斗兽场娱乐大众。西塞奥一谈起将罗马公民在十字架上钉死就义愤填膺，慷慨激昂，却对胜利之后罗马人对战俘的暴行默不作声。显然，在他的眼中，蛮夷与罗马人并非同类。与之相反，随着国家间差别日益缩小，彼此越来越相似，能够更加同情彼此的不幸，国际公法也会更加温和。

Chapter II: That Democracy Renders The Habitual Intercourse Of The Americans Simple And Easy

Democracy does not attach men strongly to each other; but it places their habitual intercourse upon an easier footing. If two Englishmen chance to meet at the Antipodes, where they are surrounded by strangers whose language and manners are almost unknown to them, they will first stare at each other with much curiosity and a kind of secret uneasiness; they will then turn away, or, if one accosts the other, they will take care only to converse with a constrained and absent air upon very unimportant subjects. Yet there is no enmity between these men; they have never seen each other before, and each believes the other to be a respectable person. Why then should they stand so cautiously apart? We must go back to England to learn the reason.

When it is birth alone, independent of wealth, which classes men in society, everyone knows exactly what his own position is upon the social scale; he does not seek to rise, he does not fear to sink. In a community thus organized, men of different castes communicate very little with each other; but if accident brings them together, they are ready to converse without hoping or fearing to lose their own position. Their intercourse is not upon a footing of equality, but it is not constrained. When moneyed aristocracy succeeds to aristocracy of birth, the case is altered. The privileges of some are still extremely great, but the possibility of acquiring those privileges is open to all: whence it follows that those who possess them are constantly haunted by the apprehension of losing them, or of other men's sharing them; those who do not yet enjoy them long to possess them at any cost, or, if they fail to appear at least to possess them—which is not impossible. As the social importance of men is no longer ostensibly and permanently fixed by blood, and is infinitely varied by wealth, ranks still exist, but it is not easy clearly to distinguish at a glance those who respectively belong to them. Secret hostilities then arise in the community; one set of men endeavor by innumerable artifices to penetrate, or to appear to penetrate, amongst those who are above them; another set are constantly in arms against these usurpers of their rights; or rather the same individual does both at once, and whilst he seeks to raise himself into a higher circle, he is always on the defensive against the intrusion of

第二章 民主是美国人之间的关系简易化

民主并不会使人们之间的关系紧密，但是会让人们的日常关系简易化。如果两个英国人偶然在西半球邂逅，而且身边尽是些语言不通、民情不同的外国人。他们首先会用好奇的目光打量彼此，各自心中暗自不安，随后便各走各路；而如果其中的一个人上前与另一个人搭讪，他们也只会小心翼翼拘谨地谈论一些无关痛痒的事情。当然他们彼此之间没有敌意，以前也互不相识，而且都认为彼此是值得尊重的人。但是为什么他们如此小心地回避彼此呢？个中的原因我们要回到英格兰去寻找。

当只靠一个人的出身而不靠财产来划分社会等级的时候，每个人都清楚地知道自己在社会阶梯上所处的位置，既不想要往上爬也不担心会掉下去。因此，在这样组织起来的社会里，不同阶层的人们彼此很少交流。但如果有什么偶然事件将他们联系起来的时候，彼此却可以坦然交谈，既不希望也不担心会失去自己的位置。他们的交流并不是建立在平等之上，但也不是强制的。当金钱贵族取代以出身为基础的贵族时，情况就发生了改变。一些人的特权依旧很大，但是几乎所有人都有机会获得这些特权。于是，拥有特权的人终日提心吊胆，唯恐失去自己的特权或是不得不与人分享。而那些没有得到特权的人则不惜一切代价想要得到它们，即使得不到特权，也会表示并不是没有可能。当人的社会重要性不再因为血统而一成不变，而是随着财富的变换而变化无常时，阶级依然会存在，但是很难一眼分清人们各自属于哪个阶层。于是，公民之间彼此悄悄敌视。一些人千方百计想要进入，或是似乎进入那些高于自己的人们的行列，而另一些人则不断战斗想要击退那些妄图

those below him.

Such is the condition of England at the present time; and I am of opinion that the peculiarity before adverted to is principally to be attributed to this cause. As aristocratic pride is still extremely great amongst the English, and as the limits of aristocracy are ill-defined, everybody lives in constant dread lest advantage should be taken of his familiarity. Unable to judge at once of the social position of those he meets, an Englishman prudently avoids all contact with them. Men are afraid lest some slight service rendered should draw them into an unsuitable acquaintance; they dread civilities, and they avoid the obtrusive gratitude of a stranger quite as much as his hatred. Many people attribute these singular anti-social propensities, and the reserved and taciturn bearing of the English, to purely physical causes. I may admit that there is something of it in their race, but much more of it is attributable to their social condition, as is proved by the contrast of the Americans.

In America, where the privileges of birth never existed, and where riches confer no peculiar rights on their possessors, men unacquainted with each other are very ready to frequent the same places, and find neither peril nor advantage in the free interchange of their thoughts. If they meet by accident, they neither seek nor avoid intercourse; their manner is therefore natural, frank, and open: it is easy to see that they hardly expect or apprehend anything from each other, and that they do not care to display, any more than to conceal, their position in the world. If their demeanor is often cold and serious, it is never haughty or constrained; and if they do not converse, it is because they are not in a humor to talk, not because they think it their interest to be silent. In a foreign country two Americans are at once friends, simply because they are Americans. They are repulsed by no prejudice; they are attracted by their common country. For two Englishmen the same blood is not enough; they must be brought together by the same rank. The Americans remark this unsociable mood of the English as much as the French do, and they are not less astonished by it. Yet the Americans are connected with England by their origin, their religion, their language, and partially by their manners; they only differ in their social condition. It may therefore be inferred that the reserve of the English proceeds from the constitution of their country much more than from that of its inhabitants.

篡夺他们权利的人。或者说是一个人在两面作战，一方面他试图冲入更高的阶层，另一方面又需要不断抵御下面阶层的侵入。

这就是英国的现状，我认为前面所说的怪现象主要就是这一原因造成的。当贵族的骄傲依然在英国人心中很重要，阶级的界限已不明确的时候，每个人都时刻害怕，唯恐自己的友善被别人利用。因为无法一下子判断他们所碰到的人所属的阶层，英国人便格外小心地避免与之接触。人们害怕别人施与的小恩惠会让自己结识与自己并不相称的熟人，并对别人的多礼心存疑窦，不喜欢陌生人贸然的恭维。许多人将这些反社会的倾向归结为英国人性格的保守和沉默寡言。我承认，这的确与英国人的性格有些关系，但是更主要的还是因为他们的社会原因。我们可以用美国人的例子来证明这一点。

在美国，不存在身份特权，财富也并没有带给富人任何特殊的权利，彼此互不相识的人会随时在同一地点相遇，在他们彼此自由交流思想的时候既不是为了带来好处也不害怕会产生什么危险。如果他们偶然相遇，他们既不会主动搭讪也不会避免交谈。因此，他们的态度总是很自然、直爽和坦率。不难发现，他们既不打算也不期待从对方那里得到什么，所以并不在意暴露更不用说去掩盖他们的地位了。他们的举止往往冷淡而严肃，却从不高傲和拘谨。如果他们一言不发，那只是因为他们心情不好不想说话，并不是因为觉得缄口不言对他们有利。在异国他乡，两个美国人会立刻成为朋友，就因为他们都是美国人。他们彼此之间没有成见，共同的祖国让他们彼此吸引。对于两个英国人而言，同样的血统还不够，他们必须属于同样的阶级。美国人与我们法国人一样深知英国人这种冷漠的态度，所以对此不足

Chapter III: Why The Americans Show So Little Sensitiveness In Their Own Country, And Are So Sensitive In Europe

The temper of the Americans is vindictive, like that of all serious and reflecting nations. They hardly ever forget an offence, but it is not easy to offend them; and their resentment is as slow to kindle as it is to abate. In aristocratic communities where a small number of persons manage everything, the outward intercourse of men is subject to settled conventional rules. Everyone then thinks he knows exactly what marks of respect or of condescension he ought to display, and none are presumed to be ignorant of the science of etiquette. These usages of the first class in society afterwards serve as a model to all the others; besides which each of the latter lays down a code of its own, to which all its members are bound to conform. Thus the rules of politeness form a complex system of legislation, which it is difficult to be perfectly master of, but from which it is dangerous for anyone to deviate; so that men are constantly exposed involuntarily to inflict or to receive bitter affronts. But as the distinctions of rank are obliterated, as men differing in education and in birth meet and mingle in the same places of resort, it is almost impossible to agree upon the rules of good breeding. As its laws are uncertain, to disobey them is not a crime, even in the eyes of those who know what they are; men attach more importance to intentions than to forms, and they grow less civil, but at the same time less quarrelsome. There are many little attentions which an American does not care about; he thinks they are not due to him, or he presumes that they are not known to be due: he therefore either does not perceive a rudeness or he forgives it; his manners become less courteous, and his character more plain and masculine.

The mutual indulgence which the Americans display, and the manly confidence with which they treat each other, also result from another deeper and more general cause, which I have already adverted to in the preceding chapter. In the United States the distinctions of rank in civil society are slight, in political society they are null; an American, therefore, does not think himself bound to pay particular attentions to any of his fellow-citizens, nor does he require such attentions from them towards himself. As he does not see that it is his interest eagerly to seek the company of any of his

为奇。但是美国人与英国人在血统、宗教、语言乃至民情都一样，他们的唯一不同之处就是社会状况。所以，由此可见，英国人的谨慎主要是因为他们的国家制度，而不是居民的性格。

第三章　为什么美国人在本国不敏感，而在欧洲却表现得非常敏感

美国人的性情，像大多数严肃自重的民族一样，是有仇必报。美国人几乎不会忘记别人对自己的冒犯，但是想要冒犯他们也不是容易的事情，因为他们的怒火来得慢去得也慢。在贵族社会，所有事务由少数几个人掌管，人们之间的公开交往都会遵循常规。于是，每个人都认为自己知道应该如何表现得谦逊有礼，而且认为其他人也同样知礼。上层阶级的这些习惯后来成为所有人的行为典范，除此之外，其他阶级也各自有其成员必须遵守的行为准则。因此，礼仪规范成为一套复杂的繁文缛节，一般很难掌握得面面俱到，但如果稍有差池就会酿出祸患。所以，人们时刻都有可能在无意之中受到侮辱或侮辱他人。但是随着阶级差别的消失，不同教育和出身的人在同一个场所相遇融合，几乎不可能就良好教养的标准达成共识。因为礼法并没有明文规定，所以不遵从礼法也算不上犯罪，甚至那些深知礼仪的人也这么认为。人们更在意的是意图而不是形式，于是人们不再那么彬彬有礼，但同时也鲜有争执。美国人并不会为一些接连不断的小殷勤所打动，因为他们认为自己不应受到这样的礼遇，或是假装不知道自己应该享用。所以，他们不会因为别人没有对自己多加礼遇而感到受了冒犯，也就更谈不上什么宽恕别人。因此，他们的举止不拘小节，性格更为直爽有男子气概。

countrymen, he is slow to fancy that his own company is declined: despising no one on account of his station, he does not imagine that anyone can despise him for that cause; and until he has clearly perceived an insult, he does not suppose that an affront was intended. The social condition of the Americans naturally accustoms them not to take offence in small matters; and, on the other hand, the democratic freedom which they enjoy transfuses this same mildness of temper into the character of the nation. The political institutions of the United States constantly bring citizens of all ranks into contact, and compel them to pursue great undertakings in concert. People thus engaged have scarcely time to attend to the details of etiquette, and they are besides too strongly interested in living harmoniously for them to stick at such things. They therefore soon acquire a habit of considering the feelings and opinions of those whom they meet more than their manners, and they do not allow themselves to be annoyed by trifles.

I have often remarked in the United States that it is not easy to make a man understand that his presence may be dispensed with; hints will not always suffice to shake him off. I contradict an American at every word he says, to show him that his conversation bores me; he instantly labors with fresh pertinacity to convince me; I preserve a dogged silence, and he thinks I am meditating deeply on the truths which he is uttering; at last I rush from his company, and he supposes that some urgent business hurries me elsewhere. This man will never understand that he wearies me to extinction unless I tell him so: and the only way to get rid of him is to make him my enemy for life.

It appears surprising at first sight that the same man transported to Europe suddenly becomes so sensitive and captious, that I often find it as difficult to avoid offending him here as it was to put him out of countenance. These two opposite effects proceed from the same cause. Democratic institutions generally give men a lofty notion of their country and of themselves. An American leaves his country with a heart swollen with pride; on arriving in Europe he at once finds out that we are not so engrossed by the United States and the great people which inhabits them as he had supposed, and this begins to annoy him. He has been informed that the conditions of society are not equal in our

　　美国人表现出的相互宽容，和彼此之间采取的大丈夫态度，有其更为深刻普遍的原因。对此，我已经在上一章做过论述。在美国的市民社会中，等级差别非常小，而在政界则根本没有等级差别。因此，一个美国人不认为自己应该对任何一位同胞礼遇有加，也不需要别人这样对待自己。因为他不认为自己的利益在于与任何一位同胞结伴，于是便认为没人想要和他结伴。没有人会因为他的地位而轻视他，而他也相信没有人会因为这个原因而轻视自己。所以，他在确认别人存心侮辱自己之前，绝不认为此人有意如此。美国人的社会状况让他们自然而然习惯于不会因为小事而感觉受到冒犯，而另一方面，他们所享有的民主自由将这种宽容的风气灌输到美国的民情之中。美国的政治制度不断促进各阶层公民的接触，驱使他们共同行动推进伟大的事业。因此，人们几乎没有时间注重繁文缛节，而且因为他们太重视和睦相处而往往不拘礼节。因此，他们很快养成一种习惯，在待人接物的时候更注重人们的感情和思想而不拘于形式，同时也不让自己为一些小事而大为光火。

　　所以，在美国我常常会发现很难让一个人明白他的出现也许会令人不快，拐弯抹角想把他打发走，往往并不奏效。我曾经对一个美国人说的话句句反驳，试图表明与他谈话让我感到不胜其烦。可是他却一次又一次找到新的论点企图说服我，后来我保持沉默一言不发，而他却认为我正在沉思他给我讲的道理。最后，当我离席而去时，他又认为我有要紧事需要去处理。这个人除非我跟他直说，否则他永远也不知道我对他烦得要死，而唯一能够摆脱他的办法就是让他成为我生活中的敌人。

　　最初，我非常惊讶，这样的一个人在来到欧洲以后竟突然之间变得如此的敏感和挑剔，以至于我常常感到要想在欧洲不得罪他，简直就跟在美国让他生气一样难。这两种截

part of the globe, and he observes that among the nations of Europe the traces of rank are not wholly obliterated; that wealth and birth still retain some indeterminate privileges, which force themselves upon his notice whilst they elude definition. He is therefore profoundly ignorant of the place which he ought to occupy in this half-ruined scale of classes, which are sufficiently distinct to hate and despise each other, yet sufficiently alike for him to be always confounding them. He is afraid of ranging himself too high—still more is he afraid of being ranged too low; this twofold peril keeps his mind constantly on the stretch, and embarrasses all he says and does. He learns from tradition that in Europe ceremonial observances were infinitely varied according to different ranks; this recollection of former times completes his perplexity, and he is the more afraid of not obtaining those marks of respect which are due to him, as he does not exactly know in what they consist. He is like a man surrounded by traps: society is not a recreation for him, but a serious toil: he weighs your least actions, interrogates your looks, and scrutinizes all you say, lest there should be some hidden allusion to affront him. I doubt whether there was ever a provincial man of quality so punctilious in breeding as he is: he endeavors to attend to the slightest rules of etiquette, and does not allow one of them to be waived towards himself: he is full of scruples and at the same time of pretensions; he wishes to do enough, but fears to do too much; and as he does not very well know the limits of the one or of the other, he keeps up a haughty and embarrassed air of reserve.

But this is not all: here is yet another double of the human heart. An American is forever talking of the admirable equality which prevails in the United States; aloud he makes it the boast of his country, but in secret he deplores it for himself; and he aspires to show that, for his part, he is an exception to the general state of things which he vaunts. There is hardly an American to be met with who does not claim some remote kindred with the first founders of the colonies; and as for the scions of the noble families of England, America seemed to me to be covered with them. When an opulent American arrives in Europe, his first care is to surround himself with all the luxuries of wealth: he is so afraid of being taken for the plain citizen of a democracy, that he adopts a hundred distorted ways of bringing

然相反的表现实际上都出于同一原因。民主制度通常会让人觉得自己的国家和自己很了不起。离开祖国来到国外的美国人内心往往充满骄傲。但是一到欧洲他们就发现我们对于美国以及居住在那里的伟大人民的看法并非他所想象的那样，这令他感到很生气。他以前就听说，在我们这半球，人们并不平等，而且现在他亲眼看到，在欧洲国家，等级差别并没有完全消除，财富和出身仍然拥有一些他说不清道不明的不定特权。因此，在已经半垮台的等级制度中，在这些分明彼此仇视相互轻视却又随时准备融合的阶级中，他完全找不到自己应有的位置。他害怕把自己的位置摆得过高，也害怕被摆的过低，这两种想法在他的脑子里不断作祟，干扰着他的一言一行。他了解欧洲的传统，在欧洲礼仪会因阶级不同而大不相同。这些昔日的作风让他大惑不解，而更令他担忧的是自己得不到应有的尊重，因为他不知道应有的尊重到底是如何。他就好像一个身边处处陷阱的人。社交对他不再是消遣，而是一项吃力的工作。他琢磨你的一举一动，察言观色，唯恐暗藏任何对他的侮辱。我很怀疑是否还有比他更拘泥于礼仪的乡绅。他力图一丝不苟地遵守所有繁文缛节，也不允许别人对自己稍有失礼。他谨小慎微同时又妄自尊大。他想要做得恰如其分，却又害怕过犹不及。而且因为他弄不清楚两者的界限，所以总是显得高傲、惺惺作态。

但这并不是全部，人心还有另一种伪装。一个美国人总是对美国盛行的平等津津乐道，并以此为祖国而骄傲。但是在他的内心深处又常常为此而遗憾，并渴望展示给人们自己是自己所吹嘘的那种普遍平等中的一个特例。几乎每个美国人都想要跟创建殖民地的第一批移民攀上点关系。在我看来，所有美国人都可以算是英国大家庭的后裔。当一个美国的富人来到欧洲时，他所关心的第一件事情，就是用奢侈来炫耀自己的财富。他不愿意人们将他

some new instance of his wealth before you every day. His house will be in the most fashionable part of the town: he will always be surrounded by a host of servants. I have heard an American complain, that in the best houses of Paris the society was rather mixed; the taste which prevails there was not pure enough for him; and he ventured to hint that, in his opinion, there was a want of elegance of manner; he could not accustom himself to see wit concealed under such unpretending forms.

These contrasts ought not to surprise us. If the vestiges of former aristocratic distinctions were not so completely effaced in the United States, the Americans would be less simple and less tolerant in their own country—they would require less, and be less fond of borrowed manners in ours.

Chapter IV: Consequences Of The Three Preceding Chapters

When men feel a natural compassion for their mutual sufferings—when they are brought together by easy and frequent intercourse, and no sensitive feelings keep them asunder—it may readily be supposed that they will lend assistance to one another whenever it is needed. When an American asks for the co-operation of his fellow-citizens it is seldom refused, and I have often seen it afforded spontaneously and with great goodwill. If an accident happens on the highway, everybody hastens to help the sufferer; if some great and sudden calamity befalls a family, the purses of a thousand strangers are at once willingly opened, and small but numerous donations pour in to relieve their distress. It often happens amongst the most civilized nations of the globe, that a poor wretch is as friendless in the midst of a crowd as the savage in his wilds: this is hardly ever the case in the United States. The Americans, who are always cold and often coarse in their manners, seldom show insensibility; and if they do not proffer services eagerly, yet they do not refuse to render them.

All this is not in contradiction to what I have said before on the subject of individualism. The two things are so far from combating each other, that I can see how they agree. Equality of conditions, whilst it makes men feel their independence, shows them their own weakness: they are free, but exposed to a thousand accidents; and experience soon teaches them that, although they do not

视为民主国家的普通公民，每天他都会千方百计地在你面前炫耀他的财富。他要住在城里最繁华的地方，身边总是有一批的仆人前呼后拥。我曾经听到一个美国人抱怨，在巴黎最好的沙龙也不过如此，那里的品位对他来说不够高雅。他还会暗示，在他看来，那里人们的仪态应该更加优雅才对。其实，他还不习惯于我们的风气，看不到隐藏在俗气外表背后的智慧。

这些对比并不应该让我们感到惊讶。如果旧贵族时代的等级差别在美国没有完全消灭，美国人在自己的国家就不会表现得那么纯朴宽容，也不需要在我们面前表现得如此矫揉造作。

第四章　前三章的总结

当人们对彼此的不幸流露出自然的同情，当他们能够随意频繁的交往，且不存在使他们相互分离的冲动时，则不难理解，人们会在必要时随时互相帮助。当一个美国人寻求同胞的合作时，很少遭到拒绝。我曾经多次看到人们这种自发的善举。如果公路上突发车祸，每个人都会积极救助受难人员；如果一个家庭突遭大难，数以千计的陌生人会慷慨解囊，纷至沓来的无数笔小捐助会帮助他们渡过难关。而在世界上一些最文明的国家，一个不幸的人则往往如同身处荒野一般在人群中孤立无援。但是在美国绝不会有这样的事情发生。美国人的举止尽管总是显得冷淡而粗野，但很少表现得冷酷无情。即使他们并没有主动热情地帮忙，也不代表他们会拒绝别人的求助。

所有这一切与我前面所说的个人主义并不矛盾。它们彼此不但绝不对立，我反而认为它们还很协调。平等在让人们感受到独立自主的同时，也让人们意识到自己的弱小。他们自由，

habitually require the assistance of others, a time almost always comes when they cannot do without it. We constantly see in Europe that men of the same profession are ever ready to assist each other; they are all exposed to the same ills, and that is enough to teach them to seek mutual preservatives, however hard-hearted and selfish they may otherwise be. When one of them falls into danger, from which the others may save him by a slight transient sacrifice or a sudden effort, they do not fail to make the attempt. Not that they are deeply interested in his fate; for if, by chance, their exertions are unavailing, they immediately forget the object of them, and return to their own business; but a sort of tacit and almost involuntary agreement has been passed between them, by which each one owes to the others a temporary support which he may claim for himself in turn. Extend to a people the remark here applied to a class, and you will understand my meaning. A similar covenant exists in fact between all the citizens of a democracy: they all feel themselves subject to the same weakness and the same dangers; and their interest, as well as their sympathy, makes it a rule with them to lend each other mutual assistance when required. The more equal social conditions become, the more do men display this reciprocal disposition to oblige each other. In democracies no great benefits are conferred, but good offices are constantly rendered: a man seldom displays self-devotion, but all men are ready to be of service to one another.

Chapter V: How Democracy Affects the Relation Of Masters And Servants

An American who had travelled for a long time in Europe once said to me, "The English treat their servants with a stiffness and imperiousness of manner which surprise us; but on the other hand the French sometimes treat their attendants with a degree of familiarity or of politeness which we cannot conceive. It looks as if they were afraid to give orders: the posture of the superior and the inferior is ill-maintained." The remark was a just one, and I have often made it myself. I have always considered England as the country in the world where, in our time, the bond of domestic service is drawn most tightly, and France as the country where it is most relaxed. Nowhere have I seen masters

却面对着无数的威胁。不久，经验教会他们，尽管他们并不总是需要他人的帮助，但随时可能有这种需要。在欧洲，我们不断看到同一行业的人们随时互助，他们都面临着同样的困难，而且无论他们在其他方面是多么铁石心肠和自私，这足以教会他们寻求互相支持。当他们之中有人陷入困境，而其他人只要做一点暂时牺牲或一些额外努力就能挽救他的时候，所有人都愿意施以援手。这并不能证明他们对这个人的命运非常关心，因为，如果他们的努力徒劳无功，他们便会立即各忙各事，完全将这件事抛到一边。但是在他们之间似乎有一种几乎不由自主的默契，每个人都有义务给别人提供暂时的援助，而每个人在困难时也都有权利要求别人的援助。如果对一个阶级的论述可以推及一个国家，大家就会明白我的想法。实际上，在民主国家的所有公民之间存在一种相似的默契。他们同样都感受到自己的弱小和可能遭遇的危险，而且他们的利益和同情心，使必要时互相帮助成为一种不成文的规定。社会越是平等，人们就越是觉得有义务互相支援。在民主国家，没有人会做出大的付出，却会经常帮助他人，人们很少表现出自我牺牲的精神，但是所有人都时刻愿意互相帮助。

第五章　美国民主对于主仆关系的影响

一个在欧洲旅游过很长时间的人曾经对我说："英国人对自己仆人表现出的那种高傲和专横的态度真让我们惊讶。但是另一方面，法国人对待仆人有时候又过于亲密和客气，也让我们不能理解。看上去就好像他们害怕支使仆人一样，上下级的关系非常不明确。"他的说法很正确，而且我自己也曾多次这样说过。我一直都认为，英国人是我们这个时代世界上主仆关系最严谨的国家，而法国则往往是最随意的国家。我从来没有见过任何国家

stand so high or so low as in these two countries. Between these two extremes the Americans are to be placed. Such is the fact as it appears upon the surface of things: to discover the causes of that fact, it is necessary to search the matter thoroughly.

No communities have ever yet existed in which social conditions have been so equal that there were neither rich nor poor, and consequently neither masters nor servants. Democracy does not prevent the existence of these two classes, but it changes their dispositions and modifies their mutual relations. Amongst aristocratic nations servants form a distinct class, not more variously composed than that of masters. A settled order is soon established; in the former as well as in the latter class a scale is formed, with numerous distinctions or marked gradations of rank, and generations succeed each other thus without any change of position. These two communities are superposed one above the other, always distinct, but regulated by analogous principles. This aristocratic constitution does not exert a less powerful influence on the notions and manners of servants than on those of masters; and, although the effects are different, the same cause may easily be traced. Both classes constitute small communities in the heart of the nation, and certain permanent notions of right and wrong are ultimately engendered amongst them. The different acts of human life are viewed by one particular and unchanging light. In the society of servants, as in that of masters, men exercise a great influence over each other: they acknowledge settled rules, and in the absence of law they are guided by a sort of public opinion: their habits are settled, and their conduct is placed under a certain control.

These men, whose destiny is to obey, certainly do not understand fame, virtue, honesty, and honor in the same manner as their masters; but they have a pride, a virtue, and an honesty pertaining to their condition; and they have a notion, if I may use the expression, of a sort of servile honor. Because a class is mean, it must not be supposed that all who belong to it are mean-hearted; to think so would be a great mistake. However lowly it may be, he who is foremost there, and who has no notion of quitting it, occupies an aristocratic position which inspires him with lofty feelings, pride, and self-respect, that fit him for the higher virtues and actions above the common. Amongst aristocratic nations it was by no means rare to find men of noble and vigorous minds in the service of the great,

的主人地位像他们那样有天壤之别。而美国人则处在这两个极端之间。这就是事情表面看上去的样子，要想发现个中的原因，就必须进行全面的梳理。

世界上从未出现过一个社会平等得没有贫富之分，主仆之别。民主并不妨碍主仆阶级的存在，却让他们的思想意识发生变化，对他们的关系进行调整。在贵族制国家，仆人来自一个不同的阶层，其成员与主人阶层一样没有什么变化。一个固定的秩序很快就确立起来。无论是在仆人还是在主人，很快便形成等级、集团和显赫的人物，而且代代相传，始终不变。这两个社会一个在上一个在下，始终保持着明显的差别，却遵守着相似的原则。这种贵族制度对于主人阶层观念和习惯的影响不亚于仆人阶层。尽管产生的影响并不相同，但不难发现原因相同。这两个阶层在国家中各自形成自己的小国家，关于对与错最终都形成自己的特定看法。他们对人生的各种行为，各有其独特的固定看法。在仆人社会，像在主人社会一样，人们彼此相互影响。他们认可固定的规范，当没有明文规定的时候，会遵循公共舆论。长期形成的习惯牢牢支配着他们的行为。

命中注定受人支使的这些人对待名誉、美德、正直和荣誉的看法肯定与他们的主人不同，但是他们也有属于自己的骄傲、美德和正直的标准。如果我可以这么说的话，他们有一种仆人的荣誉感。不要因为一个阶级卑微，就认为这个阶级所有的人都是胸无大志。如果这样认为就大错特错了。无论一个阶级多么卑微，总是会有出类拔萃且不想放弃高位的人，他们的地位与贵族类似。这让他们总是趾高气扬，妄自尊大，认为自己的德行和作为会超过常人。在贵族制国家，常常有一些心灵高尚精明强干的人为大人物服务，却没觉

who felt not the servitude they bore, and who submitted to the will of their masters without any fear of their displeasure. But this was hardly ever the case amongst the inferior ranks of domestic servants. It may be imagined that he who occupies the lowest stage of the order of menials stands very low indeed. The French created a word on purpose to designate the servants of the aristocracy—they called them lackeys. This word "lackey" served as the strongest expression, when all others were exhausted, to designate human meanness. Under the old French monarchy, to denote by a single expression a low-spirited contemptible fellow, it was usual to say that he had the "soul of a lackey"; the term was enough to convey all that was intended.

The permanent inequality of conditions not only gives servants certain peculiar virtues and vices, but it places them in a peculiar relation with respect to their masters. Amongst aristocratic nations the poor man is familiarized from his childhood with the notion of being commanded: to whichever side he turns his eyes the graduated structure of society and the aspect of obedience meet his view. Hence in those countries the master readily obtains prompt, complete, respectful, and easy obedience from his servants, because they revere in him not only their master but the class of masters. He weighs down their will by the whole weight of the aristocracy. He orders their actions—to a certain extent he even directs their thoughts. In aristocracies the master often exercises, even without being aware of it, an amazing sway over the opinions, the habits, and the manners of those who obey him, and his influence extends even further than his authority.

In aristocratic communities there are not only hereditary families of servants as well as of masters, but the same families of servants adhere for several generations to the same families of masters (like two parallel lines which neither meet nor separate); and this considerably modifies the mutual relations of these two classes of persons. Thus, although in aristocratic society the master and servant have no natural resemblance—although, on the contrary, they are placed at an immense distance on the scale of human beings by their fortune, education, and opinions—yet time ultimately binds them together. They are connected by a long series of common reminiscences, and however different they may be, they grow alike; whilst in democracies, where they are naturally almost alike, they always

得自己是仆从，他们服从主人的意志但也不怕惹恼他们。但是在仆人阶级的下层却并非如此。可以想象，仆人阶层最下层的地位必定非常卑微。法国人专门造了一个词来称呼为贵族服务的仆人，即奴才。奴才这个词是一个非常贬义的词，当人们想骂一个人下贱，却又找不到合适的词时，他们会用这个词。在法国旧君主时代，想要骂一个最卑鄙无耻之人时，常常会说他有奴才的劣根性，只这一句话就足以表达所有含义。

　　长久的不平等不但让仆人阶层形成自己独特的美德观和罪恶观，而且让他们与主人形成特殊的关系。在贵族制社会，穷人从小就形成服从的观念。无论他们将目光投向何处，看到的都是森严的社会等级和下级对上级的服从。因此，在这些国家，主人可以随时轻而易举地得到仆人毕恭毕敬的绝对服从，因为他们服从的不仅是自己的主人还有整个主人阶级。主人阶级将贵族制度的所有压力都压在他们的身上。主人支配仆人的行动，甚至在一定程度上支配他们的思想。在贵族社会主人往往是在无意之中，左右着那些服从自己的人的思想、习惯和情绪，而且他的影响力甚至超越权威。

　　在贵族社会，不仅有世袭的主人家族还有世袭的仆人家族，而且同一个仆人家族往往世代服侍同一个主人家族（就好像两条永不相交却又不分开的平行线），而这将会在很大程度上改变两个阶级之间人们的相互关系。因此，尽管在贵族社会主人和仆人没有天然的相似之处，而且财产、教育和观念上的巨大差异又令他们的处境有天壤之别，但是时间最终让他们合为一体。对于往事的一连串长久的共同回忆将他们联系起来，无论他们各自多么不同，彼此却越来越像。然而，在民主国家，主仆天生几乎没有差别，而且彼此都视对

remain strangers to each other. Amongst an aristocratic people the master gets to look upon his servants as an inferior and secondary part of himself, and he often takes an interest in their lot by a last stretch of egotism.

Servants, on their part, are not averse to regard themselves in the same light; and they sometimes identify themselves with the person of the master, so that they become an appendage to him in their own eyes as well as in his. In aristocracies a servant fills a subordinate position which he cannot get out of; above him is another man, holding a superior rank which he cannot lose. On one side are obscurity, poverty, obedience for life; on the other, and also for life, fame, wealth, and command. The two conditions are always distinct and always in propinquity; the tie that connects them is as lasting as they are themselves. In this predicament the servant ultimately detaches his notion of interest from his own person; he deserts himself, as it were, or rather he transports himself into the character of his master, and thus assumes an imaginary personality. He complacently invests himself with the wealth of those who command him; he shares their fame, exalts himself by their rank, and feeds his mind with borrowed greatness, to which he attaches more importance than those who fully and really possess it. There is something touching, and at the same time ridiculous, in this strange confusion of two different states of being. These passions of masters, when they pass into the souls of menials, assume the natural dimensions of the place they occupy—they are contracted and lowered. What was pride in the former becomes puerile vanity and paltry ostentation in the latter. The servants of a great man are commonly most punctilious as to the marks of respect due to him, and they attach more importance to his slightest privileges than he does himself. In France a few of these old servants of the aristocracy are still to be met with here and there; they have survived their race, which will soon disappear with them altogether. In the United States I never saw anyone at all like them. The Americans are not only unacquainted with the kind of man, but it is hardly possible to make them understand that such ever existed. It is scarcely less difficult for them to conceive it, than for us to form a correct notion of what a slave was amongst the Romans, or a serf in the Middle Ages. All these men were in fact, though in different degrees, results of the same cause: they are all retiring

方为陌生人。在贵族制国家，主人则总是把仆人视为自己人和下属，并在利己主义的推动下关心仆人的命运。

至于仆人，他们自己也这么认为。有时他们认为自己是主人的人，因为他们也跟主人一样认为自己是主人的附属物。在贵族制社会，仆人无法摆脱自己的从属地位，在自己之上的人，拥有永远不会失去的高爵显位。一方面是终身卑微、贫穷、任人摆布；另一方面是一辈子声名显赫、荣华富贵、颐指气使。两个阶层的境遇永远不同，但又始终接近。而将他们彼此联系起来的纽带将会伴随他们的存在而一直存在下去。在这样的窘境中，仆人最终将自己的利益观抛弃，也将自己抛弃，或者说把自己的一切交给了主人，让自己具备主人的个性，假设了一个虚构的性格。他们为有权支配他人的财富而沾沾自喜，以主人的荣誉为荣，以主人的高贵而得意扬扬，并满足于这些仰仗他人得来的荣耀。他们把这种荣耀看得往往比那些真正拥有这些的人还要重。这两种不同生活状态的奇怪结合既有些让人感动又有些让人觉得可笑。当主人的情感深入到仆人的灵魂，自然会变得狭隘和低级。前者身上高尚的东西，在后者的身上变成了虚荣和炫耀。大人物的仆人往往会摆出一副主人的派头，对特权的斤斤计较比主人更甚。在法国，还可以在各处看到一些这样的贵族老仆，他们是这类人的遗子，但是不久之后他们也会随这类人的消失而消失。在美国，我从未见过这样的人，而且他们也难以理解这类人的存在。让他们想象这种人的存在，与让我们想象古罗马的奴隶或中世纪的农奴的情景，几乎是同样困难。尽管所有的仆人，有高低之别，但他们都是同一原因的产物。他们正在从我们的视线中消失，与孕育他们的社会状

from our sight, and disappearing in the obscurity of the past, together with the social condition to which they owed their origin.

Equality of conditions turns servants and masters into new beings, and places them in new relative positions. When social conditions are nearly equal, men are constantly changing their situations in life: there is still a class of menials and a class of masters, but these classes are not always composed of the same individuals, still less of the same families; and those who command are not more secure of perpetuity than those who obey. As servants do not form a separate people, they have no habits, prejudices, or manners peculiar to themselves; they are not remarkable for any particular turn of mind or moods of feeling. They know no vices or virtues of their condition, but they partake of the education, the opinions, the feelings, the virtues, and the vices of their contemporaries; and they are honest men or scoundrels in the same way as their masters are. The conditions of servants are not less equal than those of masters. As no marked ranks or fixed subordination are to be found amongst them, they will not display either the meanness or the greatness which characterizes the aristocracy of menials as well as all other aristocracies. I never saw a man in the United States who reminded me of that class of confidential servants of which we still retain a reminiscence in Europe, neither did I ever meet with such a thing as a lackey: all traces of the one and of the other have disappeared.

In democracies servants are not only equal amongst themselves, but it may be said that they are in some sort the equals of their masters. This requires explanation in order to be rightly understood. At any moment a servant may become a master, and he aspires to rise to that condition: the servant is therefore not a different man from the master. Why then has the former a right to command, and what compels the latter to obey?—the free and temporary consent of both their wills. Neither of them is by nature inferior to the other; they only become so for a time by covenant. Within the terms of this covenant, the one is a servant, the other a master; beyond it they are two citizens of the commonwealth—two men. I beg the reader particularly to observe that this is not only the notion which servants themselves entertain of their own condition; domestic service is looked upon by masters in the same light; and the precise limits of authority and obedience are as clearly settled in

况一起消失在朦胧的过去。

平等让仆人和主人有了新的面貌，建立起新的关系。当社会状况几乎完全平等时，人们可以不断改变自己的处境。仆人和主人阶层依旧存在，但是这两个阶级的成员不再始终是同一群人，也不再是同一些家族。无论是发号施令的还是听人支使的地位都不会永远不变。因为仆人不再是一群孤立的人，他们没有专属于自己的习惯、偏见和民情，也看不到他们特有的思想变化或是情感表达。他们不知道由地位而来的善恶为何物，却与同时代的人有着相同的知识、思想、情感、美德以及恶习。他们跟他们的主人一样既有正直良民也有卑鄙小人。因为在他们之中没有明显的等级和固定的从属关系，所以看不到贵族制社会仆人阶级和其他贵族社会所常见的尊卑。我在美国从未见到一个人让我想起欧洲人尚未忘记的那些赫赫有名的忠仆；而且也没有碰到一件事让我想起奴才这个词。在美国，所有忠仆和奴才的痕迹都已消失不见。

在民主制度下，仆人之间不但彼此平等，而且可以说他们在一定程度上与主人平等。为了能正确理解这一点，有必要进行一下说明。仆人随时都可能变成主人，而且渴望成为主人。因此，仆人与主人并没有什么不同。那么，是什么让主人有权发号施令，又是什么让仆人不得不服从呢？是双方自由意志达成的暂时契约。当然，他们天生本无高低之分，只是根据契约暂时如此。按照契约的规定，一方是仆人，而另一方则为主人。但在契约的范围之外，他们是共和国的两个公民，两个平等的人。我希望读者特别留意的不仅是仆人对于自己地位的看法。主人和被雇用的人都持有这样的看法，在他们的头脑里对于命令和

the mind of the one as in that of the other.

When the greater part of the community have long attained a condition nearly alike, and when equality is an old and acknowledged fact, the public mind, which is never affected by exceptions, assigns certain general limits to the value of man, above or below which no man can long remain placed. It is in vain that wealth and poverty, authority and obedience, accidentally interpose great distances between two men; public opinion, founded upon the usual order of things, draws them to a common level, and creates a species of imaginary equality between them, in spite of the real inequality of their conditions. This all-powerful opinion penetrates at length even into the hearts of those whose interest might arm them to resist it; it affects their judgment whilst it subdues their will. In their inmost convictions the master and the servant no longer perceive any deep-seated difference between them, and they neither hope nor fear to meet with any such at any time. They are therefore neither subject to disdain nor to anger, and they discern in each other neither humility nor pride. The master holds the contract of service to be the only source of his power, and the servant regards it as the only cause of his obedience. They do not quarrel about their reciprocal situations, but each knows his own and keeps it.

In the French army the common soldier is taken from nearly the same classes as the officer, and may hold the same commissions; out of the ranks he considers himself entirely equal to his military superiors, and in point of fact he is so; but when under arms he does not hesitate to obey, and his obedience is not the less prompt, precise, and ready, for being voluntary and defined. This example may give a notion of what takes place between masters and servants in democratic communities.

It would be preposterous to suppose that those warm and deep-seated affections, which are sometimes kindled in the domestic service of aristocracy, will ever spring up between these two men, or that they will exhibit strong instances of self-sacrifice. In aristocracies masters and servants live apart, and frequently their only intercourse is through a third person; yet they commonly stand firmly by one another. In democratic countries the master and the servant are close together; they are in daily personal contact, but their minds do not intermingle; they have common occupations, hardly

服从的界限都非常明确。

当大部分公民长期以来都处于基本相同的状况，当平等已成为由来已久的公认事实时，不曾受到任何特殊力量影响的公众意识，开始对人的价值划出一定的界限，没有人会长期地处在这个界限之上或之下。虽然富贵与贫穷、权威与服从会偶然令两个人之间形成巨大的差距，但这都无关紧要，因为建立在事物常规秩序之上的公共舆论将会引导他们走向相同的水平，并不管他们实际的不平等而在他们之间创造出一种假想的平等。这种力量无比强大的舆论，最终会深入到自身利益会令其表示反对的那些人的内心，影响着他们的判断，征服了他们的意志。在他们的心灵深处主人和仆人不再感到彼此之间存在根深蒂固的差别。因此，他们不再彼此轻视憎恨，前者并不再蛮横无理，后者亦无须卑躬屈膝。主人认为契约是他权力的唯一根源，而仆人则将其视为自己服从的唯一理由。他们之间决不会为彼此的地位而争执，每个人都清楚自己的地位并恪尽职守。

在法国的军队中，士兵与军官几乎都来自相同的阶层，而且士兵也同样能够晋升为军官。除了军衔之外，士兵认为自己与长官完全平等，而且事实上也的确如此。但是，在军队之中，士兵会毫不犹豫地服从长官，而且他会随时迅速完全地执行命令，因为这种服从是出于自愿而且有明文规定。这个例子可以让我们对民主社会中的主仆关系有所认识。

如果认为贵族的家臣有时对主人表现出的那份深情厚谊，或是强烈的自我牺牲精神会出现在民主社会的主仆二人之间那将是非常可笑的。在贵族制度下，主人和仆人分开居住，有话也往往由第三者传达，但两者的关系非常牢固。在民主国家，主人和仆人之间没

ever common interests. Amongst such a people the servant always considers himself as a sojourner in the dwelling of his masters. He knew nothing of their forefathers—he will see nothing of their descendants—he has nothing lasting to expect from their hand. Why then should he confound his life with theirs, and whence should so strange a surrender of himself proceed? The reciprocal position of the two men is changed—their mutual relations must be so too.

I would fain illustrate all these reflections by the example of the Americans; but for this purpose the distinctions of persons and places must be accurately traced. In the South of the Union, slavery exists; all that I have just said is consequently inapplicable there. In the North, the majority of servants are either freedmen or the children of freedmen; these persons occupy a contested position in the public estimation; by the laws they are brought up to the level of their masters—by the manners of the country they are obstinately detruded from it. They do not themselves clearly know their proper place, and they are almost always either insolent or craven. But in the Northern States, especially in New England, there are a certain number of whites, who agree, for wages, to yield a temporary obedience to the will of their fellow-citizens. I have heard that these servants commonly perform the duties of their situation with punctuality and intelligence; and that without thinking themselves naturally inferior to the person who orders them, they submit without reluctance to obey him. They appear to me to carry into service some of those manly habits which independence and equality engender. Having once selected a hard way of life, they do not seek to escape from it by indirect means; and they have sufficient respect for themselves, not to refuse to their master that obedience which they have freely promised. On their part, masters require nothing of their servants but the faithful and rigorous performance of the covenant: they do not ask for marks of respect, they do not claim their love or devoted attachment; it is enough that, as servants, they are exact and honest. It would not then be true to assert that, in democratic society, the relation of servants and masters is disorganized: it is organized on another footing; the rule is different, but there is a rule.

It is not my purpose to inquire whether the new state of things which I have just described is inferior to that which preceded it, or simply different. Enough for me that it is fixed and determined:

有距离，经常直接接触，却从没有思想交流。他们的工作相同，但利益完全不同。在这样的国家里，仆人总认为自己是住在主人家里的寄居者。他们既不知道主人的祖先是谁，也不过问主人的后代，而且对主人也没有抱任何长期的期待，那么，他们为什么要让自己的生活与主人的生活搅在一起呢？他们那种忘我的服务精神又来自何处呢？这是因为他们彼此的地位发生了改变，因此他们的关系也必然发生变化。

我乐意用美国人的实例来证明我上述的观点。但是，为了达到这个目的，我必须严格注意人物和地点的选择。在联邦的南部，奴隶制依然存在。所以我刚刚所说的一切都不适用于这里。在北部，大多数的仆人是已获解放的奴隶或其子女。在大众的眼中，这些人的地位尚未确定。法律虽然把他们的地位提高到与主人相同的水平，而国家的民情却顽固地加以抵制。他们自己也弄不清楚自己的地位，所以他们总是表现得不是粗鲁无礼就是唯唯诺诺。但是，在北部各州，特别是在新英格兰，有一定数量的白人为了工资而愿意暂时听从自己的同胞的支使。我听说，这些白人一般都恪守职责工作认真，也并不认为自己生来就比雇用自己的人低下，并且心甘情愿地服从雇主。在我看来，他们似乎把独立和平等造就的刚毅气质，或多或少地带进仆役的工作。他们一旦选择了这样一条辛苦的生活道路，就会想通过某种间接手段逃避辛苦。他们都非常自重，从不拒绝主人自己所承诺的服从。至于主人，也只要求仆人忠诚地恪尽职守。他们不要求仆人对自己毕恭毕敬，不要求仆人的热爱或是关怀备至。作为仆人只要诚实肯干就足矣。所以说在民主社会，主仆关系杂乱无序，是不正确的。他们的关系建立在另外一套规则之上。尽管规则不同，但的确有其规则。

for what is most important to meet with among men is not any given ordering, but order. But what shall I say of those sad and troubled times at which equality is established in the midst of the tumult of revolution—when democracy, after having been introduced into the state of society, still struggles with difficulty against the prejudices and manners of the country? The laws, and partially public opinion, already declare that no natural or permanent inferiority exists between the servant and the master. But this new belief has not yet reached the innermost convictions of the latter, or rather his heart rejects it; in the secret persuasion of his mind the master thinks that he belongs to a peculiar and superior race; he dares not say so, but he shudders whilst he allows himself to be dragged to the same level. His authority over his servants becomes timid and at the same time harsh: he has already ceased to entertain for them the feelings of patronizing kindness which long uncontested power always engenders, and he is surprised that, being changed himself, his servant changes also. He wants his attendants to form regular and permanent habits, in a condition of domestic service which is only temporary: he requires that they should appear contented with and proud of a servile condition, which they will one day shake off—that they should sacrifice themselves to a man who can neither protect nor ruin them—and in short that they should contract an indissoluble engagement to a being like themselves, and one who will last no longer than they will.

Amongst aristocratic nations it often happens that the condition of domestic service does not degrade the character of those who enter upon it, because they neither know nor imagine any other; and the amazing inequality which is manifest between them and their master appears to be the necessary and unavoidable consequence of some hidden law of Providence. In democracies the condition of domestic service does not degrade the character of those who enter upon it, because it is freely chosen, and adopted for a time only; because it is not stigmatized by public opinion, and creates no permanent inequality between the servant and the master. But whilst the transition from one social condition to another is going on, there is almost always a time when men's minds fluctuate between the aristocratic notion of subjection and the democratic notion of obedience. Obedience

　　我并不想去探究我所说的这种新情况是否不如以前，或只是与以前不同。我只想说这种情况已经固定下来不容更改，因为人与人之间最重要的东西不在于遵守特定的秩序，而在于有秩序可循。但是，对于在革命的暴风骤雨中确立起来的平等所经历的，以及民主制度作为一种社会制度建立之后依然要同偏见和世俗进行艰苦斗争的那个悲惨的动乱时代，我又该说什么呢？法律和部分公共舆论都主张，仆人和主人之间并不存在天生和永恒的优劣之分。但是，这种新的思想尚未深入后者的头脑，或者不如说他从内心拒绝接受。在主人的内心深处，他认为自己是高人一等的特别之人。但是，他们不敢这么说，而是很不情愿地被拉到一般水平。所以他们在对仆人发号施令时，既胆怯，又苛刻。对于自己的仆人，他们已经不再有长期握有毫无争议权力的人们对仆人经常有的那种屈尊俯就的善良感情，而让他们自己也奇怪的是自己改变的同时他们的仆人也改变了。鉴于仆人只是暂时为他工作，他们只希望仆人形成规矩和持久的习惯，只需要对迟早要离开自己的仆人的服务表示满意和称心，为一个既不能保护也不会伤害到他们的人效劳。简而言之，他们与跟自己相似的人建立了牢固的契约，而这个契约会随人们意愿的消失而失效。

　　在贵族制国家，仆人往往并不因为受人支使而感到低贱，因为他们既不知道也想象不到其他工作，而且认为他们与主人之间存在的惊人不平等是上帝的某个神秘法则的必然的和不可避免的结果。在民主制度下，仆人也不觉得自己卑贱，因为这是他自己的选择而且只是暂时的工作，公共舆论也并不轻视他，主仆之间的不平等关系也并非永久不变。但是，当一种社会制度向另一种社会制度过渡时，人们的思想总会有一段时间在贵族观念的臣服和民主观念的服从之间摇摆不定。于是，在服从者的眼中，服从逐渐失去其道德意

then loses its moral importance in the eyes of him who obeys; he no longer considers it as a species of divine obligation, and he does not yet view it under its purely human aspect; it has to him no character of sanctity or of justice, and he submits to it as to a degrading but profitable condition. At that moment a confused and imperfect phantom of equality haunts the minds of servants; they do not at once perceive whether the equality to which they are entitled is to be found within or without the pale of domestic service; and they rebel in their hearts against a subordination to which they have subjected themselves, and from which they derive actual profit. They consent to serve, and they blush to obey; they like the advantages of service, but not the master; or rather, they are not sure that they ought not themselves to be masters, and they are inclined to consider him who orders them as an unjust usurper of their own rights. Then it is that the dwelling of every citizen offers a spectacle somewhat analogous to the gloomy aspect of political society. A secret and intestine warfare is going on there between powers, ever rivals and suspicious of one another: the master is ill-natured and weak, the servant ill-natured and intractable; the one constantly attempts to evade by unfair restrictions his obligation to protect and to remunerate—the other his obligation to obey. The reins of domestic government dangle between them, to be snatched at by one or the other. The lines which divide authority from oppression, liberty from license, and right from might, are to their eyes so jumbled together and confused, that no one knows exactly what he is, or what he may be, or what he ought to be. Such a condition is not democracy, but revolution.

Chapter VI: That Democratic Institutions And Manners Tend To Raise Rents And Shorten The Terms Of Leases

What has been said of servants and masters is applicable, to a certain extent, to landowners and farming tenants; but this subject deserves to be considered by itself. In America there are, properly speaking, no tenant farmers; every man owns the ground he tills. It must be admitted that democratic laws tend greatly to increase the number of landowners, and to diminish that of farming tenants.

义，不再认为服从是某种神圣的义务，并且仍然没有从纯人的角度去看待服从。服从于他们既不神圣，也不正义，而只是将其看成是一种不光彩，但可以获利的行为。在这个时期，一种模糊的不完整的平等观念开始在仆人的脑海中浮现。他们最初并不知道自己被赋予的平等是否可以在处于仆人的地位时获得，还是只有在摆脱仆人的地位后才能拥有，而且从内心深处对自己所处的受人支使却能带来实际利益的从属地位表示反感。他们同意受雇于人，但羞于受人支使。他们喜欢仆役工作给自己带来的好处，但不喜欢自己的主人。或者更准确地说，他们还不了解为什么自己不是主人，所以往往把对自己发号施令的人视为非法剥夺自己的权利的人。于是，每个公民的家里便出现一种现象，与政界呈现的阴暗有些类似。也就是说，在公民的家庭里，互相怀疑的敌对力量之间不断地进行明争暗斗。主人心地不良，但表面和蔼，仆人也居心叵测，难以驯服；一方不断企图通过种种不公正的限制来规避自己保护和给予报酬的义务，另一方则设法推脱其服从的义务。家政大权在两者之间摇摆，谁都想把它抢到自己的手里。在他们的眼中权威和压迫、自由和任性、权利和力量都被混为一谈。没有人知道自己到底应该是干什么的，自己会做什么，或是自己应当做什么。这样的状态不是民主，而是革命。

第六章　为什么民主制度和民情趋向于提高租金和缩短租期

我对于主人和仆人所做的论述在一定程度上也适用于地主和佃户，但是这个问题有必要进行单独论述。在美国，严格来说，并没有佃户，每个人都在自己的土地上耕作。必须承认，一般来说，民主的法制非常有利于地主数量的大幅增加和佃户数量的减少。但是，

Yet what takes place in the United States is much less attributable to the institutions of the country than to the country itself. In America land is cheap, and anyone may easily become a landowner; its returns are small, and its produce cannot well be divided between a landowner and a farmer. America therefore stands alone in this as well as in many other respects, and it would be a mistake to take it as an example.

I believe that in democratic as well as in aristocratic countries there will be landowners and tenants, but the connection existing between them will be of a different kind. In aristocracies the hire of a farm is paid to the landlord, not only in rent, but in respect, regard, and duty; in democracies the whole is paid in cash. When estates are divided and passed from hand to hand, and the permanent connection which existed between families and the soil is dissolved, the landowner and the tenant are only casually brought into contact. They meet for a moment to settle the conditions of the agreement, and then lose sight of each other; they are two strangers brought together by a common interest, and who keenly talk over a matter of business, the sole object of which is to make money.

In proportion as property is subdivided and wealth distributed over the country, the community is filled with people whose former opulence is declining, and with others whose fortunes are of recent growth and whose wants increase more rapidly than their resources. For all such persons the smallest pecuniary profit is a matter of importance, and none of them feel disposed to waive any of their claims, or to lose any portion of their income. As ranks are intermingled, and as very large as well as very scanty fortunes become more rare, every day brings the social condition of the landowner nearer to that of the farmer; the one has not naturally any uncontested superiority over the other; between two men who are equal, and not at ease in their circumstances, the contract of hire is exclusively an affair of money. A man whose estate extends over a whole district, and who owns a hundred farms, is well aware of the importance of gaining at the same time the affections of some thousands of men; this object appears to call for his exertions, and to attain it he will readily make considerable sacrifices. But he who owns a hundred acres is insensible to similar considerations, and he cares but little to win the private regard of his tenant.

美国所发生的一切变化主要应归因于其国土环境自身，而不是国家制度原因。在美国土地价格非常低廉，每个人都可以轻而易举地当上地主。但是他的土地收益有限，土地的产出不能很好地维系地主和佃户的生计。因此，美国在这一方面与其他方面一样，也很特殊，不能用其作为范例。

我认为，无论是在民主国家还是在贵族制国家，都应该存在地主和佃户，但是他们之间的关系则有非常大的差异。在贵族制国家，租种土地不但要付给地主租金，而且还要为地主服劳役；在民主国家，只要付租金就可以了。当一个家庭的地产被分割易手之后，它与土地之间的永恒关系就告一段落，而地主和佃户之间只是偶然形成的暂时契约关系。他们只会为了协调契约内容而会面，除此之外谁也看不见谁。他们是由共同利益联系起来的两个陌生人，彼此之间讨价还价做交易，而双方唯一的目标就是挣钱。

随着地产的日益分割以及财富的日益分散，社会上充斥着家道衰落的破落户和欲壑难填的暴发户。因为对于这样的人们而言，再小的利益都很重要，所以谁也不会放弃丝毫的蝇头小利，或者让自己受到丝毫的损失。随着各阶层的融合，以及巨富和赤贫越来越少，使得地主和佃户的生活状况日益接近，一方比另一方不再拥有天然的绝对优势。在两个平等和不安于现状的人之间，契约的基础除了金钱以外还能有什么呢？一个拥有万顷良田和数以百计农场的人深知同时赢得人心的重要性，为了实现这一目标他不断努力，并愿意为此做出巨大牺牲。但是对于一个只拥有几百英亩土地的人而言，则很少会有这样的想法，而且根本不在乎佃户是否对自己有好感。

An aristocracy does not expire like a man in a single day; the aristocratic principle is slowly undermined in men's opinion, before it is attacked in their laws. Long before open war is declared against it, the tie which had hitherto united the higher classes to the lower may be seen to be gradually relaxed. Indifference and contempt are betrayed by one class, jealousy and hatred by the others; the intercourse between rich and poor becomes less frequent and less kind, and rents are raised. This is not the consequence of a democratic revolution, but its certain harbinger; for an aristocracy which has lost the affections of the people, once and forever, is like a tree dead at the root, which is the more easily torn up by the winds the higher its branches have spread.

In the course of the last fifty years the rents of farms have amazingly increased, not only in France but throughout the greater part of Europe. The remarkable improvements which have taken place in agriculture and manufactures within the same period do not suffice in my opinion to explain this fact; recourse must be had to another cause more powerful and more concealed. I believe that cause is to be found in the democratic institutions which several European nations have adopted, and in the democratic passions which more or less agitate all the rest. I have frequently heard great English landowners congratulate themselves that, at the present day, they derive a much larger income from their estates than their fathers did. They have perhaps good reasons to be glad; but most assuredly they know not what they are glad of. They think they are making a clear gain, when it is in reality only an exchange; their influence is what they are parting with for cash; and what they gain in money will ere long be lost in power.

There is yet another sign by which it is easy to know that a great democratic revolution is going on or approaching. In the Middle Ages almost all lands were leased for lives, or for very long terms; the domestic economy of that period shows that leases for ninety-nine years were more frequent then than leases for twelve years are now. Men then believed that families were immortal; men's conditions seemed settled forever, and the whole of society appeared to be so fixed, that it was not supposed that anything would ever be stirred or shaken in its structure. In ages of equality, the human mind takes a different bent; the prevailing notion is that nothing abides, and man is haunted by the

贵族制度不会像一个人一样在一天之内就会死掉，其原则只有逐渐遭到人们的厌弃之后才能用法律加以打击。因此，在战争开始之前很久，上层阶级和下层阶级之间的联系纽带就已经逐渐断裂。前者对后者表现得漠不关心，不屑一顾；后者对前者则心怀嫉妒和憎恨。富人和穷人之间的交往越来越少，越来越不友善，于是租金开始上涨。但这并不是民主革命的结果，而是民主革命的前兆。因为贵族制度一旦失去人心，就好像一个棵根部已经枯死的大树，长得越高枝叶越繁茂越容易被狂风连根拔起。

最近50年来，不但是在法国而且在欧洲的大部分地区，田地的租金飞涨。在我看来，同一时期出现的工农业的显著发展不足以解释这一现象，所以我们必须求助于另一个非常有利和隐秘的原因来对此进行解释。我认为我们可以从一些欧洲国家采用的民主制度，以及或多或少激动其他各国人心的民主热情中去寻找原因。我常常听到一些英国的大地主得意扬扬地说他们现在的租金收入比他们的祖辈要高得多。也许他们有理由自鸣得意，但是他们并不知其所以然。他们认为自己得到一笔纯收入，但实际上这只是一种交换，他们是在用自己的影响力来交换金钱，他们获得金钱不久便会让他们失去一些权力。

还有另外的一个迹象让人们很容易地意识到一场伟大的民主革命正在到来。在中世纪，几乎所有的土地都是永世出租或长期出租，对于中世纪家庭经济的研究表明，以99年为期的出租往往比现在12年的更普遍。因为人们认为家庭是永存不灭的，人们的状况似乎也是一成不变的，整个社会似乎也是固定不变的，以至于人们认为不会有任何动乱会撼动或动摇社会结构。在平等时代，人们的思想发生了变化，人们普遍认为，没有什么会始终

thought of mutability. Under this impression the landowner and the tenant himself are instinctively averse to protracted terms of obligation; they are afraid of being tied up to-morrow by the contract which benefits them today. They have vague anticipations of some sudden and unforeseen change in their conditions; they mistrust themselves; they fear lest their taste should change, and lest they should lament that they cannot rid themselves of what they coveted; nor are such fears unfounded, for in democratic ages that which is most fluctuating amidst the fluctuation of all around is the heart of man.

Chapter VII: Influence Of Democracy On Wages

Most of the remarks which I have already made in speaking of servants and masters, may be applied to masters and workmen. As the gradations of the social scale come to be less observed, whilst the great sink the humble rise, and as poverty as well as opulence ceases to be hereditary, the distance both in reality and in opinion, which heretofore separated the workman from the master, is lessened every day. The workman conceives a more lofty opinion of his rights, of his future, of himself; he is filled with new ambition and with new desires, he is harassed by new wants. Every instant he views with longing eyes the profits of his employer; and in order to share them, he strives to dispose of his labor at a higher rate, and he generally succeeds at length in the attempt. In democratic countries, as well as elsewhere, most of the branches of productive industry are carried on at a small cost, by men little removed by their wealth or education above the level of those whom they employ. These manufacturing speculators are extremely numerous; their interests differ; they cannot therefore easily concert or combine their exertions. On the other hand the workmen have almost always some sure resources, which enable them to refuse to work when they cannot get what they conceive to be the fair price of their labor. In the constant struggle for wages which is going on between these two classes, their strength is divided, and success alternates from one to the other. It is even probable that in the end the interest of the working class must prevail; for the high wages which

如一，世事无常的观念占据了人们的头脑。在这种思想的作用下，地主和佃户本能地对长期义务有一种抵触，害怕自己明天的利益受到眼前利益的束缚。他们忐忑不安，不知道自己的处境什么时候会发生骤变。他们怀疑自己，唯恐一旦他们的生活方式改变，会因放弃曾经习以为常的东西而感伤。而且他们的担忧不无道理，因为在民主时代，在一切变化无常的事物中最容易改变的就是人心。

第七章　民主对工资的影响

到目前为止，我对于主仆关系的大部分论述都适用于雇主和工人。随着社会等级的划分越来越模糊，大人物的没落和小人物的崛起，贫富不再世代不变，雇主与工人之间实际和观念上的差距日益缩小。工人对自己的权利、命运和本身有了更为高级的认识，心中充满着新的抱负和渴望，新的愿望不断困扰着他们。他们时时刻刻对雇主的利益虎视眈眈。为了能够从雇主那里分享到利益，他们努力争取提高自己的劳动报酬，而且往往能达到目的。在民主国家与在其他国家一样，大部分经营各类实业的人在财力和知识上都普遍高于他们所雇佣的工人，而且他们的生意都赚钱。这样的实业家为数众多，而且各自利益不同，因此他们很难通力合作。而另一方面，当工人认为自己获得的劳动报酬不合理的时候，几乎总是有把握拒绝给雇主服务。在两个阶级之间长期不断的工资斗争中，双方的力量势均力敌，而且各有胜负。而且，甚至可以断言，工人阶级的利益很可能占据上风，因为他们已经取得的高额工资使得他们对于雇主的依赖越来越少，而且随着他们越来越独立，更容易争取更高的工资。

they have already obtained make them every day less dependent on their masters; and as they grow more independent, they have greater facilities for obtaining a further increase of wages.

I shall take for example that branch of productive industry which is still at the present day the most generally followed in France, and in almost all the countries of the world—I mean the cultivation of the soil. In France most of those who labor for hire in agriculture, are themselves owners of certain plots of ground, which just enable them to subsist without working for anyone else. When these laborers come to offer their services to a neighboring landowner or farmer, if he refuses them a certain rate of wages, they retire to their own small property and await another opportunity.

I think that, upon the whole, it may be asserted that a slow and gradual rise of wages is one of the general laws of democratic communities. In proportion as social conditions become more equal, wages rise; and as wages are higher, social conditions become more equal. But a great and gloomy exception occurs in our own time. I have shown in a preceding chapter that aristocracy, expelled from political society, has taken refuge in certain departments of productive industry, and has established its sway there under another form; this powerfully affects the rate of wages. As a large capital is required to embark in the great manufacturing speculations to which I allude, the number of persons who enter upon them is exceedingly limited: as their number is small, they can easily concert together, and fix the rate of wages as they please. Their workmen on the contrary are exceedingly numerous, and the number of them is always increasing; for, from time to time, an extraordinary run of business takes place, during which wages are inordinately high, and they attract the surrounding population to the factories. But, when once men have embraced that line of life, we have already seen that they cannot quit it again, because they soon contract habits of body and mind which unfit them for any other sort of toil. These men have generally but little education and industry, with but few resources; they stand therefore almost at the mercy of the master. When competition, or other fortuitous circumstances, lessen his profits, he can reduce the wages of his workmen almost at pleasure, and make from them what he loses by the chances of business. Should the workmen strike,

我将以现在依然在法国和几乎世界上所有国家仍然兴盛的一种实业，即种植业为例进行说明。在法国，大多数受雇务农的人本身自己也有一些土地，即使不受雇于人，也能勉强糊口。当这些人向其附近的地主或农户提供服务的时候，如果对方提出的工资不能令他们满意，他们会回家耕作自己的土地，等待更好的机会。

我认为，从总体来看，可以说工资的缓慢增长是民主社会的一个一般规律。随着社会越来越平等，工资会越来越高，而工资的不断上涨，则会反过来促使社会越来越平等。但是，在我们这个时代，却出现一个非常不幸的例外。在前面的章节中，我已经说过被挤出政界的贵族开始在实业界寻求庇护，并以另一种形式在其中确立起自己的影响，而这足以影响到工资的水平。因为创办我所述的大型实业需要大笔的资金，所以能够参与其中的人非常有限；而且因为他们的人数很少，所以他们很容易联合起来，随意规定工资。而与之相反，他们的工人则人数众多，而且数量还在不断增长，因为有时候生意会特别好，所以工资会特别高，就会将附近的人大量吸引到工厂。但是，人们一旦开始这样的生活方式，我们会注意到他们将无法再从其中脱离，因为在工厂中很快形成的身心习惯，让他们无法再适应其他的劳动。这些人普遍文化水平低，手艺差，积蓄少，因此他们几乎总是受到雇主的摆布。当竞争和其他的意外情况令其利润降低的时候，他们几乎可以随意降低工人工资，以弥补生意上的损害。而如果工人罢工，有钱的雇主则可以不受什么影响悠闲地等待着贫困迫使他们回到自己身边。然而工人不得不日复一日地劳动，否则只有死路一条，因为他们拥有的只有一双手。长期的压迫让他们一贫如洗，所以始终无法逃脱这样的因果循环。因此，在这个行业工资在时不时地突然增长之后，必然处于长期的下跌趋势，而在另

the master, who is a rich man, can very well wait without being ruined until necessity brings them back to him; but they must work day by day or they die, for their only property is in their hands. They have long been impoverished by oppression, and the poorer they become the more easily may they be oppressed: they can never escape from this fatal circle of cause and consequence. It is not then surprising that wages, after having sometimes suddenly risen, are permanently lowered in this branch of industry; whereas in other callings the price of labor, which generally increases but little, is nevertheless constantly augmented.

This state of dependence and wretchedness, in which a part of the manufacturing population of our time lives, forms an exception to the general rule, contrary to the state of all the rest of the community; but, for this very reason, no circumstance is more important or more deserving of the especial consideration of the legislator; for when the whole of society is in motion, it is difficult to keep any one class stationary; and when the greater number of men are opening new paths to fortune, it is no less difficult to make the few support in peace their wants and their desires.

Chapter VIII: Influence Of Democracy On Kindred

I have just examined the changes which the equality of conditions produces in the mutual relations of the several members of the community amongst democratic nations, and amongst the Americans in particular. I would now go deeper, and inquire into the closer ties of kindred: my object here is not to seek for new truths, but to show in what manner facts already known are connected with my subject.

It has been universally remarked, that in our time the several members of a family stand upon an entirely new footing towards each other; that the distance which formerly separated a father from his sons has been lessened; and that paternal authority, if not destroyed, is at least impaired. Something analogous to this, but even more striking, may be observed in the United States. In America the family, in the Roman and aristocratic signification of the word, does not exist. All that remains of it are a few vestiges in the first years of childhood, when the father exercises, without opposition, that

一些行业劳动报酬虽然普遍只是有小幅增长，但是始终呈现增长的趋势也并不足为奇。

我们这个时代，产业人口的悲惨的从属状况成为一般规律的一个意外，与其周围的一切形成鲜明反差。但是，正是由于这一原因，这一情况特别重要，特别需要引起立法者的注意。因为当整个社会处于动态之中时，很难有任何一个阶级保持不变。而当越来越多的人试图开辟致富新路的时候，也很难让人们安然自得地满足自己的需要和欲望。

第八章　民主对家庭的影响

刚刚我已经考察了在民主国家特别是在美国平等带来的变化对社会成员相互关系的影响。现在我要更进一步，深入到家庭内部。在此，我并不试图挖掘新的真理，而只是想要说明已知的事实与我的题目之间的关系。

人们普遍认为，在我们这个时代，家庭成员之间的关系已建立在新的基础之上，父子之间原来的距离已经缩小，而且父母的权威，尽管没有消失，但至少已经减弱。美国也有类似的情况，而且更加明显。在美国，并不存在罗马和贵族意义的"家庭"这个词。美国人在出生后的最初几年才逐渐形成家庭意识。在孩子的童年时期，父亲实行家庭专政，子女不得反抗，而子女的年幼无知，又使这种专政成为必要；于是子女们的利益，以及父亲无可争辩的优势，使这种专政成为合理合法。但是一旦美国的年轻人成年，子女对父母的服从关系便越来越松弛。从开始思想上的自主，很快变成行动上的自主。在美国，严格来说没有青年时期。少年时代一旦结束，便已是成年人，开始追求自己的人生道路。不要错

absolute domestic authority, which the feebleness of his children renders necessary, and which their interest, as well as his own incontestable superiority, warrants. But as soon as the young American approaches manhood, the ties of filial obedience are relaxed day by day: master of his thoughts, he is soon master of his conduct. In America there is, strictly speaking, no adolescence: at the close of boyhood the man appears, and begins to trace out his own path. It would be an error to suppose that this is preceded by a domestic struggle, in which the son has obtained by a sort of moral violence the liberty that his father refused him. The same habits, the same principles which impel the one to assert his independence, predispose the other to consider the use of that independence as an incontestable right. The former does not exhibit any of those rancorous or irregular passions which disturb men long after they have shaken off an established authority; the latter feels none of that bitter and angry regret which is apt to survive a bygone power. The father foresees the limits of his authority long beforehand, and when the time arrives he surrenders it without a struggle: the son looks forward to the exact period at which he will be his own master; and he enters upon his freedom without precipitation and without effort, as a possession which is his own and which no one seeks to wrest from him.

It may perhaps not be without utility to show how these changes which take place in family relations, are closely connected with the social and political revolution which is approaching its consummation under our own observation. There are certain great social principles, which a people either introduces everywhere, or tolerates nowhere. In countries which are aristocratically constituted with all the gradations of rank, the government never makes a direct appeal to the mass of the governed: as men are united together, it is enough to lead the foremost, the rest will follow. This is equally applicable to the family, as to all aristocracies which have a head. Amongst aristocratic nations, social institutions recognize, in truth, no one in the family but the father; children are received by society at his hands; society governs him, he governs them. Thus the parent has not only a natural right, but he acquires a political right, to command them: he is the author and the support of his family; but he is also its constituted ruler. In democracies, where the government picks out every

误地以为，这是一场家庭斗争的结果，儿子通过违反道德的方法获得父亲拒绝给予他的自由。促使儿子独立的习惯和原则也在同样促使父亲认为独立是其不可抗拒的权利。所以，前者丝毫没有摆脱长期束缚自己的权威之后的那种怨恨不满的情绪，而后者也没有任何失去权力之后随之而来的痛苦和愤怒的遗憾。父亲早就预见到自己权威的大限，而当大限来临的时候他心甘情愿地放权；而儿子也知道独立自主的一天必会到来，自己的自由是十拿九稳的，就像一份属于自己的财产，没人会去抢。

论述一下家庭关系发生的变化与我们眼前即将完成的社会政治革命之间的密切关系也并非一无用处。有一些重大的社会原则，不是被一个国家到处推行，就是无法容忍其存在。在等级制度森严的贵族国家，政府从不直接向被统治的大众呼吁求援，因为人们都被联结起来，最上面的人发号施令，其余人必定追随。而这也适用于家庭，和由一人统领的所有社团。实际上，在贵族制国家，社会制度只承认一家之长父亲的存在，子女则是通过父亲与社会发生关系。社会对父亲加以管束，而父亲又对家庭成员进行管束。因此，父亲不但有天赋权利而且拥有对子女发号施令的政治权利。他是家庭的缔造者，是家庭生计的维持者，也是家庭的统治者。在民主国家，政府会对每个个人进行约束，用同样的法律治理所有的人，所以不需要父亲那样的中间人。在法律的眼中，父亲只是一名比子女年纪大、有钱的社会成员。

当大部分人极不平等，而这种不平等又是永恒的时候，上级的观念便会在人们的想象中成长起来。即使法律不给予这个上级特权，习惯和公共舆论也会对此表示认可。与之相

individual singly from the mass, to make him subservient to the general laws of the community, no such intermediate person is required: a father is there, in the eye of the law, only a member of the community, older and richer than his sons.

When most of the conditions of life are extremely unequal, and the inequality of these conditions is permanent, the notion of a superior grows upon the imaginations of men: if the law invested him with no privileges, custom and public opinion would concede them. When, on the contrary, men differ but little from each other, and do not always remain in dissimilar conditions of life, the general notion of a superior becomes weaker and less distinct: it is vain for legislation to strive to place him who obeys very much beneath him who commands; the manners of the time bring the two men nearer to one another, and draw them daily towards the same level. Although the legislation of an aristocratic people should grant no peculiar privileges to the heads of families; I shall not be the less convinced that their power is more respected and more extensive than in a democracy; for I know that, whatsoever the laws may be, superiors always appear higher and inferiors lower in aristocracies than amongst democratic nations.

When men live more for the remembrance of what has been than for the care of what is, and when they are more given to attend to what their ancestors thought than to think themselves, the father is the natural and necessary tie between the past and the present—the link by which the ends of these two chains are connected. In aristocracies, then, the father is not only the civil head of the family, but the oracle of its traditions, the expounder of its customs, the arbiter of its manners. He is listened to with deference, he is addressed with respect, and the love which is felt for him is always tempered with fear. When the condition of society becomes democratic, and men adopt as their general principle that it is good and lawful to judge of all things for one's self, using former points of belief not as a rule of faith but simply as a means of information, the power which the opinions of a father exercise over those of his sons diminishes as well as his legal power.

Perhaps the subdivision of estates which democracy brings with it contributes more than anything else to change the relations existing between a father and his children. When the property

反，若人们彼此之间并没有什么差别，而且生活状况也不再始终如一，则上级的一般观念将日渐淡薄和模糊。哪怕立法者硬要把一个人安排在上级的位置让他发号施令，也只会徒劳无功，因为在这个时代民情会让这两个人彼此接近，逐渐来到同一水平。尽管一个贵族制国家的立法机构从未将特权授予一家之长，但我也不能不确信他们的权力比在民主国家更受尊重和更广泛。因为我知道无论法律规定如何，上级在贵族制国家总比在民主国家地位高，而下属则与此相反，即在前者比在后者更低。

当生活中人们更多的是缅怀过去而不是关心现在，更多的是考虑祖先的想法而不是思索自己的想法的时候，父亲就成为联系过去和现在的天然的和必然的纽带，成为将上一代和下一代连接起来的一环。于是，在贵族制度下，父亲不但是家庭内部的首长，而且是家庭传统的传承人、习惯的解释人、民情的仲裁人。他的话家庭的成员要洗耳恭听；对待他要毕恭毕敬，而且爱他要爱得诚惶诚恐。当社会情况变得民主，人们运用自己的一般原则来对一切事物做出判断，并认为这样做合情合理，而祖先的信念不再被视为行为规范，而只是作为参考时，父亲的看法对于子女的影响，与他的合法权利一样，大幅降低。

民主制度导致的分家对于现有父子关系改变的影响最为显著。当一家之主的父亲财产不多的时候，他和儿子会长期住在一起，共享现有的一切。习惯和需要让他们始终在一起，而且不得不不断交流。这必然会在家庭内部建立起一种亲密的关系，使父亲权威的绝对性下降，并且也不再讲究表面形式的尊敬。然而，在民主国家，拥有少量财产的阶级，正是在社会里能够使思想产生力量和为民情指引方向的阶级。这个阶级能够让它的意见和

of the father of a family is scanty, his son and himself constantly live in the same place, and share the same occupations: habit and necessity bring them together, and force them to hold constant communication: the inevitable consequence is a sort of familiar intimacy, which renders authority less absolute, and which can ill be reconciled with the external forms of respect. Now in democratic countries the class of those who are possessed of small fortunes is precisely that which gives strength to the notions, and a particular direction to the manners, of the community. That class makes its opinions preponderate as universally as its will, and even those who are most inclined to resist its commands are carried away in the end by its example. I have known eager opponents of democracy who allowed their children to address them with perfect colloquial equality.

Thus, at the same time that the power of aristocracy is declining, the austere, the conventional, and the legal part of parental authority vanishes, and a species of equality prevails around the domestic hearth. I know not, upon the whole, whether society loses by the change, but I am inclined to believe that man individually is a gainer by it. I think that, in proportion as manners and laws become more democratic, the relation of father and son becomes more intimate and more affectionate; rules and authority are less talked of; confidence and tenderness are oftentimes increased, and it would seem that the natural bond is drawn closer in proportion as the social bond is loosened. In a democratic family the father exercises no other power than that with which men love to invest the affection and the experience of age; his orders would perhaps be disobeyed, but his advice is for the most part authoritative. Though he be not hedged in with ceremonial respect, his sons at least accost him with confidence; no settled form of speech is appropriated to the mode of addressing him, but they speak to him constantly, and are ready to consult him day by day; the master and the constituted ruler have vanished—the father remains. Nothing more is needed, in order to judge of the difference between the two states of society in this respect, than to peruse the family correspondence of aristocratic ages. The style is always correct, ceremonious, stiff, and so cold that the natural warmth of the heart can hardly be felt in the language. The language, on the contrary, addressed by a son to his father in democratic countries is always marked by mingled freedom, familiarity and affection, which at once

意志，普遍占有统治地位；甚至最想违抗它命令的人，最后也只得听之任之随波逐流。我就曾看到一些强烈反对民主的人允许自己的孩子用完全平等的方式与自己说话。

因此，在贵族权力衰弱的同时，父母的那种严肃的、约定俗成的、合法的权威也随之消失，而一种平等的关系在家庭内部建立起来。总的来说，我不知道这样的变化是否会给社会带来损害，但我趋向于认为个人能够从中获益。我认为，随着民情和法制的日益民主，父子关系会变得越来越亲密和温情，不再那样讲究规矩和权威；彼此之间的信任和体贴也往往得到加强。似乎随着父子之间社会关系纽带的松弛，他们之间的天然联系更加紧密了。在民主的家庭里，父亲除了对子女表示关爱和向他们传授经验之外，没有任何权力。他的命令可能会遭到违抗，但他的忠告则多半很有威信。虽然子女们对他不再是毕恭毕敬，但至少对他表示信任。子女同他交谈也不需要恪守固定的礼仪，而是可以随时随地地向他请教。在这里，家长和统治者不见了，但父亲依然存在。为了能够明确两种社会在这方面的差异，只看一看贵族时代留下的一些家书就可以了。书信的语气往往是端庄、刻板和生硬的，而且字里行间冰冷得几乎无法让人心里感到一丝一毫的温暖。反之，在民主国家，儿子写给父亲的信总又表现得随意、亲切和情意绵绵，显而易见新的关系已经在家庭里建立起来。

一个相似的变革也在子女相互关系之间发生。在贵族的家庭也像在贵族制社会一样，每个人的地位早已定好。不仅是父亲在家庭里另成一级，享有广泛的特权，甚至是子女之间地位也不平等。年龄和性别，决定着他们每个人在家里的地位，保障其特有的特权。这些差别大部分都被民主制度废除或削弱。在贵族制家庭，长子能够继承大部分家产和几乎

show that new relations have sprung up in the bosom of the family.

A similar revolution takes place in the mutual relations of children. In aristocratic families, as well as in aristocratic society, every place is marked out beforehand. Not only does the father occupy a separate rank, in which he enjoys extensive privileges, but even the children are not equal amongst themselves. The age and sex of each irrevocably determine his rank, and secure to him certain privileges: most of these distinctions are abolished or diminished by democracy. In aristocratic families the eldest son, inheriting the greater part of the property, and almost all the rights of the family, becomes the chief, and, to a certain extent, the master, of his brothers. Greatness and power are for him—for them, mediocrity and dependence. Nevertheless it would be wrong to suppose that, amongst aristocratic nations, the privileges of the eldest son are advantageous to himself alone, or that they excite nothing but envy and hatred in those around him. The eldest son commonly endeavors to procure wealth and power for his brothers, because the general splendor of the house is reflected back on him who represents it; the younger sons seek to back the elder brother in all his undertakings, because the greatness and power of the head of the family better enable him to provide for all its branches. The different members of an aristocratic family are therefore very closely bound together; their interests are connected, their minds agree, but their hearts are seldom in harmony.

Democracy also binds brothers to each other, but by very different means. Under democratic laws all the children are perfectly equal, and consequently independent; nothing brings them forcibly together, but nothing keeps them apart; and as they have the same origin, as they are trained under the same roof, as they are treated with the same care, and as no peculiar privilege distinguishes or divides them, the affectionate and youthful intimacy of early years easily springs up between them. Scarcely any opportunities occur to break the tie thus formed at the outset of life; for their brotherhood brings them daily together, without embarrassing them. It is not, then, by interest, but by common associations and by the free sympathy of opinion and of taste, that democracy unites brothers to each other. It divides their inheritance, but it allows their hearts and minds to mingle together. Such is the charm of these democratic manners, that even the partisans of aristocracy are

所有权利，所以他必然成为一家之长，而且在一定程度上会成为兄弟们的主人。他尊贵有权，而兄弟们则平庸而且依附于他。然而，如果认为在贵族制国家，长子的特权只会带来好处，那就错了，因为它们还会招来兄弟们对他的忌妒和憎恨。所以，长子一般都竭力帮助他的兄弟们发财致富和获得权势。因为一个家族的繁荣必然反映在其代表的身上，所以，弟弟们也设法助兄长的所有事业一臂之力。因为一家之长的显赫和权势能够让他更好地去支持家族的各支。因而，贵族家庭成员之间的关系非常密切，尽管他们的利益休戚相关，想法也完全一致，但是他们的心却并不和谐。

民主制度也会让兄弟之间彼此依靠，但采用的方式却截然不同。根据民主的法制，所有的子女彼此完全平等，因而也彼此独立。没有任何东西迫使他们必须在一起，但也没有任何东西迫使他们互相疏远。因为他们拥有相同的血统，在同一屋檐下成长，受到同样的照顾，而且也没有任何特权使彼此不同被分为三六九等，所以他们从小很容易产生亲密无间的手足情感。因此，在成年之后，幼时建立起来的这种纽带也几乎不会受到任何事情的破坏，因为兄弟的情义只会让他们彼此日益接近，而不会令他们反目。因此，民主制度不是通过利害关系，而是利用共同的回忆以及思想和爱好的自由共鸣将兄弟们团结起来。民主制度虽然在他们之间划分家产，但能使他们的身心合一。这就是民主民情的魅力所在，甚至于贵族制度拥护者也难以抵挡，并在有过一段时间的这种体验后，再也不想回到原来贵族家庭的那种毕恭毕敬刻板的样子。如果他们能够抛弃原有的社会情况和法制，他们很乐于接受民主的家庭习惯。但是，这还牵扯到另一个问题，即不接受民主的社会情况和法

caught by it; and after having experienced it for some time, they are by no means tempted to revert to the respectful and frigid observance of aristocratic families. They would be glad to retain the domestic habits of democracy, if they might throw off its social conditions and its laws; but these elements are indissolubly united, and it is impossible to enjoy the former without enduring the latter. The remarks I have made on filial love and fraternal affection are applicable to all the passions which emanate spontaneously from human nature itself. If a certain mode of thought or feeling is the result of some peculiar condition of life, when that condition is altered nothing whatever remains of the thought or feeling. Thus a law may bind two members of the community very closely to one another; but that law being abolished, they stand asunder. Nothing was more strict than the tie which united the vassal to the lord under the feudal system; at the present day the two men know not each other; the fear, the gratitude, and the affection which formerly connected them have vanished, and not a vestige of the tie remains. Such, however, is not the case with those feelings which are natural to mankind. Whenever a law attempts to tutor these feelings in any particular manner, it seldom fails to weaken them; by attempting to add to their intensity, it robs them of some of their elements, for they are never stronger than when left to themselves.

Democracy, which destroys or obscures almost all the old conventional rules of society, and which prevents men from readily assenting to new ones, entirely effaces most of the feelings to which these conventional rules have given rise; but it only modifies some others, and frequently imparts to them a degree of energy and sweetness unknown before. Perhaps it is not impossible to condense into a single proposition the whole meaning of this chapter, and of several others that preceded it. Democracy loosens social ties, but it draws the ties of nature more tight; it brings kindred more closely together, whilst it places the various members of the community more widely apart.

Chapter IX: Education Of Young Women In The United States

No free communities ever existed without morals; and, as I observed in the former part of this work, morals are the work of woman. Consequently, whatever affects the condition of women, their

制，就无法享用民主的家庭习惯。我刚刚对于父子之爱和手足之情的描述，适用于所有从人性本身自发产生的一切情感。如果特定的思想和感情是特定社会状况的产物，那么当社会情况发生改变时，它们便不复存在。因此，法律虽然可以把两个公民紧紧联系起来，但当这项法律废除后，他们便会彼此分离。再没有比封建制度下将主仆联系起来的纽带更为紧密的了。但在如今，这两种人已各奔东西，互不相识了。曾经将他们联系起来的那些恐惧、感激、热爱的情感已经消失，甚至没有留下一点痕迹。然而，人类的天生感情却不能如此。无论法律采用什么样的方式约束这样的情感，都难以奏效；而法律想要促进这种情感时，也难以从中得到什么好处，因为这种感情只依靠本身的力量，就能永远强大。

民主制度不但几乎将所有旧的社会习惯，而且将人们接受新的社会习惯的所有障碍都已打破，进而使旧社会习惯造就的大部分感情销声匿迹。但是，对于其余的习惯民主制度只进行了改进，并不断赋予它们原来所没有的活力和美妙。也许用一句话来概括一下这一章及其前面几章的内容并非没有可能。民主制度让社会纽带松弛，却令天然纽带变得更加强韧；它在令亲缘关系不断紧密的同时，却令社会成员之间的关系更加疏远。

第九章　美国年轻女性的教育

没有一个自由社会没有其道德标准，而且正如我在本书上卷已经说过的那样，道德是由女性缔造的。因此，在我看来凡是会影响到妇女地位、习惯和思想的一切东西，都会对政治产生巨大影响。几乎在所有信奉新教的国家，年轻女性的行动都远比在信奉天主教

586 DEMOCRACY IN AMERICA · 论美国的民主

habits and their opinions, has great political importance in my eyes. Amongst almost all Protestant nations young women are far more the mistresses of their own actions than they are in Catholic countries. This independence is still greater in Protestant countries, like England, which have retained or acquired the right of self-government; the spirit of freedom is then infused into the domestic circle by political habits and by religious opinions. In the United States the doctrines of Protestantism are combined with great political freedom and a most democratic state of society; and nowhere are young women surrendered so early or so completely to their own guidance. Long before an American girl arrives at the age of marriage, her emancipation from maternal control begins; she has scarcely ceased to be a child when she already thinks for herself, speaks with freedom, and acts on her own impulse. The great scene of the world is constantly open to her view; far from seeking concealment, it is every day disclosed to her more completely, and she is taught to survey it with a firm and calm gaze. Thus the vices and dangers of society are early revealed to her; as she sees them clearly, she views them without illusions, and braves them without fear; for she is full of reliance on her own strength, and her reliance seems to be shared by all who are about her. An American girl scarcely ever displays that virginal bloom in the midst of young desires, or that innocent and ingenuous grace which usually attends the European woman in the transition from girlhood to youth. It is rarely that an American woman at any age displays childish timidity or ignorance. Like the young women of Europe, she seeks to please, but she knows precisely the cost of pleasing. If she does not abandon herself to evil, at least she knows that it exists; and she is remarkable rather for purity of manners than for chastity of mind. I have been frequently surprised, and almost frightened, at the singular address and happy boldness with which young women in America contrive to manage their thoughts and their language amidst all the difficulties of stimulating conversation; a philosopher would have stumbled at every step along the narrow path which they trod without accidents and without effort. It is easy indeed to perceive that, even amidst the independence of early youth, an American woman is always mistress of herself; she indulges in all permitted pleasures, without yielding herself up to any

的国家自主得多。这种独立性在像英国那样保留或获得自治权利的新教国家更为强大，因此，自由精神便通过政治习惯和宗教信仰深入每个家庭。在美国，新教的教义与伟大的政治自由和最民主的社会状况结合起来，而且没有一个地方的年轻女性能像美国的年轻女性那样完全独立自主。美国的年轻女性在达到适婚年龄之前很久，便开始逐步脱离母亲的监护；她们在还没有完全走出童年时期时，就已经开始独立思考，自由发表自己的见解，按照自己的意志行动。世界上的宏大场面在她们的眼前不断地展现，父母非但不想对她们有丝毫的隐藏，反而每天引导她们进行全面观察，学会用冷静正确的眼光审视它。因此，她们早已深知社会的险恶；而当她们能够清楚地看清这些险恶后，就不会再产生错觉，并能勇敢地面对它们，因为她们对自己的力量深信不疑，而且她们对自己的这份信心也得到周围人的认可。一个美国的女孩几乎从不会表现出情窦初开时期的那种处女的稚气，更不会有那种欧洲女性从女孩过渡到少女时期的那份天真无邪的优雅。美国女性，无论在任何年龄段，都很少表现出孩子气的胆小和无知。同欧洲的年轻女性一样，她们也想取悦于人，但她们清楚地知道为此需要付出什么样的代价。即使她们没有放任自己堕入邪恶，但至少她知道这世间的邪恶。显然她们更愿意追求纯洁的情操而不是高尚的思想。当我看到美国年轻女性在面对交谈中出现的困境能够巧妙从容地表达自己的思想和语言时，往往会大吃一惊，倒吸一口凉气。在一条一位哲学家会一步一跌的狭窄道路上，美国女性则可以毫无意外地安然而过。实际上，不难注意到，美国女性甚至在年纪轻轻的时候，便已自己当家做主；她们尽情享受一切被允许的享乐，却从不沉湎于其中任何一种享乐；尽管她们往往似乎随随便便，但她们理智的控制力从未失去控制。

of them; and her reason never allows the reins of self-guidance to drop, though it often seems to hold them loosely.

In France, where remnants of every age are still so strangely mingled in the opinions and tastes of the people, women commonly receive a reserved, retired, and almost cloistral education, as they did in aristocratic times; and then they are suddenly abandoned, without a guide and without assistance, in the midst of all the irregularities inseparable from democratic society. The Americans are more consistent. They have found out that in a democracy the independence of individuals cannot fail to be very great, youth premature, tastes ill-restrained, customs fleeting, public opinion often unsettled and powerless, paternal authority weak, and marital authority contested. Under these circumstances, believing that they had little chance of repressing in woman the most vehement passions of the human heart, they held that the surer way was to teach her the art of combating those passions for herself. As they could not prevent her virtue from being exposed to frequent danger, they determined that she should know how best to defend it; and more reliance was placed on the free vigor of her will than on safeguards which have been shaken or overthrown. Instead, then, of inculcating mistrust of herself, they constantly seek to enhance their confidence in her own strength of character. As it is neither possible nor desirable to keep a young woman in perpetual or complete ignorance, they hasten to give her a precocious knowledge on all subjects. Far from hiding the corruptions of the world from her, they prefer that she should see them at once and train herself to shun them; and they hold it of more importance to protect her conduct than to be over-scrupulous of her innocence.

Although the Americans are a very religious people, they do not rely on religion alone to defend the virtue of woman; they seek to arm her reason also. In this they have followed the same method as in several other respects; they first make the most vigorous efforts to bring individual independence to exercise a proper control over itself, and they do not call in the aid of religion until they have reached the utmost limits of human strength. I am aware that an education of this kind is not without danger; I am sensible that it tends to invigorate the judgment at the expense of the imagination, and

在法国，历代的残余依然不可思议地混入我们的观念和爱好，所以女性往往受到贵族时代那样的严厉管束、隐居深闺、几乎完全是修道院式的教育。然而，在民主社会建立以后，她们又立即被丢到民主社会必然的混乱之中，既得不到指导也没有支援。美国人的行为则始终如一。他们发现，在民主社会，个人的独立无疑非常重要，年轻人应当早熟，趣味不必持久，习惯可以改变，公众舆论通常应当是不定的和无力的，父权应予以削弱，夫权则应被否认。在这样的情况下，他们认为，压抑妇女内心最强烈的感情无济于事，而最稳妥的办法是教会她们自己控制这些情感的技巧。因为他们无法防止妇女的贞操暴露于危险之中，所以他们认为妇女应该自己去保卫自己的贞操，而且应该依靠的是妇女的自由意志力，而不依靠那些已经摇摇欲坠或已被推翻的保护措施。于是，他们不再向女性灌输自己的无能，而是相反想方设法地提高她们的自信心。由于他们既不可能也不希望年轻女性愚昧无知，所以他们便急于将所有的知识传授给她们。于是，他们不再向年轻女性隐瞒世间的腐败，而是更愿意让她们一目了然，并训练自己能够抵制这些腐败。他们认为，培养女性的情操比特别重视女孩子的贞洁更重要。

尽管美国是一个笃信宗教的民族，但他们并不仅仅依靠宗教来捍卫女性的贞操，而是寻求武装她们的理智。在这方面，他们所采用的方法与在其他许多方面完全一样。首先，他们竭尽所能，让个人能够对独立自主地进行很好的掌控，而且只有穷尽人为的力量之后，才求助于宗教。我注意到，这样的教育也并非完全没有危险。我也感觉到，这样的教育往往是以人们的想象力为代价来鼓励人们的判断力，使女性成为感情冷淡却有节操的妻子，却难以成为男人的爱妻和亲密伴侣。即使这样的社会比较安定和更有秩序，家庭生

to make cold and virtuous women instead of affectionate wives and agreeable companions to man. Society may be more tranquil and better regulated, but domestic life has often fewer charms. These, however, are secondary evils, which may be braved for the sake of higher interests. At the stage at which we are now arrived the time for choosing is no longer within our control; a democratic education is indispensable to protect women from the dangers with which democratic institutions and manners surround them.

Chapter X: The Young Woman In The Character Of A Wife

In America the independence of woman is irrevocably lost in the bonds of matrimony: if an unmarried woman is less constrained there than elsewhere, a wife is subjected to stricter obligations. The former makes her father's house an abode of freedom and of pleasure; the latter lives in the home of her husband as if it were a cloister. Yet these two different conditions of life are perhaps not so contrary as may be supposed, and it is natural that the American women should pass through the one to arrive at the other.

Religious peoples and trading nations entertain peculiarly serious notions of marriage: the former consider the regularity of woman's life as the best pledge and most certain sign of the purity of her morals; the latter regard it as the highest security for the order and prosperity of the household. The Americans are at the same time a puritanical people and a commercial nation: their religious opinions, as well as their trading habits, consequently lead them to require much abnegation on the part of woman, and a constant sacrifice of her pleasures to her duties which is seldom demanded of her in Europe. Thus in the United States the inexorable opinion of the public carefully circumscribes woman within the narrow circle of domestic interest and duties, and forbids her to step beyond it.

Upon her entrance into the world a young American woman finds these notions firmly established; she sees the rules which are derived from them; she is not slow to perceive that she cannot depart for an instant from the established usages of her contemporaries, without putting in jeopardy her peace of mind, her honor, nay even her social existence; and she finds the energy required for such an act

活也往往缺乏温暖。但是，这些还是等而次之的缺陷，而且为了更大的利益，可以不去计较。事情到了我们现在所说的地步，使我们只能做一种选择：必须实行民主的教育，以使妇女免遭民主的制度和民情将会给妇女带来的危害。

第十章　年轻女性怎样习得为妻之道

在美国，女性结婚以后不可避免地会失去独立性。如果一个未婚的女性在这里受到的束缚比任何其他地方都少的话，那么，她们结婚以后需要承担的义务则更为沉重。对于前者在父亲的家里可以充分地享受自由和乐趣，但是对于后者生活在丈夫的家简直如同生活在修道院。但是这两种迥然不同的生活也许并不像人们想象的那样矛盾。美国的女性能够很自然地从一种情况过渡到另一种情况。

笃信宗教的人民和重商的民族对婚姻秉持特别严肃的观念。前者认为女性循规蹈矩地生活是其道德纯良的最好保证和最显著的标志，而后者则认为这是家庭安定繁荣的最好保障。而美国人恰好既是清教徒又是重商民族。他们的宗教观念和商业习惯，最终促使他们要求女性具有自我牺牲精神，而这种要求女性为了义务而不断牺牲个人乐趣的情况在欧洲则很少见。因此，在美国无情的公共舆论将女性严格地限制在家庭利益和责任的小圈子，不得越雷池半步。

美国的年轻女性一旦进入社会，就会发现这些观念已经根深蒂固，她们看到由此而生的规则，便很快意识到自己一刻也不能与这些这个时代已经确立起来的惯例背道而驰，否则

of submission in the firmness of her understanding and in the virile habits which her education has given her. It may be said that she has learned by the use of her independence to surrender it without a struggle and without a murmur when the time comes for making the sacrifice. But no American woman falls into the toils of matrimony as into a snare held out to her simplicity and ignorance. She has been taught beforehand what is expected of her, and voluntarily and freely does she enter upon this engagement. She supports her new condition with courage, because she chose it. As in America paternal discipline is very relaxed and the conjugal tie very strict, a young woman does not contract the latter without considerable circumspection and apprehension. Precocious marriages are rare. Thus American women do not marry until their understandings are exercised and ripened; whereas in other countries most women generally only begin to exercise and to ripen their understandings after marriage.

I by no means suppose, however, that the great change which takes place in all the habits of women in the United States, as soon as they are married, ought solely to be attributed to the constraint of public opinion: it is frequently imposed upon themselves by the sole effort of their own will. When the time for choosing a husband is arrived, that cold and stern reasoning power which has been educated and invigorated by the free observation of the world, teaches an American woman that a spirit of levity and independence in the bonds of marriage is a constant subject of annoyance, not of pleasure; it tells her that the amusements of the girl cannot become the recreations of the wife, and that the sources of a married woman's happiness are in the home of her husband. As she clearly discerns beforehand the only road which can lead to domestic happiness, she enters upon it at once, and follows it to the end without seeking to turn back.

The same strength of purpose which the young wives of America display, in bending themselves at once and without repining to the austere duties of their new condition, is no less manifest in all the great trials of their lives. In no country in the world are private fortunes more precarious than in the United States. It is not uncommon for the same man, in the course of his life, to rise and sink again through all the grades which lead from opulence to poverty. American women support these

自己的安宁、名声甚至本身的社会存在都会处于危险之中。而且她们发现令自己服从这种社会规范的认识已经牢牢地树立起来，而且教育也令她们养成这样的习惯。可以说正是通过享有独立，她才学会当需要牺牲的时候能够心甘情愿毫、无怨言地做出牺牲。但是，美国女性步入繁重的婚姻生活，绝不是因为出于自己的单纯和无知而落入预设的陷阱。结婚之前人们对她们的教育让她们了解自己将来应当如何，所以她们是自愿套上婚姻枷锁的。她们鼓起勇气接受新的生活，因为这是她们自己的选择。因为在美国，父母的管束并不严，而夫妇的约束则很严格，所以年轻的女性只有在经过慎重的考虑和反复的衡量之后才会结婚。在美国，早婚现象极为罕见。因此，美国女性只有在她们的理智经过历练成熟之后才会结婚，而在其他国家，大部分的女性通常是在结婚之后才开始锻炼她们的理智并成熟起来。

然而，我丝毫不认为婚后美国女性所有生活习惯的巨大变化完全是因为受到公共舆论的束缚，她们往往是完全靠自己的意志力来做到这点。当来到择偶的时期，自由的世界观所培养和巩固起来的冷静而严肃的理智便教导美国妇女：婚后一如既往的轻浮和独立自主只能导致无尽的争吵，绝不会有乐趣；未婚女性的娱乐也不能成为已婚妇女的消遣，丈夫的家才是已婚妇女的幸福之源。因为她们事先已经看清，只有一条道路可以通向家庭幸福，于是她们一开始便走上这条道路并头也不回地一路走下去。美国少妇表现出来的能够立刻专注于新生活所带来的严格义务而毫无怨言的这种意志力，也同样反映在她们接受生活中的一切重大考验上。世界上没有一个国家的个人命运像美国人那样动荡不定。在美国，一个人一生之中浮浮沉沉，由富变穷又由穷至富的现象，并不罕见。美国妇女总是能

vicissitudes with calm and unquenchable energy: it would seem that their desires contract, as easily as they expand, with their fortunes.

The greater part of the adventurers who migrate every year to people the western wilds, belong, as I observed in the former part of this work, to the old Anglo-American race of the Northern States. Many of these men, who rush so boldly onwards in pursuit of wealth, were already in the enjoyment of a competency in their own part of the country. They take their wives along with them, and make them share the countless perils and privations which always attend the commencement of these expeditions. I have often met, even on the verge of the wilderness, with young women, who after having been brought up amidst all the comforts of the large towns of New England, had passed, almost without any intermediate stage, from the wealthy abode of their parents to a comfortless hovel in a forest. Fever, solitude, and a tedious life had not broken the springs of their courage. Their features were impaired and faded, but their looks were firm: they appeared to be at once sad and resolute. I do not doubt that these young American women had amassed, in the education of their early years, that inward strength which they displayed under these circumstances. The early culture of the girl may still therefore be traced, in the United States, under the aspect of marriage: her part is changed, her habits are different, but her character is the same.

Chapter XI: That The Equality Of Conditions Contributes To The Maintenance Of Good Morals In America

Some philosophers and historians have said, or have hinted, that the strictness of female morality was increased or diminished simply by the distance of a country from the equator. This solution of the difficulty was an easy one; and nothing was required but a globe and a pair of compasses to settle in an instant one of the most difficult problems in the condition of mankind. But I am not aware that this principle of the materialists is supported by facts. The same nations have been chaste or dissolute at different periods of their history; the strictness or the laxity of their morals depended therefore on some variable cause, not only on the natural qualities of their country, which were invariable. I do

够冷静而坚定地应对这样巨大的变化。似乎她们的欲望会随着她们的贫富随意伸缩。

正如我在本书上卷所说的，每年迁移到西部荒凉的冒险者，大部分都是早年定居在美国北部的英裔美国人。其中有许多人在故乡本已过着舒适的生活，但仍大胆地前来追逐财富。他们带着妻子，让她们与自己同甘共苦。我在西部荒漠的边缘地带，甚至常常会遇到一些在大城市的舒适环境中生长起来的少妇，她们几乎是婚后刚刚离开父母的豪华住宅，就来到林中的简陋茅屋。疾病、孤独和沉闷，都没能挫败她们的勇气。尽管她们的面容苍白憔悴，但眼神很坚毅。她们既有忧郁的表情，又有果敢的气概。我丝毫不怀疑，这些美国少妇在她们早年接受的教育中就已积聚起在这种情况下所需表现出的内在力量。因此，美国的妇女在婚后依旧能够看到他们少女时代所受教育的影子。尽管她们在生活中担当的角色已经改变，日常生活的习惯也不再相同，但她们的品质依旧如故。

第十一章　平等在美国怎样有助于维护良好的道德

一些哲学家和历史学家曾经说过或暗示过，女性的操守是随国家距离赤道的远近而增强或递减。这是回避难题最简单的方法。如果是这样的话，我们只需要一个地球仪和一个圆规，那么人性这个最难以解答的问题就可以立即迎刃而解。我认为这个唯物主义理论没有任何事实依据。同一个民族在不同的历史时期会有不同的表现，有时贞洁，有时淫荡。因此，国家的道德风尚到底是严谨还是放荡取决于一些可变因素，而并非是国家不变的地理位置。我并不否认，在特定的气候下，性的相互吸引激起的情欲特别强烈，但是我认为

not deny that in certain climates the passions which are occasioned by the mutual attraction of the sexes are peculiarly intense; but I am of opinion that this natural intensity may always be excited or restrained by the condition of society and by political institutions.

Although the travellers who have visited North America differ on a great number of points, they all agree in remarking that morals are far more strict there than elsewhere. It is evident that on this point the Americans are very superior to their progenitors the English. A superficial glance at the two nations will establish the fact. In England, as in all other countries of Europe, public malice is constantly attacking the frailties of women. Philosophers and statesmen are heard to deplore that morals are not sufficiently strict, and the literary productions of the country constantly lead one to suppose so. In America all books, novels not excepted, suppose women to be chaste, and no one thinks of relating affairs of gallantry. No doubt this great regularity of American morals originates partly in the country, in the race of the people, and in their religion: but all these causes, which operate elsewhere, do not suffice to account for it; recourse must be had to some special reason. This reason appears to me to be the principle of equality and the institutions derived from it. Equality of conditions does not of itself engender regularity of morals, but it unquestionably facilitates and increases it.

Amongst aristocratic nations birth and fortune frequently make two such different beings of man and woman, that they can never be united to each other. Their passions draw them together, but the condition of society, and the notions suggested by it, prevent them from contracting a permanent and ostensible tie. The necessary consequence is a great number of transient and clandestine connections. Nature secretly avenges herself for the constraint imposed upon her by the laws of man. This is not so much the case when the equality of conditions has swept away all the imaginary, or the real, barriers which separated man from woman. No girl then believes that she cannot become the wife of the man who loves her; and this renders all breaches of morality before marriage very uncommon: for, whatever be the credulity of the passions, a woman will hardly be able to persuade herself that she is beloved, when her lover is perfectly free to marry her and does not.

这种自然而然产生的情欲往往会因社会状况和政治制度而受到激发或是抑制。

尽管到过北美的旅游者们在很多问题上意见并不一致，但他们全都承认那里的道德风尚远比其他任何地方都严格。显然，在这一点上他们比他们的祖辈英国人强得多。只对这两个国家稍作观察，就可以确认这一事实。在英国，像在欧洲所有其他国家一样，公众舆论总是不断攻击女性的意志薄弱。于是，经常会听到哲学家和政治家扼腕叹息道德风尚不够正派，而且文学作品也在不断引导人们这样认为。在美国，所有的书籍，长篇小说也不例外，都把女性构想为冰清玉洁，没有人在书中讲述男女的风流韵事。毫无疑问，美国这种正派的道德风尚，其部分原因在于其国家、种族和宗教。但是，所有这些原因在其他地方也存在，所以还不足以说明这个问题，其中必然有一些特殊原因在起作用。在我看来，这个特殊原因就是平等及由此而来的各项制度。平等本身无法规范道德风尚，但毫无疑问它会促进并加速道德风尚的提高。

在贵族制国家，出身和财势不同的男女，往往不能结婚。情欲也许可能让他们彼此结合，但是，社会情况及由此而生的观念，却阻碍着他们结成永久的正式夫妻。因此，必然会存在大量的露水夫妻和秘密夫妻。这是大自然秘密地在对人类制定的法律施以报复。但是，当平等将所有想象的和实际存在的阻碍男女结合的所有障碍扫清之后，情形就完全不同了。于是，所有女孩都相信自己能够成为深爱着自己的男人的妻子，这使得婚前伤风败俗的行为非常罕见。因为无论情欲多么容易令人盲从，在你完全可以自由结婚却不愿娶她的时候，但你很难让一个女人确信你爱着她。

The same cause operates, though more indirectly, on married life. Nothing better serves to justify an illicit passion, either to the minds of those who have conceived it or to the world which looks on, than compulsory or accidental marriages. In a country in which a woman is always free to exercise her power of choosing, and in which education has prepared her to choose rightly, public opinion is inexorable to her faults. The rigor of the Americans arises in part from this cause. They consider marriages as a covenant which is often onerous, but every condition of which the parties are strictly bound to fulfil, because they knew all those conditions beforehand, and were perfectly free not to have contracted them.

The very circumstances which render matrimonial fidelity more obligatory also render it more easy. In aristocratic countries the object of marriage is rather to unite property than persons; hence the husband is sometimes at school and the wife at nurse when they are betrothed. It cannot be wondered at if the conjugal tie which holds the fortunes of the pair united allows their hearts to rove; this is the natural result of the nature of the contract. When, on the contrary, a man always chooses a wife for himself, without any external coercion or even guidance, it is generally a conformity of tastes and opinions which brings a man and a woman together, and this same conformity keeps and fixes them in close habits of intimacy.

Our forefathers had conceived a very strange notion on the subject of marriage: as they had remarked that the small number of love-matches which occurred in their time almost always turned out ill, they resolutely inferred that it was exceedingly dangerous to listen to the dictates of the heart on the subject. Accident appeared to them to be a better guide than choice. Yet it was not very difficult to perceive that the examples which they witnessed did in fact prove nothing at all. For in the first place, if democratic nations leave a woman at liberty to choose her husband, they take care to give her mind sufficient knowledge, and her will sufficient strength, to make so important a choice: whereas the young women who, amongst aristocratic nations, furtively elope from the authority of their parents to throw themselves of their own accord into the arms of men whom they have had neither time to know, nor ability to judge of, are totally without those securities. It is not

这个原因也同样对婚后生活产生一些间接影响。无论是在搞不正当情爱的人的眼中，还是在那些想要搞出这种不正当情爱的人的眼中，再没有什么比强迫婚姻或随机结合更能使不正当的情爱合理化了。在一个女性可以行使自由选择权，而且教育可以让她们能够做出最佳选择的国家，公共舆论对她们的错误绝不宽容。美国人苛刻的部分原因正是由此而来。他们认为婚姻是一种负有义务的契约，双方应该严格地履行所有条款，因为他们已事先知道这些条款，并完全拥有拒不缔约的自由。

让夫妇对婚姻忠诚的义务，也使得对婚姻的忠诚更加容易。在贵族制国家，结婚的目的与其说是两个人的结合，不如说是双方财产的结合。因此，有时他们在订婚的时候，男方已经上学读书，而女方还在被哺乳。所以并不奇怪，以双方的财产联合为目的的夫妇往往无法同心。这是这种契约的本质自然而然的结果。相反，当一个男人总是能自己选择妻子，不会受到外来干扰甚至诱导的时候，一致的爱好和观念往往会让一男一女彼此接近。这种一致性又可以让他们始终保持固定的亲密关系。

我们的祖先对于婚姻曾有一种古怪的看法。因为他们注意到那时不多的自由恋爱结婚几乎都是以悲剧收场，于是他们便断言这类事情听凭当事人的心意是极为危险的。在他们看来，萍水相逢可能比精挑细选更好。但是，不难发现，他们所见证的事例什么也证明不了。首先，如果民主国家允许女性自由选择配偶，必然会设法先让女性具备相应的知识和足够坚强的意志力，从而能够做出如此重要的选择；然而贵族制国家的少女，在不顾父母的权威而私奔，委身于一个她们既无时间了解，又无能力判断其好坏的男子时，这些保

surprising that they make a bad use of their freedom of action the first time they avail themselves of it; nor that they fall into such cruel mistakes, when, not having received a democratic education, they choose to marry in conformity to democratic customs. But this is not all. When a man and woman are bent upon marriage in spite of the differences of an aristocratic state of society, the difficulties to be overcome are enormous. Having broken or relaxed the bonds of filial obedience, they have then to emancipate themselves by a final effort from the sway of custom and the tyranny of opinion; and when at length they have succeeded in this arduous task, they stand estranged from their natural friends and kinsmen: the prejudice they have crossed separates them from all, and places them in a situation which soon breaks their courage and sours their hearts. If, then, a couple married in this manner are first unhappy and afterwards criminal, it ought not to be attributed to the freedom of their choice, but rather to their living in a community in which this freedom of choice is not admitted.

Moreover it should not be forgotten that the same effort which makes a man violently shake off a prevailing error, commonly impels him beyond the bounds of reason; that, to dare to declare war, in however just a cause, against the opinion of one's age and country, a violent and adventurous spirit is required, and that men of this character seldom arrive at happiness or virtue, whatever be the path they follow. And this, it may be observed by the way, is the reason why in the most necessary and righteous revolutions, it is so rare to meet with virtuous or moderate revolutionary characters. There is then no just ground for surprise if a man, who in an age of aristocracy chooses to consult nothing but his own opinion and his own taste in the choice of a wife, soon finds that infractions of morality and domestic wretchedness invade his household: but when this same line of action is in the natural and ordinary course of things, when it is sanctioned by parental authority and backed by public opinion, it cannot be doubted that the internal peace of families will be increased by it, and conjugal fidelity more rigidly observed.

Almost all men in democracies are engaged in public or professional life; and on the other hand the limited extent of common incomes obliges a wife to confine herself to the house, in order to watch in person and very closely over the details of domestic economy. All these distinct and

障则一无所有。因此，她们在第一次运用自由意志时就出现了失误，并在从未受过民主教育就运用民主习惯来选择婚姻时，铸下如此大错，并不足为奇。但是，还不止于此。当一男一女想要冲破贵族社会所造成的差异而结合时，需要克服的困难还有很多。在打破或削弱父母之命的束缚之后，他们还要做最后的努力去让自己摆脱习俗和专横舆论的影响。最后，当他们费尽九牛二虎之力达成心愿时，还会被亲朋好友疏远。偏见将他们与所有人隔离开来，将他们置于身心俱痛的境地。因此，即使这样结婚的一对夫妻一开始就很不幸，而且后来还可能犯错，那也不应该归咎于他们的自由选择，而是应当归咎于他们所生活的不允许自由选择婚姻的社会。

此外，不应该忘记，粗暴地为避免一个人不犯一般错误而做的努力往往同时会驱使其失去理智。敢于向自己所处的时代和国家的观念宣战，无论其事业如何正义，都需要在精神上做好进行暴力和冒险的斗争的准备。而具有这种性格的人，不管他走什么样的道路，都很少能够得到幸福或是有善举。顺便提一下，这也是在一些最必要的和最正义的革命中罕有温和正直的革命家的原因所在。因此，即使生活在贵族时代只听从自己的意愿和爱好选择妻子的人，婚后不久就见异思迁而乱搞或出现悲剧，也实在无须惊讶。但是，如果这种结合能按照自然常规的秩序进行，并受到父母的权威的认可和舆论的赞扬，则毫无疑问，家庭内部会更加和谐，夫妻之间会更加忠诚。

在民主国家，几乎所有的男人都参与政治生活，或从事某种职业；而另一方面，有限的家庭的收入迫使妻子不得不待在家中，以便亲自料理家务，精心管理家庭财产。所有这

compulsory occupations are so many natural barriers, which, by keeping the two sexes asunder, render the solicitations of the one less frequent and less ardent—the resistance of the other more easy.

Not indeed that the equality of conditions can ever succeed in making men chaste, but it may impart a less dangerous character to their breaches of morality. As no one has then either sufficient time or opportunity to assail a virtue armed in self-defence, there will be at the same time a great number of courtesans and a great number of virtuous women. This state of things causes lamentable cases of individual hardship, but it does not prevent the body of society from being strong and alert: it does not destroy family ties, or enervate the morals of the nation. Society is endangered not by the great profligacy of a few, but by laxity of morals amongst all. In the eyes of a legislator, prostitution is less to be dreaded than intrigue.

The tumultuous and constantly harassed life which equality makes men lead, not only distracts them from the passion of love, by denying them time to indulge in it, but it diverts them from it by another more secret but more certain road. All men who live in democratic ages more or less contract the ways of thinking of the manufacturing and trading classes; their minds take a serious, deliberate, and positive turn; they are apt to relinquish the ideal, in order to pursue some visible and proximate object, which appears to be the natural and necessary aim of their desires. Thus the principle of equality does not destroy the imagination, but lowers its flight to the level of the earth. No men are less addicted to reverie than the citizens of a democracy; and few of them are ever known to give way to those idle and solitary meditations which commonly precede and produce the great emotions of the heart. It is true they attach great importance to procuring for themselves that sort of deep, regular, and quiet affection which constitutes the charm and safeguard of life, but they are not apt to run after those violent and capricious sources of excitement which disturb and abridge it.

I am aware that all this is only applicable in its full extent to America, and cannot at present be extended to Europe. In the course of the last half-century, whilst laws and customs have impelled several European nations with unexampled force towards democracy, we have not had occasion to

些不同且各自必须承担的义务，就像一道道天然的屏障妨碍着性生活，使一方的性冲动日益减少且兴致大不如前，而另一方的抵制也更加容易。

实际上，平等并不能保证男人忠贞不贰，但可以让男人伤风败俗的行为不那么危险。因为这时谁也没有时间和机会去对他人是否想保持贞操评头论足，于是便在出现大量交际花的同时涌现出众多的具有节操的女性。这种情况虽然造成个人可悲的不幸，但并不妨碍整个社会变得活跃和坚强。它既不会破坏家庭纽带，又不会造成整个国家的道德沦丧。让社会陷入危机的不是某些人的放荡不羁，而是所有人道德的普遍堕落。在立法者的眼中，卖淫远远没有私通可怕。

平等让人们过上的这种喧闹和奔波的生活，不但让人无暇沉湎于谈情说爱，而且还通过一个更为隐秘可靠的办法让人避开谈情说爱。生活在民主时代的所有人，或多或少都有点工商阶级的思维习惯；他们的思维严谨、慎重而实际，而且往往会为了追求眼前目标而将理想弃之不顾，并将其视为自己天然的和必然的向往。因此，平等的原则并不会破坏人们的想象力，只是让它更加现实。没有任何国家的公民比民主国家的公民更不愿幻想，他们之中几乎没有人会做通常事前令人心潮跌宕的悠闲孤独的冥想。的确，他们十分重视追求可以使生活美好安定的深厚、普通而恬静的情感，但往往不愿意追求那些会干扰到生活并使生命缩短的强烈的并反复无常的激情。

我知道，所有这些只适用于美国，目前还不能推广到欧洲。最近半个世纪以来，法律和习惯虽以史无前例的力量推动许多欧洲国家走向民主，但我们依然可以看到这些国家的男女

observe that the relations of man and woman have become more orderly or more chaste. In some places the very reverse may be detected: some classes are more strict—the general morality of the people appears to be more lax. I do not hesitate to make the remark, for I am as little disposed to flatter my contemporaries as to malign them. This fact must distress, but it ought not to surprise us. The propitious influence which a democratic state of society may exercise upon orderly habits, is one of those tendencies which can only be discovered after a time. If the equality of conditions is favorable to purity of morals, the social commotion by which conditions are rendered equal is adverse to it. In the last fifty years, during which France has been undergoing this transformation, that country has rarely had freedom, always disturbance. Amidst this universal confusion of notions and this general stir of opinions—amidst this incoherent mixture of the just and unjust, of truth and falsehood, of right and might—public virtue has become doubtful, and private morality wavering. But all revolutions, whatever may have been their object or their agents, have at first produced similar consequences; even those which have in the end drawn the bonds of morality more tightly began by loosening them. The violations of morality which the French frequently witness do not appear to me to have a permanent character; and this is already betokened by some curious signs of the times.

Nothing is more wretchedly corrupt than an aristocracy which retains its wealth when it has lost its power, and which still enjoys a vast deal of leisure after it is reduced to mere vulgar pastimes. The energetic passions and great conceptions which animated it heretofore, leave it then; and nothing remains to it but a host of petty consuming vices, which cling about it like worms upon a carcass. No one denies that the French aristocracy of the last century was extremely dissolute; whereas established habits and ancient belief still preserved some respect for morality amongst the other classes of society. Nor will it be contested that at the present day the remnants of that same aristocracy exhibit a certain severity of morals; whilst laxity of morals appears to have spread amongst the middle and lower ranks. So that the same families which were most profligate fifty years ago are nowadays the most exemplary, and democracy seems only to have strengthened the

关系并没有因此而变得更为正派和纯真。在某些地方，甚至出现相反的情形。有些阶级在这个问题上很严肃，但整个国家的普遍道德水准则在下降。我会毫不犹豫地指出这一点，因为我既不想谄媚同时代的人，也不想中伤他们。这样的事实的确让人伤心，但也不必惊恐。民主的社会对有序习惯的有利影响，是需要经过一段时间之后才能显示出效果的现象之一。如果平等有利于道德风尚的净化，那么，社会在酝酿这种平等时呈现的混乱，则对其不利。近50年来，法国的面貌不断变化，但我们并没有获得很多自由，可动乱却时常发生。在观念普遍混乱，舆论摇摆不定的时候，在是非、真假、功过混淆难辨的时期，社会公德遭到怀疑，个人道德摇摇欲坠。但是，所有的革命，无论其目的何在，由什么人进行，最初的结果都是一样的，甚至那些以加强道德而结束的革命，在开始的时候也松弛了道德。在我看来，法国人屡见不鲜的道德动荡将会长期继续下去，而且一些不同寻常的征兆已经开始出现。

再也没有比这些贵族更加腐败透顶的了，他们在失去权力后仍然保留着财富，在享尽低俗消遣之后，依然拥有大量的闲暇。此前鼓舞他们的热烈激情和伟大思想已经弃他们而去，剩下的只有一大堆很小但腐蚀性很大的恶习，好像集聚在尸体上的苍蝇一样，紧紧地附着在他们身上。没有任何人否认，上个世纪的法国贵族极其放荡，然而传统的习惯和古老的信仰让对道德的尊重能够在其他阶级保留下来。而且也没有任何人会不认同，在我们这个时代，贵族的残余表现出一定程度的道德严肃性，而道德的放纵则在社会的中下阶层日益扩散。结果，50年前最为放荡的家庭，如今却成为家庭典范，民主似乎只巩固了贵族阶级的道德。法国大革命，通过分割贵族的财产，强迫他们把注意力集中在自己的私事

morality of the aristocratic classes. The French Revolution, by dividing the fortunes of the nobility, by forcing them to attend assiduously to their affairs and to their families, by making them live under the same roof with their children, and in short by giving a more rational and serious turn to their minds, has imparted to them, almost without their being aware of it, a reverence for religious belief, a love of order, of tranquil pleasures, of domestic endearments, and of comfort; whereas the rest of the nation, which had naturally these same tastes, was carried away into excesses by the effort which was required to overthrow the laws and political habits of the country. The old French aristocracy has undergone the consequences of the Revolution, but it neither felt the revolutionary passions nor shared in the anarchical excitement which produced that crisis; it may easily be conceived that this aristocracy feels the salutary influence of the Revolution in its manners, before those who achieve it. It may therefore be said, though at first it seems paradoxical, that, at the present day, the most anti-democratic classes of the nation principally exhibit the kind of morality which may reasonably be anticipated from democracy. I cannot but think that when we shall have obtained all the effects of this democratic Revolution, after having got rid of the tumult it has caused, the observations which are now only applicable to the few will gradually become true of the whole community.

Chapter XII: How The Americans Understand The Equality Of The Sexes

I Have shown how democracy destroys or modifies the different inequalities which originate in society; but is this all? or does it not ultimately affect that great inequality of man and woman which has seemed, up to the present day, to be eternally based in human nature? I believe that the social changes which bring nearer to the same level the father and son, the master and servant, and superiors and inferiors generally speaking, will raise woman and make her more and more the equal of man. But here, more than ever, I feel the necessity of making myself clearly understood; for there is no subject on which the coarse and lawless fancies of our age have taken a freer range.

There are people in Europe who, confounding together the different characteristics of the sexes, would make of man and woman beings not only equal but alike. They would give to both the same

和家庭，迫使他们与子女住在同一屋檐下，简而言之使他们的头脑比以前更为清晰和严肃，在不知不觉之中让贵族学会尊重宗教信仰，热爱秩序、平凡的娱乐、天伦之乐以及家庭幸福。然而，本来拥有这些爱好的其他阶层，却被为推翻法制和政治习惯而做的努力所席卷，变得毫无节制。旧的法国贵族只承受了大革命的后果，既没有感受到革命的激情，也并未感染到革命之前通常会有的无政府主义的兴奋。所以，不妨这样设想：他们感觉到这场革命对自己的生活方式产生的健康影响，比那些从事革命的人要早。因此，尽管乍听来有点骇人听闻，但可以说，今天国家中最反民主的阶级表现出大部分民主理所当然的道德。所以，我只能认为，当我们已经取得民主革命的所有成果时，并在消除革命带来的混乱之后，只被少数人视为真理的一些东西就将逐渐成为整个社会的真理。

第十二章　美国人怎样理解男女平等

我已经说过民主如何破坏或改变社会所造成的各种不平等。但这就是全部吗？或者民主最后是否会影响到至今似乎始终以人性为基础的重大的男女不平等呢？我认为，让父子关系、主仆关系以及一般而言的上下级关系越来越平等的社会变化，必然会提高女性地位，并逐渐让男女变得越来越平等。但是，在这里，我感觉非常有必要清楚地说明我的看法，因为没有一个题目比这个题目更可以让当代人展开天马行空的想象。

在欧洲，有些人模糊男女性别的特征，而鼓吹男女不但平等，而且完全相同。他们赋予男女同样的职责，强加给他们同样的义务，并给予他们同样的权利，即在职业、享乐和事务

functions, impose on both the same duties, and grant to both the same rights; they would mix them in all things—their occupations, their pleasures, their business. It may readily be conceived, that by thus attempting to make one sex equal to the other, both are degraded; and from so preposterous a medley of the works of nature nothing could ever result but weak men and disorderly women. It is not thus that the Americans understand that species of democratic equality which may be established between the sexes. They admit, that as nature has appointed such wide differences between the physical and moral constitution of man and woman, her manifest design was to give a distinct employment to their various faculties; and they hold that improvement does not consist in making beings so dissimilar do pretty nearly the same things, but in getting each of them to fulfil their respective tasks in the best possible manner. The Americans have applied to the sexes the great principle of political economy which governs the manufactures of our age, by carefully dividing the duties of man from those of woman, in order that the great work of society may be the better carried on.

In no country has such constant care been taken as in America to trace two clearly distinct lines of action for the two sexes, and to make them keep pace one with the other, but in two pathways which are always different. American women never manage the outward concerns of the family, or conduct a business, or take a part in political life; nor are they, on the other hand, ever compelled to perform the rough labor of the fields, or to make any of those laborious exertions which demand the exertion of physical strength. No families are so poor as to form an exception to this rule. If on the one hand an American woman cannot escape from the quiet circle of domestic employments, on the other hand she is never forced to go beyond it. Hence it is that the women of America, who often exhibit a masculine strength of understanding and a manly energy, generally preserve great delicacy of personal appearance and always retain the manners of women, although they sometimes show that they have the hearts and minds of men.

Nor have the Americans ever supposed that one consequence of democratic principles is the subversion of marital power, of the confusion of the natural authorities in families. They hold that every association must have a head in order to accomplish its object, and that the natural head of

等一切方面将他们混为一谈。不难想见,妄图使一种性别与另一种性别完全相等,反而会适得其反损害到双方。如此可笑地不顾两性的天性让他们各自做违反天性的事情,必然只会造就一些柔弱的男人和无法无天的女人。因此,这不是美国人所理解的两性之间建立的民主的平等。他们认为,既然大自然使男女在身心方面存在巨大差异,显然是要让他们各自利用自己的不同特点。而且他们确信,进步并不在于让不同性别的人去做几乎相同的事情,而是要让他们用最好的方式各司其职。美国人已经将指导当今工业的伟大政治经济学原则应用到两性方面,通过对男女的职责进行细致的划分,以便于伟大的社会工作能够更好地继续下去。

世界上没有哪个国家能够像美国那样注重划清两性之间的行动界线,让两性在同步前进的同时始终走在不同的道路上。美国妇女从不关心家庭以外的事务,或是涉足商业,参与政治生活;而另一方面也没有人会强迫妇女下地干粗活,或是任何重体力劳动。没有一个家庭穷到破例的地步。一方面,美国妇女无法走出的家务劳动的宁静小圈子,而另一方面也从没有人要强迫她们走出去。因此,美国妇女尽管常常表现出男子般的理解力和颇有男子气概的毅力,而且尽管有时候她们的头脑和心胸不让须眉,但无论是外表还是举止依旧普遍保持着女性的娇柔。

美国人从来没有想到民主原则会导致夫权的颠覆和家庭权威混乱的后果。他们认为,为了实现目标,每个团体都必须有一个领导,而丈夫就是夫妻这个小团体的天然领导。因此,美国人并不否认丈夫对其配偶的支配权,并且主张夫妻这个小团体,与大社会一样,民主的目的在于对必要的权利进行规范和合法化,而不是颠覆所有的权利。这并非是一种

the conjugal association is man. They do not therefore deny him the right of directing his partner; and they maintain, that in the smaller association of husband and wife, as well as in the great social community, the object of democracy is to regulate and legalize the powers which are necessary, not to subvert all power. This opinion is not peculiar to one sex, and contested by the other: I never observed that the women of America consider conjugal authority as a fortunate usurpation of their rights, nor that they thought themselves degraded by submitting to it. It appeared to me, on the contrary, that they attach a sort of pride to the voluntary surrender of their own will, and make it their boast to bend themselves to the yoke, not to shake it off. Such at least is the feeling expressed by the most virtuous of their sex; the others are silent; and in the United States it is not the practice for a guilty wife to clamor for the rights of women, whilst she is trampling on her holiest duties.

It has often been remarked that in Europe a certain degree of contempt lurks even in the flattery which men lavish upon women: although a European frequently affects to be the slave of woman, it may be seen that he never sincerely thinks her his equal. In the United States men seldom compliment women, but they daily show how much they esteem them. They constantly display an entire confidence in the understanding of a wife, and a profound respect for her freedom; they have decided that her mind is just as fitted as that of a man to discover the plain truth, and her heart as firm to embrace it; and they have never sought to place her virtue, any more than his, under the shelter of prejudice, ignorance, and fear. It would seem that in Europe, where man so easily submits to the despotic sway of women, they are nevertheless curtailed of some of the greatest qualities of the human species, and considered as seductive but imperfect beings; and (what may well provoke astonishment) women ultimately look upon themselves in the same light, and almost consider it as a privilege that they are entitled to show themselves futile, feeble, and timid. The women of America claim no such privileges.

Again, it may be said that in our morals we have reserved strange immunities to man; so that there is, as it were, one virtue for his use, and another for the guidance of his partner; and that, according to the opinion of the public, the very same act may be punished alternately as a crime or only as a fault.

性别所独有而受到另一性别反对的看法。我从没见过美国妇女认为丈夫行使其权利就是侵夺她们的权利，而且她们也从不将服从视为一种屈辱。而且恰恰相反，在我看来她们把心甘情愿放弃自己的主见视为一种荣誉，是值得夸耀而不是要摆脱的东西。这至少是最具美德的美国妇女的感受，至于其他美国妇女，她们并未发表意见。另外，在美国，当一个有罪的妻子践踏自己最神圣的义务时，绝不会叫嚣着主张自己的女权。

在欧洲，人们常常说，甚至男人对女人极尽奉承之能事，也总会带有一些轻视。尽管欧洲男人往往表现得像女人的奴隶，但可以看得出，他们从来没有发自内心地认为女性与他们平等。在美国，男人很少恭维女性，但他们每天都在证明他们对女性的尊重。他们往往对妻子的智力表现出充分的信心，并十分尊重她的自由。他们认定女人的头脑跟男人的一样能够发现纯正的真理，而且心胸也足够坚定能够拥抱这种真理。他们从来没有试图用成见掩盖她们的美德，用女性的无知和胆小来证明自己的德行比配偶高。然而，在男人如此容易受到女人左右的欧洲，他们却似乎要剥夺女性作为人类的某些主要属性。他们认为女性虽然很有魅力，但并不是完美的人；而且更令人惊奇的是，女性最终对自己也持有同样的看法，并将表现自己的无用、脆弱和胆小视为自己的特权。美国妇女却从不会要求这种权利。

而且，我们还可以说，按照我们的道德标准男人实际上保有一种奇怪的豁免权，以至于好像一套道德规范是专为男人而定，而另一套道德规范则是专为其配偶所定，而且按照公共舆论，同一种行为在女性身上出现就是犯罪，而在男人身上出现则不过是过错。然而，美国人则没有这种权利和义务的不公平分配，在他们看来，诱奸者和受害者是同样不

The Americans know not this iniquitous division of duties and rights; amongst them the seducer is as much dishonored as his victim. It is true that the Americans rarely lavish upon women those eager attentions which are commonly paid them in Europe; but their conduct to women always implies that they suppose them to be virtuous and refined; and such is the respect entertained for the moral freedom of the sex, that in the presence of a woman the most guarded language is used, lest her ear should be offended by an expression. In America a young unmarried woman may, alone and without fear, undertake a long journey.

The legislators of the United States, who have mitigated almost all the penalties of criminal law, still make rape a capital offence, and no crime is visited with more inexorable severity by public opinion. This may be accounted for; as the Americans can conceive nothing more precious than a woman's honor, and nothing which ought so much to be respected as her independence, they hold that no punishment is too severe for the man who deprives her of them against her will. In France, where the same offence is visited with far milder penalties, it is frequently difficult to get a verdict from a jury against the prisoner. Is this a consequence of contempt of decency or contempt of women? I cannot but believe that it is a contempt of one and of the other.

Thus the Americans do not think that man and woman have either the duty or the right to perform the same offices, but they show an equal regard for both their respective parts; and though their lot is different, they consider both of them as beings of equal value. They do not give to the courage of woman the same form or the same direction as to that of man; but they never doubt her courage: and if they hold that man and his partner ought not always to exercise their intellect and understanding in the same manner, they at least believe the understanding of the one to be as sound as that of the other, and her intellect to be as clear. Thus, then, whilst they have allowed the social inferiority of woman to subsist, they have done all they could to raise her morally and intellectually to the level of man; and in this respect they appear to me to have excellently understood the true principle of democratic improvement. As for myself, I do not hesitate to avow that, although the women of the United States are confined within the narrow circle of domestic life, and their situation is in some respects one of

光彩的。事实上，美国男人很少像欧洲男人那样向女性百般献殷勤，但他们常常会用实际行动表示他们认为女性是贞洁娴雅的。他们非常尊重女性的精神自由，以至于女性在场的时候，每个人都会小心措辞，唯恐言语有失让她们听到感到不快的言辞。在美国，一个未婚的年轻姑娘独自长途旅行而不会感到害怕。

美国的立法者尽管减轻了刑法典中的几乎所有的刑罚，但是强奸罪依然可以被判死刑，而且公众舆论对这种犯罪的声讨也最为严厉。因为美国人最为珍视女性的名节，最为尊重女性的自由，所以他们认为对于违背女性意愿剥夺其节操的人应该施以最严厉的惩罚。在法国，这种犯罪则被判得很轻，而且往往很难见到陪审团做出有罪裁定。这样的结果到底是因为轻视女性的节操还是轻视女性呢？而我只能认为，是两者兼而有之。

因此，尽管美国人不认为男人和女人有同样的义务和权利去做同样的事情，但对他们各自的角色表示同样的尊重。而且他们认为男女的命运虽然不同，但作为人具有同等的价值。他们并不认为女性的勇气与男性的勇气具有相同的形式，也不认为女性应该像男性那样运用自己的勇气，但他们从未置疑女性的勇气。即使他们始终认为男人及其配偶不应当始终用同样的方式运用他们各自的智慧和理解力，但至少认为女性的理解力与男性的同样可靠，女性的智慧与男性的同样清晰。因此，美国人在让女性处于社会下层的同时，竭尽所能将她们的道德和智力提高到与男人相同的水平。在这方面，依我看他们真正理解了民主进步的含义。至于我自己，我会毫不犹豫地公开承认，尽管美国的女性被限制在家庭生活的小圈子，而且在一定程度上还具有很大的依附性，但我从来没有见过其他地方的女性

extreme dependence, I have nowhere seen woman occupying a loftier position; and if I were asked, now that I am drawing to the close of this work, in which I have spoken of so many important things done by the Americans, to what the singular prosperity and growing strength of that people ought mainly to be attributed, I should reply—to the superiority of their women.

Chapter XIII: That The Principle Of Equality Naturally Divides The Americans Into A Number Of Small Private Circles

It may probably be supposed that the final consequence and necessary effect of democratic institutions is to confound together all the members of the community in private as well as in public life, and to compel them all to live in common; but this would be to ascribe a very coarse and oppressive form to the equality which originates in democracy. No state of society or laws can render men so much alike, but that education, fortune, and tastes will interpose some differences between them; and, though different men may sometimes find it their interest to combine for the same purposes, they will never make it their pleasure. They will therefore always tend to evade the provisions of legislation, whatever they may be; and departing in some one respect from the circle within which they were to be bounded, they will set up, close by the great political community, small private circles, united together by the similitude of their conditions, habits, and manners.

In the United States the citizens have no sort of pre-eminence over each other; they owe each other no mutual obedience or respect; they all meet for the administration of justice, for the government of the State, and in general to treat of the affairs which concern their common welfare; but I never heard that attempts have been made to bring them all to follow the same diversions, or to amuse themselves promiscuously in the same places of recreation. The Americans, who mingle so readily in their political assemblies and courts of justice, are wont on the contrary carefully to separate into small distinct circles, in order to indulge by themselves in the enjoyments of private life. Each of them is willing to acknowledge all his fellow-citizens as his equals, but he will only receive a very limited number of them amongst his friends or his guests. This appears to me to be very natural.

有她们这样高的地位。如果有人问我，既然我即将完成本书，讲了美国人已经做过的那么多的重大事情，那么这个国家惊人的繁荣和国力的蒸蒸日上主要应当归功于什么呢，我的回答会是，这个国家女性的出类拔萃。

第十三章　平等自然而然将美国人分为许多私人小团体

也许可以这样认为，民主制度的最终的必然结果就是，让全体公民的私人生活像在政治生活一样融合起来，并迫使所有人过上相同的生活，但这将是对于源自民主的平等极为粗陋蛮横的理解。没有任何社会状况或是法制能够让人们相似得在教育、财富和爱好上没有一点差别。尽管不同的人有时候会发现他们会出于相同的目的而联合起来，但是他们不会从中感到快乐。因此，他们无论如何都会始终想要逃避立法条文的约束，在某一方面摆脱他们被规定的活动范围。于是，他们会凭借相似的条件、习惯和品德结成小的私人团体，并与大的政治团体共存。

在美国公民之间没有高低之分，既不需要彼此服从也不需要彼此尊重。他们共同执法，共同治国，总之，他们共同处理与所有人有关的共同事务。但是，我从来没听说有人主张大家以同样方式去消遣，或混迹于同一娱乐场所。在政治集会和法庭经常混在一起的美国人，相反，在私人生活方面小心翼翼地各自分成许多很不同的小圈子，以便于充分享受私人生活的乐趣。每个公民都认可所有同胞一律平等，但只认可其中极少数的人作为的朋友和客人。随着公共生活圈子的扩大，可以料想私人交往的范围将被压缩。我非但不

In proportion as the circle of public society is extended, it may be anticipated that the sphere of private intercourse will be contracted; far from supposing that the members of modern society will ultimately live in common, I am afraid that they may end by forming nothing but small coteries.

Amongst aristocratic nations the different classes are like vast chambers, out of which it is impossible to get, into which it is impossible to enter. These classes have no communication with each other, but within their pale men necessarily live in daily contact; even though they would not naturally suit, the general conformity of a similar condition brings them nearer together. But when neither law nor custom professes to establish frequent and habitual relations between certain men, their intercourse originates in the accidental analogy of opinions and tastes; hence private society is infinitely varied. In democracies, where the members of the community never differ much from each other, and naturally stand in such propinquity that they may all at any time be confounded in one general mass, numerous artificial and arbitrary distinctions spring up, by means of which every man hopes to keep himself aloof, lest he should be carried away in the crowd against his will. This can never fail to be the case; for human institutions may be changed, but not man: whatever may be the general endeavor of a community to render its members equal and alike, the personal pride of individuals will always seek to rise above the line, and to form somewhere an inequality to their own advantage.

In aristocracies men are separated from each other by lofty stationary barriers; in democracies they are divided by a number of small and almost invisible threads, which are constantly broken or moved from place to place. Thus, whatever may be the progress of equality, in democratic nations a great number of small private communities will always be formed within the general pale of political society; but none of them will bear any resemblance in its manners to the highest class in aristocracies.

Chapter XIV: Some Reflections On American Manners

Nothing seems at first sight less important than the outward form of human actions, yet there is

认为现代社会的成员最终会在生活上一模一样，反而担心他们最终会形成许多小团体。

在贵族制国家，不同的阶级都是一个个不同的大会所，其本阶级成员不但无法出来，而且其他阶级的成员也休想进去。这些阶级之间互不来往，但在每个阶级内部，人们的往来则必不可少，而且即使他们彼此的天性并不协调，但普遍一致的相似的状况会让他们越来越接近。但是当法律和习惯都没有公开表示在某些人之间建立频繁的和经常的关系的时候，偶然的观点和爱好的一致，会对建立这种关系发挥作用。因此，私人团体变化万千。在民主制度下，公民之间永远不会出现太大的差别，因此自然感到互相接近得随时都可能融合为一体，于是便人为随意地制定许多不同并希望凭借这些不同而避开他人，唯恐身不由己地随波逐流。这样的情况可能永远无法改变，因为人们的制度可能会改变，但是人本身不会改变。无论一个社会做出怎样大的努力确保公民的平等和相同，个人的荣誉感总是试图要使自己鹤立鸡群，并形成一种对己有利的不平等。

在贵族制度下，人们被岿然不动的高高壁垒隔开；在民主制度下，人们被许多细得几乎看不见的线隔开，尽管这些线会随时断开，但它们也在不断变换位置重新联结。因此，无论平等发展到何种地步，在民主国家政治社会的大范围之内总会形成大量的私人小团体，但是，它们之中没有任何一个会具有与贵族社会上层阶级相似的行为风尚。

第十四章　对美国人行为风尚的思考

初看起来，人们的外在行为似乎并不是那么重要，然而人们对于这些表象的重视程度

nothing upon which men set more store: they grow used to everything except to living in a society which has not their own manners. The influence of the social and political state of a country upon manners is therefore deserving of serious examination. Manners are, generally, the product of the very basis of the character of a people, but they are also sometimes the result of an arbitrary convention between certain men; thus they are at once natural and acquired. When certain men perceive that they are the foremost persons in society, without contestation and without effort—when they are constantly engaged on large objects, leaving the more minute details to others—and when they live in the enjoyment of wealth which they did not amass and which they do not fear to lose, it may be supposed that they feel a kind of haughty disdain of the petty interests and practical cares of life, and that their thoughts assume a natural greatness, which their language and their manners denote. In democratic countries manners are generally devoid of dignity, because private life is there extremely petty in its character; and they are frequently low, because the mind has few opportunities of rising above the engrossing cares of domestic interests. True dignity in manners consists in always taking one's proper station, neither too high nor too low; and this is as much within the reach of a peasant as of a prince. In democracies all stations appear doubtful; hence it is that the manners of democracies, though often full of arrogance, are commonly wanting in dignity, and, moreover, they are never either well disciplined or accomplished.

The men who live in democracies are too fluctuating for a certain number of them ever to succeed in laying down a code of good breeding, and in forcing people to follow it. Every man therefore behaves after his own fashion, and there is always a certain incoherence in the manners of such times, because they are moulded upon the feelings and notions of each individual, rather than upon an ideal model proposed for general imitation. This, however, is much more perceptible at the time when an aristocracy has just been overthrown than after it has long been destroyed. New political institutions and new social elements then bring to the same places of resort, and frequently compel to live in common, men whose education and habits are still amazingly dissimilar, and this renders the motley composition of society peculiarly visible. The existence of a former strict code of good

却超过一切，除非生活在一个没有自己行为风尚的社会。因此，一个国家社会和政治状况对于行为风尚的影响特别值得仔细研究。一般来说，行为风尚是一个民族特征最为基础的产物，但它们有时候也是某些人之间约定俗成的结果，因此，行为风尚既是与生俱来的，也是后天习得的。当一些人认为自己可以不费周折和不经努力便可在社会出人头地时，当他们不断感到自己有大事要做而将一些琐碎小事留给别人去做时，以及当他们自己享受这并非由自己积累起来的财富而且毫不担心会失去这些财富时，可以想见他们对小小的利益和生活上的实际需要是多么傲慢地不屑一顾，而且他们的思想呈现出一种自然而然的伟大，并通过他们的语言和举止流露出来。在民主国家，人们的行为风尚一般并不高贵，因为私人生活的特点就是极为琐碎，而且往往还很低俗，因为人们只忙于家事，很少有机会讲究这些。行为风尚的真正尊严在于能够表现得得体，不卑不亢，而这一点，无论是农民还是王公都能做到。在民主国家，所有人的地位似乎会受到质疑，所以尽管人们的举止往往很傲慢，但普遍不高贵。此外，民主国家的人们的举止既没有受到严格的规范，也没有经过严格的训练。

生活在民主制度下的人过于好动，以至于有些人很难养成彬彬有礼的举止，即使养成也无法长期遵守。因此，每个人总是按照自己的意愿随意行动，所以经常会出现不连贯的表现，因为每个人的举止主要是根据个人的思想和感情铸成，而不是对理想典范的普遍模仿。而且，这一点在贵族制度刚被推翻时会比在贵族制度被推翻很久以后表现得更为明显。于是，新的政治制度和新的社会因素，促使教育程度和习惯有天壤之别的人们会聚在同一地点，并迫使他们共同生活，从而使社会的形形色色特别显眼。人们依然还记得从前

breeding is still remembered, but what it contained or where it is to be found is already forgotten. Men have lost the common law of manners, and they have not yet made up their minds to do without it; but everyone endeavors to make to himself some sort of arbitrary and variable rule, from the remnant of former usages; so that manners have neither the regularity and the dignity which they often display amongst aristocratic nations, nor the simplicity and freedom which they sometimes assume in democracies; they are at once constrained and without constraint.

This, however, is not the normal state of things. When the equality of conditions is long established and complete, as all men entertain nearly the same notions and do nearly the same things, they do not require to agree or to copy from one another in order to speak or act in the same manner: their manners are constantly characterized by a number of lesser diversities, but not by any great differences. They are never perfectly alike, because they do not copy from the same pattern; they are never very unlike, because their social condition is the same. At first sight a traveller would observe that the manners of all the Americans are exactly similar; it is only upon close examination that the peculiarities in which they differ may be detected.

The English make game of the manners of the Americans; but it is singular that most of the writers who have drawn these ludicrous delineations belonged themselves to the middle classes in England, to whom the same delineations are exceedingly applicable: so that these pitiless censors for the most part furnish an example of the very thing they blame in the United States; they do not perceive that they are deriding themselves, to the great amusement of the aristocracy of their own country.

Nothing is more prejudicial to democracy than its outward forms of behavior: many men would willingly endure its vices, who cannot support its manners. I cannot, however, admit that there is nothing commendable in the manners of a democratic people. Amongst aristocratic nations, all who live within reach of the first class in society commonly strain to be like it, which gives rise to ridiculous and insipid imitations. As a democratic people does not possess any models of high breeding, at least it escapes the daily necessity of seeing wretched copies of them. In democracies manners are never so refined as amongst aristocratic nations, but on the other hand they are never

严格的礼仪典范，但已经忘却它有什么内容，从何而来。人们已经失去共同的行为准则，但还没有下定决心弃它而去，但是每个人又试图利用旧规矩的断壁残垣为自己构建起某种任意且随时变化的行为准则。于是，行为风尚再也没有贵族时期呈现出的整齐划一和高贵威严，而且也不像民主时期有时呈现的那样朴素大方。它们既受拘束又不受拘束。

然而，这并不是事情的正常状态。当平等长期全面地确立，而且所有的人都有着几乎同样的观念并做着几乎同样的工作，彼此之间并不需要互相商量或模仿来保持言行上的一致时，他们的举止虽有很多细小的差别，但没有什么大的不同。他们永远不会一模一样，因为他们并没有模仿同一个模式。他们也永远不会有大的差别，因为他们的社会状况相同。一个来到美国的旅行者，乍看之下，会觉得所有美国人的举止完全一样，只有经过仔细观察，才能发觉他们彼此之间的细微差别。

英国人总爱嘲笑美国人的举止，但奇怪的是，做如此滑稽描述的大部分作家，他们本人也属于有同样滑稽之举的英国中产阶级。因此，这些笔下毫不留情的挖苦者们往往也都是他们所指摘的美国人那些举止的身体力行者。他们没有感觉到他们正在自己嘲弄自己，而让本国的贵族觉得可笑。

再没有什么比人们的外在举止更不利于民主的了。许多人宁愿容忍民主的缺陷，而不肯支持民主的行为风尚。但是，我并不认为民主国家的行为风尚毫无可取之处。在贵族制国家，所有能够接近上层阶级的人，普遍都力图向其靠拢，对他们进行荒唐可笑的模仿。因为民主国家的人民没有任何高贵血统可以来模仿，所以他们至少每天不必看到那些可悲的模

so coarse. Neither the coarse oaths of the populace, nor the elegant and choice expressions of the nobility are to be heard there: the manners of such a people are often vulgar, but they are neither brutal nor mean. I have already observed that in democracies no such thing as a regular code of good breeding can be laid down; this has some inconveniences and some advantages. In aristocracies the rules of propriety impose the same demeanor on everyone; they make all the members of the same class appear alike, in spite of their private inclinations; they adorn and they conceal the natural man. Amongst a democratic people manners are neither so tutored nor so uniform, but they are frequently more sincere. They form, as it were, a light and loosely woven veil, through which the real feelings and private opinions of each individual are easily discernible. The form and the substance of human actions often, therefore, stand in closer relation; and if the great picture of human life be less embellished, it is more true. Thus it may be said, in one sense, that the effect of democracy is not exactly to give men any particular manners, but to prevent them from having manners at all.

The feelings, the passions, the virtues, and the vices of an aristocracy may sometimes reappear in a democracy, but not its manners; they are lost, and vanish forever, as soon as the democratic revolution is completed. It would seem that nothing is more lasting than the manners of an aristocratic class, for they are preserved by that class for some time after it has lost its wealth and its power—nor so fleeting, for no sooner have they disappeared than not a trace of them is to be found; and it is scarcely possible to say what they have been as soon as they have ceased to be. A change in the state of society works this miracle, and a few generations suffice to consummate it. The principal characteristics of aristocracy are handed down by history after an aristocracy is destroyed, but the light and exquisite touches of manners are effaced from men's memories almost immediately after its fall. Men can no longer conceive what these manners were when they have ceased to witness them; they are gone, and their departure was unseen, unfelt; for in order to feel that refined enjoyment which is derived from choice and distinguished manners, habit and education must have prepared the heart, and the taste for them is lost almost as easily as the practice of them. Thus not only a

仿。在民主国家，人们的举止从来不像贵族制国家那样讲究，但也从来不粗野。在这里，既听不到老百姓的粗野咒骂，也听不到贵族那种满口珠玑的高贵谈吐。在这样一个国家，人们的举止尽管往往略显粗陋但决不粗野和卑鄙。我曾经说过，在民主国家并没有高雅的礼仪规范，而这虽然会带来不便，但也会带来好处。在贵族制国家，一套套的礼仪规范将同样的仪态加诸每个人身上。它们不顾这些人的个人性格让同一阶级所有成员的举止看起来完全相同。它们粉饰每个人并将人的本性掩盖起来。在民主国家，人们的举止既没有受到约束，也不是如此整齐划一，但往往发自内心。在这里，人们的仪表就像一层织得很轻薄稀疏的纱，通过它人们可以很容易地看到每个人的真正情感和个人想法。因此，人们行动的方式和实质往往非常一致，而且即使它所渲染的人生图景不够绚丽，但更为真实。因此，从某种意义上也可以说，民主的作用并不是赋予人们一定的行为风尚，而是阻止人们形成一定的行为风尚。

贵族的情感、激情、美德和恶行有时会在一个民主国家再现，但贵族的行为风尚则绝无可能。民主革命一旦彻底完成，它们便不复存在永远消失。似乎没有什么东西能够比贵族阶级的行为风尚更加持久，因为它会在这个阶级丧失其财富和权势之后，依然可以持续一段时间；然而，似乎又没有什么东西能够比它还要脆弱，因为它一旦消失便踪迹全无，以至于很难说它曾经存在过。社会情况的变化造就了这个足足需要几代人才能完成的奇迹。贵族制度的主要特点会在贵族制度消亡之后被历史传承；但是其高雅精致的行为方式，则会随着贵族制度的崩溃而被人们立即遗忘。人们只要看不到这样的行为方式就不会再想起它。它已经消逝，而且它的消失既没有人看到，也没有人感觉到，因为要体会来自精致高贵举止的美好享受，人们必须首先在习惯上和教育上做好思想准备，而人们对于这

democratic people cannot have aristocratic manners, but they neither comprehend nor desire them; and as they never have thought of them, it is to their minds as if such things had never been. Too much importance should not be attached to this loss, but it may well be regretted.

I am aware that it has not unfrequently happened that the same men have had very high-bred manners and very low-born feelings: the interior of courts has sufficiently shown what imposing externals may conceal the meanest hearts. But though the manners of aristocracy did not constitute virtue, they sometimes embellish virtue itself. It was no ordinary sight to see a numerous and powerful class of men, whose every outward action seemed constantly to be dictated by a natural elevation of thought and feeling, by delicacy and regularity of taste, and by urbanity of manners. Those manners threw a pleasing illusory charm over human nature; and though the picture was often a false one, it could not be viewed without a noble satisfaction.

Chapter XV: Of The Gravity Of The Americans, And Why It Does Not Prevent Them From Often Committing Inconsiderate Actions

Men who live in democratic countries do not value the simple, turbulent, or coarse diversions in which the people indulge in aristocratic communities: such diversions are thought by them to be puerile or insipid. Nor have they a greater inclination for the intellectual and refined amusements of the aristocratic classes. They want something productive and substantial in their pleasures; they want to mix actual fruition with their joy. In aristocratic communities the people readily give themselves up to bursts of tumultuous and boisterous gayety, which shake off at once the recollection of their privations: the natives of democracies are not fond of being thus violently broken in upon, and they never lose sight of their own selves without regret. They prefer to these frivolous delights those more serious and silent amusements which are like business, and which do not drive business wholly from their minds. An American, instead of going in a leisure hour to dance merrily at some place of public resort, as the fellows of his calling continue to do throughout the greater part of Europe, shuts

种美好享受的爱好则会轻易消失就好像人们曾经很容易地做到一样。因此，不但民主国家的人民不会有贵族的行为风尚，而且他们既不理解也不会渴望拥有贵族的行为风尚。因为他们想象不出它的样子。在他们的意识之中，这样的行为风尚似乎从来没有存在过。对于这样的损失不应当过于在意，但也的确令人遗憾。

我意识到，举止十分高雅但其感情却十分庸俗的人并不罕见，在法庭上能够清晰地看到，堂堂的外表之下往往隐藏着最为卑鄙的心肠。但是，尽管贵族的行为风尚不能算作美德，但有时的确可以粉饰美德。很少会看到一个人数众多力量强大的阶级会有如此表现，他们往往会用每个外在举动来显示其感情和思想与生俱来的高尚，其爱好的精致和规范，其举止的文雅。贵族的行为风尚使人们对人性产生美好的错觉，尽管其所呈现的图景往往是虚伪的，但看到它的时候总是让人有一种高尚的满足感。

第十五章　美国人的严肃性，以及为什么它不能防止美国人做出有欠考虑的事情

生活在民主国家的人们并不重视贵族社会老百姓所热衷的那些洲淳朴的、喧闹的和粗俗的消遣，他们认为这样的消遣过于幼稚和无聊。而且对于贵族阶级的高雅精致的娱乐也不喜欢。他们想要在享乐中获得某些富有成效和实际的东西，并且希望寓实利于享乐之中。在贵族制社会，人们很容易沉溺于喧闹的欢乐之中，以暂时忘却生活中的苦难。而民主社会的居民不喜欢这样的得意忘形，他们总是对自己失控后悔不已。他们更喜欢同工作相似而且不会让他们把工作抛到脑后的那种严肃安静的娱乐。一个美国人，不会像欧洲大部分国家那些与他同行的人常常做的那样，在工作之余来到某个公共场所跳舞娱乐，而是

himself up at home to drink. He thus enjoys two pleasures; he can go on thinking of his business, and he can get drunk decently by his own fireside.

I thought that the English constituted the most serious nation on the face of the earth, but I have since seen the Americans and have changed my opinion. I do not mean to say that temperament has not a great deal to do with the character of the inhabitants of the United States, but I think that their political institutions are a still more influential cause. I believe the seriousness of the Americans arises partly from their pride. In democratic countries even poor men entertain a lofty notion of their personal importance: they look upon themselves with complacency, and are apt to suppose that others are looking at them, too. With this disposition they watch their language and their actions with care, and do not lay themselves open so as to betray their deficiencies; to preserve their dignity they think it necessary to retain their gravity.

But I detect another more deep-seated and powerful cause which instinctively produces amongst the Americans this astonishing gravity. Under a despotism communities give way at times to bursts of vehement joy; but they are generally gloomy and moody, because they are afraid. Under absolute monarchies tempered by the customs and manners of the country, their spirits are often cheerful and even, because as they have some freedom and a good deal of security, they are exempted from the most important cares of life; but all free peoples are serious, because their minds are habitually absorbed by the contemplation of some dangerous or difficult purpose. This is more especially the case amongst those free nations which form democratic communities. Then there are in all classes a very large number of men constantly occupied with the serious affairs of the government; and those whose thoughts are not engaged in the direction of the commonwealth are wholly engrossed by the acquisition of a private fortune. Amongst such a people a serious demeanor ceases to be peculiar to certain men, and becomes a habit of the nation.

We are told of small democracies in the days of antiquity, in which the citizens met upon the public places with garlands of roses, and spent almost all their time in dancing and theatrical

宁可把自己关在家里独酌。这样，他就可以把两种享乐合二为一，既可以继续想着他的生意，又可以在自己的壁炉边酒意浓浓。

我曾经以为英国人是地球上最严肃的民族，但自从我见到美国人以后便改变了我的看法。我并不是说气质对于美国居民的性格不会产生重要的影响，但我认为政治制度对他们性格的影响更大。我相信美国人的严肃部分是来源于他们骄傲。在民主国家，甚至穷人也非常看重自己的个人重要性。他为自己自鸣得意，而且往往认为别人也会这样看待他。在这种心情的支配下，他对自己的言行非常谨慎，绝不会忘乎所以，以免暴露自己的缺点。为了保持自己的自尊，他们认为有必要保持严肃。

但我发觉还有一个更为深层的强大的因素激发起美国人这种本能的令人吃惊的严肃性。在专制社会，人们会时不时地纵情欢乐，但一般来说，他们总是郁郁寡欢闷闷不乐，这是因为他们害怕。在王权受到习惯和民情抑制的君主国家，人们的精神往往很平和愉悦，因为他们享有一定的自由和极大的保障，不必为生活而过分担忧。但是，所有自由的人民都是严肃的，因为他们的思想习惯于陷入对事业危机和困难的思索。这对于已形成民主社会的自由国家的人民来说，尤其如此。于是，在各个阶级都有大量的人不断参与国家大事，而那些不想考虑联邦利益的人，则专心致力于增加个人财富，因此，在这样的国家，严肃的作风不再为某些人所特有，而成为一种民族习性。

人们告诉我们在古代的一些小共和国，公民会戴着玫瑰花环聚会在公共场所，并几乎把所有的时间都消磨在跳舞和观看戏剧上面。我既不相信有这样的共和国存在也不相信柏拉图鼓吹的共和国。如果事实真如他们所说的那样，我可以毫不犹豫地肯定，这些所设想的

amusements. I do not believe in such republics any more than in that of Plato; or, if the things we read of really happened, I do not hesitate to affirm that these supposed democracies were composed of very different elements from ours, and that they had nothing in common with the latter except their name. But it must not be supposed that, in the midst of all their toils, the people who live in democracies think themselves to be pitied; the contrary is remarked to be the case. No men are fonder of their own condition. Life would have no relish for them if they were delivered from the anxieties which harass them, and they show more attachment to their cares than aristocratic nations to their pleasures.

I am next led to inquire how it is that these same democratic nations, which are so serious, sometimes act in so inconsiderate a manner. The Americans, who almost always preserve a staid demeanor and a frigid air, nevertheless frequently allow themselves to be borne away, far beyond the bound of reason, by a sudden passion or a hasty opinion, and they sometimes gravely commit strange absurdities. This contrast ought not to surprise us. There is one sort of ignorance which originates in extreme publicity. In despotic States men know not how to act, because they are told nothing; in democratic nations they often act at random, because nothing is to be left untold. The former do not know—the latter forget; and the chief features of each picture are lost to them in a bewilderment of details.

It is astonishing what imprudent language a public man may sometimes use in free countries, and especially in democratic States, without being compromised; whereas in absolute monarchies a few words dropped by accident are enough to unmask him forever, and ruin him without hope of redemption. This is explained by what goes before. When a man speaks in the midst of a great crowd, many of his words are not heard, or are forthwith obliterated from the memories of those who hear them; but amidst the silence of a mute and motionless throng the slightest whisper strikes the ear.

In democracies men are never stationary; a thousand chances waft them to and fro, and their life is always the sport of unforeseen or (so to speak) extemporaneous circumstances. Thus they are often

共和国与我们所说的共和国的构成要素必然大相径庭。除了名称一样以外，两者肯定毫无共同之处。但是也千万不要以为生活在民主制度下终日辛勤劳动的人会觉得自己可悲。情况刚好相反。没有任何地方的人能像他们那样对自己的处境感到满意。如果他们没有任何需要操劳的事情，反而会觉得人生没有滋味。他们对于操劳的喜爱比贵族对于享受的喜爱还要更甚。

接下来，我不禁思索，行事如此严肃的民主国家的人民为什么会有时候做事有欠思考。然而，几乎总是保持举止沉稳态度冷静的美国人，往往却难以自制，在心血来潮或轻率判断之下失去理智，有时还会做出一些荒唐之举。我们不应该为这样对比而惊讶。有一种无知正是源于知之过多。在专制国家，人们不知道该如何行事，因为没有人告诉他们；而在民主国家，人们往往会随意行事，因为人们把一切都告诉了他们。前者什么也不知道，而后者则把知道的东西都忘了。这两幅画面的主要特点都是只有轮廓而缺少细节。

令人感到惊讶的是，在自由国家，特别是在民主国家，公职人员时不时地出言不逊并不会对其有什么影响；然而在君主专制国家，公职人员偶然的失言便足以令他丢掉官职，永远无法挽回。这一点已经被以往许多的事件证明。当一个人面对乱哄哄的一大群人讲话的时候，他的许多话人们没有听到，而且即使听到了，也会马上被忘掉，然而当一个人面对一群洗耳恭听的人讲话时，哪怕声音轻得不能再轻，人们也能听到。

在民主国家，人们永远不会始终保持不变，太多的机会让他们飘忽不定，他们的生活几乎总是被一种不可预见的力量，或许可以称之为即兴的力量所左右。因此，他们往往会去做一些他们还没有完全学会的事情，去说一些他们还没有完全理解的话，去从事一些他们没有经过长期学习做好准备的工作。在贵族制国家，每个人的一生只有唯一一个不懈追

obliged to do things which they have imperfectly learned, to say things they imperfectly understand, and to devote themselves to work for which they are unprepared by long apprenticeship. In aristocracies every man has one sole object which he unceasingly pursues, but amongst democratic nations the existence of man is more complex; the same mind will almost always embrace several objects at the same time, and these objects are frequently wholly foreign to each other: as it cannot know them all well, the mind is readily satisfied with imperfect notions of each.

When the inhabitant of democracies is not urged by his wants, he is so at least by his desires; for of all the possessions which he sees around him, none are wholly beyond his reach. He therefore does everything in a hurry, he is always satisfied with "pretty well," and never pauses more than an instant to consider what he has been doing. His curiosity is at once insatiable and cheaply satisfied; for he cares more to know a great deal quickly than to know anything well: he has no time and but little taste to search things to the bottom. Thus then democratic peoples are grave, because their social and political condition constantly leads them to engage in serious occupations; and they act inconsiderately, because they give but little time and attention to each of these occupations. The habit of inattention must be considered as the greatest bane of the democratic character.

Chapter XVI: Why The National Vanity Of The Americans Is More Restless And Captious Than That Of The English

All free nations are vainglorious, but national pride is not displayed by all in the same manner. The Americans in their intercourse with strangers appear impatient of the smallest censure and insatiable of praise. The most slender eulogium is acceptable to them; the most exalted seldom contents them; they unceasingly harass you to extort praise, and if you resist their entreaties they fall to praising themselves. It would seem as if, doubting their own merit, they wished to have it constantly exhibited before their eyes. Their vanity is not only greedy, but restless and jealous; it will grant nothing, whilst it demands everything, but is ready to beg and to quarrel at the same time. If I

求的目标；但是在民主国家，人们的生活则非常复杂，一个人往往同时怀有几个目标，而且这些目标往往完全互不相干。因为他们不能对每个目标都有清晰的认识，所以很容易满足于一知半解。

民主国家的居民即使不会被贫困所迫，至少也会受到欲望的驱使。因为他们看到自己周围的一切财富，都是唾手可得。因此，他们做所有的事情都是急急忙忙，往往满足于差不多就好，而且从来不曾做片刻的停留去思考一下自己已经做了些什么。他们的好奇心永无止境，却又很容易满足，因为他们只想尽快地知道更多的东西，而不想深入地认识这些东西。他们既没有时间也没有兴趣追根究底。因此，民主国家的人民之所以严肃是因为他们的社会和政治状况不断促使他们必须认真工作。而他们之所以有时行为有欠考虑，则是因为他们能够投入给每一项工作的时间和精力都非常有限。注意力不集中的习惯，应被视为民主特点之中最大的缺陷。

第十六章　为什么美国人的民族自负心比英国人的更为轻浮和沽名钓誉

所有的自由人民都非常自负，但民族自豪感的表现形式却并不相同。美国人在与外国人交谈的时候，无法容忍一星半点的批评，但对溢美之词却从不嫌多。不管多么微不足道的褒奖，他们都觉得非常受用；不管多么高的评价，他们也不会觉得满足。他们不断地纠缠，想让你多赞美他们几句，即使你置之不理，他们也会自吹自擂一番。似乎他们是因为对自己的优点存疑，所以总想让别人在他们面前多夸赞他们几句。他们的自负心不但贪婪，而且轻浮善妒。他们的这种自负心只许进不许出，既想沽名又想钓誉。如果我对一个

say to an American that the country he lives in is a fine one, "Ay," he replies, "there is not its fellow in the world." If I applaud the freedom which its inhabitants enjoy, he answers, "Freedom is a fine thing, but few nations are worthy to enjoy it." If I remark the purity of morals which distinguishes the United States, "I can imagine," says he, "that a stranger, who has been struck by the corruption of all other nations, is astonished at the difference." At length I leave him to the contemplation of himself; but he returns to the charge, and does not desist till he has got me to repeat all I had just been saying. It is impossible to conceive a more troublesome or more garrulous patriotism; it wearies even those who are disposed to respect it.

Such is not the case with the English. An Englishman calmly enjoys the real or imaginary advantages which in his opinion his country possesses. If he grants nothing to other nations, neither does he solicit anything for his own. The censure of foreigners does not affect him, and their praise hardly flatters him; his position with regard to the rest of the world is one of disdainful and ignorant reserve: his pride requires no sustenance, it nourishes itself. It is remarkable that two nations, so recently sprung from the same stock, should be so opposite to one another in their manner of feeling and conversing.

In aristocratic countries the great possess immense privileges, upon which their pride rests, without seeking to rely upon the lesser advantages which accrue to them. As these privileges came to them by inheritance, they regard them in some sort as a portion of themselves, or at least as a natural right inherent in their own persons. They therefore entertain a calm sense of their superiority; they do not dream of vaunting privileges which everyone perceives and no one contests, and these things are not sufficiently new to them to be made topics of conversation. They stand unmoved in their solitary greatness, well assured that they are seen of all the world without any effort to show themselves off, and that no one will attempt to drive them from that position. When an aristocracy carries on the public affairs, its national pride naturally assumes this reserved, indifferent, and haughty form, which is imitated by all the other classes of the nation.

美国人说他的国家很好，他会回答说："的确如此，世界上没有任何一个国家能比得上它！"如果我再赞美美国人所享有的自由，他又回答说："自由是珍贵的东西！但没有几个国家配得上拥有它。"如果我说美国的民风淳朴，他接着说："我能想象得出，一个曾在其他一切国家目睹贪污腐化现象的外国人，必然会对这样完全不同的淳朴民情大吃一惊。"最后，我让他自己沉思一下；他却叫我回到原来的话题上，不让我把刚才说过的话重复一遍决不罢休。这种令人生厌的喋喋不休的爱国精神简直超乎人们的想象，甚至连称赞这种精神的人也会感到厌烦。

但英国人并不这样。英国人对本国确有的优点或是自认为有的优点总是能够平静以对。他们不称赞别的国家，所以也不要求别人称赞自己的国家。外国人的指责不会对他们有任何影响，而他们的赞扬也不会让他们得意扬扬。对于其余的世界他们总是保持着一种傲慢无知的态度。他们的自豪感不需要别人培养，而是自己给自己提供养料。两个族源基本相同的民族，在言谈举止上却如此迥异着实让人吃惊不小。

在贵族制国家，达官显贵们享有莫大的特权，而他们的骄傲也正是来源于此，所以不必依靠历数本国的优点去培养。因为他们的特权是继承下来的，所以将其视为自身的一部分，或者至少是与生俱来的天赋权利。因此，他们对自己的优越性能泰然处之，所以做梦也想不到要在人前炫耀自己那些人所共知也无人质疑的特权。这些特权对他们而言丝毫没有新鲜感所以根本构不成话题。他们岿然不动，独享尊荣，深知不必炫耀自己也会引起世人的注意，并坚信没有人想要把他们从这样的地位赶下去。在贵族处理公共事务的时候，其民族自豪感会自然而然地采取这种矜持、冷淡和傲慢的形式，而国内的其余所有阶级也会随之效仿。

When, on the contrary, social conditions differ but little, the slightest privileges are of some importance; as every man sees around himself a million of people enjoying precisely similar or analogous advantages, his pride becomes craving and jealous, he clings to mere trifles, and doggedly defends them. In democracies, as the conditions of life are very fluctuating, men have almost always recently acquired the advantages which they possess; the consequence is that they feel extreme pleasure in exhibiting them, to show others and convince themselves that they really enjoy them. As at any instant these same advantages may be lost, their possessors are constantly on the alert, and make a point of showing that they still retain them. Men living in democracies love their country just as they love themselves, and they transfer the habits of their private vanity to their vanity as a nation. The restless and insatiable vanity of a democratic people originates so entirely in the equality and precariousness of social conditions, that the members of the haughtiest nobility display the very same passion in those lesser portions of their existence in which there is anything fluctuating or contested. An aristocratic class always differs greatly from the other classes of the nation, by the extent and perpetuity of its privileges; but it often happens that the only differences between the members who belong to it consist in small transient advantages, which may any day be lost or acquired. The members of a powerful aristocracy, collected in a capital or a court, have been known to contest with virulence those frivolous privileges which depend on the caprice of fashion or the will of their master. These persons then displayed towards each other precisely the same puerile jealousies which animate the men of democracies, the same eagerness to snatch the smallest advantages which their equals contested, and the same desire to parade ostentatiously those of which they were in possession. If national pride ever entered into the minds of courtiers, I do not question that they would display it in the same manner as the members of a democratic community.

Chapter XVII: That The Aspect Of Society In The United States Is At Once Excited And Monotonous

It would seem that nothing can be more adapted to stimulate and to feed curiosity than the

反之，当人们的社会状况差别不大时，一点点的特权也非常重要。当每个人看到自己周围上百万的人都享有与自己完全相同或类似的优势时，他们的自豪感就会变成贪婪和嫉妒，会执著于微不足道的利益，并尽其所能地捍卫它们。在民主国家，人们的生活状况起伏不断，因此他们所拥有的优势几乎总是刚刚才取得，结果总会想要去炫耀自己的优势，让别人和自己确信自己确实享有这些优势。因为这些优势随时都有可能失去，所以他们总是惴惴不安，想要显示自己依然还保有它们。生活在民主国家的人，爱国家犹如爱自己，并将他们个人的自负心转变成民族自负心。民主国家人民无休止的永不满足的自负心，完全源自社会的平等和状况的不稳定，以至于一些最高尚的人在生活当中的一些小事情发生变动时，也会显示出同样的情绪。贵族阶级凭借其广泛和持久的特权因而与其他阶级大不相同。但有时候贵族成员之间也常常会出现小的暂时的优势差异，这些优势随时都有可能失去或得到。但是，强大贵族阶级的成员们，有时为了争夺主上随心所欲赐予的一点无关紧要的特权，而聚集到首都或宫廷互相攻击。这时，他们所表现出来的那种幼稚的嫉妒会让民主制度下的人都感到可笑，为得到一点小利而互不相让，并竭力证明他们也应享有同样的特权。一旦朝臣们的心中产生民族自豪感，我毫不怀疑，他们也会像民主国家的人一样炫耀。

第十七章　美国的社会面貌为什么千变万化又单调一致

似乎任何东西也不如美国的社会面貌更适于激发和满足人们的好奇心。人们的命运、观念和国家的法律，在这里都在永无休止地变化。可以说由于人们用双手每天都在改造大

aspect of the United States. Fortunes, opinions, and laws are there in ceaseless variation: it is as if immutable nature herself were mutable, such are the changes worked upon her by the hand of man. Yet in the end the sight of this excited community becomes monotonous, and after having watched the moving pageant for a time the spectator is tired of it. Amongst aristocratic nations every man is pretty nearly stationary in his own sphere; but men are astonishingly unlike each other—their passions, their notions, their habits, and their tastes are essentially different: nothing changey, but everything differs. In democracies, on the contrary, all men are alike and do things pretty nearly alike. It is true that they are subject to great and frequent vicissitudes; but as the same events of good or adverse fortune are continually recurring, the name of the actors only is changed, the piece is always the same. The aspect of American society is animated, because men and things are always changing; but it is monotonous, because all these changes are alike.

Men living in democratic ages have many passions, but most of their passions either end in the love of riches or proceed from it. The cause of this is, not that their souls are narrower, but that the importance of money is really greater at such times. When all the members of a community are independent of or indifferent to each other, the co-operation of each of them can only be obtained by paying for it: this infinitely multiplies the purposes to which wealth may be applied, and increases its value. When the reverence which belonged to what is old has vanished, birth, condition, and profession no longer distinguish men, or scarcely distinguish them at all: hardly anything but money remains to create strongly marked differences between them, and to raise some of them above the common level. The distinction originating in wealth is increased by the disappearance and diminution of all other distinctions. Amongst aristocratic nations money only reaches to a few points on the vast circle of man's desires—in democracies it seems to lead to all. The love of wealth is therefore to be traced, either as a principal or an accessory motive, at the bottom of all that the Americans do: this gives to all their passions a sort of family likeness, and soon renders the survey of them exceedingly wearisome. This perpetual recurrence of the same passion is monotonous; the peculiar methods by which this passion seeks its own gratification are no less so.

自然，不可改变的大自然似乎本身也在变化。然而，最终社会的这种千变万化反而会显得单调一致，而且，在观看这种变幻莫测的盛会一段时间之后，观众便会感到厌烦。在贵族制国家，每个人几乎完全固定在自己的活动领域，但彼此之间却存在巨大的差异，他们的感情、观念、习惯和爱好截然不同。什么都没有变化，但一切又完全不同。相反，在民主国家，所有人几乎相同，做的工作也几乎一样。的确，人们会随着社会的巨大和不断的变化而沉浮，同样的成功和失败不断上演，改变的只有演员的名字，而剧情则始终如一。美国社会面貌千变万化，因为那里的人和物都在不断变化；但它又单调一致，因为所有的变化都是千篇一律。

生活在民主时代的人热情洋溢，但他们大部分的热情不是以爱财为目的就是出于爱财。造成这种现象的原因并不是他们的精神狭隘，而是因为在那样的时代金钱的重要性的确非常之大。当社会所有公民都彼此独立漠不关心的时候，相互的合作只有通过金钱才能达成。这就使财富的作用无限扩大，财富的价值不断增加。当古老的尊严不复存在，出身、地位和职业也不再是区分人的标准，或者说人们再无高低贵贱之分时，金钱依然能够在人们之间制造显著差异，让一些人高人一等。基于财富的差异，随着其他差别的消失和缩小而不断增加。在贵族制国家，金钱只是人庞大欲望圈上的某几个点；而在民主国家，金钱则好像是整个欲望圈。因此，我们会发现爱财既是美国人行动的主要动机也是次要动机，是美国人一切行动的终极目的。这让他们所有的激情看上去都如出一辙，不久就会让人感到极为厌倦。同样的热情不断地再现，就会让人感到单调；而且满足这种热情的每个

In an orderly and constituted democracy like the United States, where men cannot enrich themselves by war, by public office, or by political confiscation, the love of wealth mainly drives them into business and manufactures. Although these pursuits often bring about great commotions and disasters, they cannot prosper without strictly regular habits and a long routine of petty uniform acts. The stronger the passion is, the more regular are these habits, and the more uniform are these acts. It may be said that it is the vehemence of their desires which makes the Americans so methodical; it perturbs their minds, but it disciplines their lives.

The remark I here apply to America may indeed be addressed to almost all our contemporaries. Variety is disappearing from the human race; the same ways of acting, thinking, and feeling are to be met with all over the world. This is not only because nations work more upon each other, and are more faithful in their mutual imitation; but as the men of each country relinquish more and more the peculiar opinions and feelings of a caste, a profession, or a family, they simultaneously arrive at something nearer to the constitution of man, which is everywhere the same. Thus they become more alike, even without having imitated each other. Like travellers scattered about some large wood, which is intersected by paths converging to one point, if all of them keep, their eyes fixed upon that point and advance towards it, they insensibly draw nearer together—though they seek not, though they see not, though they know not each other; and they will be surprised at length to find themselves all collected on the same spot. All the nations which take, not any particular man, but man himself, as the object of their researches and their imitations, are tending in the end to a similar state of society, like these travellers converging to the central plot of the forest.

Chapter XVIII: Of Honor In The United States And In Democratic Communities

It would seem that men employ two very distinct methods in the public estimation of the actions of their fellowmen; at one time they judge them by those simple notions of right and wrong which are diffused all over the world; at another they refer their decision to a few very special notions which belong exclusively to some particular age and country. It often happens that these two rules

具体过程，也同样单调。

在像美国一样的秩序井然的立宪民主国家，人们不能依靠战争、假公济私或通过政治手段没收财产的方法致富，所以爱财之心会驱使大多数人投身工商业。但是，这些追求往往会带来巨大的混乱和灾难，因为没有严格规范的习惯和长期划一的行动，就无法实现工商业的繁荣。经营工商业的热情越高，这些习惯也越规范，行动也越能整齐划一。可以说正是美国人强烈的欲望才能使他们如此有条不紊。这种欲望虽然令他们心绪不宁，但安顿了他们的生活。

在这里我关于美国的所有叙述，实际上也几乎适用于我们当代所有人。多样性正从人类社会消失，同样的行为、思考和情感模式出现在世界各个角落。这不仅使各国之间的交往日益频繁，彼此的模仿日益准确，而且使每个国家的人们逐步放弃了本阶级、本行业、本家族所特有的观念和感情，同时变得更加接近到处一样的人的本质。因此，他们即使不互相模仿也会变得越来越像。他们就像分散在一片大森林里的旅行者，而在这个森林里纵横交错的所有道路最终都通向同一个地点，如果所有人的目标都是这个地点，并始终朝这个地点走去，那么，即使他们不互相寻找，也看不到彼此，哪怕互不相识，也会在不知不觉之中彼此越来越近。而当他们最终在同一地点相遇之后，则会大吃一惊。不以特定的人而以人本身作为学习和模仿对象的所有国家，最终往往会像汇合在林中的旅行者一样，达到相似的社会状况。

第十八章　关于美国和民主社会的荣誉

人们似乎采用两种截然不同的标准去公断他人的行为，有时，他们会按照全世界普遍

differ; they sometimes conflict: but they are never either entirely identified or entirely annulled by one another. Honor, at the periods of its greatest power, sways the will more than the belief of men; and even whilst they yield without hesitation and without a murmur to its dictates, they feel notwithstanding, by a dim but mighty instinct, the existence of a more general, more ancient, and more holy law, which they sometimes disobey although they cease not to acknowledge it. Some actions have been held to be at the same time virtuous and dishonorable—a refusal to fight a duel is a case in point.

I think these peculiarities may be otherwise explained than by the mere caprices of certain individuals and nations, as has hitherto been the customary mode of reasoning on the subject. Mankind is subject to general and lasting wants that have engendered moral laws, to the neglect of which men have ever and in all places attached the notion of censure and shame: to infringe them was "to do ill"—"to do well" was to conform to them. Within the bosom of this vast association of the human race, lesser associations have been formed which are called nations; and amidst these nations further subdivisions have assumed the names of classes or castes. Each of these associations forms, as it were, a separate species of the human race; and though it has no essential difference from the mass of mankind, to a certain extent it stands apart and has certain wants peculiar to itself. To these special wants must be attributed the modifications which affect in various degrees and in different countries the mode of considering human actions, and the estimate which ought to be formed of them. It is the general and permanent interest of mankind that men should not kill each other: but it may happen to be the peculiar and temporary interest of a people or a class to justify, or even to honor, homicide.

Honor is simply that peculiar rule, founded upon a peculiar state of society, by the application of which a people or a class allot praise or blame. Nothing is more unproductive to the mind than an abstract idea; I therefore hasten to call in the aid of facts and examples to illustrate my meaning.

I select the most extraordinary kind of honor which was ever known in the world, and that which we are best acquainted with, viz., aristocratic honor springing out of feudal society. I shall explain

的简单的是非观念去判断；有时，又会根据特定时代特定国家所特有的观念去评判。这两种标准往往并不相同，有时甚至相互抵触；但是，它们永远不会被完全混淆，也不能完全相互抵消。荣誉，在其力量最为强大的时候，比信仰对人们意志的影响还要大；甚至在人们会毫不犹豫和决无怨言地服从信仰的时候，也会靠着一种模糊但很强大的本能，感到一个更为普遍、古老和神圣的行为规范的存在。尽管他们有时会违背它，但始终承认它的存在。有些行为，既可以被认为是美德，又可以被认为是耻辱。比如，拒绝决斗的行为，就属于这种情况。

我认为，人们也可以用某些个人和某些国家的反复无常来解释这些特别现象，而且迄今为止大家一直都在这么做。道德规范是人类一直以来普遍的需要，无论在何时何地只要罔顾它就会受到指责和耻笑。违反道德规范的行为，就是作恶；遵守道德规范的行为，就是为善。在整个人类的大团体之中，形成一些名为国家的较小团体，而在这个小团体之内，又被进一步划分出一些更小的名为阶级或等级的团体。每一个这样的团体都自成为人类中的一个特殊种属，尽管它与整个人类并没有本质的区别，但在一定程度上它独立存在，而且有其自身特殊的需要。而这些特殊的需要，在不同国家不同程度地影响着对人类行为方式的看法，并根据这些看法形成各自的评价。人们彼此之间不相互残杀是人类普遍的和永恒的利益。然而，某个国家或阶级需要捍卫的特殊的和暂时的利益，或者是某种荣誉有可能碰巧刚好是杀人。

荣誉简单地来说是特殊的标准，它建立在特定的社会状况之上，以供一个国家或一个阶级用来确定哪些应该获得褒奖哪些应该受到指责。抽象的观念对于人的思想最没有意

it by means of the principle already laid down, and I shall explain the principle by means of the illustration. I am not here led to inquire when and how the aristocracy of the Middle Ages came into existence, why it was so deeply severed from the remainder of the nation, or what founded and consolidated its power. I take its existence as an established fact, and I am endeavoring to account for the peculiar view which it took of the greater part of human actions. The first thing that strikes me is, that in the feudal world actions were not always praised or blamed with reference to their intrinsic worth, but that they were sometimes appreciated exclusively with reference to the person who was the actor or the object of them, which is repugnant to the general conscience of mankind. Thus some of the actions which were indifferent on the part of a man in humble life, dishonored a noble; others changed their whole character according as the person aggrieved by them belonged or did not belong to the aristocracy. When these different notions first arose, the nobility formed a distinct body amidst the people, which it commanded from the inaccessible heights where it was ensconced. To maintain this peculiar position, which constituted its strength, it not only required political privileges, but it required a standard of right and wrong for its own especial use. That some particular virtue or vice belonged to the nobility rather than to the humble classes—that certain actions were guiltless when they affected the villain, which were criminal when they touched the noble—these were often arbitrary matters; but that honor or shame should be attached to a man's actions according to his condition, was a result of the internal constitution of an aristocratic community. This has been actually the case in all the countries which have had an aristocracy; as long as a trace of the principle remains, these peculiarities will still exist; to debauch a woman of color scarcely injures the reputation of an American—to marry her dishonors him.

In some cases feudal honor enjoined revenge, and stigmatized the forgiveness of insults; in others it imperiously commanded men to conquer their own passions, and imposed forgetfulness of self. It did not make humanity or kindness its law, but it extolled generosity; it set more store on liberality than on benevolence; it allowed men to enrich themselves by gambling or by war, but not by labor; it preferred great crimes to small earnings; cupidity was less distasteful to it than avarice; violence

义，所以我要尽快求助事实和实例来证明我的看法。

我选择世界上有史以来最特别的一种荣誉作为例子，这就是我们所熟知的封建社会的贵族荣誉。一方面会用我已经说过的观点来对其进行说明，另一面我还会用例子来说明我的观点。在这里我并不打算探讨中世纪的贵族是何时以及如何出现的，为什么它与国家其余部分之间存在如此之深的鸿沟，以及是什么确立和巩固了它的权力。我把它的存在看成既成事实，并尽力说明它为什么要用极为特殊的眼光去看待人们的大部分行为。首先让我感到惊讶的是，在封建社会，人们的行为永远不会因其固有的价值而被赞扬或指责，而有时完全是单凭行为的主体和客体来进行评判，所以往往与人类的普遍良知相矛盾。因此，一些在老百姓看来无关紧要的行为，则会令贵族感到耻辱；而另一些行为的性质则会因为行为的受害者是否属于贵族而完全不同。这种差别对待的观念一旦确立，贵族阶级便会从人民之中独立出来，坐到高高在上的位置。为了维护自己力量所在的特殊地位，贵族阶级不仅需要有政治特权，而且需要自己特有的是非标准，也就是专属于贵族所有而不适用于平民阶级的善与恶。特定的行为施于平民则无罪，而施于贵族则要受到惩罚，而且这些惩罚往往很随意。但是，根据一个人的地位来断定其行为的荣辱，是贵族社会内部制度的结果。事实上，所有曾经有过贵族阶级的国家都是如此。只要贵族制度的残余仍在，这种奇特的现象就不会消失。例如，诱奸一个有色人种姑娘不会令一个美国男人名誉扫地，但是娶这个姑娘为妻则会让他无脸见人。

在某些情况下，封建主义的荣誉主张复仇，并将宽恕视为屈辱；而在另一些情况下，

it often sanctioned, but cunning and treachery it invariably reprobated as contemptible. These fantastical notions did not proceed exclusively from the caprices of those who entertained them. A class which has succeeded in placing itself at the head of and above all others, and which makes perpetual exertions to maintain this lofty position, must especially honor those virtues which are conspicuous for their dignity and splendor, and which may be easily combined with pride and the love of power. Such men would not hesitate to invert the natural order of the conscience in order to give those virtues precedence before all others. It may even be conceived that some of the more bold and brilliant vices would readily be set above the quiet, unpretending virtues. The very existence of such a class in society renders these things unavoidable.

The nobles of the Middle Ages placed military courage foremost amongst virtues, and in lieu of many of them. This was again a peculiar opinion which arose necessarily from the peculiarity of the state of society. Feudal aristocracy existed by war and for war; its power had been founded by arms, and by arms that power was maintained; it therefore required nothing more than military courage, and that quality was naturally exalted above all others; whatever denoted it, even at the expense of reason and humanity, was therefore approved and frequently enjoined by the manners of the time. Such was the main principle; the caprice of man was only to be traced in minuter details. That a man should regard a tap on the cheek as an unbearable insult, and should be obliged to kill in single combat the person who struck him thus lightly, is an arbitrary rule; but that a noble could not tranquilly receive an insult, and was dishonored if he allowed himself to take a blow without fighting, were direct consequences of the fundamental principles and the wants of military aristocracy.

Thus it was true to a certain extent to assert that the laws of honor were capricious; but these caprices of honor were always confined within certain necessary limits. The peculiar rule, which was called honor by our forefathers, is so far from being an arbitrary law in my eyes, that I would readily engage to ascribe its most incoherent and fantastical injunctions to a small number of fixed and invariable wants inherent in feudal society.

If I were to trace the notion of feudal honor into the domain of politics, I should not find it more

它又专横地命令人们自我克制、忘我。它不要求仁慈和温存，但颂扬宽宏大量；它重视心胸开阔甚于广施善行；它允许人们靠赌博战争发财，但不允许人们靠劳动致富；它宁愿罪恶滔天而不愿追逐小利；它厌恶吝啬甚于厌恶贪婪；它时常鼓励暴力但始终鄙视奸诈和背叛。这些离奇古怪的观念，并非只是拥有这些想法的人们的异想天开。一个取得领导地位并高于其他一切阶级，并始终竭尽全力保持其高高在上的地位的阶级，必然特别尊重那些能够彰显其伟大和显赫，以及能轻而易举把其骄傲与权力欲结合起来的美德。为了能够将这些美德呈现在其他阶级面前，他们这些人会毫不犹豫地违背天理良心。我们甚至可以想象，一些厚颜无耻和臭名昭彰的恶行会被置于温和纯朴的美德之上。这样一个阶级在社会的存在必然会做出倒行逆施之举。

中世纪的贵族将战斗的勇气视为最高的美德，并认为它可以取代众多美德。这也是一种特定社会状况所带来的特殊观念。封建贵族靠战争起家，并且为战争而存在。他们的武器就是力量，并靠武器来维持权力。因此，他们最需要的莫过于战斗的勇气，于是这样的品德受到的追捧自然要高过其他一切品德。因此，只要能够显示出战斗勇气的行为，哪怕是以理性和人性为代价，都会受到认可而且往往还是出于命令。这就是主要的原则，至于人们肆意而生的念头，只能作用于细枝末节。一个人认为挨一记耳光是不可容忍的耻辱，必须要与轻轻打了他一下的那个人单打独斗，将其置于死地，这只是他个人的自行判断；但一个贵族之所以不能忍受耻辱，并在挨打之后不还手便会名誉扫地，则是军事贵族的基本原则和其本身的需要。

difficult to explain its dictates. The state of society and the political institutions of the Middle Ages were such, that the supreme power of the nation never governed the community directly. That power did not exist in the eyes of the people: every man looked up to a certain individual whom he was bound to obey; by that intermediate personage he was connected with all the others. Thus in feudal society the whole system of the commonwealth rested upon the sentiment of fidelity to the person of the lord: to destroy that sentiment was to open the sluices of anarchy. Fidelity to a political superior was, moreover, a sentiment of which all the members of the aristocracy had constant opportunities of estimating the importance; for every one of them was a vassal as well as a lord, and had to command as well as to obey. To remain faithful to the lord, to sacrifice one's self for him if called upon, to share his good or evil fortunes, to stand by him in his undertakings whatever they might be—such were the first injunctions of feudal honor in relation to the political institutions of those times. The treachery of a vassal was branded with extraordinary severity by public opinion, and a name of peculiar infamy was invented for the offence which was called "felony."

On the contrary, few traces are to be found in the Middle Ages of the passion which constituted the life of the nations of antiquity—I mean patriotism; the word itself is not of very ancient date in the language. Feudal institutions concealed the country at large from men's sight, and rendered the love of it less necessary. The nation was forgotten in the passions which attached men to persons. Hence it was no part of the strict law of feudal honor to remain faithful to one's country. Not indeed that the love of their country did not exist in the hearts of our forefathers; but it constituted a dim and feeble instinct, which has grown more clear and strong in proportion as aristocratic classes have been abolished, and the supreme power of the nation centralized. This may be clearly seen from the contrary judgments which European nations have passed upon the various events of their histories, according to the generations by which such judgments have been formed. The circumstance which most dishonored the Constable de Bourbon in the eyes of his contemporaries was that he bore arms against his king: that which most dishonors him in our eyes, is that he made war against his country; we brand him as deeply as our forefathers did, but for different reasons.

因此，在一定程度上说荣誉具有任意性，有其一定的道理。但是，荣誉的任意性往往会超出它特定的必要限界。在我眼中，被我们祖先称为荣誉的那些特别规则绝不是肆意而定，我可以轻而易举地把封建社会固有的不多的固定不变的需要和那些不连贯的异想天开的规定联系起来。

如果我从政治方面去追踪封建社会的荣誉，则解释其政令也不再是什么难事。中世纪的社会情况和政治制度就是国家政权从不直接治理人民。也就是说人民不知道国家政权为何物，每个人只抬头仰望他必须服从的那个人，并通过这个中间人同其他所有的人发生联系。因此，在封建社会，整个国家制度都是建立在属民对其领主的忠心之上。人们的忠心一旦被摧毁，整个国家便会立即陷入无政府状态。此外，对政治首领的忠诚，也是所有贵族成员每天用来的判断其重要性的标准，因为他们每个人既是领主又是家臣，既能发号施令又要俯首听命。忠于领主，必要时为其牺牲，与其同甘共苦，无论其做什么都要拥护他，这就是那些时代封建主义的荣誉与政治制度的关系准则。臣属的背叛会受到舆论极为严厉的口诛笔伐。人们还专为这样的行为起了一个臭名昭著的骂名，叫作变节。

然而，在中世纪已经很难看到古代国家生命的一种激情的痕迹，即爱国心，而这个词本身并不是一个古老词汇。封建制度让人们看不到国家，并认为爱国家没有多大的必要。国家被人们遗忘在人们对个人的热爱之中。因此，封建主义荣誉的制度从来不要求效忠国家。但这实际上并不能说我们的祖先心中没有对祖国的热爱，但他们对国家的热爱只是一种模糊微弱的本能，但随着贵族阶级的没落、国家的中央集权，对国家的热爱越来越明确，

I have chosen the honor of feudal times by way of illustration of my meaning, because its characteristics are more distinctly marked and more familiar to us than those of any other period; but I might have taken an example elsewhere, and I should have reached the same conclusion by a different road. Although we are less perfectly acquainted with the Romans than with our own ancestors, yet we know that certain peculiar notions of glory and disgrace obtained amongst them, which were not solely derived from the general principles of right and wrong. Many human actions were judged differently, according as they affected a Roman citizen or a stranger, a freeman or a slave; certain vices were blazoned abroad, certain virtues were extolled above all others. "In that age," says Plutarch in the life of Coriolanus, "martial prowess was more honored and prized in Rome than all the other virtues, insomuch that it was called virtus, the name of virtue itself, by applying the name of the kind to this particular species; so that virtue in Latin was as much as to say valor." Can anyone fail to recognize the peculiar want of that singular community which was formed for the conquest of the world?

Any nation would furnish us with similar grounds of observation; for, as I have already remarked, whenever men collect together as a distinct community, the notion of honor instantly grows up amongst them; that is to say, a system of opinions peculiar to themselves as to what is blamable or commendable; and these peculiar rules always originate in the special habits and special interests of the community. This is applicable to a certain extent to democratic communities as well as to others, as we shall now proceed to prove by the example of the Americans. Some loose notions of the old aristocratic honor of Europe are still to be found scattered amongst the opinions of the Americans; but these traditional opinions are few in number, they have but little root in the country, and but little power. They are like a religion which has still some temples left standing, though men have ceased to believe in it. But amidst these half-obliterated notions of exotic honor, some new opinions have sprung up, which constitute what may be termed in our days American honor. I have shown how the Americans are constantly driven to engage in commerce and industry. Their origin, their social condition, their political institutions, and even the spot they inhabit, urge them irresistibly

越来越强。这种情况，在欧洲各国不同时代人们根据其评判标准对一些史实做出的截然相反的评价上，可以看得非常清楚。在波旁王朝同时代的人们眼中，波旁王朝元帅们最可耻的行为就是他们率领军队攻打国王；然而在我们眼中，他们最可耻的行为则是他们同自己的国家作战。虽然我们和我们的祖先都给他们深深打上了相同的烙印，但原因却各不相同。

我之所以选择封建时代的荣誉来说明我的观点，是因为它的特点比其他时代荣誉的特点更鲜明，我们也更熟悉。当然我还可以举出其他的例证，用不同的方法也能得出同样的结论。尽管我们对罗马人不如对我们祖先的了解深，但我们知道他们特有的荣辱观念，并非只来自一般的善恶观念。他们的许多行为，会因其是罗马公民或外国人，是自由人或奴隶，而做出不同的评判。在海外他们表扬某些恶行，并把某些美德说得高于其他一切美德。普卢塔克在《科里奥拉努斯传》中曾说："在那个时代，英勇在罗马比其他所有美德都荣耀和值得赞美。他们把勇敢称为美德，使美德这个普通名词具有专门的含义。所以，在拉丁文中美德也有勇敢的意思。"有谁会看不出为征服世界而形成的这个国家的特别需要呢？

每个国家都能给我们提供类似的现象，因为正如我已经说过的那样，人们一旦形成独特的团体，他们的荣誉观念便会立即形成，也就是说形成他们所特有的对于应褒或应贬的事物所持的一套看法，而这些特别的规定则总是源于其团体的特殊习惯和利益。这在一定范围之内不但适用于民主社会也适用于其他社会。现在我们将以美国人为例进行说明。欧洲旧贵族荣誉的一些观念依然能够零星地在美国人的思想中看到。但这些传统观念已经非常有限，而且也没有深植在这个国家，影响力也不大。它们就好像一些已经无人信仰的宗

in this direction. Their present condition is then that of an almost exclusively manufacturing and commercial association, placed in the midst of a new and boundless country, which their principal object is to explore for purposes of profit. This is the characteristic which most peculiarly distinguishes the American people from all others at the present time. All those quiet virtues which tend to give a regular movement to the community, and to encourage business, will therefore be held in peculiar honor by that people, and to neglect those virtues will be to incur public contempt. All the more turbulent virtues, which often dazzle, but more frequently disturb society, will on the contrary occupy a subordinate rank in the estimation of this same people: they may be neglected without forfeiting the esteem of the community—to acquire them would perhaps be to run a risk of losing it.

　　The Americans make a no less arbitrary classification of men's vices. There are certain propensities which appear censurable to the general reason and the universal conscience of mankind, but which happen to agree with the peculiar and temporary wants of the American community: these propensities are lightly reproved, sometimes even encouraged; for instance, the love of wealth and the secondary propensities connected with it may be more particularly cited. To clear, to till, and to transform the vast uninhabited continent which is his domain, the American requires the daily support of an energetic passion; that passion can only be the love of wealth; the passion for wealth is therefore not reprobated in America, and provided it does not go beyond the bounds assigned to it for public security, it is held in honor. The American lauds as a noble and praiseworthy ambition what our own forefathers in the Middle Ages stigmatized as servile cupidity, just as he treats as a blind and barbarous frenzy that ardor of conquest and martial temper which bore them to battle. In the United States fortunes are lost and regained without difficulty; the country is boundless, and its resources inexhaustible. The people have all the wants and cravings of a growing creature; and whatever be their efforts, they are always surrounded by more than they can appropriate. It is not the ruin of a few individuals which may be soon repaired, but the inactivity and sloth of the community at large which would be fatal to such a people. Boldness of enterprise is the foremost cause of its rapid progress, its strength, and its greatness. Commercial business is there like a vast lottery, by which a small number

教，剩下的只有庙宇。在那些具有异国情调的或明或暗的荣誉观念中，出现了一些新的观念，可以称之为我们这个时代的美国荣誉感。我已经说过，美国人是如何不断地被推动从事工商业的。他们的出身，社会情况，政治制度，甚至居住地区，都在不断促使他们朝这个方向走。所以他们目前情况就是在一片广阔无垠的新国土上建立起一个几乎以获利为主要目标的只搞工商业的社会。当今，这就是美国人与所有其他国家人们之间的最为不同的特征。因此，所有能够规范社会正常发展和有利于工商业的安稳的德行，都受到这个国家的特别尊重，忽略这些德行则必然招致公众的鄙视。而一切往往令人目眩的躁动的德行，却又总是会给社会带来动荡，所以这个国家的人民对其评价反而不高。人们可以忽略这些德行而不致失去同胞对他们的尊重，但硬要表现这些德行，则会得不偿失。

　　美国人对恶行的判断则不那么武断。一些看起来受到人类普遍理性和良心非难的嗜好，却刚好符合美国社会特殊和暂时的需要。对于这些嗜好美国人只是稍作责难，甚至有时还会加以鼓励。例如，美国人对爱财之心及随之而来的一些嗜好的看法就非常典型。为了开垦、耕耘和改造这个归他们所有的人迹罕至的广袤大陆，美国人时刻需要充沛的激情来支撑自己，而这种激情只能是爱财之心。因此，爱财在美国不会遭人非难，而且只要不超过为维护公共安全而为它设定的界限，甚至还很光荣。为美国人所赞颂的高尚的值得称道的抱负正是被我们中世纪的祖先称为卑鄙可耻的贪欲，而他们口中盲目的野蛮的狂热则是促使我们中世纪的祖先投入新战斗的征服和好战的热情。在美国，财富去得容易来得快。国土无限辽阔，资源取之不尽用之不竭。人民有每个活着的人所拥有的一切需求和欲

of men continually lose, but the State is always a gainer; such a people ought therefore to encourage and do honor to boldness in commercial speculations. But any bold speculation risks the fortune of the speculator and of all those who put their trust in him. The Americans, who make a virtue of commercial temerity, have no right in any case to brand with disgrace those who practise it. Hence arises the strange indulgence which is shown to bankrupts in the United States; their honor does not suffer by such an accident. In this respect the Americans differ, not only from the nations of Europe, but from all the commercial nations of our time, and accordingly they resemble none of them in their position or their wants.

In America all those vices which tend to impair the purity of morals, and to destroy the conjugal tie, are treated with a degree of severity which is unknown in the rest of the world. At first sight this seems strangely at variance with the tolerance shown there on other subjects, and one is surprised to meet with a morality so relaxed and so austere amongst the selfsame people. But these things are less incoherent than they seem to be. Public opinion in the United States very gently represses that love of wealth which promotes the commercial greatness and the prosperity of the nation, and it especially condemns that laxity of morals which diverts the human mind from the pursuit of well-being, and disturbs the internal order of domestic life which is so necessary to success in business. To earn the esteem of their countrymen, the Americans are therefore constrained to adapt themselves to orderly habits—and it may be said in this sense that they make it a matter of honor to live chastely.

On one point American honor accords with the notions of honor acknowledged in Europe; it places courage as the highest virtue, and treats it as the greatest of the moral necessities of man; but the notion of courage itself assumes a different aspect. In the United States martial valor is but little prized; the courage which is best known and most esteemed is that which emboldens men to brave the dangers of the ocean, in order to arrive earlier in port—to support the privations of the wilderness without complaint, and solitude more cruel than privations—the courage which renders them almost insensible to the loss of a fortune laboriously acquired, and instantly prompts to fresh exertions to make another. Courage of this kind is peculiarly necessary to the maintenance and prosperity of the

望，无论他们如何努力，周围总是布满他们还没有掌握的财富。对于这样的民族而言，个别人的倾家荡产会很快得到恢复，但是整个社会的游手好闲将会是致命的。经营企业所表现出魄力，是其迅速发展、国力强大和四海扬威的最主要原因。在这里，做生意就像买彩票，少数人总是不断输钱，而国家却永远是赢家。因此，商业投机的魄力便受到这个国家人民的青睐和尊重。但是，所有大胆的经营，又都会让投机者及信任他的人的财富陷于风险之中。把冒险经商视为美德的美国人，在任何情况下都不会觉得这样做的人丢脸。因此，美国对破产倒闭的商人表现出特别的宽容，他们的荣誉并不会因为这样的意外而受到损害。在这方面，美国人不但与欧洲各国不同，而且与我们这个时代所有商业国家都不同，相应地，他们在地位和需要上也与其他国家的人民完全不同。

在美国，所有败坏民风淳朴破坏婚姻纽带的劣行都会受到世界上最严厉的惩罚。乍一看，这似乎与他们在其他方面表现出的宽容极为不协调。同一个民族，奉行既放纵又严肃的道德，也会令人感到吃惊。但是，所有这些事情似乎又不是表面上看起来的那样毫无联系。美国的公共舆论对有利于工业发展和国家繁荣的爱财之心只是轻轻地鞭挞，而对于转移人们追求幸福之心和会干扰到事业成功必不可少的家庭内部秩序的放纵行为却大加口诛笔伐。因此，为了赢得国人的尊重，美国人不得不服从通行的习惯。从这个意义上可以认为他们把做一个纯洁无瑕的人视为荣誉。

美国人的荣誉观与欧洲公认的荣誉观有一点是一致的，即勇气是美德之首，是人必不可少的最高尚的德行，但他们对勇气的看法则各不相同。在美国，好战的勇气不会受到颂

American communities, and it is held by them in peculiar honor and estimation; to betray a want of it is to incur certain disgrace.

I have yet another characteristic point which may serve to place the idea of this chapter in stronger relief. In a democratic society like that of the United States, where fortunes are scanty and insecure, everybody works, and work opens a way to everything: this has changed the point of honor quite round, and has turned it against idleness. I have sometimes met in America with young men of wealth, personally disinclined to all laborious exertion, but who had been compelled to embrace a profession. Their disposition and their fortune allowed them to remain without employment; public opinion forbade it, too imperiously to be disobeyed. In the European countries, on the contrary, where aristocracy is still struggling with the flood which overwhelms it, I have often seen men, constantly spurred on by their wants and desires, remain in idleness, in order not to lose the esteem of their equals; and I have known them submit to ennui and privations rather than to work. No one can fail to perceive that these opposite obligations are two different rules of conduct, both nevertheless originating in the notion of honor.

What our forefathers designated as honor absolutely was in reality only one of its forms; they gave a generic name to what was only a species. Honor therefore is to be found in democratic as well as in aristocratic ages, but it will not be difficult to show that it assumes a different aspect in the former. Not only are its injunctions different, but we shall shortly see that they are less numerous, less precise, and that its dictates are less rigorously obeyed. The position of a caste is always much more peculiar than that of a people. Nothing is so much out of the way of the world as a small community invariably composed of the same families (as was for instance the aristocracy of the Middle Ages), whose object is to concentrate and to retain, exclusively and hereditarily, education, wealth, and power amongst its own members. But the more out of the way the position of a community happens to be, the more numerous are its special wants, and the more extensive are its notions of honor corresponding to those wants. The rules of honor will therefore always be less numerous amongst a people not divided into castes than amongst any other. If ever any nations are constituted in which

扬。最好的和最值得称赞的勇气是敢于乘风破浪早日抵达港口,是毫无怨言地忍受荒漠中的艰苦以及比艰苦更让人痛苦的寂寞。这样的勇气能够让他们在不知不觉之中失去辛苦积攒的财富之后,能立即重新努力去积累新的财富。这种勇气对美国社会的存在和繁荣极为必要,所以在美国社会备受尊重和推崇,而流露出缺乏这种勇气,则必然被人看不起。

我还要指出另一个特点来突出本章的中心思想。在像美国这样的民主社会,财富不多而且也不稳定,因此,每个人都劳动,劳动可以开辟通往一切的道路。这让人们的荣誉观产生翻天覆地的转变,而新的荣誉观反对游手好闲。在美国我有时会碰到一些有钱的年轻人,尽管就个人而言他们不愿干任何累活,但依然不得不干点什么。他们的家庭和财富,能够让他们不必工作也可以过得悠闲自在,但公共舆论却禁止如此,所以他们也只有服从。相反,在贵族依然与反对他们的洪流不懈斗争的欧洲,我却常常看到一些人,尽管不断为贫困所迫,但为了不在与自己同样的人之中失去尊严而继续游手好闲。他们宁愿忍受无聊贫困也不愿工作。不会有哪个人看不出在这两种截然相反的劳动观中存在两种完全不同的行为规范,而它们又都源于各自不同的荣誉观。

我们祖先所标榜的荣誉,实际上只是荣誉的形式之一。并赋予类概念种概念的内涵。因此,无论是民主时代还是贵族时代都有荣誉观,但不难发现它在民主时代呈现出一种不同的表现形式。在民主时代,不仅关于荣誉的规定有所不同,而且我们还会很快发现,这些规定的数量也并不多,并不明确,而且执行得也并不严格。在一个民族之中等级始终处于非常特殊的地位。全世界毫无例外地都存在往往是由同一家族组成的小团体(比如中世

it may even be difficult to find any peculiar classes of society, the notion of honor will be confined to a small number of precepts, which will be more and more in accordance with the moral laws adopted by the mass of mankind. Thus the laws of honor will be less peculiar and less multifarious amongst a democratic people than in an aristocracy. They will also be more obscure; and this is a necessary consequence of what goes before; for as the distinguishing marks of honor are less numerous and less peculiar, it must often be difficult to distinguish them. To this, other reasons may be added. Amongst the aristocratic nations of the Middle Ages, generation succeeded generation in vain; each family was like a never-dying, ever-stationary man, and the state of opinions was hardly more changeable than that of conditions. Everyone then had always the same objects before his eyes, which he contemplated from the same point; his eyes gradually detected the smallest details, and his discernment could not fail to become in the end clear and accurate. Thus not only had the men of feudal times very extraordinary opinions in matters of honor, but each of those opinions was present to their minds under a clear and precise form.

This can never be the case in America, where all men are in constant motion; and where society, transformed daily by its own operations, changes its opinions together with its wants. In such a country men have glimpses of the rules of honor, but they have seldom time to fix attention upon them.

But even if society were motionless, it would still be difficult to determine the meaning which ought to be attached to the word "honor." In the Middle Ages, as each class had its own honor, the same opinion was never received at the same time by a large number of men; and this rendered it possible to give it a determined and accurate form, which was the more easy, as all those by whom it was received, having a perfectly identical and most peculiar position, were naturally disposed to agree upon the points of a law which was made for themselves alone. Thus the code of honor became a complete and detailed system, in which everything was anticipated and provided for beforehand, and a fixed and always palpable standard was applied to human actions. Amongst a democratic nation, like the Americans, in which ranks are identified, and the whole of society forms one single

纪的贵族）。而这种小团体的目的就是把文化、财富和权力都集中保留在自己成员手中，并永远垄断和继承下去。但是，一个团体的地位越高，特别的需要就越大，与其需要相一致的荣誉观也就越广。因此，在没有等级区分的国家荣誉的规定往往比其他国家要更少。如果出现任何阶级都难以存在的国家，那么荣誉的规定必然会减少到为数不多的几条，而这些规定则会越来越接近人民大众所采用的道德准则。因此，在民主国家，荣誉的规定必然不会像在贵族制国家那样特殊和五花八门。当然，它们也更为含糊，而这正是上述原因的必然结果。因为当荣誉的显著标志越来越少，越来越不特殊的时候，它必然往往会变得难以识别。当然对此还有另外一些原因需要补充。在中世纪的贵族制国家，人们只是徒劳地代代相传，每个家族就像一个永远不死而又一动不动的人，人们的思想状况并没有比他们的生活状况发生更多的变化。于是，每个人眼前的东西总是一成不变，总是从同一观点出发进行思考。他们的眼睛慢慢地深入到最微小的细节，而他们的洞察力，最终也会毫无疑问地变得清晰明确。因此，封建时代的人不仅有其极为特殊的荣辱观，而且他们还能把每一个观点清晰准确地呈现在自己的头脑中。

在美国则绝不会出现这样的情况，因为在这里所有人都处于运动之中，每天在其自身作用下不断变化的社会，也在改变它的观念和需要。在这样的国家，对于荣誉的规则人们只会看上几眼，而很少有时间专注于它。

但即使社会静止不动，依然很难界定荣誉一词应有的含义。在中世纪，因为每个阶级都有自己的荣誉观，所以从未出现同时为绝大多数人所接受的荣誉观，而这使得各阶级形

mass, composed of elements which are all analogous though not entirely similar, it is impossible ever to agree beforehand on what shall or shall not be allowed by the laws of honor. Amongst that people, indeed, some national wants do exist which give rise to opinions common to the whole nation on points of honor; but these opinions never occur at the same time, in the same manner, or with the same intensity to the minds of the whole community; the law of honor exists, but it has no organs to promulgate it.

The confusion is far greater still in a democratic country like France, where the different classes of which the former fabric of society was composed, being brought together but not yet mingled, import day by day into each other's circles various and sometimes conflicting notions of honor—where every man, at his own will and pleasure, forsakes one portion of his forefathers' creed, and retains another; so that, amidst so many arbitrary measures, no common rule can ever be established, and it is almost impossible to predict which actions will be held in honor and which will be thought disgraceful. Such times are wretched, but they are of short duration.

As honor, amongst democratic nations, is imperfectly defined, its influence is of course less powerful; for it is difficult to apply with certainty and firmness a law which is not distinctly known. Public opinion, the natural and supreme interpreter of the laws of honor, not clearly discerning to which side censure or approval ought to lean, can only pronounce a hesitating judgment. Sometimes the opinion of the public may contradict itself; more frequently it does not act, and lets things pass.

The weakness of the sense of honor in democracies also arises from several other causes. In aristocratic countries, the same notions of honor are always entertained by only a few persons, always limited in number, often separated from the rest of their fellow-citizens. Honor is easily mingled and identified in their minds with the idea of all that distinguishes their own position; it appears to them as the chief characteristic of their own rank; they apply its different rules with all the warmth of personal interest, and they feel (if I may use the expression) a passion for complying with

成稳定明确的荣誉观成为可能；而且因为所有人都会对其表示认可所以更容易形成特定一致的立场，于是自然愿意接受专为他们规定的法律条款。所以，荣誉的规定就成为一部完备而详尽的法典，它将所有的预见到的东西都提前安排妥当，成为衡量人们行为的固定而明确的标准。在像美国这样的民主国家，阶级已经消失，全社会已成为一个统一的整体，其成员虽不完全相同但都很相似，因此无法事先依照荣誉的规定，明确指出哪些行为被允许和哪些行为不被允许。的确，在这个国家人民的内部，存在着某些全国性的需要促使全国形成共同的荣誉观，但这些观念不会同时产生，而且产生方式也不会相同，对全体公民思想的影响程度也不一样。因此，在民主国家，荣誉的规定的确存在，但没有任何一个机关会来颁布。

在像法国一样的民主国家，情况会更为混乱。在法国，构成旧社会的各个阶级还未彼此融合便被混合在一起，形形色色而且有时互相冲突的荣誉观日复一日进入彼此的圈子。而且，在我们国家每个人都会按照自己的意愿随意丢弃祖先的一部分观点并保存另一部分观点，以至于在如此多的随意标准下，无法建立荣誉的共同规范；也几乎不可能事先规定应该以哪些行为为荣或以哪些行为为耻。这是一个令人痛苦的时期，但不会持续太久。

在民主国家，因为荣誉的定义不够清晰，其影响力自然也不强。因为一项没有得到公认的规范很难得到准确而坚定的实行。公共舆论，作为荣誉规范天然权威的解释者，因为它也无法认清应该根据什么去褒贬，所以只能犹豫不决地做出判断。有时公共舆论甚至自相矛盾，而更多的时候往往置之不理和听之任之。

民主制度下荣誉感之所以相对较弱，还有一些其他原因。在贵族制国家，持有相同的

its dictates. This truth is extremely obvious in the old black-letter lawbooks on the subject of "trial by battel." The nobles, in their disputes, were bound to use the lance and sword; whereas the villains used only sticks amongst themselves, "inasmuch as," to use the words of the old books, "villains have no honor." This did not mean, as it may be imagined at the present day, that these people were contemptible; but simply that their actions were not to be judged by the same rules which were applied to the actions of the aristocracy.

It is surprising, at first sight, that when the sense of honor is most predominant, its injunctions are usually most strange; so that the further it is removed from common reason the better it is obeyed; whence it has sometimes been inferred that the laws of honor were strengthened by their own extravagance. The two things indeed originate from the same source, but the one is not derived from the other. Honor becomes fantastical in proportion to the peculiarity of the wants which it denotes, and the paucity of the men by whom those wants are felt; and it is because it denotes wants of this kind that its influence is great. Thus the notion of honor is not the stronger for being fantastical, but it is fantastical and strong from the selfsame cause.

Further, amongst aristocratic nations each rank is different, but all ranks are fixed; every man occupies a place in his own sphere which he cannot relinquish, and he lives there amidst other men who are bound by the same ties. Amongst these nations no man can either hope or fear to escape being seen; no man is placed so low but that he has a stage of his own, and none can avoid censure or applause by his obscurity. In democratic States on the contrary, where all the members of the community are mingled in the same crowd and in constant agitation, public opinion has no hold on men; they disappear at every instant, and elude its power. Consequently the dictates of honor will be there less imperious and less stringent; for honor acts solely for the public eye—differing in this respect from mere virtue, which lives upon itself contented with its own approval.

If the reader has distinctly apprehended all that goes before, he will understand that there is a close and necessary relation between the inequality of social conditions and what has here been

荣誉观的人往往人数不多，数量有限，而且往往同其他人格格不入。因此，他们的荣誉观可以非常容易地与他们所特有的思想保持一致并合而为一。在他们看来，这是他们本阶级的一个主要的特征。他们利用这些不同的荣誉规定积极为自己的利益服务，而且（如果我可以这样说的话）他们还感到有一种激情促使自己服从这些规定。当我们看到中世纪习惯法有关以决斗来断定是非的内容时，会感到我所说的特别真实。在贵族之间发生纠纷的时候，以长矛和剑作为决斗的武器；而平民之间则只能用棍棒，用习惯法的话来说：“鉴于平民没有荣誉”。它的意思并非我们今天所想象的那样，认为这些人卑贱，而只是想表明不能用评判贵族行为的标准来评判平民的行为。

乍看起来令人吃惊的是，荣誉感处于支配地位的时候，其规定往往也最为离奇古怪，以至于它越是有违常理越是容易被人遵守，甚至有时会让人由此认定荣誉的规定越是荒谬，力量也越为强大。实际上，强大和荒谬的原因相同，而不是一个是另一个的原因。少数人的需要越是特殊，荣誉观也越是离奇古怪，而人们越是感到它的缺乏，其影响力也越大。因此，荣誉观并不是因为其离奇古怪而强大，而是离奇古怪和强大都来自同一原因。

此外，在贵族制国家，所有等级各不相同，但都固定不变。每个人在其活动范围内都有其无法放弃的位置，他与那些受到同样纽带束缚的人们生活在一起。在这样的国家，没有人会担心或害怕而生活不下去，而且不管一个人的地位多么卑微都有自己的舞台，此外，也没有人会因为身份卑微而能逃过褒贬。而在民主国家，情形则刚好相反。在这里，所有社会成员都混杂在一起，不断往来，公共舆论对人们没有影响，因为他们可以马上隐藏起来，逃避它的影响。因此，荣誉在民主国家没有那么专横，也没有那么严厉。因为荣誉只是给人看

styled honor—a relation which, if I am not mistaken, had not before been clearly pointed out. I shall therefore make one more attempt to illustrate it satisfactorily. Suppose a nation stands apart from the rest of mankind: independently of certain general wants inherent in the human race, it will also have wants and interests peculiar to itself: certain opinions of censure or approbation forthwith arise in the community, which are peculiar to itself, and which are styled honor by the members of that community. Now suppose that in this same nation a caste arises, which, in its turn, stands apart from all the other classes, and contracts certain peculiar wants, which give rise in their turn to special opinions. The honor of this caste, composed of a medley of the peculiar notions of the nation, and the still more peculiar notions of the caste, will be as remote as it is possible to conceive from the simple and general opinions of men.

Having reached this extreme point of the argument, I now return. When ranks are commingled and privileges abolished, the men of whom a nation is composed being once more equal and alike, their interests and wants become identical, and all the peculiar notions which each caste styled honor successively disappear: the notion of honor no longer proceeds from any other source than the wants peculiar to the nation at large, and it denotes the individual character of that nation to the world. Lastly, if it be allowable to suppose that all the races of mankind should be commingled, and that all the peoples of earth should ultimately come to have the same interests, the same wants, undistinguished from each other by any characteristic peculiarities, no conventional value whatever would then be attached to men's actions; they would all be regarded by all in the same light; the general necessities of mankind, revealed by conscience to every man, would become the common standard. The simple and general notions of right and wrong only would then be recognized in the world, to which, by a natural and necessary tie, the idea of censure or approbation would be attached. Thus, to comprise all my meaning in a single proposition, the dissimilarities and inequalities of men gave rise to the notion of honor; that notion is weakened in proportion as these differences are obliterated, and with them it would disappear.

的，与纯洁的德行不同，而德行则是依靠本身而存在，并从自我认同之中获得满足。

如果读者已经完全理解上述所有内容，就必然会发现不平等和我们这里所说的荣誉之间存在着密切的必然的关系。如果我没有说错的话，这种关系以前还从没有人明确指出过。因此，我还要再努力一下把它说得清清楚楚。假设一个民族孤立于其他人类，除了人类固有的特定一般需要，它还会有自己的特别需要和利益，而且特定的专属于他们自己的及其社会成员称之为荣誉的荣辱观也会很快在其社会形成。现在假设在这个国家内部出现一个独立于周围的其他一切阶级的阶级，并有其独特的需要，这就会令它产生特别的观点。那么这个阶级的荣誉观则是由本民族独特的观点和本阶级更加独特的观点混合而成，将与人类单纯的和一般的观点相差十万八千里。

我的论述即将结束，现在再回过头来进行总结。当各阶级互相融合，特权遭到废除的时候，社会全体成员变得越来越平等，越来越相似，他们的利益和需要也变得越来越一致，而各阶级所独有的荣誉观将会相继消失。荣誉观的来源除了本民族自身的需要以外，不会再有其他来源，而且每个民族的荣誉观都有自己的个性。最后，如果可以假设所有的种族将会融为一体，世界上的所有国家最终会产生相同的利益和需要，彼此之间不会再有任何显著区别，对于人们的行为也不再有传统的评判。于是，人们的所有行为都要按照同样的标准对待，而通过良心向每个人揭示的人类一般需要将成为共同标准。于是，这种朴素简单的是非观念在全世界得到认可，而通过天然和必然的纽带，荣辱观也必将与之相连。因此，用一句话来概括我全部的思想就是，人们之间的差异和不平等造就了荣誉观，而荣誉观会随差异和不平等的缩小而减弱，最后同它们一起消失。

Chapter XIX: Why So Many Ambitious Men And So Little Lofty Ambition Are To Be Found In The United States

The first thing which strikes a traveller in the United States is the innumerable multitude of those who seek to throw off their original condition; and the second is the rarity of lofty ambition to be observed in the midst of the universally ambitious stir of society. No Americans are devoid of a yearning desire to rise; but hardly any appear to entertain hopes of great magnitude, or to drive at very lofty aims. All are constantly seeking to acquire property, power, and reputation— few contemplate these things upon a great scale; and this is the more surprising, as nothing is to be discerned in the manners or laws of America to limit desire, or to prevent it from spreading its impulses in every direction. It seems difficult to attribute this singular state of things to the equality of social conditions; for at the instant when that same equality was established in France, the flight of ambition became unbounded. Nevertheless, I think that the principal cause which may be assigned to this fact is to be found in the social condition and democratic manners of the Americans.

All revolutions enlarge the ambition of men: this proposition is more peculiarly true of those revolutions which overthrow an aristocracy. When the former barriers which kept back the multitude from fame and power are suddenly thrown down, a violent and universal rise takes place towards that eminence so long coveted and at length to be enjoyed. In this first burst of triumph nothing seems impossible to anyone: not only are desires boundless, but the power of satisfying them seems almost boundless, too. Amidst the general and sudden renewal of laws and customs, in this vast confusion of all men and all ordinances, the various members of the community rise and sink again with excessive rapidity; and power passes so quickly from hand to hand that none need despair of catching it in turn. It must be recollected, moreover, that the people who destroy an aristocracy have lived under its laws; they have witnessed its splendor, and they have unconsciously imbibed the feelings and notions which it entertained. Thus at the moment when an aristocracy is dissolved, its spirit still pervades the mass of the community, and its tendencies are retained long after it has been defeated. Ambition is

第十九章　为什么美国人大多胸怀抱负却鲜有大志

在美国，引起旅行者注意的第一件事就是，不计其数的人们不断试图改进自己原有的条件；而引人注意的第二件事则是在这个人们普遍地怀有抱负的社会之中，怀有大志的人却非常罕见。没有美国人不求上进，但也几乎看不到人们有远大的抱负。所有人都不断地想要获得财富、权力和名誉，但很少有人有志于伟大事业，而且更让人感到惊讶的是美国的民情和法制对人的欲望及其向各方面发展的肆意没有任何限制。这种奇怪现象似乎很难归咎于社会状况的平等，因为在法国平等一经确立，便立即让一些人产生无限的野心。我认为，出现这种情况的主要原因应该从美国的社会情况和民主民情中去寻找。

所有的革命都会令人们的野心膨胀，而推翻贵族制度的革命尤其如此。当原来阻碍广大群众获得名誉和权力的障碍被突然推倒，便出现一股一窝蜂似的追逐人们垂涎已久的而且终于能够享有的名利和权势的热潮。在最初胜利的鼓舞下，人们觉得没有什么办不到。不但欲望爆棚，而且用来满足欲望的权力也几乎永无止境。在法制和习惯的这场突然的大变动中，在所有人和所有制度的大混乱中，社会各色成员快速地起起伏伏，权力走马灯似地不断易手以至于每个人都认为将会轮到自己掌权。此外，也不要忘记，摧毁贵族制度的人都曾经生活在其法制之下，都曾亲眼见证它的辉煌，所以在不知不觉之中也沾染上贵族的情感和观念。因此，当贵族制度瓦解的一刻，其精神依然弥漫在群众之中，而在它被完全打倒之后，其残余还会长期存在下去。因此，只要民主革命持续下去，人们的野心会一直爆棚；而在民主革命完成之后，这种野心依然会持续一段时间。因为人们对自己曾经目睹的那些惊天动地的大事件的记忆不会在一天之内消失，而革命所激起的热情也不会随着

therefore always extremely great as long as a democratic revolution lasts, and it will remain so for some time after the revolution is consummated. The reminiscence of the extraordinary events which men have witnessed is not obliterated from their memory in a day. The passions which a revolution has roused do not disappear at its close. A sense of instability remains in the midst of re-established order: a notion of easy success survives the strange vicissitudes which gave it birth; desires still remain extremely enlarged, when the means of satisfying them are diminished day by day. The taste for large fortunes subsists, though large fortunes are rare: and on every side we trace the ravages of inordinate and hapless ambition kindled in hearts which they consume in secret and in vain.

At length, however, the last vestiges of the struggle are effaced; the remains of aristocracy completely disappear; the great events by which its fall was attended are forgotten; peace succeeds to war, and the sway of order is restored in the new realm; desires are again adapted to the means by which they may be fulfilled; the wants, the opinions, and the feelings of men cohere once more; the level of the community is permanently determined, and democratic society established. A democratic nation, arrived at this permanent and regular state of things, will present a very different spectacle from that which we have just described; and we may readily conclude that, if ambition becomes great whilst the conditions of society are growing equal, it loses that quality when they have grown so. As wealth is subdivided and knowledge diffused, no one is entirely destitute of education or of property; the privileges and disqualifications of caste being abolished, and men having shattered the bonds which held them fixed, the notion of advancement suggests itself to every mind, the desire to rise swells in every heart, and all men want to mount above their station: ambition is the universal feeling.

But if the equality of conditions gives some resources to all the members of the community, it also prevents any of them from having resources of great extent, which necessarily circumscribes their desires within somewhat narrow limits. Thus amongst democratic nations ambition is ardent and continual, but its aim is not habitually lofty; and life is generally spent in eagerly coveting small objects which are within reach. What chiefly diverts the men of democracies from lofty ambition is

革命的终结而终结。对于秩序没有一种稳定感。成功来之容易的思想，在导致成功的动乱平息之后依然存在。欲望依然很大，但满足欲望的手段日益减少。发大财的欲望依然存在，但能够发大财的却很少。结果，我们看到到处都是毫无节制的不幸的野心，而失败的痛苦则悄悄隐藏在人们的心中。

然而，最终斗争的余威消失殆尽，贵族制度的残余踪迹全无。人们已经忘记自消自灭的大事件，和平取代了战争，秩序重新建立起来，欲望与实现欲望的手段重新相互适应，人们的需要、思想和感情又一次凝聚在一起，人们实现彼此平等，民主社会得以确立。一个民主国家，如果能够永远维持这种状态，那么将会呈现出与我方才所描述的截然不同的情景；而且我们能轻而易举地得出结论，社会越来越平等，人们的野心也会变大，则当平等实现之后，野心也不再变大。由于财富的分散和知识的普及，没人能完全独占教育和财富。一些阶级的特权和另一些阶级无资格享有特权的现象消失，人们打破使他们固定不变的束缚，前进的思想浮现在人们的脑海，而高升的欲望在人们心中膨胀，所有人都想能更进一步，人们普遍怀有抱负之心。

但是，即使平等赋予所有社会成员一定数量的财富，但也会阻碍他们拥有巨额财富。这种情况必然在很大程度上把人们的欲望限制在相对狭小的范围之内。因此，在民主国家，抱负总是热烈而持久，但目标往往不太高；人们一生往往只是热烈地追求可以实现的小目标。让民主国家的人鲜有大抱负的主要原因，并不是他们的缺乏财富，而是他们每天忙于致富的努力过于激烈。他们竭尽所能想要取得一些微不足道的成就，这就必然会迅速

not the scantiness of their fortunes, but the vehemence of the exertions they daily make to improve them. They strain their faculties to the utmost to achieve paltry results, and this cannot fail speedily to limit their discernment and to circumscribe their powers. They might be much poorer and still be greater. The small number of opulent citizens who are to be found amidst a democracy do not constitute an exception to this rule. A man who raises himself by degrees to wealth and power, contracts, in the course of this protracted labor, habits of prudence and restraint which he cannot afterwards shake off. A man cannot enlarge his mind as he would his house. The same observation is applicable to the sons of such a man; they are born, it is true, in a lofty position, but their parents were humble; they have grown up amidst feelings and notions which they cannot afterwards easily get rid of; and it may be presumed that they will inherit the propensities of their father as well as his wealth. It may happen, on the contrary, that the poorest scion of a powerful aristocracy may display vast ambition, because the traditional opinions of his race and the general spirit of his order still buoy him up for some time above his fortune. Another thing which prevents the men of democratic periods from easily indulging in the pursuit of lofty objects, is the lapse of time which they foresee must take place before they can be ready to approach them. "It is a great advantage," says Pascal, "to be a man of quality, since it brings one man as forward at eighteen or twenty as another man would be at fifty, which is a clear gain of thirty years." Those thirty years are commonly wanting to the ambitious characters of democracies. The principle of equality, which allows every man to arrive at everything, prevents all men from rapid advancement.

In a democratic society, as well as elsewhere, there are only a certain number of great fortunes to be made; and as the paths which lead to them are indiscriminately open to all, the progress of all must necessarily be slackened. As the candidates appear to be nearly alike, and as it is difficult to make a selection without infringing the principle of equality, which is the supreme law of democratic societies, the first idea which suggests itself is to make them all advance at the same rate and submit to the same probation. Thus in proportion as men become more alike, and the principle of equality is more peaceably and deeply infused into the institutions and manners of the country, the rules of

限制他们的洞察力和能力。他们可能会变穷，但抱负依旧不减。民主国家少数的富裕公民，也不会例外地逃脱这一规则。一个逐步累积起财富和权力的人，在这旷日持久的努力中他们养成无法摆脱的办事谨慎和自我节制的习惯。人们不能像扩建房屋似的扩大自己的思想境界。这种人的儿子也是这样。的确，他们出生在大富之家，可他们的父母曾经历贫寒，所以他们在这样的思想和情感的影响下长大，而且很难摆脱这种影响，因此，可以认为他们在继承父亲的财产的同时，也继承了父亲的爱好。相反，权倾一时的贵族的最落魄的子孙倒是往往能展现出雄心壮志，因为贵族的传统观念及其阶级的普遍精神依然会在一段时间内鼓励他们暂时忍受现实的处境。民主时代阻碍人们胸怀大志去完成宏伟事业的另一个原因是，他们在有能力完成这项事业之前天年已尽。帕斯卡尔说过："名门出身的一大好处是能让一个人在18岁或20岁时就可以达到另一个人在50岁时达到的地步，他显然节省了30年。"民主国家野心勃勃的人通常并没有这样的30年去实现他们的大愿。平等可以让每个人得到一切，但也妨碍人们迅速地壮大自己。

在民主社会与在其他社会一样，只有少数人可以发大财，而且因为通往财富的道路毫无差别地向每个人敞开，所以所有人的前进速度必然无可避免地缓慢下来。此外，因为所有竞争参与者看起来几乎完全相同，而且在不破坏民主社会最高法则平等原则的前提下很难进行甄选，所以人们首先想到的办法是让所有人以同样的速度前进并通过测试。因此，随着人们越来越相似，平等的原则便和平地、广泛地渗入国家的体制和民情，前进的规则也越来越缺乏灵活性，速度也变得越来越慢，快速达到一定高度也变得越发困难。因为憎恨特权

advancement become more inflexible, advancement itself slower, the difficulty of arriving quickly at a certain height far greater. From hatred of privilege and from the embarrassment of choosing, all men are at last constrained, whatever may be their standard, to pass the same ordeal; all are indiscriminately subjected to a multitude of petty preliminary exercises, in which their youth is wasted and their imagination quenched, so that they despair of ever fully attaining what is held out to them; and when at length they are in a condition to perform any extraordinary acts, the taste for such things has forsaken them.

In China, where the equality of conditions is exceedingly great and very ancient, no man passes from one public office to another without undergoing a probationary trial. This probation occurs afresh at every stage of his career; and the notion is now so rooted in the manners of the people that I remember to have read a Chinese novel, in which the hero, after numberless crosses, succeeds at length in touching the heart of his mistress by taking honors. A lofty ambition breathes with difficulty in such an atmosphere.

The remark I apply to politics extends to everything; equality everywhere produces the same effects; where the laws of a country do not regulate and retard the advancement of men by positive enactment, competition attains the same end. In a well-established democratic community great and rapid elevation is therefore rare; it forms an exception to the common rule; and it is the singularity of such occurrences that makes men forget how rarely they happen. Men living in democracies ultimately discover these things; they find out at last that the laws of their country open a boundless field of action before them, but that no one can hope to hasten across it. Between them and the final object of their desires, they perceive a multitude of small intermediate impediments, which must be slowly surmounted: this prospect wearies and discourages their ambition at once. They therefore give up hopes so doubtful and remote, to search nearer to themselves for less lofty and more easy enjoyments. Their horizon is not bounded by the laws but narrowed by themselves.

I have remarked that lofty ambitions are more rare in the ages of democracy than in times of

及选择的尴尬，所以所有人无论其能力如何都要经历同样严酷的考验。所有人都要经过小小的预备训练，浪费了他们的青春，消耗了他们的想象力，以至于他们对于自己有望获得的好处感到完全绝望。最终当他们有能力做出一番大事业的时候，对此已完全失去了兴致。

在中国，平等具有悠久的历史。人们只有进行科举考试，才能够从一个官职升迁到另一个官职。这样的考试会伴随其职业生涯的每个阶段，而且这样的观念已经深入民情。我记得曾在一本中国的小说中读到，书中的主人公在经历过无数次的挫折之后，终于金榜题名并赢得女主人公的芳心。在这样的氛围中，人们很难怀有大志向。

我就政治问题所做的论述也适用于其他一切问题。平等在所有地方都会产生同样的效果。对官职晋升并未依法进行明确规定或管理的国家，采用考试竞争也能达到同样的效果。因此，在一个组织非常良好的民主社会，快速大幅度的晋升很少见，是有违常规的例外。这种情况罕见得甚至使人忘记了它是少有的现象。生活在民主时代的人终于认识到这些事情。最终，他们发现国家的法律为他们开辟了无限的活动空间，但谁也不可能奢望一步登天。在他们和自己的最终目标之间，他们注意到有许许多多小障碍有待一步步克服。这个前景使他们望而生畏，感到泄气。因此，他们放弃这种遥远而渺茫的希望，转而寻找离他们更近的虽不远大但容易实现的目标。因此他们的视野并不是受到法律的限制，而是受到自己的限制。

我曾经说过，远大的志向在民主时代比在贵族时代要更为罕见。而且，我还要再补充一点：在民主时代尽管有这些天然障碍的干扰，但远大的志向依旧存在，只是其特点有所不同。在贵族时代，志向的前程往往很远大，但其范围早已被限定。在民主时代，志向的

aristocracy: I may add that when, in spite of these natural obstacles, they do spring into existence, their character is different. In aristocracies the career of ambition is often wide, but its boundaries are determined. In democracies ambition commonly ranges in a narrower field, but if once it gets beyond that, hardly any limits can be assigned to it. As men are individually weak—as they live asunder, and in constant motion—as precedents are of little authority and laws but of short duration, resistance to novelty is languid, and the fabric of society never appears perfectly erect or firmly consolidated. So that, when once an ambitious man has the power in his grasp, there is nothing he may noted are; and when it is gone from him, he meditates the overthrow of the State to regain it. This gives to great political ambition a character of revolutionary violence, which it seldom exhibits to an equal degree in aristocratic communities. The common aspect of democratic nations will present a great number of small and very rational objects of ambition, from amongst which a few ill-controlled desires of a larger growth will at intervals break out: but no such a thing as ambition conceived and contrived on a vast scale is to be met with there.

I have shown elsewhere by what secret influence the principle of equality makes the passion for physical gratifications and the exclusive love of the present predominate in the human heart: these different propensities mingle with the sentiment of ambition, and tinge it, as it were, with their hues. I believe that ambitious men in democracies are less engrossed than any others with the interests and the judgment of posterity; the present moment alone engages and absorbs them. They are more apt to complete a number of undertakings with rapidity than to raise lasting monuments of their achievements; and they care much more for success than for fame. What they most ask of men is obedience—what they most covet is empire. Their manners have in almost all cases remained below the height of their station; the consequence is that they frequently carry very low tastes into their extraordinary fortunes, and that they seem to have acquired the supreme power only to minister to their coarse or paltry pleasures.

I think that in our time it is very necessary to cleanse, to regulate, and to adapt the feeling of

范围往往比较狭小，但一经突破，几乎不会再受任何限制。因为，在民主国家，个人的力量很薄弱，而且各自为政，经常变动，而且因为先例并没有什么权威，法律也容易改变，所以对新鲜事物的抵抗力很弱，社会组织结构无法完全确立或是得到充分的巩固。因此，一旦怀有野心的人大权在握，他们便敢为所欲为；而他们在失去权力之后，便会图谋颠覆国家重新掌权。因此，伟大的政治抱负往往具有暴力革命的性质，然而在贵族社会却很少出现这样的情况。在民主国家，一个人最初通常会有许多非常合理的小志向，但随后其不断膨胀衍化成一种时不时会爆发的难以掌控的欲望。与自身条件相适应的远大而有节制的志向，民主国家的人几乎没有。

我曾在别的地方指出过平等对于追求物质享受的激情和已掌控人心的只顾眼前的热情的潜在影响。这些不同的偏好和雄心壮志相结合，也使雄心壮志沾染上它们的色彩。我认为，在民主社会胸怀大志的人，不会像其他社会的人那样全神贯注于子孙后代的利益和规划，他们只会把注意力和精力投注在此刻。他们更愿意能快速地完成很多的小事，而不愿去做能让自己名垂千古的大事业，对于他们而言更重要的是成功而不是名誉。他们所提出的最重要的是服从，最喜欢的是统治。他们的行为举止，几乎总是表现得不如他们的社会地位那样高贵。结果，他们在拥有巨额财富时往往会表现出非常低级的趣味，而且获得最高权力似乎也只是为了满足粗陋猥琐的享乐。

我认为，在我们这个时代有必要洁化、规范和调节人们的抱负；而且退化和过分抑制人们的野心是极其危险的。我们应当尝试为其划定不得逾越的极限，但在其范围之内则不应过分抑制其发展。我承认，我对民主社会胆大妄为的担心比对人们欲望过大担心要更

ambition, but that it would be extremely dangerous to seek to impoverish and to repress it over-much. We should attempt to lay down certain extreme limits, which it should never be allowed to outstep; but its range within those established limits should not be too much checked. I confess that I apprehend much less for democratic society from the boldness than from the mediocrity of desires. What appears to me most to be dreaded is that, in the midst of the small incessant occupations of private life, ambition should lose its vigor and its greatness—that the passions of man should abate, but at the same time be lowered, so that the march of society should every day become more tranquil and less aspiring. I think then that the leaders of modern society would be wrong to seek to lull the community by a state of too uniform and too peaceful happiness; and that it is well to expose it from time to time to matters of difficulty and danger, in order to raise ambition and to give it a field of action. Moralists are constantly complaining that the ruling vice of the present time is pride. This is true in one sense, for indeed no one thinks that he is not better than his neighbor, or consents to obey his superior: but it is extremely false in another; for the same man who cannot endure subordination or equality, has so contemptible an opinion of himself that he thinks he is only born to indulge in vulgar pleasures. He willingly takes up with low desires, without daring to embark in lofty enterprises, of which he scarcely dreams. Thus, far from thinking that humility ought to be preached to our contemporaries, I would have endeavors made to give them a more enlarged idea of themselves and of their kind. Humility is unwholesome to them; what they most want is, in my opinion, pride. I would willingly exchange several of our small virtues for this one vice.

Chapter XX: The Trade Of Place-Hunting In Certain Democratic Countries

In the United States as soon as a man has acquired some education and pecuniary resources, he either endeavors to get rich by commerce or industry, or he buys land in the bush and turns pioneer. All that he asks of the State is not to be disturbed in his toil, and to be secure of his earnings. Amongst the greater part of European nations, when a man begins to feel his strength and to extend

甚。在我看来最可怕的是，人们不断忙于私人生活的琐碎之中，抱负会失去其活力和伟大；人们的激情既没有昂扬也没有低落，社会的前进的步伐日复一日变得更加安宁但也更缺乏大志。因此我认为：现代社会的领导人要是想通过单调和平静幸福的状态让整个社会昏昏欲睡，将是错误的；而是应当让整个社会时不时面临一些困难和危险，以便激发人们的奋进之心和为他们提供大显身手的舞台。道德家们不断地埋怨，现代人的主要恶习就是骄傲。从某种意义上来说，这是对的，因为的确没有一个人认为自己不如别人，或满足于听命于上司；但是，从另一个意义来讲，这样说又是非常错误的，因为同一个人不可能同时既忍受从属的地位，又享受平等，但他也可能产生自卑的想法，认为自己只能享受低俗的乐趣。他愿意热衷于平凡的欲求，不敢涉足高尚的事业，甚至连想也不敢想。因此，我认为绝不应当向我们的同时代的人鼓吹谦逊，而是应该努力让他们扩大对自己及与其同类的他人的认识。谦逊对他们毫无裨益，在我看来他们最需要的是骄傲。我宁可用我们一些小小的美德，来换取这个恶习。

第二十章　民主国家谋求官职的问题

在美国，一个公民只要受过一定教育和获得一些财富，不是通过经营工商业谋求致富，或买荒地开垦。对于政府他唯一的要求就是不要干扰他的辛勤劳动，保障他的劳动所得。在欧洲大部分国家，当一个人开始感到自己的力量并试图实现自己的愿望时，他第一个想到的是谋求公职。这两种截然不同的结果出自同一个原因，值得我们在此花时间加以研究。

当公职的位置不多、待遇不高和变化不断，而经营工商业的门路很多并利润丰厚时，

his desires, the first thing that occurs to him is to get some public employment. These opposite effects, originating in the same cause, deserve our passing notice.

When public employments are few in number, ill-paid and precarious, whilst the different lines of business are numerous and lucrative, it is to business, and not to official duties, that the new and eager desires engendered by the principle of equality turn from every side. But if, whilst the ranks of society are becoming more equal, the education of the people remains incomplete, or their spirit the reverse of bold—if commerce and industry, checked in their growth, afford only slow and arduous means of making a fortune—the various members of the community, despairing of ameliorating their own condition, rush to the head of the State and demand its assistance. To relieve their own necessities at the cost of the public treasury, appears to them to be the easiest and most open, if not the only, way they have to rise above a condition which no longer contents them; place-hunting becomes the most generally followed of all trades. This must especially be the case, in those great centralized monarchies in which the number of paid offices is immense, and the tenure of them tolerably secure, so that no one despairs of obtaining a place, and of enjoying it as undisturbedly as a hereditary fortune.

I shall not remark that the universal and inordinate desire for place is a great social evil; that it destroys the spirit of independence in the citizen, and diffuses a venal and servile humor throughout the frame of society; that it stifles the manlier virtues: nor shall I be at the pains to demonstrate that this kind of traffic only creates an unproductive activity, which agitates the country without adding to its resources: all these things are obvious. But I would observe, that a government which encourages this tendency risks its own tranquillity, and places its very existence in great jeopardy. I am aware that at a time like our own, when the love and respect which formerly clung to authority are seen gradually to decline, it may appear necessary to those in power to lay a closer hold on every man by his own interest, and it may seem convenient to use his own passions to keep him in order and in silence; but this cannot be so long, and what may appear to be a source of strength for a certain time

平等的思想每天都会制造新的急切的渴望，促使人们经营工商业，而不是为官一任。但是，当社会等级越来越平等，人们受到的教育尚不完善或是有羞臊心理，而且发展受到阻碍的工商业只能缓慢艰难地给人们带来财富时，社会上的各色公民会在感到依靠自身的力量来改善处境无望的同时蜂拥到政府首长那里寻求帮助。似乎对他们来说用国库的钱来缓解自己的生活所需，即使不是唯一的办法，至少也是让他们自己改变不满意的现有处境的最容易和最可靠的办法。于是，谋求官职成为最普遍的歪门邪道。在那些实行中央集权的君主国家，情况尤其如此。在这样的国家，领取薪俸的官员人数极多，而且任期非常有保证，以至于人人都想得到一个官职，并想要像享用继承到的财产一样安稳地做官。

不用我说，这种普遍过度的求官热是一大社会弊端，它侵蚀了公民的独立精神，让贿赂和奴性在全国上下弥漫开来，并会扼杀光明正大的美德。而且更不用我着力指出，这样的歪门邪道只能产生有害的结果，只会扰乱国家而不会给国家带来任何好处，因为这一切都显而易见。但是，我要指出，鼓励这种倾向的政府会让自己的安定受到危险，甚至会让自己遭到灭亡的厄运。我意识到，在像我们这样的时代，原来对于权威的热爱和尊敬正在消失，掌权者可能认为有必要从本身的利益出发加紧控制每个人，并且觉得利用人们的激情让他们遵守秩序保持沉默是最便捷的办法，但是这并不会持久，而且在某个特定的时期似乎是力量源泉的东西，最终必然会成为困境和衰弱的主要原因。

在民主国家也和其他国家一样，公职人员的数量最终总有一个限度，但是在这些国家，追求官职的人数量却没有上限，而且随着社会日益平等还会不可抑制地持续逐步递增，只有人口数量的限制才能对其产生抑制作用。因此，当公职成为人们一展抱负的唯一

will assuredly become in the end a great cause of embarrassment and weakness.

Amongst democratic nations, as well as elsewhere, the number of official appointments has in the end some limits; but amongst those nations, the number of aspirants is unlimited; it perpetually increases, with a gradual and irresistible rise in proportion as social conditions become more equal, and is only checked by the limits of the population. Thus, when public employments afford the only outlet for ambition, the government necessarily meets with a permanent opposition at last; for it is tasked to satisfy with limited means unlimited desires. It is very certain that of all people in the world the most difficult to restrain and to manage are a people of solicitants. Whatever endeavors are made by rulers, such a people can never be contented; and it is always to be apprehended that they will ultimately overturn the constitution of the country, and change the aspect of the State, for the sole purpose of making a clearance of places. The sovereigns of the present age, who strive to fix upon themselves alone all those novel desires which are aroused by equality, and to satisfy them, will repent in the end, if I am not mistaken, that they ever embarked in this policy: they will one day discover that they have hazarded their own power, by making it so necessary; and that the more safe and honest course would have been to teach their subjects the art of providing for themselves.

Chapter XXI: Why Great Revolutions Will Become More Rare

A people which has existed for centuries under a system of castes and classes can only arrive at a democratic state of society by passing through a long series of more or less critical transformations, accomplished by violent efforts, and after numerous vicissitudes; in the course of which, property, opinions, and power are rapidly transferred from one hand to another. Even after this great revolution is consummated, the revolutionary habits engendered by it may long be traced, and it will be followed by deep commotion. As all this takes place at the very time at which social conditions are becoming more equal, it is inferred that some concealed relation and secret tie exist between the principle of equality itself and revolution, insomuch that the one cannot exist without giving rise to the other.

On this point reasoning may seem to lead to the same result as experience. Amongst a people

出口时，政府最后必然遭到长期的反对，因为政府需要用有限的手段去满足人们无限的渴望。可以非常肯定的是，全世界的人当中最难控制和驾驭的人就是待业求职的人。无论统治者怎样努力，都无法满足这些人的要求。因此，必须时刻留意这些人，他们仅仅为了达到官职空缺这一目的，最终要推翻国家制度，改变国家的面貌。因此，如果没有错的话我认为，全神贯注致力于平等所激起的那些新的欲望并使其得到满足的当今统治者们，最后必然为采用这种策略而后悔。他们终有一天会发现，把自己的权力用于这样的需要非常危险，而最稳妥可靠的办法应当是教会被统治者自力更生的技术。

第二十一章　为什么大规模革命越来越少

一个生活在等级或阶级制度下几个世纪的国家，只有经过一系列长期的或大或小的关键转变，借助于暴力，并在财产、观点和权力等相继出现多次剧变之后，才能达到民主的社会情况。甚至在这场大规模的革命完成之后，由革命而来的革命习惯还会长期存在下去，而且还会有一些深重的动乱随之而来。因为所有这一切都发生在社会状况越来越平等的时期，所以人们便由此推断，在平等和革命之间存在着某种潜藏的关系或秘密的纽带，以至于一个的存在必须伴随另一个的出现。

就这一点，推理似乎与经验的结果相吻合。在等级彼此接近平等的国家，没有一种明显的纽带把人们联系起来，或是使他们固定在所处的位置。任何人都没有永享的权利，或发号施令的权力，也没有被迫处于受人支配的地位，但每一个受过一些教育拥有一些财

whose ranks are nearly equal, no ostensible bond connects men together, or keeps them settled in their station. None of them have either a permanent right or power to command—none are forced by their condition to obey; but every man, finding himself possessed of some education and some resources, may choose his won path and proceed apart from all his fellow-men. The same causes which make the members of the community independent of each other, continually impel them to new and restless desires, and constantly spur them onwards. It therefore seems natural that, in a democratic community, men, things, and opinions should be forever changing their form and place, and that democratic ages should be times of rapid and incessant transformation.

But is this really the case? does the equality of social conditions habitually and permanently lead men to revolution? does that state of society contain some perturbing principle which prevents the community from ever subsiding into calm, and disposes the citizens to alter incessantly their laws, their principles, and their manners? I do not believe it; and as the subject is important, I beg for the reader's close attention. Almost all the revolutions which have changed the aspect of nations have been made to consolidate or to destroy social inequality. Remove the secondary causes which have produced the great convulsions of the world, and you will almost always find the principle of inequality at the bottom. Either the poor have attempted to plunder the rich, or the rich to enslave the poor. If then a state of society can ever be founded in which every man shall have something to keep, and little to take from others, much will have been done for the peace of the world. I am aware that amongst a great democratic people there will always be some members of the community in great poverty, and others in great opulence; but the poor, instead of forming the immense majority of the nation, as is always the case in aristocratic communities, are comparatively few in number, and the laws do not bind them together by the ties of irremediable and hereditary penury. The wealthy, on their side, are scarce and powerless; they have no privileges which attract public observation; even their wealth, as it is no longer incorporated and bound up with the soil, is impalpable, and as it were invisible. As there is no longer a race of poor men, so there is no longer a race of rich men; the latter spring up daily from the multitude, and relapse into it again. Hence they do not form a distinct class,

富的人都会发现可以选择自己的道路，并同其他所有人分开独自前进。令所有社会成员彼此独立的这一原因，同样也在不断促使他们产生新的难以满足的欲望，并驱使他们不断向前。因此，人们似乎可以理所当然地认为，在民主社会，人、事物和观念的外貌和地位始终都在不断地变化，民主时代就是快速不断变化的时代。

但真实情况果真如此吗？社会的平等会促使人们习惯性地、永远地革命下去吗？平等的社会状况中蕴含某种动乱的根源妨碍社会持久安定，并驱使公民不断改变他们的法律、主张和民情吗？我并不这么认为，而且鉴于这个问题很重要，我请读者对此给予特别的关注。几乎所有改变国家面貌的革命，不是巩固就是会破坏不平等。撇开造成人类世界大动乱的次要原因不谈，最后你几乎总是能够发现是不平等在作祟，无论是穷人想夺取富人的财富，还是富人想要奴役穷人。因此，如果一个社会能够一直处于每个人都有某些东西在手，而很少去别人那里获取的状态，那无疑将会对世界和平做出重大贡献。我注意到，在一个大民主国家中，总是有一些人极为贫困，而另一些人则十分富有。但是，穷人并没有像在贵族社会里那样构成民族的绝大多数，而总是人数相对很少，法律也没有规定他们必须祖祖辈辈永远贫困下去。而在富人那一面，他们则是一盘散沙，毫无力量。他们没有引人瞩目的特权，甚至他们的财富也不再与土地合而为一或与土地联系在一起，而是一些看不到摸不着的东西。如同不再有穷人世家一样，富人世家也不复存在，在芸芸众生之中每天都会有富人诞生，同样也不断有富人重新变回芸芸众生。因此，他们并未形成一个可以独立的容易确认的掠夺阶级。此外，因为他们与同胞大众之间有着千丝万缕的隐秘联系，

which may be easily marked out and plundered; and, moreover, as they are connected with the mass of their fellow-citizens by a thousand secret ties, the people cannot assail them without inflicting an injury upon itself. Between these two extremes of democratic communities stand an innumerable multitude of men almost alike, who, without being exactly either rich or poor, are possessed of sufficient property to desire the maintenance of order, yet not enough to excite envy. Such men are the natural enemies of violent commotions: their stillness keeps all beneath them and above them still, and secures the balance of the fabric of society. Not indeed that even these men are contented with what they have gotten, or that they feel a natural abhorrence for a revolution in which they might share the spoil without sharing the calamity; on the contrary, they desire, with unexampled ardor, to get rich, but the difficulty is to know from whom riches can be taken. The same state of society which constantly prompts desires, restrains these desires within necessary limits: it gives men more liberty of changing and less interest in change.

　　Not only are the men of democracies not naturally desirous of revolutions, but they are afraid of them. All revolutions more or less threaten the tenure of property: but most of those who live in democratic countries are possessed of property—not only are they possessed of property, but they live in the condition of men who set the greatest store upon their property. If we attentively consider each of the classes of which society is composed, it is easy to see that the passions engendered by property are keenest and most tenacious amongst the middle classes. The poor often care but little for what they possess, because they suffer much more from the want of what they have not, than they enjoy the little they have. The rich have many other passions besides that of riches to satisfy; and, besides, the long and arduous enjoyment of a great fortune sometimes makes them in the end insensible to its charms. But the men who have a competency, alike removed from opulence and from penury, attach an enormous value to their possessions. As they are still almost within the reach of poverty, they see its privations near at hand, and dread them; between poverty and themselves there is nothing but a scanty fortune, upon which they immediately fix their apprehensions and their

所以人民在攻击他们时不可避免地会伤害到自己。在民主社会的两极之间，还有无数的几乎完全相同的人们，他们既不贫穷，也不富有，他们拥有的财产令他们渴望社会的秩序，但也没有达到令人嫉妒的程度。这些人是暴力动乱的天然敌人。他们的稳定使处于他们之下和之上的人都保持不动，并能确保社会机体的平衡。这并不是说这些人对自己所拥有的已经感到满足，或是对他们能够分享到好处而又不受损失的革命有一种天生的痛恨。恰恰相反，他们对发财致富有着无可比拟的热情，但使他们为难的是，他们知道这会侵夺某些人的财富。不断促使人们产生新欲望的社会情况，也同样会把这些欲望限制在必要的范围之内。它赋予人们更多变革的自由，但减少了人们对变革的兴趣。

　　民主制度下的人们，不仅不是从心里渴望革命，而且还很害怕革命。所有的革命都会或多或少地威胁到既得的财产，而大多数生活在民主国家的人都拥有财产。他们不但拥有财产，而且生活在人人都十分尊重他们财产的环境中。如果我们仔细观察一下社会上的每个阶级，很容易看到由财产而来的激情在中产阶级身上表现得最为强烈和顽强。穷人往往并不关心他们所拥有的财物，因为他们从匮乏中感受到的痛苦远超过其享有的少量财物带来的满足。富人除了爱财之外，还有其他许多需要得到满足的激情，而且长期艰苦地经营巨额财富之后，有时反而让他们感觉不到财富的魅力。但是，既非巨富又非极贫的小康之人，则对自己的财富极为重视。因为他们离贫穷并不太远，感到贫穷近在咫尺，令他们感到非常害怕，在贫穷和他们自己之间只有一点微薄的财富，于是他们把自己的担心和希望都寄托在这点家产上。他们每天都希望能够从家产中获得更多的利益，通过不断不失时机地关注自己的家产，他们夜以继日地努力使家产增加，所以对家产更加依恋。把极小部分

hopes. Every day increases the interest they take in it, by the constant cares which it occasions; and they are the more attached to it by their continual exertions to increase the amount. The notion of surrendering the smallest part of it is insupportable to them, and they consider its total loss as the worst of misfortunes. Now these eager and apprehensive men of small property constitute the class which is constantly increased by the equality of conditions. Hence, in democratic communities, the majority of the people do not clearly see what they have to gain by a revolution, but they continually and in a thousand ways feel that they might lose by one.

I have shown in another part of this work that the equality of conditions naturally urges men to embark in commercial and industrial pursuits, and that it tends to increase and to distribute real property: I have also pointed out the means by which it inspires every man with an eager and constant desire to increase his welfare. Nothing is more opposed to revolutionary passions than these things. It may happen that the final result of a revolution is favorable to commerce and manufactures; but its first consequence will almost always be the ruin of manufactures and mercantile men, because it must always change at once the general principles of consumption, and temporarily upset the existing proportion between supply and demand. I know of nothing more opposite to revolutionary manners than commercial manners. Commerce is naturally adverse to all the violent passions; it loves to temporize, takes delight in compromise, and studiously avoids irritation. It is patient, insinuating, flexible, and never has recourse to extreme measures until obliged by the most absolute necessity. Commerce renders men independent of each other, gives them a lofty notion of their personal importance, leads them to seek to conduct their own affairs, and teaches how to conduct them well; it therefore prepares men for freedom, but preserves them from revolutions. In a revolution the owners of personal property have more to fear than all others; for on the one hand their property is often easy to seize, and on the other it may totally disappear at any moment—a subject of alarm to which the owners of real property are less exposed, since, although they may lose the income of their estates, they may hope to preserve the land itself through the greatest vicissitudes. Hence the former are

家产分给别人的想法，在他们看来完全不可想象。他们把损失全部家产视为最大的不幸。由于平等的不断加强，这些热心保护并唯恐丧失家产的小笔财富所有者的数量不断增加。因此，在民主社会，大多数的人民看不清革命会给他们带来的好处，而是时时刻刻感到革命会从各个方面给他们带来损失。

我在这本书的另一个地方说过，平等会自然而然驱使人们从事工商业，并会促使地产的不断增加和日益分化。我也曾指出，平等会鼓励每个人热烈地，不断地追求幸福。再没有什么比这些更能抵制革命激情的了。革命的最终结果可能会有利于工商业，但它的最初的后果往往是令工商业者倾家荡产，因为革命一开始必然会首先改变消费的一般原则，暂时使供需关系紊乱。此外，据我所知再没有什么比商业道德与革命道德更为对立了。商业自然而然会反对一切狂热的激情，它爱见风使舵，喜欢妥协，并竭力避免激怒人。它有忍性，善于巴结奉迎，有韧性，而且除非万不得已绝不采取极端手段。商业让人们彼此独立，并对自己自视甚高，促使人们自己处理自己的工作，并教会人们成功之道。因此，商业为人们的自由做好准备，却让他们远离革命。在革命之中，动产的所有者比其他所有人都要更加害怕，因为一方面他们的财产往往容易被查封，另一方面又随时有完全消失的可能。然而，不动产的所有者就不会这么害怕，因为尽管他们可能会失去土地的收益，但是依然有希望在大动荡之后保住土地本身。因此，前者对于革命动荡的惧怕比后者更甚。因此，随着国家个人动产数量的增加及其种类增多，革命会越少。此外，不管人们从事什么行业，拥有何种财产，所有人都有一个共同点，那就是没有一个人满足于现有的财产，所有人都一直努力千方百计地增加财富。对任何一个人一生中的任意一段人生进行考察会发

much more alarmed at the symptoms of revolutionary commotion than the latter. Thus nations are less disposed to make revolutions in proportion as personal property is augmented and distributed amongst them, and as the number of those possessing it increases. Moreover, whatever profession men may embrace, and whatever species of property they may possess, one characteristic is common to them all. No one is fully contented with his present fortune—all are perpetually striving in a thousand ways to improve it. Consider any one of them at any period of his life, and he will be found engaged with some new project for the purpose of increasing what he has; talk not to him of the interests and the rights of mankind: this small domestic concern absorbs for the time all his thoughts, and inclines him to defer political excitement to some other season. This not only prevents men from making revolutions, but deters men from desiring them. Violent political passions have but little hold on those who have devoted all their faculties to the pursuit of their well-being. The ardor which they display in small matters calms their zeal for momentous undertakings.

From time to time indeed, enterprising and ambitious men will arise in democratic communities, whose unbounded aspirations cannot be contented by following the beaten track. Such men like revolutions and hail their approach; but they have great difficulty in bringing them about, unless unwonted events come to their assistance. No man can struggle with advantage against the spirit of his age and country; and, however powerful he may be supposed to be, he will find it difficult to make his contemporaries share in feelings and opinions which are repugnant to t all their feelings and desires.

It is a mistake to believe that, when once the equality of conditions has become the old and uncontested state of society, and has imparted its characteristics to the manners of a nation, men will easily allow themselves to be thrust into perilous risks by an imprudent leader or a bold innovator. Not indeed that they will resist him openly, by well-contrived schemes, or even by a premeditated plan of resistance. They will not struggle energetically against him, sometimes they will even applaud him—but they do not follow him. To his vehemence they secretly oppose their inertia; to his

现，为了增加自己拥有的财富他会不断拟订新计划，而对他们大讲人类的利益和权利则是枉费口舌，因为他们把所有的时间和精力都投入到琐碎的自家小事上面，并总是要另找时间去考虑政治热潮。这不仅能阻止人们进行革命，还能让他们打消革命的念头。狂热的政治激情，很少能够打动那些全心投入追求幸福的人，他们在小事上表现的狂热，平复了他们对大事业的热情。

不错，在民主社会，有时也出现一些有魄力野心勃勃的人，常规道路根本无法满足他们无限的欲望。这些人喜欢革命，并为革命欢呼雀跃！但是，除非有意外事件助其一臂之力，否则他们也很难发动起革命。没有人能够在与其时代和国家精神的斗争中获得好处。而且无论他认为自己有多么强大，也难以使同时代人的接受与他们所有人的愿望和感情相悖的情感和思想。

因此，不要认为一旦平等成了永久不争的事实，并赋予民情它的特点，人们就会轻易地跟着一个鲁莽的领袖或一位大胆的革新家投身冒险之路。但人们也的确不能通过深思熟虑的谋划，或者通过事先安排好的抵抗计划，对其表示公开反对。人们不会同他们进行激烈的斗争，有时甚至还会为他们鼓掌喝彩，但绝不会追随他们。人们悄悄地用自己的惰性抵制他们的狂热，用自己的保守主义态度抵制他们的革命倾向，用自己平凡的爱好抵制他们冒险家的热情，用自己的良知抵制他们的天才，用自己的散文抵制他们的诗篇。通过千辛万苦的努力，他们会让人们在一时之间应声而起，但不久人们就会离他们而去，而他们自己也会因为自身的重量而跌倒在地。他们用尽全身解数唤起这些态度冷淡和漫不经心的群众，最终却发现自己无能为力，这并不是因为他们被征服，而是因为他们成了孤家寡人。

revolutionary tendencies their conservative interests; their homely tastes to his adventurous passions; their good sense to the flights of his genius; to his poetry their prose. With immense exertion he raises them for an instant, but they speedily escape from him, and fall back, as it were, by their own weight. He strains himself to rouse the indifferent and distracted multitude, and finds at last that he is reduced to impotence, not because he is conquered, but because he is alone.

I do not assert that men living in democratic communities are naturally stationary; I think, on the contrary, that a perpetual stir prevails in the bosom of those societies, and that rest is unknown there; but I think that men bestir themselves within certain limits beyond which they hardly ever go. They are forever varying, altering, and restoring secondary matters; but they carefully abstain from touching what is fundamental. They love change, but they dread revolutions. Although the Americans are constantly modifying or abrogating some of their laws, they by no means display revolutionary passions. It may be easily seen, from the promptitude with which they check and calm themselves when public excitement begins to grow alarming, and at the very moment when passions seem most roused, that they dread a revolution as the worst of misfortunes, and that every one of them is inwardly resolved to make great sacrifices to avoid such a catastrophe. In no country in the world is the love of property more active and more anxious than in the United States; nowhere does the majority display less inclination for those principles which threaten to alter, in whatever manner, the laws of property. I have often remarked that theories which are of a revolutionary nature, since they cannot be put in practice without a complete and sometimes a sudden change in the state of property and persons, are much less favorably viewed in the United States than in the great monarchical countries of Europe: if some men profess them, the bulk of the people reject them with instinctive abhorrence. I do not hesitate to say that most of the maxims commonly called democratic in France would be proscribed by the democracy of the United States. This may easily be understood: in America men have the opinions and passions of democracy, in Europe we have still the passions and opinions of revolution. If ever America undergoes great revolutions, they will be brought about

　　我并不认为生活在民主社会的人天生不好动；而且我认为事实恰恰相反，始终有一种永恒的运动在这样的社会之中起支配作用，让人们不知休息为何物。但我相信，人们的活动总有不可逾越的一定界限。他们每天都在对次要的东西进行改变、变化或重建，并小心翼翼地不去触动根本的东西。他们热爱变化，但惧怕革命。尽管美国人不断修订或废除他们的某些法律，但绝不会表现出革命的激情。当公众的骚动开始构成威胁的时候，甚至在公众的激情极为高涨的时刻，他们会立刻止步并冷静下来。从中不难发现，他们害怕革命，视革命为最大的不幸，每个人都暗下决定，为了避免这样的灾难愿意做出重大的牺牲。世界上没有一个国家比美国更热爱所有权并为其担惊受怕，也没有一个国家像美国那样绝大多数的人都反对以任何方式威胁改变所有权制度的学说。我经常说，具有革命性质的理论，只有通过完全彻底的和有时是突然的财产和人现状的改变才能实现的时候，在美国不会像在欧洲的那些大君主国那样受到无限的欢迎。即使有人主张这样的理论，群众本能的反感也会对其抵制。我会毫不犹豫地说，在法国往往称为民主的那些名言，大部分都会被美国的民主所谴责。这一点不难理解，在美国，人们拥有民主的思想和激情；而在欧洲，人们所有的依旧是革命的激情和思想。如果有一天美国发生大规模的革命，必然是因居住在美国土地上的黑人而起。也就是说，造成这种革命的原因不是地位的平等，而是地位的不平等。

　　当社会平等的时候，每个人都独立生活，将公众置于脑后。如果民主国家的统治者们不去纠正这个致命的倾向或者认为它能使公民戒除政治激情并远离革命而助长它，那他们最终将会作茧自缚，遭到本想避免的恶果，而且终有一天，当某些人的破坏性激情得到大多数人的愚昧利己主义和胆怯心理的帮助时，最终会迫使整个社会经历异常的变故。在民

by the presence of the black race on the soil of the United States—that is to say, they will owe their origin, not to the equality, but to the inequality, of conditions.

When social conditions are equal, every man is apt to live apart, centred in himself and forgetful of the public. If the rulers of democratic nations were either to neglect to correct this fatal tendency, or to encourage it from a notion that it weans men from political passions and thus wards off revolutions, they might eventually produce the evil they seek to avoid, and a time might come when the inordinate passions of a few men, aided by the unintelligent selfishness or the pusillanimity of the greater number, would ultimately compel society to pass through strange vicissitudes. In democratic communities revolutions are seldom desired except by a minority; but a minority may sometimes effect them. I do not assert that democratic nations are secure from revolutions; I merely say that the state of society in those nations does not lead to revolutions, but rather wards them off. A democratic people left to itself will not easily embark in great hazards; it is only led to revolutions unawares; it may sometimes undergo them, but it does not make them; and I will add that, when such a people has been allowed to acquire sufficient knowledge and experience, it will not suffer them to be made. I am well aware that it this respect public institutions may themselves do much; they may encourage or repress the tendencies which originate in the state of society. I therefore do not maintain, I repeat, that a people is secure from revolutions simply because conditions are equal in the community; but I think that, whatever the institutions of such a people may be, great revolutions will always be far less violent and less frequent than is supposed; and I can easily discern a state of polity, which, when combined with the principle of equality, would render society more stationary than it has ever been in our western apart of the world.

The observations I have here made on events may also be applied in part to opinions. Two things are surprising in the United States—the mutability of the greater part of human actions, and the singular stability of certain principles. Men are in constant motion; the mind of man appears almost unmoved. When once an opinion has spread over the country and struck root there, it would seem that no power on earth is strong enough to eradicate it. In the United States, general principles

主社会，只有少数想要革命，但少数有时候也可能制造革命。但这并不是说民主国家可以避免革命，而是说这种国家的社会情况不会导致革命，或者不如说可以使人们远离革命。凡是靠自己的民主国家的人民不会轻易冒巨大的风险，他们只会在无意之间被卷入革命。他们有时也会经历革命，但这种革命并非他们所制造。而且我要再补充一句，当这样国家的人民获得充分的知识和经验，时便不会纵容革命的出现。我已充分意识到，在这方面公共制度本身可以起到很大的作用，它们会对来自社会情况的各种趋势起着促进或抑制的作用。因此，我再重复一遍，我并不认为一个国家仅仅因为社会平等就能避免革命的发生；但我认为，无论这样的国家实行什么制度，那里的大革命始终会远没有想象的那么暴力和频繁。而且，我能很容易地发现，当这样的政治情况与平等结合时，便会让社会达到西方世界前所未有的安定。

我就事实所做的描述也部分适用于思想观念。在美国，有两件事使人感到惊奇，即人们大部分活动的流动性和某些原则的稳定性。人们不断地流动，而他们的思想却几乎一动不动。一旦某种观念在美国的土地上传播并扎根，似乎地球上再没有任何力量能够把它根除。在美国，宗教、哲学、道德，甚至政治方面的通行学说从未发生改变，或者至少是以隐秘的而且往往难以察觉的方式进行改变。在人和事物这种变幻不定的环境中，甚至一些最粗野的偏见消除的速度也缓慢得令人难以置信。我听说，观念和情感的不断变化是民主的本性和习惯。对于那些古代的全体公民会集到一个公共场所聆听一位演说家鼓噪的小共和国来说，情况也许的确如此。但是，在位于大洋彼岸的伟大民主共和国里，我却丝毫没

in religion, philosophy, morality, and even politics, do not vary, or at least are only modified by a hidden and often an imperceptible process: even the grossest prejudices are obliterated with incredible slowness, amidst the continual friction of men and things. I hear it said that it is in the nature and the habits of democracies to be constantly changing their opinions and feelings. This may be true of small democratic nations, like those of the ancient world, in which the whole community could be assembled in a public place and then excited at will by an orator. But I saw nothing of the kind amongst the great democratic people which dwells upon the opposite shores of the Atlantic Ocean. What struck me in the United States was the difficulty in shaking the majority in an opinion once conceived, or of drawing it off from a leader once adopted. Neither speaking nor writing can accomplish it; nothing but experience will avail, and even experience must be repeated. This is surprising at first sight, but a more attentive investigation explains the fact. I do not think that it is as easy as is supposed to uproot the prejudices of a democratic people—to change its belief—to supersede principles once established, by new principles in religion, politics, and morals—in a word, to make great and frequent changes in men's minds. Not that the human mind is there at rest—it is in constant agitation; but it is engaged in infinitely varying the consequences of known principles, and in seeking for new consequences, rather than in seeking for new principles. Its motion is one of rapid circumvolution, rather than of straightforward impulse by rapid and direct effort; it extends its orbit by small continual and hasty movements, but it does not suddenly alter its position.

　　Men who are equal in rights, in education, in fortune, or, to comprise all in one word, in their social condition, have necessarily wants, habits, and tastes which are hardly dissimilar. As they look at objects under the same aspect, their minds naturally tend to analogous conclusions; and, though each of them may deviate from his contemporaries and from opinions of his own, they will involuntarily and unconsciously concur in a certain number of received opinions. The more attentively I consider the effects of equality upon the mind, the more am I persuaded that the intellectual anarchy which we witness about us is not, as many men suppose, the natural state of democratic nations. I think it is rather to be regarded as an accident peculiar to their youth, and that

有看到过这样的现象。在美国，让我感到惊讶的是，要动摇多数放弃他们所认定的观念，或抛弃他们所选定的领袖是何等之难。无论是演讲还是写书都无济于事，只有亲身经验才能发挥作用，而且甚至亲身经验也需要反复的验证。乍一看，这的确让人吃惊，但经过深入研究之后，便可一探究竟。我并不认为，根除民主国家的偏见，改变其信仰，用宗教、政治、道德的一套新原则取代已经确立的原则，简而言之，就是让人们的思想时常经历大规模的变化，会像想象的那样容易。这不是说，在民主国家人们的思想处于停滞状态，实际上它在不断活动，不过它并不是在探求新的原则，而是在永无止境地改变已知原则的结果。它不是快速地径直向前冲，而是围着自己快速地打转。它用匆忙不断的小动作扩大自己的活动半径，但绝不会突然改变自己的活动范围。

　　权利、教育和财富相同的人，简而言之，就是社会状况相同的人，其需要、习惯和爱好必然也相差无几。因为他们看待事物的角度相同，所以他们的思想会自然而然得出相同的结论。尽管每个人的观念都可能与同时代人以及自己的观念产生偏离，但他们会不知不觉地形成一定数量的共同观念。我越是对平等对思想活动的影响做深入的观察，就越是深信我们所看到的智力活动的混乱并非如有些人认为的那样是民主国家的自然状态。我认为，更应该将其视为民主国家青年时期所特有的偶然现象，只会发生在人们已经冲破原先将其捆绑在一起的纽带，但出身、教育和习惯上仍存在很大不同的过渡时期。因此，在过渡时期，只要人们还保留着非常不同的观念、倾向和爱好，什么也无法阻止他们公开表现出来。但随着人们日趋相同，人们的主要观点将会日益相似。在我看来，这是普遍永久的

it only breaks out at that period of transition when men have already snapped the former ties which bound them together, but are still amazingly different in origin, education, and manners; so that, having retained opinions, propensities and tastes of great diversity, nothing any longer prevents men from avowing them openly. The leading opinions of men become similar in proportion as their conditions assimilate; such appears to me to be the general and permanent law—the rest is casual and transient.

I believe that it will rarely happen to any man amongst a democratic community, suddenly to frame a system of notions very remote from that which his contemporaries have adopted; and if some such innovator appeared, I apprehend that he would have great difficulty in finding listeners, still more in finding believers. When the conditions of men are almost equal, they do not easily allow themselves to be persuaded by each other. As they all live in close intercourse, as they have learned the same things together, and as they lead the same life, they are not naturally disposed to take one of themselves for a guide, and to follow him implicitly. Men seldom take the opinion of their equal, or of a man like themselves, upon trust. Not only is confidence in the superior attainments of certain individuals weakened amongst democratic nations, as I have elsewhere remarked, but the general notion of the intellectual superiority which any man whatsoever may acquire in relation to the rest of the community is soon overshadowed. As men grow more like each other, the doctrine of the equality of the intellect gradually infuses itself into their opinions; and it becomes more difficult for any innovator to acquire or to exert much influence over the minds of a people. In such communities sudden intellectual revolutions will therefore be rare; for, if we read aright the history of the world, we shall find that great and rapid changes in human opinions have been produced far less by the force of reasoning than by the authority of a name. Observe, too, that as the men who live in democratic societies are not connected with each other by any tie, each of them must be convinced individually; whilst in aristocratic society it is enough to convince a few—the rest follow. If Luther had lived in an age of equality, and had not had princes and potentates for his audience, he would perhaps have found it more difficult to change the aspect of

法则，而其余的则都是偶然的和过渡的东西。

　　我认为，在民主社会，任何人都很难突然之间构筑一个与同时代人所接受的思想体系截然不同的思想体系。即使有这样的一位革新家出现，我认为他也难以找到倾听者，更不要说听信者了。在人们彼此几乎平等的时候，人们无法轻易说服彼此。因为大家都彼此亲密交流，在一起学习同样的东西，过着同样的生活，所以自然不愿意从中选出一个人当领导并盲目地追随于他。人们很少信服与自己平等或相同的人的话。在民主国家，人们不但对某些个人卓越学识的信心下降，而且正如我在本书其他地方所说的那样，任何人相对于其余所有人可能存在智力优越性的一般观念，不久也会失去光彩。随着人们越来越彼此相同，智力平等的学说逐渐渗入人们的观念，无论什么样的革新家，都难以对全国人民的精神产生或施加更大的影响。因此，在这样的社会，突然智力革命极为罕见，因为如果我们浏览一下世界史就会发现，让人们的观念发生重大迅速转变的远非理性的力量，而是名望的权威。而且还要注意到，因为生活在民主社会的人彼此之间没有任何纽带相连，所以要对每个人逐个说服。然而在贵族社会，只要让一些人信服就足够了，因为其余的人都会追随于他。如果路德生活在平等时代，既没有领主也没有王侯做他的听众，他可能会发现改变欧洲的面貌要遭遇更多的困难。这并不是说民主时代的人天生坚信自己的见解，或是信仰牢不可破。他们也往往会产生在他们眼中谁也无法解决的疑问。在这样的时候，人们的思想有时愿意改变方位，但因为没有任何东西对其加以推动和引导，所以仍在原地来回徘徊，毫无进展。

Europe. Not indeed that the men of democracies are naturally strongly persuaded of the certainty of their opinions, or are unwavering in belief; they frequently entertain doubts which no one, in their eyes, can remove. It sometimes happens at such times that the human mind would willingly change its position; but as nothing urges or guides it forwards, it oscillates to and fro without progressive motion.

Even when the reliance of a democratic people has been won, it is still no easy matter to gain their attention. It is extremely difficult to obtain a hearing from men living in democracies, unless it be to speak to them of themselves. They do not attend to the things said to them, because they are always fully engrossed with the things they are doing. For indeed few men are idle in democratic nations; life is passed in the midst of noise and excitement, and men are so engaged in acting that little remains to them for thinking. I would especially remark that they are not only employed, but that they are passionately devoted to their employments. They are always in action, and each of their actions absorbs their faculties: the zeal which they display in business puts out the enthusiasm they might otherwise entertain for idea. I think that it is extremely difficult to excite the enthusiasm of a democratic people for any theory which has not a palpable, direct, and immediate connection with the daily occupations of life: therefore they will not easily forsake their old opinions; for it is enthusiasm which flings the minds of men out of the beaten track, and effects the great revolutions of the intellect as well as the great revolutions of the political world. Thus democratic nations have neither time nor taste to go in search of novel opinions. Even when those they possess become doubtful, they still retain them, because it would take too much time and inquiry to change them— they retain them, not as certain, but as established.

There are yet other and more cogent reasons which prevent any great change from being easily effected in the principles of a democratic people. I have already adverted to them at the commencement of this part of my work. If the influence of individuals is weak and hardly perceptible amongst such a people, the power exercised by the mass upon the mind of each individual is extremely great—I have already shown for what reasons. I would now observe that it is wrong to

甚至在赢得一个民主国家的人民的信任之后，想要赢得他们的关注依然并不轻松。如果不是谈他们本身的事情，想让生活在民主国家的人们静心聆听非常困难。他们之所以不注意听别人对他们讲话是因为他们总是忙于自己的事情。事实上，在民主国家，游手好闲的人极少。人们生活在繁忙喧闹的环境之中，人们忙得不行几乎没有时间去思考。我想特别指出的是，他们不只是忙于工作，而是全身心地投入工作。他们不停地在活动，而且对每一行动都全神贯注。他们在事业上表现出的热情，扑灭了他们有可能燃起的思想之火。我认为，很难激起民主国家人民对于任何与他们日常生活实践没有明显的、直接的和迫切联系的某一理论的热情。因此，他们不会轻易放弃旧的观念，因为能使人的精神脱离常规并完成思想大革命和政治大革命的，正是热情。因此，民主国家的人民既没有时间也没有兴趣追求新的观念。甚至当他们对现有观念产生怀疑的时候，依然会固守它们，因为要改变观念需要太多的时间和反复的探索。人们之所以要保留原有的观念，并不是因为它们可靠，而是因为它们已经确立。

还有另外一些更为强大的原因阻碍民主国家的原则发生重大的变化。在本书的绪言里我已经指出过这些原因。即使个人的影响力微弱并几乎无法察觉，人民大众对每个人精神的影响力却极为巨大。至于原因我已经说过。在这里我想要指出，认为这完全取决于政府的形式，而且多数的政治影响力一旦消失其精神影响力也将随之消失，这样的观点并不正确。在贵族社会，个人往往拥有高贵的品格和强大的力量，但当他们发现自己与大多数同胞相抵触时，他们会退回到能让自己自省自慰的自己的圈子。而在民主社会情况则并非

suppose that this depends solely upon the form of government, and that the majority would lose its intellectual supremacy if it were to lose its political power. In aristocracies men have often much greatness and strength of their own: when they find themselves at variance with the greater number of their fellow-countrymen, they withdraw to their own circle, where they support and console themselves. Such is not the case in a democratic country; there public favor seems as necessary as the air we breathe, and to live at variance with the multitude is, as it were, not to live. The multitude requires no laws to coerce those who think not like itself: public disapprobation is enough; a sense of their loneliness and impotence overtakes them and drives them to despair.

Whenever social conditions are equal, public opinion presses with enormous weight upon the mind of each individual; it surrounds, directs, and oppresses him; and this arises from the very constitution of society, much more than from its political laws. As men grow more alike, each man feels himself weaker in regard to all the rest; as he discerns nothing by which he is considerably raised above them, or distinguished from them, he mistrusts himself as soon as they assail him. Not only does he mistrust his strength, but he even doubts of his right; and he is very near acknowledging that he is in the wrong, when the greater number of his countrymen assert that he is so. The majority do not need to constrain him—they convince him. In whatever way then the powers of a democratic community may be organized and balanced, it will always be extremely difficult to believe what the bulk of the people reject, or to profess what they condemn.

This circumstance is extraordinarily favorable to the stability of opinions. When an opinion has taken root amongst a democratic people, and established itself in the minds of the bulk of the community, it afterwards subsists by itself and is maintained without effort, because no one attacks it. Those who at first rejected it as false, ultimately receive it as the general impression; and those who still dispute it in their hearts, conceal their dissent; they are careful not to engage in a dangerous and useless conflict. It is true, that when the majority of a democratic people change their opinions, they may suddenly and arbitrarily effect strange revolutions in men's minds; but their opinions do not change without much difficulty, and it is almost as difficult to show that they are changed.

如此。在这里，公众的拥护就像我们呼吸的空气一样必不可少，而与群众背道而驰，可以说根本无法生活下去。群众不必用法律强迫那些与自己想法不同的人，公众的谴责就已足够。孤独和无能为力的感觉很快向他们袭来，让他们感到绝望。

一旦社会状况平等，公共舆论就会对每个人的思想产生巨大的压力，会包围、指导并控制每个人。这主要是因为社会组织本身，而非政治法令。随着人们彼此越来越相似，每个人感到相对于其他所有人自己变得越来越虚弱。他看到自己毫无出众之处，只要人们开始反对便会怀疑自己。而且不但开始怀疑自己的力量，而且开始怀疑自己的权利，并当绝大多数人说他错了的时候，他会几乎完全认错。多数根本不需强制他，只需要让他信服。因此，民主社会不管采用什么样的力量来组织和保持平衡，人们始终难以相信群众所反对的东西或是宣扬群众所谴责的东西。

这样的情况特别有利于人们观念的稳定。当一种观念在民主国家扎根，并在大多数人的头脑中确立起来的时候，它便能依靠自己的力量毫不费力地存在下去，因为没有人会反对它。那些最初斥其为谬误的人，最终也会因为大家都接受而接受；而那些内心依然抗拒它的人，也会隐藏起自己的不满，小心翼翼地避免一场危险无谓的斗争。的确，当民主国家的多数改变其观念时，可能突然之间随意地在人们的思想世界掀起一场奇怪的革命。但是，多数的观念不会轻易改变，而确认它已经改变，也同样并不容易。

时间和事件，或个人独立的思考活动，有时会动摇或破坏一种观念，但表面上却看不出任何变化。这种观念不会受到人们公开的挑战，也没有人谋划对其发动战争，但是其

Time, events, or the unaided individual action of the mind, will sometimes undermine or destroy an opinion, without any outward sign of the change. It has not been openly assailed, no conspiracy has been formed to make war on it, but its followers one by one noiselessly secede—day by day a few of them abandon it, until last it is only professed by a minority. In this state it will still continue to prevail. As its enemies remain mute, or only interchange their thoughts by stealth, they are themselves unaware for a long period that a great revolution has actually been effected; and in this state of uncertainly they take no steps—they observe each other and are silent. The majority have ceased to believe what they believed before; but they still affect to believe, and this empty phantom of public opinion in strong enough to chill innovators, and to keep them silent and at respectful distance. We live at a time which has witnessed the most rapid changes of opinion in the minds of men; nevertheless it may be that the leading opinions of society will ere long be more settled than they have been for several centuries in our history: that time is not yet come, but it may perhaps be approaching. As I examine more closely the natural wants and tendencies of democratic nations, I grow persuaded that if ever social equality is generally and permanently established in the world, great intellectual and political revolutions will become more difficult and less frequent than is supposed. Because the men of democracies appear always excited, uncertain, eager, changeable in their wills and in their positions, it is imagined that they are suddenly to abrogate their laws, to adopt new opinions, and to assume new manners. But if the principle of equality predisposes men to change, it also suggests to them certain interests and tastes which cannot be satisfied without a settled order of things; equality urges them on, but at the same time it holds them back; it spurs them, but fastens them to earth;—it kindles their desires, but limits their powers. This, however, is not perceived at first; the passions which tend to sever the citizens of a democracy are obvious enough; but the hidden force which restrains and unites them is not discernible at a glance.

Amidst the ruins which surround me, shall I dare to say that revolutions are not what I most fear coming generations? If men continue to shut themselves more closely within the narrow circle of

追随者一个接一个悄然离开，日复一日都有一些人弃它而去，直到最后，只有少数人依然信奉它。但在这样的情况下，它依然盛行。因为它的反对者们始终保持沉默，或者只是秘密地交流思想，因此在很长一段时间内他们还不能确信一场大革命实际上已在进行，所以仍在迟疑而一动不动。他们彼此观察，默不作声。大多数人已经不再相信原来他们所相信的东西，但依然佯装相信。这种公共舆论毫无意义的假象足以让革新者心灰意冷，保持沉默，被人敬而远之。我们正生活在一个人们的思想发生急剧变化的时代。但是不久以后，社会的主流观念也许会比我们历史的过去几个世纪以来的基本观念都要稳定。尽管这个时候还尚未到来，但它可能正在朝我们走来。随着对民主国家人民自然需要和本性的深入研究，我愈加确信，如果平等在世界上全面永久地确立起来，思想和政治大革命的出现将远比人们想象的困难和罕有。因为民主国家的人表面看来似乎始终活跃，不断变化，总在忙活，会随时改变自己的主意和地位，所以会让人觉得他们要随时废除他们的法律，接受新的观念和采用新的习惯。但即使平等的原则会促使人发生变化，也会告诉人们要想满足自己的利益和爱好，安定的环境必不可少。平等在推动人们前进的同时又阻止他们的前进；在激励人们奋起的同时又让他们脚踏实地。它燃起人们的欲望，却限制了人的能力。然而，这无法一下子就能看清，会促使民主国家公民彼此隔离的激情往往非常显眼，而能让他们团结合作的潜在力量则无法一眼就看出。

身处一片革命带来的废墟之中的我，是否还敢说革命并不是我对未来几代人最大的担忧？如果人们继续将自己关闭在窄小的家庭利益的小圈子，并永无休止地追求这种利益，

domestic interests and to live upon that kind of excitement, it is to be apprehended that they may ultimately become inaccessible to those great and powerful public emotions which perturb nations—but which enlarge them and recruit them. When property becomes so fluctuating, and the love of property so restless and so ardent, I cannot but fear that men may arrive at such a state as to regard every new theory as a peril, every innovation as an irksome toil, every social improvement as a stepping-stone to revolution, and so refuse to move altogether for fear of being moved too far. I dread, and I confess it, lest they should at last so entirely give way to a cowardly love of present enjoyment, as to lose sight of the interests of their future selves and of those of their descendants; and to prefer to glide along the easy current of life, rather than to make, when it is necessary, a strong and sudden effort to a higher purpose. It is believed by some that modern society will be ever changing its aspect; for myself, I fear that it will ultimately be too invariably fixed in the same institutions, the same prejudices, the same manners, so that mankind will be stopped and circumscribed; that the mind will swing backwards and forwards forever, without begetting fresh ideas; that man will waste his strength in bootless and solitary trifling; and, though in continual motion, that humanity will cease to advance.

Chapter XXII: Why Democratic Nations Are Naturally Desirous Of Peace, And Democratic Armies Of War

The same interests, the same fears, the same passions which deter democratic nations from revolutions, deter them also from war; the spirit of military glory and the spirit of revolution are weakened at the same time and by the same causes. The ever-increasing numbers of men of property—lovers of peace, the growth of personal wealth which war so rapidly consumes, the mildness of manners, the gentleness of heart, those tendencies to pity which are engendered by the equality of conditions, that coolness of understanding which renders men comparatively insensible to the violent and poetical excitement of arms—all these causes concur to quench the military spirit. I think it may be admitted as a general and constant rule, that, amongst civilized nations, the warlike

可以预见他们最终不会再产生那种会扰乱国家但能使人民前进和革新的伟大的强有力的无私情操。当财富变得如此不稳定，而爱财之心又如此激烈和迫切的时候，我无法不担心人们最终会达到视一切新的理论为灾难，视一切革新为轻举妄动，视一切社会进步为通向革命的台阶的地步，并唯恐被卷进去而一动不动。我承认我害怕，唯恐人们最后会完全屈服于眼前的享乐，以至于看不到自己将来的利益和子孙的利益，宁愿轻松自在地沿着命运的轨迹前进，而不愿在必要的时候毅然决然地做出努力达到更高的目标。人们认为新社会每天都在改变它的面貌，至于我，则害怕它会最终不可改变地固守原来的制度、偏见和民情，结果，人类不再进步反而将自己束缚，思想在原地徘徊永远不会创造出新的思想。人们将精力浪费在一些无益的独立的活动之上，尽管他们不断在活动，但整个人类却停止了进步。

第十二十章　为什么民主国家的人民自然渴望和平而民主国家的军队自然渴望战争

促使民主国家人民打消革命念头的那些利益、恐惧和激情，同样也促使他们远离战争。在同一原因的作用下，尚武精神和革命精神同时被削弱。持续增长的不动产所有者数量，和平的爱好者，会迅速毁于炮火的动产数量，民情的纯朴，人心的温存，平等所激发的同情心，以及会让人们对来自战争的诗意般的强烈激情无动于衷的冷静理智，所有这些因素会共同抑制尚武精神。在文明国家随着社会越来越平等，好战的激情将越来越罕见和越来越不强烈的现象可以被视为一个普遍的常规。然而，战争是所有国家，无论是民主国家或其他国家，都可能卷入的不幸事件。无论它们多么热爱和平，都必须随时做好准备抵

passions will become more rare and less intense in proportion as social conditions shall be more equal. War is nevertheless an occurrence to which all nations are subject, democratic nations as well as others. Whatever taste they may have for peace, they must hold themselves in readiness to repel aggression, or in other words they must have an army.

Fortune, which has conferred so many peculiar benefits upon the inhabitants of the United States, has placed them in the midst of a wilderness, where they have, so to speak, no neighbors: a few thousand soldiers are sufficient for their wants; but this is peculiar to America, not to democracy. The equality of conditions, and the manners as well as the institutions resulting from it, do not exempt a democratic people from the necessity of standing armies, and their armies always exercise a powerful influence over their fate. It is therefore of singular importance to inquire what are the natural propensities of the men of whom these armies are composed.

Amongst aristocratic nations, especially amongst those in which birth is the only source of rank, the same inequality exists in the army as in the nation; the officer is noble, the soldier is a serf; the one is naturally called upon to command, the other to obey. In aristocratic armies, the private soldier's ambition is therefore circumscribed within very narrow limits. Nor has the ambition of the officer an unlimited range. An aristocratic body not only forms a part of the scale of ranks in the nation, but it contains a scale of ranks within itself: the members of whom it is composed are placed one above another, in a particular and unvarying manner. Thus one man is born to the command of a regiment, another to that of a company; when once they have reached the utmost object of their hopes, they stop of their own accord, and remain contented with their lot. There is, besides, a strong cause, which, in aristocracies, weakens the officer's desire of promotion. Amongst aristocratic nations, an officer, independently of his rank in the army, also occupies an elevated rank in society; the former is almost always in his eyes only an appendage to the latter. A nobleman who embraces the profession of arms follows it less from motives of ambition than from a sense of the duties imposed on him by his birth. He enters the army in order to find an honorable employment for the idle years of his youth, and to be able to bring back to his home and his peers some honorable recollections of military life;

御入侵，换句话说，就是必须要有一支军队。

身处荒漠之中也就是说没有邻居的幸运带给美国居民民众多得天独厚的优势。也就是说，少量的士兵就足以满足他们的需要。但这只适用于美国，而不适用于民主。平等、民情以及由此而来的各项制度，并不会让民主国家免除建立军队的义务，而且它的军队还往往会对其命运产生重大影响。因此，研究一下军队人员的自然本质非常重要。在贵族制国家，特别是那些全凭出身来确定等级的国家，军队也像国家一样存在不平等。军官是贵族，而士兵是农奴。一个应征是为了发号施令，而另一个则是为了服从。因此，在贵族制国家的军队之中，士兵个人的野心非常有限，而军官的野心则永无止境。贵族阶层不但是国家等级阶梯中的一个，而且在其内部也有自己的等级阶梯。阶梯上的等级一个比一个高，而且永远保持不变。因此，一个人生来注定要去指挥一个团，而另一个人则要去指挥一个连。他们一旦达到他们所希望的极限之后便会自动停止，满足于自己的命运。此外，还有一个有力的因素抑制贵族制国家军官的晋升欲望。在贵族制国家，军官除了在军队中有军阶以外，在社会上还属于上层阶级。在他们眼里，前者不过是后者的附属品。贵族之所以要从戎并非是为了高升，而是家庭出身的一种义务。他们之所以参军，是为了光荣地度过无所事事的年轻时光，并把军中生活的一些光荣回忆带回家庭和与自己同样的人们中间，但他们的主要目的绝不是借此发财、成名或掌权，因为他们本身已经有这些优势，无须离家就可以享有这一切。

在民主国家的军队，所有士兵都有机会升任军官，这就使人普遍产生晋升的欲望，并

but his principal object is not to obtain by that profession either property, distinction, or power, for he possesses these advantages in his own right, and enjoys them without leaving his home.

In democratic armies all the soldiers may become officers, which makes the desire of promotion general, and immeasurably extends the bounds of military ambition. The officer, on his part, sees nothing which naturally and necessarily stops him at one grade more than at another; and each grade has immense importance in his eyes, because his rank in society almost always depends on his rank in the army. Amongst democratic nations it often happens that an officer has no property but his pay, and no distinction but that of military honors: consequently as often as his duties change, his fortune changes, and he becomes, as it were, a new man. What was only an appendage to his position in aristocratic armies, has thus become the main point, the basis of his whole condition. Under the old French monarchy officers were always called by their titles of nobility; they are now always called by the title of their military rank. This little change in the forms of language suffices to show that a great revolution has taken place in the constitution of society and in that of the army. In democratic armies the desire of advancement is almost universal: it is ardent, tenacious, perpetual; it is strengthened by all other desires, and only extinguished with life itself. But it is easy to see, that of all armies in the world, those in which advancement must be slowest in time of peace are the armies of democratic countries. As the number of commissions is naturally limited, whilst the number of competitors is almost unlimited, and as the strict law of equality is over all alike, none can make rapid progress— many can make no progress at all. Thus the desire of advancement is greater, and the opportunities of advancement fewer, there than elsewhere. All the ambitious spirits of a democratic army are consequently ardently desirous of war, because war makes vacancies, and warrants the violation of that law of seniority which is the sole privilege natural to democracy.

We thus arrive at this singular consequence, that of all armies those most ardently desirous of war are democratic armies, and of all nations those most fond of peace are democratic nations: and, what makes these facts still more extraordinary, is that these contrary effects are produced at the same time by the principle of equality.

极大助长了军事野心。就军官而言，他们看不到有什么东西自然而然地必然强迫他们停止于某一军阶而无法升迁。而且在他们眼中，每个军阶都极为重要，因为他们在社会上的地位总是要依靠他们在军队中的等级。在民主国家，军官往往除了薪金以外没有其他收入，除了军功荣誉以外不会享有其他荣誉。于是，他们的义务改变之后，命运也会随之改变，成为一个全新的人。因此，在贵族制国家军队中只是附属品的东西，在民主国家的军队中成为主要的东西，是军官一切的基础。在法国的旧君主时代，人们总是称呼军官的贵族头衔，很少用他们的军衔。而在现代，只称他们的军衔。这个语言习惯的小小变化足以说明在社会制度和军事制度当中已经发生了巨大的革命。在民主国家的军队，晋升的欲望不但非常普遍，而且很热切、执著和永久。它随着其他所有欲望的上升而上升，生命不息欲望不止。但是，也不难发现，在世界各国的军队中，和平时期军队的晋升速度最为缓慢的必然是民主国家的军队。军职的席位本来就有限，同时竞争者则数不胜数。而且严格的平等原则适用于所有的人，所以没人能够得到迅速晋升，许多人甚至晋升无望。因此，晋升的欲望大大高于其他国家，而晋升的机会则远远不如其他国家。结果，民主国家军队中所有野心勃勃的人，都渴望战争，因为战争能够制造军官的空缺，还可以打破民主制度所特有的按年资晋升的规定。

因此，我们可以得出一个奇怪的结论：在所有国家的军队中，最热衷于战争的军队是民主国家的军队；而在所有国家的人民中，最热爱和平的人民则是民主国家的人民。这种反常现象的成因，使平等同时产生了这两个对立的结果。

All the members of the community, being alike, constantly harbor the wish, and discover the possibility, of changing their condition and improving their welfare: this makes them fond of peace, which is favorable to industry, and allows every man to pursue his own little undertakings to their completion. On the other hand, this same equality makes soldiers dream of fields of battle, by increasing the value of military honors in the eyes of those who follow the profession of arms, and by rendering those honors accessible to all. In either case the inquietude of the heart is the same, the taste for enjoyment as insatiable, the ambition of success as great—the means of gratifying it are alone different.

These opposite tendencies of the nation and the army expose democratic communities to great dangers. When a military spirit forsakes a people, the profession of arms immediately ceases to be held in honor, and military men fall to the lowest rank of the public servants: they are little esteemed, and no longer understood. The reverse of what takes place in aristocratic ages then occurs; the men who enter the army are no longer those of the highest, but of the lowest rank. Military ambition is only indulged in when no other is possible. Hence arises a circle of cause and consequence from which it is difficult to escape: the best part of the nation shuns the military profession because that profession is not honored, and the profession is not honored because the best part of the nation has ceased to follow it. It is then no matter of surprise that democratic armies are often restless, ill-tempered, and dissatisfied with their lot, although their physical condition is commonly far better, and their discipline less strict than in other countries. The soldier feels that he occupies an inferior position, and his wounded pride either stimulates his taste for hostilities which would render his services necessary, or gives him a turn for revolutions, during which he may hope to win by force of arms the political influence and personal importance now denied him. The composition of democratic armies makes this last-mentioned danger much to be feared. In democratic communities almost every man has some property to preserve; but democratic armies are generally led by men without property, most of whom have little to lose in civil broils. The bulk of the nation is naturally much more afraid of revolutions than in the ages of aristocracy, but the leaders of the army much

因彼此相似，所有社会成员都不断抱有希望，并发现改变自己处境和改善自己福利的可能性。这促使他们热爱和平，因为和平有利于工商业，能够让每个人达成自己的小小事业。另一方面，平等同样会令从事戎马生活的人更加重视军事荣誉的价值，让所有的官兵都有机会染指这种荣誉，以至于士兵做梦都想上战场。在这两种不同情况之下，人心同样地躁动，对享受的爱好同样难以满足，成功的野心同样地勃勃，只不过满足各自野心的手段有所不同。

国家和军队中这种背道而驰的倾向会让民主社会面临巨大的危险。当人民丧失尚武精神的时候，从军便立即失去荣光，军人就会沦为最底层的公务人员。人们不太尊敬他们，也不再了解他们。于是，便出现同贵族时代完全相反的情况。从军的公民不再是身居高位的公民，而是一些最微不足道的人。一个人只有走投无路的时候才愿意去从军。于是就会形成一个难以摆脱的恶性循环。国家的精英不愿从军，因为这一行不光荣；而这一行之所以不光荣，则是因为国家的精英不愿从军。因此，不必惊讶民主国家的军队尽管物质条件比其他国家军队一般来说要更好，纪律不如其他国家军队那样严明，但往往情绪低落、怨声载道。士兵感到自己的地位低下，受到挫伤的自尊心让他们爱上没有他们就无法进行的战争，或促使他们转向革命，因为凭借手中的武器他们有希望赢得人们本拒绝给予他们的政治权力和个人尊严。民主国家军队的构成，使引发革命的危险变得更加可怕。在民主社会，几乎每个人都有需要保护的财产；但是，民主国家的军队往往是无产者领导，他们当中的大多数人在内乱期间几乎没有什么可以失去。在民主时代，人民群众自然比在贵族时

less so.

Moreover, as amongst democratic nations (to repeat what I have just remarked) the wealthiest, the best educated, and the most able men seldom adopt the military profession, the army, taken collectively, eventually forms a small nation by itself, where the mind is less enlarged, and habits are more rude than in the nation at large. Now, this small uncivilized nation has arms in its possession, and alone knows how to use them: for, indeed, the pacific temper of the community increases the danger to which a democratic people is exposed from the military and turbulent spirit of the army. Nothing is so dangerous as an army amidst an unwarlike nation; the excessive love of the whole community for quiet continually puts its constitution at the mercy of the soldiery. It may therefore be asserted, generally speaking, that if democratic nations are naturally prone to peace from their interests and their propensities, they are constantly drawn to war and revolutions by their armies. Military revolutions, which are scarcely ever to be apprehended in aristocracies, are always to be dreaded amongst democratic nations. These perils must be reckoned amongst the most formidable which beset their future fate, and the attention of statesmen should be sedulously applied to find a remedy for the evil.

When a nation perceives that it is inwardly affected by the restless ambition of its army, the first thought which occurs is to give this inconvenient ambition an object by going to war. I speak no ill of war: war almost always enlarges the mind of a people, and raises their character. In some cases it is the only check to the excessive growth of certain propensities which naturally spring out of the equality of conditions, and it must be considered as a necessary corrective to certain inveterate diseases to which democratic communities are liable. War has great advantages, but we must not flatter ourselves that it can diminish the danger I have just pointed out. That peril is only suspended by it, to return more fiercely when the war is over; for armies are much more impatient of peace after having tasted military exploits. War could only be a remedy for a people which should always be athirst for military glory. I foresee that all the military rulers who may rise up in great democratic nations, will find it easier to conquer with their armies, than to make their armies live at peace after

代更惧怕革命，但军队的首脑们却并不太害怕革命。

另外，在民主国家，最富有、最有教养和最有能力的人很少从军，所以军队最后成为一个独立的小国。在这里，人们的思想往往更为狭隘，习惯更为粗野。现在，这个不文明的小国却掌握着武器，而且只有它会运用武器。正是民主社会和平的心态加剧了军队好战尚武的精神给国家带来的危险。没有什么会比一个不好战国家的军队更危险的了；全社会对于安宁的过度热爱，则会促使他们把整个社会都交给士兵去支配。因此，可以断言，一般来说，如果民主国家出于自己的利益和本性而自然而然爱好和平，那么它们则是被其军队不断地拖向战争和革命。军人政变在贵族制国家几乎从未有过，而民主国家却整天为此提心吊胆。在困扰民主国家未来命运的所有危险之中，这种危险最为可怕。政治家必须时刻把自己的注意力放在寻找消除这种危险的办法上面。

当一个国家注意到军队的野心蠢蠢欲动而影响到内部安宁的时候，首先想到的就是为这个令人讨厌的野心提供一个发动战争的借口。我并无意诽谤战争。战争几乎总是能够开阔一个民族的思想，提升其品格。在有些情况下，战争是能够遏止平等自然造成的某些倾向过分发展的唯一手段，是纠正民主社会根深蒂固的某些恶疾的必不可少的一剂良药。战争虽然有很大的好处，但也不能对其过度追捧，认为它可以根除我方才指出的危险。战争只能暂时延缓这种危险，而当战争过后危险会更为疯狂地卷土重来，而军队则因为品尝到战争的甜头，更加不愿意容忍和平。战争只是崇尚军功的民族解决困难的办法。我可以预言，所有民主大国里涌现出来的军事首脑们，会发现率军出征远比在胜利之后让军队和平

conquest. There are two things which a democratic people will always find very difficult—to begin a war, and to end it.

Again, if war has some peculiar advantages for democratic nations, on the other hand it exposes them to certain dangers which aristocracies have no cause to dread to an equal extent. I shall only point out two of these. Although war gratifies the army, it embarrasses and often exasperates that countless multitude of men whose minor passions every day require peace in order to be satisfied. Thus there is some risk of its causing, under another form, the disturbance it is intended to prevent. No protracted war can fail to endanger the freedom of a democratic country. Not indeed that after every victory it is to be apprehended that the victorious generals will possess themselves by force of the supreme power, after the manner of Sylla and Caesar: the danger is of another kind. War does not always give over democratic communities to military government, but it must invariably and immeasurably increase the powers of civil government; it must almost compulsorily concentrate the direction of all men and the management of all things in the hands of the administration. If it lead not to despotism by sudden violence, it prepares men for it more gently by their habits. All those who seek to destroy the liberties of a democratic nation ought to know that war is the surest and the shortest means to accomplish it. This is the first axiom of the s cience.

One remedy, which appears to be obvious when the ambition of soldiers and officers becomes the subject of alarm, is to augment the number of commissions to be distributed by increasing the army. This affords temporary relief, but it plunges the country into deeper difficulties at some future period. To increase the army may produce a lasting effect in an aristocratic community, because military ambition is there confined to one class of men, and the ambition of each individual stops, as it were, at a certain limit; so that it may be possible to satisfy all who feel its influence. But nothing is gained by increasing the army amongst a democratic people, because the number of aspirants always rises in exactly the same ratio as the army itself. Those whose claims have been satisfied by the creation of new commissions are instantly succeeded by a fresh multitude beyond all power of

地生活下去更容易。有两件事总会让民主国家觉得很难办：一件是开始战争，另一件是结束战争。

此外，即使战争对民主国家有特别的好处，那另一方面也会使民主国家面临昔日的贵族制国家同样未曾放在心上的某些危险。现在，我只谈其中的两种危险。尽管战争满足了军队的要求，但令每天都需要和平来满足自己小激情的无数人民群众感到尴尬和愤怒。因此，战争从另一方面导致了它本应防止的动乱。所有旷日持久的战争都必然会给民主国家的自由带来巨大的危害。这并不是说在每次胜利之后，获胜的将军们会像罗马的苏拉和恺撒那样取得最高权力，其危险是另一种。战争并不总是会让民主社会出现军人政府，但必然不可改变地无限加强文官政府的权力。它差不多必定要把管理万民和处理万机的大权集中到这个政府手中。即使它不会凭借武力突然实现专制，也会依靠习惯势力温和地让人们做好专制的准备。所有妄图毁灭民主国家自由的人都应该知道，战争是达到这个目的最可靠和最简便的办法。这是第一条科学定理。

当官兵的野心引起人民恐慌的时候，一个显而易见的解决之道就是通过增加军队的人数来扩大军官的编制。但这只能解燃眉之急，会在未来将国家推入更深的困境。在贵族制社会，扩军会产生持久的影响，因为在这里，只有一类人有军事野心，而每个人的野心也会到一定程度便会停止，因此有可能满足所有野心勃勃的人。但是，在民主国家，扩军则没有任何好处，因为随军队人数增加，野心勃勃之人的数量也在不断上涨。被许诺有空缺时就职的人上任以后，不久又会出现一批欲望没有得到满足的人，而那些刚刚上任的人

satisfaction; and even those who were but now satisfied soon begin to crave more advancement; for the same excitement prevails in the ranks of the army as in the civil classes of democratic society, and what men want is not to reach a certain grade, but to have constant promotion. Though these wants may not be very vast, they are perpetually recurring. Thus a democratic nation, by augmenting its army, only allays for a time the ambition of the military profession, which soon becomes even more formidable, because the number of those who feel it is increased. I am of opinion that a restless and turbulent spirit is an evil inherent in the very constitution of democratic armies, and beyond hope of cure. The legislators of democracies must not expect to devise any military organization capable by its influence of calming and restraining the military profession: their efforts would exhaust their powers, before the object is attained.

The remedy for the vices of the army is not to be found in the army itself, but in the country. Democratic nations are naturally afraid of disturbance and of despotism; the object is to turn these natural instincts into well-digested, deliberate, and lasting tastes. When men have at last learned to make a peaceful and profitable use of freedom, and have felt its blessings—when they have conceived a manly love of order, and have freely submitted themselves to discipline—these same men, if they follow the profession of arms, bring into it, unconsciously and almost against their will, these same habits and manners. The general spirit of the nation being infused into the spirit peculiar to the army, tempers the opinions and desires engendered by military life, or represses them by the mighty force of public opinion. Teach but the citizens to be educated, orderly, firm, and free, the soldiers will be disciplined and obedient. Any law which, in repressing the turbulent spirit of the army, should tend to diminish the spirit of freedom in the nation, and to overshadow the notion of law and right, would defeat its object: it would do much more to favor, than to defeat, the establishment of military tyranny.

After all, and in spite of all precautions, a large army amidst a democratic people will always be a source of great danger; the most effectual means of diminishing that danger would be to reduce the army, but this is a remedy which all nations have it not in their power to use.

很快也会渴望新的升迁，因为民主国家公民阶层的那种不安在军队中也同样普遍。人们想要到达的不是一个特定的军阶，而是不断地晋升。尽管他们的欲望并不算太大，但一个一个接踵而来。因此，民主国家通过扩军只能在一时之间满足军人的野心，但不久以后，他们的野心会变得更为可怕，因为想得到晋升的人越来越多。我认为不安和躁动的精神是民主国家军队组织本身固有的不愿根除的弊端。民主国家的立法者们不要期待能够制定一套可以依靠自己的力量安抚和抑制军人情绪的军事制度。哪怕他们为此殚精竭虑也只能白费功夫。

能够医治军队恶疾的良方不是军队本身，而是国家。民主国家天生害怕动乱和专制。只要使军队的天然本性转化为审慎的、理智的和稳重的爱好，问题就可迎刃而解。当人们最终学会和平有益地运用自由，并体会到自由的好处，当他们对秩序的热爱有男子般的气魄，并自愿地服从纪律时，他们入伍从军就会不知不觉地和似乎是违反本意地把这些习惯和品质带进军队。国家的一般精神一旦渗入军队特有的精神，由军队生活而来的观点和欲望就会被缓和，或是依靠公共舆论的强大力量将其抑制下去。有了有知识、守纪律、意志坚定和爱好自由的公民，才会有纪律严明和服从命令的士兵。任何法律，在抑制军队叛乱精神的同时，往往会压制整个国家的自由精神，从而法律和权利的观念会黯然失色，结果必然会适得其反。它不但不会消灭军人暴政，反而会有利于军人暴政的确立。

不管采取什么预防措施，民主国家的庞大的军队终究是一大祸根，而消除这个祸根最有效r办法就是裁军，但这又是所有国家都有力量采用的解决之法。

Chapter XXIII: Which Is The Most Warlike And Most Revolutionary Class In Democratic Armies?

It is a part of the essence of a democratic army to be very numerous in proportion to the people to which it belongs, as I shall hereafter show. On the other hand, men living in democratic times seldom choose a military life. Democratic nations are therefore soon led to give up the system of voluntary recruiting for that of compulsory enlistment. The necessity of their social condition compels them to resort to the latter means, and it may easily be foreseen that they will all eventually adopt it. When military service is compulsory, the burden is indiscriminately and equally borne by the whole community. This is another necessary consequence of the social condition of these nations, and of their notions. The government may do almost whatever it pleases, provided it appeals to the whole community at once: it is the unequal distribution of the weight, not the weight itself, which commonly occasions resistance. But as military service is common to all the citizens, the evident consequence is that each of them remains but for a few years on active duty. Thus it is in the nature of things that the soldier in democracies only passes through the army, whilst among most aristocratic nations the military profession is one which the soldier adopts, or which is imposed upon him, for life.

This has important consequences. Amongst the soldiers of a democratic army, some acquire a taste for military life, but the majority, being enlisted against their will, and ever ready to go back to their homes, do not consider themselves as seriously engaged in the military profession, and are always thinking of quitting it. Such men do not contract the wants, and only half partake in the passions, which that mode of life engenders. They adapt themselves to their military duties, but their minds are still attached to the interests and the duties which engaged them in civil life. They do not therefore imbibe the spirit of the army—or rather, they infuse the spirit of the community at large into the army, and retain it there. Amongst democratic nations the private soldiers remain most like civilians: upon them the habits of the nation have the firmest hold, and public opinion most influence. It is by the instrumentality of the private soldiers especially that it may be possible to

第二十三章　民主国家军队中最好战和最革命的阶级

民主国家军队的一个特性是从人口数量与兵员人数的比例来说，人数非常庞大，其原因我会在以后进行说明。另一方面，生活在民主时代的人很少选择在军中供职。因此，民主国家过不了多久就不得不放弃自愿入伍的募兵制，而采用强制入伍的征兵制。出于本国社会状况的要求，它们被迫采用后一种制度，而且不难预见，最终所有人都要应征入伍。当服军役是强制义务时，就必然要毫无差别地由全体公民平等地分担。这是这些国家社会状况及其观念的另一个必然结果。这些国家的政府，只要向全体人民呼吁，几乎可以做成它所想做的任何事。一般来说，引起反抗的是负担分配的不平等，而不是负担本身。但是，因为全体公民都要服兵役，所以显然每个人都要在军队里服役几年。因此，民主国家的士兵只是军队的过客，然而，在大部分贵族制国家，当兵却是士兵所选定或被迫接受的终生职业。

这种情况造成了重要的后果。在民主国家军队的士兵中，有些人很热爱军队生活，但大多数人从军则并非出自本意，甚至时刻准备返回家园，所以没有严肃地对待服兵役的义务，只是想着离开军队。这些人没有什么要求，也没有染上半点这种职业带来的欲望。他们让自己适应军中生活，但脑子里想的总是市民生活的利益和责任。因此，他们不但没有尚武精神，反而将社会的公民精神带入军队并在军队里保持这种精神。在民主国家，普通士兵仍然保存着公民的本色，国家的习惯对他们的影响根深蒂固，公共舆论对他们的影响举足轻重。士兵们可以特别自诩的是，如果对自由的热爱和对权利的尊重曾经被成功地灌输给全体人民，现在他们有可能将这些观念渗透到民主国家的军队。贵族制国家的情况则

infuse into a democratic army the love of freedom and the respect of rights, if these principles have once been successfully inculcated on the people at large. The reverse happens amongst aristocratic nations, where the soldiery have eventually nothing in common with their fellow-citizens, and where they live amongst them as strangers, and often as enemies. In aristocratic armies the officers are the conservative element, because the officers alone have retained a strict connection with civil society, and never forego their purpose of resuming their place in it sooner or later: in democratic armies the private soldiers stand in this position, and from the same cause.

It often happens, on the contrary, that in these same democratic armies the officers contract tastes and wants wholly distinct from those of the nation—a fact which may be thus accounted for. Amongst democratic nations, the man who becomes an officer severs all the ties which bound him to civil life; he leaves it forever; he has no interest to resume it. His true country is the army, since he owes all he has to the rank he has attained in it; he therefore follows the fortunes of the army, rises or sinks with it, and henceforward directs all his hopes to that quarter only. As the wants of an officer are distinct from those of the country, he may perhaps ardently desire war, or labor to bring about a revolution at the very moment when the nation is most desirous of stability and peace. There are, nevertheless, some causes which allay this restless and warlike spirit. Though ambition is universal and continual amongst democratic nations, we have seen that it is seldom great. A man who, being born in the lower classes of the community, has risen from the ranks to be an officer, has already taken a prodigious step. He has gained a footing in a sphere above that which he filled in civil life, and he has acquired rights which most democratic nations will ever consider as inalienable. He is willing to pause after so great an effort, and to enjoy what he has won. The fear of risking what he has already obtained damps the desire of acquiring what he has not got. Having conquered the first and greatest impediment which opposed his advancement, he resigns himself with less impatience to the slowness of his progress. His ambition will be more and more cooled in proportion as the increasing distinction of his rank teaches him that he has more to put in jeopardy. If I am not mistaken, the least warlike, and also the least revolutionary part, of a democratic army, will always

刚好相反，在那里士兵最终与自己的同胞毫无共同之处，如陌生人般形同陌路，甚至往往彼此敌视。在贵族制国家的军队，军官是保守派，因为只有他们同市民社会保持紧密的联系，而且从来没有放弃迟早要回市民社会恢复原来地位的想法。在民主国家的军队，士兵也有同样的想法，而且其原因也完全相同。

相反，在民主国家军队的内部，军官们往往会养成与全国人民完全不同的爱好和欲望。这种现象并不难解释。在民主国家，成为军官的人便已切断与市民生活的所有联系，并永久地离开市民生活，而且也丝毫不想再回到过去。他真正的祖国是军队，因为他所获得的一切都取决于他的军阶。因此，他随着军队命运的浮沉而浮沉，将今后自己所有的希望都寄托在这里。因为军官的需要与国家的需要不同，所以在国家极度渴望和平稳定的时候，他有可能非常渴望战争或是努力想要发动一场革命。然而，有一些因素可以抑制军官躁动的尚武好战的精神。尽管民主国家的人们的野心很普遍而且层出不穷，但正如我们所见它并不强大。出生在社会下层的人，在军队经过几次晋升后成为军官，这已是惊人之举。在军队之中，他已经取得比他在市民社会中要高得多的地位，并获得大部分民主国家一直以来都认为不可出让的权利。在经过一番艰苦努力之后，他会很乐于休息片刻，享用已经获得的一切。但因为害怕失去已经获得的东西，所以对尚未得到的东西的渴望便不再强烈。在征服阻碍自己晋升的第一个和最大的障碍之后，他便对后来缓慢的晋升更有耐性。随着军阶的不断提升，危险也越来越大，于是他的野心也越来越萎缩。如果我没说错的话，民主国家军队中最不好战和最缺乏革命精神的始终会是高级指挥官。

be its chief commanders.

But the remarks I have just made on officers and soldiers are not applicable to a numerous class which in all armies fills the intermediate space between them—I mean the class of non-commissioned officers. This class of non-commissioned officers which have never acted a part in history until the present century, is henceforward destined, I think, to play one of some importance. Like the officers, non-commissioned officers have broken, in their minds, all the ties which bound them to civil life; like the former, they devote themselves permanently to the service, and perhaps make it even more exclusively the object of all their desires: but non-commissioned officers are men who have not yet reached a firm and lofty post at which they may pause and breathe more freely, ere they can attain further promotion. By the very nature of his duties, which is invariable, a non-commissioned officer is doomed to lead an obscure, confined, comfortless, and precarious existence; as yet he sees nothing of military life but its dangers; he knows nothing but its privations and its discipline—more difficult to support than dangers: he suffers the more from his present miseries, from knowing that the constitution of society and of the army allow him to rise above them; he may, indeed, at any time obtain his commission, and enter at once upon command, honors, independence, rights, and enjoyments. Not only does this object of his hopes appear to him of immense importance, but he is never sure of reaching it till it is actually his own; the grade he fills is by no means irrevocable; he is always entirely abandoned to the arbitrary pleasure of his commanding officer, for this is imperiously required by the necessity of discipline: a slight fault, a whim, may always deprive him in an instant of the fruits of many years of toil and endeavor; until he has reached the grade to which he aspires he has accomplished nothing; not till he reaches that grade does his career seem to begin. A desperate ambition cannot fail to be kindled in a man thus incessantly goaded on by his youth, his wants, his passions, the spirit of his age, his hopes, and his age, his hopes, and his fears. Non-commissioned officers are therefore bent on war—on war always, and at any cost; but if war be denied them, then they desire revolutions to suspend the authority of established regulations, and to enable them, aided by the general confusion and the political passions of the time, to get rid of their superior officers and

但是，我刚才就军官和士兵所做的论述，并不适用于所有的军队中介于军官和士兵之间的那些阶层，即军士阶层。直到19世纪之前，军士阶层在历史上从未扮演过重要角色，但是我认为从今往后他们注定要在历史上发挥重要作用。同军官一样，军士们在思想上已经同市民社会断绝所有关系；而且也同军官一样，他们也全身心投入军事生涯；甚至比军官还要更甚地把全部希望都寄托在此。但是，军士们还没有达到一个较高的稳固地位，在更进一步之前还不能停下来舒舒服服地喘口气。但是军士义务的本质永远不会改变，所以他们注定要过默默无闻、备受限制、很不舒适和生死难料的生活。因此，在他们眼中只会看到军队生活的危险重重。他们只知道艰苦和服从，而这比危险更难以忍受。他们之所以能够忍受眼前的痛苦，是因为他们知道社会和军队的制度能够让自己摆脱这些痛苦。而且他们的确会随时当上军官，并可以立即发号施令，获得荣誉、独立、权力乃至享受。他们所希望得到的东西不但对他们非常重要，而且在实际拿到手以前，他们不敢确信一定能够拿到。他们的军阶也并非一成不变。他们每天都要任凭长官随意摆布，因为军队的纪律要求他们必须这样做。一点点小错误，或一时的心血来潮，往往会立刻葬送他们多年心血积累下的成果。在他们熬到所向往的军阶之前，可以说他们一无所获。只有在取得军官军阶之后，他们的职业生涯似乎才刚刚开始。因为不断地受到青春、需要、激情、时代精神、希望、时代及其恐惧心理的刺激，他们必然会燃起铤而走险的野心。因此，军士一心想要进行战争，而且不计代价始终不渝。但是如果人们反对战争，于是他们就寄希望于能够使典章制度失去权威的革命，并借助混乱的局势和时代的政治激情来除掉他们的长官并取而

to take their places. Nor is it impossible for them to bring about such a crisis, because their common origin and habits give them much influence over the soldiers, however different may be their passions and their desires.

It would be an error to suppose that these various characteristics of officers, non-commissioned officers, and men, belong to any particular time or country; they will always occur at all times, and amongst all democratic nations. In every democratic army the non-commissioned officers will be the worst representatives of the pacific and orderly spirit of the country, and the private soldiers will be the best. The latter will carry with them into military life the strength or weakness of the manners of the nation; they will display a faithful reflection of the community: if that community is ignorant and weak, they will allow themselves to be drawn by their leaders into disturbances, either unconsciously or against their will; if it is enlightened and energetic, the community will itself keep them within the bounds of order.

Chapter XXIV: Causes Which Render Democratic Armies Weaker Than Other Armies At The Outset Of A Campaign, And More Formidable In Protracted Warfare

Any army is in danger of being conquered at the outset of a campaign, after a long peace; any army which has long been engaged in warfare has strong chances of victory: this truth is peculiarly applicable to democratic armies. In aristocracies the military profession, being a privileged career, is held in honor even in time of peace. Men of great talents, great attainments, and great ambition embrace it; the army is in all respects on a level with the nation, and frequently above it. We have seen, on the contrary, that amongst a democratic people the choicer minds of the nation are gradually drawn away from the military profession, to seek by other paths, distinction, power, and especially wealth. After a long peace—and in democratic ages the periods of peace are long—the army is always inferior to the country itself. In this state it is called into active service; and until war has altered it, there is danger for the country as well as for the army.

代之。而这并非没有可能，因为无论他们的激情和欲望与士兵有多么大的不同，但他们与士兵共同的出身和习惯让其对士兵能够产生更大的影响力。

如果认为军官、军士以及士兵各自呈现的迥然不同的特点为一个时代或一个国家所特有，那就错了。这种现象会出现在任何时代和任何民主国家。在所有民主国家的军队，军士是国家和平秩序风气的最坏代表，而士兵则是最好代表。士兵将国家民情的优点或缺点都带进军队，忠实地反映出社会的面貌。如果士兵无知而软弱，他们会在不知不觉之中，或是违背本意的情况下，任由长官将其拉去搞叛乱。而如果士兵有知识够坚强，他们可以约束长官遵守秩序。

第二十四章　民主国家军队在战争初期比其他国家军队软弱，而在战争持续下去后更为强韧的原因

任何一支在长期和平之后的军队，在战争伊始都有被击败的危险。而任何长期作战的军队则都有很大的获胜机会。这一真理特别适用于民主国家的军队。在贵族制国家，军职是特权职业，甚至在和平时期也享有荣誉。往往是有才华、有学问和有野心的人从事这一行。军队在各方面都不低于全国的平均水平，而且往往高于这一水平。然而在民主国家我们所看到的情况则刚好相反。国家的精英都弃它而去，通过其他的途径去谋求荣誉和权力，特别是财富。在长期的和平之后，而且在民主国家和平时期特别长，军队的水平往往低于国家的水平。在这样的状态下军队参战，不仅对国家而且对军队都有危险，在战争使这种状态发生改变之前，危险将始终存在。

I have shown that in democratic armies, and in time of peace, the rule of seniority is the supreme and inflexible law of advancement. This is not only a consequence, as I have before observed, of the constitution of these armies, but of the constitution of the people, and it will always occur. Again, as amongst these nations the officer derives his position in the country solely from his position in the army, and as he draws all the distinction and the competency he enjoys from the same source, he does not retire from his profession, or is not super-annuated, till towards the extreme close of life. The consequence of these two causes is, that when a democratic people goes to war after a long interval of peace all the leading officers of the army are old men. I speak not only of the generals, but of the non-commissioned officers, who have most of them been stationary, or have only advanced step by step. It may be remarked with surprise, that in a democratic army after a long peace all the soldiers are mere boys, and all the superior officers in declining years; so that the former are wanting in experience, the latter in vigor. This is a strong element of defeat, for the first condition of successful generalship is youth: I should not have ventured to say so if the greatest captain of modern times had not made the observation. These two causes do not act in the same manner upon aristocratic armies: as men are promoted in them by right of birth much more than by right of seniority, there are in all ranks a certain number of young men, who bring to their profession all the early vigor of body and mind. Again, as the men who seek for military honors amongst an aristocratic people, enjoy a settled position in civil society, they seldom continue in the army until old age overtakes them. After having devoted the most vigorous years of youth to the career of arms, they voluntarily retire, and spend at home the remainder of their maturer years.

A long peace not only fills democratic armies with elderly officers, but it also gives to all the officers habits both of body and mind which render them unfit for actual service. The man who has long lived amidst the calm and lukewarm atmosphere of democratic manners can at first ill adapt himself to the harder toils and sterner duties of warfare; and if he has not absolutely lost the taste for arms, at least he has assumed a mode of life which unfits him for conquest.

Amongst aristocratic nations, the ease of civil life exercises less influence on the manners of

我曾经说过，民主国家的军队，在和平时期，年资是晋升的最高的和不可撼动的制度。正如我曾指出的那样，这不仅仅是军队制度的结果，也是国家制度的结果，因此，这样的现象会始终存在。而且，在这些国家中军官在国家的地位完全取决于他们在军队的地位，因为他们所享有的荣华富贵也都来自这个地位，所以他们只有到死才会离开或退出军界。这两个原因造成的后果就是，当民主国家的军队在经历长期的和平走上战场的时候，所有的指挥人员均已老迈。我所说的不仅仅是将军，还包括一直以来原地踏步或一步一步爬上去的军士。人们会惊讶地发现，在长期和平之后的民主军队中，所有士兵都是孩子，而所有的长官都已垂暮，以至于士兵缺乏经验，长官精力不足。这是失败的重要原因，因为成功将领的首要条件就是年轻。如果不是近代的一位最伟大的统帅指出过这一点，我还不敢这样说。这两个因素在贵族制国家的军队则并不算是以同样的方式在发挥作用。因为人们获得晋升的主要依据是家庭出身而不是年资，因此在各个军阶都有一定数量的年轻人，他们将最充沛的体力和精力全部带进战争。另外，在贵族制国家谋求军事荣誉的人，在市民社会都拥有不变的地位，所以很少有人在年老的时候才离开军队。他们在把精力最充沛的年华献给军队之后，便自动退伍，回到家乡享受余生。

长期的和平不仅让民主国家的军队充斥着年老的军官，而且让所有军官的身心养成不适应于实战的习惯。长期生活在民主温和平静氛围中的人们，开始很难适应战争的艰苦工作和严峻任务。而且即使他还没有失去担任军职的兴趣，但至少已经养成不适宜征战的生活方式。

在贵族制国家，市民生活的安逸对军队作风的影响不大，因为在这些国家，是贵族在

the army, because amongst those nations the aristocracy commands the army: and an aristocracy, however plunged in luxurious pleasures, has always many other passions besides that of its own well-being, and to satisfy those passions more thoroughly its well-being will be readily sacrificed.

I have shown that in democratic armies, in time of peace, promotion is extremely slow. The officers at first support this state of things with impatience, they grow excited, restless, exasperated, but in the end most of them make up their minds to it. Those who have the largest share of ambition and of resources quit the army; others, adapting their tastes and their desires to their scanty fortunes, ultimately look upon the military profession in a civil point of view. The quality they value most in it is the competency and security which attend it: their whole notion of the future rests upon the certainty of this little provision, and all they require is peaceably to enjoy it. Thus not only does a long peace fill an army with old men, but it is frequently imparts the views of old men to those who are still in the prime of life.

I have also shown that amongst democratic nations in time of peace the military profession is held in little honor and indifferently followed. This want of public favor is a heavy discouragement to the army; it weighs down the minds of the troops, and when war breaks out at last, they cannot immediately resume their spring and vigor. No similar cause of moral weakness occurs in aristocratic armies: there the officers are never lowered either in their own eyes or in those of their countrymen, because, independently of their military greatness, they are personally great. But even if the influence of peace operated on the two kinds of armies in the same manner, the results would still be different. When the officers of an aristocratic army have lost their warlike spirit and the desire of raising themselves by service, they still retain a certain respect for the honor of their class, and an old habit of being foremost to set an example. But when the officers of a democratic army have no longer the love of war and the ambition of arms, nothing whatever remains to them.

I am therefore of opinion that, when a democratic people engages in a war after a long peace, it incurs much more risk of defeat than any other nation; but it ought not easily to be cast down by

指挥军队，而贵族，尽管过着穷奢极侈的生活，但除了追求幸福的激情以外，还往往拥有一些其他的激情，而且为了能够充分满足这些激情，他们愿意随时牺牲自己的幸福。

我已经说过，和平时期的民主军队中，军阶的晋升极为缓慢。军官们起初对这种情况没有耐性，他们焦躁不安，牢骚满腹，心灰意冷，但最后大部分人决心忍受下去。而那些野心很大和有办法的人则离开了军队，其余的人则进行自我调整使自己的爱好和欲望与他们的命运相适应，最终以市民的眼光来看待军职。他们认为军职最可贵之处在于它所带来的舒适和安定。他们对未来的全部设想都建立在这一点小小保障之上，他们所需要的就是能够平平安安地享受这些。因此，长期的和平不仅会让民主国家的军队充满年老的军官，而且还会不断把老年人的观念传输给年轻力壮的军官。

我也说过，在和平时期的民主国家，军职不会带来很高的荣誉，人们也不会蜂拥而至。公众的这种态度，是压在军人头上的一块又重又大的石头，极大地挫伤军队的士气。当战争终于爆发的时候，士气不可能立即恢复得活力十足。在贵族制国家的军队中则不会出现同样的这种挫败士气的原因。在这里，军官的地位无论是在他们自己眼中还是在其同胞眼中，从来都不低下，因为除了他们军队的伟大之外，他们本人也很伟大。但即使和平对这两种军队会产生相同的影响，其结果依旧不同。当贵族制国家军队的军官失去战斗精神并不愿意靠军职发迹的时候，他们仍会尊重本阶级的荣誉和身先士卒的古老习惯。但是，当民主国家军队的军官不再好战并不再抱有晋升的野心时，那么什么都不会被保留下来。

因此，我认为民主国家在长期和平之后投入战争，失败的危险会比其他国家都要大得多。但它不会轻而易举一蹶不振，因为随着战争时间的拉长，其军队胜利的概率也在不断

its reverses, for the chances of success for such an army are increased by the duration of the war. When a war has at length, by its long continuance, roused the whole community from their peaceful occupations and ruined their minor undertakings, the same passions which made them attach so much importance to the maintenance of peace will be turned to arms. War, after it has destroyed all modes of speculation, becomes itself the great and sole speculation, to which all the ardent and ambitious desires which equality engenders are exclusively directed. Hence it is that the selfsame democratic nations which are so reluctant to engage in hostilities, sometimes perform prodigious achievements when once they have taken the field. As the war attracts more and more of public attention, and is seen to create high reputations and great fortunes in a short space of time, the choicest spirits of the nation enter the military profession: all the enterprising, proud, and martial minds, no longer of the aristocracy solely, but of the whole country, are drawn in this direction. As the number of competitors for military honors is immense, and war drives every man to his proper level, great generals are always sure to spring up. A long war produces upon a democratic army the same effects that a revolution produces upon a people; it breaks through regulations, and allows extraordinary men to rise above the common level. Those officers whose bodies and minds have grown old in peace, are removed, or superannuated, or they die. In their stead a host of young men are pressing on, whose frames are already hardened, whose desires are extended and inflamed by active service. They are bent on advancement at all hazards, and perpetual advancement; they are followed by others with the same passions and desires, and after these are others yet unlimited by aught but the size of the army. The principle of equality opens the door of ambition to all, and death provides chances for ambition. Death is constantly thinning the ranks, making vacancies, closing and opening the career of arms.

There is moreover a secret connection between the military character and the character of democracies, which war brings to light. The men of democracies are naturally passionately eager to acquire what they covet, and to enjoy it on easy conditions. They for the most part worship chance, and are much less afraid of death than of difficulty. This is the spirit which they bring to commerce

增加。当冗长的战争最终使全体公民无法从事和平劳动并毁了他们的小小事业时，他们就会把投注在和平上的激情转投给战争。战争在破坏一切之后，成为独一无二的伟大事业，平等造就的一切炙热的强烈的激情全部集中到战争上来。这就是为什么如此勉强奔赴战场的民主国家人民一旦拿起武器，有时就会在战场上取得惊人成就的原因。随着战争越来越吸引所有人的视线，以及在军队中短时间内便可功成名就并创造出巨大财富，全国的精英纷纷投身军队。所有有魄力的、骄傲的以及尚武的人士，而且不再只是贵族，而是整个国家都被吸引过来。由于竞争军事荣誉的人数量巨大，战争又迫使每个人发挥其应有的才智，所以必然会涌现出伟大的将领。长期的战争对民主国家军队产生的影响，与革命对民主国家产生的影响一样，它会打破常规，让杰出的人才脱颖而出。而那些在和平时期身体和思想就已经衰老的军官不是离开军队，就是退休或死去。一批在战争中壮大起来的青年人接替了他们的职位。这些年轻人满怀激情，坚持把战争打下去。他们不惜一切代价力求晋升，而且实际上也在不断晋升。在他们身后，一大批年轻人正在大踏步而来。他们不顾一切地向前，勇往直前。在他们的身后还有一批怀有同样激情和欲望的人紧随其后。而在他们的身后还有另外的一批人，只要军队没有限制，这样的人将一批一批不断涌现。平等为所有人敞开抱负之门，而死亡又为野心提供了契机。死亡让军官数量不断减少，制造空缺，在关闭晋升之门的同时又将其打开。

此外，在军人的特征和民主国家的特征之间，还存有一种隐秘的联系，只能在战争中才能发现。民主国家的人，自然热切地渴望获得他们所垂涎的东西，然后舒舒服服地享受。他们之中大部分人崇尚冒险，怕穷不怕死，并将这种精神带入工商业，而且他们也把

and manufactures; and this same spirit, carried with them to the field of battle, induces them willingly to expose their lives in order to secure in a moment the rewards of victory. No kind of greatness is more pleasing to the imagination of a democratic people than military greatness—a greatness of vivid and sudden lustre, obtained without toil, by nothing but the risk of life. Thus, whilst the interests and the tastes of the members of a democratic community divert them from war, their habits of mind fit them for carrying on war well; they soon make good soldiers, when they are roused from their business and their enjoyments. If peace is peculiarly hurtful to democratic armies, war secures to them advantages which no other armies ever possess; and these advantages, however little felt at first, cannot fail in the end to give them the victory. An aristocratic nation, which in a contest with a democratic people does not succeed in ruining the latter at the outset of the war, always runs a great risk of being conquered by it.

Chapter XXV: Of Discipline In Democratic Armies

It is a very general opinion, especially in aristocratic countries, that the great social equality which prevails in democracies ultimately renders the private soldier independent of the officer, and thus destroys the bond of discipline. This is a mistake, for there are two kinds of discipline, which it is important not to confound. When the officer is noble and the soldier a serf—one rich, the other poor—the former educated and strong, the latter ignorant and weak—the strictest bond of obedience may easily be established between the two men. The soldier is broken in to military discipline, as it were, before he enters the army; or rather, military discipline is nothing but an enhancement of social servitude. In aristocratic armies the soldier will soon become insensible to everything but the orders of his superior officers; he acts without reflection, triumphs without enthusiasm, and dies without complaint: in this state he is no longer a man, but he is still a most formidable animal trained for war.

A democratic people must despair of ever obtaining from soldiers that blind, minute, submissive, and invariable obedience which an aristocratic people may impose on them without difficulty. The

同样的精神带到战场，为了能在瞬间取得胜利，宁愿冒生命的危险。没有哪种伟大能够比战场上的伟大更能满足民主国家人民想象中的伟大，一种只要甘冒生命危险而无须艰苦劳动便可大放异彩一下子得到的伟大。因此，当民主国家人民的利益和爱好驱使他们远离战争时，他们的思想习惯却能让他们把仗打得有声有色。当他们从自己的事业和享受中苏醒过来后，很快就会成为好士兵。如果说和平对民主国家的军队特别有害，那么，战争则可保证其得到其他任何军队所没有得到过的好处。尽管这些好处起初不易察觉，但最终必然会给他们带来胜利。一个贵族制国家在与一个民主国家交战的时候，如果不能在最初阶段成功击垮对方，那么被对方征服的危险将大大增加。

第二十五章　民主国家军队的纪律

一个非常普遍的观点，特别是在贵族制国家非常普遍的观点认为，民主国家盛行的广泛的社会平等，最终会让士兵不听军官的指挥，从而破坏纪律的约束。这样的看法并不正确。因为实际上存在两种纪律，切不可混淆。当军官是贵族，士兵是农奴时，一个富一个穷，前者聪明能干后者愚昧无能，所以两者之间很容易确立最严格的服从关系。可以说，士兵在入伍之前就已服从军队纪律，或者不如说，军队的纪律不过是社会奴役的放大。在贵族制国家的军队，士兵很快会变得除了长官的命令以外对什么事都麻木不仁。他们只行动不思考，不会因为胜利而兴奋，战死也毫无怨言。在这种状态下，他不再是一个人，而成为一个被训练去打仗的可怕动物。

对于民主国家而言，永远不要指望能够从士兵那里得到贵族制国家可以轻易加诸其士

state of society does not prepare them for it, and the nation might be in danger of losing its natural advantages if it sought artificially to acquire advantages of this particular kind. Amongst democratic communities, military discipline ought not to attempt to annihilate the free spring of the faculties; all that can be done by discipline is to direct it; the obedience thus inculcated is less exact, but it is more eager and more intelligent. It has its root in the will of him who obeys: it rests not only on his instinct, but on his reason; and consequently it will often spontaneously become more strict as danger requires it. The discipline of an aristocratic army is apt to be relaxed in war, because that discipline is founded upon habits, and war disturbs those habits. The discipline of a democratic army on the contrary is strengthened in sight of the enemy, because every soldier then clearly perceives that he must be silent and obedient in order to conquer.

The nations which have performed the greatest warlike achievements knew no other discipline than that which I speak of. Amongst the ancients none were admitted into the armies but freemen and citizens, who differed but little from one another, and were accustomed to treat each other as equals. In this respect it may be said that the armies of antiquity were democratic, although they came out of the bosom of aristocracy; the consequence was that in those armies a sort of fraternal familiarity prevailed between the officers and the men. Plutarch's lives of great commanders furnish convincing instances of the fact: the soldiers were in the constant habit of freely addressing their general, and the general listened to and answered whatever the soldiers had to say: they were kept in order by language and by example, far more than by constraint or punishment; the general was as much their companion as their chief. I know not whether the soldiers of Greece and Rome ever carried the minutiae of military discipline to the same degree of perfection as the Russians have done; but this did not prevent Alexander from conquering Asia—and Rome, the world.

Chapter XXVI: Some Considerations On War In Democratic Communities

When the principle of equality is in growth, not only amongst a single nation, but amongst several

兵身上的那种盲目的、分毫不差的、唯唯诺诺的、始终如一的服从。因为社会情况不会让士兵如此，而如果民主国家要想人为地获得这种优势，必然要冒失去其固有优势的危险。在民主社会，军队纪律不应当试图消灭人们的自由精神，而所要做的则是利用纪律对其进行引导，因此，军队纪律规定的服从并不十分周密，但很粗放和简明。这种服从以服从者的意志为基础，它不仅基于人的本能，而且还基于他的理智。因此，当危险使服从成为必要的时候，服从者往往会自愿严格服从。贵族制国家军队的纪律在战争中往往容易松弛，因为这种纪律基于习惯，而战争则会打乱这些习惯。相反，民主国家军队的纪律会在大敌当前的时候更加巩固，因为每个士兵都清楚地意识到，为了取胜他必须默默服从。

那些依靠战争来实现宏伟事业的国家，只知道我所讲的纪律。在古代的国家中，军队只征召自由人和公民入伍，这些人彼此之间没有大的差别，习惯于平等地对待彼此。就这一点来看，可以说古代国家的军队是民主的，尽管其成员都来自贵族内部。结果，在这些军队中，官兵之间普遍情同手足。读完普卢塔克的《名人传》，你就会对此深信不疑。士兵们常常与将军们畅所欲言；将军们也愿意倾听士兵们的意见，而且有问必答。将军们通过谈话和示范来领导士兵，远比利用约束和惩罚要好得多。可以说将军既是士兵的伙伴，又是士兵的长官。我不知道古希腊和古罗马的士兵是否也曾像如今的俄国人一样一丝不苟地遵守军纪，但这并没有妨碍亚历山大征服亚洲，罗马征服世界。

第二十六章　对民主社会战争的思考

当平等的原则不仅在一个国家发展，而是像现在的欧洲一样在邻近的几个国家同时发

neighboring nations at the same time, as is now the case in Europe, the inhabitants of these different countries, notwithstanding the dissimilarity of language, of customs, and of laws, nevertheless resemble each other in their equal dread of war and their common love of peace. It is in vain that ambition or anger puts arms in the hands of princes; they are appeased in spite of themselves by a species of general apathy and goodwill, which makes the sword drop from their grasp, and wars become more rare. As the spread of equality, taking place in several countries at once, simultaneously impels their various inhabitants to follow manufactures and commerce, not only do their tastes grow alike, but their interests are so mixed and entangled with one another that no nation can inflict evils on other nations without those evils falling back upon itself; and all nations ultimately regard war as a calamity, almost as severe to the conqueror as to the conquered. Thus, on the one hand, it is extremely difficult in democratic ages to draw nations into hostilities; but on the other hand, it is almost impossible that any two of them should go to war without embroiling the rest. The interests of all are so interlaced, their opinions and their wants so much alike, that none can remain quiet when the others stir. Wars therefore become more rare, but when they break out they spread over a larger field. Neighboring democratic nations not only become alike in some respects, but they eventually grow to resemble each other in almost all. This similitude of nations has consequences of great importance in relation to war.

If I inquire why it is that the Helvetic Confederacy made the greatest and most powerful nations of Europe tremble in the fifteenth century, whilst at the present day the power of that country is exactly proportioned to its population, I perceive that the Swiss are become like all the surrounding communities, and those surrounding communities like the Swiss: so that as numerical strength now forms the only difference between them, victory necessarily attends the largest army. Thus one of the consequences of the democratic revolution which is going on in Europe is to make numerical strength preponderate on all fields of battle, and to constrain all small nations to incorporate themselves with large States, or at least to adopt the policy of the latter. As numbers are the determining cause of victory, each people ought of course to strive by all the means in its power to bring the greatest

展时，这些不同国家的居民，尽管有着语言、习惯和法制的不同，却都同样地惧怕战争和爱好和平。野心和愤怒让君主们拿起武器，而人民普遍持有的那种漠不关心和袖手旁观的态度，又使他们做出让步，丢下手中的宝剑，于是，战争越来越少。随着平等在几个国家同时传播，各国的居民一起涌向工商业，不仅他们的爱好日趋一致，而且他们的利益也彼此交融，以至于任何国家加诸他国的危害都必然会回到自己身上。最终，所有国家无论是征服者还是被征服者都视战争为灾难。因此，一方面，在民主时代难以将各国拖入战争；而另一方面，几乎不可能只有两个国家交战而不牵涉其他国家。各国之间的利益互相交织，它们的观念和需要也非常相似，以至于其他国家坐立不安的时候，没有任何一个国家能平心静气。因此，战争越来越少，但战争一旦爆发，战场必然会越来越扩大。邻近的民主国家，不仅会在我所说的某些方面变得相似，而且最终会在各个方面越来越像。这种国家间的相似性会对战争产生重大影响。

如果我去探究为什么15世纪的瑞士联邦曾让欧洲一些最伟大最强大的国家发抖，而如今瑞士的国力则完全与其人口数成正比，我会发现瑞士人已变得同邻国的人们一样，而邻国的人们也变得同瑞士人一样，所以现在他们之间的差别只是人口的多寡，而胜利必然属于兵多将广的国家。因此，依然在欧洲进行的民主革命的后果之一就是，人们重视战场上的兵力优势，迫使所有小国与大国合并，或至少采取大国的政策。因为兵力是胜负的决定性因素，所以每个国家都想尽一切办法尽可能多地往战场派兵。在部队里可以招募到像瑞士的步兵和16世纪法国的骑兵那样比其他兵种都要优越的精锐兵种时，人们认为没有必要招募大

possible number of men into the field. When it was possible to enlist a kind of troops superior to all others, such as the Swiss infantry or the French horse of the sixteenth century, it was not thought necessary to raise very large armies; but the case is altered when one soldier is as efficient as another.

The same cause which begets this new want also supplies means of satisfying it; for, as I have already observed, when men are all alike, they are all weak, and the supreme power of the State is naturally much stronger amongst democratic nations than elsewhere. Hence, whilst these nations are desirous of enrolling the whole male population in the ranks of the army, they have the power of effecting this object: the consequence is, that in democratic ages armies seem to grow larger in proportion as the love of war declines. In the same ages, too, the manner of carrying on war is likewise altered by the same causes. Machiavelli observes in "The Prince," "that it is much more difficult to subdue a people which has a prince and his barons for its leaders, than a nation which is commanded by a prince and his slaves." To avoid offence, let us read public functionaries for slaves, and this important truth will be strictly applicable to our own time.

A great aristocratic people cannot either conquer its neighbors, or be conquered by them, without great difficulty. It cannot conquer them, because all its forces can never be collected and held together for a considerable period: it cannot be conquered, because an enemy meets at every step small centres of resistance by which invasion is arrested. War against an aristocracy may be compared to war in a mountainous country; the defeated party has constant opportunities of rallying its forces to make a stand in a new position. Exactly the reverse occurs amongst democratic nations: they easily bring their whole disposable force into the field, and when the nation is wealthy and populous it soon becomes victorious; but if ever it is conquered, and its territory invaded, it has few resources at command; and if the enemy takes the capital, the nation is lost. This may very well be explained: as each member of the community is individually isolated and extremely powerless, no one of the whole body can either defend himself or present a rallying point to others. Nothing is strong in a democratic country except the State; as the military strength of the State is destroyed by the destruction of the army, and its civil power paralyzed by the capture of the chief city, all that remains

量的兵员；但是，当一个士兵与另一个士兵的战斗力相差无几时，情况就会发生改变。

导致新需要出现的原因，也同样提供了满足新需要的方法。正如我已经指出的那样，当所有人彼此相似，所有人也同样软弱，所以国家的力量在民主国家自然大大强于其他国家。因此，当这种国家想要召集全体男性公民入伍时，也有能力办到。结果，在民主时代，随着人们尚武精神的减弱，军队的规模却在不断扩大。在这样的时代，作战的方法也由于同样的原因而发生改变。马基雅维里在其《君主论》里说道："征服以一个君主及其诸侯为首领的国家，要比征服由一个君主及其奴隶治理的国家困难得多。"为了避免冒犯他人，我们不妨将"奴隶"改为"公仆"。这样，这一重要的真理就会完全适用于我们这个时代。

一个伟大的贵族国家，无论是征服邻国还是被其征服，都极为困难。它之所以难以征服邻国，是因为它无法长期集结全国的力量；而它之所以难以被邻国征服，则是因为敌人每前进一步都会遭到小防御据点的抵抗，从而阻碍它的前进。在贵族制国家作战犹如在山地国家作战，战败者随时有机会在新的阵地集结力量。而在民主国家，情况则完全相反。民主国家可以轻而易举地把所有可用的兵力投入战场，而如果国家富强人口众多，则不久就会取得胜利。然而，它一旦遭到侵略，敌人深入其国土，则可以调动的资源就会非常有限。而如果敌人占领了它的首都，国家也就随之灭亡。这很容易解释，因为民主国家的个人彼此孤立，非常软弱，既无力自卫，更无法支援他人。在民主国家，力量最强大的就是国家。当国家的军事力量一旦因为被击溃而消失，行政力量也因首都被攻占而瘫痪时，所剩下的只有一群既无组织又无力量的群众，他们无法抵御有组织的力量的入侵。我注意

is only a multitude without strength or government, unable to resist the organized power by which it is assailed. I am aware that this danger may be lessened by the creation of provincial liberties, and consequently of provincial powers, but this remedy will always be insufficient. For after such a catastrophe, not only is the population unable to carry on hostilities, but it may be apprehended that they will not be inclined to attempt it. In accordance with the law of nations adopted in civilized countries, the object of wars is not to seize the property of private individuals, but simply to get possession of political power. The destruction of private property is only occasionally resorted to for the purpose of attaining the latter object. When an aristocratic country is invaded after the defeat of its army, the nobles, although they are at the same time the wealthiest members of the community, will continue to defend themselves individually rather than submit; for if the conqueror remained master of the country, he would deprive them of their political power, to which they cling even more closely than to their property. They therefore prefer fighting to subjection, which is to them the greatest of all misfortunes; and they readily carry the people along with them because the people has long been used to follow and obey them, and besides has but little to risk in the war. Amongst a nation in which equality of conditions prevails, each citizen, on the contrary, has but slender share of political power, and often has no share at all; on the other hand, all are independent, and all have something to lose; so that they are much less afraid of being conquered, and much more afraid of war, than an aristocratic people. It will always be extremely difficult to decide a democratic population to take up arms, when hostilities have reached its own territory. Hence the necessity of giving to such a people the rights and the political character which may impart to every citizen some of those interests that cause the nobles to act for the public welfare in aristocratic countries.

It should never be forgotten by the princes and other leaders of democratic nations, that nothing but the passion and the habit of freedom can maintain an advantageous contest with the passion and the habit of physical well-being. I can conceive nothing better prepared for subjection, in case of defeat, than a democratic people without free institutions.

Formerly it was customary to take the field with a small body of troops, to fight in small

到，这种危险可以通过创建地方自由，并由此建立地方政权而得以缓和，但这种办法往往并不足够。因为在这样一场大灾之后，不但人民无法再继续作战，而且他们恐怕连想都不敢想。根据文明国家所认可的国际法，战争的目的并非是掠夺私人的财产，而是要夺取政权。破坏私人财产只是为了达到后一个目的才偶尔为之。当贵族制国家在军队战败之后被敌军入侵时，贵族尽管是社会最富有的成员，但宁愿单独继续抵抗而不愿投降。因为如果征服者成为国家的主人，就会剥夺他们所有的政治权力，而他们对政治权力重视程度要甚于财产。因此，他们宁愿继续战斗，而不愿被征服，因为被征服对他们来说是最大的不幸。而且，他们能够随时把人民组织起来，因为人民长期以来已经习惯于追随并服从于他们，而且在战争中自己几乎也没有什么好损失的。相反，在平等盛行的国家，每个公民只享有很少的政治权力，而且往往一点也没有；另一方面，所有人都是独立的，都拥有害怕失去的财产，因此，与贵族制国家的人民不同，他们害怕被征服，但更害怕战争。当战火蔓延到民主国家的土地时，很难判断它的人民是否会拿起武器。因此，有必要赋予这种国家的人民以权利和政治意识，从而使每个公民感到自己也享有某些促使贵族制国家的贵族为公共利益而战的类似利益。

民主国家的君主和其他领袖们应该永远不要忘记，自由的激情和习惯能够最有效地抵制追求物质享受的激情和习惯。我认为，假如战败，再也没有比不以自由制度为基础的民主国家更容易被征服的了。

以前，战场上交战双方投入的兵力都不太多，交战规模也比较小，并进行长期常规的

engagements, and to make long, regular sieges: modern tactics consist in fighting decisive battles, and, as soon as a line of march is open before the army, in rushing upon the capital city, in order to terminate the war at a single blow. Napoleon, it is said, was the inventor of this new system; but the invention of such a system did not depend on any individual man, whoever he might be. The mode in which Napoleon carried on war was suggested to him by the state of society in his time; that mode was successful, because it was eminently adapted to that state of society, and because he was the first to employ it. Napoleon was the first commander who marched at the head of an army from capital to capital, but the road was opened for him by the ruin of feudal society. It may fairly be believed that, if that extraordinary man had been born three hundred years ago, he would not have derived the same results from his method of warfare, or, rather, that he would have had a different method.

I shall add but a few words on civil wars, for fear of exhausting the patience of the reader. Most of the remarks which I have made respecting foreign wars are applicable a fortiori to civil wars. Men living in democracies are not naturally prone to the military character; they sometimes assume it, when they have been dragged by compulsion to the field; but to rise in a body and voluntarily to expose themselves to the horrors of war, and especially of civil war, is a course which the men of democracies are not apt to adopt. None but the most adventurous members of the community consent to run into such risks; the bulk of the population remains motionless. But even if the population were inclined to act, considerable obstacles would stand in their way; for they can resort to no old and well-established influence which they are willing to obey—no well-known leaders to rally the discontented, as well as to discipline and to lead them—no political powers subordinate to the supreme power of the nation, which afford an effectual support to the resistance directed against the government. In democratic countries the moral power of the majority is immense, and the physical resources which it has at its command are out of all proportion to the physical resources which may be combined against it. Therefore the party which occupies the seat of the majority, which speaks in its name and wields its power, triumphs instantaneously and irresistibly over all private resistance; it does not even give such opposition time to exist, but nips it in the bud. Those who in such nations

围攻。而在现代往往采取决定性战役的战术，一开战就是大规模的战斗，直奔敌方的首都，以便一举结束战斗。据说，拿破仑是这套新战术的发明者。这套战术不可能只依靠一个人的力量就能发明，不管他是什么人。拿破仑采用的战术模式是其所处时代的社会情况给他的提示。这种模式很成功，因为它非常适应当时的社会状况，而且因为他首次将这种战术应用于战争。拿破仑是第一个率军长驱直入从一个国家的首都打到另一个国家首都的人。但是，为他敞开的这条道路实际上是封建社会的崩溃。我们可以认为，如果这位杰出的人物出生在300年前，他的战术不会产生同样的效果，或者不如说他可能会采取完全不同的战术。

我想就内战问题再补充几句，但也担心读者会感到不耐烦。就对外战争我所做的论述，大部分也充分有理由适用于内战。生活在民主国家的人，天生不具备尚武精神。当他们被迫上战场的时候，有时候也具有这样的精神。但是，发自内心自愿上战场冒险特别是内战，往往决非民主国家的人想要采取的行动。只有社会最具冒险精神的成员，才肯同意冒这种风险，而民主国家的大部分群众则不会采取任何行动。即使人民愿意行动，仍然有重重阻碍挡在前面，因为他们找不到自己愿意服从的早已确立已久的权威，没有公认的领袖来集结、约束和指挥想要行动起来的人们，也没有国家政权领导下的政治力量去有效地支持政府进行抵抗。在民主国家，多数的道德力量巨大，而多数拥有的物质力量，也是为了抵制它而首先可以联合起来的力量所无法比的。因此，占据多数席位的党派，以多数的名义并利用多数的权力发言，可以毫不费力地瞬间打败所有个别的抵抗。这些党派甚至不给个别抵抗诞生的机会，而将其扼杀在萌芽阶段。因此，在这样的国家，试图通过武力进行革命的人，

seek to effect a revolution by force of arms have no other resource than suddenly to seize upon the whole engine of government as it stands, which can better be done by a single blow than by a war; for as soon as there is a regular war, the party which represents the State is always certain to conquer. The only case in which a civil war could arise is, if the army should divide itself into two factions, the one raising the standard of rebellion, the other remaining true to its allegiance. An army constitutes a small community, very closely united together, endowed with great powers of vitality, and able to supply its own wants for some time. Such a war might be bloody, but it could not be long; for either the rebellious army would gain over the government by the sole display of its resources, or by its first victory, and then the war would be over; or the struggle would take place, and then that portion of the army which should not be supported by the organized powers of the State would speedily either disband itself or be destroyed. It may therefore be admitted as a general truth, that in ages of equality civil wars will become much less frequent and less protracted.

除了出其不意地攻占整个政府机关以外，别无他法。这样的办法远比发动战争要好得多。因为一旦开始常规战争，代表国家的党派几乎总是能够取得胜利。只有军队自身分成两派，一派举起叛旗，而另一派继续效忠政府的时候，才会发生内战。军队本身就是一个小社会，组织严密，具有强大的生命力，而且能在一段时间内自给自足。这样的战争很可能会流血，但不会持续很久，因为叛军通过显示自己的力量，或初战的胜利，就能接管政府，于是战争随之结束；或者因为战争一开始，没有得到政府有组织的力量支持的那一派军队很快自行土崩瓦解或被消灭。因此，可以将平等时代内战将会变得非常稀少和短促视为一个普遍真理。

Book Four: Influence Of Democratic Opinions On Political Society

Chapter I: That Equality Naturally Gives Men A Taste For Free Institutions

I should imperfectly fulfil the purpose of this book, if, after having shown what opinions and sentiments are suggested by the principle of equality, I did not point out, ere I conclude, the general influence which these same opinions and sentiments may exercise upon the government of human societies. To succeed in this object I shall frequently have to retrace my steps; but I trust the reader will not refuse to follow me through paths already known to him, which may lead to some new truth.

The principle of equality, which makes men independent of each other, gives them a habit and a taste for following, in their private actions, no other guide but their own will. This complete independence, which they constantly enjoy towards their equals and in the intercourse of private life, tends to make them look upon all authority with a jealous eye, and speedily suggests to them the notion and the love of political freedom. Men living at such times have a natural bias to free institutions. Take any one of them at a venture, and search if you can his most deep-seated instincts; you will find that of all governments he will soonest conceive and most highly value that government, whose head he has himself elected, and whose administration he may control. Of all the political effects produced by the equality of conditions, this love of independence is the first to strike the observing, and to alarm the timid; nor can it be said that their alarm is wholly misplaced, for

第四篇　民主观念对政治社会的影响

第一章　平等自然让人爱好自由

如果我在阐述由平等而来的思想和情感之后，未能指出这些观念和情感对人类社会政治管理产生哪些普遍影响，那么，我就没能很好地完成著作本书的目的。为了能做到这一点，我需要不断地回顾已经走过的路，但是我相信读者们会继续追随着我一起走过那些已经熟悉的通往新的真理的道路。

让人彼此独立的平等原则，也让人们养成只按个人意志活动的习惯和爱好。他们在与自己平等的人交往的过程中以及作为个人生活习惯而永远享有的这种完全独立，往往令其对所有权威投以嫉妒的目光，并很快激起关于政治自由的思想和对于政治自由的爱好。因此，生活在这样时代的人，对于自由制度有一种天生的热爱。随便找一个人问一问，如果可以的话去探究一下他的内心最深处的本能，便会发现在所有的政府中，他会首先考虑并予以最高评价的政府是经他选举产生首脑而且其行动受他监督的政府。在平等造就的一切政治效果中，对独立的热爱最先引起人们注目，而且会令懦弱的人感到害怕。我们不能说

anarchy has a more formidable aspect in democratic countries than elsewhere. As the citizens have no direct influence on each other, as soon as the supreme power of the nation fails, which kept them all in their several stations, it would seem that disorder must instantly reach its utmost pitch, and that, every man drawing aside in a different direction, the fabric of society must at once crumble away.

I am, however, persuaded that anarchy is not the principal evil which democratic ages have to fear, but the least. For the principle of equality begets two tendencies; the one leads men straight to independence, and may suddenly drive them into anarchy; the other conducts them by a longer, more secret, but more certain road, to servitude. Nations readily discern the former tendency, and are prepared to resist it; they are led away by the latter, without perceiving its drift; hence it is peculiarly important to point it out. For myself, I am so far from urging as a reproach to the principle of equality that it renders men untractable, that this very circumstance principally calls forth my approbation. I admire to see how it deposits in the mind and heart of man the dim conception and instinctive love of political independence, thus preparing the remedy for the evil which it engenders; it is on this very account that I am attached to it.

Chapter II: That The Notions Of Democratic Nations On Government Are Naturally Favorable To The Concentration Of Power

The notion of secondary powers, placed between the sovereign and his subjects, occurred naturally to the imagination of aristocratic nations, because those communities contained individuals or families raised above the common level, and apparently destined to command by their birth, their education, and their wealth. This same notion is naturally wanting in the minds of men in democratic ages, for converse reasons: it can only be introduced artificially, it can only be kept there with difficulty; whereas they conceive, as it were, without thinking upon the subject, the notion of a sole and central power which governs the whole community by its direct influence. Moreover in politics, as well as in philosophy and in religion, the intellect of democratic nations is peculiarly open to simple and general notions. Complicated systems are repugnant to it, and its favorite conception is

他们的恐惧完全错了，因为无政府状态在民主国家比在其他国家有其更为可怕的一面。因为公民之间彼此没有直接影响，所以一旦令所有人各在其位的国家政权不复存在，似乎混乱的状态必然会立刻达到顶峰，每个人各奔东西，社会组织必然即刻崩溃。

但是，我确信无政府状态不是民主时代应主要忧虑的弊端，而是最不需要忧虑的弊端。因为平等会产生两种倾向：一种倾向会直接引导人们独立，并有可能让人们突然陷入无政府状态；另一种倾向则会促使人们沿着一条漫长、隐秘但确实的道路走向奴役。人们很容易看清第一种倾向，并加以抵制；却在不知不觉中被第二种倾向引向歧途。因此，特别需要指出这第二种倾向。至于我，则绝不是想要指责平等如何让人们桀骜不驯，而是主要想要对其造就的状况大加赞美。我很乐于看到平等如何在人们的思想中积淀下政治独立的模糊概念和本能的冲动，并为纠正其所产生的弊端准备好解决之道。正是基于这一点，我才热爱平等。

第二章　民主国家对于政府的观点自然有利于中央集权

在君主和臣民之间存在次级权力的观点，会自然而然出现在贵族制国家人民的头脑之中，因为这些社会中存在高于一般水平的个人和家族，而且其出身、教育和财富显然注定他们要发号施令。由于相反的原因，同样的观念并不天生存在于平等时代人们的思想之中，而只能人为地将这样的观点引入平等时代，并需要克服极大的困难才能使其保留下来。然而，他们无须深思就会产生由政府直接领导全社会的单一的中央权力的观念。此

that of a great nation composed of citizens all resembling the same pattern, and all governed by a single power.

The very next notion to that of a sole and central power, which presents itself to the minds of men in the ages of equality, is the notion of uniformity of legislation. As every man sees that he differs but little from those about him, he cannot understand why a rule which is applicable to one man should not be equally applicable to all others. Hence the slightest privileges are repugnant to his reason; the faintest dissimilarities in the political institutions of the same people offend him, and uniformity of legislation appears to him to be the first condition of good government. I find, on the contrary, that this same notion of a uniform rule, equally binding on all the members of the community, was almost unknown to the human mind in aristocratic ages; it was either never entertained, or it was rejected. These contrary tendencies of opinion ultimately turn on either side to such blind instincts and such ungovernable habits that they still direct the actions of men, in spite of particular exceptions. Notwithstanding the immense variety of conditions in the Middle Ages, a certain number of persons existed at that period in precisely similar circumstances; but this did not prevent the laws then in force from assigning to each of them distinct duties and different rights. On the contrary, at the present time all the powers of government are exerted to impose the same customs and the same laws on populations which have as yet but few points of resemblance. As the conditions of men become equal amongst a people, individuals seem of less importance, and society of greater dimensions; or rather, every citizen, being assimilated to all the rest, is lost in the crowd, and nothing stands conspicuous but the great and imposing image of the people at large. This naturally gives the men of democratic periods a lofty opinion of the privileges of society, and a very humble notion of the rights of individuals; they are ready to admit that the interests of the former are everything, and those of the latter nothing. They are willing to acknowledge that the power which represents the community has far more information and wisdom than any of the members of that community; and that it is the duty, as well as the right, of that power to guide as well as govern each private citizen.

If we closely scrutinize our contemporaries, and penetrate to the root of their political opinions,

外，在政治方面，跟在哲学和宗教方面一样，民主国家人民的头脑特别喜欢接受简单的一般观念。他们不喜欢复杂的制度，并认为一个大国由同一模式的公民组成和由一个权力当局领导最好。

在平等的时代，单一的中央权力观念产生之后，下一个自然而然出现在人们思想中的观念就是统一的立法观念。因为每个人都看到自己与周围的人没有多大差别，所以无法理解为什么适用于一个人的法规不能同样地适用于其他所有人。因此，最微不足道的特权，也会让他们从理性上感到厌恶，同一国家最微小的政治制度上的差异，也会令他们感到不快，在他们看来，立法的统一是好政府的首要条件。与之相反，我发现，在贵族制时代，人们的头脑中从来没有过对全体社会成员同等地实行统一法制的观念，人们对此不是反感就是拒绝。这两种互相对立的思想倾向，最终都变成盲目的本能和无法驾驭的习惯，至今仍在支配人们的行动，尽管有个别例外情况存在。虽然中世纪各国状况存在巨大的差异，但各国有时依然存在一定数量完全相同的人，但这并不能够妨碍各国实行的法律为每个人规定不同的义务和相异的权利。相反，在今天这个时代，所有国家的政府却竭力将同样的习惯和同样的法律推行到并没有多少相同点的全体居民身上。随着一个国家的状况越来越平等，个人似乎越来越渺小，而社会却越来越壮大。或者不如说，变得彼此越来越相似的每个公民消失在群众之中，除了整个民族形象的高大宏伟之外，再也看不到什么闪光点。这自然让民主时代的人们对社会的特权有高尚的看法，而对个人权利则持卑微的观点。他们乐于承认社会的利益重如泰山，而个人的利益则轻如鸿毛。他们也很愿意承认，代表社

we shall detect some of the notions which I have just pointed out, and we shall perhaps be surprised to find so much accordance between men who are so often at variance. The Americans hold, that in every State the supreme power ought to emanate from the people; but when once that power is constituted, they can conceive, as it were, no limits to it, and they are ready to admit that it has the right to do whatever it pleases. They have not the slightest notion of peculiar privileges granted to cities, families, or persons: their minds appear never to have foreseen that it might be possible not to apply with strict uniformity the same laws to every part, and to all the inhabitants. These same opinions are more and more diffused in Europe; they even insinuate themselves amongst those nations which most vehemently reject the principle of the sovereignty of the people. Such nations assign a different origin to the supreme power, but they ascribe to that power the same characteristics. Amongst them all, the idea of intermediate powers is weakened and obliterated: the idea of rights inherent in certain individuals is rapidly disappearing from the minds of men; the idea of the omnipotence and sole authority of society at large rises to fill its place. These ideas take root and spread in proportion as social conditions become more equal, and men more alike; they are engendered by equality, and in turn they hasten the progress of equality.

In France, where the revolution of which I am speaking has gone further than in any other European country, these opinions have got complete hold of the public mind. If we listen attentively to the language of the various parties in France, we shall find that there is not one which has not adopted them. Most of these parties censure the conduct of the government, but they all hold that the government ought perpetually to act and interfere in everything that is done. Even those which are most at variance are nevertheless agreed upon this head. The unity, the ubiquity, the omnipotence of the supreme power, and the uniformity of its rules, constitute the principal characteristics of all the political systems which have been put forward in our age. They recur even in the wildest visions of political regeneration: the human mind pursues them in its dreams. If these notions spontaneously arise in the minds of private individuals, they suggest themselves still more forcibly to the minds of princes. Whilst the ancient fabric of European society is altered and dissolved, sovereigns acquire

会的力量比任何一个社会成员都更加有知识和有智慧，所以它有义务有权利引导并统治每个公民。

如果我们仔细研究一下我们同时代的人，并探寻他们政治见解的根源，就会察觉到我刚刚所谈到的某些观念，并可能会惊奇地发现如此不同的人们之间竟是如此的一致。美国人认为，在每个州里，最高权力都应当来自人民，但是当这一权力一旦形成，人们便会意识到它是无限的，并心甘情愿认可它有权去做想做的一切。人们完全没有要赋予城市、家庭或个人特权的观念。他们的头脑从未想到过有可能不严格地将同样的法律运用到各个地方和全体居民。但是，这样的观念在欧洲正在逐渐蔓延开来，甚至渗透到最激烈反对人民主权学说的国家之中。这些国家的最高权力的来源与美国不同，但对权力特点的看法却与美国的一样。在所有这些国家中，中间权力的观念被模糊和弱化。特定个人固有的权利思想正迅速从人们的脑海里消失，取而代之的是无限唯一的社会权威的思想。随着社会状况越来越平等，人们越来越相似，这些思想逐渐生根并蔓延。他们由平等而生，又反过来加速平等的发展。

在法国，我所讲的革命比欧洲其他任何国家都走得更远，所以这些观念已经完全深入人心。如果我们仔细聆听法国不同政党的主张，会发现没有任何一个政党不接受它们。大部分政党都指责政府工作不利，但所有政党却都认为政府应当继续工作下去并参与所有进行中的活动。甚至那些激烈反对政府的人对此也频频点头表示认可。最高权力的一致性、普遍性和全能性，以及制度的统一性，是我们这个时代所有政治制度的主要特征，甚至在

new conceptions of their opportunities and their duties; they learn for the first time that the central power which they represent may and ought to administer by its own agency, and on a uniform plan, all the concerns of the whole community. This opinion, which, I will venture to say, was never conceived before our time by the monarchs of Europe, now sinks deeply into the minds of kings, and abides there amidst all the agitation of more unsettled thoughts.

Our contemporaries are therefore much less divided than is commonly supposed; they are constantly disputing as to the hands in which supremacy is to be vested, but they readily agree upon the duties and the rights of that supremacy. The notion they all form of government is that of a sole, simple, providential, and creative power. All secondary opinions in politics are unsettled; this one remains fixed, invariable, and consistent. It is adopted by statesmen and political philosophers; it is eagerly laid hold of by the multitude; those who govern and those who are governed agree to pursue it with equal ardor: it is the foremost notion of their minds, it seems inborn. It originates therefore in no caprice of the human intellect, but it is a necessary condition of the present state of mankind.

Chapter III: That The Sentiments Of Democratic Nations Accord With Their Opinions In Leading Them To Concentrate Political Power

If it be true that, in ages of equality, men readily adopt the notion of a great central power, it cannot be doubted on the other hand that their habits and sentiments predispose them to recognize such a power and to give it their support. This may be demonstrated in a few words, as the greater part of the reasons, to which the fact may be attributed, have been previously stated. As the men who inhabit democratic countries have no superiors, no inferiors, and no habitual or necessary partners in their undertakings, they readily fall back upon themselves and consider themselves as beings apart. I had occasion to point this out at considerable length in treating of individualism. Hence such men can never, without an effort, tear themselves from their private affairs to engage in public business; their natural bias leads them to abandon the latter to the sole visible and permanent representative of the interests of the community, that is to say, to the State. Not only are they naturally wanting in

各种千奇百怪的政治思想之中也能看到，人在做梦的时候都在追求这些东西。如果这些观念会自发地出现在个人的头脑之中，那么，它必然更容易出现在君主们的思想之中。在欧洲社会古老的组织正在改变和消失的同时，君主们对自己的机遇和责任也有了新的概念。他们第一次知道，他们所代表的中央权力可以并应当按照统一的计划亲自管理所有国家事务和所有的人。我敢说这种观念是我们这个时代以前的欧洲君主们从来没有想到过的，而现在却深深印在君主的脑海，在各种变化无常的观念之中坚如磐石。

因此，我们同时代的人，并非想象的那样有很大的意见分歧。尽管他们不断地争论主权应当归谁所有，但他们已就主权的责任和权利达成一致。所有的人都认为政府应该是一种独一无二、奉天承运和具有创造力的权力。政治上的所有次级观念都变化无常，唯有此观念是固定的、不变的、始终如一的。它为政治家和政治哲学家所接受，为群众所热烈拥护。统治者和被统治者都同样地热烈追求它。它是才出现在人们思想中的观念，却好像由来已久。因此，它不是人类智慧任意的产物，而是人类目前思想情况的必然要求。

第三章　民主国家人民的感情和思想一致引导他们走向中央集权

如果在平等时代人们的确容易接受建立强大中央政权的思想，那么，另一方面就不应当怀疑，他们的习惯和感情已经让他们提前具备认可这一权力并给予其支持的倾向。现在只用几句话来进行说明，因为造成这一现象的大部分理由已在前面做过陈述。因为生活在民主国家的人没有高低贵贱之分，而且也没有长久的不可缺少的伙伴，所以他们会随时

a taste for public business, but they have frequently no time to attend to it. Private life is so busy in democratic periods, so excited, so full of wishes and of work, that hardly any energy or leisure remains to each individual for public life. I am the last man to contend that these propensities are unconquerable, since my chief object in writing this book has been to combat them. I only maintain that at the present day a secret power is fostering them in the human heart, and that if they are not checked they will wholly overgrow it.

I have also had occasion to show how the increasing love of well-being, and the fluctuating character of property, cause democratic nations to dread all violent disturbance. The love of public tranquillity is frequently the only passion which these nations retain, and it becomes more active and powerful amongst them in proportion as all other passions droop and die. This naturally disposes the members of the community constantly to give or to surrender additional rights to the central power, which alone seems to be interested in defending them by the same means that it uses to defend itself. As in ages of equality no man is compelled to lend his assistance to his fellow-men, and none has any right to expect much support from them, everyone is at once independent and powerless. These two conditions, which must never be either separately considered or confounded together, inspire the citizen of a democratic country with very contrary propensities. His independence fills him with self-reliance and pride amongst his equals; his debility makes him feel from time to time the want of some outward assistance, which he cannot expect from any of them, because they are all impotent and unsympathizing. In this predicament he naturally turns his eyes to that imposing power which alone rises above the level of universal depression. Of that power his wants and especially his desires continually remind him, until he ultimately views it as the sole and necessary support of his own weakness. This may more completely explain what frequently takes place in democratic countries, where the very men who are so impatient of superiors patiently submit to a master, exhibiting at once their pride and their servility.

The hatred which men bear to privilege increases in proportion as privileges become more scarce

自我反省，并进行独立思考。在讨论个人主义时我曾非常详细地谈过这一点。因此，把这些人的注意力从个人的事业转移到公共事务不可能轻而易举。他们的自然倾向促使他们将公共事务交给唯一可见的永久存在的公共利益的代表去管理，也就是说是国家。他们不但天生对公共事务不感兴趣，而且往往没有时间去管理。在民主时代，个人生活非常忙碌活跃，满是欲望和工作，以至于每个人几乎没有任何精力和闲暇留给公共生活。我绝不认为这些倾向不可克服，因为我写此书的主要目的就是与它们进行斗争。我只认为，在今天这个时代，有一种隐秘的力量在人们心中培养这些倾向，如果不加以抑制，必然会占据人心。

我也曾指出，对幸福与日俱增的热爱和财富不动产化的特点使得民主国家的人民惧怕一些暴动。爱好社会安宁之心往往是民主国家人民留下的唯一政治激情，并随其他激情的萎缩和消失而越发活跃和强大。这自然会促使社会成员不断向中央政权给予或出让一些额外的权利，并认为似乎只有中央政权才有兴趣采用捍卫它自己的办法来捍卫他们。因为，在平等时代，没人有援助他人的义务，也没人有权利要求他人的支援，所以每个人既独立又软弱。这两种既不能分开而论又不能混为一谈的情况，使民主国家的公民具有了十分矛盾的性格。他们的独立，让他们自力更生并在与自己平等的人们往来时充满自豪感；而他们的软弱，又让他们时不时地感到需要他人的支援，然而他们又不能对此有所指望，因为大家都同样软弱和冷漠。在这样的困境中，他们自然会将视线转向那个在这种普遍感到无能为力的情况下唯一能够超然屹立的伟大力量。他们的需要，特别是他们的欲望，不断提醒他们这个伟大力量，最终他们将其视为自身弱点的唯一和必要的依靠。这可以更为充分地解释在民主国家不断发生的现象，无法忍受有人高人一等的人们却能耐心忍受长官的支

and less considerable, so that democratic passions would seem to burn most fiercely at the very time when they have least fuel. I have already given the reason of this phenomenon. When all conditions are unequal, no inequality is so great as to offend the eye; whereas the slightest dissimilarity is odious in the midst of general uniformity: the more complete is this uniformity, the more insupportable does the sight of such a difference become. Hence it is natural that the love of equality should constantly increase together with equality itself, and that it should grow by what it feeds upon. This never-dying, ever-kindling hatred, which sets a democratic people against the smallest privileges, is peculiarly favorable to the gradual concentration of all political rights in the hands of the representative of the State alone. The sovereign, being necessarily and incontestably above all the citizens, excites not their envy, and each of them thinks that he strips his equals of the prerogative which he concedes to the crown. The man of a democratic age is extremely reluctant to obey his neighbor who is his equal; he refuses to acknowledge in such a person ability superior to his own; he mistrusts his justice, and is jealous of his power; he fears and he contemns him; and he loves continually to remind him of the common dependence in which both of them stand to the same master. Every central power which follows its natural tendencies courts and encourages the principle of equality; for equality singularly facilitates, extends, and secures the influence of a central power.

In like manner it may be said that every central government worships uniformity: uniformity relieves it from inquiry into an infinite number of small details which must be attended to if rules were to be adapted to men, instead of indiscriminately subjecting men to rules: thus the government likes what the citizens like, and naturally hates what they hate. These common sentiments, which, in democratic nations, constantly unite the sovereign and every member of the community in one and the same conviction, establish a secret and lasting sympathy between them. The faults of the government are pardoned for the sake of its tastes; public confidence is only reluctantly withdrawn in the midst even of its excesses and its errors, and it is restored at the first call. Democratic nations often hate those in whose hands the central power is vested; but they always love that power itself.

使，在表现出傲慢的同时又表现得很屈从。

　　随着特权的减少和缩小，人们对特权的憎恶愈加强烈，以至于民主的激情似乎在燃料最少的时候反而燃烧得最为热烈。前面我已经对这种现象产生的原因做过说明。当社会状况极不平等的时候，最大的不平等也不刺眼；而在普遍统一的时候，最微小的差异也会引起不快。这种一致性越是完全，一点点的不同便更加让人难以忍受。因此，对平等的热爱会随着平等本身的发展而同步增强，而当这种热爱得到满足后又会促进平等的发展，这是自然而然的事情。促使民主国家人民反对任何特权的这种永存的始终炙热的憎恶，特别有利于一切政治权力逐步集中到国家的唯一代表手里。地位必然无可争议地高于所有公民的国家元首，并不会引起人们的嫉妒，因为每个人都认为与他平等的人可以取消他们从国家元首那里取得的任何特权。民主时代的人非常不愿服从与自己平等的邻人的指点，拒绝承认其能力在自己之上，不相信他的正直，嫉妒他的权力，既害怕又瞧不起邻人，并喜欢不断提醒他们双方都属于同一个主人管辖。顺应其天性的每个中央权力，都喜欢和鼓励平等，因为平等特别便于扩大和巩固中央权力的影响力。

　　可以说每个中央政府都崇拜一致性，因为一致性可以使政府不必制定无数的细则，而如果不对所有的人规定同一制度，而对不同人采用不同的制度，则必须对其进行详细规定。因此，政府爱公民之所爱，并自然恨公民之所恨。民主国家的这种共同的感情，不断将每个公民和国家元首团结在同一信念之下，并在他们之间建立起隐秘而永久的同情。因为有着相同的爱好，政府的缺点会得到谅解，甚至只有当政府做得太过分或犯了错误时，公民才不情不愿地不再信任政府；而且只要政府一声令下，人们又会马上恢复对它的信

Thus, by two separate paths, I have reached the same conclusion. I have shown that the principle of equality suggests to men the notion of a sole, uniform, and strong government: I have now shown that the principle of equality imparts to them a taste for it. To governments of this kind the nations of our age are therefore tending. They are drawn thither by the natural inclination of mind and heart; and in order to reach that result, it is enough that they do not check themselves in their course. I am of opinion, that, in the democratic ages which are opening upon us, individual independence and local liberties will ever be the produce of artificial contrivance; that centralization will be the natural form of government.

Chapter IV: Of Certain Peculiar And Accidental Causes Which Either Lead A People To Complete Centralization Of Government, Or Which Divert Them From It

If all democratic nations are instinctively led to the centralization of government, they tend to this result in an unequal manner. This depends on the particular circumstances which may promote or prevent the natural consequences of that state of society—circumstances which are exceedingly numerous; but I shall only advert to a few of them. Amongst men who have lived free long before they became equal, the tendencies derived from free institutions combat, to a certain extent, the propensities superinduced by the principle of equality; and although the central power may increase its privileges amongst such a people, the private members of such a community will never entirely forfeit their independence. But when the equality of conditions grows up amongst a people which has never known, or has long ceased to know, what freedom is (and such is the case upon the Continent of Europe), as the former habits of the nation are suddenly combined, by some sort of natural attraction, with the novel habits and principles engendered by the state of society, all powers seem spontaneously to rush to the centre. These powers accumulate there with astonishing rapidity, and the State instantly attains the utmost limits of its strength, whilst private persons allow themselves to sink as suddenly to the lowest degree of weakness.

The English who emigrated three hundred years ago to found a democratic commonwealth on the shores of the New World, had all learned to take a part in public affairs in their mother-country; they

任。民主国家的人民虽然往往憎恨那些手握中央政权的人，但他们对于这个政权本身始终非常爱护。

因此，通过两条不同的道路，我得出同一结论。我曾指出，平等使人产生单一、一致和强大政府的思想，现在我又指出，平等使人们热爱这样的政府，因此，这样的政府是我们这个时代的发展趋势，人们在其思想和感情自然倾向的驱使下向这个方面迈进。只要不加阻止，人们就可以抵达目的地。我认为，在展现于我们面前的民主时代，个人独立和地方自由始终是人为的产物，而中央集权则是政府的自然趋势。

第四章　导致民主国家走上中央集权或避免中央集权的几个特殊和偶然因素

如果所有民主国家都本能地建立中央集权政府，那么它们也往往会采取不同的方式。这取决于该国促进或阻碍社会情况自然发展的特殊状况。这种特殊状况举不胜举，我只想略述一二。在平等之前长期生活于自由之中的人们那里，源于自由制度的趋势在一定程度上会与平等造成的倾向发生冲突。尽管中央政权可以在这样的国家增加自己的特权，但社会中的个人永远也不会放弃自己的独立。但是，当平等在一个从来不知道或长期以来不知道自由为何物的国家（比如在欧洲大陆）发展起来的时候，由于某种自然吸引力的作用，民族古老的习惯突然与社会情况造成的新习惯和新原则结合起来，导致所有的权力似乎自发地向中央集中。这些权力以惊人的速度集聚到中央，国家立刻达到其强大的极限，而个人则被突然之间推到弱小的极限。

were conversant with trial by jury; they were accustomed to liberty of speech and of the press—to personal freedom, to the notion of rights and the practice of asserting them. They carried with them to America these free institutions and manly customs, and these institutions preserved them against the encroachments of the State. Thus amongst the Americans it is freedom which is old—equality is of comparatively modern date. The reverse is occurring in Europe, where equality, introduced by absolute power and under the rule of kings, was already infused into the habits of nations long before freedom had entered into their conceptions.

I have said that amongst democratic nations the notion of government naturally presents itself to the mind under the form of a sole and central power, and that the notion of intermediate powers is not familiar to them. This is peculiarly applicable to the democratic nations which have witnessed the triumph of the principle of equality by means of a violent revolution. As the classes which managed local affairs have been suddenly swept away by the storm, and as the confused mass which remains has as yet neither the organization nor the habits which fit it to assume the administration of these same affairs, the State alone seems capable of taking upon itself all the details of government, and centralization becomes, as it were, the unavoidable state of the country. Napoleon deserves neither praise nor censure for having centred in his own hands almost all the administrative power of France; for, after the abrupt disappearance of the nobility and the higher rank of the middle classes, these powers devolved on him of course: it would have been almost as difficult for him to reject as to assume them. But no necessity of this kind has ever been felt by the Americans, who, having passed through no revolution, and having governed themselves from the first, never had to call upon the State to act for a time as their guardian. Thus the progress of centralization amongst a democratic people depends not only on the progress of equality, but on the manner in which this equality has been established.

At the commencement of a great democratic revolution, when hostilities have but just broken out between the different classes of society, the people endeavors to centralize the public administration in the hands of the government, in order to wrest the management of local affairs from the aristocracy. Towards the close of such a revolution, on the contrary, it is usually the conquered

二百年前登上新大陆海岸建立民主共和国的英国人，都已在母国养成参与公共事务的习惯。他们熟悉陪审制度，习惯言论出版自由，以及人身自由，并具有权利观念和行使权利的经验。他们把这些自由制度和刚毅的民情带到美洲，并利用这些制度让自己免遭政府的侵犯。因此，在美国人那里，自由是古老的，而平等则是相对现代的。欧洲的情况则刚好相反。在欧洲，由专制王权引入的并在国王统治下的平等，早已在自由进入人们思想之前很久，便已渗透到人民的习惯。

我已经说过，在民主国家，人们认为政府是统一的中央政权的当然代表，而对于中间权力则一无所知。这特别适用于通过暴力革命确立平等原则胜利的民主国家。因为管理地方事务的阶级突然之间被革命的风暴一扫而光，而被留下的混乱的群众既无组织，也没有适用于管理这些事务的习惯，所以似乎只有国家才能担负起处理所有政府事务的重任，于是，中央集权便成为必然的事实。对于将法国几乎所有行政大权揽于手中的拿破仑既不值得赞扬，也不必斥责，因为在贵族和大资产阶级突然消失之后，这些权力便当然落到他的手里。对他而言，当时无论是拒绝这些权力还是接受这些权力，都几乎同样困难。美国人就从来没有感受过这种必要性，因为他们没有经历过革命，一开始就自己治理自己，从不需要国家做自己的临时监护人。因此，中央集权在民主国家的发展，不仅有赖于平等的进步，而且有赖于平等确立的方式。

在一场伟大的民主革命开始之初，当不同的阶级之间刚刚展开斗争的时候，人民努力把公共行政权力集中到中央政府手中，以便于从贵族手中夺取地方事务的管理权。相反，

aristocracy that endeavors to make over the management of all affairs to the State, because such an aristocracy dreads the tyranny of a people which has become its equal, and not unfrequently its master. Thus it is not always the same class of the community which strives to increase the prerogative of the government; but as long as the democratic revolution lasts there is always one class in the nation, powerful in numbers or in wealth, which is induced, by peculiar passions or interests, to centralize the public administration, independently of that hatred of being governed by one's neighbor, which is a general and permanent feeling amongst democratic nations. It may be remarked, that at the present day the lower orders in England are striving with all their might to destroy local independence, and to transfer the administration from all points of the circumference to the centre; whereas the higher classes are endeavoring to retain this administration within its ancient boundaries. I venture to predict that a time will come when the very reverse will happen.

These observations explain why the supreme power is always stronger, and private individuals weaker, amongst a democratic people which has passed through a long and arduous struggle to reach a state of equality than amongst a democratic community in which the citizens have been equal from the first. The example of the Americans completely demonstrates the fact. The inhabitants of the United States were never divided by any privileges; they have never known the mutual relation of master and inferior, and as they neither dread nor hate each other, they have never known the necessity of calling in the supreme power to manage their affairs. The lot of the Americans is singular: they have derived from the aristocracy of England the notion of private rights and the taste for local freedom; and they have been able to retain both the one and the other, because they have had no aristocracy to combat.

If at all times education enables men to defend their independence, this is most especially true in democratic ages. When all men are alike, it is easy to found a sole and all-powerful government, by the aid of mere instinct. But men require much intelligence, knowledge, and art to organize and to maintain secondary powers under similar circumstances, and to create amidst the independence and individual weakness of the citizens such free associations as may be in a condition to struggle against tyranny without destroying public order.

在革命接近尾声的时候，失败的贵族往往试图将所有事务的管理权交给国家，因为贵族害怕已变得与自己平等而且往往成为自己主人的人民实行暴政。因此，并不总是社会同一阶级力求加强政府的特权，但只要民主革命继续下去，国家之中总会出现一个在人数或财富上强大的阶级，它在不同于民主国家普遍永久存在的对被邻国统治的憎恨的特殊心理和自身利益的作用下，想要把国家的管理大权集于中央。可以看到，今天英国的下层阶级正竭尽全力摧毁地方独立并将各地的行政权转归中央，而上层阶级则试图在其古老封地保留这些行政权。我敢预言，总有一天会出现完全相反的情景。

这些论述足以说明，为什么一个经过长期艰苦斗争之后实现平等的社会与公民一开始便已平等的民主社会相比，往往其社会力量更为强大，而个人力量更为弱小。美国人的例子完全能够充分证明这一事实。美国的居民从未按特权分成不同等级，他们也从来不知道主人与仆人的相互关系，而且因为他们既不害怕，又不憎恨彼此，所以从来不知道有必要请求最高权力来管理他们的事务。美国人的命运非常特殊：他们从英国的贵族那里承袭了个人权利的观念和对地方自由的爱好，并将两者保存下来，因为他们用不着同贵族进行斗争。

如果教育在任何时候都能帮助人们捍卫自己的独立，那么，在民主时代尤其是真理。当人们全部相同的时候，仅在本能的驱使下就可以很容易地建立一个单一的全能的政府。但是，人们需要具备丰富的智慧、知识和技巧才能在这种环境下组织和维护次级权力，并在公民都独立且软弱无力的情况下建立既可以反抗暴政又可以维持秩序的自由社团。

Hence the concentration of power and the subjection of individuals will increase amongst democratic nations, not only in the same proportion as their equality, but in the same proportion as their ignorance. It is true, that in ages of imperfect civilization the government is frequently as wanting in the knowledge required to impose a despotism upon the people as the people are wanting in the knowledge required to shake it off; but the effect is not the same on both sides. However rude a democratic people may be, the central power which rules it is never completely devoid of cultivation, because it readily draws to its own uses what little cultivation is to be found in the country, and, if necessary, may seek assistance elsewhere. Hence, amongst a nation which is ignorant as well as democratic, an amazing difference cannot fail speedily to arise between the intellectual capacity of the ruler and that of each of his subjects. This completes the easy concentration of all power in his hands: the administrative function of the State is perpetually extended, because the State alone is competent to administer the affairs of the country. Aristocratic nations, however unenlightened they may be, never afford the same spectacle, because in them instruction is nearly equally diffused between the monarch and the leading members of the community.

The pacha who now rules in Egypt found the population of that country composed of men exceedingly ignorant and equal, and he has borrowed the science and ability of Europe to govern that people. As the personal attainments of the sovereign are thus combined with the ignorance and democratic weakness of his subjects, the utmost centralization has been established without impediment, and the pacha has made the country his manufactory, and the inhabitants his workmen.

I think that extreme centralization of government ultimately enervates society, and thus after a length of time weakens the government itself; but I do not deny that a centralized social power may be able to execute great undertakings with facility in a given time and on a particular point. This is more especially true of war, in which success depends much more on the means of transferring all the resources of a nation to one single point, than on the extent of those resources. Hence it is chiefly in war that nations desire and frequently require to increase the powers of the central government. All men of military genius are fond of centralization, which increases their strength; and all men of centralizing genius are fond of war, which compels nations to combine all their powers in the

因此，中央集权和个人服从在民主国家不仅会随平等的普及而增强，还会随公民的开化而增强。的确，在不很开化的时代，政府往往缺乏对人民实行专制统治的知识，而人民也同样缺乏如何摆脱专制的知识。但是，对双方而言其后果截然不同。无论民主国家的人民多么粗鲁，统治他们的中央政权从来不会完全没有一点知识，因为它能随时从全国汲取它所发现的少量知识为己所用，而且如果必要还可以到国外寻求帮助。这就能很容易地将所有权力集中到国家手中。国家的行政权力将不断扩大，因为只有国家能够胜任行政管理工作。贵族制国家，无论其多么不开化，也永远不会出现这样的情况，因为在贵族制国家，君主及其社会主要公民几乎同样都受过教育。

现在统治埃及的帕夏发现他的人民极为愚昧和平等，于是便借鉴欧洲的科学和经验统治人民。当君主的个人学识与臣民的愚昧和民主的弱点相结合，极度的中央集权便可毫无障碍地确立起来，于是帕夏把国家变成他的工厂，把臣民变成他的工人。

我认为政府的极度中央集权最终会让社会失去活力，因此，在一段时间之后还会使政府本身软弱无能。但是，我并不否认集权的社会力量在特定的时期和特定地点可以轻易实现巨大的事业。对于战争来说，尤其如此，因为战争的胜负主要依赖于将全国所有资源迅速投入到一点的技能，其次才取决于资源的多寡。因此，主要在战争时期，国家特别渴望并需要不断增加中央政府的权力。所有的军事天才都喜欢中央集权，因为中央集权可以增强他们的力量；而所有的中央集权天才都喜欢战争，因为战争会迫使国家将所有权力集中

hands of the government. Thus the democratic tendency which leads men unceasingly to multiply the privileges of the State, and to circumscribe the rights of private persons, is much more rapid and constant amongst those democratic nations which are exposed by their position to great and frequent wars, than amongst all others.

I have shown how the dread of disturbance and the love of well-being insensibly lead democratic nations to increase the functions of central government, as the only power which appears to be intrinsically sufficiently strong, enlightened, and secure, to protect them from anarchy. I would now add, that all the particular circumstances which tend to make the state of a democratic community agitated and precarious, enhance this general propensity, and lead private persons more and more to sacrifice their rights to their tranquility. A people is therefore never so disposed to increase the functions of central government as at the close of a long and bloody revolution, which, after having wrested property from the hands of its former possessors, has shaken all belief, and filled the nation with fierce hatreds, conflicting interests, and contending factions. The love of public tranquillity becomes at such times an indiscriminating passion, and the members of the community are apt to conceive a most inordinate devotion to order.

I have already examined several of the incidents which may concur to promote the centralization of power, but the principal cause still remains to be noticed. The foremost of the incidental causes which may draw the management of all affairs into the hands of the ruler in democratic countries, is the origin of that ruler himself, and his own propensities. Men who live in the ages of equality are naturally fond of central power, and are willing to extend its privileges; but if it happens that this same power faithfully represents their own interests, and exactly copies their own inclinations, the confidence they place in it knows no bounds, and they think that whatever they bestow upon it is bestowed upon themselves.

The attraction of administrative powers to the centre will always be less easy and less rapid under the reign of kings who are still in some way connected with the old aristocratic order, than under new princes, the children of their own achievements, whose birth, prejudices, propensities, and habits

到政府手中。因此，促使人们不停扩大国家特权并限制个人权利的民主趋势，在不断面临大规模战争危险的民主国家，要比在其他所有国家发展得更为迅速和持久。

我已经说过，对于动乱的恐惧和对幸福的热爱如何在不知不觉中促使民主国家中央政府的职能增加，以至于中央政府自以为足够强大、开明和巩固，是能够防止国家陷入无政府状态的唯一力量。几乎无须我补充大家就会知道，所有会导致民主国家动荡不安和岌岌可危的特殊社会情况都会加强中央集权的这种一般倾向，并驱使个人为了社会安定而越来越多地牺牲自己的权利。因此，一个国家在刚刚结束一场长期的流血的革命之后，绝不会增加中央政权的职能，而且这场革命在把财产从其原所有者手中夺过来之后，动摇了所有人的信念，让整个国家充满疯狂的仇恨、利害冲突和党派倾轧。在这样的时刻，对社会安定的爱好变成一种盲目的激情，而公民对秩序则产生一种反常的热爱。

上面我只考察了几个促进中央集权的偶然原因，而主要的偶然原因我还没有谈到。在民主国家会将一切事务管理权交到统治者手中的最首要的偶然原因，就是统治者本人的出身和爱好。生活在民主时代的人自然喜欢中央政权，并愿意扩大其特权；但如果这个政权能忠实地代表他们的利益，准确地展现他们的爱好，那么他们对这个政权的信任将是无限的，并认为无论他们赋予政权什么实际上都是赋予他们自己。

与旧贵族制度仍然保持某些联系的国王在实行行政集权时，往往不如出身、成见、本性和习惯等方面似乎与平等有不可分割联系的自创新业的国王那么容易和迅速。我并不是说生活在民主时代的贵族出身的国王们不想实行中央集权。我认为他们对于实行中央集

appear to bind them indissolubly to the cause of equality. I do not mean that princes of aristocratic origin who live in democratic ages do not attempt to centralize; I believe they apply themselves to that object as diligently as any others. For them, the sole advantages of equality lie in that direction; but their opportunities are less great, because the community, instead of volunteering compliance with their desires, frequently obeys them with reluctance. In democratic communities the rule is that centralization must increase in proportion as the sovereign is less aristocratic. When an ancient race of kings stands at the head of an aristocracy, as the natural prejudices of the sovereign perfectly accord with the natural prejudices of the nobility, the vices inherent in aristocratic communities have a free course, and meet with no corrective. The reverse is the case when the scion of a feudal stock is placed at the head of a democratic people. The sovereign is constantly led, by his education, his habits, and his associations, to adopt sentiments suggested by the inequality of conditions, and the people tend as constantly, by their social condition, to those manners which are engendered by equality. At such times it often happens that the citizens seek to control the central power far less as a tyrannical than as an aristocratical power, and that they persist in the firm defence of their independence, not only because they would remain free, but especially because they are determined to remain equal. A revolution which overthrows an ancient regal family, in order to place men of more recent growth at the head of a democratic people, may temporarily weaken the central power; but however anarchical such a revolution may appear at first, we need not hesitate to predict that its final and certain consequence will be to extend and to secure the prerogatives of that power. The foremost or indeed the sole condition which is required in order to succeed in centralizing the supreme power in a democratic community, is to love equality, or to get men to believe you love it. Thus the science of despotism, which was once so complex, is simplified, and reduced as it were to a single principle.

Chapter V: That Amongst The European Nations Of Our Time The Power Of Governments Is Increasing, Although The Persons Who Govern Are Less Stable

On reflecting upon what has already been said, the reader will be startled and alarmed to find that

权的迫切程度与其他君主一样。对他们而言，平等的好处就在于此。但是，他们的胜算不高，因为公民并非自愿服从他们的欲望，而往往是勉强服从他们的要求。在民主社会，最高统治者越是没有贵族气派，中央集权的可能性就越大。一个古老王朝的国王站在贵族面前，因为君主天生的成见与贵族天生的成见完全一致，贵族社会所固有的弊端可以自由发展，并且无药可救。当封建世家的后裔成为民主国家的领导时，情况则会相反。君主在自身教育、习惯和传统的影响下，不断倾向不平等所造成的情感；而人民则在自己社会情况的作用下，不断追求源自平等的民情。这时，公民们往往试图抑制中央政权，并视其为贵族的政权，甚至暴君的政权。于是他们会坚定地捍卫自己的独立，这不仅是因为他们要保留自由，而且更因为他们要保留平等。为了能够让新人领导民主国家而推翻旧王朝的革命，可能会暂时削弱中央政权。但无论这样的革命在其最初看起来如何无法无天，我们都可以毫不犹豫地预言，其最终的必然结果将会扩大和保护这个政权的特权。为了能够在民主社会成功实现政治权力的集中，首要的也可以说是唯一的必要条件，就是要热爱平等或是让人们相信自己热爱平等。因此，曾经非常复杂的专制之术，已经变得简单，并被简化成为一个单一的原则。

第五章　当今尽管欧洲国家最高统治者的地位不够稳固但是政府的权力却不断增加

玩味一下已经谈过的东西，必然会奇怪和吃惊于在欧洲似乎所有的一切都会促使政府特权的无限扩大，以及个人所享有权利的日益软弱，日益处于从属地位，日益岌岌可危。

678

in Europe everything seems to conduce to the indefinite extension of the prerogatives of government, and to render all that enjoyed the rights of private independence more weak, more subordinate, and more precarious. The democratic nations of Europe have all the general and permanent tendencies which urge the Americans to the centralization of government, and they are moreover exposed to a number of secondary and incidental causes with which the Americans are unacquainted. It would seem as if every step they make towards equality brings them nearer to despotism. And indeed if we do but cast our looks around, we shall be convinced that such is the fact. During the aristocratic ages which preceded the present time, the sovereigns of Europe had been deprived of, or had relinquished, many of the rights inherent in their power. Not a hundred years ago, amongst the greater part of European nations, numerous private persons and corporations were sufficiently independent to administer justice, to raise and maintain troops, to levy taxes, and frequently even to make or interpret the law. The State has everywhere resumed to itself alone these natural attributes of sovereign power; in all matters of government the State tolerates no intermediate agent between itself and the people, and in general business it directs the people by its own immediate influence. I am far from blaming this concentration of power, I simply point it out.

At the same period a great number of secondary powers existed in Europe, which represented local interests and administered local affairs. Most of these local authorities have already disappeared; all are speedily tending to disappear, or to fall into the most complete dependence. From one end of Europe to the other the privileges of the nobility, the liberties of cities, and the powers of provincial bodies, are either destroyed or upon the verge of destruction. Europe has endured, in the course of the last half-century, many revolutions and counter-revolutions which have agitated it in opposite directions: but all these perturbations resemble each other in one respect—they have all shaken or destroyed the secondary powers of government. The local privileges which the French did not abolish in the countries they conquered, have finally succumbed to the policy of the princes who conquered the French. Those princes rejected all the innovations of the French Revolution except centralization: that is the only principle they consented to receive from such a source. My object

欧洲的民主国家具有所有促使美国人走向中央集权的一般倾向和长期趋势。此外，他们还有许多为美国人所不曾拥有的促进中央集权的次要和偶然因素。可以说它们每向平等迈进一步，就更接近专制一步。如果我们环顾一下四周，就会发现事实的确如此。在以前的贵族时代，欧洲君主固有的许多权利已经相继被剥夺或自动放弃。距今不到100年以前，在大部分欧洲国家，许多个人或团体就已经非常独立到可以自行审理案件、募兵、养兵、收税，甚至常常自己制定或解释法律的地步。现在，国家已经在各地收回这些本专属于国家主权的权力，不再允许在自己与人民之间存在中间人插手有关国家管理的一切事务，并亲自对公民进行全面领导。我并不想指责这种中央集权，不过是想指出这样的事实而已。

在同一时期，在欧洲存在大量代表地方利益和管理地方事务的次级政权。现在，这些地方当局大部分已经消失，剩下的也正在迅速消失，或是完全听命于中央。在欧洲各地，领主的特权、城市的自由和地方行政权，不是已经消失，就是在崩溃的边缘。近半个世纪以来，欧洲经历了多次革命和反革命。但所有这些动乱都有一个共同之处，即它们都动摇或破坏了地方的次级政权。法国人并没有废除其所征服国家的地方特权，而是最终被征服法国的君主们所消灭。这些君主们把革命所创造的一切新鲜事物全部抛弃，除了中央集权以外，这是他们唯一认可的源自革命的东西。我所想要指出的是，在我们这个时代相继从某些阶级、团体和个人手里夺来的各种权力并没有用来服务于在更为民主的基础上建立新的次级政权，而是无一例外地全部集中到君主手中。各国对最低级的公民进行着越来越直接的领导，并对他们每个人的小事也越来越亲自管理。几乎所有欧洲的慈善事业原先都由

is to remark, that all these various rights, which have been successively wrested, in our time, from classes, corporations, and individuals, have not served to raise new secondary powers on a more democratic basis, but have uniformly been concentrated in the hands of the sovereign. Everywhere the State acquires more and more direct control over the humblest members of the community, and a more exclusive power of governing each of them in his smallest concerns. Almost all the charitable establishments of Europe were formerly in the hands of private persons or of corporations; they are now almost all dependent on the supreme government, and in many countries are actually administered by that power. The State almost exclusively undertakes to supply bread to the hungry, assistance and shelter to the sick, work to the idle, and to act as the sole reliever of all kinds of misery. Education, as well as charity, is become in most countries at the present day a national concern. The State receives, and often takes, the child from the arms of the mother, to hand it over to official agents: the State undertakes to train the heart and to instruct the mind of each generation. Uniformity prevails in the courses of public instruction as in everything else; diversity, as well as freedom, is disappearing day by day. Nor do I hesitate to affirm, that amongst almost all the Christian nations of our days, Catholic as well as Protestant, religion is in danger of falling into the hands of the government. Not that rulers are over-jealous of the right of settling points of doctrine, but they get more and more hold upon the will of those by whom doctrines are expounded; they deprive the clergy of their property, and pay them by salaries; they divert to their own use the influence of the priesthood, they make them their own ministers—often their own servants—and by this alliance with religion they reach the inner depths of the soul of man.

But this is as yet only one side of the picture. The authority of government has not only spread, as we have just seen, throughout the sphere of all existing powers, till that sphere can no longer contain it, but it goes further, and invades the domain heretofore reserved to private independence. A multitude of actions, which were formerly entirely beyond the control of the public administration, have been subjected to that control in our time, and the number of them is constantly increasing. Amongst aristocratic nations the supreme government usually contented itself with managing and

个人或团体掌控；现在它们几乎都依附于国家政权，而且在某些国家实际上完全由国家管理。向饥饿者施舍面包，救济和收容病残，安排无业者就业，几乎全由国家办理。国家几乎成为所有灾难的唯一救济者，给饥饿者提供面包，给病人提供帮助和庇护，给失业者提供工作。现在，在大多数国家，教育同慈善一样，已经成为国家的事业。国家从母亲的怀抱接过而且往往是要过孩子，交给官方代理机构，国家承担起陶冶每一代人情操和教育每一代人思想的责任。同其他制度一样，教育制度也是统一的，多样性与自由一样正在日渐消失。所以我会毫不犹豫地断言，在我们这个时代几乎所有基督教国家，无论是天主教还是新教，宗教都面临被政府掌控的危险。这并不是说统治者过分嫉妒教会自行决定教义的权力，而是说他们日益加强对教义宣讲者意志的控制。他们剥夺教士的财产，取而代之向其支付薪金，把教士的影响力为己所用。他们任命神职人员为自己的教士，而且往往是自己的仆从，并与宗教联手深入到每个人灵魂的深处。

　　但这只是整幅图画的一个侧面而已。正如我们已经看到的那样，政府的权威不仅扩大到现有权力的所有领域，而且这并不能让它感到满足，它还要更进一步，侵入到迄今从未染指过的个人独立的领域。以前完全不受政府控制的许多行动，在我们这个时代已经被政府所控制，而且其数量依然不断上涨。在贵族制国家，最高政权往往只满足于管理和监督公民与国家荣誉有直接和显著关系的事务，但在其余的方面公民则可自行处理。在这些国家，政府往往似乎忘记了个人的错误和苦难会危害到国家的繁荣，忘记了防止个人破产有时候也是国家的义务。我们这个时代的民主国家则刚好倒向另一个极端。显然，大多数我

superintending the community in whatever directly and ostensibly concerned the national honor; but in all other respects the people were left to work out their own free will. Amongst these nations the government often seemed to forget that there is a point at which the faults and the sufferings of private persons involve the general prosperity, and that to prevent the ruin of a private individual must sometimes be a matter of public importance. The democratic nations of our time lean to the opposite extreme. It is evident that most of our rulers will not content themselves with governing the people collectively: it would seem as if they thought themselves responsible for the actions and private condition of their subjects—as if they had undertaken to guide and to instruct each of them in the various incidents of life, and to secure their happiness quite independently of their own consent. On the other hand private individuals grow more and more apt to look upon the supreme power in the same light; they invoke its assistance in all their necessities, and they fix their eyes upon the administration as their mentor or their guide.

I assert that there is no country in Europe in which the public administration has not become, not only more centralized, but more inquisitive and more minute it everywhere interferes in private concerns more than it did; it regulates more undertakings, and undertakings of a lesser kind; and it gains a firmer footing every day about, above, and around all private persons, to assist, to advise, and to coerce them. Formerly a sovereign lived upon the income of his lands, or the revenue of his taxes; this is no longer the case now that his wants have increased as well as his power. Under the same circumstances which formerly compelled a prince to put on a new tax, he now has recourse to a loan. Thus the State gradually becomes the debtor of most of the wealthier members of the community, and centralizes the largest amounts of capital in its own hands. Small capital is drawn into its keeping by another method. As men are intermingled and conditions become more equal, the poor have more resources, more education, and more desires; they conceive the notion of bettering their condition, and this teaches them to save. These savings are daily producing an infinite number of small capitals, the slow and gradual produce of labor, which are always increasing. But the greater part of this money would be unproductive if it remained scattered in the hands of its owners.

们这个时代的统治者都不只满足于治理整个国家，他们似乎认为自己对臣民的行为和命运负有责任，并承担起在人生各阶段指导和指点每个人的义务，而且在必要时，还会不顾人们的个人意愿去教导他们如何获得幸福。另一方面，老百姓也越来越这样看待政府，他们恳请政府给予援助，并视政府为导师和向导，时刻关注着它。

我敢说在欧洲与以往相比，所有国家的政府不仅越来越中央集权，而且越来越插手公民个人私事，它管的事情越来越多，越来越细。每天站在公民的身边或是头上对其予以帮助、引导并对他们发号施令。以前，君主靠自己土地的收入或赋税生活。现在，情况则完全不同，他的需求和权力都已增加。在同样的情况下，以前，君主如有需要会制定新的赋税，而现在他则会举债。于是，国家逐渐成为社会大多数富人的债务人，并将大量资金集中到自己手里。至于小额资金，它会用另一种办法吸纳到手中。当人们日益融合，日益平等，穷人开始拥有更多的资源，受到更多的教育，产生更多的欲求，于是便开始产生改善现状的想法，并学会用储蓄的办法实现这一目的。这样，储蓄每天会制造出无数的小额资金，是慢慢积累起来的劳动果实，而且其数额不断增加。但是，如果这么多钱分散在个人手里，不会产生任何收益。这种情况便催生了一种慈善组织，如果我没有错的话，它不久就会成为我们最重要的政治机构之一。一些慈善人士想到，把穷人的储蓄集中起来，使之产生效益。在某些国家，这种慈善团体仍然完全与国家无关；但几乎在大多数国家，所有这些团体都表现出被政府合并的趋势；而且在有些国家，已经被政府所取代，政府亲自担起将数以百万计的劳动阶级人民的日常储蓄集中于一处，并独自经营让其生息的庞大任

This circumstance has given rise to a philanthropic institution, which will soon become, if I am not mistaken, one of our most important political institutions. Some charitable persons conceived the notion of collecting the savings of the poor and placing them out at interest. In some countries these benevolent associations are still completely distinct from the State; but in almost all they manifestly tend to identify themselves with the government; and in some of them the government has superseded them, taking upon itself the enormous task of centralizing in one place, and putting out at interest on its own responsibility, the daily savings of many millions of the working classes. Thus the State draws to itself the wealth of the rich by loans, and has the poor man's mite at its disposal in the savings banks. The wealth of the country is perpetually flowing around the government and passing through its hands; the accumulation increases in the same proportion as the equality of conditions; for in a democratic country the State alone inspires private individuals with confidence, because the State alone appears to be endowed with strength and durability. Thus the sovereign does not confine himself to the management of the public treasury; he interferes in private money matters; he is the superior, and often the master, of all the members of the community; and, in addition to this, he assumes the part of their steward and paymaster.

The central power not only fulfils of itself the whole of the duties formerly discharged by various authorities—extending those duties, and surpassing those authorities—but it performs them with more alertness, strength, and independence than it displayed before. All the governments of Europe have in our time singularly improved the science of administration: they do more things, and they do everything with more order, more celerity, and at less expense; they seem to be constantly enriched by all the experience of which they have stripped private persons. From day to day the princes of Europe hold their subordinate officers under stricter control, and they invent new methods for guiding them more closely, and inspecting them with less trouble. Not content with managing everything by their agents, they undertake to manage the conduct of their agents in everything; so that the public administration not only depends upon one and the same power, but it is more and more confined to one spot and concentrated in the same hands. The government centralizes its agency whilst it

务。于是，国家通过举债吸纳富人的资金，通过储蓄银行可以随意支配穷人的存款。国家的财富会一直在政府的操纵下不断循环，并随着平等的增强而不断增加。因为在民主国家，只有政府能获得人们的信任，因为只有政府才拥有力量和持久性。因此，统治者不但掌握着公共财产，而且还在干预私人财产。他是每个公民的上司，而且往往也是他们的主人，另外，他还是公民的管家和账房先生。

中央政权不但将原来各个权力当局的所有职权揽入手中，而且对其进一步扩大，超越了原有职权，但是，其运行却比原来更灵活、有力和独立。我们这个时代欧洲所有国家的政府已经对行政科学进行改进，能够做更多的事情，而且能够更有条理、更迅速、更经济地完成每件事情。他们似乎在不断地利用从个人那里得到的知识丰富自己。欧洲君主们对其所辖地区的常驻代表进行着越来越严格的管理，并且发明出新的方法以便于对他们进行直接领导监督。欧洲的君主们不满足于通过他们的代表管理一切事务，于是便直接插手这些事务。结果，公共行政不但依赖于同一权力，而且越来越被限定在同一地方和被控制在同一些人手中里。政府在集中其活动的同时增强自己的特权。因此，力量得到双倍增加。

在对大多数欧洲国家古代司法制度的考察中，有两件事情特别引人注意，即司法权的独立和司法权的权限。法院不但几乎负责审理所有私人纠纷，而且在许多案件中还扮演着个人与国家之间仲裁人的角色。在这里我不想谈某些国家法院所篡夺的政治和行政职权，而只想谈各国法院普遍拥有的司法权。在大多数欧洲国家，存在并始终存在许多大部分与一般财产权有关的个人权利，这些权利受到法院的保护，没有法院授权国家不得剥

increases its prerogative—hence a twofold increase of strength.

In examining the ancient constitution of the judicial power, amongst most European nations, two things strike the mind—the independence of that power, and the extent of its functions. Not only did the courts of justice decide almost all differences between private persons, but in very many cases they acted as arbiters between private persons and the State. I do not here allude to the political and administrative offices which courts of judicature had in some countries usurped, but the judicial office common to them all. In most of the countries of Europe, there were, and there still are, many private rights, connected for the most part with the general right of property, which stood under the protection of the courts of justice, and which the State could not violate without their sanction. It was this semi-political power which mainly distinguished the European courts of judicature from all others; for all nations have had judges, but all have not invested their judges with the same privileges. Upon examining what is now occurring amongst the democratic nations of Europe which are called free, as well as amongst the others, it will be observed that new and more dependent courts are everywhere springing up by the side of the old ones, for the express purpose of deciding, by an extraordinary jurisdiction, such litigated matters as may arise between the government and private persons. The elder judicial power retains its independence, but its jurisdiction is narrowed; and there is a growing tendency to reduce it to be exclusively the arbiter between private interests. The number of these special courts of justice is continually increasing, and their functions increase likewise. Thus the government is more and more absolved from the necessity of subjecting its policy and its rights to the sanction of another power. As judges cannot be dispensed with, at least the State is to select them, and always to hold them under its control; so that, between the government and private individuals, they place the effigy of justice rather than justice itself. The State is not satisfied with drawing all concerns to itself, but it acquires an ever-increasing power of deciding on them all without restriction and without appeal.

There exists amongst the modern nations of Europe one great cause, independent of all those which have already been pointed out, which perpetually contributes to extend the agency or to

夺。正是这种半政治性权力是欧洲国家法院与所有其他国家法院的主要差异。因为其他所有国家都有法官，但都没有赋予法官同样的特权。如果考察一下人们所说的欧洲自由民主国家以及其他国家中正在发生的事情，就会发现在旧的普通法院身边，新的法院在各地层出不穷，以便于专门审理国家与公民间可能发生的纠纷。原有的法院依旧保持独立，但它们的审判权限变窄，并出现只充当个人利益冲突仲裁者的发展趋势。特别法院的数量不断增加，它们的职权也在相应增加。因此，政府越来越无须由另一个权力机关对其政策和权利指手画脚。尽管政府不能绕过法官，但它至少可以选任法官，并始终能够掌控他们。也就是说，在政府和私人之间设立了一个貌似主持正义，实质上偏袒政府的司法机构。由此可见，国家并未满足于总揽一切事务，它还想要不断获得可自行决定而不被控诉和上诉的力量。

在现代欧洲国家中，除了我已经指出的原因之外，还有一个重要的原因始终促使最高当局的活动范围和特权的不断扩大，尽管它还并未引起人们的充分注意。这个原因就是社会平等带来的工业发展。工业一般会将大量的人集中在同一地方，于是在这些人之间建立起新的复杂的关系。工业让他们时而突然暴富，时而突然一贫如洗，这样的突然变化，会危害到社会的安定。最后还会出现这些工作损害受益者和靠此糊口者的健康乃至生命的情况。因此，工业阶级比社会其他阶级更需要制度、监督和控制，所以政府的权力自然会随这一阶级的壮大而增加。

这是一项可以普遍应用的真理。接下来我想谈的是与欧洲各国特别有关的部分。在多

strengthen the prerogative of the supreme power, though it has not been sufficiently attended to: I mean the growth of manufactures, which is fostered by the progress of social equality. Manufactures generally collect a multitude of men of the same spot, amongst whom new and complex relations spring up. These men are exposed by their calling to great and sudden alternations of plenty and want, during which public tranquillity is endangered. It may also happen that these employments sacrifice the health, and even the life, of those who gain by them, or of those who live by them. Thus the manufacturing classes require more regulation, superintendence, and restraint than the other classes of society, and it is natural that the powers of government should increase in the same proportion as those classes.

This is a truth of general application; what follows more especially concerns the nations of Europe. In the centuries which preceded that in which we live, the aristocracy was in possession of the soil, and was competent to defend it: landed property was therefore surrounded by ample securities, and its possessors enjoyed great independence. This gave rise to laws and customs which have been perpetuated, notwithstanding the subdivision of lands and the ruin of the nobility; and, at the present time, landowners and agriculturists are still those amongst the community who must easily escape from the control of the supreme power. In these same aristocratic ages, in which all the sources of our history are to be traced, personal property was of small importance, and those who possessed it were despised and weak: the manufacturing class formed an exception in the midst of those aristocratic communities; as it had no certain patronage, it was not outwardly protected, and was often unable to protect itself.

Hence a habit sprung up of considering manufacturing property as something of a peculiar nature, not entitled to the same deference, and not worthy of the same securities as property in general; and manufacturers were looked upon as a small class in the bulk of the people, whose independence was of small importance, and who might with propriety be abandoned to the disciplinary passions of princes. On glancing over the codes of the middle ages, one is surprised to see, in those periods of personal independence, with what incessant royal regulations manufactures were hampered, even in

个世纪以前，只有贵族拥有土地，并有能力捍卫土地。因此，围绕地产有许多的保障，其所有者享有极大的独立。于是，在土地被分割和贵族没落之后，依然有一些法律和习惯在起作用。而今天，地主和农户仍然是最容易逃过中央政权控制的公民。在能够从中找到我们所有历史根源的贵族时代，不动产不受重视，其所有者也受到轻视，而且势单力薄；工业阶级成为贵族社会里的一个例外。因为他们没有保护人，所以无法得到保护，而且也往往不能自保。

因此，人们便习惯性地认为工业财产具有特殊的性质，不能给予其与一般财产同样的重视和保护，而且从事工业的人被视为社会中一个单独的小阶级，他们的独立不受重视，君主一不高兴便会把他们踢开。浏览一下中世纪的法典，人们会惊讶地看到，在那些个人独立的时代，皇家法规对工业不断干涉，甚至对工业的最细小的细节也要管。就这一点来看，中央集权的积极和细致程度已经达到登峰造极。在此以后，世界上发生了一场大革命，尚处萌芽之中的工业财产逐渐发展遍布整个欧洲，工业阶级通过其他阶级的残余日益壮大了自己的队伍，而且其人数、重要性和财富还在增加，并将一直增加下去。几乎所有并不属于这个阶级的人，至少也在某些方面与其发生联系。这个原先被视为例外阶级的阶级，现在有可能会变成即使不是唯一也是主要阶级，但是，其原来所形成的政治思想和政治习惯依旧没有改变。这些思想和习惯之所以没有改变，不仅是因为它们陈旧，而且还因为它们刚好与我们这个时代新的观念和一般习惯完全吻合。因此，工业财产的权利并未随其重要性的增加而扩大，工业阶级也并没有随其队伍的壮大而越来越独立，相反，它把

their smallest details: on this point centralization was as active and as minute as it can ever be. Since that time a great revolution has taken place in the world; manufacturing property, which was then only in the germ, has spread till it covers Europe: the manufacturing class has been multiplied and enriched by the remnants of all other ranks; it has grown and is still perpetually growing in number, in importance, in wealth. Almost all those who do not belong to it are connected with it at least on some one point; after having been an exception in society, it threatens to become the chief, if not the only, class; nevertheless the notions and political precedents engendered by it of old still cling about it. These notions and these precedents remain unchanged, because they are old, and also because they happen to be in perfect accordance with the new notions and general habits of our contemporaries. Manufacturing property then does not extend its rights in the same ratio as its importance. The manufacturing classes do not become less dependent, whilst they become more numerous; but, on the contrary, it would seem as if despotism lurked within them, and naturally grew with their growth. As a nation becomes more engaged in manufactures, the want of roads, canals, harbors, and other works of a semi-public nature, which facilitate the acquisition of wealth, is more strongly felt; and as a nation becomes more democratic, private individuals are less able, and the State more able, to execute works of such magnitude. I do not hesitate to assert that the manifest tendency of all governments at the present time is to take upon themselves alone the execution of these undertakings; by which means they daily hold in closer dependence the population which they govern.

On the other hand, in proportion as the power of a State increases, and its necessities are augmented, the State consumption of manufactured produce is always growing larger, and these commodities are generally made in the arsenals or establishments of the government. Thus, in every kingdom, the ruler becomes the principal manufacturer; he collects and retains in his service a vast number of engineers, architects, mechanics, and handicraftsmen. Not only is he the principal manufacturer, but he tends more and more to become the chief, or rather the master of all other manufacturers. As private persons become more powerless by becoming more equal, they can effect nothing in manufactures without combination; but the government naturally seeks to place these

专制引入自己的内部，并让其随自身的发展而发展。国家越是工业化，就越是需要有利于致富的道路、运河、港口及其他半公共性质的工程；而国家越是民主，私人就越难以进行这样的工程，而国家就越是有能力进行这样浩大的工程。我会毫不犹豫地断言，现在各国政府已经出现独揽这些工程的明显趋势，通过这样的方式他们让人民对自己的依赖性与日俱增。

另一方面，随着国家力量的增强以及需求的增加，国家本身对工业品的消耗也在不断上涨。这些工业品一般都由国家的兵工厂和工厂制造。因此，在每个王国，统治者成为重要的工业家。他招揽一大批工程师、建筑师、技师和技工为自己服务。他不仅是头号的工业家，而且越来越想主持或者毋宁说是控制其他一切产业。因为随着平等的发展，个人变得越来越无能为力，所以不联合就无法在工业方面有所作为。但是，政府自然想把这些联合组织置于自己的掌控之下。

必须承认，被称为联合组织的这些集合体，比原先的个人要更为强大和可怕，而且对其所要承担的责任也更少。因此，不允许其像私人那样拥有较大的独立性，似乎是合理的。

统治者们往往更倾向于这样的政策，因为他们自身的倾向促使他们如此。在民主国家，只有通过联合人民才能对中央政权进行有效的抵制，因此中央政府始终不喜欢不受其控制的结社。而且特别值得一提的是，在民主国家，人们本身往往对结社怀有恐怖感和嫉妒心理，从而妨碍自己捍卫对其必不可少的社团。在全体公民普遍的软弱和不稳定之中，

combinations under its own control.

It must be admitted that these collective beings, which are called combinations, are stronger and more formidable than a private individual can ever be, and that they have less of the responsibility of their own actions; whence it seems reasonable that they should not be allowed to retain so great an independence of the supreme government as might be conceded to a private individual.

Rulers are the more apt to follow this line of policy, as their own inclinations invite them to it. Amongst democratic nations it is only by association that the resistance of the people to the government can ever display itself: hence the latter always looks with ill-favor on those associations which are not in its own power; and it is well worthy of remark, that amongst democratic nations, the people themselves often entertain a secret feeling of fear and jealousy against these very associations, which prevents the citizens from defending the institutions of which they stand so much in need. The power and the duration of these small private bodies, in the midst of the weakness and instability of the whole community, astonish and alarm the people; and the free use which each association makes of its natural powers is almost regarded as a dangerous privilege. All the associations which spring up in our age are, moreover, new corporate powers, whose rights have not been sanctioned by time; they come into existence at a time when the notion of private rights is weak, and when the power of government is unbounded; hence it is not surprising that they lose their freedom at their birth. Amongst all European nations there are some kinds of associations which cannot be formed until the State has examined their by-laws, and authorized their existence. In several others, attempts are made to extend this rule to all associations; the consequences of such a policy, if it were successful, may easily be foreseen. If once the sovereign had a general right of authorizing associations of all kinds upon certain conditions, he would not be long without claiming the right of superintending and managing them, in order to prevent them from departing from the rules laid down by himself. In this manner, the State, after having reduced all who are desirous of forming associations into dependence, would proceed to reduce into the same condition all who belong to associations already formed—that is to say, almost all the men who are now in existence. Governments thus appropriate to themselves,

这些个人小团体的力量和持久性让人们感到吃惊和不安，而且每个团体对其天然力量的自由应用都被视为是一种危险的特权。此外，我们这个时代出现的所有社团都是新的法人权利，其权利也并非时代赋予，它们产生于个人权利观念薄弱和国家权力无限的时代。因此，它们自诞生之后就失去自由，并不足为奇。在所有欧洲国家，有几种社团未经国家审查和授权不得成立，而有些国家则试图将这样的制度应用于所有社团。这种办法如果成功的话，其后果不难预见。如果一旦统治者拥有按一定条件批准各种社团成立的一般权力，用不了多久他就会宣布自己对社团的监督和管理权，以防止它们背离自己制定的规则。通过这样的方式，国家在让所有想要成立社团的人从属于自己之后，还要把已经成立社团的人置于自己的控制之下。也就是说，把现有的几乎所有的人都控制起来。于是，政府将我们这个时代工业在世界上创造出来的大部分新力量都据为己有或为己所用。工业控制我们，而他们控制工业。

我特别重视我刚刚所述的一切，以至于唯恐我在想把意思表达得更清楚时未能表达得淋漓尽致。如果读者认为我用来支持自己观点的例子不够充分或不够恰当，认为我对中央政权的扩张过于夸张，而另一方面又低估了个人独立依然保有的活动半径，那么我请您将书放下片刻，仔细玩味一下我试图向读者说明的东西，仔细考察一下在法国和其他国家正在发生的事情，同自己周围的人聊一聊，最后再思索一下，如果您在我的引导下或通过其他途径没有达到我想引导您去的地方，那么我就大错而特错了。读者会发现，在过去的半个世纪，中央集权在各地以千百种不同的方式发展起来。战争、革命、征服都会促进中

and convert to their own purposes, the greater part of this new power which manufacturing interests have in our time brought into the world. Manufacturers govern us—they govern manufactures.

I attach so much importance to all that I have just been saying, that I am tormented by the fear of having impaired my meaning in seeking to render it more clear. If the reader thinks that the examples I have adduced to support my observations are insufficient or ill-chosen—if he imagines that I have anywhere exaggerated the encroachments of the supreme power, and, on the other hand, that I have underrated the extent of the sphere which still remains open to the exertions of individual independence, I entreat him to lay down the book for a moment, and to turn his mind to reflect for himself upon the subjects I have attempted to explain. Let him attentively examine what is taking place in France and in other countries—let him inquire of those about him—let him search himself, and I am much mistaken if he does not arrive, without my guidance, and by other paths, at the point to which I have sought to lead him. He will perceive that for the last half-century, centralization has everywhere been growing up in a thousand different ways. Wars, revolutions, conquests, have served to promote it: all men have labored to increase it. In the course of the same period, during which men have succeeded each other with singular rapidity at the head of affairs, their notions, interests, and passions have been infinitely diversified; but all have by some means or other sought to centralize. This instinctive centralization has been the only settled point amidst the extreme mutability of their lives and of their thoughts.

If the reader, after having investigated these details of human affairs, will seek to survey the wide prospect as a whole, he will be struck by the result. On the one hand the most settled dynasties shaken or overthrown—the people everywhere escaping by violence from the sway of their laws—abolishing or limiting the authority of their rulers or their princes—the nations, which are not in open revolution, restless at least, and excited—all of them animated by the same spirit of revolt: and on the other hand, at this very period of anarchy, and amongst these untractable nations, the incessant increase of the prerogative of the supreme government, becoming more centralized, more adventurous, more absolute, more extensive—the people perpetually falling under the control of the public administration—led insensibly to surrender to it some further portion of their individual

央集权的发展，所有人都为中央集权的扩大出努力。在此期间，人们走马灯似的一个接着一个相继掌权，他们的观念、利益和热情千变万化，各不相同，但他们都想通过这样或那样的某种方式寻求中央集权。在人们生活和思想的极度变化中，这种本能的中央集权是唯一一个固定的点。

如果读者研究过人类这些详情之后，试图通观全局，必然会被其所看到的结果惊呆。一方面，最为稳固的王朝不是摇摇欲坠就是相继垮台，各国人民通过暴力手段摆脱法律对自己的禁锢，废除或限制其领主或君主的权威，没有发生革命的国家至少也感到不安和恐惧，所有人都受到同样的反叛精神的鼓舞。另一方面，在这样的无政府状态下，在这些人民桀骜不驯的国家中，最高权力的特权不断增加，变得日益集中，日益胆大妄为，日益专制，日益扩大，于是人民将始终处于国家行政机关的控制之下，不知不觉、一点点地将自己的独立让与国家，这些刚刚打倒王权和把国王踩在脚下的人，却越来越对新政权的一个小小办事员谄媚奉迎俯首听命。因此，在我们这个时代，似乎有两种截然相反的革命正在进行：一个在不断削弱政权，另一个则不断巩固政权。在我们历史上还没有任何时期，政权既如此软弱，又如此强大。但是，当对整个世界的局势进行观察时，便会发现这两种革命似乎紧密联系在一起，它们系出同源，走在不同的路线，但最后将人们引到同一地点。我还要再次重复我已在本书许多地方多次提到和指出的一点：千万不要把平等本身和平等最终确立的社会情况和法制的革命混为一谈，这就是人们之所以对几乎所有现象表示惊讶

independence, till the very men, who from time to time upset a throne and trample on a race of kings, bend more and more obsequiously to the slightest dictate of a clerk. Thus two contrary revolutions appear in our days to be going on; the one continually weakening the supreme power, the other as continually strengthening it: at no other period in our history has it appeared so weak or so strong. But upon a more attentive examination of the state of the world, it appears that these two revolutions are intimately connected together, that they originate in the same source, and that after having followed a separate course, they lead men at last to the same result. I may venture once more to repeat what I have already said or implied in several parts of this book: great care must be taken not to confound the principle of equality itself with the revolution which finally establishes that principle in the social condition and the laws of a nation: here lies the reason of almost all the phenomena which occasion our astonishment. All the old political powers of Europe, the greatest as well as the least, were founded in ages of aristocracy, and they more or less represented or defended the principles of inequality and of privilege. To make the novel wants and interests, which the growing principle of equality introduced, preponderate in government, our contemporaries had to overturn or to coerce the established powers. This led them to make revolutions, and breathed into many of them, that fierce love of disturbance and independence, which all revolutions, whatever be their object, always engender. I do not believe that there is a single country in Europe in which the progress of equality has not been preceded or followed by some violent changes in the state of property and persons; and almost all these changes have been attended with much anarchy and license, because they have been made by the least civilized portion of the nation against that which is most civilized. Hence proceeded the two-fold contrary tendencies which I have just pointed out. As long as the democratic revolution was glowing with heat, the men who were bent upon the destruction of old aristocratic powers hostile to that revolution, displayed a strong spirit of independence; but as the victory or the principle of equality became more complete, they gradually surrendered themselves to the propensities natural to that condition of equality, and they strengthened and centralized their governments. They had sought to be free in order to make themselves equal; but in proportion as equality was more established by the aid of freedom, freedom itself was thereby rendered of more

的原因所在。欧洲所有古老的政权，无论是最强大的还是最弱小的，都建立在贵族时代，或多或少地代表或维护不平等和特权的原则。为了能够让平等带来的新需要和新利益在政府中占据优势，我们同时代的人不得不推翻和压制现有的旧政权。这必然促使人们进行革命，并赋予人们无论以什么为目的的革命都会产生的那种对动乱和独立的强烈热爱。我认为，没有哪个欧洲国家平等的发展，不是在经历过财产状况和人民状况的激烈变化之后或紧随这种变化之后才发展起来的，而且几乎所有这些变化都伴随严重的无政府状态和胡作非为，因为这些变化是由国家中反对最有教养的人的最没教养的那些人发动起来的。因此，便出现了我刚刚所指出的那两种截然相反的倾向。只要民主革命热潮还在，那些志在摧毁敌对民主革命的原有贵族政权的人们，便会表现出强大的独立精神，但随着胜利的到来和平等越来越完全，他们逐渐服从这个平等的自然本性，并努力巩固国家权力使之中央集权化。他们为了实现平等而寻求自由，但随着平等在自由的帮助下进一步确立，自由反而更难获得。

一个国家的这两种状况有时会同时并存。上一代法国人就曾证明一个民族如何在与贵族权威的斗争以及对一切王权表示藐视的同时在社会建立起惊人的暴政，从而向世界传授在赢得独立的同时又失去独立的方法。在我们这个时代，人们看到旧政权在四处崩溃，所有旧势力的苟延残喘，一切旧障碍的坍塌，眼前的一切让最精明的人也无所适从。他们只注意到发生在眼前的不可思议的革命，并以为人类将永远陷入无政府状态。如果他们看到

difficult attainment.

These two states of a nation have sometimes been contemporaneous: the last generation in France showed how a people might organize a stupendous tyranny in the community, at the very time when they were baffling the authority of the nobility and braving the power of all kings—at once teaching the world the way to win freedom, and the way to lose it. In our days men see that constituted powers are dilapidated on every side—they see all ancient authority gasping away, all ancient barriers tottering to their fall, and the judgment of the wisest is troubled at the sight: they attend only to the amazing revolution which is taking place before their eyes, and they imagine that mankind is about to fall into perpetual anarchy: if they looked to the final consequences of this revolution, their fears would perhaps assume a different shape. For myself, I confess that I put no trust in the spirit of freedom which appears to animate my contemporaries. I see well enough that the nations of this age are turbulent, but I do not clearly perceive that they are liberal; and I fear lest, at the close of those perturbations which rock the base of thrones, the domination of sovereigns may prove more powerful than it ever was before.

Chapter VI: What Sort Of Despotism Democratic Nations Have To Fear

I had remarked during my stay in the United States, that a democratic state of society, similar to that of the Americans, might offer singular facilities for the establishment of despotism; and I perceived, upon my return to Europe, how much use had already been made by most of our rulers, of the notions, the sentiments, and the wants engendered by this same social condition, for the purpose of extending the circle of their power. This led me to think that the nations of Christendom would perhaps eventually undergo some sort of oppression like that which hung over several of the nations of the ancient world. A more accurate examination of the subject, and five years of further meditations, have not diminished my apprehensions, but they have changed the object of them. No sovereign ever lived in former ages so absolute or so powerful as to undertake to administer by his own agency, and without the assistance of intermediate powers, all the parts of a great empire: none

这场革命的最终结果，他们的恐惧会是另一番样子。至于我自己，我坦白承认，我并不相信那种似乎在鼓舞当代人的自由精神。我已经充分见识到这个时代国家的巨变，但并没有清楚地看到他们的自由，并担心在动摇王权根基的那些动乱结束之后，统治者的权力会变得比以往都更为强大。

第六章　民主国家害怕哪种专制

在美国逗留期间，我已经注意到像美国那样的民主社会情况会为专制的建立提供非常便利的条件。而在我回到欧洲后则发现，欧洲大部分君主已经在利用这种社会情况产生的思想、感情和需要来扩大他们的权力范围。这使我想到，基督教国家也许最后也要遭受某种类似古代一些国家经历过的那种压迫。对这一问题的细致研究，以及五年来的反复思考，并未能减轻我的忧虑，但令我忧虑的对象发生改变。在以往的时代，从来没有一位君主专制和强大的能够在没有次级政权的帮助而依靠自己的地方政府治理整个帝国；也从来没有一位君主试图让全体臣民毫无差别地一律服从统一的制度并亲自对每个社会成员进行约束和管理。人们从来没有过这样的念头，而即使任何人产生这样的想法，知识的不足，治理方法的不完善，而且特别是不平等带来的天然障碍，会迅速阻碍如此庞大计划的实行。在罗马皇帝的势力达到鼎盛时，罗马帝国的不同民族依然保有彼此各不相同的习惯和风俗；尽管他们服从同一君主，但大部分地区实行自治，并拥有许多强大而兴旺的大都市；尽管帝国的全部统治权都集中在皇帝一人之手，并在必要时可以独断一切，然而大部

ever attempted to subject all his subjects indiscriminately to strict uniformity of regulation, and personally to tutor and direct every member of the community. The notion of such an undertaking never occurred to the human mind; and if any man had conceived it, the want of information, the imperfection of the administrative system, and above all, the natural obstacles caused by the inequality of conditions, would speedily have checked the execution of so vast a design. When the Roman emperors were at the height of their power, the different nations of the empire still preserved manners and customs of great diversity; although they were subject to the same monarch, most of the provinces were separately administered; they abounded in powerful and active municipalities; and although the whole government of the empire was centred in the hands of the emperor alone, and he always remained, upon occasions, the supreme arbiter in all matters, yet the details of social life and private occupations lay for the most part beyond his control. The emperors possessed, it is true, an immense and unchecked power, which allowed them to gratify all their whimsical tastes, and to employ for that purpose the whole strength of the State. They frequently abused that power arbitrarily to deprive their subjects of property or of life: their tyranny was extremely onerous to the few, but it did not reach the greater number; it was fixed to some few main objects, and neglected the rest; it was violent, but its range was limited.

But it would seem that if despotism were to be established amongst the democratic nations of our days, it might assume a different character; it would be more extensive and more mild; it would degrade men without tormenting them. I do not question, that in an age of instruction and equality like our own, sovereigns might more easily succeed in collecting all political power into their own hands, and might interfere more habitually and decidedly within the circle of private interests, than any sovereign of antiquity could ever do. But this same principle of equality which facilitates despotism, tempers its rigor. We have seen how the manners of society become more humane and gentle in proportion as men become more equal and alike. When no member of the community has much power or much wealth, tyranny is, as it were, without opportunities and a field of action. As all fortunes are scanty, the passions of men are naturally circumscribed—their imagination limited, their

分的社会生活细节和个人日常生活都不受其控制。的确，罗马皇帝拥有巨大的无可争辩的权力，能够让其肆意妄为，并可以为一己私欲而动用全国的力量。他们不断肆意滥用权力蛮横地剥夺臣民的财产或生命。他们的暴政对某些人来说极为沉重，但并未扩及大多数人；暴政的对象只是几个重大人物，不会波及他人。暴政尽管残酷，但是范围有限。

但是似乎如果专制在我们这个时代的民主国家确立起来，它有可能会具有不同的特点。它的范围会更广，方式会更温和；不折磨人便可屈人之志。我不怀疑，在像我们今天这样文明平等的时代，统治者们能够比任何古代的君主更为轻松地把所有政治权力集于手中，并习惯性地、坚决地干涉私人利益的领域。但利于专制出现的平等，同样也能抑制专制的活力。我们已经看到，随着人们的日益相似和平等，民情如何变得越来越具人性和温和。当没有任何社会成员拥有巨大的力量和财富时，专制也没有机会和活动的舞台。如果所有人的财富都有限，人们的激情自然会受到抑制，其想象力也必然有限，享乐也必然朴素。这种普遍的节制也会节制统治者本人，并将其毫无节制的欲望限制在一定的范围。

除了来自社会情况本质自身的原因外，我还可以举出许多不在我讨论范之内的原因。但是，我并想不超出自己所划定的范围。在群情极度沸腾和出现重大危机的特定时刻，民主政府可能变得暴戾，甚至残忍，但这种危险极为少见和短暂。当我想到现代人并不炙热的激情、温和的民情、广泛的知识、对宗教信仰的虔诚、道德的良好、端正而勤奋的习惯以及对是非善恶的明辨，所担心的便不再是他们会遭到统治者的暴政，而是更担心他们会遭受监护人的暴政。因此我认为，威胁民主国家的那种压迫，与迄今为止世界上出现过的

pleasures simple. This universal moderation moderates the sovereign himself, and checks within certain limits the inordinate extent of his desires.

Independently of these reasons drawn from the nature of the state of society itself, I might add many others arising from causes beyond my subject; but I shall keep within the limits I have laid down to myself. Democratic governments may become violent and even cruel at certain periods of extreme effervescence or of great danger: but these crises will be rare and brief. When I consider the petty passions of our contemporaries, the mildness of their manners, the extent of their education, the purity of their religion, the gentleness of their morality, their regular and industrious habits, and the restraint which they almost all observe in their vices no less than in their virtues, I have no fear that they will meet with tyrants in their rulers, but rather guardians. I think then that the species of oppression by which democratic nations are menaced is unlike anything which ever before existed in the world: our contemporaries will find no prototype of it in their memories. I am trying myself to choose an expression which will accurately convey the whole of the idea I have formed of it, but in vain; the old words "despotism" and "tyranny" are inappropriate: the thing itself is new; and since I cannot name it, I must attempt to define it.

I seek to trace the novel features under which despotism may appear in the world. The first thing that strikes the observation is an innumerable multitude of men all equal and alike, incessantly endeavoring to procure the petty and paltry pleasures with which they glut their lives. Each of them, living apart, is as a stranger to the fate of all the rest—his children and his private friends constitute to him the whole of mankind; as for the rest of his fellow-citizens, he is close to them, but he sees them not—he touches them, but he feels them not; he exists but in himself and for himself alone; and if his kindred still remain to him, he may be said at any rate to have lost his country. Above this race of men stands an immense and tutelary power, which takes upon itself alone to secure their gratifications, and to watch over their fate. That power is absolute, minute, regular, provident, and mild. It would be like the authority of a parent, if, like that authority, its object was to prepare men for manhood; but it seeks on the contrary to keep them in perpetual childhood: it is well content that the people should rejoice, provided they think of nothing but rejoicing. For their happiness

任何压迫均不相同，当代的人们将无法在他们的记忆中找到这样的原型。我正试图寻找一个能准确表达我头脑中形成的对这种压迫的完整概念，却徒劳无果。专制或暴政都不合适。这个事物本身是新的，而且因为我无法给其命名，所以就要努力对其说明。

我试图描绘出现在世界上的这种专制会有怎样的新特点。我首先注意到的是无数相同而平等的人，终日不断为追求内心小小的庸俗享乐而奔波。他们每个人都离群索居，似乎其他所有人的命运都与他无关，他们的孩子和亲友对他而言就是整个人类。至于其他同胞，即使与其并肩而战，他们也不屑一顾；尽管与其进行接触，也感觉不到这些人存在。每个人都独立生存，并且只为自己而生存。如果说他们还有至亲好友，那么至少可以说他们已经不再拥有祖国。在这样的一群人之上，存在着一个只负责保证他们的享乐和关注他们命运的强大的守护力量。这股力量是绝对的，无微不至的，极其认真的，很有预见，而且非常温和的。它就像是以教导人如何长大成人为目的的父权。但它想做的刚好相反，只是想把人永远当成孩子。它喜欢公民享乐，而且认为只要设法享乐就可以了。为了人民的幸福，这样的政府愿意付出辛苦，但它要充当公民幸福唯一的代理人和仲裁人。它可以保障公民安全，预见并满足公民的需要，为公民的享乐提供方便，指挥公民的主要活动，领导公民的工商业，规定公民的遗产继承，并分配公民的遗产。这岂不是完全不让公民开动脑筋和为生计而操劳吗？因此，公民终日无所事事，很少运用和不太运用自己的自由意志。它将人们的意志活动限制在狭小的范围，并逐渐剥夺人们自我活动能力。平等让人养

such a government willingly labors, but it chooses to be the sole agent and the only arbiter of that happiness: it provides for their security, foresees and supplies their necessities, facilitates their pleasures, manages their principal concerns, directs their industry, regulates the descent of property, and subdivides their inheritances—what remains, but to spare them all the care of thinking and all the trouble of living? Thus it every day renders the exercise of the free agency of man less useful and less frequent; it circumscribes the will within a narrower range, and gradually robs a man of all the uses of himself. The principle of equality has prepared men for these things: it has predisposed men to endure them, and oftentimes to look on them as benefits.

After having thus successively taken each member of the community in its powerful grasp, and fashioned them at will, the supreme power then extends its arm over the whole community. It covers the surface of society with a net-work of small complicated rules, minute and uniform, through which the most original minds and the most energetic characters cannot penetrate, to rise above the crowd. The will of man is not shattered, but softened, bent, and guided: men are seldom forced by it to act, but they are constantly restrained from acting: such a power does not destroy, but it prevents existence; it does not tyrannize, but it compresses, enervates, extinguishes, and stupefies a people, till each nation is reduced to be nothing better than a flock of timid and industrious animals, of which the government is the shepherd. I have always thought that servitude of the regular, quiet, and gentle kind which I have just described, might be combined more easily than is commonly believed with some of the outward forms of freedom; and that it might even establish itself under the wing of the sovereignty of the people. Our contemporaries are constantly excited by two conflicting passions; they want to be led, and they wish to remain free: as they cannot destroy either one or the other of these contrary propensities, they strive to satisfy them both at once. They devise a sole, tutelary, and all-powerful form of government, but elected by the people. They combine the principle of centralization and that of popular sovereignty; this gives them a respite; they console themselves for being in tutelage by the reflection that they have chosen their own guardians. Every man allows himself to be put in leading-strings, because he sees that it is not a person or a class of persons, but the people at large that holds the end of his chain. By this system the people shake off their state

成接受这一切的习惯，不但迫使人们忍受这一切，往往还让人们把这一切视为恩惠。

于是，在统治者相继把每个社会成员置于自己的掌控下，并按照自己的意愿塑造他们之后，便将其权力的触手伸向整个社会。他用一张织就详尽、细微、全面和统一规则的网将社会覆盖，即使最具独创精神和坚强意志的人也无法冲破这张网让自己出类拔萃。人的意志没有遭到践踏，但被软化、驯服和引导。人们很少在其胁迫下行动，但不断受到其限制。这样的一股力量它并不破坏，但阻碍新生事物的存在；它不实行暴政，但限制和压制人，使人精神颓靡、意志消沉和麻木不仁，直到最后全体人民都变成一群胆小而勤奋的牲畜，而政府则成为牧人。我一直认为，我刚刚所描述的这种严明、平静和温和的奴役，可能往往会比人们想象的更容易披上自由的外衣，甚至可以在人民主权的幌子下建立起来。我们现代人不断在这两种互相对立的激情的驱使下，一方面想要有人指导，而另一方面又希望保持自由。因为人们无法放弃这两种相反倾向之中的任何一个，所以他们力求能够同时满足它们。于是，他们设计出一种唯一的、具有监护性质的、无所不能的，但是经人民选举产生的政府形式。他们把中央集权和人民主权结合起来，使自己得到一些缓解。他们认为监护人是自己所选，所以安于被人监护。每个人都能忍受捆在身上的链子，因为他们看到握着链子另一端的不是一个人，也不是一个阶级，而是人民自己。在这种制度下，他们在刚刚摆脱依附状态后，又为自己选定新的主人再次回到原来的状态。如今，很多人对这种行政专制与人民主权的妥协很满意，并认为自己在将自由托付给国家权力之后，个人

of dependence just long enough to select their master, and then relapse into it again. A great many persons at the present day are quite contented with this sort of compromise between administrative despotism and the sovereignty of the people; and they think they have done enough for the protection of individual freedom when they have surrendered it to the power of the nation at large. This does not satisfy me: the nature of him I am to obey signifies less to me than the fact of extorted obedience.

I do not however deny that a constitution of this kind appears to me to be infinitely preferable to one, which, after having concentrated all the powers of government, should vest them in the hands of an irresponsible person or body of persons. Of all the forms which democratic despotism could assume, the latter would assuredly be the worst. When the sovereign is elective, or narrowly watched by a legislature which is really elective and independent, the oppression which he exercises over individuals is sometimes greater, but it is always less degrading; because every man, when he is oppressed and disarmed, may still imagine, that whilst he yields obedience it is to himself he yields it, and that it is to one of his own inclinations that all the rest give way. In like manner I can understand that when the sovereign represents the nation, and is dependent upon the people, the rights and the power of which every citizen is deprived, not only serve the head of the State, but the State itself; and that private persons derive some return from the sacrifice of their independence which they have made to the public. To create a representation of the people in every centralized country, is therefore, to diminish the evil which extreme centralization may produce, but not to get rid of it. I admit that by this means room is left for the intervention of individuals in the more important affairs; but it is not the less suppressed in the smaller and more private ones. It must not be forgotten that it is especially dangerous to enslave men in the minor details of life. For my own part, I should be inclined to think freedom less necessary in great things than in little ones, if it were possible to be secure of the one without possessing the other. Subjection in minor affairs breaks out every day, and is felt by the whole community indiscriminately. It does not drive men to resistance, but it crosses them at every turn, till they are led to surrender the exercise of their will. Thus their spirit is gradually broken and their character enervated; whereas that obedience, which is exacted

自由就能得到充分的保证。但是这并不能令我感到满意。在我看来，主人的本性远不及强制服从的事实重要。

然而，我并不否认，这种政体远比那种把所有政府权力都集中交给一个不负责任的人或团体来管理的政体要好上不知多少。在民主专制可能采用的各种形式中，后一种无疑是最糟糕的。当统治者经选举产生，或受到真正经选举产生的独立立法机构监督的时候，他对于个人的压迫往往要更大，却很少让人感到羞耻，因为当每个人在受到压迫和限制之后，会依然想象他所服从的实际上是自己，而牺牲其他一切也正是他自己意志的一种表现。我能够理解，当统治者代表国家并依靠人民的时候，剥夺每个公民的力量和权利不但是为国家首脑服务，而且也是为国家本身服务，而个人在为公共而牺牲自己的独立之后也会得到某些补偿。因此，在一个非常集权的国家建立人民代表制度，可以减少极端中央集权可能带来的弊端，但无法将其根除。我承认，通过这样的方式可以给个人提供参与国家大事的空间，但很少能对小事和私人施加影响。千万不能忘记，在生活琐事上奴役人民尤其危险。至于我，则趋向于认为，如果两者不能兼顾的话，自由的必要性在大事上远不及在小事上。小事上的服从每天都会出现，而且所有公民无一例外都能感受到。尽管它并不会促使人们反抗，但是在一直牵绊着人们，直到其放弃运用自己的意志。因此，人们的精神之火慢慢熄灭，心灵之光渐渐暗淡。然而，对大事的服从尽管严格，但极为罕见，而且绝不同于奴役，只会有一些特定的人受苦。鼓励已经如此依附于中央政权的人们时不时地选举这个政权的代表，是徒劳无益的；这种罕见的暂时的自由意志的行使，无论其如何重

on a few important but rare occasions, only exhibits servitude at certain intervals, and throws the burden of it upon a small number of men. It is in vain to summon a people, which has been rendered so dependent on the central power, to choose from time to time the representatives of that power; this rare and brief exercise of their free choice, however important it may be, will not prevent them from gradually losing the faculties of thinking, feeling, and acting for themselves, and thus gradually falling below the level of humanity. I add that they will soon become incapable of exercising the great and only privilege which remains to them. The democratic nations which have introduced freedom into their political constitution, at the very time when they were augmenting the despotism of their administrative constitution, have been led into strange paradoxes. To manage those minor affairs in which good sense is all that is wanted—the people are held to be unequal to the task, but when the government of the country is at stake, the people are invested with immense powers; they are alternately made the playthings of their ruler, and his masters—more than kings, and less than men. After having exhausted all the different modes of election, without finding one to suit their purpose, they are still amazed, and still bent on seeking further; as if the evil they remark did not originate in the constitution of the country far more than in that of the electoral body. It is, indeed, difficult to conceive how men who have entirely given up the habit of self-government should succeed in making a proper choice of those by whom they are to be governed; and no one will ever believe that a liberal, wise, and energetic government can spring from the suffrages of a subservient people. A constitution, which should be republican in its head and ultra-monarchical in all its other parts, has ever appeared to me to be a short-lived monster. The vices of rulers and the ineptitude of the people would speedily bring about its ruin; and the nation, weary of its representatives and of itself, would create freer institutions, or soon return to stretch itself at the feet of a single master.

Chapter VII: Continuation Of The Preceding Chapters

I believe that it is easier to establish an absolute and despotic government amongst a people in which the conditions of society are equal, than amongst any other; and I think that if such a

要，都无法防止他们逐渐失去独立思考、感受和行动的能力，于是，慢慢下降到人类的一般水平之下。我还要补充一下，他们不久就将无法行使他们仅有的重大唯一特权。把自由制度引进政治领域并同时加强行政领域专制的民主国家，必然会出现一些非常离奇的现象。一些只凭常识就可以处理好的小事，人民被认为没有能力办理；但在事关国家政务的问题时，人民又被赋予无限权力。于是，人民时而成为统治者的玩偶，时而又成为他们的主人；而统治者的权力时而比国王还大，时而又不如普通老百姓。在历经各种选举制度而未找到符合其心意的制度之后，他们依然感到吃惊，并依然继续寻找，似乎他们所发现的弊端并不是来自本国的政治制度，而是来自选举制度。的确很难想象，已经完全失去自治习惯的人，如何能够成功地选出将要治理他们的人，而且也不会有人相信，一个自由、精明和活力充沛的政府会由处于奴隶状态的人民选举而出。在我看来，一个上层为共和制而其余部分为极端君主制的政体必然是一个短命的怪物。统治者的腐败和人民的无能，会迅速令其倒台。而对自己和自己的代表感到厌烦的国家，会创造出更为自由的制度，或是不久便会重新匍匐在一个独夫的脚下。

第七章　以上各章的延续

我认为在社会状况平等的国家比其他任何国家更容易建立绝对专制的政府；而且如果这样的政府一旦在这样的国家建立，它不但要压迫人民，而且最终会剥夺人类一些最可贵的品质。因此，在我看来专制在民主时代特别可怕。我认为在任何时候我都爱自由，但

government were once established amongst such a people, it would not only oppress men, but would eventually strip each of them of several of the highest qualities of humanity. Despotism therefore appears to me peculiarly to be dreaded in democratic ages. I should have loved freedom, I believe, at all times, but in the time in which we live I am ready to worship it. On the other hand, I am persuaded that all who shall attempt, in the ages upon which we are entering, to base freedom upon aristocratic privilege, will fail—that all who shall attempt to draw and to retain authority within a single class, will fail. At the present day no ruler is skilful or strong enough to found a despotism, by re-establishing permanent distinctions of rank amongst his subjects: no legislator is wise or powerful enough to preserve free institutions, if he does not take equality for his first principle and his watchword. All those of our contemporaries who would establish or secure the independence and the dignity of their fellow-men, must show themselves the friends of equality; and the only worthy means of showing themselves as such, is to be so: upon this depends the success of their holy enterprise. Thus the question is not how to reconstruct aristocratic society, but how to make liberty proceed out of that democratic state of society in which God has placed us.

These two truths appear to me simple, clear, and fertile in consequences; and they naturally lead me to consider what kind of free government can be established amongst a people in which social conditions are equal. It results from the very constitution of democratic nations and from their necessities, that the power of government amongst them must be more uniform, more centralized, more extensive, more searching, and more efficient than in other countries. Society at large is naturally stronger and more active, individuals more subordinate and weak; the former does more, the latter less; and this is inevitably the case. It is not therefore to be expected that the range of private independence will ever be as extensive in democratic as in aristocratic countries—nor is this to be desired; for, amongst aristocratic nations, the mass is often sacrificed to the individual, and the prosperity of the greater number to the greatness of the few. It is both necessary and desirable that the government of a democratic people should be active and powerful: and our object should not be to render it weak or indolent, but solely to prevent it from abusing its aptitude and its strength.

在我们这个时代，我甚至要崇拜它。而且，我确信在我们正在迈进的时代，所有试图将自由建立在贵族特权之上的人，以及所有试图将权威交给一个阶级独掌的人，都必将失败。凡是想在唯一的阶级里建立并保持权威的人，也将遭到失败。当今，没有任何一个统治者足够强大和有本领到能通过在臣民之间重新确立永久的阶级差别来建立专制统治；也没有一个议员高明和强大到能不以平等为第一原则和号召来维护自由制度。因此，我们这个时代所有想要确立并保障同胞独立尊严的人，必然是平等的朋友，而唯一能够证明自己是平等之友的办法就是平等待人，而他们的神圣事业的成败也完全取决于此。因此，问题不在于如何重建贵族社会，而在于怎样从上帝让我们生活其中的民主社会的内部发掘自由。

在我看来，这两项真理会带来简单而明确的众多结果，并自然而然地引导我去思索哪种自由政府可以在社会状况平等的国家建立。民主国家政府权力之所以比其他国家更为统一、集中、广泛、彻底和高效，是民主国家制度本身及其国家需要的结果。社会自然而然更为活跃和强大，而个人则比较驯服和软弱。也就是说，社会做的事情多，个人做的事情少，而且这种情况不可避免。因此，不要指望个人独立的范围在民主国家会像在贵族制国家那样广泛，而且这也并不是人们所渴望的，因为在贵族制国家群众往往要为某个人而牺牲，而且绝大多数人往往要为某些人的荣华而牺牲自己的财富。民主国家政府的积极和强大不但是必需的，而且是人们所渴望的，而且我们的目的并不是使中央政权变得软弱而懒散，而只是要防止它滥用自己的能力和权力。

在贵族时代保障个人独立最有力的因素是君主不独揽治理公民的职责，而是把部分职

The circumstance which most contributed to secure the independence of private persons in aristocratic ages, was, that the supreme power did not affect to take upon itself alone the government and administration of the community; those functions were necessarily partially left to the members of the aristocracy: so that as the supreme power was always divided, it never weighed with its whole weight and in the same manner on each individual. Not only did the government not perform everything by its immediate agency; but as most of the agents who discharged its duties derived their power not from the State, but from the circumstance of their birth, they were not perpetually under its control. The government could not make or unmake them in an instant, at pleasure, nor bend them in strict uniformity to its slightest caprice—this was an additional guarantee of private independence. I readily admit that recourse cannot be had to the same means at the present time: but I discover certain democratic expedients which may be substituted for them. Instead of vesting in the government alone all the administrative powers of which corporations and nobles have been deprived, a portion of them may be entrusted to secondary public bodies, temporarily composed of private citizens: thus the liberty of private persons will be more secure, and their equality will not be diminished.

The Americans, who care less for words than the French, still designate by the name of "county" the largest of their administrative districts: but the duties of the count or lord-lieutenant are in part performed by a provincial assembly. At a period of equality like our own it would be unjust and unreasonable to institute hereditary officers; but there is nothing to prevent us from substituting elective public officers to a certain extent. Election is a democratic expedient which insures the independence of the public officer in relation to the government, as much and even more than hereditary rank can insure it amongst aristocratic nations. Aristocratic countries abound in wealthy and influential persons who are competent to provide for themselves, and who cannot be easily or secretly oppressed: such persons restrain a government within general habits of moderation and reserve. I am very well aware that democratic countries contain no such persons naturally; but something analogous to them may be created by artificial means. I firmly believe that an aristocracy cannot again be founded in the world; but I think that private citizens, by combining together, may

权交给其他贵族成员，所以中央政权总是分权的，无法对每个人予以同样的重视并用同样的方式加以管理。政府不但不独揽一切，而且大部分承担这些职责的代理人的权力也并非来自国家，而是来自他们的家庭出身，所以他们始终不受国家的控制。政府随时随意任免这些人，也无法迫使他们统一服从自己的指挥。这也是对个人独立的额外保障。我深知，在我们这个时代不能依靠这样的办法，但是我发现一些可以取代这种办法的民主措施。即不将从各团体或贵族那里剥夺的管理权全部交给政府，而取而代之以将一部分的权力交给由普通公民临时组成的次级团体。这样，个人自由将得到更多保障，而他们的平等也不会被削弱。

不像法国人那样注意措辞的美国人，依然用county（县）一词来称呼州之下的最大行政单位，而其部分职责却由州议会代行。在我们这样的平等时代，世袭官员的设立既不公正也不合理，但不妨在一定的范围内用官员选任的办法取而代之。选举是民主制度的权宜之计，并能够像贵族制国家的官员世袭那样，同样甚至可以更好地保障公职人员相对于政府的独立性。贵族制国家有钱有势的人很多，他们生活富裕，不会轻易受到秘密压迫。这些人可以使政府在态度上温和与谨慎。我完全知道，民主国家自然不会有这样的人；但可以人为地创造出与其类似的人物。我深信，世界上再也不会存在贵族制度；但我认为，通过公民个人的联合，也可能形成相当于贵族性质的非常富裕、有影响和强大的社团。通过这样的方式就可以获得贵族强大的政治优势，同时又不具有贵族制度的不公正性和危险。以政治、工业和商业，乃至科学和文艺为目的的社团，是不能随意处置或肆意迫害的既有

constitute bodies of great wealth, influence, and strength, corresponding to the persons of an aristocracy. By this means many of the greatest political advantages of aristocracy would be obtained without its injustice or its dangers. An association for political, commercial, or manufacturing purposes, or even for those of science and literature, is a powerful and enlightened member of the community, which cannot be disposed of at pleasure, or oppressed without remonstrance; and which, by defending its own rights against the encroachments of the government, saves the common liberties of the country.

In periods of aristocracy every man is always bound so closely to many of his fellow-citizens, that he cannot be assailed without their coming to his assistance. In ages of equality every man naturally stands alone; he has no hereditary friends whose co-operation he may demand—no class upon whose sympathy he may rely: he is easily got rid of, and he is trampled on with impunity. At the present time, an oppressed member of the community has therefore only one method of self-defence—he may appeal to the whole nation; and if the whole nation is deaf to his complaint, he may appeal to mankind: the only means he has of making this appeal is by the press. Thus the liberty of the press is infinitely more valuable amongst democratic nations than amongst all others; it is the only cure for the evils which equality may produce. Equality sets men apart and weakens them; but the press places a powerful weapon within every man's reach, which the weakest and loneliest of them all may use. Equality deprives a man of the support of his connections; but the press enables him to summon all his fellow-countrymen and all his fellow-men to his assistance. Printing has accelerated the progress of equality, and it is also one of its best correctives.

I think that men living in aristocracies may, strictly speaking, do without the liberty of the press: but such is not the case with those who live in democratic countries. To protect their personal independence I trust not to great political assemblies, to parliamentary privilege, or to the assertion of popular sovereignty. All these things may, to a certain extent, be reconciled with personal servitude—but that servitude cannot be complete if the press is free: the press is the chiefest democratic instrument of freedom.

Something analogous may be said of the judicial power. It is a part of the essence of judicial

力量又有知识的公民，通过维护自己的权利免遭政府的侵犯，也保护了公民全体的自由。

在贵族时代，每个人都与许多同胞有密切的联系，所以他们一旦受到攻击，这些人就会来帮助他。在平等时代，每个人自然而然彼此孤立。他们既没有可以求援的世代好友，又没有会予以其同情可以仰赖的阶级。他们容易被抛弃，被随意践踏而不受惩罚。因此，在我们这个时代，受到压迫的社会成员只有一种手段可以保护自己，这就是向全国呼吁，而如果全国上下都对此充耳不闻，则只能向全人类呼吁。然而，他们用来进行呼吁的唯一手段就是报刊。因此，出版自由在民主国家比在其他任何国家都无限可贵，它是由平等衍生而出的弊端的唯一解药。平等让人彼此孤立和变得虚弱，但报刊是每一个最弱小最孤独的人都可以利用的强大武器。平等剥夺了亲友对每个人的支持，报刊却可以召唤所有本国同胞乃至全人类。印刷术加速了平等的发展，而同时也是平等最好的矫正手段之一。

我认为，严格来说生活在贵族制下的人们可以不需要出版自由，然而生活在民主制度下的人们却不行。我不相信大规模的政治集会、议会的特权和人民主权的宣言能够保证民主国家人民的个人独立。所有这一切，在一定程度内可以与对个人的奴役相妥协，而如果出版是自由的，这种奴役就不可能是彻底的，所以报刊是民主保护自由的最主要手段。

谈到司法权，也有一些类似之处。处理私人利益纠纷和专注于研究其处理的每件小事，是司法权的本质，而司法权的另一本质是从不主动援助受压迫者，却始终会为向其求援的最微贱者不断提供援助。无论这些人本身多么软弱，他们总是可以要求法官听取他们的控诉并予以答复，因为这是司法制度本身所固有。因此，在政府不断关注和插手个人最

power to attend to private interests, and to fix itself with predilection on minute objects submitted to its observation; another essential quality of judicial power is never to volunteer its assistance to the oppressed, but always to be at the disposal of the humblest of those who solicit it; their complaint, however feeble they may themselves be, will force itself upon the ear of justice and claim redress, for this is inherent in the very constitution of the courts of justice. A power of this kind is therefore peculiarly adapted to the wants of freedom, at a time when the eye and finger of the government are constantly intruding into the minutest details of human actions, and when private persons are at once too weak to protect themselves, and too much isolated for them to reckon upon the assistance of their fellows. The strength of the courts of law has ever been the greatest security which can be offered to personal independence; but this is more especially the case in democratic ages: private rights and interests are in constant danger, if the judicial power does not grow more extensive and more strong to keep pace with the growing equality of conditions.

Equality awakens in men several propensities extremely dangerous to freedom, to which the attention of the legislator ought constantly to be directed. I shall only remind the reader of the most important amongst them. Men living in democratic ages do not readily comprehend the utility of forms: they feel an instinctive contempt for them—I have elsewhere shown for what reasons. Forms excite their contempt and often their hatred; as they commonly aspire to none but easy and present gratifications, they rush onwards to the object of their desires, and the slightest delay exasperates them. This same temper, carried with them into political life, renders them hostile to forms, which perpetually retard or arrest them in some of their projects. Yet this objection which the men of democracies make to forms is the very thing which renders forms so useful to freedom; for their chief merit is to serve as a barrier between the strong and the weak, the ruler and the people, to retard the one, and give the other time to look about him. Forms become more necessary in proportion as the government becomes more active and more powerful, whilst private persons are becoming more indolent and more feeble. Thus democratic nations naturally stand more in need of forms than other nations, and they naturally respect them less. This deserves most serious attention. Nothing is more

微不足道的行动，同时个人又软弱得无力自保和孤立得无法指望同胞支援的时代，这种权力特别适合自由的需要。法院的力量永远都是个人独立的最大保障，而且在民主时代尤其如此。在民主时代，如果司法权不能随平等的加强而不断扩大和强壮，那么个人的权利和利益就不断处于危险之中。

平等唤醒了人身上一些对自由十分有害的癖好，对此立法者应当时常予以关注。在此，我只谈其中最主要的几个。生活在民主时代的人，不容易了解规章制度的功用，对其有一种本能的轻视，至于原因我已经在其他地方讲过。规章制度会激起人们的轻视，而且往往是憎恨。因为人们通常只想轻易获得眼前的满足，于是迫不及待地冲向他们渴望的目标，而且稍有挫折就会感到失望。这样的性格被带入政治生活后，便对始终阻碍拖延他们实现某些计划的规章制度怀有敌意。但是，民主时代的人对规章制度的反感，正是其有利于自由之处，因为规章的主要优势在于其可以在强者和弱者之间、统治者和人民之间筑起一道屏障，可以将一方拖住，而让另一方有时间仔细筹划对策。随着政府越来越积极和强大，同时个人变得越来越懒散和软弱，规章制度越来越必不可少。因此，民主国家的人民自然而然比其他国家的人民更需要规章制度，但他们天生又不太尊重规章制度。这是一个特别值得注意的问题。再没有什么事情比我们当代大多数人傲慢地轻视规章制度这个问题更可悲的了，因为在我们这个时代，最小的规章制度问题也具有前所未有的重要性。人类许多最重大的利益都仰赖他们。我认为，尽管生活在贵族时代的政治家有时会肆意轻视规章制度，并常常会凌驾其之上，但今天各国的政治家们则对最细小的规章制度都非常尊

pitiful than the arrogant disdain of most of our contemporaries for questions of form; for the smallest questions of form have acquired in our time an importance which they never had before: many of the greatest interests of mankind depend upon them. I think that if the statesmen of aristocratic ages could sometimes contemn forms with impunity, and frequently rise above them, the statesmen to whom the government of nations is now confided ought to treat the very least among them with respect, and not neglect them without imperious necessity. In aristocracies the observance of forms was superstitious; amongst us they ought to be kept with a deliberate and enlightened deference.

Another tendency, which is extremely natural to democratic nations and extremely dangerous, is that which leads them ta despise and undervalue the rights of private persons. The attachment which men feel to a right, and the respect which they display for it, is generally proportioned to its importance, or to the length of time during which they have enjoyed it. The rights of private persons amongst democratic nations are commonly of small importance, of recent growth, and extremely precarious—the consequence is that they are often sacrificed without regret, and almost always violated without remorse. But it happens that at the same period and amongst the same nations in which men conceive a natural contempt for the rights of private persons, the rights of society at large are naturally extended and consolidated: in other words, men become less attached to private rights at the very time at which it would be most necessary to retain and to defend what little remains of them. It is therefore most especially in the present democratic ages, that the true friends of the liberty and the greatness of man ought constantly to be on the alert to prevent the power of government from lightly sacrificing the private rights of individuals to the general execution of its designs. At such times no citizen is so obscure that it is not very dangerous to allow him to be oppressed—no private rights are so unimportant that they can be surrendered with impunity to the caprices of a government. The reason is plain:—if the private right of an individual is violated at a time when the human mind is fully impressed with the importance and the sanctity of such rights, the injury done is confined to the individual whose right is infringed; but to violate such a right, at the present day, is deeply to corrupt the manners of the nation and to put the whole community in jeopardy, because the very

重，只在万不得已的情况下才会有所疏忽。在贵族制度下，存在迷信规章制度的现象；而我们则应当对其始终保持谨慎明智的尊重。

对民主国家而言，另一个非常自然又非常危险的趋势就是促使人鄙视和看轻个人权利。人们之所以热爱一种权利并对这种权利表示尊重，一般来说不是因为其重要就是因为人们长期享有它们。民主国家的个人权利往往不具有很大重要性，多为最近出现而且极不稳定。结果，人们往往会毫无遗憾地放弃，而且受到侵犯也不会一直怀恨在心。但是，有时候在人们天生轻视个人权利的时代和国家，社会权力会自然而然得到扩大和巩固。也就是说，在最需要保持和捍卫其仅有的权利的时候，人们便不再那么重视个人权利。因此，特别是在当今民主时代，人类自由和伟大的真正朋友，应当不断提防并设法防止国家权力为全面推行其计划而轻易牺牲个人权利。在这样的时代，没有任何一个人渺小得不会面临受到压迫的危险，也没有任何个人权利微不足道得可能拱手交给专横的政府。其理由很简单，在个人的私人权利被认为重要而神圣的时代，侵害只会波及受到侵害的人，但在今天这个时代，侵犯这种权利就是严重败坏国家的民情，并置整个社会于危险之中，因为这种权利的观念在我们之中会逐渐变质并消失。

无论革命的性质和目的为何，以及在哪里发生，都有其特定的一些习惯、观念和弊端，会必然在长期的革命之中产生并得到推广。当任何一个国家，在短期之内，统治者、舆论和法制不断变换，其人民最终也会养成喜欢变动的爱好，并对暴力迅速带来的所有变化都习以为常。因此，他们自然而然轻视每天都被证明毫无效力的规章制度，而只是在无

notion of this kind of right constantly tends amongst us to be impaired and lost.

There are certain habits, certain notions, and certain vices which are peculiar to a state of revolution, and which a protracted revolution cannot fail to engender and to propagate, whatever be, in other respects, its character, its purpose, and the scene on which it takes place. When any nation has, within a short space of time, repeatedly varied its rulers, its opinions, and its laws, the men of whom it is composed eventually contract a taste for change, and grow accustomed to see all changes effected by sudden violence. Thus they naturally conceive a contempt for forms which daily prove ineffectual; and they do not support without impatience the dominion of rules which they have so often seen infringed. As the ordinary notions of equity and morality no longer suffice to explain and justify all the innovations daily begotten by a revolution, the principle of public utility is called in, the doctrine of political necessity is conjured up, and men accustom themselves to sacrifice private interests without scruple, and to trample on the rights of individuals in order more speedily to accomplish any public purpose.

These habits and notions, which I shall call revolutionary, because all revolutions produce them, occur in aristocracies just as much as amongst democratic nations; but amongst the former they are often less powerful and always less lasting, because there they meet with habits, notions, defects, and impediments, which counteract them: they consequently disappear as soon as the revolution is terminated, and the nation reverts to its former political courses. This is not always the case in democratic countries, in which it is ever to be feared that revolutionary tendencies, becoming more gentle and more regular, without entirely disappearing from society, will be gradually transformed into habits of subjection to the administrative authority of the government. I know of no countries in which revolutions re more dangerous than in democratic countries; because, independently of the accidental and transient evils which must always attend them, they may always create some evils which are permanent and unending. I believe that there are such things as justifiable resistance and legitimate rebellion: I do not therefore assert, as an absolute proposition, that the men of democratic ages ought never to make revolutions; but I think that they have especial reason to hesitate before

奈之下才遵守他们目睹的不断被人们违反的规章制度。因为公正和道德的普通观念不再足以解释并证明革命每天带来的所有革新，所以社会效益原则被引入，政治必要性的学说被召唤，于是人们习惯于自愿牺牲个人私利和践踏个人权利，以便能更为快速地实现所有公共目标。

我之所以称这些习惯和思想为革命的习惯和思想，是因为无论是在贵族制国家还是在民主国家，所有革命中都会造就这些习惯和思想，但在前者它们往往没有那么有力那么持久。因为所有贵族制国家，它们受到原有习惯、思想、缺陷和障碍的抵制。结果，随着革命的结束，它们便随之消失，而国家又重新回到原来的政治道路。但在民主国家则并不总是如此。在这里，人们始终害怕已经变得越来越温和、规范却没有完全从社会消失的革命倾向，会改头换面逐渐成为政府的行政习惯。我不知道还有什么国家的革命比民主国家的革命更危险，因为除了民主国家时常出现的偶然和暂时的灾难之外，他们还经常会制造长期的、永无休止的灾难。我相信会出现公正的抵抗和正当的造反。因此，我无法断言，民主时代的人永远不会革命，但我认为他们有特殊的理由在发动革命之前三思而行，并感到与其诉诸如此危险的救治手段，不如忍受目前的诸多委屈。

最后，我将用一个一般观点来做总结。这一观点不仅囊括本章所讲述的所有个别观点，而且还涵盖本书旨在讲述的大部分观点。在我们之前的贵族时代，个人权力极大，而社会权威则极为弱势，社会轮廓本身也模糊不清，混杂着统治公民的不同权力。因此，这个时代人们把主要力量用在加强、扩大以及保障社会权力；而另一方面，则用在将个人独

they embark in them, and that it is far better to endure many grievances in their present condition than to have recourse to so perilous a remedy.

I shall conclude by one general idea, which comprises not only all the particular ideas which have been expressed in the present chapter, but also most of those which it is the object of this book to treat of. In the ages of aristocracy which preceded our own, there were private persons of great power, and a social authority of extreme weakness. The outline of society itself was not easily discernible, and constantly confounded with the different powers by which the community was ruled. The principal efforts of the men of those times were required to strengthen, aggrandize, and secure the supreme power; and on the other hand, to circumscribe individual independence within narrower limits, and to subject private interests to the interests of the public. Other perils and other cares await the men of our age. Amongst the greater part of modern nations, the government, whatever may be its origin, its constitution, or its name, has become almost omnipotent, and private persons are falling, more and more, into the lowest stage of weakness and dependence. In olden society everything was different; unity and uniformity were nowhere to be met with. In modern society everything threatens to become so much alike, that the peculiar characteristics of each individual will soon be entirely lost in the general aspect of the world. Our forefathers were ever prone to make an improper use of the notion, that private rights ought to be respected; and we are naturally prone on the other hand to exaggerate the idea that the interest of a private individual ought always to bend to the interest of the many. The political world is metamorphosed: new remedies must henceforth be sought for new disorders. To lay down extensive, but distinct and settled limits, to the action of the government; to confer certain rights on private persons, and to secure to them the undisputed enjoyment of those rights; to enable individual man to maintain whatever independence, strength, and original power he still possesses; to raise him by the side of society at large, and uphold him in that position— these appear to me the main objects of legislators in the ages upon which we are now entering. It would seem as if the rulers of our time sought only to use men in order to make things great; I wish that they would try a little more to make great men; that they would set less value on the work,

立限制在更为狭小的范围之内，并致力于让个人利益服从公共利益。而等待我们这个时代人们的则是另一种危险和另一种忧虑。在绝大部分现代国家，政府无论其出身、体制或名号如何，几乎都拥有无限权力；而个人则越来越沦落成为最软弱和最有依附性的人。在以前的社会，事情则完全不是这个样子。在那里，在任何地方都看不到统一或一致。在现代社会里，所有一切都迫使人们变得相似，以至于每个人的独有特点不久后将完全消失在千人一面的世界。我们的祖先往往滥用个人权利应受到尊重的观点，而我们则自然而然喜欢夸大个人利益应始终服从多数人利益的观点。政治世界正在变化，因此今后必须寻找新的办法来解决新的无序。对于政府的行为必须要划定广泛而明确固定的界限，为了赋予个人特定的权利并确保个人能够无可争议地享有这些权利，为能使个人保持无论怎样的独立、影响力和独创精神，让个人与社会平起平坐并对其地位予以支持，在我看来，这些就是我们正迈进的这个时代立法者的主要目标。我们这个时代的统治者们似乎只想利用人们去完成伟大的事业。我希望他们能多花点工夫去造就伟大的人物，少点重视工作多点重视工作的人，并永远不要忘记，当国家中的每个人都很软弱的时候，国家本身也不可能长期繁荣，而且也无法找到一种社会政权形式或组织结构，能让由一群懦弱无力的公民组成的社会造就精力充沛的国家。

我发现在我们现代人之中存在两种对立的但同样有害的观点。一些人只注意到平等原则造就的无政府状态的倾向。他们害怕自己的自由意志，即自己害怕自己。另一些人尽管人数不多，但更有知识，则持有另一种不同看法。除了那条始自平等最终通向无政府状

and more upon the workman; that they would never forget that a nation cannot long remain strong when every man belonging to it is individually weak, and that no form or combination of social polity has yet been devised, to make an energetic people out of a community of pusillanimous and enfeebled citizens.

I trace amongst our contemporaries two contrary notions which are equally injurious. One set of men can perceive nothing in the principle of equality but the anarchical tendencies which it engenders: they dread their own free agency—they fear themselves. Other thinkers, less numerous but more enlightened, take a different view: besides that track which starts from the principle of equality to terminate in anarchy, they have at last discovered the road which seems to lead men to inevitable servitude. They shape their souls beforehand to this necessary condition; and, despairing of remaining free, they already do obeisance in their hearts to the master who is soon to appear. The former abandon freedom, because they think it dangerous; the latter, because they hold it to be impossible. If I had entertained the latter conviction, I should not have written this book, but I should have confined myself to deploring in secret the destiny of mankind. I have sought to point out the dangers to which the principle of equality exposes the independence of man, because I firmly believe that these dangers are the most formidable, as well as the least foreseen, of all those which futurity holds in store: but I do not think that they are insurmountable. The men who live in the democratic ages upon which we are entering have naturally a taste for independence: they are naturally impatient of regulation, and they are wearied by the permanence even of the condition they themselves prefer. They are fond of power; but they are prone to despise and hate those who wield it, and they easily elude its grasp by their own mobility and insignificance. These propensities will always manifest themselves, because they originate in the groundwork of society, which will undergo no change: for a long time they will prevent the establishment of any despotism, and they will furnish fresh weapons to each succeeding generation which shall struggle in favor of the liberty of mankind. Let us then look forward to the future with that salutary fear which makes men keep watch and ward for freedom, not with that faint and idle terror which depresses and enervates the heart.

态的道路以外，他们最终发现另一条让人们不可避免走向奴役的小路。他们提前将自己的灵魂塑造得符合这种必然的奴役，并因为已对自由绝望，便在心中开始崇拜不久即将出现的主人。前者放弃自由是因为他们认为自由危险，而后者之所以放弃自由是因为他们认定自由无法实现。如果我秉持后者的观点，那么我应该不会写这本书，而是在内心悄悄为我们人类的命运而扼腕叹息。我之所以试图指出平等原则给人的独立带来的危害，是因为我坚信这些危害是未来所有隐患中最可怕的，也是最无法预见的。但我并不认为它们无法克服。生活在我们正在进入的民主时代的人，天生爱好独立，自然无可奈何地忍受着限制，而且他们甚至对自己选定的心仪的社会状况的始终不变而感到厌倦。他们喜欢权力，但又轻视和憎恨行使权力的人，并凭借自己的渺小和流动性轻易逃脱权力的控制。这些癖好将会在人们身上经常反复出现，因为它们来自始终不会改变的社会情况。在很长一段时期内，它们会阻止任何一种专制的确立，并赋予为人类自由而斗争的前赴后继的每一代人新的武器。因此，在展望未来的时候，让我们怀着可以使人们始终警惕并为自由而斗争的有益的忧虑，而不要抱有会令人沮丧而无力的虚弱无能的恐惧。

第八章 综述

在我结束这项已经进行许久的研究之前，我很乐于再综述一下现代社会的各种特点，并最后评判一下民主原则对人类命运产生的一般影响。但是，这项工作的艰巨性让我有些犹豫；在如此重大的题目面前，我感到自己的视野不够宽阔，理性也难以胜任。我试图描

Chapter VIII: General Survey Of The Subject

Before I close forever the theme that has detained me so long, I would fain take a parting survey of all the various characteristics of modern society, and appreciate at last the general influence to be exercised by the principle of equality upon the fate of mankind; but I am stopped by the difficulty of the task, and in presence of so great an object my sight is troubled, and my reason fails. The society of the modern world which I have sought to delineate, and which I seek to judge, has but just come into existence. Time has not yet shaped it into perfect form: the great revolution by which it has been created is not yet over: and amidst the occurrences of our time, it is almost impossible to discern what will pass away with the revolution itself, and what will survive its close. The world which is rising into existence is still half encumbered by the remains of the world which is waning into decay; and amidst the vast perplexity of human affairs, none can say how much of ancient institutions and former manners will remain, or how much will completely disappear. Although the revolution which is taking place in the social condition, the laws, the opinions, and the feelings of men, is still very far from being terminated, yet its results already admit of no comparison with anything that the world has ever before witnessed. I go back from age to age up to the remotest antiquity; but I find no parallel to what is occurring before my eyes: as the past has ceased to throw its light upon the future, the mind of man wanders in obscurity. Nevertheless, in the midst of a prospect so wide, so novel and so confused, some of the more prominent characteristics may already be discerned and pointed out. The good things and the evils of life are more equally distributed in the world: great wealth tends to disappear, the number of small fortunes to increase; desires and gratifications are multiplied, but extraordinary prosperity and irremediable penury are alike unknown. The sentiment of ambition is universal, but the scope of ambition is seldom vast. Each individual stands apart in solitary weakness; but society at large is active, provident, and powerful: the performances of private persons are insignificant, those of the State immense. There is little energy of character; but manners are mild, and laws humane. If there be few instances of exalted heroism or of virtues of the highest, brightest, and purest temper, men's habits are regular, violence is rare, and cruelty almost unknown. Human

绘并品评的现代世界的社会不过刚刚出现，还没有足够的时间使之完全成形，而使之产生的大革命还没有结束。而在我们这个时代所发生的一切当中，还几乎不可能看清哪些东西会随革命本身的结束而消失，而哪些又会在革命结束之后继续存在下去。新兴的世界还有一半深陷在正处于衰败世界的废墟之中；而且，在纷繁复杂的人类事务之中，没有人能说得清楚会有多少古老的制度和习俗能够劫后余生，又有多少会消失殆尽。尽管发生在社会情况、法制、观念和人们感情方面的革命依然还远未结束，但其后果已远非世界迄今为止发生的任何事情可比。我一个时代一个时代地向上一直追溯到最遥远的古代，但始终没有发现一个与眼前所发生的变化相似的变化。因为过去已经无法再为未来提供借鉴，所以人类的思想正在黑暗中摸索。然而，在这片如此广阔、新奇和混乱的前景之中，一些更为突出的特征已经表现出来。在世界上，善与恶的分布更为平等，各占一半。巨富已经不见，小康之家日益增加。人们的渴望和享受成倍增加，但无以复加的繁荣和无可救药的贫困都同样不存在。人们普遍都有野心，但胸怀大志者不多。每个人都孤立而软弱，但整个社会却活跃、有远见并强大，个人做小事，而国家做大事。个性的光辉已难以闪耀，但民情温和，立法人性。即使没有什么崇高的英雄主义，以及最高尚、最光辉和最纯洁的美德的示范，人们的习惯依然纯朴，暴力现象极为罕见，而残酷几乎更是闻所未闻。人的寿命越来越长，财富越来越有保障。生活虽然不光辉迤逦，但异常安逸舒适。既没有过于高雅也没有过于庸俗的享乐；而且也不讲究繁文缛节，也没有低级趣味的嗜好。既看不到饱学之士，也没有愚昧无知的平民。天才越来越少，但知识越来越普及。人类思想的发展依靠的

existence becomes longer, and property more secure: life is not adorned with brilliant trophies, but it is extremely easy and tranquil. Few pleasures are either very refined or very coarse; and highly polished manners are as uncommon as great brutality of tastes. Neither men of great learning, nor extremely ignorant communities, are to be met with; genius becomes more rare, information more diffused. The human mind is impelled by the small efforts of all mankind combined together, not by the strenuous activity of certain men. There is less perfection, but more abundance, in all the productions of the arts. The ties of race, of rank, and of country are relaxed; the great bond of humanity is strengthened. If I endeavor to find out the most general and the most prominent of all these different characteristics, I shall have occasion to perceive, that what is taking place in men's fortunes manifests itself under a thousand other forms. Almost all extremes are softened or blunted: all that was most prominent is superseded by some mean term, at once less lofty and less low, less brilliant and less obscure, than what before existed in the world.

When I survey this countless multitude of beings, shaped in each other's likeness, amidst whom nothing rises and nothing falls, the sight of such universal uniformity saddens and chills me, and I am tempted to regret that state of society which has ceased to be. When the world was full of men of great importance and extreme insignificance, of great wealth and extreme poverty, of great learning and extreme ignorance, I turned aside from the latter to fix my observation on the former alone, who gratified my sympathies. But I admit that this gratification arose from my own weakness: it is because I am unable to see at once all that is around me, that I am allowed thus to select and separate the objects of my predilection from among so many others. Such is not the case with that almighty and eternal Being whose gaze necessarily includes the whole of created things, and who surveys distinctly, though at once, mankind and man. We may naturally believe that it is not the singular prosperity of the few, but the greater well-being of all, which is most pleasing in the sight of the Creator and Preserver of men. What appears to me to be man's decline, is to His eye advancement; what afflicts me is acceptable to Him. A state of equality is perhaps less elevated, but it is more just; and its justice constitutes its greatness and its beauty. I would strive then to raise myself to this point

是所有人类微小努力的共同推动，而不是某几个人的强大推动。在所有的文艺作品之中，杰作虽不常见，但数量却大增。种族、阶级、国家的各种束缚越来越松弛，而人类的大团结却得到加强。如果我试图从所有这些不同特征中找出最普遍和最显著的特征，我会认为其表现在人们财产形式的千变万化上。几乎所有的极端现象都趋于缓和。所有那些最突出的东西都会被普通的东西所取代，它们与世界上曾经存在过的类似东西相比，既不高也不低，既不光彩也不逊色。

我环顾四周无数众生，他们彼此相似，既没有人出类拔萃也没有人落于人后，如此普遍统一的情景不仅让我感到悲伤和心寒，而且为已不复存在的社会状况感到遗憾。当世界充满大人物和小人物、巨富和赤贫、饱学之士和愚昧的人的时候，我总是会把视线从后者转向前者，而且并对他们充满同情。但是，我知道这种情绪来自我自身的弱点，因为我无法同时观察周围所有的一切，于是只能从如此众多的对象之中选择和分离出我最喜欢的对象。然而，全能和永恒的上帝则并非如此，他的目光必然遍及所有事物，并一下子就能同时把整个人类和每个人看得清清楚楚。我们自然相信，在造物主和人类守护者眼中令其欣喜的并不是少数人的荣华富贵，而是所有人的更大的幸福。因此，在我看来是人类衰退的东西，在上帝看来则是进步的东西，令我感到不快的事物，是他所钟爱。平等也许并不怎么崇高，但它非常正义，它的正义让它变得伟大和美丽。我要努力让自己的观念达到上帝的高度，并从这一观念去考察和判断世间的事物。

世界上还没有人能够绝对全面地断言，世界的新状况比旧状况要更好，但已经可以轻

of the divine contemplation, and thence to view and to judge the concerns of men.

No man, upon the earth, can as yet affirm absolutely and generally, that the new state of the world is better than its former one; but it is already easy to perceive that this state is different. Some vices and some virtues were so inherent in the constitution of an aristocratic nation, and are so opposite to the character of a modern people, that they can never be infused into it; some good tendencies and some bad propensities which were unknown to the former, are natural to the latter; some ideas suggest themselves spontaneously to the imagination of the one, which are utterly repugnant to the mind of the other. They are like two distinct orders of human beings, each of which has its own merits and defects, its own advantages and its own evils. Care must therefore be taken not to judge the state of society, which is now coming into existence, by notions derived from a state of society which no longer exists; for as these states of society are exceedingly different in their structure, they cannot be submitted to a just or fair comparison. It would be scarcely more reasonable to require of our own contemporaries the peculiar virtues which originated in the social condition of their forefathers, since that social condition is itself fallen, and has drawn into one promiscuous ruin the good and evil which belonged to it.

But as yet these things are imperfectly understood. I find that a great number of my contemporaries undertake to make a certain selection from amongst the institutions, the opinions, and the ideas which originated in the aristocratic constitution of society as it was: a portion of these elements they would willingly relinquish, but they would keep the remainder and transplant them into their new world. I apprehend that such men are wasting their time and their strength in virtuous but unprofitable efforts. The object is not to retain the peculiar advantages which the inequality of conditions bestows upon mankind, but to secure the new benefits which equality may supply. We have not to seek to make ourselves like our progenitors, but to strive to work out that species of greatness and happiness which is our own. For myself, who now look back from this extreme limit of my task, and discover from afar, but at once, the various objects which have attracted my more attentive investigation upon my way, I am full of apprehensions and of hopes. I perceive mighty

易察觉到它们的不同。贵族制国家体制所固有的一些善和恶，与现代人的性格格格不入，因此不能为人们所接受。前者全然不知的一些好的倾向和坏的嗜好，在后者看来却自然而然。某些从一方的想象中自发产生的思想，却被另一方所排斥。它们就像两个完全不同的人一样，各有各的优点和缺点，各有各的优势和弊端。因此，必须特别注意，不要用源自已经消失的社会状况的观点去判断正在形成的社会。因为这两种社会其结构截然不同，所以无法进行公正公平的比较。要求我们这个时代的人具有适合他们祖先的社会情况的美德，也绝不合理，因为原有的社会情况已经崩溃，而其原有的一切善与恶，也随之陷入混乱。

但是，因为这些情况现在还无法充分了解，我注意到，于是大多数当代人便从源自旧贵族制社会的制度、观念和思想中进行选择。他们会随意放弃其中一部分，而将留下的另一部分植入新世界。我认为，这些人正在浪费时间和他们的经历干一件徒劳无功的事情。保留不平等赋予人类的那些特殊好处并不是目的，而确保平等可能会带给人们的新利益才是目的之所在。我们不必试图让自己与祖辈相同，而是应当努力表现出我们自己所特有的伟大和幸福。至于我自己，在我的讨论行将结束之时，远远地回顾一下曾在我的研究之路上引起我极大关注的所有不同对象，我既充满恐惧又满怀希望。我注意到一些巨大的危险，但并非无药可救；一些重大的弊端，却也可以规避或缓解。因此，我更坚定地认为，只要民主国家愿意，就能建成高尚而繁荣的社会。我意识到，许多当代人认为从此以后，人民在世上从未做过自己的主人，他们必然要服从某种来自外部条件、种族、土地和气候

dangers which it is possible to ward off—mighty evils which may be avoided or alleviated; and I cling with a firmer hold to the belief, that for democratic nations to be virtuous and prosperous they require but to will it. I am aware that many of my contemporaries maintain that nations are never their own masters here below, and that they necessarily obey some insurmountable and unintelligent power, arising from anterior events, from their race, or from the soil and climate of their country. Such principles are false and cowardly; such principles can never produce aught but feeble men and pusillanimous nations. Providence has not created mankind entirely independent or entirely free. It is true that around every man a fatal circle is traced, beyond which he cannot pass; but within the wide verge of that circle he is powerful and free: as it is with man, so with communities. The nations of our time cannot prevent the conditions of men from becoming equal; but it depends upon themselves whether the principle of equality is to lead them to servitude or freedom, to knowledge or barbarism, to prosperity or to wretchedness.

的难以克服和无法理解的力量的支配。这是一种错误的消极观念，只会让人永远软弱，国家永远懦弱。上帝创造的人类，既非完全独立又非完全自由。的确，在每个人的周围都有一个他所无法逾越的命运注定的圈子，但是在这个圈子广泛的范围之内，他依然强大而自由。如同一个人一样，一个国家也是如此。我们这个时代的国家无法阻止国内平等的发展，至于平等最终会将其引向奴役还是自由，文明还是野蛮，繁荣还是贫困，还是由它们自己说了算。

APPENDIX

Appendix A

For information concerning all the countries of the West which have not been visited by Europeans, consult the account of two expeditions undertaken at the expense of Congress by Major Long. This traveller particularly mentions, on the subject of the great American desert, that a line may be drawn nearly parallel to the 20th degree of longitude (meridian of Washington), beginning from the Red River and ending at the River Platte. From this imaginary line to the Rocky Mountains, which bound the valley of the Mississippi on the west, lie immense plains, which are almost entirely covered with sand, incapable of cultivation, or scattered over with masses of granite. In summer, these plains are quite destitute of water, and nothing is to be seen on them but herds of buffaloes and wild horses. Some hordes of Indians are also found there, but in no great numbers. Major Long was told that in travelling northwards from the River Platte you find the same desert lying constantly on the left; but he was unable to ascertain the truth of this report. However worthy of confidence may be the narrative of Major Long, it must be remembered that he only passed through the country of which he speaks, without deviating widely from the line which he had traced out for his journey.

Appendix B

South America, in the region between the tropics, produces an incredible profusion of climbing

附录

A

有关欧洲人尚未涉足的所有西部地区的相关信息，可以参看朗少校在国会资助下所进行的考察的两次报告。对于美国的大沙漠，他特别指出，可以紧靠东经20° （以华盛顿为0°）并与这条经线几乎平行，从鲁日河为起点到普拉特河为终点画一条线。从这条假想的线到密西西比河谷的西侧落基山脉之间，存在一些面积巨大的平地，这里几乎完全被沙子所覆盖，寸草不生，并有花岗岩的石块散落在各处。夏天这里极度缺水，除了许多成群的野牛和野马什么也看不到。也有一些印第安人部落在这里，但每个部落的人数不多。朗少校听人说，沿普拉特河向北，其左岸也常会看到这样的沙漠，但他未能亲自考察证实这一传闻。郎少校的描述是值得信任的。但不应忘记，他只是穿越了他所说的地区，而没有走到他所经过的路线的两侧做反复细致的考察。

B

在南美的南北回归线之间的地区，到处都是大量的攀缘植物，仅在安的列斯群岛一

plants, of which the flora of the Antilles alone presents us with forty different species. Among the most graceful of these shrubs is the passion-flower, which, according to Descourtiz, grows with such luxuriance in the Antilles, as to climb trees by means of the tendrils with which it is provided, and form moving bowers of rich and elegant festoons, decorated with blue and purple flowers, and fragrant with perfume. The Mimosa scandens (Acacia a grandes gousses) is a creeper of enormous and rapid growth, which climbs from tree to tree, and sometimes covers more than half a league.

Appendix C

The languages which are spoken by the Indians of America, from the Pole to Cape Horn, are said to be all formed upon the same model, and subject to the same grammatical rules; whence it may fairly be concluded that all the Indian nations sprang from the same stock. Each tribe of the American continent speaks a different dialect; but the number of languages, properly so called, is very small, a fact which tends to prove that the nations of the New World had not a very remote origin. Moreover, the languages of America have a great degree of regularity, from which it seems probable that the tribes which employ them had not undergone any great revolutions, or been incorporated voluntarily or by constraint, with foreign nations. For it is generally the union of several languages into one which produces grammatical irregularities. It is not long since the American languages, especially those of the North, first attracted the serious attention of philologists, when the discovery was made that this idiom of a barbarous people was the product of a complicated system of ideas and very learned combinations. These languages were found to be very rich, and great pains had been taken at their formation to render them agreeable to the ear. The grammatical system of the Americans differs from all others in several points, but especially in the following:—Some nations of Europe, amongst others the Germans, have the power of combining at pleasure different expressions, and thus giving a complex sense to certain words. The Indians have given a

地，就有美洲野藤40多种。其中最优美的就要属鸡蛋果藤。德库蒂兹在其记述安的列斯群岛植物界的著作中说，它们利用自身生长的卷须爬上大树，在林中形成一条条拱廊或柱廊。这些拱廊或柱廊，其间点缀着蓝色和紫色的美丽花朵，散发着优雅的香气。大豆荚金合欢，是一种非常粗的藤本植物。它生长快速，从一棵树爬向另一棵树，有时可以蔓延半里约以上。

C

美洲印第安人所说的语言，从北极圈一直到合恩角，据说都基于同样的句式和同样的语法规则。因此，基本上可以得出结论，所有的印第安人为同一血统。美洲大陆的每个部落，都操着自己不同的方言。但是，符合严格定义的语言却为数很少，这一事实可以用来证明新大陆的各民族并没有非常古老的起源。然而，美洲土著的语言在很大程度上很有规律，由此可以推断，似乎现存的各个部落还未经历过巨大的革命，或是自愿和非自愿地与外来民族混合。因为一般来说，几种语言合而为一后，必然出现语法规则的混乱。不久，美洲的土著语言，特别是北美的土著语言，首先得到语言学家的认真研究。他们发现，野蛮人的土语是一套非常复杂的思想体系的产物，并组织得极其合理。此外，这种语言极其丰富，而且在创制的时候还特别注意到听觉的可变性。美洲语言的语法体系，在许多方面与其他语言大不相同，特别是在下列方面。欧洲的一些民族，除了德国之外，可以随意把不同的表达联结起来，因此有些词可以表示许多复杂的意思。印第安语则将这一特点加以惊人地扩大，甚至到达只用一个词就能表达一大堆概念的地步。利用杜邦索先生在

most surprising extension to this power, so as to arrive at the means of connecting a great number of ideas with a single term. This will be easily understood with the help of an example quoted by Mr. Duponceau, in the "Memoirs of the Philosophical Society of America": A Delaware woman playing with a cat or a young dog, says this writer, is heard to pronounce the word kuligatschis, which is thus composed: k is the sign of the second person, and signifies "thou" or "thy"; uli is a part of the word wulit, which signifies "beautiful," "pretty"; gat is another fragment, of the word wichgat, which means "paw"; and, lastly, schis is a diminutive giving the idea of smallness. Thus in one word the Indian woman has expressed "Thy pretty little paw." Take another example of the felicity with which the savages of America have composed their words. A young man of Delaware is called pilape. This word is formed from pilsit, "chaste," "innocent"; and lenape, "man"; viz., "man in his purity and innocence." This facility of combining words is most remarkable in the strange formation of their verbs. The most complex action is often expressed by a single verb, which serves to convey all the shades of an idea by the modification of its construction. Those who may wish to examine more in detail this subject, which I have only glanced at superficially, should read:—

1. The correspondence of Mr. Duponceau and the Rev. Mr. Hecwelder relative to the Indian languages, which is to be found in the first volume of the "Memoirs of the Philosophical Society of America," published at Philadelphia, 1819, by Abraham Small; vol. i. p. 356-464.

2. The "Grammar of the Delaware or the Lenape Language," by Geiberger, and the preface of Mr. Duponceau. All these are in the same collection, vol. iii.

3. An excellent account of these works, which is at the end of the sixth volume of the American Encyclopaedia.

Appendix D

See in Charlevoix, vol. i. p. 235, the history of the first war which the French inhabitants of

《美国哲学学会报告》中引用的例子，可以轻松说明这一点。一个特拉华族的妇女在逗弄一只小猫或小狗时，会听到她反复说kuligatschis。而这就是一个由数个词合成的词。其中的k 代表第二人称，意为"你"或"你的"；uli 读作ouli（乌利），是wulit 一词的中段，意为"美丽的"和"可爱的"；gat 是wichgat 一词的末段，意为"爪子"；最后的schis，读作chise（西斯），是一个表示小形的爱称词尾。因此，印第安妇女只用一词，就表达了"你可爱的小爪子"这层意思。这里，还有一个例子更能令人信服他所说明的美洲蛮族是善于联结他们的单词的。一个特拉华族的男青年自称pilape。这个词是由pilsii（意为"纯洁的""无辜的"）和lenape（意为"人"）组成的。就是说，他自称是"纯洁的人"。这种把几个词连缀起来的特点，尤其常见于动词的合成方面。一个非常复杂的动作，往往只用一个动词来表示。意思上的几乎一切细微差别，都能用动词和改变动词的词形表示出来。想要详细了解我只是略微提及的这个问题的人，可以阅读：

1. 杜邦索先生与赫克维尔德牧师关于印第安语的通信。这封通信载于阿伯拉罕·斯莫尔主编的1819年在费城出版的《美国哲学学会报告》第1卷第356~464页。

2. 盖伯格的《特拉华语或勒纳普语语法》以及杜邦索先生的序言。此书共三卷。

3. 《美国百科全书》第6卷末尾所收上述语法书的摘要。

D

参见夏尔瓦的《新法兰西的历史》〔全称为《新法兰西的历史与通志以及奉王命去北

Canada carried on, in 1610, against the Iroquois. The latter, armed with bows and arrows, offered a desperate resistance to the French and their allies. Charlevoix is not a great painter, yet he exhibits clearly enough, in this narrative, the contrast between the European manners and those of savages, as well as the different way in which the two races of men understood the sense of honor. When the French, says he, seized upon the beaver-skins which covered the Indians who had fallen, the Hurons, their allies, were greatly offended at this proceeding; but without hesitation they set to work in their usual manner, inflicting horrid cruelties upon the prisoners, and devouring one of those who had been killed, which made the Frenchmen shudder. The barbarians prided themselves upon a scrupulousness which they were surprised at not finding in our nation, and could not understand that there was less to reprehend in the stripping of dead bodies than in the devouring of their flesh like wild beasts. Charlevoix, in another place (vol. i. p. 230), thus describes the first torture of which Champlain was an eyewitness, and the return of the Hurons into their own village. Having proceeded about eight leagues, says he, our allies halted; and having singled out one of their captives, they reproached him with all the cruelties which he had practised upon the warriors of their nation who had fallen into his hands, and told him that he might expect to be treated in like manner; adding, that if he had any spirit he would prove it by singing. He immediately chanted forth his death-song, and then his war-song, and all the songs he knew, "but in a very mournful strain," says Champlain, who was not then aware that all savage music has a melancholy character. The tortures which succeeded, accompanied by all the horrors which we shall mention hereafter, terrified the French, who made every effort to put a stop to them, but in vain. The following night, one of the Hurons having dreamt that they were pursued, the retreat was changed to a real flight, and the savages never stopped until they were out of the reach of danger. The moment they perceived the cabins of their own village, they cut themselves long sticks, to which they fastened the scalps which had fallen to their share, and carried them in triumph. At this sight, the women swam to the canoes, where they received the bloody scalps from the hands of their husbands, and tied them round their necks. The warriors offered one of these horrible trophies to Champlain; they also presented him with some bows and arrows—the only

美旅行日记》（共6卷，巴黎，1744年）］的第1卷第235页，载有1610年加拿大法国人对易洛魁人的第一次战争历史。尽管易洛魁人的武器只是弓箭，但却对法国人及其盟友进行殊死抵抗。夏尔瓦虽然并非写作高手，但对这段历史的描述已足够清晰地展示出欧洲人和野蛮人品德的对比，以及两个种族对待荣誉的不同态度。他写到，当法国人纷纷争抢卧死疆场的易洛魁人的海狸皮衣之时，他们的盟友休伦人则对此行径大为不满。但他们毫不犹豫地对俘虏施以他们习以为常的酷刑，并将一个被他们杀死的人狼吞虎咽，这着实让法国人胆寒。野蛮人以无私不贪为荣，对我们没有这种想法甚为惊讶，而且无法理解为什么像吃野兽的肉一样吃死人的肉要比扒死人的衣服受到更多的斥责。夏尔瓦在第1卷的另一处，即在第230页，还曾转述过尚普兰首次目睹的割肉酷刑和休伦人回到自己村舍时的情景。他说：在走了8里约以后，我们的盟友停了下来。他们从俘虏中选出一个，对他施以他们的同族战士落到这个俘虏的所在部族手中时受过的一切酷刑，并告诉他，他的结局理应如此；并补充道，如果他有勇气，可以用歌声伴奏来证明。这个俘虏立即唱起战歌，而且把他所会的一切歌都唱完，歌声十分悲怆。尚普兰说，他还从不知道野蛮人的音乐竟有如此悲伤的调子。这种处死办法还伴以我们随后即将谈到的各种酷刑，这可吓坏了法国人。他们想要阻止这一切但徒劳无益。当天夜里，一个休伦人梦到他们受到追击，撤退简直变成了逃命：而野蛮人紧追不舍，完全把危险置之度外。他们一望见自己的村舍，立即砍了一些长竿子，把各自分得的被处死的俘虏的头皮拴在竿头，以示凯旋。见到此景，妇女们纷纷跳进水里登上独木舟，从自己丈夫的手里接过血淋淋的头皮，围在自己的脖子上。一个战士

spoils of the Iroquois which they had ventured to seize—entreating him to show them to the King of France. Champlain lived a whole winter quite alone among these barbarians, without being under any alarm for his person or property.

Appendix E

Although the Puritanical strictness which presided over the establishment of the English colonies in America is now much relaxed, remarkable traces of it are still found in their habits and their laws. In 1792, at the very time when the anti-Christian republic of France began its ephemeral existence, the legislative body of Massachusetts promulgated the following law, to compel the citizens to observe the Sabbath. We give the preamble and the principal articles of this law, which is worthy of the reader's attention: "Whereas," says the legislator, "the observation of the Sunday is an affair of public interest; inasmuch as it produces a necessary suspension of labor, leads men to reflect upon the duties of life, and the errors to which human nature is liable, and provides for the public and private worship of God, the creator and governor of the universe, and for the performance of such acts of charity as are the ornament and comfort of Christian societies:—Whereas irreligious or light-minded persons, forgetting the duties which the Sabbath imposes, and the benefits which these duties confer on society, are known to profane its sanctity, by following their pleasures or their affairs; this way of acting being contrary to their own interest as Christians, and calculated to annoy those who do not follow their example; being also of great injury to society at large, by spreading a taste for dissipation and dissolute manners; Be it enacted and ordained by the Governor, Council, and Representatives convened in General Court of Assembly, that all and every person and persons shall on that day carefully apply themselves to the duties of religion and piety, that no tradesman or labourer shall exercise his ordinary calling, and that no game or recreation shall be used on the Lord's Day, upon pain of forfeiting ten shillings.

"That no one shall travel on that day, or any part thereof, under pain of forfeiting twenty shillings;

将一件这样令人生畏的战利品送给尚普兰，还送给他几张弓、几支箭，还将原本打算自己留下的那张仅有的易洛魁人皮，托尚普兰呈给法兰西国王。他只身在这些野蛮人中间生活了整整一个冬天，没有受到任何人身和财产侵害。

E

虽然在美洲英国殖民地建立之初占有支配地位的清教徒的清规戒律如今已不再那样严格，但在他们的习惯和法律上仍能看到一些明显的痕迹。在1792年反对基督教的法兰西共和国开始其昙花一现的时候，马萨诸塞的立法团便公布了一项法律强制公民遵守礼拜日。下面引述该法律的序言和主要条款，值得读者一读：

鉴于遵守礼拜日是一项公益活动，能够让劳动得到必要的暂停，并引导人们反思人生的意义以及人类不可避免的错误，让人们独自和集体礼拜宇宙的创造者和统治　者上帝，并使人们专心于这种使基督教社会增辉和安宁的善行。

鉴于不虔诚信教或轻佻浮华的人会忘记礼拜日应尽的义务和社会给予他们的好处，而亵渎神明沉湎于自己的享乐或事务；鉴于这样的行为有违基督徒固有的义务，会干扰到不仿效他们的人，从而给整个社会带来极大伤害，使放荡浪费之风蔓延。

参议院和众议院兹命令如下：

第一条　在礼拜日，任何人不得在自己的店铺或作坊里做活。在这一天，任何人也不得从事任何劳动和公务，不得出席任何音乐会、舞会或观看任何性质的演出，不得进行任何种

that no vessel shall leave a harbour of the colony; that no persons shall keep outside the meeting-house during the time of public worship, or profane the time by playing or talking, on penalty of five shillings.

"Public-houses shall not entertain any other than strangers or lodgers, under penalty of five shillings for every person found drinking and abiding therein.

"Any person in health, who, without sufficient reason, shall omit to worship God in public during three months, shall be condemned to a fine of ten shillings.

"Any person guilty of misbehaviour in a place of public worship, shall be fined from five to forty shillings.

"These laws are to be enforced by the tything-men of each township, who have authority to visit public-houses on the Sunday. The innkeeper who shall refuse them admittance, shall be fined forty shillings for such offence.

"The tything-men are to stop travellers, and require of them their reason for being on the road on Sunday; anyone refusing to answer, shall be sentenced to pay a fine not exceeding five pounds sterling. If the reason given by the traveller be not deemed by the tything-man sufficient, he may bring the traveller before the justice of the peace of the district." (Law of March 8, 1792; General Laws of Massachusetts, vol. i. p. 410.)

On March 11, 1797, a new law increased the amount of fines, half of which was to be given to the informer. (Same collection, vol. ii. p. 525.) On February 16, 1816, a new law confirmed these same measures. (Same collection, vol. ii. p. 405.) Similar enactments exist in the laws of the State of New York, revised in 1827 and 1828. (See Revised Statutes, Part I. chapter 20, p. 675.) In these it is declared that no one is allowed on the Sabbath to sport, to fish, to play at games, or to frequent houses where liquor is sold. No one can travel, except in case of necessity. And this is not the only trace which the religious strictness and austere manners of the first emigrants have left behind them in the American laws. In the Revised Statutes of the State of New York, vol. i. p. 662, is the following clause:—

类的狩猎、游戏或娱乐，违者罚款。罚款的金额每次不低于10先令，但也不超过20先令。

第二条　外出旅行者和车船驾驶者，除非必要，不得在礼拜日出行。违者处以与第一条相同的罚款。

第三条　小酒馆主、小店铺主和小客栈主应阻止本乡镇的定居居民在礼拜日于其店铺逗留娱乐或办事。如有违反，店主和客人同被罚款，而且可以吊销店主的执照。

第四条　身体健康而又无正当理由在三个月内少向上帝进行一次公开礼拜的人，要被罚款10先令。

第五条　在教堂的围墙以内做出不当行为的人，要处以5至10先令的罚款。

第六条　乡镇的十户长（Tithingmen）负责执行本法。他们有权在礼拜日巡视旅店或公共场所。拒绝十户长进本店铺巡视的店主，将处以40先令的罚款。十户长有权拘留旅客，查问其在礼拜日滞留于旅途的理由。拒不回答的人，将处以金额可达5英镑的罚款。如果旅客回答的理由没有使十户长满意，十户长可将此旅客送交县的治安法官处理。（1792年3月8日法令，载《马萨诸塞普通法》第1卷第410页）

1797年3月11日，一项新法律提高了罚款的金额，罚金的一半归告密者所有。（见上述法令汇编第1卷第525页）1816年2月16日，一项新法律批准了这些措施。（见上述法令汇编第2卷第405页）在1827年和1828年纽约州修订的法律之中，也有类似的条款（见《增订纽约州法令集》第1编第20章第675页）。其中规定，在礼拜日任何人不得打猎、钓鱼、游戏，或是不断出入出售酒类的场所。而且除非必要，任何人不得在礼拜日出行。而这并非

"Whoever shall win or lose in the space of twenty-four hours, by gaming or betting, the sum of twenty-five dollars, shall be found guilty of a misdemeanour, and upon conviction shall be condemned to pay a fine equal to at least five times the value of the sum lost or won; which shall be paid to the inspector of the poor of the township. He that loses twenty-five dollars or more may bring an action to recover them; and if he neglects to do so the inspector of the poor may prosecute the winner, and oblige him to pay into the poor's box both the sum he has gained and three times as much besides."

The laws we quote from are of recent date; but they are unintelligible without going back to the very origin of the colonies. I have no doubt that in our days the penal part of these laws is very rarely applied. Laws preserve their inflexibility, long after the manners of a nation have yielded to the influence of time. It is still true, however, that nothing strikes a foreigner on his arrival in America more forcibly than the regard paid to the Sabbath. There is one, in particular, of the large American cities, in which all social movements begin to be suspended even on Saturday evening. You traverse its streets at the hour at which you expect men in the middle of life to be engaged in business, and young people in pleasure; and you meet with solitude and silence. Not only have all ceased to work, but they appear to have ceased to exist. Neither the movements of industry are heard, nor the accents of joy, nor even the confused murmur which arises from the midst of a great city. Chains are hung across the streets in the neighborhood of the churches; the half-closed shutters of the houses scarcely admit a ray of sun into the dwellings of the citizens. Now and then you perceive a solitary individual who glides silently along the deserted streets and lanes. Next day, at early dawn, the rolling of carriages, the noise of hammers, the cries of the population, begin to make themselves heard again. The city is awake. An eager crowd hastens towards the resort of commerce and industry; everything around you bespeaks motion, bustle, hurry. A feverish activity succeeds to the lethargic stupor of yesterday; you might almost suppose that they had but one day to acquire wealth and to enjoy it.

初代移民的宗教精神和严肃习俗在法律上的唯一痕迹。在纽约州的增订法律集第1卷第662页，可以见到如下的条款：

任何因赌博或打赌而在24小时内输或赢25美元者，即被视为犯有轻罪，并依据证据处以至少其所赢或所输金额5倍的罚款。这笔罚款将交由乡镇济贫工作视察员收管。输25美元或以上的人可以向法院申诉。如不申诉，则济贫工作视察员可以作为赢方，收下输方的输款和相当于输款3倍的罚款，供济贫工作使用。

我们所引用的这几项法律都是最近的，但如果不追溯到殖民地始建之初，人们就不能理解这些法律。我毫不怀疑，在我们这个时代，这些法律的刑事部分很少得到应用。当国家的民情已随时代的发展而变化时，法律却依然没有改变。然而，严守礼拜日的做法，最令初到美国的外国人感到无比惊讶也是事实。特别是美国有一个大城市，一到星期六晚上整个社会就开始停止运动。如果你在本以为成年人应该忙于工作和青年人应该享乐的时间在这座城市走一走，感到的只有孤独和寂静。不但所有的人都停止了工作，而且连他们的影子都看不到。既没有工业生产的隆隆声，也没有人们的欢声笑语，甚至都听不到闹市区的喧嚣声。生活的锁链捆绑在教堂的周围，半掩的百叶窗，只容阳光一缕一缕地射进居民的室内。时不时地你会看到寂寞的人影静静地穿过空旷的街道和小路。次日清晨，车辆的辘辘声，铁锤的敲打声，人们的喊叫声，才又开始传入人们的耳朵。城市苏醒了。热切的人群匆忙地涌向城市的工商业中心；你身边的一切都在行动，精神焕发，匆匆忙忙。在昨天麻木不仁的昏睡之后，人们又开始兴奋地活动，直奔财富和享乐，好像过了今天就没有明天似的。

Appendix F

It is unnecessary for me to say, that in the chapter which has just been read, I have not had the intention of giving a history of America. My only object was to enable the reader to appreciate the influence which the opinions and manners of the first emigrants had exercised upon the fate of the different colonies, and of the Union in general. I have therefore confined myself to the quotation of a few detached fragments. I do not know whether I am deceived, but it appears to me that, by pursuing the path which I have merely pointed out, it would be easy to present such pictures of the American republics as would not be unworthy the attention of the public, and could not fail to suggest to the statesman matter for reflection. Not being able to devote myself to this labor, I am anxious to render it easy to others; and, for this purpose, I subjoin a short catalogue and analysis of the works which seem to me the most important to consult.

At the head of the general documents which it would be advantageous to examine I place the work entitled "An Historical Collection of State Papers, and other authentic Documents, intended as Materials for a History of the United States of America," by Ebenezer Hasard. The first volume of this compilation, which was printed at Philadelphia in 1792, contains a literal copy of all the charters granted by the Crown of England to the emigrants, as well as the principal acts of the colonial governments, during the commencement of their existence. Amongst other authentic documents, we here find a great many relating to the affairs of New England and Virginia during this period. The second volume is almost entirely devoted to the acts of the Confederation of 1643. This federal compact, which was entered into by the colonies of New England with the view of resisting the Indians, was the first instance of union afforded by the Anglo-Americans. There were besides many other confederations of the same nature, before the famous one of 1776, which brought about the independence of the colonies.

Each colony has, besides, its own historic monuments, some of which are extremely curious; beginning with Virginia, the State which was first peopled. The earliest historian of Virginia was its

F

不必我说，在这一章我并不打算讲述美国历史。我唯一的目的就是让读者了解早期移民的观念和民情对各殖民地和整个联邦命运的影响。因此，我只会引用一些相关的片段。我不知道这样做是否正确，但我认为，通过我所指出的这条唯一道路，能够轻而易举地呈现出会引起一般读者注意，并必然会引起政治家思考的画面。尽管我无法投身这项工作，但我至少愿意为别人提供方便。因此，我认为应当在这里列出一篇简短的书目，并对我觉得最适合引用的几部著作进行简要的分析。

在可供引用的大量一般性文献中，我首先要推荐埃伯尼泽·哈泽德编的收有各州文件和其他可靠文献的《美利坚合众国历史资料汇编》。这部汇编于1792年在费城出版，在第1卷中收录有英国国王颁给移民的全部特许状的全文，以及各殖民地政府自成立以来的主要法规。此外，我们还发现大量有关这一时期新英格兰和弗吉尼亚事务的官方文件。第2卷几乎全部是关于1643年联盟法案的文件。其中有新英格兰各殖民地之间为抵抗印第安人而结成的联盟的公约，这是英裔美国人宣布联合的第一个实例。直到1776年北美殖民地宣布独立，还有很多与此性质相同的联盟。

此外，各殖民地还有自己的历史文献，而且有些还十分珍贵。我们首先从弗吉尼亚这个最早开始有人居住的州开始。弗吉尼亚最早的历史学家就是其缔造者约翰·斯密斯船长。斯密斯船长给我们留下一部名为《弗吉尼亚和新英格兰通史》的十六开本著作，1627

founder, Captain John Smith. Captain Smith has left us an octavo volume, entitled "The generall Historie of Virginia and New England, by Captain John Smith, sometymes Governor in those Countryes, and Admirall of New England"; printed at London in 1627. The work is adorned with curious maps and engravings of the time when it appeared; the narrative extends from the year 1584 to 1626. Smith's work is highly and deservedly esteemed. The author was one of the most celebrated adventurers of a period of remarkable adventure; his book breathes that ardor for discovery, that spirit of enterprise, which characterized the men of his time, when the manners of chivalry were united to zeal for commerce, and made subservient to the acquisition of wealth. But Captain Smith is most remarkable for uniting to the virtues which characterized his contemporaries several qualities to which they were generally strangers; his style is simple and concise, his narratives bear the stamp of truth, and his descriptions are free from false ornament. This author throws most valuable light upon the state and condition of the Indians at the time when North America was first discovered.

The second historian to consult is Beverley, who commences his narrative with the year 1585, and ends it with 1700. The first part of his book contains historical documents, properly so called, relative to the infancy of the colony. The second affords a most curious picture of the state of the Indians at this remote period. The third conveys very clear ideas concerning the manners, social conditions, laws, and political customs of the Virginians in the author's lifetime. Beverley was a native of Virginia, which occasions him to say at the beginning of his book, that he entreats his readers not to exercise their critical severity upon it, since, having been born in the Indies, he does not aspire to purity of language. Notwithstanding this colonial modesty, the author shows throughout his book the impatience with which he endures the supremacy of the mother-country. In this work of Beverley are also found numerous traces of that spirit of civil liberty which animated the English colonies of America at the time when he wrote. He also shows the dissensions which existed among them, and retarded their independence. Beverley detests his Catholic neighbors of Maryland even more than he hates the English government: his style is simple, his narrative interesting, and apparently trustworthy.

年在伦敦出版。这部著作附有多幅珍贵的地图和一些标有制作日期的版画。这位历史学家从1584年一直写到1626年。斯密斯的著作得到高度的尊重。作者是在那个以冒险而著称的时代中，最为著名的冒险家之一。在他的书中，我们可以体会到冒险开发的热情，那个时代人们所特有的进取精神，以及混有经商致富味道的行侠仗义气息。但是，在斯密斯船长身上表现得最突出的，是他除具有同时代人的美德之外，还具备他们当中的大部分人所没有的一些品质。他的文章简练明确，叙事真实，丝毫不矫揉造作。这位作者非常清楚地向我们展示了北美在被发现伊始印第安人当时的状况。

第二位可供咨询的历史学家是贝弗利，他的记述始于1585年，止于1700年。其著作的第1章记载了殖民在摇篮时期的历史文献。第2章则展示出印第安人在这个遥远时期的最珍贵的生活情景。第3章清晰地传递出有关弗吉尼亚当时的民情、社会情况、法律和政治习惯的思想。贝弗利出生于弗吉尼亚，所以他在一开始就恳请读者不要以过于严格的批判观点来审视自己的著作，因为出生在印第安人土地上的自己没有专注过语言的纯洁性。尽管这位移民后代谦虚地表示自己做得不够，但在整部著作中，他始终情不自禁地维护母国的最高主权。在贝弗利的著作中，我们还可以看到当时曾经鼓舞美洲殖民地英国人的那种公民自由精神的诸多痕迹，还可以看到各殖民地之间长期以来存在的并且一直延续到独立时的不睦。贝弗利憎恨其邻居马里兰的天主教徒，这种憎恨甚至比对英国政府的憎恨还要更甚。他的文风简洁，叙述有趣，令人信服。

我在美国还读过另外一本值得参阅的著作，是威廉·斯蒂思写的《弗吉尼亚最初发现

I saw in America another work which ought to be consulted, entitled "The History of Virginia," by William Stith. This book affords some curious details, but I thought it long and diffuse. The most ancient as well as the best document to be consulted on the history of Carolina, is a work in small quarto, entitled "The History of Carolina," by John Lawson, printed at London in 1718. This work contains, in the first part, a journey of discovery in the west of Carolina; the account of which, given in the form of a journal, is in general confused and superficial; but it contains a very striking description of the mortality caused among the savages of that time both by the smallpox and the immoderate use of brandy; with a curious picture of the corruption of manners prevalent amongst them, which was increased by the presence of Europeans. The second part of Lawson's book is taken up with a description of the physical condition of Carolina, and its productions. In the third part, the author gives an interesting account of the manners, customs, and government of the Indians at that period. There is a good deal of talent and originality in this part of the work. Lawson concludes his history with a copy of the charter granted to the Carolinas in the reign of Charles II. The general tone of this work is light, and often licentious, forming a perfect contrast to the solemn style of the works published at the same period in New England. Lawson's history is extremely scarce in America, and cannot be procured in Europe. There is, however, a copy of it in the Royal Library at Paris.

From the southern extremity of the United States, I pass at once to the northern limit; as the intermediate space was not peopled till a later period. I must first point out a very curious compilation, entitled "Collection of the Massachusetts Historical Society," printed for the first time at Boston in 1792, and reprinted in 1806. The collection of which I speak, and which is continued to the present day, contains a great number of very valuable documents relating to the history of the different States in New England. Among them are letters which have never been published, and authentic pieces which had been buried in provincial archives. The whole work of Gookin, concerning the Indians, is inserted there.

I have mentioned several times in the chapter to which this note relates, the work of Nathaniel Norton entitled "New England's Memorial"; sufficiently, perhaps, to prove that it deserves the

与定居开发史》。此书提供了许多珍贵的细节内容，但我认为它太过冗长。有关卡罗来纳州历史的最早和最好的著作就是约翰·劳森所著的一部十六开本的薄书《卡罗来纳史》，于1718年在伦敦出版。在这部著作的第一部分记述了西卡罗来纳的发现之旅。这部书采用旅行游记的手法写成，叙述一般比较无序和肤浅。但对当时野蛮部落中流行的天花和酗酒所造成的荒废情景描写得相当深刻，并对这些部落风行的因欧洲人的到来而不断加剧的道德败坏行为记述得饶有风趣。劳森著作的第二部分专门对卡罗来纳的自然状况和物产加以描述。而在第三部分，作者则生动地描述了当时印第安人的风尚、习俗和组织管理。该书的这一部分显示出作者的才华和独到之处。劳森的这部历史，写到查理二世时期赐给卡罗来纳以特许状为止。整部著作的笔调轻快，而且往往有些骇人，与同一时期新英格兰出版的著作深沉的笔调形成鲜明的对比。劳森的这部历史在美国非常罕见，而在欧洲更是难以找到。然而，在巴黎的皇家图书馆还有一部孤本。

我曾从美国的最南部一直游历到最北部，其间的广大地区直到很晚以后才有移民居住。我必须首先介绍一部非常有价值的汇编，名为《马萨诸塞历史学会论丛》，于1792年在波士顿首次出版，后来在1806年又有再版。我所说的这部论丛，直到今天仍在继续编辑，记录了有关新英格兰各州历史的大量极具价值的文献，其中有尚未公开发表的信件和地方档案馆收藏的原始文件。古金主编的这部论丛，也收录有关于印第安人的材料。

在本章中我已经多次提到纳撒尼尔·莫尔顿的名为《新英格兰回忆录》的著作。在这里，我只想补充一句：凡想了解新英格兰历史的人，都应当读一读这部著作。莫尔顿的著

attention of those who would be conversant with the history of New England. This book is in octavo, and was reprinted at Boston in 1826.

The most valuable and important authority which exists upon the history of New England, is the work of the Rev. Cotton Mather, entitled "Magnalia Christi Americana, or the Ecclesiastical History of New England, 1620-1698, 2 vols. 8vo, reprinted at Hartford, United States, in 1820." The author divided his work into seven books. The first presents the history of the events which prepared and brought about the establishment of New England. The second contains the lives of the first governors and chief magistrates who presided over the country. The third is devoted to the lives and labors of the evangelical ministers who, during the same period, had the care of souls. In the fourth the author relates the institution and progress of the University of Cambridge (Massachusetts). In the fifth he describes the principles and the discipline of the Church of New England. The sixth is taken up in retracing certain facts, which, in the opinion of Mather, prove the merciful interposition of Providence in behalf of the inhabitants of New England. Lastly, in the seventh, the author gives an account of the heresies and the troubles to which the Church of New England was exposed. Cotton Mather was an evangelical minister who was born at Boston, and passed his life there. His narratives are distinguished by the same ardor and religious zeal which led to the foundation of the colonies of New England. Traces of bad taste sometimes occur in his manner of writing; but he interests, because he is full of enthusiasm. He is often intolerant, still oftener credulous, but he never betrays an intention to deceive. Sometimes his book contains fine passages, and true and profound reflections, such as the following:—

"Before the arrival of the Puritans," says he (vol. i. chap. iv.), "there were more than a few attempts of the English to people and improve the parts of New England which were to the northward of New Plymouth; but the designs of those attempts being aimed no higher than the advancement of some worldly interests, a constant series of disasters has confounded them, until there was a plantation erected upon the nobler designs of Christianity: and that plantation though it has had more adversaries than perhaps any one upon earth, yet, having obtained help from God, it continues to this

作为三十二开本，于1826年在波士顿再版。

现存有关新英格兰历史的最具价值和最重要的权威著作就是大教士科顿·马瑟的《基督教美洲传教史，或1620—1698年新英格兰教会史》。这部书为三十二开本，共两卷，1820年在美国的哈特福德再版。作者将此书分为七册。第一册呈现了新英格兰筹建和建设的历史。第二册记述主持新英格兰事务的几位早期的总督和主要行政官员的生平。第三册专注于当时指导人们思想的福音会牧师们的生平和事迹。在第四册，作者叙述了剑桥（在马萨诸塞）大学成立和发展的过程。在第五册他描述了新英格兰教会的教义和教规。第六册讲述了据马瑟说是表明上帝向新英格兰居民施福的某些事件。最后，在第七册，作者讲述了当时存在的异端邪说和新英格兰教会面对的动乱。马瑟是一个出生在波士顿的福音会牧师，并在此度过一生。他的著作充满促成新英格兰殖民地建成的那种宗教热心和激情。他的文笔时常会暴露出不够典雅的缺陷，但这不可避免，因为他想只靠宗教的热情去打动读者。他过于偏执，而且经常过于轻信，但他从不是故意欺骗。有时，他的著作中也有精彩的片段和真实深刻的思想。比如，下面的这一段：

"在清教徒到来之前，英国人曾多次尝试向我们现在居住的地方移居，但是人们好像对能够得到的物质利益没有过高的希望，于是一连串的困难，让他们不断受挫。而在崇高的宗教思想的推动和支持下来到美洲的人，决不会如此。虽然这些人遇到的敌人远比任何殖民地的创建者遇到的敌人要强大得多，但他们能够坚持自己的信念，以致使他们创建的东西依然存在于今天。"马瑟在其严肃的笔触之中，有时也会有一些温情脉脉的描写。比

day." Mather occasionally relieves the austerity of his descriptions with images full of tender feeling: after having spoken of an English lady whose religious ardor had brought her to America with her husband, and who soon after sank under the fatigues and privations of exile, he adds, "As for her virtuous husband, Isaac Johnson,

He tryed

To live without her, liked it not, and dyed."

Mather's work gives an admirable picture of the time and country which he describes. In his account of the motives which led the Puritans to seek an asylum beyond seas, he says:—"The God of Heaven served, as it were, a summons upon the spirits of his people in the English nation, stirring up the spirits of thousands which never saw the faces of each other, with a most unanimous inclination to leave all the pleasant accommodations of their native country, and go over a terrible ocean, into a more terrible desert, for the pure enjoyment of all his ordinances. It is now reasonable that, before we pass any further, the reasons of his undertaking should be more exactly made known unto posterity, especially unto the posterity of those that were the undertakers, lest they come at length to forget and neglect the true interest of New England. Wherefore I shall now transcribe some of them from a manuscript, wherein they were then tendered unto consideration:

"General Considerations for the Plantation of New England

"First, It will be a service unto the Church of great consequence, to carry the Gospel unto those parts of the world, and raise a bulwark against the kingdom of Antichrist, which the Jesuits labour to rear up in all parts of the world.

"Secondly, All other Churches of Europe have been brought under desolations; and it may be feared that the like judgments are coming upon us; and who knows but God hath provided this place to be a refuge for many whom he means to save out of the general destruction?

"Thirdly, The land grows weary of her inhabitants, insomuch that man, which is the most precious of all creatures, is here more vile and base than the earth he treads upon; children, neighbours, and friends, especially the poor, are counted the greatest burdens, which, if things were right, would be

如，他谈到一位英国妇女，在宗教热情的鼓舞下同她的丈夫一起来到美洲，但不久以后便无法忍受流亡生活的艰难困苦。然后他接着说："至于她的道德高尚的丈夫，却试图独自一人留在那里，但他并未能活下来，最终死去。"

马瑟的著作对他所描述的时代和地区进行了极佳的描绘。他在对促使清教徒到大洋彼岸寻找避难所的动机的叙述中谈道："上帝向我们当中居住于英国的人提出号召。上帝在号召无数不相识的人的时候，要求他们下定决心放弃在故乡的安适生活，横渡波涛汹涌的大洋，到那还是令人生畏的荒野去安家立业；而这样做的唯一目的，就是无条件地服从上帝的戒命。"他接着说："在做长篇大论之前，应当说明一下他们是出于什么动机进行这种冒险的，以使后代清楚地知道他们的动机，而尤为重要的，是提醒我们今天的人怀念他们，切勿忘记祖先追求的目的，不要减少对新英格兰的真正关心。因此，我要在这里介绍一部手稿里谈到的某些人的当时动机。

"第一个动机：为教会做出最大的贡献，即向世界的这一部分（北美）传播福音，建起一所保卫基督徒的堡垒，以反对企图在世界的其余部分建立统治的非基督徒。

"第二个动机：欧洲的其余所有教会已被破坏，害怕上帝也会这样来惩罚我们的教会，故决心开辟这个地方（新英格兰），为大多数人提供免遭大破坏的避难场所。

"第三个动机：我们所在的国度好像在折磨居民，最珍视财物的人却最轻视他们所踏的土地。人们视有子女、邻居和朋友为最沉重的累赘，他们尽力躲开穷人。如果事物按照这样的秩序发展，最能创造享乐的人要被排挤出这个世界。

the chiefest of earthly blessings.

"Fourthly, We are grown to that intemperance in all excess of riot, as no mean estate almost will suffice a man to keep sail with his equals, and he that fails in it must live in scorn and contempt: hence it comes to pass, that all arts and trades are carried in that deceitful manner and unrighteous course, as it is almost impossible for a good upright man to maintain his constant charge and live comfortably in them.

"Fifthly, The schools of learning and religion are so corrupted, as (besides the unsupportable charge of education) most children, even the best, wittiest, and of the fairest hopes, are perverted, corrupted, and utterly overthrown by the multitude of evil examples and licentious behaviours in these seminaries.

"Sixthly, The whole earth is the Lord's garden, and he hath given it to the sons of Adam, to be tilled and improved by them: why, then, should we stand starving here for places of habitation, and in the meantime suffer whole countries, as profitable for the use of man, to lie waste without any improvement?

"Seventhly, What can be a better or nobler work, and more worthy of a Christian, than to erect and support a reformed particular Church in its infancy, and unite our forces with such a company of faithful people, as by timely assistance may grow stronger and prosper; but for want of it, may be put to great hazards, if not be wholly ruined?

"Eighthly, If any such as are known to be godly, and live in wealth and prosperity here, shall forsake all this to join with this reformed Church, and with it run the hazard of an hard and mean condition, it will be an example of great use, both for the removing of scandal and to give more life unto the faith of God's people in their prayers for the plantation, and also to encourage others to join the more willingly in it."

Further on, when he declares the principles of the Church of New England with respect to morals, Mather inveighs with violence against the custom of drinking healths at table, which he denounces as a pagan and abominable practice. He proscribes with the same rigor all ornaments for the hair used

"第四个动机：我们的放纵行为已经达到极点，好像有钱才能在同类中保持应有的地位，而无钱就要被人轻视。因此，各行各业的人都去寻找不道德的致富门路，从而便宜了因为有钱而能荒淫无耻生活的富人。

"第五个动机：讲授科学和宗教知识的学校办得太差，以致使大部分儿童，特别是最优秀和最有才华的儿童以及人们认为最有成才希望的儿童，在耳闻目睹大量坏榜样和周围的腐化现象的影响下学坏。

"第六个动机：大地是上帝的花园，他把大地赐给他的儿子亚当去耕种，而我们为什么要让自己因为没有土地而饿死，并叫这片本来应当供人使用的广阔土地无人居住和荒芜不毛呢？

"第七个动机：要成立一个革新的教会，并从成立之初就支持它；要把我们的力量与一个虔诚的民族的力量联合起来，以巩固和发展这个教会，使它摆脱那些没有这种支持就可能成为它的大灾大难的危险。对于一个基督徒来说，有什么工作能比这项工作更为高尚和壮丽的呢？有什么事业能比这项事业更值得做的呢？

"第八个动机：一个信仰虔诚并在这里（英国）享有荣华富贵的人如能放弃因致力建设这个革新的教会而获得的好处，并愿意分担苦难，他将为人们做出一个伟大而高尚的榜样，使人们学习他在向上帝为殖民地祷告时表示自己的虔诚信仰，并把大多数人联合过来。"

后面，他在谈到新英格兰教会有关道德方面的原则时，强烈反对在宴会上为健康而干杯的做法，并将其斥为异教徒的可憎习俗。他也同样激烈地反对妇女对头发进行任何装饰，

by the female sex, as well as their custom of having the arms and neck uncovered. In another part of his work he relates several instances of witchcraft which had alarmed New England. It is plain that the visible action of the devil in the affairs of this world appeared to him an incontestable and evident fact.

This work of Cotton Mather displays, in many places, the spirit of civil liberty and political independence which characterized the times in which he lived. Their principles respecting government are discoverable at every page. Thus, for instance, the inhabitants of Massachusetts, in the year 1630, ten years after the foundation of Plymouth, are found to have devoted Pound 400 sterling to the establishment of the University of Cambridge. In passing from the general documents relative to the history of New England to those which describe the several States comprised within its limits, I ought first to notice "The History of the Colony of Massachusetts," by Hutchinson, Lieutenant-Governor of the Massachusetts Province, 2 vols. 8vo. The history of Hutchinson, which I have several times quoted in the chapter to which this note relates, commences in the year 1628, and ends in 1750. Throughout the work there is a striking air of truth and the greatest simplicity of style: it is full of minute details. The best history to consult concerning Connecticut is that of Benjamin Trumbull, entitled "A Complete History of Connecticut, Civil and Ecclesiastical," 1630-1764, 2 vols. 8vo, printed in 1818 at New Haven. This history contains a clear and calm account of all the events which happened in Connecticut during the period given in the title. The author drew from the best sources, and his narrative bears the stamp of truth. All that he says of the early days of Connecticut is extremely curious. See especially the Constitution of 1639, vol. i. ch. vi. p. 100; and also the Penal Laws of Connecticut, vol. i. ch. vii. p. 123.

"The History of New Hampshire," by Jeremy Belknap, is a work held in merited estimation. It was printed at Boston in 1792, in 2 vols. 8vo. The third chapter of the first volume is particularly worthy of attention for the valuable details it affords on the political and religious principles of the Puritans, on the causes of their emigration, and on their laws. The following curious quotation is given from a sermon delivered in 1663:—"It concerneth New England always to remember that they

以及她们袒胸露臂的时尚着装。在其著作的其他章节中，他还谈到几个曾使整个新英格兰震惊的妖魔作怪的事例。显然在他看来，恶魔在这个世界兴妖作怪，是千真万确的事实。

马瑟的著作中有多处展示出其所生活的时代所特有的追求公民自由和政治独立的精神，而他们的治理原则在每一页中都能看得到。比如，马萨诸塞的居民，在1630年，即普利茅斯殖民地建立十年之后，用400英镑创办剑桥大学。如果我们从新英格兰的全史转而研究新英格兰各州的历史，则首先应当提到马萨诸塞地方副总督哈钦森的《马萨诸塞殖民地史》。此书为三十二开本，共两卷。哈坎森的这部著作，我在本章中多次引用，其叙述始自1628年，终于1750年。全书真实可信，文笔简练朴实，是一部内容翔实的历史著作。关于康涅狄格的历史，值得推荐的最好著作是本杰明·特朗布尔的《康涅狄格全史：世俗史和宗教史，1630—1764》。此书为三十二开本，共两卷，于1818年在纽黑文出版。这部史书清晰沉着地描述了在书名所指这段时期康涅狄格发生的所有重大事件。作者引用了珍贵的历史文献，而且叙述确切。他对于康涅狄格早期的所有描述十分有趣。尤其应当读一读第1卷第5章《1639年的康涅狄格》第100页，以及第1卷第7章《康涅狄格的刑法》第123页。

杰理米·贝尔纳普的《新罕布什尔史》是一部值得给予高度评价的著作。此书为三十二开本，共两卷，于1792年在波士顿出版。第1卷第3章特别值得一读。因为在这一章里，作者对于清教徒的政治原则和宗教教义及他们的移居原因和法律，做了极其详细的叙述。下面引用的是1663年一段布道讲话：　"新英格兰要永久记住它的创建目的在于宗教，而不在于商业。人们在前进中要坚持清教徒的教义和纪律。因此，商人和一个铜板一个铜

are a plantation religious, not a plantation of trade. The profession of the purity of doctrine, worship, and discipline, is written upon her forehead. Let merchants, and such as are increasing cent. per cent., remember this, that worldly gain was not the end and design of the people of New England, but religion. And if any man among us make religion as twelve, and the world as thirteen, such an one hath not the spirit of a true New Englishman." The reader of Belknap will find in his work more general ideas, and more strength of thought, than are to be met with in the American historians even to the present day.

Among the Central States which deserve our attention for their remote origin, New York and Pennsylvania are the foremost. The best history we have of the former is entitled "A History of New York," by William Smith, printed at London in 1757. Smith gives us important details of the wars between the French and English in America. His is the best account of the famous confederation of the Iroquois.

With respect to Pennsylvania, I cannot do better than point out the work of Proud, entitled "The History of Pennsylvania, from the original Institution and Settlement of that Province, under the first Proprietor and Governor, William Penn, in 1681, till after the year 1742," by Robert Proud, 2 vols. 8vo, printed at Philadelphia in 1797. This work is deserving of the especial attention of the reader; it contains a mass of curious documents concerning Penn, the doctrine of the Quakers, and the character, manners, and customs of the first inhabitants of Pennsylvania. I need not add that among the most important documents relating to this State are the works of Penn himself, and those of Franklin.

Appendix G

We read in Jefferson's "Memoirs" as follows:—
"At the time of the first settlement of the English in Virginia, when land was to be had for little or nothing, some provident persons having obtained large grants of it, and being desirous of maintaining

板攒钱的人也不要忘记，创建这些殖民地的目的在于宗教，而不在于金钱。如果我们当中有人在评价世界和宗教时认为世界值13，而宗教只值12，那么，这个人就不具有新英格兰人的真正精神。"读者从贝尔纳普的著作里可以看到，他甚至比至今研究美国历史的其他作者更多地提到普遍观念并强调思想的力量。

在我们所研究的已经存在很久的几个主要州中，纽约州和宾夕法尼亚州最为突出。关于纽约州的历史，最好的一部著作是威廉·斯密斯的《纽约史》。于1757年在伦敦出版。斯密斯为我们提供了英法两国在美洲战争的重要细节。在研究美国史的所有著作中，它对著名的易洛魁联盟的描述最为详尽。

关于宾夕法尼亚的历史，最好的推荐莫过于罗伯特·普劳特的《宾夕法尼亚自创建与定居：1861年威廉·佩恩就第一任领主与总督直至1742年以后的历史》。此书为三十二开本，共两卷，于1797年在费城出版。这部书值得读者特别注意，它收录有关佩恩的大批珍贵文献，谈到了教友会的教义，以及宾夕法尼亚早期移民的性格、风尚和习惯。不必说，在研究宾夕法尼亚的主要著作中，佩恩本人和富兰克林的著作也必不可少。

G

杰斐逊在自传中写道："英国人在弗吉尼亚建立殖民地之初，土地所能向人们提供的产品还少得可怜或是一无所有的时候，一些有远见的人便获得了大量的租让地，并为了保持家庭的荣华富贵，而把财产传给后代。财产一代一代传给同姓人，从而产生一些独特的

the splendor of their families, entailed their property upon their descendants. The transmission of these estates from generation to generation, to men who bore the same name, had the effect of raising up a distinct class of families, who, possessing by law the privilege of perpetuating their wealth, formed by these means a sort of patrician order, distinguished by the grandeur and luxury of their establishments. From this order it was that the King usually chose his councillors of state."

In the United States, the principal clauses of the English law respecting descent have been universally rejected. The first rule that we follow, says Mr. Kent, touching inheritance, is the following:—If a man dies intestate, his property goes to his heirs in a direct line. If he has but one heir or heiress, he or she succeeds to the whole. If there are several heirs of the same degree, they divide the inheritance equally amongst them, without distinction of sex. This rule was prescribed for the first time in the State of New York by a statute of February 23, 1786. (See Revised Statutes, vol. iii. Appendix, p. 48.) It has since then been adopted in the Revised Statutes of the same State. At the present day this law holds good throughout the whole of the United States, with the exception of the State of Vermont, where the male heir inherits a double portion. (Kent's "Commentaries," vol. iv. p. 370.) Mr. Kent, in the same work, vol. iv. p. 1-22, gives a historical account of American legislation on the subject of entail: by this we learn that, previous to the Revolution, the colonies followed the English law of entail. Estates tail were abolished in Virginia in 1776, on a motion of Mr. Jefferson. They were suppressed in New York in 1786, and have since been abolished in North Carolina, Kentucky, Tennessee, Georgia, and Missouri. In Vermont, Indiana, Illinois, South Carolina, and Louisiana, entail was never introduced. Those States which thought proper to preserve the English law of entail, modified it in such a way as to deprive it of its most aristocratic tendencies. "Our general principles on the subject of government," says Mr. Kent, "tend to favor the free circulation of property."

It cannot fail to strike the French reader who studies the law of inheritance, that on these questions the French legislation is infinitely more democratic even than the American. The American law makes an equal division of the father's property, but only in the case of his will not being known; "for

家族集团。它们依法享有永久保持财富的特权，进而依靠自己州的强大和富饶而形成显赫的贵族阶层。而国王也照例从这个阶层中选派州议员。"

在美国，英国法律有关遗产继承的主要规定全部被否定。肯特先生说，我们在遗产继承上遵循的第一个规定是：如果一个人死后没有留下遗嘱，其财产由直接亲属继承；如他只有一个男性或一个女性继承人，他或她则可继承全部遗产；如有数名同顺序的继承人，则不分性别，在他们之中平均分配遗产。最初，纽约州以1786年2月23日法令通过这项规定，后来又进行过修订（见《增订纽约州法令集》第3卷，附录，第48页）。今天，美国各州几乎都采用这项规定，只是佛蒙特州例外，在那里男性继承人可得到双份遗产（见《美国法释义》第4卷第375页）。肯特先生在该书第4卷第1~22页，叙述了美国的限嗣继承立法史。据此我们了解到，在美国独立前，各殖民地都采用英国的限嗣继承法。后来，在杰斐逊的提议下，弗吉尼亚于1776年废除遗产限嗣继承制度。纽约州也于1786年废除这种制度。随后，北卡罗来纳、肯塔基、田纳西、佐治亚和密苏里，也相继废除限嗣继承法。而在佛蒙特、印第安纳、伊利诺伊、南卡罗来纳和路易斯安那，则从来就没有采用过限嗣继承制度。认为应当保留英国限嗣继承法的各州，也对其进行修订，去掉其中的贵族倾向。肯特先生写道："我们有关国家管理的一般原则是致力于促进财产的自由流通。"

研究美国遗产继承法的法国人必然会注意到，在这些问题上法国的立法比美国还要无限民主。美国的法律规定子女平分父亲的遗产，但父亲须并未另立遗嘱，因为纽约州的法律规定（《增订纽约州法令集》，第3卷，附录，第51页）："在纽约州，因为每个人都有

every man," says the law, "in the State of New York (Revised Statutes, vol. iii. Appendix, p. 51), has entire liberty, power, and authority, to dispose of his property by will, to leave it entire, or divided in favor of any persons he chooses as his heirs, provided he do not leave it to a political body or any corporation." The French law obliges the testator to divide his property equally, or nearly so, among his heirs. Most of the American republics still admit of entails, under certain restrictions; but the French law prohibits entail in all cases. If the social condition of the Americans is more democratic than that of the French, the laws of the latter are the most democratic of the two. This may be explained more easily than at first appears to be the case. In France, democracy is still occupied in the work of destruction; in America, it reigns quietly over the ruins it has made.

Appendix H

Summary Of The Qualifications Of Voters In The United States As They Existed In 1832

All the States agree in granting the right of voting at the age of twenty-one. In all of them it is necessary to have resided for a certain time in the district where the vote is given. This period varies from three months to two years.

As to the qualification: in the State of Massachusetts it is necessary to have an income of Pound 3 or a capital of Pound 60. In Rhode Island, a man must possess landed property to the amount of $133.

In Connecticut, he must have a property which gives an income of $17. A year of service in the militia also gives the elective privilege.

In New Jersey, an elector must have a property of Pound 50 a year.

In South Carolina and Maryland, the elector must possess fifty acres of land.

In Tennessee, he must possess some property.

In the States of Mississippi, Ohio, Georgia, Virginia, Pennsylvania, Delaware, New York, the only necessary qualification for voting is that of paying the taxes; and in most of the States, to serve in the militia is equivalent to the payment of taxes. In Maine and New Hampshire any man can vote who is

完全的自由、权利和资格按照自己的意愿处理其财产，即对某一政治机构或社会团体留下遗言，将其财产全部或部分遗赠给某人。"法国的法律则规定立遗嘱人可将其财产平分或近于平分与继承人和受遗赠人。现在，美国的大部分州还实行限嗣继承制度，但对其进行了严格的限制。但是，法国的法律在任何情况下都不允许限嗣继承。美国的社会情况比我们的民主，而我们的法律则比他们的民主。这最能说明一个值得人们深思的问题，即：在法国，民主安于遭受破坏；而在美国，民主能在废墟之上泰然自立。

H

美国的选举资格概要

各州均赋予年满21岁的人选举权。各州均要求选举人应在其参加选举的地区居住超过一定的期限。这一期限从3个月到2年不等。

关于财产资格：在马萨诸塞州，选举人必须有3英镑收入或60英镑的资产。在罗得岛，选举人必须拥有价值133美元的地产。在康涅狄格，选举人必须拥有能够获得17美元收入的财产。在民兵中服役一年，也可享有选举权。在新泽西，选举人应有50英镑财产。在南卡罗来纳和马里兰，选举人必须拥有50英亩土地。在田纳西，选举人必须拥有某一种数量足够的财产。在密西西比州、俄亥俄州、佐治亚州、弗吉尼亚州、宾夕法尼亚州、特拉华州和纽约州，获得选举权的唯一的必要资格就是纳税。而在大部分州，在民兵服役也等同于纳税。在缅因和新罕布什尔，凡未被列入赤贫名单者均可有选举权。最后，在密苏里

not on the pauper list.

Lastly, in the States of Missouri, Alabama, Illinois, Louisiana, Indiana, Kentucky, and Vermont, the conditions of voting have no reference to the property of the elector.

I believe there is no other State besides that of North Carolina in which different conditions are applied to the voting for the Senate and the electing the House of Representatives. The electors of the former, in this case, should possess in property fifty acres of land; to vote for the latter, nothing more is required than to pay taxes.

Appendix I

The small number of custom-house officers employed in the United States, compared with the extent of the coast, renders smuggling very easy; notwithstanding which, it is less practised than elsewhere, because everybody endeavors to repress it. In America there is no police for the prevention of fires, and such accidents are more frequent than in Europe; but in general they are more speedily extinguished, because the surrounding population is prompt in lending assistance.

Appendix K

It is incorrect to assert that centralization was produced by the French Revolution; the revolution brought it to perfection, but did not create it. The mania for centralization and government regulations dates from the time when jurists began to take a share in the government, in the time of Philippele-Bel; ever since which period they have been on the increase. In the year 1775, M. de Malesherbes, speaking in the name of the Cour des Aides, said to Louis XIV:—

". . . Every corporation and every community of citizens retained the right of administering its own affairs; a right which not only forms part of the primitive constitution of the kingdom, but has a still higher origin; for it is the right of nature, and of reason. Nevertheless, your subjects, Sire,

州、亚拉巴马州、伊利诺伊州、路易斯安那州、印第安纳州、肯塔基州和佛蒙特州，选举资格则与财产无关。

我相信，除了北卡罗来纳州，没有哪个州对参议员选举人资格的规定与众议员会有所不同。在那里，前者的选举人要拥有50英亩土地，而后者只要纳税即可。

I

美国实行关税保护政策，所以少数海关人员和大部分海岸地区最容易走私，但却并不像在其他国家那样肆无忌惮，因为任何人都可以缉私。在美国没有消防警察，所以火灾多于欧洲，但一般来说可以被快速扑灭，因为周围的居民会迅速赶赴火灾现场提供帮助。

K

声称中央集权是法国大革命的产物并不正确。法国大革命完善了中央集权但并没有创造中央集权。在法国，对中央集权的爱好和对典章制度的狂信，可以追溯到法学家进入政府的时期，即腓力四世统治法国的时代。从那时起，这两种倾向不断发展。1775年，马尔泽尔布先生在以最高税务法院的名义向路易十六国王进言时说道：

"……每个公民社团或村镇都保有自己管理自己事务的权利；这项权利不但应该写进王国的第一部宪法里，而且还是一项很古老的权利；因为它是天赋的合情合理的权利。然而，陛下，您臣民的这项权利已经被剥夺，我们不得不说：在这方面，您的管理工作已经

have been deprived of it; and we cannot refrain from saying that in this respect your government has fallen into puerile extremes. From the time when powerful ministers made it a political principle to prevent the convocation of a national assembly, one consequence has succeeded another, until the deliberations of the inhabitants of a village are declared null when they have not been authorized by the Intendant. Of course, if the community has an expensive undertaking to carry through, it must remain under the control of the sub-delegate of the Intendant, and, consequently, follow the plan he proposes, employ his favorite workmen, pay them according to his pleasure; and if an action at law is deemed necessary, the Intendant's permission must be obtained. The cause must be pleaded before this first tribunal, previous to its being carried into a public court; and if the opinion of the Intendant is opposed to that of the inhabitants, or if their adversary enjoys his favor, the community is deprived of the power of defending its rights. Such are the means, Sire, which have been exerted to extinguish the municipal spirit in France; and to stifle, if possible, the opinions of the citizens. The nation may be said to lie under an interdict, and to be in wardship under guardians." What could be said more to the purpose at the present day, when the Revolution has achieved what are called its victories in centralization?

In 1789, Jefferson wrote from Paris to one of his friends:—"There is no country where the mania for over-governing has taken deeper root than in France, or been the source of greater mischief." (Letter to Madison, August 28, 1789.) The fact is, that for several centuries past the central power of France has done everything it could to extend central administration; it has acknowledged no other limits than its own strength. The central power to which the Revolution gave birth made more rapid advances than any of its predecessors, because it was stronger and wiser than they had been; Louis XIV committed the welfare of such communities to the caprice of an intendant; Napoleon left them to that of the Minister. The same principle governed both, though its consequences were more or less remote.

幼稚透顶。自从几位有权势的大臣提出不准召集国民议会的政治原则以来，官员们便上行下效，以致村镇的居民不经总督的批准，什么决定也不能做出。因此，如果某个村镇要想花钱办一项事业，就得去恳求总督的下属官员，从而要根据官员同意的计划进行，雇用他们喜欢的工人，按照他们的指示支付工资；如果村镇有人要打官司，也得经总督批准，即在向法院起诉之前，要把案件先送到那里进行初审。如果总督的意见同要打官司的居民相反，或诉讼的对方是总督的亲信，村镇就失去保卫自己权利的能力。总督老爷就是通过这些办法尽力在法国窒息全部地方自治精神的，而如果有可能，则必将从公民的心中除掉这种精神。也可以说，全国人民都被置于禁令之下，并给他们指定了监护人。"怎么今天还能说法国大革命在中央集权方面所做的一切是所谓征服呢？

1789年杰斐逊在巴黎给一位友人写信说："我们的国家绝不是一个统治的狂热像法国那样根深蒂固并造成许多灾难的国家。"（这是1789年8月28日致麦迪逊的信）实际上，几个世纪以来，法国的中央政权所做的一切都是为了扩大中央行政集权；在这方面，它的权力从来没有受到过限制。法国大革命造就的中央政权，在这一点上比任何以往的先行者走得都更远，因为它比它们更有力量，更有学识。比如，路易十四只是使村镇生活的一切服从于一位总督的享乐；而拿破仑则是使其服从于一位大臣。两者的指导原则相同，只是后来的发展有大有小。

Appendix L

The immutability of the constitution of France is a necessary consequence of the laws of that country. To begin with the most important of all the laws, that which decides the order of succession to the throne; what can be more immutable in its principle than a political order founded upon the natural succession of father to son? In 1814, Louis XVIII had established the perpetual law of hereditary succession in favor of his own family. The individuals who regulated the consequences of the Revolution of 1830 followed his example; they merely established the perpetuity of the law in favor of another family. In this respect they imitated the Chancellor Meaupou, who, when he erected the new Parliament upon the ruins of the old, took care to declare in the same ordinance that the rights of the new magistrates should be as inalienable as those of their predecessors had been. The laws of 1830, like those of 1814, point out no way of changing the constitution: and it is evident that the ordinary means of legislation are insufficient for this purpose. As the King, the Peers, and the Deputies, all derive their authority from the constitution, these three powers united cannot alter a law by virtue of which alone they govern. Out of the pale of the constitution they are nothing: where, when, could they take their stand to effect a change in its provisions? The alternative is clear: either their efforts are powerless against the charter, which continues to exist in spite of them, in which case they only reign in the name of the charter; or they succeed in changing the charter, and then, the law by which they existed being annulled, they themselves cease to exist. By destroying the charter, they destroy themselves. This is much more evident in the laws of 1830 than in those of 1814. In 1814, the royal prerogative took its stand above and beyond the constitution; but in 1830, it was avowedly created by, and dependent on, the constitution. A part, therefore, of the French constitution is immutable, because it is united to the destiny of a family; and the body of the constitution is equally immutable, because there appear to be no legal means of changing it. These remarks are not applicable to England. That country having no written constitution, who can assert when its constitution is changed?

L

法国宪法的不变性，是其国家法制的必然结果。首先从所有法律中最重要的法律，即王位继承的法律为例来说明。有什么法律比这个以父传子继的自然顺序为基础的政治规定在原则上更不可改变的呢？1814年，路易十八确立了有利于其家族的永久的政治继承权的法律。为1830年革命善后的那些人仿效了路易十八的做法，只是把这个政治继承权转给另一个家族。在拥立新王朝时，他们则效仿了大法官莫普，他曾在旧最高法院的废墟上建立新最高法院时，没有忘记在国王的诏令中写进新的大法官也同他们的前任一样不可罢免。1830年的法律也同1814年的法律一样，没有提到修改宪法的问题。而且，显然一般的立法手段不足以达到这一目的。因为国王、贵族院议员和众议院议员的权力都来自宪法，所以这三权怎么可能联合起来对其权力唯一依靠的法律进行修改呢？离开了宪法，他们就什么都不是。那么，在什么条件下他们才会修改宪法呢？下述两种条件必居其一：不是在他们无力反对人民能够不按他们的意愿，但却是以他们的名义继续实行宪法的某些条款的时候；就是在他们借以掌权的法律不复存在，他们自己不再有什么地位，而要求改变宪法的时候。因为他们自己破坏了宪法，于是便自取灭亡了。这一点，1830年的宪法比1814年的宪法表现得更加清楚。在1814年，王权凌驾于宪法之外或以上；而在1830年，王权则由宪法赋予，并依靠宪法而存在。因此，法国宪法的这个部分没有变动，因为它与一个家族的命运联系在一起；法国宪法的整体也同样没有变动，因为人们似乎没有找到修改宪法的合法手段。这些论述都不适用于英国。英国没有成文的宪法，谁能说英国修改过成文宪法呢？

Appendix M

The most esteemed authors who have written upon the English Constitution agree with each other in establishing the omnipotence of the Parliament. Delolme says: "It is a fundamental principle with the English lawyers, that Parliament can do everything except making a woman a man, or a man a woman." Blackstone expresses himself more in detail, if not more energetically, than Delolme, in the following terms:—"The power and jurisdiction of Parliament, says Sir Edward Coke (4 Inst. 36), 'is so transcendent and absolute that it cannot be confined, either for causes or persons, within any bounds.' And of this High Court, he adds, may be truly said, 'Si antiquitatem spectes, est vetustissima; si dignitatem, est honoratissima; si jurisdictionem, est capacissima.' It hath sovereign and uncontrollable authority in the making, confirming, enlarging, restraining, abrogating, repealing, reviving, and expounding of laws, concerning matters of all possible denominations; ecclesiastical or temporal; civil, military, maritime, or criminal; this being the place where that absolute despotic power which must, in all governments, reside somewhere, is intrusted by the constitution of these kingdoms. All mischiefs and grievances, operations and remedies, that transcend the ordinary course of the laws, are within the reach of this extraordinary tribunal. It can regulate or new-model the succession to the Crown; as was done in the reign of Henry VIII and William III. It can alter the established religion of the land; as was done in a variety of instances in the reigns of King Henry VIII and his three children. It can change and create afresh even the constitution of the kingdom, and of parliaments themselves; as was done by the Act of Union and the several statutes for triennial and septennial elections. It can, in short, do everything that is not naturally impossible to be done; and, therefore some have not scrupled to call its power, by a figure rather too bold, the omnipotence of Parliament."

M

最受尊重的研究英国宪法的著名学者，争先恐后地论述过议会的这种无限权威。德洛姆说过："英国法学家所坚信的基本原则就是，议会除了不能把女人变成男人或把男人变成女人以外，什么都能做到。"布莱克斯通说得虽然没有这么坚定，但说得更具体。下面就是他所说的："爱德华·科克爵士认为议会的权力和司法权（第4项第36款），无论是对人，还是对事，都极为非凡和绝对，以至任何限制都禁止不了它的活动。他补充说，对于这个最高的法院简直可以说是：Si antiquitatem spectes, est vetustissima; si dignitatem, esthonoratissima; si jurisdictionem, est capacissima.（论资格，它最古老；论荣誉，它最光荣；论权力，它最强大）在制定、通过、扩大使用、停用、废除、恢复使用和解释教会法令或世俗法令、民法、军事法、海运法、刑法等名目众多的法律方面，议会享有至高无上和不受监督的权力；而授予议会以这种可以左右政府各部门的绝对权力的，正是这个王国的宪法。凡是申冤和要求赔偿损失的案件，都可越过普通法院而送到这个特殊的法院去解决。它能修改或重新订立王位继承法，比如亨利八世和威廉三世，就是由它拥上王位的。它能改变国家已经确立信奉的教派，比如在亨利八世及其三个子女统治时期，就有过这种改变的先例。它可以修改和改变王国的宪法和议会本身，比如它曾为通过英格兰与苏格兰的联合法案，以及三年和七年举行一次选举的各项法令，而这样做过。简而言之，它能做到本来所无法做到的一切，所以使用自己权力的时候无所顾忌，可以说过于大胆地表现了议会的无所不能。"

Appendix N

There is no question upon which the American constitutions agree more fully than upon that of political jurisdiction. All the constitutions which take cognizance of this matter, give to the House of Delegates the exclusive right of impeachment; excepting only the constitution of North Carolina, which grants the same privilege to grand juries. (Article 23.) Almost all the constitutions give the exclusive right of pronouncing sentence to the Senate, or to the Assembly which occupies its place.

The only punishments which the political tribunals can inflict are removal, or the interdiction of public functions for the future. There is no other constitution but that of Virginia (p. 152), which enables them to inflict every kind of punishment. The crimes which are subject to political jurisdiction are, in the federal constitution (Section 4, Art. 1); in that of Indiana (Art. 3, paragraphs 23 and 24); of New York (Art. 5); of Delaware (Art. 5), high treason, bribery, and other high crimes or offences. In the Constitution of Massachusetts (Chap. I, Section 2); that of North Carolina (Art. 23); of Virginia (p. 252), misconduct and maladministration. In the constitution of New Hampshire (p. 105), corruption, intrigue, and maladministration. In Vermont (Chap. 2, Art. 24), maladministration. In South Carolina (Art. 5); Kentucky (Art. 5); Tennessee (Art. 4); Ohio (Art. 1, 23, 24); Louisiana (Art. 5); Mississippi (Art. 5); Alabama (Art. 6); Pennsylvania (Art. 4), crimes committed in the non-performance of official duties. In the States of Illinois, Georgia, Maine, and Connecticut, no particular offences are specified.

Appendix O

It is true that the powers of Europe may carry on maritime wars with the Union; but there is

N

美国各州的宪法，就有关政治审判制度方面的规定最为一致。各州的宪法都包含这种制度，并将起诉的专有权交给州众议院，只有北卡罗来纳州是一个例外，它将这一权力赋予大陪审团（第23条）。几乎所有州的宪法，都把政治审判的专有权授予州参议院或有州参议员列席的审判团。

政治法院能够做出的处罚，只有撤职或不准再任公职。只有弗吉尼亚州的宪法允许政治法院可出各种不同的处罚。提交政治审判的罪行有：联邦宪法第2条第4项、印第安纳州宪法第3条第23项和第24项、纽约州宪法第5条和特拉华州宪法第5条规定的叛国罪、贿赂罪和其他重罪或轻罪；根据马萨诸塞州宪法第1章第2条、北卡罗来纳州宪法第23条和弗吉尼亚州宪法第252页规定的渎职罪和玩忽职守罪；新罕布什尔州宪法第105页规定的贿赂罪、医疗事故罪和玩忽职守罪；佛蒙特州宪法第2章第24条规定的玩忽职守罪；南卡罗来纳州宪法第5条、肯塔基州宪法第5条、田纳西州宪法第4条、俄亥俄州宪法第1条第23项和第24项、路易斯安那州宪法第5条、密西西比州宪法第5条、亚拉巴马州宪法第6条和宾夕法尼亚州宪法第4条规定的渎职罪。而在伊利诺伊州、佐治亚州、缅因州和康涅狄格州的宪法则并没有列举出罪名。

O

的确，欧洲列强可以与美国进行大规模的海战，但对美国而言，应对海战总比陆战

always greater facility and less danger in supporting a maritime than a continental war. Maritime warfare only requires one species of effort. A commercial people which consents to furnish its government with the necessary funds, is sure to possess a fleet. And it is far easier to induce a nation to part with its money, almost unconsciously, than to reconcile it to sacrifices of men and personal efforts. Moreover, defeat by sea rarely compromises the existence or independence of the people which endures it. As for continental wars, it is evident that the nations of Europe cannot be formidable in this way to the American Union. It would be very difficult to transport and maintain in America more than 25,000 soldiers; an army which may be considered to represent a nation of about 2,000,000 of men. The most populous nation of Europe contending in this way against the Union, is in the position of a nation of 2,000,000 of inhabitants at war with one of 12,000,000. Add to this, that America has all its resources within reach, whilst the European is at 4,000 miles distance from his; and that the immensity of the American continent would of itself present an insurmountable obstacle to its conquest.

Appendix P

The first American journal appeared in April, 1704, and was published at Boston. See "Collection of the Historical Society of Massachusetts," vol. vi. p. 66. It would be a mistake to suppose that the periodical press has always been entirely free in the American colonies: an attempt was made to establish something analogous to a censorship and preliminary security. Consult the Legislative Documents of Massachusetts of January 14, 1722. The Committee appointed by the General Assembly (the legislative body of the province) for the purpose of examining into circumstances connected with a paper entitled "The New England Courier," expresses its opinion that "the tendency of the said journal is to turn religion into derision and bring it into contempt; that it mentions the sacred writers in a profane and irreligious manner; that it puts malicious interpretations upon the conduct of the ministers of the Gospel; and that the Government of his Majesty is insulted, and the

要来得容易得多，危险也要小得多。海战只需要一种武力。同意向政府提供必要资金的商业国家，必然可以拥有强大的舰队。而且诱导人们几乎在不知不觉中牺牲金钱比让他们心甘情愿牺牲个人生命和人力要容易得多。此外，海战的失利很少会损害战败国的生存和独立。至于陆战，欧洲国家显然不能给美国造成可怕的危险。即使对于一支代表拥有200万人口大国的军队，向美国运送并在那里供养2.5万名士兵也实在非常困难。如果一个这样的欧洲大国同美国交战，就等于一个拥有200万人口的国家同拥有1200万人口的国家打仗。而且，美国坐拥所有物资，而欧洲的给养远在4000英里之外，而且美国的辽阔土地本身就是征服它所无法逾越的障碍。

P

美国的第一份报纸，于1704年4月在波士顿出版。参见《马萨诸塞历史学会集刊》第6卷第66页，波士顿，1880年。如果认为期刊的出版在美国历来完全自由那就错了。在那里，也曾设立过预先检查和提交保证金之类的制度。马萨诸塞州1722年1月14日法令就有这类规定。州下院（立法机构）任命的检查新闻工作的"新英格兰报刊委员会"表示："被告的报纸有嘲弄宗教和使人轻视宗教的倾向，准许一些著名作者在上面发表亵渎宗教和对神不敬的文章，诬蔑传播福音的教士的行为，辱骂国王陛下的政府，扰乱本地的和平与安宁，所以本委员会建议：禁止该报出版人兼发行人詹姆斯·富兰克林继续出版和发行该报；令其将要发表的一切文章送交本地行政长官审查；责成萨福克县治安法官令富兰克林

peace and tranquillity of the province disturbed by the said journal. The Committee is consequently of opinion that the printer and publisher, James Franklin, should be forbidden to print and publish the said journal or any other work in future, without having previously submitted it to the Secretary of the province; and that the justices of the peace for the county of Suffolk should be commissioned to require bail of the said James Franklin for his good conduct during the ensuing year." The suggestion of the Committee was adopted and passed into a law, but the effect of it was null, for the journal eluded the prohibition by putting the name of Benjamin Franklin instead of James Franklin at the bottom of its columns, and this manoeuvre was supported by public opinion.

Appendix Q

The Federal Constitution has introduced the jury into the tribunals of the Union in the same way as the States had introduced it into their own several courts; but as it has not established any fixed rules for the choice of jurors, the federal courts select them from the ordinary jury list which each State makes for itself. The laws of the States must therefore be examined for the theory of the formation of juries. See Story's "Commentaries on the Constitution," B. iii. chap. 38, p. 654-659; Sergeant's "Constitutional Law," p. 165. See also the Federal Laws of the years 1789, 1800, and 1802, upon the subject. For the purpose of thoroughly understanding the American principles with respect to the formation of juries, I examined the laws of States at a distance from one another, and the following observations were the result of my inquiries. In America, all the citizens who exercise the elective franchise have the right of serving upon a jury. The great State of New York, however, has made a slight difference between the two privileges, but in a spirit quite contrary to that of the laws of France; for in the State of New York there are fewer persons eligible as jurymen than there are electors. It may be said in general that the right of forming part of a jury, like the right of electing representatives, is open to all the citizens: the exercise of this right, however, is not put indiscriminately into any hands. Every year a body of municipal or county magistrates—

先生交纳保证金并担保自己今后一年之内循规蹈矩。"委员会的建议被采纳并得到通过成为法律，但却未产生任何效果。因为报纸在边栏将发行人詹姆斯·富兰克林的姓名改为本杰明·富兰克林而逃过禁令，而且这样的花招得到舆论的支持。

Q

像各州在本州法院实行陪审制度一样，联邦宪法也将陪审制度引入联邦系统法院，但是，却没有对如何推选陪审员做出具体的规定。联邦法院从各州自行选定的常任陪审员中选取陪审员。因此，要根据各州的法律来对美国陪审制度的原理进行说明。参见：斯托里《美国宪法释义》第3卷第38章第654~659页；萨金特《美国宪法》第165页，以及1789年、1800年和1802年联邦有关这个问题颁布的法令。为了能够充分了解美国陪审制度形成的原则，我查阅了几个彼此相距很远的州的法律。下面就是我从中得出的研究结果。在美国，凡是有选举权的公民都可以担任陪审员。然而，在纽约这样的大州，推选人的法定资格与陪审员的法定资格略有不同，但其精神与法国法律的精神相抵触，因为纽约州陪审员的法定资格比选举人的法定资格规定的要低。总的来说，在美国，推选陪审员的权利，与推选议员的权利一样，面向所有公民。但是，这项权利的行使，并不是毫无差别地交到所有人手中。每年，乡镇或选举区的行政当局请有权推选陪审员的人，在新英格兰是请乡镇的行政委员，在纽约州是请乡镇行政长官，在俄亥俄州是请遗孤财产保管人，在路易斯安那州是请县长，为本地区推选一定人数的有权充任陪审员和预计有此种能力的公民为陪审员。

called "selectmen" in New England, "supervisors" in New York, "trustees" in Ohio, and "sheriffs of the parish" in Louisiana—choose for each county a certain number of citizens who have the right of serving as jurymen, and who are supposed to be capable of exercising their functions. These magistrates, being themselves elective, excite no distrust; their powers, like those of most republican magistrates, are very extensive and very arbitrary, and they frequently make use of them to remove unworthy or incompetent jurymen. The names of the jurymen thus chosen are transmitted to the County Court; and the jury who have to decide any affair are drawn by lot from the whole list of names. The Americans have contrived in every way to make the common people eligible to the jury, and to render the service as little onerous as possible. The sessions are held in the chief town of every county, and the jury are indemnified for their attendance either by the State or the parties concerned. They receive in general a dollar per day, besides their travelling expenses. In America, the being placed upon the jury is looked upon as a burden, but it is a burden which is very supportable. See Brevard's "Digest of the Public Statute Law of South Carolina," vol. i. pp. 446 and 454, vol. ii. pp. 218 and 338; "The General Laws of Massachusetts, revised and published by authority of the Legislature," vol. ii. pp. 187 and 331; "The Revised Statutes of the State of New York," vol. ii. pp. 411, 643, 717, 720; "The Statute Law of the State of Tennessee," vol. i. p. 209; "Acts of the State of Ohio," pp. 95 and 210; and "Digeste general des Actes de la Legislature de la Louisiane."

Appendix R

If we attentively examine the constitution of the jury as introduced into civil proceedings in England, we shall readily perceive that the jurors are under the immediate control of the judge. It is true that the verdict of the jury, in civil as well as in criminal cases, comprises the question of fact and the question of right in the same reply; thus—a house is claimed by Peter as having been

而即使这些官员本人当选为陪审员也不会引起人们的不信任。他们的权力，同大多数州行政官员一样，非常广泛和专制，并往往利用这些权力罢免不合格的无能的陪审员。将如此选出的陪审员的名单送交县法院，然后用抽签的办法从中选出有权参加各种案件审理的陪审团。美国人通过一切办法让普通人可以参加陪审团，并尽可能减轻陪审团的负担。法院在每个县的县城开庭审理案件，陪审团的出席会受到州或相关方的保护。陪审员的报酬一般为除旅行费外，一天一美元。在美国，人们把做陪审员看成是一项负担，但这项负担并不难完成。参见布雷瓦德《南卡罗来纳州法令汇编》第2卷第338页，第1卷第454和第456页，第2卷第218页。参见立法机构编辑和出版的《马萨诸塞普通法》第2卷第331页和第187页。参见《增订纽约州法令集》第2卷第411页、第643页、第717页和第720页。参见《田纳西州法令集》第1卷第209页。参见《俄亥俄州法令集》第95页和第210页。参见《路易斯安那州立法汇编》第2卷第55页。

R

当我们仔细研究英国民事陪审制度时，必然会发现陪审员处于法官的控制之下。的确，陪审团对民事案件和刑事案件所做的裁定，也包括事实问题和权利问题。例如：有一所住宅，彼得声称自己对其拥有所有权，因为他花钱购买了它，这就是事实问题。而被告方则称，出售人没有行为能力，这就是权利问题。这就是需要解决的法律问题。陪审团对刑事案件的判决只要有利于被告，英国人就同意陪审团的判决没有错误；但在民事方面，英国人则不这么认为。法官可以拒绝接受陪审团的裁定，驳回给陪审员重新审理。如果法

purchased by him: this is the fact to be decided. The defendant puts in a plea of incompetency on the part of the vendor: this is the legal question to be resolved. But the jury do not enjoy the same character of infallibility in civil cases, according to the practice of the English courts, as they do in criminal cases. The judge may refuse to receive the verdict; and even after the first trial has taken place, a second or new trial may be awarded by the Court. See Blackstone's "Commentaries," book iii. ch. 24.

Appendix S

I find in my travelling journal a passage which may serve to convey a more complete notion of the trials to which the women of America, who consent to follow their husbands into the wilds, are often subjected. This description has nothing to recommend it to the reader but its strict accuracy:

". . . From time to time we come to fresh clearings; all these places are alike; I shall describe the one at which we have halted to-night, for it will serve to remind me of all the others.

"The bell which the pioneers hang round the necks of their cattle, in order to find them again in the woods, announced our approach to a clearing, when we were yet a long way off; and we soon afterwards heard the stroke of the hatchet, hewing down the trees of the forest. As we came nearer, traces of destruction marked the presence of civilized man; the road was strewn with shattered boughs; trunks of trees, half consumed by fire, or cleft by the wedge, were still standing in the track we were following. We continued to proceed till we reached a wood in which all the trees seemed to have been suddenly struck dead; in the height of summer their boughs were as leafless as in winter; and upon closer examination we found that a deep circle had been cut round the bark, which, by stopping the circulation of the sap, soon kills the tree. We were informed that this is commonly the first thing a pioneer does; as he cannot in the first year cut down all the trees which cover his new parcel of land, he sows Indian corn under their branches, and puts the trees to death in order to

官把陪审团的判决搁置起来，不予复审，则诉讼还没有完全结束，因为他有办法抵制陪审团的判决。主要的方法是，要求法院撤销原判和成立新的陪审团。实际上，这样的要求很少得到满足，而且他以后也再没有办法。我就亲眼看到过这样的事情。参见布莱克斯通著作第3卷第24章。

S

在我的旅行日志中，一些段落所记载的内容足以说明肯追随丈夫们前往荒凉地区的美国女性所常常要经受的考验。之所以要将这几段内容介绍给读者，完全是出去其可靠的真实性：

"……我们时不时的会碰到一些新开垦的土地，所有这样的地方都很相似。我所要描述的就是今晚我们将要停留的地方，因为这里让我想起曾经到过的其他地方。

为了能够在树林中找到自家的牲畜，拓荒者给牲畜的脖子挂上铃铛。在我们离居民点还很远的时候，便可循着这铃声一路前行。接着不久，我们就能听到树林里传来斧头伐木的声音。随着我们不断的前进，伐木的痕迹告诉我们这里有文明人在劳作。一路上堆满了被砍掉的树枝。树木被砍伐后剩下的树桩以及被火烧焦后残留的树干，还依然立在我们走过的道路上。我们继续往前走，直到来到一片林子旁，这里的树木好像都突然得了暴病而枯死。正值盛夏时节，这些树木的枝子却犹如冬日一般一片叶子的影子都看不到。凑近这些树木仔细观察我们才发现树干上有一圈树皮被砍掉后留下的深深的痕迹。这样树液的循环就被切断，树木就会很快枯死。我们得知这是拓荒者循例要做的第一件事情。因为在第

prevent them from injuring his crop. Beyond this field, at present imperfectly traced out, we suddenly came upon the cabin of its owner, situated in the centre of a plot of ground more carefully cultivated than the rest, but where man was still waging unequal warfare with the forest; there the trees were cut down, but their roots were not removed, and the trunks still encumbered the ground which they so recently shaded. Around these dry blocks, wheat, suckers of trees, and plants of every kind, grow and intertwine in all the luxuriance of wild, untutored nature. Amidst this vigorous and various vegetation stands the house of the pioneer, or, as they call it, the log house. Like the ground about it, this rustic dwelling bore marks of recent and hasty labor; its length seemed not to exceed thirty feet, its height fifteen; the walls as well as the roof were formed of rough trunks of trees, between which a little moss and clay had been inserted to keep out the cold and rain.

"As night was coming on, we determined to ask the master of the log house for a lodging. At the sound of our footsteps, the children who were playing amongst the scattered branches sprang up and ran towards the house, as if they were frightened at the sight of man; whilst two large dogs, almost wild, with ears erect and outstretched nose, came growling out of their hut, to cover the retreat of their young masters. The pioneer himself made his appearance at the door of his dwelling; he looked at us with a rapid and inquisitive glance, made a sign to the dogs to go into the house, and set them the example, without betraying either curiosity or apprehension at our arrival.

"We entered the log house: the inside is quite unlike that of the cottages of the peasantry of Europe: it contains more than is superfluous, less than is necessary. A single window with a muslin blind; on a hearth of trodden clay an immense fire, which lights the whole structure; above the hearth a good rifle, a deer's skin, and plumes of eagles' feathers; on the right hand of the chimney a map of the United States, raised and shaken by the wind through the crannies in the wall; near the map, upon a shelf formed of a roughly hewn plank, a few volumes of books—a Bible, the six first books of Milton, and two of Shakespeare's plays; along the wall, trunks instead of closets; in the centre of the room a rude table, with legs of green wood, and with the bark still upon them, looking as if they

一年，他们没办法将自己那片土地上所有的树木都伐倒，并且还要在其间种植玉米，为了不让树木影响到玉米的生长，于是让树木枯死。走过这片还尚未开垦完的田地，我们马上看到了主人的房舍。主人的小屋坐落在一块比周围其余地方开垦的都要好的多土地中央。在这片遭到人们滥伐的林子里，树木被砍倒而树根却还没有被清除，树干倒伏在前不久还绿树成荫的土地上。在这片荒地的周围，小麦，初生的柞树以及各种植物竞相生长交错在这片尚未被驯服的土地。拓荒者的房子，也就是人们说的"圆木小屋"，就位于这片茂盛的植被之中。跟这片土地一样，这座乡村小屋也流露着才刚刚匆匆完工的痕迹。房子似乎高不够30英尺，宽也不过15英尺。屋子的墙和顶也都是原木搭建，之间的缝隙用干草和上泥巴来堵住，这样既防寒又防雨。

当夜幕降临的时候，我们决定向房子的主人借宿一夜。一听到我们的脚步声，在四处散落着破树枝的林子里玩耍的小孩，立即起身跑向家里，好像很怕生的样子。这时，两条犹如野狗一般的大狗，竖着耳朵伸长了脖子，狂吠着从农舍里跑出来，似乎是在掩护小主人们的撤退。拓荒者本人此时来到了屋门前，好奇的朝我们瞟了一眼，打手势让狗回屋，并向他们示范，我们的到来并未引起他的恐慌和不安。

我们走进木屋，发现这里的陈设跟欧洲农舍的完全不同，摆放了很多多余的东西，而必需品则很少。一个窗户上挂着细布窗帘，土坯搭成的壁炉上放着一盏大灯照亮整个屋子，在其上方还挂着一支来复枪，一张鹿皮和一串鹰的羽毛。在壁炉烟囱的右侧挂着一张美国地图，被从墙缝吹进来的风吹的直晃荡。在地图旁边，一个粗糙木板搭成的架子上放着几本书。一本是《圣经》，还有六本弥尔顿最早的长诗，以及两本莎士比亚的戏剧。沿

grew out of the ground on which they stood; but on this table a tea-pot of British ware, silver spoons, cracked tea-cups, and some newspapers.

"The master of this dwelling has the strong angular features and lank limbs peculiar to the native of New England. It is evident that this man was not born in the solitude in which we have met with him: his physical constitution suffices to show that his earlier years were spent in the midst of civilized society, and that he belongs to that restless, calculating, and adventurous race of men, who do with the utmost coolness things only to be accounted for by the ardor of the passions, and who endure the life of savages for a time, in order to conquer and civilize the backwoods.

"When the pioneer perceived that we were crossing his threshold, he came to meet us and shake hands, as is their custom; but his face was quite unmoved; he opened the conversation by inquiring what was going on in the world; and when his curiosity was satisfied, he held his peace, as if he were tired by the noise and importunity of mankind. When we questioned him in our turn, he gave us all the information we required; he then attended sedulously, but without eagerness, to our personal wants. Whilst he was engaged in providing thus kindly for us, how came it that in spit of ourselves we felt our gratitude die upon our lips? It is that our host whilst he performs the duties of hospitality, seems to be obeying an irksome necessity of his condition: he treats it as a duty imposed upon him by his situation, not as a pleasure. By the side of the hearth sits a woman with a baby on her lap: she nods to us without disturbing herself. Like the pioneer, this woman is in the prime of life; her appearance would seem superior to her condition, and her apparel even betrays a lingering taste for dress; but her delicate limbs appear shrunken, her features are drawn in, her eye is mild and melancholy; her whole physiognomy bears marks of a degree of religious resignation, a deep quiet of all passions, and some sort of natural and tranquil firmness, ready to meet all the ills of life, without fearing and without braving them. Her children cluster about her, full of health, turbulence, and energy: they are true children of the wilderness; their mother watches them from time to time with mingled melancholy and joy: to look at their strength and her languor, one might imagine that

着墙放着几个木箱代替了壁橱，屋子的中间摆放这一张做工极粗糙的桌子，桌腿是用刚刚砍下的树枝做的，上面的树皮还没剥去，看起来它们似乎是从地里长出来的一样。然而桌子的上面却摆放着英式的茶壶，银制的勺子，破了口的茶杯，还有几张报纸。

房子的主人脸上棱角分明，四肢袖长，是典型的新英格兰人。显然，他并不是出生在这片我们与其相遇的蛮荒之地，因为他的举止足以说明他早年生活在文明社会，而且属于那种不安于现状，精于计算，具有冒险精神的人。这类人能够极为冷静的处理专靠热情发动起来的事物，而且为了能够征服和开化蛮荒之地，他们宁愿过上一段时间的野蛮生活。

当拓荒者意识到我们是想要跨进他家门槛的时候，便迎上前来习惯性的与我们打招呼握手。但是他脸上表情则显得无动于衷，一开口便打听世界上发生的事情，待好奇心得到满足之后，于是又不再做声，似乎早已厌倦世俗的聒噪和纠缠。当轮到我们开口提问时，他对我们的问题知无不言，但随后尽管他依然努力满足我们的需要，但多少有些心不在焉。在他如此诚意待客的时候，为什么又会觉得感激的言辞难以启齿呢？这是因为待客于他似乎是在履行职责，似乎是命运的安排令人不快却又必须遵从。他认为这是他现在处境赋予自己的义务，而不是一件快事。

在壁炉的旁边，一个女人坐在哪里将一个男孩抱在膝上。她只是向我们点点头并未加入我们的谈话。像拓荒者一样，女人也正值盛年，她的举止外貌显得比她的处境要更优雅，她的衣着也在诉说她对服饰的热爱丝毫未减。但是她的四肢已不复往日的纤细，面容也显得有些疲惫，目光温和而忧郁。她的外貌整体上给人留下这样一种印象：她因笃信宗教而安于天命，情感宁静而热烈，以及某种莫名的与生俱来的坚毅，让她能够随时准备面

the life she has given them has exhausted her own, and still she regrets not what they have cost her. The house inhabited by these emigrants has no internal partition or loft. In the one chamber of which it consists, the whole family is gathered for the night. The dwelling is itself a little world—an ark of civilization amidst an ocean of foliage: a hundred steps beyond it the primeval forest spreads its shades, and solitude resumes its sway."

Appendix T

It is not the equality of conditions which makes men immoral and irreligious; but when men, being equal, are at the same time immoral and irreligious, the effects of immorality and irreligion easily manifest themselves outwardly, because men have but little influence upon each other, and no class exists which can undertake to keep society in order. Equality of conditions never engenders profligacy of morals, but it sometimes allows that profligacy to show itself.

Appendix U

Setting aside all those who do not think at all, and those who dare not say what they think, the immense majority of the Americans will still be found to appear satisfied with the political institutions by which they are governed; and, I believe, really to be so. I look upon this state of public opinion as an indication, but not as a demonstration, of the absolute excellence of American laws. The pride of a nation, the gratification of certain ruling passions by the law, a concourse of circumstances, defects which escape notice, and more than all the rest, the influence of a majority which shuts the mouth of all cavillers, may long perpetuate the delusions of a people as well as those of a man. Look at England throughout the eighteenth century. No nation was ever more prodigal of self-applause, no people was ever more self-satisfied; then every part of its constitution was right—

对生活中的所有不幸，而且既不害怕也不会轻视它们。她的孩子们簇拥在她的身边，健康、活波而且精力充沛。他们是这里土生土长的孩子，他们的母亲看着他们时不时的流露出忧郁却又欢喜的神情。看着结实的孩子们和他们疲惫的母亲，不难想象她为孩子们的成长如何费尽心血，而且为自己付出的代价毫不吝惜。移民者们就住在这样既无隔断又无阁楼房子里。在这样的一间大屋里，全家人每夜同眠在一处。这间小屋自成一个小世界，是飘荡在林海中的文明方舟。仅仅在百步之外，原始森林又开始遮天蔽日，荒凉又重新归来。"

T

让人们道德沦丧不笃信宗教的并不是身分的平等。但是当平等的人们道德沦丧不再笃信宗教的时候，不道德和无信仰的影响就特别容易表现出来。因为人们彼此间几乎无法在相互影响，没有任何一个阶级能够担起维护社会秩序的责任。身分的平等并不会让道德沦丧，而是有时会让道德的沦丧呈现出来。

U

将所有那些压根什么都不想以及那些不敢说出自己想法的人放在一边，你会发现绝大多数的美国人对现行的政治制度似乎表示满意，而且我也相信他们的确是满意的。我认为这样的舆论倾向是美国法制十分优秀的表现，而非是它优秀的证明。民族自豪感，立法的对于某些激情，偶然事件以及隐秘弊端的满足，而且特别是能够堵住反对派悠悠之口的多数的利益，会长期给这个民族和人民带来一种错觉。现在我们来看一下18世纪的英国。从

everything, even to its most obvious defects, was irreproachable: at the present day a vast number of Englishmen seem to have nothing better to do than to prove that this constitution was faulty in many respects. Which was right?—the English people of the last century, or the English people of the present day?

The same thing has occurred in France. It is certain that during the reign of Louis XIV the great bulk of the nation was devotedly attached to the form of government which, at that time, governed the community. But it is a vast error to suppose that there was anything degraded in the character of the French of that age. There might be some sort of servitude in France at that time, but assuredly there was no servile spirit among the people. The writers of that age felt a species of genuine enthusiasm in extolling the power of their king; and there was no peasant so obscure in his hovel as not to take a pride in the glory of his sovereign, and to die cheerfully with the cry "Vive le Roi!" upon his lips. These very same forms of loyalty are now odious to the French people. Which are wrong?—the French of the age of Louis XIV, or their descendants of the present day?

Our judgment of the laws of a people must not then be founded Future Condition Of Three Races In The United States exclusively upon its inclinations, since those inclinations change from age to age; but upon more elevated principles and a more general experience. The love which a people may show for its law proves only this:—that we should not be in too great a hurry to change them.

Appendix V

In the chapter to which this note relates I have pointed out one source of danger: I am now about to point out another kind of peril, more rare indeed, but far more formidable if it were ever to make its appearance. If the love of physical gratification and the taste for well-being, which are naturally suggested to men by a state of equality, were to get entire possession of the mind of a democratic people, and to fill it completely, the manners of the nation would become so totally opposed to

来没有任何一个民族像那时候的英国一样那么的喜欢自我吹捧，也从来没有人民如他们一样对自己感到那么的满意。于是乎认为自己制度样样都好，即使是最显眼的缺陷也是无可指摘的。而如今，大量的英国人似乎都认为他们的制度在很多方面都存在瑕疵。那么到底谁才是对的呢？18世纪的英国人还是如今的英国人呢？

同样的事情也发生在法国。毫无疑问，在路易十四统治时期，绝大多数民众都全心全意的热爱当时统治社会的政府。但是据此而贬低那个时代法国人的人格就大错特错了。在那个时代，法国人也许受到了某种奴役，但是可以肯定人民并没有奴性的思想。那个时代的作家对于颂扬王权有一种真挚的热情。在他的笔下，没有农民会如此的不明事理而不去颂扬至高无上的王权，而且还会高呼着"国王万岁"而含笑九泉。而这样的愚忠恰恰为如今的法国人所深恶痛绝。这又是谁错了？路易十四时期的法国人还是作为他们后人的我们呢？

所以对于一个国家法律的评判不能只凭着人民的喜好，因为人民的喜好会随时代的变化而变化，而是应该依据其更为重要的原则和普遍的经验。人民对其法制的拥护只能证明我们不应该匆忙的改变现有的法律。

V

在这个注释所在的文章里，我只提到一种危险。现在，我要指出另外一种极为罕见，而一旦出现便极为可怕的危机。如果平等让人们自然而然产生的对于物质享受和舒适生活的热爱会完全占据并牢牢控制住他们的思想，那么这个国家将变得不再尚武，甚至军队都

military tastes, that perhaps even the army would eventually acquire a love of peace, in spite of the peculiar interest which leads it to desire war. Living in the midst of a state of general relaxation, the troops would ultimately think it better to rise without efforts, by the slow but commodious advancement of a peace establishment, than to purchase more rapid promotion at the cost of all the toils and privations of the field. With these feelings, they would take up arms without enthusiasm, and use them without energy; they would allow themselves to be led to meet the foe, instead of marching to attack him. It must not be supposed that this pacific state of the army would render it adverse to revolutions; for revolutions, and especially military revolutions, which are generally very rapid, are attended indeed with great dangers, but not with protracted toil; they gratify ambition at less cost than war; life only is at stake, and the men of democracies care less for their lives than for their comforts. Nothing is more dangerous for the freedom and the tranquillity of a people than an army afraid of war, because, as such an army no longer seeks to maintain its importance and its influence on the field of battle, it seeks to assert them elsewhere. Thus it might happen that the men of whom a democratic army consists should lose the interests of citizens without acquiring the virtues of soldiers; and that the army should cease to be fit for war without ceasing to be turbulent. I shall here repeat what I have said in the text: the remedy for these dangers is not to be found in the army, but in the country: a democratic people which has preserved the manliness of its character will never be at a loss for military prowess in its soldiers.

Appendix W

Men connect the greatness of their idea of unity with means, God with ends: hence this idea of greatness, as men conceive it, leads us into infinite littleness. To compel all men to follow the same course towards the same object is a human notion;—to introduce infinite variety of action, but so combined that all these acts lead by a multitude of different courses to the accomplishment of one great design, is a conception of the Deity. The human idea of unity is almost always barren; the

会爱好和平而反对因为特定的利益而将其拖入战争。生活在这样舒适的环境下，士兵们最终将宁愿在和平环境里缓慢而轻松的一步步晋升，而不愿在战场上以艰难险阻为代价得到迅速晋升。有了这样的情绪，他们不会热情满满的拿起武器，精力充沛的挥舞起来，于是他们非但不会迎敌而上反而会引狼入室。但是一定不能由此认定处于这样和平氛围的军队必然会反对革命。因为革命，特别是军事革命，往往非常迅速并伴随极大的危险，但无需旷日持久的艰苦付出。与战争相比，只需付出较小的代价就能满足人们的野心。生命是唯一需要付出的代价，而对于民主国家的人而言舒适的生活显然比生命更为重要。对于一个自由宁静的国家，没有什么事情比军队害怕战争更怕的了。因为这样的军队不再想要在战场上证明自己的重要性和影响力，而是寻求其他地方来表现。因此，民主国家军队的官兵有可能失去军人的美德而罔顾公民的利益，而军队也不再有战斗力，并不断发生骚乱。这里我要重复一下我在书中所说过的话：解决这些危险的方法不在军队而在国家。一个具有英雄气概的民主国家的士兵永远也不会失去善战的英勇。

W

人认为统一思想的伟大之处在于手段，而神认为在于目的。因此，这样的伟大观只会关注无穷无尽的小事。迫使所有的人遵循同样的道路奔向同样的目标是人的观点，而引导千变万化的行动，并将其整合的如此之好让所有的行动能够通过许许多多不同的道路去完成一幅伟大蓝图的是神的观点。人类思想的统一性几乎总是贫瘠而无趣，而神的统一性观

divine idea pregnant with abundant results. Men think they manifest their greatness by simplifying the means they use; but it is the purpose of God which is simple—his means are infinitely varied.

Appendix X

A democratic people is not only led by its own tastes to centralize its government, but the passions of all the men by whom it is governed constantly urge it in the same direction. It may easily be foreseen that almost all the able and ambitious members of a democratic community will labor without 2 ceasing to extend the powers of government, because they all hope at some time or other to wield those powers. It is a waste of time to attempt to prove to them that extreme centralization may be injurious to the State, since they are centralizing for their own benefit. Amongst the public men of democracies there are hardly any but men of great disinterestedness or extreme mediocrity who seek to oppose the centralization of government: the former are scarce, the latter powerless.

Appendix Y

I have often asked myself what would happen if, amidst the relaxation of democratic manners, and as a consequence of the restless spirit of the army, a military government were ever to be founded amongst any of the nations of the present age. I think that even such a government would not differ very much from the outline I have drawn in the chapter to which this note belongs, and that it would retain none of the fierce characteristics of a military oligarchy. I am persuaded that, in such a case, a sort of fusion would take place between the habits of official men and those of the military service. The administration would assume something of a military character, and the army some of the usages of the civil administration. The result would be a regular, clear, exact, and absolute system of government; the people would become the reflection of the army, and the community be drilled like a garrison.

点则往往孕育出丰硕的成果。人通过简化他们所运用的手段而彰显自己的伟大，而神的目标则很简单，就是让手段千变万化。

X

民主国家之所以走向中央集权并不仅仅是因为其爱好使然，而且还有领导它的人也不断将其推向同一个方向。不难预见，民主国家里几乎所有才能出众野心勃勃的人都会不遗余力的扩大政府的权力，因为他们都盼望有朝一日能够大权在握。试图向他们证明极端中央集权可能会损害国家利益，简直就是浪费时间，因为他们是为自己的利益而集权。在民主国家的公仆中，反对中央集权的几乎不是大公无私之人就是平庸之辈，前者凤毛麟角，而后者无权无势。

Y

我常常问自己，在民主社会如此温和的民情中，并在军队情绪不稳的作用下，在当今这个时代如果某些国家出现军政府，其结果将会怎样？我认为甚至这样的政府不会出现在本注所在的章节里所描绘的现象，也不会保留任何军事寡头政治的野蛮作风。我深信在这种情况下，文官的习惯和武官的习惯将产生某种融合，行政管理方面会呈现出某种军人特质，而军队则会采用某些文官的行事习惯。结果就会出现一个有条不紊、纪律严明、条理分明以及绝对专制的政府体制。人民成为军地的影子，而社会则被训练的如一座营房。

Appendix Z

It cannot be absolutely or generally affirmed that the greatest danger of the present age is license or tyranny, anarchy or despotism. Both are equally to be feared; and the one may as easily proceed as the other from the selfsame cause, namely, that "general apathy," which is the consequence of what I have termed "individualism": it is because this apathy exists, that the executive government, having mustered a few troops, is able to commit acts of oppression one day, and the next day a party, which has mustered some thirty men in its ranks, can also commit acts of oppression. Neither one nor the other can found anything to last; and the causes which enable them to succeed easily, prevent them from succeeding long: they rise because nothing opposes them, and they sink because nothing supports them. The proper object therefore of our most strenuous resistance, is far less either anarchy or despotism than the apathy which may almost indifferently beget either the one or the other.

Z

不能绝对笼统的断言当今时代最大的危机就是胡作非为或暴政，就是无政府状态或专制。这些东西都同样令人害怕，而且两者都会因为同样的原因而轻而易举的出现，而原因就是普遍的漠不关心，也就是我所说过的个人主义的结果。正是因为这种普遍漠不关心现象的存在，今天集结了一些军队的执政府能够实行压迫，而以后，一个能够纠集起三十人队伍的政党也能实行压迫。无论前者还是后者都不能长久的存在下去，能让他们轻而易举获得成功的原因，也同样会阻碍他们长久的成功。他们之所以崛起是因为没人反对他们，而他们的垮台也正是因为没有人支持他们。因此，我们最应该展开艰苦抵抗的对象绝非无政府状态或专制，而是漠不关心，因为它会毫无分别的引起无政府状态或专制。